sisterhood
is powerful

AN ANTHOLOGY

OF WRITINGS

FROM THE WOMEN'S

LIBERATION MOVEMENT

For FAITH, my mother.
With love. Finally.

sisterhood
is powerful

AN ANTHOLOGY

OF WRITINGS

FROM THE WOMEN'S

LIBERATION MOVEMENT

EDITED BY ROBIN MORGAN

RANDOM HOUSE · NEW YORK

ACKNOWLEDGEMENTS

The collectivity, cooperation, and lack of competition (even from sisters who were also putting together collections on women's liberation) that marked the process of creating this book are proof of how radically different the women's movement is from male-dominated movements. Sisters, all over the country, some of whom I have not yet met in person, were of invaluable help in acting as regional contacts, and as sources of information, material, encouragement, and editorial suggestions. I am especially grateful to my intrepid editor, Jane Seitz, and to the following sisters in struggle: Nell Allen, Pam Allen, Jane Alpert, Sandy Barnert, Connie Brown, Peggy Dobbins, Victoria Dudley, Pat Fineran, Laura Furman, Gilda, Ruth Glass, Nancy Hawley, Joreen, Joanna Krotz, Judy Leavitt, Joan Lester, Molly Malcolm, Cicely Nichols, Maxine Orris, Wendy Roberts, Kathie Sarachilde, Faye Schreibman, Linda Seese, Judy Stamper, Sally Stein, Nancy Stokely, Marilyn Salzman Webb, Penelope Weiss, Judith Weston, and Laura X.

Some mention, albeit brief, should also go to three men: Kenneth Pitchford, Blake Jamal Pitchford, and John J. Simon (Jane Seitz's editorial assistant at Random House). Without such men, "this book would not have been possible." On the other hand, it would not have been necessary.

The Editor's thanks also go to:

The Voice of The Women's Liberation Movement, where "The 51 Percent Minority Group" first appeared.

The Florida Paper on Women's Liberation, which first printed Beverly Jones' article.

Ramparts Magazine, for permission to print the revised, lengthened version of Susan Lydon's "The Politics of Orgasm."

The Journal of the American Psychoanalytical Association, for "A Theory on Female Sexuality," by Dr. Mary Jane Sherfey.

The American Journal of Psychotherapy, for permission to reprint excerpts from "A Psychiatrist's View" by Dr. Natalie Shainess.

Come Out, which printed an earlier version of Martha Shelley's "Notes of A Radical Lesbian."

New American Review, and Doubleday & Company, Inc., for permission to use excerpts from Kate Millet's forthcoming book, *Sexual Politics*, a longer selection of which was published in *NAR*.

Harper & Row, Publishers, Inc., for permission to reprint "Sadie and Maude" from the *Selected Poems* of Gwendolyn Brooks, Copyright 1945 by Gwendolyn Brooks Blakely.

Leviathan, which first published Alice de Rivera's "On De-Segregating Stuyvesant High" and Marge Piercy's "The Grand Coolie Damn."

El Grito del Norte, which first printed Enriqueta Vasquez's article on the Chicana.

Women: A Journal of Liberation, for permission to reprint the following: "Self-Defense for Women" by Pascalé/Moon/Tanner; "For Witches" by Susan Sutheim; "Elegy for Jayne Mansfield" by Karen Lindsey; "Poem" by Janet Russo.

Rat for "A Chant for My Sisters" by Marilyn Lowen Fletcher, and for various photographs.

Motive Magazine, for permission to reprint the following: "Must I Marry" by Lynn Strongin; "The Playground" by Leah Fritz; "Going Through Changes" by Jean Tepperman.

A Journal of Female Liberation for Roxanne Dunbar's "Female Liberation As The Basis For Sexual Revolution," and for Jayne West's "Poem."

Encounter for Sylvia Plath's poem "The Jailor."

Maurice Girodias and Olympia Press for the use of excerpts from Valerie Solanis's *SCUM Manifesto*.

Liberation News Service for research and photographs.

CONTENTS

HISTORICAL DOCUMENTS

vi / APPENDIX

INTRODUCTION: THE WOMEN'S REVOLUTION

This book is an action. It was conceived, written, edited, copy-edited, proofread, designed, and illustrated by women. (The process broke down for the first time at the printer's, that industry being one of the many which are all but completely closed to women.*) During the year that it took to collectively create this anthology, we women involved had to face specific and very concrete examples of our oppression, with regard to the book itself, that simply would not have occurred in putting together any other kind of collection. Because of the growing consciousness of women's liberation, and, in some cases, because of articles that women wrote for the book, there were not a few "reprisals": five personal relationships were severed, two couples were divorced and one separated, one woman was forced to withdraw her article, by the man she lived with; another's husband kept rewriting the piece until it was unrecognizable as her own; many of the articles were late, and the deadline kept being pushed further ahead, because the

*I have just learned that the book is being set by a computer, keypunched by women. Breakthrough!—Ed.

authors had so many other pressures on them—from housework to child care to jobs. More than one woman had trouble finishing her piece because it was so personally painful to commit her gut feelings to paper. We were also delayed by occurrences that would not have been of even peripheral importance to an anthology written by men: three pregnancies, one miscarriage, and one birth—plus one abortion and one hysterectomy. Speaking from my own experience, which is what we learn to be unashamed of doing in women's liberation, during the past year I twice survived the almost-dissolution of my marriage, was fired from my job (for trying to organize a union and for being in women's liberation), gave birth to a child, worked on a women's newspaper, marched and picketed, breast-fed the baby, was arrested on a militant women's liberation action, spent some time in jail, stopped wearing makeup and shaving my legs, started learning Karate, and changed my politics completely. That is, I became, somewhere along the way, a "feminist" committed to a Women's Revolution.

Since this political change is one that has been, is being, and will be shared by many other women, it should be explained. In my case, what it meant is that, when I first began work on this book, I considered myself a radical woman who regarded the Women's Liberation Movement as an important "wing" of the Left; as a tool, perhaps, for organizing as-yet apolitical women into what has been loosely called the "Movement"—which I now refer to as the male-dominated counterfeit Left. I was a so-called "politico," who shied away from admitting (on any but a superficial level) that *I* was oppressed, and who put all other causes above and ahead of my own, castigating myself with liberal guilt and doing Lady Bountiful actions about other people's oppression. This left me conveniently on top, and in a seat of relative power, because it isn't until you begin to fight in your own cause that you *a)* become really committed to winning, and *b)* become a genuine ally of other people struggling for their freedom. I also nurtured a secret contempt for other women who weren't as strong, free, and respected (by men) as I thought I was (that's called "identifying yourself with the oppressor," and it's analogous to a black person feeling compelled to have "processed" hair). Especially threatening were the women who admitted that they were simply unable to cope with the miserable situation we were all in, and needed each other and a whole movement to change that.

Well, somewhere during that year, I became such a woman—and it's been a radicalizing experience. I still don't fully know how it came about. Surely having a baby was part of it—the delight and excitement, and then the utter exhaustion, especially during those first three months. Surely being in women's liberation small groups—talking and action—raised my consciousness. Somehow, though, this book seems to have been most responsible. All of us who worked on it in a variety of ways had to read and think and talk about the condition of women until we began to dream about the subject, literally. The suffering and courage and humor and rage and intelligence and endurance that spilled out from the pages that came in from different women! The facts we came up against, the statistics! The history we learned, the political sophistication we discovered, the insights into our own lives that dawned on us! I couldn't believe—still can't—how angry I could become, from deep down and way back, something like a five-thousand-year-buried anger.

It makes you very sensitive—raw, even—this consciousness. Everything, from the verbal assault on the street, to a "well-meant" sexist joke your husband tells, to the lower pay you get at work (for doing the same job a man would be paid more for), to television commercials, to rock-song lyrics, to the pink or blue blanket they put on your infant in the hospital nursery, to speeches by male "revolutionaries" that reek of male supremacy—everything seems to barrage your aching brain, which has fewer and fewer protective defenses to screen such things out. You begin to see how all-pervasive a thing is sexism—the definition of and discrimination against half the human species by the other half. Once started, the realization is impossible to stop, and it packs a daily wallop. *To deny that you are oppressed is to collaborate in your oppression. To collaborate in your oppression is a way of denying that you're oppressed—particularly when the price of refusing to collaborate is execution.*

Two maddening examples having to do with this book: I had insisted on working with women at Random House, and it was agreed that my two editors (women) and myself would have no interference from the men. Of course, what none of us foresaw was that neither of my editors had any real power in the male-dominated hierarchy of the house, and so were forced into a position of "interceding" with those who could enforce the decisions—men. Some of the men were openly meddlesome, and others, even with the best intentions of being politically "correct," couldn't resist an itsy-bitsy suggestion here or a teeny-weeny manipulation there, in a way they would never had dreamt of had an all-women team not been involved. And we, in turn, were forced to be dependent on them; they had the skills, the authority, the plain old power. (At this moment, an industry-wide women's group is forming in publishing to protest just such inequities—women are eighty percent of the work force in publishing, and all at the bottom of the pyramid.) After a while of this intrigue, none of us were speaking to each other. Not until we women met separately, to thrash the whole thing out as best we could, were we able to continue. Vibrations hum in the atmosphere still.

Another infuriating instance of male supremacy (plus plain old capitalist possessiveness and greed) broke over us when the manuscript was already being printed. The original title for the anthology was to have been *The Hand That Cradles The Rock*, which we all liked for its at-least triple entendre. Advance notices in catalogs, etc., had already gone out with this title when the attorneys for S.J. Perelman (a famous elderly humorist whom I now find totally lacking in wit) informed us that Mr. Perelman had written a story some decades ago with that title, and that he would get an injunction to keep us from distributing the books if we used that name. Would you believe it? Really. *Who* would have remembered Mr. Perelman's story, especially those of us who had never heard of it in the first place? Would an acknowledgement satisfy such pettiness? Nope. No silly women were going to mess around with *his* title. So, we were forced to change the title. Not that I now mind, having convinced myself that Sisterhood must be *very* Powerful for us to have even survived, let alone finished this damned book.(The monies from the book's sales, by the way, will go to the women's movement, for day-care and abortion projects, bail and defense funds, etc.)

Another difficulty in this project was caused by the quicksilver growth and change of the Women's Liberation Movement. Although we kept updating our material, the leaflets and manifestoes, especially, already seem historical documents. By the time you read this, some groups listed in the Appendix might have changed form or name, and judging from the astonishing rate at which new groups are proliferating around the country—indeed, the world—our list can hardly be considered exhaustive or definitive.So, too, with the list of women's liberation publications; the movement produces voluminous amounts of literature, and a complete list would be impossible here.

There is also a blessedly uneven quality noticeable in the book, which I, for one, delight in. There is a certain kind of linear, tight, dry, boring, male super-consistency that we are beginning to reject. That's why this collection combines all sorts of articles, poems, graphics, and sundry papers. There are the well-documented, statistically solid pieces and the intensely personal experiences. (Women's liberation is the first radical movement to base its politics—in fact, create its politics—out of concrete personal experiences. We've learned that those experiences are *not* our private hang-ups. They are shared by every woman, and are therefore political. The theory, then, comes out of human feeling, not out of textbook rhetoric. *That's* truly revolutionary, as anyone knows who's ever listened to abstract political speeches.) No one article is meant to be "representative" of anything other than some part of all women. The women's movement is a non-hierarchical one. It does things collectively and experimentally. It is also the first movement that has the potential of cutting across all class, race, age, economic, and geographical barriers—since women in every group must play essentially the same role, albeit with different sets and costumes: the multiple role of wife, mother, sexual object, baby-producer, "supplementary-income statistic," help-mate, nurturer, hostess, etc. To reflect this potential, con-tributors from those different groups speak in this book—and frequently disagree with each other.

There are different forms of consciousness present. Some of the sisters still use the appellation "chick" while most would glare down any man who used the word. Some see the enemy as the System solely, and others point out that men can't get off that easily, since they created the System and preserve it. Some women preferred to use pseudonyms, others used their husband's or father's (so-called "maiden") names, others used only their first names or newly invented "freedom" last names. Each contributor wrote her own short biography in the Contributor's Notes at the back of the book, and these paragraphs are as varied and revealing as the articles themselves. Although some of the articles have appeared elsewhere and may be widely known in or out of the movement, most are printed here for the first time, and many are by sisters who have not had the chance to write on women's liberation before. The whole book is intended to reflect the wide spectrum of political theory and action in women's liberation; there will be, I hope, an entire book on each aspect mentioned herein and more—by some-one else at some other point. What we have tried to put together is a sort of introduction to the movement: why we are, what we are, what we have done, where we might be going, but told in our own words, not those of the distorting mass media.

A word about two of the articles. First, it could be asked why we included a piece on women and the Catholic Church, but nothing on other religions and the way they regard women. The answer is that although every organized patriarchal religion works overtime to contribute its own brand of mysogyny to the myth of woman-hate, woman-fear, and woman-evil, the Roman Catholic Church also carries the immense power of very directly affecting women's lives everywhere by its stand against birth control and abortion, and by its use of skillful and wealthy lobbies to prevent legislative change. It is an obscenity—an all-male hierarchy, celibate or not, that presumes to rule on the lives and bodies of millions of women. *That* is why we have an article on the Catholic Church.

Second, about the article on China's gestures toward women's liberation in the process of their revolution. Why China? Other post-revolutionary countries, with cultures nearer to our own might have done as well, or better, for this book. Possibly. But China seemed important because it is the largest revolutionary nation in the world (the largest nation, period) and one in which the lives of approximately one-fourth of the human population have been drastically changed. It is also the most (astonishingly) ongoing revolution; it hardly seems to stop for breath between leaps and phases. But the piece was most important for this collection because women in pre-revolutionary China were treated as sub-animals, let alone sub-humans. Infant girls were buried alive or left exposed to the elements—no one wanted to raise worthless females. Shanghai and Peking were the prostitution capitals of the world. Women were bought and sold. Their feet were bound, a custom which probably had its origin in practicality: you can't run away on feet that have been deliberately deformed. China today is still a male-supremacist nation, but the condition of women has, in a very short time, become infinitely better. Charlotte Bonny

Cohen's examination of China is important to our thinking because it shows how people *can* change, but how intrepid male supremacy is.

Elsewhere, Connie Brown and Jane Seitz have summarized the historical perspectives regarding women during the last century, which set the stage for a new feminist movement. Also, Joreen has laid out a staggering set of facts and statistics on the oppression of women, which certainly make it clear why we are not happy with our lot. But why a women's movement, and why now?

Every time drastic change has shaken the established social order, some drive for women's rights has surfaced—only to be put down, or told to "wait until after," after the revolution or whatever else concerned the men. The women's suffrage movement in the United States grew out of the drive to abolish slavery. The current women's movement was begun largely, although not completely, by women who had been active in the civil-rights movement, in the anti-war movement, in student movements, and in the Left generally. There's something contagious about demanding freedom, especially where women, who comprise the oldest oppressed group on the face of the planet, are concerned. Thinking we were involved in the struggle to build a new society, it was a slowly dawning and depressing realization that we were doing the same work and playing the same roles *in* the Movement as out of it: typing the speeches that men delivered, making coffee but not policy, being accessories to the men whose politics would supposedly replace the Old Order. But whose New Order? Not ours, certainly. Marge Piercy writes about the experiences of women in the male Left very movingly in "The Grand Coolie Damn," so I won't go into the agonizing ambivalences of that situation here.

Suffice it to say that women, who had been struggling on a one-to-one basis with their men, began to see that some sort of solidarity was necessary, or insanity would result. (Perhaps the most vicious weapon used against women is the psychological line that tells us, "If you're not satisfied with your life, if you can't *adjust* to the feminine role, then something is wrong with *you*; you're frigid, neurotic, castrating, hung-up, a Lesbian, a bitch." This is one tactic they've never been able to use successfully on black people, because that oppression has always been so blatant—but what happens to women ranges from the most subtle to the most brutal, and they've tried to convince us that we want it that way. The argument is "convincingly" reinforced by very real threats, economic, emotional, and social.)

In 1964, Ruby Doris Smith Robinson, a young black woman who was a founder of SNCC (then the Student Non-violent Coordinating Committee) wrote a paper on the position of women in that organization. It was laughed at and dismissed. In 1965, Casey Hayden and Mary King, two white women who had been active in SNCC and other civil-rights organizations for years, wrote an article on women in the Movement for the now-defunct journal *Studies on the Left*. Women began to form caucuses within the Movement organizations where they worked; men's reactions ranged from fury to derision. In 1966, women who demanded that a plank on women's liberation be inserted in the SDS (Students for a Democratic Society) resolution that year were pelted with tomatoes and thrown out of the convention. But the caucuses went on forming, and gradually became small groups all on their own, as women more and more came to see the necessity of an independent women's movement, creating its own theory, politics, tactics, and directing itself toward goals in its own self-interest (which was also the self-interest of more than half the world's population).

Synchronistically, the National Organization for Women (NOW) was formed, in 1966. One of its founders was Betty Friedan, author of *The Feminine Mystique*. A civil-rights organization pledged to "bring women into full participation in the mainstream of American society . . . exercising all the privileges and responsibilities thereof in truly equal partnership with men," NOW's membership was mostly comprised of middle- and upper-middle-class women (*and men;* it is almost the only group in the women's movement that allows male members), professional, middle-aged, white women. The organization, which now has members in every state of the union, as well as about fifty chapters in twenty-four states, has been called (by some, affectionately; by others, pejoratively) "the NAACP of the women's movement" because it fights *within* the System, lobbying legislators, concentrating on job discrimination, etc. NOW helped win the airline stewardesses' fight against mandatory retirement when a woman married or reached the age of thirty-five; the group was also almost solely responsible for the Equal Employment Opportunities Commission ruling that segregated male-female help-wanted ads in newspapers were discriminatory and illegal. They have worked hard to change abortion laws and to call attention to educational discrimination against women.

NOW is essentially an organization that wants reforms about the second-class citizenship of women—and this is where it differs drastically from the rest of the Women's Liberation Movement. Its composite membership (and remember the men) determines, of course, its politics, which are not radical. An ecumenical view (which I hold on alternate Tuesdays and Fridays) would see that such an organization is extremely valid and important; it reaches a certain constituency that is never going to be reached by, say, a group called WITCH, or The Coat Hangers, and it does valuable work, as well. On certain Mondays and Thursdays, however, I fear for the women's movement's falling into precisely the same trap as did our foremothers, the suffragists: creating a bourgeois feminist movement that never quite dared enough, never questioned enough, never really reached out beyond its own class and race. For example, with a few courageous exceptions, most of the suffragists refused to examine the family as a structure oppressive to women. Because of this type of failure, they wound up having to settle for the vote. We now see what that got us. The only hope of a new feminist movement is some kind of only now barely emerging politics of *revolutionary feminism*, which some people are trying to explore in this anthology.

That politics comes from what has been called "rap sessions," "bitch sessions," or "consciousness-raising" which the small groups of radical women began to form around 1966–67. The technique attracted a lot of ridicule from men; it seems that when the Chinese used such a technique, "Speak Pains to Recall Pains," it was right-on revolutionary, but when women used it, it was "group therapy" or a "hen party." Kathie Sarachild, one of the first women to formulate consciousness-raising as it applies to women's groups, breaks down the technique along the following lines (of necessity abbreviated here):

I. The "bitch session" cell group
   A. Ongoing consciousness expansion
      1. Personal recognition and testimony
      2. Personal testimony—methods of group practice
         a. Going around the room with key questions on key topics
         b. Speaking out experience at random
         c. Cross-examination
      3. Relating and generalizing individual testimony

   B. Classic forms of resisting consciousness, *or* How to avoid facing the awful truth:
      Including
         Anti-womanism
         Glorification of the Oppressor
         Excusing or Feeling Sorry for the Oppressor
         Romantic Fantasies
         "An Adequate Personal Solution"
         Self-cultivation, Rugged Individualism
         Self-blame
         Ultra-militancy, etc.

   C. "Starting to stop"—overcoming repressions and delusions

      a. Reasons for repressing one's own consciousness
        1. Fear of feeling one's past wasted and meaningless
        2. Fear of despair for the future, etc.
      b. Analyzing which fears are valid and which invalid
      c. Discussing possible methods of struggle in a historical context, an individual context, and a group context. Daring to share one's experiences with the group

D. Understanding and developing radical feminist theory
Using the above techniques to begin to understand our oppression
Analyzing whatever privileges we have; white skin, education, class, etc. and see how these help perpetuate our oppression and that of others

E. Consciousness-raiser (organizer) training—so that every woman in a given "bitch session" cell group herself becomes an "organizer" in turn, of other groups

II. Consciousness-raising actions

III. Organizing
Helping new people start groups
Intra-group communication and actions
    Monthly meetings
    Conferences

Some groups in the Women's Liberation Movement used consciousness-raising techniques only for a few months before moving into direct actions; others remained primarily talk groups and/or study groups; still others developed along both lines, probably the most healthy combination of "theory correcting practice, practice correcting theory."

In November of 1967, thousands of women participated in the Jeanette Rankin Brigade March on Washington to protest the Vietnam War. There, a group of radical women, alienated by the dignified Establishment aura of the march, split off to discuss the possibilities of building an autonomous women's movement. Over the next year, brought into clearer focus by women's liberation meetings at various "liberated" colleges (such as Columbia, that spring and summer), such a movement began to emerge.

At present, there are women's groups (or cells), some with names, some without, some in confederations, some named after the night on which they meet, in every major city in the United States, and in many cities of secondary and tertiary size. Large cities like New York, Chicago, or Los Angeles tend to have between fifty to two hundred groups alone (New York has over two hundred small groups at last count—and growing rapidly). Every university in which there has been even a modicum of student activity, radical or otherwise, has a women's liberation group already functioning on campus or in formation. High-school women are organizing, and OWL (Older Women's Liberation) has come into existence to meet the needs of those women we tend to dismiss as our mothers until we realize that they're also our sisters. There are women's liberation groups in Canada, England, France, Mexico, Japan, Sweden, Germany, Holland, Finland, Tanzania, Australia, and other countries I'll no doubt hear about the minute it's too late to include them in this Introduction.

Alternative institutions are springing up: women's liberation child-care centers and cooperative nurseries; all-women's communes; halfway houses for women separating, divorcing, or recently widowed; abortion counseling and referral services; women's liberation books, magazines, newspapers and theater groups that can create our own new media, and bail funds to free our political prisoners—among them, prostitutes.

Until recently, the movement seemed to be composed mostly of young white women from middle-class backgrounds (more about this later). But this is beginning to change, partly because the general consciousness about the oppression of women is spreading through all groups and classes, and partly because the women's movement has set itself the task of analyzing divisions (race, class, age, hetero- and homosexuality) that keep us apart from each other, and is working very concretely to break down those divisions.

Black women, who are obviously doubly oppressed, have, for the most part, chosen to fight beside their black brothers, fighting racism as a priority oppression. But male chauvinism is rampant in the Black Liberation Movement, as well, and there are now women's caucuses forming within black organizations. The SNCC Black Women's Liberation Committee was probably the first; groups of women in the Black Panther Party are getting together, too.* Women's liberation cells have, separately and together, been working toward what would be a perfectly organic alliance with welfare rights organizations, which are made up of women, most of whom are black and brown. We share a common root as *women*, much more natural to both groups than the very *machismo* style of male-dominated organizations, black, brown, *and* white.

There are three articles by black sisters in this book written specifically about the oppression of black women; it was important to have more than one or two voices speak for so many sisters, and in differing ways. (This is also the reason for there being three different short pieces on high-school women, and two on female homosexuality. These are all areas in which the women's movement is only beginning to explore itself, and it is of vital importance that we not take a simplistic view about *any* group of women, including ourselves.)

The Women's Liberation Movement is the only radical movement I know of today which is dealing with the issue of class—*on a concrete as well as a theoretical basis.* A number of people have written about the "caste and class" analysis: that women could be class enemies but remain caste sisters. Women function as a caste because we class-climb or class-descend *via* our men, and because, in our inter-class and intra-class functions, we still take our definitions *from* men —and those definitions are always that of appendages. Thus

---

*Two recent developments of major importance are: the new Black Women's Alliance, and the "Machismo is Fascism" statement by Puerto Rican women in the Young Lords Party.

the ruling-class woman has no real power herself—she is merely the exquisitely decorated property of a man rich enough to have one slave who does absolutely nothing. Other people do things for her, and they are, of course, poor black and brown and white women. Nevertheless, it is still the "job" of the upper-class woman to "supervise" these tasks: the menu-planning, endless shopping, genteel hostess routine—which is just a diamond-studded variation of the usual female role.

Caste and class analysis notwithstanding, women from working-class backgrounds have been alienated by what has seemed to be a middle-class women's movement. Only recently, people have begun to discover that the women's movement *is* diverse in class origins. One reason for the previous image was that working-class women are of course compelled to strain after middle-class values (what mothers call "marrying well," and sociologists call "upward mobility"), and to *act* middle-class. We all began to discover that a large percentage of the movement comes from working-class backgrounds. Concurrently, as different small groups began to do consciousness-raising on the issues of class and race, whole new areas of political insight opened up in terms of the different forms of oppression experienced by ourselves and our sisters.

Class oppression clearly was alive and well within the movement itself, and a number of groups took definite steps to confront and change this process. The Feminists, a New York group, was the first to put into operation practices meant to engender real equality within their group. The Feminists found that, despite continually proclaimed sisterhood and egalitarianism, their own group was divided between those women whose class and economic backgrounds had enabled them to get better educations, be more articulate (and therefore dominate meetings), and those women who had been denied such privileges, and who felt (and in reality were) intimidated and easily manipulated by their "better equipped" sisters. This group initiated The Lot System and The Disc System, as attempted remedies for the problem. The Lot System consisted of two sets of lots (for *creative tasks* like writing papers, dealing with the media, attending conferences, etc., and *work tasks*, like answering the mail, getting literature mimeographed, etc.), and each person drew for each task. The two different lots were used so as to make it impossible for anyone to draw the same type twice in a row. The Disc System is an ingenious creation designed to keep some women from monopolizing meetings while others hardly said a word. Each member begins the meeting with a certain number of discs (say, twenty), and every time she speaks, other than to answer a simple "Yes" or "No," she must spend one disc. The first time this system was tried, the apocryphal story goes, no one in the room had any discs left after fifteen minutes. The second meeting was slow almost to silence because everyone was hoarding her discs. Gradually, the device worked its way into everyone's consciousness as a symbol for the need to listen to each other, and not interrupt or monopolize the conversation. It is an important incentive, too, for shy women to learn to speak up. The process is, of course, a continuing one, and the two systems have been adopted by a number of other groups, sometimes with variations of their own. Some other groups reject the systematic approach as being too mechanical, too "gimmicky," and are working in their own ways to create egalitarianism within the group and a collective consciousness as women.

As some of the women who eventually founded the New York Radical Feminists wrote in an earlier leaflet, "Women are the only oppressed people whose biological, emotional, and social life is totally bound to that of the oppressors. We must provide a place for women to be friends, exchange personal griefs, and give their sisters moral support—in short, develop group consciousness."

It is now the spring of 1970. During the past few months,

wildcat strikes by women workers at General Electric, Bendix, and the New York Bell Telephone Company surprised both management and labor; the women felt they had been sold out by the union, which was more concerned about its male members. The first serious woman jockey was pelted by rocks before a major race. Housewives in Stockton, California, went on strike for wages and for a clear definition of their "job"—in writing. Women's caucuses have been formed or are forming in the American Political Science Association, the Anthropological Association, the Modern Language Association, the History Association, and the American Association for the Advancement of Science, among other established professional gatherings. Welfare mothers have been disrupting welfare centers all over the country to protest the bureaucracy that robs them of human dignity. Roman Catholic women are in revolt over the Pill, and Catholic nuns demand greater autonomy from the male clerical hierarchy. Instead of delivering her expected grateful goodbye speech on television, the outgoing Miss USA exposes the commercial way in which she has been used, and denounces her exploiters. Women are marching, picketing, and mounting a variety of actions against abortion laws in every state. Boycotts have been started against billionaire corporations like Procter & Gamble or Lever Brothers, which manipulate women as consumers but are blatantly discriminatory in their own hiring and salary practices. Each television network, and all the major magazines, have had stories on the Women's Liberation Movement—almost all of them written by women because of the movement policy of speaking only to female reporters. Women's Liberation Centers are being set up by local groups all around the country, to try to deal with the women who are pouring into the movement every day. Nurses are organizing. Women in the Armed Forces are organizing. Women have attacked, disrupted, seized, or completely taken over certain media institutions: *Rat* and *High School Free Press*, two major underground radical newspapers, have been

taken over completely by women. *Newsweek* women employees brought suit against the magazine for discrimination in salaries, promotions, and assignments. The "mill-in"
at the *Ladies' Home Journal* gained, if not a liberated *Journal*,
a concession to have at least a liberated supplement in a
future issue of the magazine. And in the first "occupation
and barricade" action done by women, the executive offices
of Grove Press were seized and held for six hours until
police were called in. (The sisters were charged with felo-
nies.) The women at Grove were demanding that the millions of dollars earned from pornographic books that
degrade women go to set up child-care centers for community and working mothers, a bail fund to free prostitutes,
and training programs to prepare women for decent and
well-paying jobs. Other demands were that the huge profits
made from books written by black and Latin American
revolutionaries go to the black and Spanish-speaking communities, to be distributed by the women of those communities.

Meanwhile, a blue-ribbon Presidential panel on the status
of women (a panel headed by, of course, two men!) turned
in a report warning that women were getting angry, and
that unless the government began to act quickly against
sexist discriminatory practices, a new "feminist movement
that preaches revolution" could become a danger to the
established order. Later that month, Nixon solved the
whole problem. He created the first two women generals
(of the Army) and invaded Cambodia, slaughtering students
at Kent State, Augusta, and Jackson on the way. As usual,
the women generals had nothing to say about it; they weren't asked. Col. Jeanne Holmes (the highest ranking
woman in the Air Force) recently wrote that there was a
revolution brewing among women in the military; she implied that any organization that so discriminates within itself (against women) could hardly be other than oppressive
in its general policies.

We know that it is not enough to look around in awe at

the rising tide of anger over the lack of "women's rights." We know that we want something more, much more, than the same gray, meaningless, alienating jobs that men are forced to sacrifice their lives to—on the contrary, the technology is such that, if we weren't concerned with sending back color pictures from the moon and were concerned with putting machines to work creatively, no one would have to do those jobs, and no one would have to starve without them. We know that the vote proved useless for our needs (perhaps for those of men, too). We know that the so-called sexual revolution was only another new form of oppression for women. The invention of the Pill made millions for the drug companies, made guinea pigs of us, and made us all the more "available" as sexual objects; if a woman didn't want to go to bed with a man *now*, she must be hung-up. It was inconceivable, naturally, that she might not like the man, or the Pill, or for that matter, sex. We know that "hip culture" and "radical life style"—whatever those mean—have been hip and radical for the men, but filled with the same old chores, harassment, and bottling-up of inner rage for the women, as usual.

But what *do* we want? That's what they always ask us, as if they had expected us, like tidy housekeepers, to come up in five short years with the magic remedy cleanser that will wipe clean the unbelievable mess men have created from their position of power during the past five thousand years.

We're beginning to grope toward some analyses that feel right. We know that two evils clearly pre-date corporate capitalism, and have post-dated socialist revolutions: *sexism* and *racism*—so we know that a male-dominated socialist revolution in economic and even cultural terms, were it to occur tomorrow, would be *no* revolution, but only another coup d'état among men. We know that many historians, scientists, and anthropologists (among them, Briffault, Morgan, Mead, Levi-Strauss, Childe, Montague, Gorer, and Benedict) note a connection between the concept of property-ownership (primitive capitalism) and the oppression of women. Anthropology has also taught us that women probably invented agriculture, were the first to domesticate animals, invented the concept of weaving and of pottery, and (according to Gordon Childe) invented language, which filled a need in their communal work (rather than the necessary silence of the hunters). Anthropologists continue to turn up examples which prove that competitive, aggressive, warlike cultures are those in which sexual stereotypes are most polarized, while those social structures allowing for an overlap of roles and functions between men and women (in tasks, childrearing, decision-making, etc.) tend to be collectivist, cooperative, and peaceful. There are numerous theories about early matriarchal societies, and how and when they were overthrown; some of these are explored elsewhere in this anthology.

One thing does seem clearer as time goes on: the nuclear family unit is oppressive to women (*and* children, *and* men). The woman is forced into a totally dependent position, paying for her keep with an enormous amount of emotional and physical labor which is not even considered work. As Margaret Benston points out, "In sheer quantity, household labor, including child care, constitutes a huge amount of socially necessary production. Nevertheless, in a society based on commodity production, it is not usually considered as 'real work' since it is outside of trade and the marketplace ... In a society in which money determines value, women are a group who work outside the money economy." In essence, women are still back in feudal times.We work outside capitalism, as unpaid labor—and it is the structure of the family that makes this possible, since the employer pays only the husband and, in fact, gets the rest of the family's services for free. (The word "family" comes from the Oscan *famel*, a servant, slave, or possession. The word "father"—*pater*—means owner, possessor, master. The Roman *pater familias* was thus an "owner of slaves." It is a phrase we use with affection even today.) Well over a hundred years ago, Alexis de Tocqueville, on visiting the United States, wrote that it seemed to him a "spermatic economy," revolving totally around its men and isolating its women to the functions of either ornament or workhorse. It's an apt description for 1970.

But if the family as it now exists, with its paranoiac possessiveness of wife and of children, its isolation, and its plain unviability (one out of three American marriages ends in divorce), if this family disappears, what will it be replaced with, and who will determine that? It's obvious that when men think up alternatives (such as divorce or "just living together" or communal living) those alternatives have been know to royally louse women up, so that this time we must create the alternatives that *we* want, those we imagine to be in our self-interest. I, for one, think that some form of extended family structure (something like the old Jewish or Italian families, though not along blood lines, but living companions of choice) might be an answer. The way in which women have so far been used in "alternate culture" communes, however, has made me extremely wary. Instead of cooking Betty Crocker casseroles in Scarsdale, she's stirring brown rice in Arizona or on the Lower East Side, and instead of being the "property" of one man, she's now the "property" of all the men in the collective. It's a thoroughly terrifying subject to explore: what *are* our alternatives?

No one, clearly, has any answers yet, although a host of possibilities present themselves to confuse us all even further. Living alone? Living in mixed communes with men and women? Living in all-women communes? Having children? Not having children? Raising them collectively, or in the old family structure? The father and/or other men sharing equally in child care, or shouldering it entirely, or not being permitted any participation? Homosexuality as a viable political alternative which straight women must begin to recognize as such? More—homosexuality, or bisexuality, as a beautiful affirmation of human *sexuality*, without all those absurd prefixes? Test-tube births? Masturbation? Womb transplants? Gender control of the fetus? (*That* is an appalling idea in the context of a male-supremacist society such as our current one—in which everyone would prefer having boy babies, while females would be bred only to be further breeders!) Parthenogenesis? Why? Why not?

It has made me slightly dizzy trying to list them all—and I must have missed some—and there are others not even dreamed of yet. The only thing I know for certain is that *this* time we women must seize control over our own lives and try, in the process, to salvage the planet from the ecological disaster and nuclear threat created by male-oriented power nations. It is not a small job, and it does seem as if women's work is never done.

Meanwhile, a worldwide revolution is already taking place: Third World peoples, black and brown peoples, are rising up and demanding an end to their neo-colonial status under the economic empire of the United States. The blood of Vietnam, Laos, and Cambodia is mixing with the blood of Jackson, Watts, and Detroit. *How,* we are asked, *can you talk about the comparatively insignificant oppression of women, when set beside the issues of racism and imperialism?*

This is a male-supremacist question. Not only because of its arrogance, but because of its ignorance. First, it dares to weigh and compute human suffering, and it places oppressed groups in competition with each other (an old, and very capitalistic, trick: divide and conquer). Second, the question fails to even minimally grasp the profoundly radical analysis beginning to emerge from revolutionary feminism: that capitalism, imperialism, and racism are *symptoms* of male supremacy—sexism.

Racism as a major contradiction, for example, is surely based on the first "alienizing" act: the basic primary contradiction that occurred with the enslavement of half the human species by the other half. I think it no coincidence that all the myths of creation, in all religions, have to do with a "fall from grace" simultaneously with the emergence of set sexual roles.

It also seems obvious that half of all oppressed peoples,

black, brown, and otherwise, are *women,* and that I, as a not-starving white American woman living in the very belly of the beast, must fight for those sisters to *survive* before we can even talk together as oppressed women. (Example: in Biafra, most of the millions who died of starvation were women and children. But men were well-fed, since the army needed them kept in good fighting health. That is the essence of male thinking at its most arrogant, *machismo,* militaristic, and *patr*iotic. That is sexism.)

More and more, I begin to think of a worldwide Women's Revolution as the only hope for life on the planet. It follows, then, that where women's liberation is, *there* is, for me, the genuine radical movement; I can no more countenance the co-optive lip-service of the male-dominated Left which still stinks of male supremacy than I can countenance the class bias and racism of that male "Movement." I haven't the faintest notion what possible revolutionary role white heterosexual men could fulfill, since they are the very embodiment of reactionary-vested-interest-power. But then, I have great difficulty examining what men in general could possibly do about all this. In addition to doing the shitwork that women have been doing for generations, possibly not exist? No, I really don't mean that. Yes, I really do. Never mind, that's another whole book.

What I began to say earlier, though, was that the differences between "politico" and "feminist" women (as with other divisions of class, race, age, occupation, etc.) are possibly smokescreens, defenses from seeing a frightening truth, resistances to a consciousness that no matter what we are, say, do, or believe, there is no getting away from the shared, primary oppression of being female in a patriarchal world.

You, sister, reading this: I have no earthly way of knowing if you are already involved in women's liberation, and if so, how deeply; perhaps you have never yet been to one women's meeting, but only read and heard things about the movement in magazines and on TV; perhaps you find you have picked up the book out of anger, or defiance, or on a dare, or from genuine curiosity, or cynical amusement—or even as part of your job or your school course. I hope this book means something to you, makes some real change in your heart and head—and I take a terrific risk in saying such a corny thing, because I don't mean it as any sort of "hope you liked the book" statement. No, I mean it desperately, because if we who have put this together have failed you somehow, then we have failed ourselves seriously—because *you* are women's liberation. This is not a movement one "joins." There are no rigid structures or membership cards. The Women's Liberation Movement exists where three or four friends or neighbors decide to meet regularly over coffee and talk about their personal lives. It also exists in the cells of women's jails, on the welfare lines, in the supermarket, the factory, the convent, the farm, the maternity ward, the streetcorner, the old ladies' home, the kitchen, the steno pool, the bed. It exists in your mind, and in the political and personal insights that you can contribute to change and shape and help its growth. It is frightening. It is very exhilarating. It is creating history, or rather, *herstory.*

And anyway, you cannot escape it.

Last week, a woman I had known and worked with, went underground. The following message is meant for her, for myself, and for you.

Letter To A Sister Underground

Dear Jane:

It's funny, now, to write like this:
a letter I don't even dare shape like one
(not that you'll probably ever read it, which may be
the reason it can now be written);
sprawled in a prosey poem
unlike the poems you often asked to see
but which I somehow never brought around.
Well, it's a poem, or non-poem, because

I don't write what I once called poems anymore—
the well-wrought kind that you and I
might once have critically discussed over a gentle lunch
where we were both in former incarnations "bright young
editors."
Instead, I write, or try to, between actions
(which hardly leaves much time but that's okay)
things about women, my sisters and myself
in the hope that some small ticking insight
from the page which is the one place I don't lie
ignites a fuse of righteous bitterness
in a woman (my sister or myself)
that can flash into an action no one—least of all me—
could have foreseen erupting.
One thing I know:
there is no atom that is not political,
and poetry can be quite dangerous propaganda,
especially since all worthwhile propaganda
ought to move its readers like a poem.
Graffiti do that; so do some songs,
and rarely, poems on a page.

I should say, though, there's something probably
very "incorrect" here: this non-poem non-letter
ought to go unsigned and
ought to be addressed to Pat Swinton,
Mary Moylan, Bernardine Dohrn, the double Kathys,
and all the other so-called 'women underground'—
except that Women's Liberation has taught me
not to be afraid
of being incorrect, and most of all, of being personal.
Some of those sisters I never met at all
and of the ones I know, I know you best.
So fuck it, I'll be personal.

The other point—which is the reason (good as any other)
for this message cast adrift in a bottle sent to
where you never would be anyway even if I did know
where you are which couldn't matter less
is that it doesn't mean one damn disguise
which woman I address this to, or how I sign it,
since all of us are underground.
Each sister wearing masks of Revlonclairolplaytex
does it to survive.

Each sister faking orgasm under the System's very concrete bulk
at night, does it to survive.

Our smiles and glances,
the ways we walk, sit, laugh, the games we must play
with men and even oh my Ancient Mother God the games
we must play among ourselves—these are the ways we pass
unnoticed, by the Conquerors.
They're always watching,
invisibly electroded in our brains,
to be certain we implode our rage against each other
and not explode it against them:
the times we rip and tear at the twin
for what we have intricately defended in ourselves;
the mimicry of male hierarchy, male ego,
male possessiveness, leader/follower, doer/thinker, butch/femme
yes also when we finally learn to love each other physically.
Roles to survive a death-in-life until
that kind of life becomes worthless enough
to risk losing even precious It.

Yesterday, Margaret Mead,
(who was one of my earliest heroes,
for what she learned and wrote about women
in other cultures, for how she proved that we
are not inherently submissive types),
yesterday, in some bullshit seminar
on Women for Peace in Southeast Asia
which some of us had turned into a rap on women and revolution,
Margaret Mead swept in and yelled at me that
women were perhaps inherently so violent that there's
no evidence we might ever stop if we began to kill.
Therefore, the eminent sister had concluded,
this women's revolution must not take place,
we ought not to provoke (dig that) men to be violent
against us, and ought not to unleash our own just anger
at our own oppression. This revolution-talk
in general upsets her: we might be bringing fascism
down upon us—blacks, Latins, Asians, but especially
women, are provoking fascism. My early hero
now writes regularly for *Redbook*, to survive, no doubt.
Still, she knows, *she knows,*
that women are underground,
thousands of years in hiding, and only now

beginning to surface. Ready.

Our subterranean grapevine, which men, like fools, call gossip,
has always been efficient.
Our sabotage has ranged from witches' research
into herbal poisons to secretaries' spilling coffee on the files
to housewives' passive resistance
in front of their soap-opera screens
to housemaids' accidentally breaking china
to mothers' teaching their children to love *them*
a little bit better than their fathers. And more.
Our rebellions, like the Turkish harem revolts,
have been (as was Nat Turner's) frequent, brave,
isolated one from the other, bloody—and buried,
both in reality and in the history books.
Each time we went into the exile of our women's lives again,
changed our faces and bodies and voices (that's called Fashion),
and passed.
Each time we went back to whispering and waiting.
Each time social change broke across men, we called out,
only to get back each time a reply

rape, beatings, murder, desertion, ridicule, or loving concern

that, in essence, women should be seen and not heard.
At last, when the man has all but destroyed Our species,
Our sister earth, Our children that we made in Our own holy
bodies,
at last we are beginning to be shrill as banshees
and to act.
To be heard and not seen?
There is an ancient Chinese proverb, long long before
Mao's Quotations, that says
    A man should be careful not to arouse the anger of a woman,
    for he has to sleep sometime—and with his eyes closed.

I remember our ongoing dialectic
(which confused a lot of people—most of all, us)
as it groped its ungainly way toward trust:
you, a "politico"; me, a "feminist";
both of us, after all, just women.
Because what you were really forced to plead guilty to
was the crime of being female and daring to dislike the role.
Because you would be put in a separate prison from the man
you love/hate,

and I am put in the same cage with the man
I love/hate.
Because you once said you knew you were "a mercenary
in someone else's revolution—that of men—
paid with the coin of male approval,"
but that you had to move right now in any way you could,
even if that way was not your own fight
and even if some of your sisters would rather
be volunteers in our own people's army,
whatever that might mean (including everything),
now and later.
Because I mourned that we seemed to have just missed
each other in time—
except that it all becomes whole eventually, you know,
and I look forward to our meeting on the same side
of some totally unexpected barricade, as enlistees of course,
each carrying the one weapon the other most needed at that
moment.

Perhaps it's unfair, or at least indiscreet,
to say all these things now,
but all's fair in love and war,
and this is both.

How to close such a message?
I miss you.
We are all as well as can be expected.
Hope you are fine and
having a wonderful time.
Don't send a picture postcard when you can.
Stay hidden.
Come back to us.
We'll join you.
Don't accept rides from strange men,
and remember that all men are strange as hell.
Think of us sometimes, my sister.
Forget us, my friend.
Watch for me when you look in the mirror;
I see you all the time.
Take care of ourselves.
See you soon.
            In sisterhood, in struggle,
                    and all that,
            but mostly because

I think I love you,

Robin

P.S. : I dreamt the other night
that Blake was *your* baby, whom you'd left
for safekeeping with us. It's true, you know.

May 1970 New York City

sisterhood
is powerful

AN ANTHOLOGY

OF WRITINGS

FROM THE WOMEN'S

LIBERATION MOVEMENT

"YOU'VE COME A LONG WAY, BABY": HISTORICAL PERSPECTIVES

Connie Brown and Jane Seitz

The difficulty of learning about the history of women in America is that, for the most part, it is an unwritten history of millions of private lives, whose voices, those that were recorded at all, are scattered and buried in journals and letters. It isn't hard to find out what men thought of us—their ideas about women are accessible through the laws they passed and maintained, denying or restricting women's civil and property rights, through the religions they organized and practiced, through their literature. Women did write novels, essays, poems, magazine articles, but most of these are long out of print, and the task of digging up those old sources is still ahead of us.

There is the exception, of course, of the women's rights movement, which belongs to recorded history. Although, like the history of black people, it has long been suppressed, its documents—letters, speeches, newspapers, tracts—are available in various libraries and collections, and allow us a direct contact with the lives and the ideas of the nineteenth-century feminists. Because those women stepped out of private life into the public arena where recorded events take place, they created for us a brief "history," recognized by men in their books. (The Beards' *Basic History of the United States* has almost ten pages on the women's rights movement!)

But that movement is only a small part of our history. We need to know much more—about the women on plantations, on the lonely farms, in factories, schools, labor unions —in order to reclaim our past from obscurity, to rediscover our heroines, to understand our present. Our historical introduction to this anthology is necessarily superficial. It is written for other women as an introduction to the idea that we *have* a history.

> Man and wife are one person, but understand in what manner. When a small brooke or little river incorporateth with Rhodanus or the Thames, the poor rivulet looseth its name, it is carried and recarried with the new associate, it beareth no sway, it possetheth nothing during coverture . . . To a married woman, her new self is her superior, her companion, her master.

This poetic description of the status of married women comes from seventeenth-century British Common Law. The law itself, and the view of women it implied, defined the legal position of women in America from the arrival of the first settlers until well into the second half of the nineteenth century. Woman's intellectual and physical inferiority to man was taken for granted. God and nature had clearly ordained her social inferiority.

Whatever their class origin in England, whatever their motivation for coming to the Colonies, the lives of the early settlers in America were shaped by the severe difficulties of survival. There was endless work to be done, and women worked to the limit of their strength beside their husbands, planting, harvesting, tending stock, as well as doing their traditional work of cooking, spinning, weaving and sewing. It was only later, as the country expanded and the population grew, that the activities and status of women underwent modification according to geographic region, class position, and the demands of a changing economy.

New England, until well after the Revolution, was a place of small self-sufficient farms and towns, where life was dominated by the church and its Puritan theology, expressed in secular terms by the Protestant ethic. Man must work as hard as he can and if he is among God's elect, his efforts will be rewarded with earthly success. He must not squander such rewards, however, but return his profits to his enterprise and thus continue to earn further rewards. Sexuality, which would have threatened the singleminded drive of the community, indeed sensuality of any kind, was condemned as sinful. Women who did their duty had much to look forward to in Heaven, and on earth they played a vital role that went far beyond child rearing and housekeeping.

On a family farm the boundary between home and the fields, between men's and women's spheres, was indistinct, and productive work was done in both. There was no distinction between breadwinner and dependent consumers, and prestige attaching to work was more evenly divided between men and women than later, when industrialization brought about a separation between home and productive work. Thus, Mollie Pitcher, Deborah Garnett, and the hundreds of women who, during the Revolutionary War, formed anti-tea leagues, attacked stores where merchants hoarded scarce necessities, even picked up guns and fought, were respectable representatives of a tradition which provided, within the strict limitations of female propriety, room for a woman to be self-reliant and brave.

In that time however, and especially in the New England colonies, for a woman to deviate from her assigned role either sexually or intellectually was to violate the word of God as interpreted by the male-dominated church, and to risk the vengeance of the small, unified community she lived in. The punishment would be the scarlet letter, hanging in Salem, or the religious exile to which the church and civil courts of the Massachusetts Bay Colony sentenced Anne Hutchinson, when the influence of her quiet preaching about the primacy of individual conscience and the "indwelling Christ" threatened their rigid hierarchy. A woman's well-being depended on finding a kind and solvent husband, and avoiding scandal. In 1775, Thomas Paine wrote:

> Even in countries where they may be esteemed the most happy, [women are] constrained in their desires in the disposal of their goods, robbed of freedom and will by the laws, the slaves of opinion, which rules them with absolute sway and construes the slightest appearances into guilt; surrounded on all sides by judges who are at once tyrants and their seducers.

After the turn of the century, with industrialization and expansion, the moral strictures of the founding Puritans came to have less influence over men. The pursuit of money and power took time, and they spent more and more hours away from home, expecting from their wives, nonetheless, service without question or competition.

While the work and family patterns of the American man were changing, so were the demands on the American woman. In Colonial times, women ran self-sufficient domestic factories, producing, among other things, clothes, candles, soap, quilts and mattresses. With industrialization, however, and the adoption of such inventions as the spinning jenny and the power loom, women's energies and talents were increasingly exploited for profit. Many industries employed women, some in the home, some in the factories, and especially as the migration westward produced shortages of manpower. The owners of spinning and weaving factories sought out women and children in the belief that their smaller hands were more suited to the work than those of men. These women, typically, were underpaid. According to an account in the *Boston Courier* in 1829, women earned only one-fourth what men did:

Competition for the few places left open to her has occasioned a reduction in the estimated value of her labor, utility has fallen below the minimum and is no longer adequate to present comfortable subsistence much less to the necessary provision against age and infirmity, or the everyday contingencies of morality.

In 1833, women working at home earned as little as $1.25 per week; annual income for a woman was as little as $58.50 for full-time work. In the mills, work often began at 4:30 A.M. and continued until sunset. Women and children in these factories earned from $1.00 to $3.00 per week minus a boarding fee for lodgings provided by the companies.

To add to the troubles of the woman worker, the idea remained fixed that the real and happy province of the woman was the home. Despite long and arduous labors at a job, a woman was expected to assume household chores, thus fulfilling her "natural role" as wife and mother. If she were exhausted by leading both lives, her exhaustion was an expression of the natural physical inferiority of women.

Beginning in the 1820's, many short-lived organizations for home-working women were formed, such as the United Tailoresses Society of New York and the Lady Shoe Binders of Lynn, Massachusetts. These early efforts failed at least in part because the women, isolated and inexperienced, received little support from the men's groups of their trade and even less support from their own male relations.

Some women managed to survive the battle: the first strike by women took place in Pawtucket, Rhode Island, in 1824, and these women were joined by men with similar grievances. Dover, New Hampshire, was the scene of another women-led strike. The feelings of the factory women are represented in this strike song sung by the women workers in Lowell, Massachusetts, in 1845:

Oh, isn't it a pity, such a pretty girl as I
Should be sent into a factory to pine away and die?
Oh I cannot be a slave

I will not be a slave
For I'm so fond of liberty
That I cannot be a slave

Though women continued to strike, they were poorly organized and they accomplished little. Sarah Bagley, a mill-worker of Lowell, Massachusetts, was one of the first women to attempt to organize women workers on a large scale. Through newspaper articles and public speeches, she aroused and mobilized women in other mills. To company officials' attacks she replied:

> What! Deprive us, after working thirteen hours, of the poor privilege of finding fault—of saying our lot is a hard one . . . We will make the name of him who dares the act, stink with every wind, from all points of the compass. His name shall be a by-word among all laboring men, and he shall be hissed in the streets, and in all the cities of this widespread republic, for our name is legion though our oppression is great.

By 1846, Mrs. Bagley's followers were recognized by laboring men, and three women became directors, along with five men, of the New England Labor Reform League. These women, rejecting the conventions of public propriety, effectively testified before the first Massachusetts legislative committee on labor. Though Sarah Bagley's group made little progress against the politicians and factory owners, its efforts were part of a long battle which ultimately achieved some benefits for women. Nonetheless, women who work in factories today are still paid substantially less than men.

The development in the Southern colonies of tobacco, and later cotton, plantations provided different roles, and a different image for women. Unlike the hardworking Puritan women of New England, the wives of planters lived in leisure, and devoted their time to domestic management and to hospitable functions—a luxury made possible, of course, by slave labor, particularly that of the black women who raised the children and did the housework. It is difficult to separate fact from male fantasy in describing the lives of Southern white women. The well-known elevated image of woman as the center and focus of the larger myth of Southern chivalry resulted in what W. J. Cash calls:

> . . . downright gyneolatry. She was the South's palladium, this Southern woman—the shield-bearing Athena gleaming whitely in the clouds, the standard for its rallying, the mystic symbol of its nationality in face of the foe . . . Merely to mention her was to send strong men into tears—or shouts . . .
> "Woman!!!! The center and circumference, diameter and periphery, *sine tangent* and *secant* of all our affections!" Such was the toast which brought twenty great cheers from the audience at the celebration of Georgia's one-hundredth anniversary in the 1830's.[1]

Undoubtedly, the feeling invested in this worship of white women owes its fervor and its religious quality partly to the white men's "guilty conscience" over forcibly taking their pleasure on their female slaves. It is significant also that this romanticized image arose in literature, particularly in a rash of sentimental plantation novels, simultaneously with the growth in the North of abolitionism and the beginnings of feminism. In a study of Southern plantation ideology, William Taylor says:

> . . . it is impossible to read widely in the literature of the South without gaining the impression that Southern women in a certain sense were being bought off, offered half a loaf in the hope that they would not demand more. One or two incidents, such as the defection of the aristocratic Grimké sisters of Charleston to abolition and militant feminism, were widely commented upon, but the strait jacket of rigid convention in which Southern women lived, and men knew they lived, probably composed the principal threat. Stripped to its barest essentials the deference shown to them in the form of Southern chivalry was the deference ordinarily shown to an honored but distrusted servant.[2]

Whatever the uses of the myth, the percentage of South-

---

1. W. J. Cash, *The Mind of the South* (New York: Vintage Books), p. 89.
2. William Taylor, *Cavalier and Yankee* (New York: Anchor Books, 1961), p. 72.

ern women who were well-born or well-married enough to find a spot on the pedestal was, of course, small. But the myth, particularly after the Civil War, served the important social and political purpose of giving white men of all classes an object to protect against the imagined lust of the black man, at once reinforcing and justifying a vicious racism. A white woman who, lined and haggard at thirty, had worked eighteen hours a day and borne child after child, was still perched, in her man's imagination, on the pedestal, with a black male hand reaching for her. To protect her virtue was the focus and rationale for the poorest white sharecropper's fear and hatred of a black man who, poor as himself, perhaps farmed the land of the same plantation owner.

During the first half of the nineteenth century thousands of families left their Eastern homes to follow the frontier westward. As in early Colonial times women had to work long hours beside their husbands, cultivating the land, as well as doing housework, cooking, spinning, weaving, and sewing.

The rigid moral doctrine which had governed the patriarchal Puritan family had been diluted over two centuries. Unlike the close and homogeneous community of the Puritans, the frontier was settled by isolated families from a wide variety of backgrounds. In this atmosphere of social mobility, where a wife was likely to be chosen for her strength and skill, where life was dangerous and widows were often left to run a farm alone, women gained some new advantages. Most Western states did not duplicate Eastern laws prohibiting women from owning property, and they were the first to grant state suffrage to women.

These indications of greater freedom for frontier women should not, however, be exaggerated. All values in this rough, if more egalitarian, society were established by men, and women were expected to conform to their definitions. Serious matters were masculine matters and were discussed by the men in the saloons of the West, which only a "bad" woman would enter.

European travelers to the United States, accustomed to a great deal of social mingling of the sexes, at least in their upper classes, remarked on the peculiar social segregation of men from women in all parts of America. Mrs. Trollope, an Englishwoman who spent several years in Cincinnati in the 1820's, remarked that:

> In America, with the exception of dancing, which is almost wholly confined to the unmarried of both sexes, all the enjoyments of the men are found in the absence of the women. They dine, they play cards, they have musical meetings, they have suppers, all in large parties, but all without women.[3]

Mrs. Trollope found that American men of all classes were obsessed solely with politics and making money, activities from which women were, of course, excluded even more strictly than from male social life. Women were occupied with housework, and with religion, the one province they were allowed, even encouraged, to explore. The astonishing multiplication of religious sects and cults which swept the entire country during the first half of the nineteenth century was the immediate result of this channelling of women's energies. Mrs. Trollope's description of an Indiana camp meeting, although not flattering to the women whose prayers she witnessed, suggests their profound mental and physical frustration, and shows how cynically these misdirected outpourings were used by male preachers:

> . . . about a hundred persons, nearly all females, came forward uttering howlings and groans so terrible that I shall never cease to shudder when I recall them. They appeared to drag each other forward, and on the word being given "let us pray" they all fell on their knees; but this posture was soon changed for others that permitted greater scope for the convulsive movement of their limbs; and they were soon all lying on the ground in an indescribable confusion of heads and legs. They threw about their limbs with such incessant and violent motion, that I was every instant expecting some serious accident to occur . . . Hysterical sobbings, convulsive groans, shrieks, and

3. Frances Trollope, *Domestic Manners of the Americans* (New York: Vintage Books, 1960), p. 156.

screams of the most appalling sort burst forth on all sides. Many of these wretched creatures were beautiful young females. The preachers moved about among them, at once exciting and soothing their agonies. I heard the muttered "sister, dear sister." I saw the insidious lips approach the cheeks of the unhappy girls.[4]

The trend toward increased democratization in the first half of the nineteenth century, the expanding frontier and the migration of country people to cities which accompanied industrialization, combined to produce a crisis of identity among statesmen, writers, clergymen, professionals—those who saw themselves as the inheritors and interpreters of the new republic. What were to be the limitations on individual enterprise? What were to be the civilizing influences on the wild frontier? What was to be the rationalization for the blood-sucking plantation system now expanding into Missouri, Arkansas, Texas? The stern Puritan had been transformed into the rapacious Yankee businessman, while the aristocratic Virginia gentleman was declining into effete libertinism. If the mercenary and self-aggrandizing impulse which was behind the rapid expansion of the country and its economy were to go unchecked—what then would become of the high principles on which the country claimed its legitimacy?

An answer of sorts, if not a satisfactory one, was found in Woman. In novels, in sermons, in political speeches, in popular magazines such as Sarah Hale's *Godey Ladies' Book*, woman was seen as the source of all those virtues which could hold within bounds the necessary but dangerous instincts of acquisitiveness in men. In a circular way, woman in her sanctified family domain became not only the restraining moral force on men's greed, but the justification of and excuse for that impulse. Some women, perhaps most, accepted this glorification, unprecedented in American history, and accepted the confined and tedious existence it implied. But some did not.

4. *Ibid.*, pp. 172–173.

If Woman, as guardian of the hearth, carrier of tradition, influencer of morality, became a salve for men's consciences and a symbol of stability in a turbulent time, the same social turbulence had the effect of raising questions, in the minds of some women, about that image. In the 1830's, a period of expanding democratic rights for white men, the women's rights movement had its beginning.

Even in this atmosphere of questioning, however, the women's rights movement did not emerge at first as a self-conscious, independent movement. It had its immediate origins in another search for human rights—abolitionism. Excluded from the anti-slavery societies which were proliferating in the 1830's in the towns of New England, in New York, and in Philadelphia, women formed their own societies, and thus had their first experience in organizing and public speaking. Although the role that countless women played in the operation of the underground railway, harboring and transporting runaway slaves, required courage and ingenuity, their entrance into public affairs called for a defiance of prejudices deeply entrenched in themselves, as well as in the society, that was perhaps more taxing to them than physical danger. Women simply did not speak in public. With the exception of the Quakers, who allowed women to speak freely in Meeting, and ordained them as ministers, churches continued to practice the rule of St. Paul: "Let the women learn in silence with all subjection . . . I suffer not a woman to teach, nor to usurp authority over men, but to be in silence." However glorified by preachers and politicians in their "proper sphere," women were scolded, ridiculed and stoned when they attempted to transcend it by speaking against slavery.

Two sisters from a North Carolina slave-holding family, Sarah and Angelina Grimké, were the first to take that step. After moving to Philadelphia and becoming Quakers, they began to write anti-slavery articles, and then to accept invitations to address women's groups. Soon they were speaking publicly to large mixed audiences. A typical response

was this Pastoral Letter from the Council of Congregation-
alist Ministers of Massachusetts:

> We invite your attention to the dangers which at present seem
> to threaten the female character with widespread and perma-
> nent injury. The appropriate duties and influence of women are
> clearly stated in the New Testament . . . The power of woman
> is her dependence, flowing from the consciousness of that
> weakness which God has given her for her protection.
> We appreciate the unostentatious prayers of woman in ad-
> vancing the cause of religion at home and abroad . . . and in all
> such associated efforts as become the modesty of her sex . . . But
> when she assumes the place and tone of man as a public re-
> former . . . she yields the power which God has given her for
> her protection, and her character becomes unnatural. If the
> vine, whose strength and beauty is to lean on the trellis-work,
> and half conceal its cluster, thinks to assume the independence
> and the overshadowing nature of the elm, it will not only cease
> to bear fruit, but fall in shame and dishonor in to the dust.[5]

The Grimké sisters took these attacks seriously, being
religious women themselves, and explained at length how
Christ's teachings had been misinterpreted by men to oppress women. Their central interest at first was in the abolition of slavery, and they saw their own oppression as
women as an obstacle to accomplishing their real work. "I
ask no favors for my sex. I surrender not our claim to equality. All I ask of our brethren is that they will take their feet
from off our necks, and permit us to stand upright on the
ground which God has designed us to occupy."[6]

Following the example of these sisters, women began in
large numbers to speak, to organize meetings, and to carry
on petition drives. And the hostility aroused by the combination of outrages—abolitionism and women talking about
it—taught them to recognize their own oppression in the
image of the slave: "The investigation of the rights of the
slave have led me to a better understanding of my own. I
have found the anti-slavery cause to be the high school of

---

5. Eleanor Flexner, *Century of Struggle* (Cambridge: Belknap Press, 1968) p. 45.
6. *Ibid.*, p. 47.

morals in our land—the school in which *human rights* are more fully investigated, and better understood and taught, than any other."[7]

The possibility of a new view of a woman's proper role was one of the important effects of the work of such heroic black women as Harriet Tubman and Sojourner Truth, who, in their fight against slavery, transcended the traditional boundaries of their sex to such an extent that Harriet Tubman, in her work on the underground railroad, became by reputation a mythical figure of unknown sex, known only as "Moses."

The women's rights movement had its official beginning in 1848, when several hundred women and sympathetic men met at Seneca Falls in upstate New York for a convention called by two active abolitionists, Elizabeth Cady Stanton and Lucretia Mott. The Seneca Falls Declaration of Rights and Sentiments remained for years the single most important document for the women's movement, and still speaks eloquently more than a century later:

> The history of mankind is a history of repeated injuries and usurpations on the part of men toward women, having in direct object the establishment of an absolute tyranny over her. To prove this, let facts be submitted to a candid world.
>
> He has never permitted her to exercise her inalienable right to the elective franchise.
>
> He has compelled her to submit to laws, in the formation of which she has no voice . . .
>
> Having deprived her of this first right of a citizen, the elective franchise, thereby leaving her without representation in the halls of legislation, he has oppressed her on all sides.
>
> He has made her, if married, in the eye of the law, civilly dead.
>
> He has taken from her all right in property, even to the wages she earns.
>
> . . . In the covenant of marriage, she is compelled to promise obedience to her husband, he becoming, to all intents and pur-

7. In Aileen Kraditor, *Up From the Pedestal*, (Chicago: Quadrangle Books, 1968), p. 62.

poses, her master—the law giving him power to deprive her of her liberty, and to administer chastisement.

. . . He has monopolized nearly all the profitable employ-ments, and from those she is permitted to follow, she receives but a scanty remuneration. He closes against her all the avenues to wealth and distinction which he considers most honorable to himself. As a teacher of theology, medicine, or law, she is not known.

. . . He has created a false public sentiment by giving to the world a different code of morals for men and women, by which moral delinquencies which exclude women from society, are not only tolerated, but deemed of little account in men.

He has usurped the prerogative of Jehovah himself, claiming it as his right to assign to her a sphere of action, when that belongs to her conscience and to her God. . .

He has endeavored, in every way he could, to destroy her confidence in her own powers, to lessen her self-respect, and to make her willing to lead an abject and dependent life.

The Seneca Falls Declaration is couched in the typical enlightenment terms of basic and inalienable human rights. Its language is that of the Declaration of Independence, on which it was modeled. It gives a clear picture of women's civil status at the time it was written, and at the same time protests the psychological subjugation of women by men. Its program is an attack on the laws and customs that deny full citizenship and equal economic opportunity to women. Although it conveys a vivid sense of the depth, pervasive-ness, and subtlety of women's oppression, as well as of its legal manifestations, it conspicuously avoids an analysis of the family, and of the connection between women's pri-mary responsibilities there, and her exclusion from public life. To question the sacred rightness of the family, and women's place in it, would have brought upon these women a storm of outrage far beyond what they actually suffered. Feminist imagination, which envisaged radically new forms of dress, rebelled at the traditional marriage ceremony and the surrender of the maiden name, attacked established reli-gion and male dominance of education and the professions —the fearless feminist imagination balked at an attack on the family. Although the early feminists can not be accused of the mistake of the later ones in concentrating solely on the ballot as the key to equality, they dared only to insist on sharing public life with men—not to insist on men's sharing the burdens of home and family.

The Civil War and Reconstruction were periods of great social upheaval, and forced record numbers of women into positions away from home. In both North and South, farms and factories functioned because of female labor. The enormous growth of industry due to the demands of a country at war created a new need for workers, and women went to work in greater and greater numbers. For the first time, women entered government office jobs in large numbers, and became a majority in the teaching profession.

The changes wrought in the society by the war made it impossible for women to return to their pre-war ideas and occupations. Many women had proved their capabilities to themselves and others, and they began to expand their movement and their fight. Led by Susan B. Anthony, Elizabeth Cady Stanton, and Lucy Stone, they gradually brought about changes in the laws prohibiting women to hold property, sue and be sued in court, and those laws which gave men complete sovereignty over their wives and children. At the same time, women entered the professions. Mount Holyoke, the first college for women, was established, and Smith, Vassar, and Bryn Mawr followed soon thereafter.

Until the outbreak of the Civil War, the women's movement continued to draw strength from the abolitionist movement, and to be closely associated with it spiritually and organizationally. During the war itself, most feminist agitation ceased while the women worked for victory for the North. However, if the feminists temporarily lent their energies to what they felt was a "larger cause," the ground was being prepared for a new growth of feminism after the war.

The most prominent organizations devoted to women's rights—the militant National Women's Suffrage Associa-

tion (NWSA), headed by Elizabeth Cady Stanton and Susan
B. Anthony, and the more respectable American Woman
Suffrage Association (AWSA)—both concentrated their energies on the question of the franchise. The lack of the vote
was a symptom of women's exclusion from the society and
not its cause; yet it was such a powerful symbol that the
suffragists expected, and the anti-suffragists feared, liberating results out of all proportion to what finally came about
when women were granted the vote.

Two strains—self-serving discourses on the natural capacities and incapacities of women, and a real fear of the damage to the family and to men if women became political and
social equals—ran throughout the anti-suffrage arguments.
As Orestes Brownson wrote in "The Woman Question":

> The conclusive objection to the political enfranchisement of
> women is, that it would weaken and finally break up and de-
> stroy the Christian family. The social unit is the family, not the
> individual; and the greatest danger to American society is, that
> we are rapidly becoming a nation of individuals, without family
> ties of affection . . . We are daily losing the faith, the virtues, and
> the manners without which the family cannot be sustained; and
> when the family goes, the nation goes too, or ceases to be worth
> preserving.
>
> Extend now to women suffrage and eligibility; give them the
> political right to vote and to be voted for; render it feasible for
> them to enter the arena of political strife . . . and what remains
> of the family union will soon be dissolved. The wife may es-
> pouse one political party and the husband another, and it may
> well happen that the husband and wife may be rival candidates
> for the same office and one or the other doomed to the mortifi-
> cation of defeat. Will political rivalry increase the mutual affec-
> tion of husband and wife for each other . . . or will it not carry
> into the bosom of the family all the strife, discord, anger and
> division of the political canvass.[8]

Unfortunately, these fears were not prophetic. Women did
not vote differently from their men; apart from the issue of
temperance, there has been no issue on which women have
voted as a separate group.

8. In Kraditor, *op. cit.*, p. 193.

If the anti-suffragists were wrong in attaching great importance to the vote, they had real insight into the connection between women's liberation and the dissolution of the family. Certainly they were closer to the real issues than the overwhelming majority of suffragists—white middle-class women who accepted most of the society's attitudes toward a woman's role. These women agreed that childrearing was entirely their responsibility, that the family was sacred, and they accepted the praise for their higher moral nature which is the reverse rhetoric of sexism: "We who are more virtuous will have a purifying influence on politics."

As the women's movement concentrated more on the vote, it lost sight of the simple, forceful argument for equality based on the idea of natural rights as expounded by the Declaration of Independence, an argument that had been reinforced by the fight against slavery. The NWSA and AWSA, long split over methods and goals, were reunited on the basis of a surrender on the part of the more militant NWSA. The number of women in the suffrage organizations increased toward the end of the century, but the movement continued to recruit only middle-class women, who shared their husbands' fears that the huge numbers of poor immigrants—Irish, Italian, and Eastern European—would weaken the political power of the established classes. The women turned to a narrow and vicious, but persuasive, argument of expedience: that it was insulting to them, educated and true Americans, that ignorant, low-born foreigners should be able to vote while they could not; that if they were given the vote, the number of true Americans would be doubled and the forces of law and order strengthened. In 1894, a year before she became a national officer in the NAWSA, Carrie Chapman Catt made this statement:

> This government is menaced by a great danger . . . That danger lies in the votes possessed by the males in the slums of the cities, and the ignorant foreign vote which was sought to be bought up by each party, to make political success . . . In the mining districts the danger has already reached this point—

miners are supplied with arms, watching with greedy eyes for the moment when they can get in their greedy work of despoiling the wealth of the country. The hoodlums of Chicago gave us a forecast of their intent to reproduce the horrors of the Old World when their numbers are sufficiently increased, and every shipload of foreigners brings them nearer to their object. These men hold the government of the large cities in the hollow of their hands. There is but one way to avert the danger—cut off the vote of the slums and give to woman, who is bound to suffer all, and more than man can, of the evils his legislation has brought upon the nation, the power of protecting herself that man has secured for himself—the ballot.[9]

A similar line of reasoning was used by Southern suffragists who became active in the 1890's. They saw the enfranchisement of women, together with property and educational qualifications on the vote for both races, as a means of ensuring the perpetuation of white supremacy. There was some conflict with the old-guard Northern suffragists, but sympathy from the newer leadership led to strengthened bonds between the Northern and Southern movements.

The conservatism of the suffrage movement during the last part of the nineteenth century reflects the class division increasingly felt with rapid industrialization and the influx of immigrants. Middle-class xenophobia and hysteria, stirred by the growth of trade unions, the militant railroad workers' and miners' strikes, and the Haymarket riots in Chicago, identified militancy with anarchy and later with communism. Demonstrations and protest actions of all kinds disappeared from the suffrage movement. The energies of the suffrage organizations, both on the national and state levels, went into state campaigns consisting of speaking tours, petition drives, and lobbying. In thirty years, there were four hundred and eighty campaigns in thirty-three states attempting to force the states to hold referendums. This work resulted in only seventeen referendums, two of which (Colorado and Idaho) were successful.

The populist 1890's brought an upsurge of socialism and

9. Kraditor, *op. cit.*, p. 261.

trade unionism, which eventually influenced the women's suffrage movement. The number of working women grew from approximately four million in 1890 to almost seven-and-a-half million in 1910. Although the largest proportion were domestic or other service workers, there were great numbers of women working in industry—predominantly garment trades and textile manufacturing, in New York, Philadelphia, and the mill towns of New Jersey and Massachusetts. Wages were one-third of those for men performing comparable labor, and ranged from $2.00 to $6.00 a week. Hundreds of thousands of women, unorganized by any union, worked on their feet far into the night, packed into filthy, poorly lit, unventilated fire traps.

It was inevitable that some of the reforming zeal of the period should focus on the plight of these working women. Although no motion in that direction was evident in the established women's suffrage organizations, some women took action on behalf of the working women. Jane Addams of Hull House, and the wealthy Frances Kelley (a lawyer, a socialist, first woman Chief Inspector of Factories in Illinois, and from 1905 to 1906 Vice President of the NAWSA), pushed directly for legislation to protect factory women and urged the women of the suffrage movement to realize that the entrance of working women into the suffrage movement would strengthen the cause of suffrage.

Although there was an obvious link between women's rights and unionism, few American suffrage leaders recognized it. British leaders, unlike their American sisters, recognized the common issues and embraced them. From its inception in 1903, the Women's Social and Political Union (WSPU), the strongest women's organization in England, included many working-class women.

Led by Emmeline Pankhurst (already well-known as a social reformer) and Christabel Pankhurst, organization began in Lancashire and Yorkshire. One of the early recruits,

Anne Kinney, described the double oppression of working women:

I grew up in the midst of women and girls in the works and I saw the hard lives of women and children about me. I noticed the great difference made in the treatment of men and women in the factory, difference in conditions, difference in wages, difference in status. I realized this difference not only in the factory but also in the home. I saw men and women and boys and girls all working hard during the day in the same hot stifling factories. Then when work was over, I noticed that it was the mothers who hurried home; who fetched the child who had been put out to nurse, prepared the tea for the husband, did the cleaning, baking, washing, sewing, and nursing. I noticed that when the husband ran home, his day's work was over, he took his tea and then went to join his friends in the club or in the public houses, or in the cricket or football field, and I used to ask myself why this was so. Why was the mother the drudge of the family, and not the complement and equal.[10]

The WSPU was militant from the start and increased its militancy with each confrontation. The first such confrontation took place in 1905 at a Liberal Party meeting when Anne Kinney and several others were attacked, thrown out of the hall, and finally arrested. Three days later, upon their release from jail, there was a large demonstration for suffrage.

A pattern of disrupting meetings, arrests, and rallies continued throughout 1906–07. "Rise Up Women" had become a familiar cry to the English. Tactics were expanded to include working in the countryside to defeat the Liberal Party which had refused to take a parliamentary stand in favor of the vote for women, as well as marches on Parliament. The confrontations between the militant women and the police at these marches were violent. Line after line of women was attacked by mounted police. Sixty-five women and two men were arrested during one of the first marches. "One thing is certain," said Christabel Pankhurst, "there

10. E. Sylvia Pankhurst, *The Suffragette*, (London: Gay and Hancock, 1911), p. 74.

can be no going back for us, and more will happen if we do not get justice."

In 1908, the Third Women's Parliament met and again decided to march on Parliament to demand that the members recognize the women's question. Some attempted to sneak into the building by jumping into a truck that drove close to the Parliament's doors; others came up the river in boats, shouting their compaints to onlookers. Fifty women were arrested that day, but there was no response from Parliament. Public opinion, however, was aroused in favor of the women, in favor, at least initially, of their spirit.

The cycle of action and punishment continued, and punishment grew more severe. A series of hunger strikes by the imprisoned women led to forced-feeding, and the great public outcry at this cruelty helped to hasten the final favorable vote in Parliament to grant women suffrage. After this victory, the English movement, which had been organized around this single issue, was absorbed into general reform movements.[11]

In 1907, Harriet Stanton Blatch, a daughter of Elizabeth Cady Stanton, returned from a twenty-year stay in England, where she had worked with the Pankhursts. She judged it impossible to revitalize the NAWSA and formed her own group which initiated the famous women's suffrage parades in New York, the first outdoor meetings, and attempted to interest trade-union women and suffragists in each other. If the mass meetings were somewhat effective, the attempt to unite the two classes of women was largely unsuccessful. Few middle-class women were objective enough or politically acute enough to recognize the necessity of abandoning the class prejudices of their men. It is hard to imagine working-class women, whose main interest was in survival, sympathizing with the singular importance placed on the vote, which must have seemed to be a middle-class luxury, a paper victory. Unlike English women,

11. Today, however, the Women's Liberation Movement in England is growing both within the trade unions and among middle-class women.

American women did not have an ideological framework for social change, a framework which would have shown the necessity of a connection between the poor working conditions and low wages of the working women and the lack of political power of all women.

It was not until factory women acted to improve their conditions that substantial support emerged among middle-class suffragists. The organizing of women workers progressed slowly until two International Ladies Garment Workers Union (ILGWU) shops in New York and Philadelphia struck in September of 1909. Thirty thousand workers, ten times the number expected by the organization, joined the strike, seventy-five percent of them women between the ages of sixteen and thirty. Throughout a cold winter these women picketed, held mass meetings, and built their union, sometimes at a rate of one thousand new members in a day. The picket lines were attacked by police and there were dozens of arrests. The courts were not sympathetic: one judge informed a striker: "You are on strike against God and Nature, whose prime law it is that man shall earn his bread in the sweat of his brow. You are on strike against God."[12]

A link between the strike and the suffrage movement was provided by the Women's Trade Union League (WTUL), a group comprised of women union leaders and middle-class reformers (all of them also suffragists). The WTUL saw to publicity and raised thousands of dollars for strike funds.

Although some contact had been made between the two classes, the ILGWU strike was seen principally as a workers' struggle, only secondarily as a women's struggle.[13]

No alliance of working-class women and middle-class women survived the enfranchisement of women. Neither side was fully aware of the importance and the potential of a united women's force.

12. Flexner, p. 243.
13. The ILGWU leadership today is predominantly male and white, while the majority of its members are black and Puerto Rican women.

The support for the trade-union movement by prominent suffragists did not, then, represent any great broadening of either movement. It did reflect a growing interest among the suffragist leadership in various reforming causes. A change also came about in the tactics of the suffragists. A group of younger women split from the NAWSA and formed the Congressional Suffrage Union (CSU). Learning from their British sisters, the CSU held vigils at the White House, picketed, went to jail, went on hunger strikes, and were force-fed, bringing new publicity and new spirit to their cause. When five thousand women marched in Washington, D.C., in 1913, an angry mob attacked them, and a National Guard regiment was called out to protect the women.

This activity helped to revive interest in the women's suffrage amendment, an interest which had been languishing for over a decade. Meanwhile, the old NAWSA pulled itself together and in 1916 launched a four-year campaign on federal, state, and local levels to get the federal amendment passed by Congress and ratified by the state legislatures. It took an enormous effort on the part of hundreds of thousands of women. This was the last stage of a battle which had already been won in the minds of most Americans. Women were voting already in many states, and their massive entry into public life during the war years made their enfranchisement inevitable. Opposition in state legislatures and Congress arose mainly in New England and New Jersey and in the South, and was expressed as a matter of states' rights. It was based partly on the new identification of the suffragists with progressive causes, partly on the fear men really felt that women would bring their homely virtues into politics and stir up trouble, and partly also on the fear that such an enormous shift in numbers of voters might alter control of political machines. The Northern senators who voted against women's suffrage also voted against the income tax and the direct primary and the taxation of war profits. In the South, where Jim Crow voting laws had long since deprived black people of the vote, politicans feared any new attention to democratic rights. In 1918, Senator Smith of South Carolina told the Senate:

> I warn every man here today that when the test comes, as it will come, when the clamor for Negro rights shall have come, that you senators from the South voting for it have started it here this day . . . If it was a crime to enfranchise the male half of this race, why is it not a crime to enfranchise the other half? . . . By thus adding the word "sex" to the 15th amendment, you have just amended it to liberate them all, when it was perfectly competent for the legislatures of the several states to frame their laws as to preserve our civilization without entangling legislation involving women of the black race.[14]

Today the American woman can vote, get an education, and own property. The feminist movement accomplished this much. Of course, working-class women, black women, Mexican and Indian women have seen few changes in their long history of poverty, limited options, and humiliating dependence on an alien and greedy economy. Women have found that their subjugation goes far beyond the formal denial of civil rights. Women have obtained one limited objective after another, discovering again and again that liberation still lay ahead. The achievements of each successive movement have served to advance their status somewhat, to raise their ambitions, and to re-enlighten them each time about the nature of their struggle.

After World War I came the "emancipation of women" of which being able to vote was one aspect. Now all women could do what only "bad" women had done: show their legs, drink, smoke, go about with men without a chaperone. In intellectual and bohemian circles it was permissible to sleep with a man to whom one wasn't married. It became the rule, rather than the exception, for upper-middle-class women to go to college, and more women received Ph.D.'s in 1930 than ever before—or since. Getting married ceased to mean

14. Flexner, pp.303–304.

the end of social life for women. The figure of the young matron disappeared from American life, and the race to stay young began.

Difficult as it is to sort out and weigh the benefits and burdens of our "emancipation," one thing is clear. Somehow, what occurred was a terrible, cynical undercutting and buying off of the concepts of sexual, political, and economic liberation, and their replacement by new, more versatile forms of servitude. Isadora Duncan dreamed of, and practiced, a beautiful freedom of the body in dance and sex. Margaret Sanger tried to put into every woman's hands the power to choose whether and when to bear children.

The record numbers of female college graduates notwithstanding, economic independence and a career and a life of her own were still out of reach for the average woman, and, as a result, the new sexual freedom was used as "feminine attractions" have always been used, to purchase security from men.

In the Victorian era, before "sexual emancipation," the Virtuous Woman and the Prostitute were distinct and separate. The good, asexual wife may have felt bitterly deprived at the thought of her husband in the arms of a prostitute, but she was wrong if she envied the prostitute. The body's pleasure cannot be used to purchase security, either by a wife or by the prostitute who, notoriously, fakes pleasure to please her customer and earn more money. The Victorian wife who stifled her sexuality to buy her security at least was spared the hypocrisy of pretended pleasure.

Liberation would obviously dispense with the cruel dichotomy of sex and virtue, but instead after "emancipation" the roles were maintained, even combined. Now a woman must, to hold her man, act *both* the prostitute and the homebody, mistress and mother. The image of this good/bad woman has varied over the years—from flapper to the Playboy bunny who looks like the girl next door, or the housewife-sex kitten of TV commercials. A good girl, whose grandmother would have refused to kiss her fiance until the engagement was sealed, now has to decide "how far to go" on each date to keep her reputation poised between prudish and loose. The decision has to be based on the need to keep a man's respect while maintaining his sexual interest—her own needs and feelings must come second. Our pleasure and our womanhood are still defined by what men want from us.

There are, of course, practical reasons for this state of affairs. We would not need to distort and disguise ourselves and our sex if we did not still need to purchase from men what should be ours by right—equal opportunity for making money, for doing work we like, and equal responsibility on the part of individual men, and from the society, for taking care of the children. Sex and love have been so contaminated for women by economic dependence that the package deal of love and marriage looks like a con and a shill. We will not be able to sort out what we do want from men and what we want to give them until we know that our own physical and psychological survival—at home and at work—does not depend on men. Like all oppressed peoples, we need, first of all, *self-determination*.

i

THE OPPRESSED
MAJORITY:
THE WAY IT IS

Know Your Enemy: A Sampling of Sexist Quotes

The glory of a man is knowledge, but the glory of a woman is to renounce knowledge. —Chinese proverb

Do not trust a good woman, and keep away from a bad one. —Portugese proverb

Women are sisters nowhere. —West African proverb

Whenever a woman dies there is one quarrel less on earth. —German proverb

Never trust a woman, even though she has given you ten sons. —Chinese proverb

In childhood a woman must be subject to her father; in youth, to her husband; when her husband is dead, to her sons. A woman must never be free of subjugation.
                    —*The Hindu Code of Manu, V*

I thank thee, O Lord, that thou hast not created me a woman. —Daily Orthodox Jewish Prayer (for a male)

There is a good principle which created order, light, and

man, and an evil principle which created chaos, darkness, and woman.   —Pythagoras

We may thus conclude that it is a general law that there should be naturally ruling elements and elements naturally ruled . . . the rule of the freeman over the slave is one kind of rule; that of the male over the female another . . . the slave is entirely without the faculty of deliberation; the female indeed possesses it, but in a form which remains inconclusive . . .   —Aristotle (*Politics*)

If thy wife does not obey thee at a signal and a glance, separate from her.   —*Sirach* 25:26

When a woman thinks . . . she thinks evil.   —Seneca

Creator of the heavens and the earth, He has given you wives from among yourselves to multiply you, and cattle male and female. Nothing can be compared with Him.
                    —*Holy Koran of Islam*

And the rib, which the Lord God had taken from man, made he a woman and brought her unto the man. And Adam said, This is now bone of my bone, and flesh of my flesh; she shall be called Woman, because she was taken out of Man.   —*Genesis* 2:22–23

How can he be clean that is born of a woman?
                    —*Job*, 4:4

Suffer women once to arrive at an equality with you, and they will from that moment become your superiors.
                    —Cato the Elder, 195 B.C.

Let the women learn in silence with all subjection . . . I suffer not a woman to usurp authority over men, but to be in silence.   —St. Paul

Wives, submit yourselves unto your husbands . . . for the husband is the head of the wife, even as Christ is the head of the church.   —*Ephesians* 5:23–24

The five worst infirmities that afflict the female are in-docility, discontent, slander, jealousy, and silliness . . . Such is the stupidity of woman's character, that it is incumbent upon her, in every particular, to distrust herself and to obey her husband. —*Confucian Marriage Manual*

God created Adam lord of all living creatures, but Eve spoiled it all. —Martin Luther

All witchcraft comes from carnal lust, which is in women insatiable.
> —Kramer and Sprenger, Inquisitors (*Malleus Maleficarum, c.* 1486)

A man in general is better pleased when he has a good dinner than when his wife talks Greek.
> —Samuel Johnson

The whole education of women ought to be relative to men. To please them, to be useful to them, to make themselves loved and honored by them, to educate them when young, to care for them when grown, to counsel them, to console them, and to make life sweet and agreeable to them—these are the duties of women at all times and what should be taught them from their infancy.
> —Jean Jacques Rousseau

Women have no moral sense; they rely for their behavior upon the men they love. —La Bruyere

Most women have no characters at all.
> —Alexander Pope

I never knew a tolerable woman to be fond of her own sex.
> —Jonathan Swift

Man for the field and woman for the hearth:
Man for the sword and for the needle she:
Man with the head and woman with the heart:
Man to command and woman to obey;
All else confusion. —Alfred, Lord Tennyson

Men are men, but Man is a woman.

—G. K. Chesterton

Nature intended women to be our slaves . . . they are our property; we are not theirs. They belong to us, just as a tree that bears fruit belongs to a gardener. What a mad idea to demand equality for women! . . . Women are nothing but machines for producing children.

—Napoleon Bonaparte

To men a man is but a mind. Who cares what face he carries or what he wears? But woman's body *is* the woman.

—Ambrose Bierce

Regard the society of women as a necessary unpleasantness of social life, and avoid it as much as possible.

—Count Leo Tolstoy

A woman who is guided by the head and not the heart is a social pestilence: she has all the defects of the passionate and affectionate woman, with none of her compensations; she is without pity, without love, without virtue, without sex.   —Honoré de Balzac

And a woman is only a woman but a good cigar is a smoke.

—Rudyard Kipling

Women have great talent, but no genius, for they always remain subjective.   —Arthur Schopenhauer

One must have loved a woman of genius to comprehend the happiness of loving a fool.   —Talleyrand

If the feminine abilities were developed to the same degree as those of the male, her (woman's) maternal organs would suffer and we should have a repulsive and useless hybrid.
—P.J. Moebius (German scientist, 1907)

The great question that has never been answered, and which I have not yet been able to answer despite my thirty years of research into the feminine soul, is: What does a woman want?   —Sigmund Freud

The woman's fundamental status is that of her husband's wife, the mother of his children.   —Talcott Parsons

Man's superiority will be shown, not in the fact that he has enslaved his wife, but that *he* has made her free.
                                                        —Eugene V. Debs

Women should receive a higher education, not in order to become doctors, lawyers, or professors, but to rear their offspring to be valuable human beings.
                              —Alexis Carrel, *Man, the Unknown*

Woman as a person enjoys a dignity equal with men, but she was given different tasks by God and by Nature which perfect and complete the work entrusted to men.
                                                    —Pope John XXIII

The only position for women in SNCC is prone.
                                        —Stokeley Carmichael, 1966

It would be preposterously naive to suggest that a B.A. can be made as attractive to girls as a marriage license.
              —Dr. Grayson Kirk (former President, Columbia
                                                        University)

Women, in general, want to be loved for what they are and men for what they accomplish. The first for their looks and charm, the latter for their actions.   —Theodor Reik

My secretary is a lovable slave.
              —Morris Ernst, attorney, on the 50th Anniversary
                  of his having hired Paula Gross, secretary.

The only alliance I would make with the Women's Liberation Movement is in bed.—Abbie Hoffman

Women are usually more patient in working at unexciting, repetitive tasks . . . Women on the average have more passivity in the inborn core of their personality . . . I believe women are designed in their deeper instincts to get more pleasure out of life—not only sexually but socially, occupa-

tionally, maternally—when they are not aggressive. To put it another way I think that when women are encouraged to be competitive too many of them become disagreeable.
                            —Dr. Benjamin M. Spock, *Decent and Indecent*

Women? I guess they ought to exercise Pussy Power.
                                      —Eldridge Cleaver, 1968

AND

A woman's place is in the home/Housewives are such dull people/Women's talk is all chatter/Intelligent women are emasculating/If you're so smart why aren't you married?/-Can you type?/If you want to make decisions in this family, go out and earn a paycheck yourself/Working women are unfeminine/A smart woman never shows her brains/It is a woman's duty to make herself attractive/All women think about are clothes/Women are always playing hard to get/No man likes an easy woman/Women should be struck regularly, like gongs/Women like to be raped/Women are always crying about something/Women don't understand the value of a dollar/Women executives are castrating bitches/Don't worry your pretty little head about it/Dumb broad/It is glorious to be the mother of all mankind/A woman's work is never done/All you do is cook and clean and sit around all day/Women are only interested in trapping some man/A woman who can't hold a man isn't much of a woman/Women hate to be with other women/Women are always off chattering with each other/Some of my best friends are women . . .

THE 51 PERCENT MINORITY GROUP:
A STATISTICAL ESSAY

Joreen

Women are 51 percent of the population. That is the only category in which they constitute 51 percent. In virtually every other, their share is grossly disproportionate.

Women's position in the labor market is outlined with a few statistics from the Women's Bureau of the Labor Department: 37 percent of all women of working age are in the labor force and they constitute 35 percent of all workers. But they are highly concentrated in the underpaid and menial jobs. Women are 70 percent of all clerical workers, 99 percent of all private household workers, 55 percent of all other service workers, and 27 percent of all factory workers. Only 14 percent of all working women are employed as professional or technical workers.

The result of this pattern is that the median income of white women, employed full time, is lower than that of Negro men, employed full time. The median income of black women, victims of both race *and* sex discrimination, is lower still. This is despite the fact that the median education of both groups of women is higher than that of their male counterparts.

Their unemployment rate is also higher, although the only people counted in these figures are those actively seeking work. According to the Women's Bureau, "Since no account is taken of the many who have given up job hunting because it seemed hopeless, these figures may be deceptively low." The over-all unemployment rate for women is 6.2 percent, compared with 4.7 percent for men. The highest unemployment rate of all is found in non-white women between 18 and 20 years of age. Over 31 percent cannot find work.

Income differences are not accounted for solely by differences in occupations because even within the same occupations the median income of women employees runs considerably lower than that of men. For example, among sales workers, full-time women workers earn 40.4 percent the salaries of men. Among clerical workers they earn 66.2 percent, and among professional workers they earn 64.2 percent. Only twenty-five states have equal pay for equal work laws, and these are not vigorously enforced. They are also frequently circumvented by giving the woman's job a lesser title than that of the man.

It is generally assumed that with increased skills and increased education the income differentials between women and men disappear. Yet an examination of some highly skilled professions shows the contrary. *Chemical and Engineering News* did a study of chemists' salaries in the fall of 1968, which showed that, with seniority held constant, women with Ph.D's made less than men with only B.A.'s. James J. White recently conducted an analysis of every woman graduate from a law school in the last ten years compared with a similar male group. With every variable he could think of controlled for, the figures still showed that a year after graduation the average man earned 20 percent more than the woman lawyer, and ten years later he earned 200 percent more.

In 1964, the National Education Association collected data on the salaries of the teaching staff of all colleges and universities. Women represented 13 percent of the faculties that year. But their median income, for 9 full months of teaching, ran $1,500 below that of men. This is partially accounted for by the fact that women constitute 25 percent of all untenured positions and only 12 percent of the tenured ones. But a breakdown by position shows that the median income of women is lower than that of men at all positions from instructor to professor. In fact, the differential is greatest at the level of full professors.

These figures do not necessarily mean that individual

institutions or companies maintain separate salary schedules for women and men of comparable experience and ability. Rather, the differences are most often due to the fact that the higher paying, generally more prestigious organizations, prefer not to hire women at all. Therefore, women must seek employment elsewhere, at whatever salaries they can get.

The general belief, used to justify the lower pay given to women, is that theirs is a luxury income, which supplements that of their husbands. Yet 35 percent of all women of marriageable age are not married and study after study has shown that most women, married or not, work out of economic necessity. In fact, more than one-fifth of the sixty-five million women in this country aged sixteen and over live in poverty. Ten percent of the nation's families are headed only by a woman, but 40 percent of the families classified as poor have female heads.

This situation is exacerbated not only by low wages but by the fact that forty-three states limit the number of hours a woman can work—generally to eight per day. Passed at the turn of the century in an attempt to curb sweat-shop exploitation, this "protective" legislation prevents women from earning overtime pay and promotions to jobs requiring overtime. Other states limit the amount of weight a woman can carry on the job. The limits run from ten to thirty-five pounds (the weight of a small child) and for some reason factories tend to have weight requirements more often for supervisory jobs than for menial ones. These laws, also, are more often protective of men. Many of them are now being challenged in the courts.[1]

1. In *Menqelkoch et al.* v. *the Industrial Welfare Commission of California and North American Aviation Inc.*, the defending corporation admitted that women were denied overtime and promotions to positions requiring overtime and justified their actions by the California maximum hours law. In *Roiq* v. *Southern Bell Telephone and Telegraph Co.*, the plaintiffs are protesting that their current job is exempt from the Louisiana maximum hours law but that the higher paying job to which they were denied promotion is not. *Weeks* v. *Southern Bell Telephone and Telegraph* is challenging the Georgia weightlifting law. In *Bowe* v. *Colgate Palmolive Co.*, a lower court ruled that a company could establish maximum weightlifting restrictions on higher paying jobs even though its plant and the plaintiffs were located

Women with degrees don't fare much better. Although 70 percent of all women with degrees work, only 2 percent are executives. Forty percent teach and over 20 percent are employed in clerical, sales, or factory jobs. The median income of working women with degrees is 51 percent that of men with degrees.

These economic facts of life have always been shrouded by the belief that "things are getting better." But in reality, while the percentage of women in the labor force increases steadily, the gap between the incomes of full-time men and women workers has been widening at the rate of 1/2 percent a year for at least the last fifteen years. According to Mary Keyserling, Director of the Women's Bureau, "Occupationally women are relatively more disadvantaged today than they were twenty-five years ago. . . This deterioration has occurred despite the increase in women's share of total employment over the same period and the rising number of women who enroll in and graduate from institutions of higher education."

For fifteen to twenty years after women were given the vote, their participation in every field expanded rapidly. A higher percentage of the major jobs in every field, and of every degree from B.A. to Ph.D. were granted to women in 1930 than in 1960. Then, in the late 1930's and 1940's the reaction set in and the era of the "feminine mystique" began. This course parallels that of the black man after the passage of the 13th and 14th Amendments. Negroes also experienced a wide expansion of opportunities during Reconstruction until the advent of the Jim Crow laws created a new form of slavery.

And like the Negro, women have once again begun to revolt. Consciousness that women are still second-class citizens has been growing at least since the establishment in 1961 of the Commission on the Status of Women by President Kennedy. Created at the urging of Esther Peterson of the Women's Bureau, and Eleanor Roosevelt, in its short life

in a state (Indiana) which did not have such laws. Plaintiffs are appealing.

time the Commission came out with several reports docu-
menting just how thoroughly women are still denied many
rights and opportunities. A Citizen's Advisory Council and
fifty state commissions have continued this information
gathering. But the best single source of information on
women is the Women's Bureau of the Labor Department.
Set up after the passage of the 19th Amendment, it has
quietly been putting out voluminous reports and pamphlets
for years, and will give single copies free on request. The
Handbook on Women Workers is the only book of graphs and
statistics guaranteed to raise a woman reader's blood pressure.

The Commission's reports came out in 1963. But they had
little effect on federal legislation. The inclusion of the word
"sex" in Title VII of the 1964 Civil Rights Act was put there
as a joke by octogenarian representative Howard W. Smith
of Virginia. As documented in the first chapter of Caroline
Bird's book *Born Female: The High Cost of Keeping Women
Down* (David McKay Co., New York, 1968), it was opposed
by all the liberals on the ground that it would make the
whole Civil Rights Act more difficult to pass—but it stayed
in, anyway.

Since then, that little word has gone on to plague the
Equal Employment Opportunities Commission. Set up to
handle complaints of race discrimination, the EEOC was
totally unprepared to deal with the complaints of sex discrimination that flooded the agency. Forty percent of all
complaints are about sex discrimination. According to Rep.
Martha W. Griffiths of Michigan, the EEOC "started out by
casting disrespect and ridicule on the law." She later decided that their "wholly negative attitude toward the sex
provisions of Title VII" had changed—for the worse. The
Executive Director of the Commission stated that the sex
provision was a "fluke" and "conceived out of wedlock."

After several years of pressure by feminist groups, the
EEOC decided the women were serious and even entitled
to some of the same rights as Negroes under the law. Al-

though Title VII had clearly prohibited discrimination in employment on the basis of an "individual's race, color, religion, sex or national origin," the EEOC had maintained that this meant newspapers could not segregate want-ads by race but could do so by sex. This supported the traditional practice of listing the better jobs under the "men wanted" section where women were unlikely to look, and made it difficult to discover that dually listed.jobs offer salaries to women about 20 percent below those offered to men.

In August of 1968, they changed their ruling and ordered the newspapers to desegregate their want-ads by December 1, 1968. The American Newspaper Publishers Association and the *Washington Star* promptly filed suit. ANPA claimed that compliance would hurt job seekers, employers and newspapers and that "newspapers and their advertisers are unwilling to depart so radically from a successful system." The newspaper publishers lost, but have not complied with the ruling while they are appealing the decision.

By now it should be evident that with 51 percent of the population, women are the nation's largest minority group. The mythology that women are inferior and need to be protected by men went out with the mythology about the superiority of the Aryan race. But the *Kinder, Kuche,* and *Kirche* philosophy that it supported has not entirely receded with it. It has only been transformed into a more sophisticated version.

With increased prosperity, increased education, and increased freedom from unplanned pregnancies, women have been moving out of the home and into the world in greater and greater numbers. Men have welcomed them, but only if they maintain their place as auxiliaries to men. The current attitude is that of what Caroline Bird calls "the New Masculinists." They are all "for updating women's traditional role, providing their jobs don't change the lives of men." That is, women are welcome at work as long as they are in supplementary positions, assisting men, not competing with them.

This attitude is reflected in an occupational structure which refuses to admit more than a token number of women to any major positions and virtually none at all to those where they would have authority over men. While doing the research for her book, Bird interviewed several hundred "successful" women and discovered that virtually every one had either made it through a loophole or was significantly better qualified than a man in a comparable position. *Harvard Business Review* once decided to do a survey of opportunities for women as business executives. They concluded that there were hardly any. Scan the masthead of any magazine or the faculty listings of any university catalog. The higher you look, the fewer women there are.

The general attitude toward women is also solidly enshrined in law[2] which reflects the English common law tradition that "the husband and wife are as one and that one is the husband." In many states, a woman's income and property are under the control of her husband. In most states she cannot use her maiden name if he should object or maintain a separate domicile for tax and voting purposes. Even the prostitution laws discriminate. Soliciting is an offense in 34 states, but customers are subject to prosecution in only 14 states. Nonetheless, prostitutes are jailed in every state, and customers (i.e. men) are prosecuted virtually not at all. It might also be added that brothels are prohibited in all states except Arizona and Nevada, and in those states cannot be established near a main street, church, or school.

Nor does the law permit a woman control of her own body for non-pecuniary purposes. Many states continue to restrict the dispersal of birth-control information and devices and despite recent liberalizations in some states, hospital abortions are still for the rich. Few people pay much attention to the fact that more American women die each year from medically unsafe abortions than the number of American soldiers who die annually in Vietnam.

2. See "Does the Law Oppress Women?" by Diane Schulder, p. 139——Ed.

Study after study has shown that the children of working women are not harmed by the fact that their mothers work —and frequently benefit from it—but employed mothers are still harrassed with guilt that they are shirking their maternal responsibilities. Because this is the only industrialized nation in the world which does not provide public child-care services, working women, whose over-all median income is less than $1,500 per year, must pay out most of it in babysitting fees.

The egregious situation of American women has gone unheralded by all but a few for so long because our culture has never been particularly interested in what happened to women. As Gunnar Myrdal once commented, our values and concerns are those of the white male. In a little noted Appendix to his monumental study of the American Negro, he wrote that when a legal status had to be found for Negro slaves in the seventeenth century, "the nearest and most natural analogy was the status of women." Both groups "were placed under the jurisdiction of paternal power," and their main function was defined as freeing the white male from menial concerns.

To maintain them in their place, both groups were also rigidly stereotyped. Factual support for these stereotypes has begun to break down, but the attitudes and social structures behind them has not yet gone. The Masters and Johnson milestone study, *Human Sexual Response* (Little, Brown, Boston, 1966), shattered the foundation for the myth that women are sexually passive. But passivity, in mind as well as body, is still deemed a feminine characteristic. Sex roles differ with each culture, but all cultures carefully shape children from birth to fit accepted concepts of masculine and feminine behavior and to believe that these concepts have some eternal validity.

The social sciences claim to study people. But in fact they spend very little time studying the female half of the population except to discern the ways in which it differs from the male. In the multitude of "sex-difference" studies all that has been discovered is that: 1) individual differences are greater than sex differences, i.e., sex is just one of the multitude of characteristics which define a human being and 2) virtually all ability differences do not appear until a child enters school, and increase with age. Even these seem to be more strongly correlated with child-rearing practices and social expectations than sex.

Nonetheless, the hazy myths about women and the traditional beliefs of the proper sex-roles continue to prevail. A woman's only important function, for which she is "naturally" made, is held to be that of wife and mother. If she wants a career she is told to choose between that and motherhood, because she cannot do both well and society refuses to provide her with the structural means of handling both roles. Men are never asked to choose between their career and fatherhood; it is assumed that they can do both and the two roles are defined as complementary.

In this sphere as all others, the social structures are set up to benefit men, and women are judged by male standards. Our values require a woman to succeed in "a man's world," but do not provide such minimal compensations as day-care centers or tax relief to hire babysitters. Time off for vacations, sick-leave, or the draft is allowed for without loss of job or seniority, but pregnancy or child-care needs will often cost a woman both. Underlying these problems is a family structure in which the responsibilities and pleasures of home and work are not shared equitably.

Reinforcing these social structures are conceptions of women and social attitudes about their capabilities so pervasive that we rarely think about them. They are reflected in our movies, our fiction, our advertising, and our opinions. They act as invisible bonds which are greater than chains because they are not understood to exist.

It is these attitudes and these structures which must be changed if women are to be liberated. And it is only by organizing that this can be done. Men will not liberate women; women must free themselves. They have waited too long as it is. Now the largest minority group is getting angry. Women are tired of working for everyone's liberation except their own.

THE DYNAMICS OF MARRIAGE AND MOTHERHOOD

Beverly Jones

No one would think of judging a marriage by its first hundred days. To be sure there are cases of sexual trauma, of sudden and violent misunderstandings, but in general all is happiness; the girl has finally made it; the past is but a bad dream. All good things are about to come to her. And then reality sets in. It can be held off a little as long as they are both students and particularly if they have money, but sooner or later it becomes entrenched. The man moves to ensure his position of power and dominance.

There are several more or less standard pieces of armament used in this assault upon wives, but the biggest gun is generally the threat of divorce or abandonment. With a plucky woman a man may actually feel it necessary to openly and repeatedly toy with this weapon, but usually it is sufficient simply to keep it in the house undercover somewhere. We all know the bit, we have heard it and all the others I am about to mention on television marital comedies and in night-club jokes; it is supposed to be funny.

The husband says to the wife who is about to go somewhere that doesn't meet with his approval, "If you do, you need never come back." Or later, when the process is more complete and she is reduced to frequent outbreaks of begging, he slams his way out of the house claiming that she is trying to destroy him, that he can no longer take these endless, senseless scenes, that "This isn't a marriage, it's a meat grinder." Or he may simply lay down the law that goddamn it, her first responsibility is to her family and he will not permit or tolerate something or other. If she wants to maintain the marriage she is simply going to have to accommodate herself.

There are thousands of variations on this theme and it is really very clever the way male society creates for women this premarital hell so that some man can save her from it and control her ever after by the threat of throwing her back. Degrading her further, the final crisis is usually averted or postponed by a tearful reconciliation in which the wife apologizes for her shortcomings, namely the sparks of initiative still left to her.

The other crude and often open weapon that a man uses to control his wife is the threat of force or force itself. Though this weapon is not necessarily used in conjunction with the one described above, it presupposes that a roman is more frightened of returning to an unmarried state than she is of being beaten about one way or another. How can one elaborate on such a threat? At a minimum it begins by a man's paling or flushing, clenching his fists at his sides or gritting his teeth, perhaps making lurching but controlled motions, or wild threatening ones while he states his case. In this circumstance it is difficult for a woman to pursue the argument which is bringing about the reaction, usually an argument for more freedom, respect, or equality in the marital situation. And, of course, the conciliation of this scene, even if he has beaten her, may require his apology, but also hers for provoking him. After a while the conditioning becomes so strong that a slight change of color on his part, or a slight stiffening of stance (nothing observable to an outsider) suffices to quiet her or keep her in line. She turns off or detours mechanically, like a robot, not even herself aware of the change, or only momentarily and almost subliminally.

But these are gross and vulgar techniques. There are many more, subtle and intricate, which in the long run are even more devastating. Take, for instance, the ploy of keeping women from recognizing their intelligence by not talking to them in public. After marriage this technique is extended and used on a woman in her own home.

At breakfast a woman speaks to her husband over or through the morning paper. Which he clutches firmly in his hands. Incidentally, he reserves the right to see the paper first and to read the sections in order of his preference. The assumption is, of course, that he has a more vested interest in world affairs and a superior intelligence with which to grasp the relevance of daily news. The women's section of the paper is called that, not only because it contains the totality of what men want women to be concerned with, but also because it is the only section permitted to women at certain times of the day.

I can almost hear you demur. Now she has gone too far. What supersensitivity to interpret the morning paper routine as a deliberate put-down. After all, a woman has the whole day to read the paper and a man must get to work. I put it to you that this same situation exists when they both work or when the wife works and the husband is still a student, assuming he gets up for breakfast, and on Sundays. What we are describing here is pure self-indulgence. A minor and common, though none the less enjoyable, exercise in power. A flexing of the male prerogative.

Perhaps the best tip-off to the real meaning of the daily paper act comes when a housewife attempts to solve the problem by subscribing to two papers. This is almost invariably met with resistance on the part of the man as being an unnecessary and frivolous expense, never mind whether they can afford it. And if his resistance doesn't actually forestall the second subscription he attempts to monopolize the front sections of both papers! This is quite a complicated routine but, assuming the papers are not identical, it can be done and justified.

However, we were talking about conversation and noted that it was replaced by the paper in the morning. In the evening men attempt to escape through more papers, returning to work, working at home, reading, watching television, going to meetings, etc. But eventually they have to handle the problem some other way because their wives are desperate for conversation, for verbal interchange.

To understand this desperation you have to remember that women before marriage have on the whole only superficial, competitive, and selfish relationships with one another. Should one of them have a genuine relationship, it is more likely with a male than a female. After marriage a woman stops courting her old unmarried or married female sidekicks. They have served their purpose, to tide her over. And there is the fear, often well founded, that these females will view her marriage less as a sacrament than a challenge, that they will stalk her husband as fair game, that they will outshine her, or in some other way lead to the disruption of her marriage.

Her husband will not tolerate the hanging around of any past male friends, and that leaves the woman isolated. When, as so often happens, after a few years husband and wife move because he has graduated, entered service, or changed jobs, her isolation is complete. Now all ties are broken. Her husband is her only contact with the outside world, aside, of course, from those more or less perfunctory contacts she has at work, if she works.

So she is desperate to talk with her husband because she must talk with *someone* and he is all she has. To tell the truth, a woman doesn't really understand the almost biologic substructure to her desperation. She sees it in psychological terms. She thinks that if her husband doesn't talk to her he doesn't love her or doesn't respect her. She may even feel that this disrespect on his part is causing her to lose her own self-respect (a fair assumption since he is her only referent). She may also feel cheated and trapped because she understood that in return for all she did for him in marriage she was to be allowed to live vicariously, and she cannot do that if he will not share his life.

What she does not understand is that she cannot go on

thinking coherently without expressing those thoughts and having them accepted, rejected, or qualified in some manner. This kind of feedback is essential to the healthy functioning of the human mind. That is why solitary confinement is so devastating. It is society's third-rung "legal deterrent," ranking just below capital punishment and forced wakefulness, or other forms of torture that lead to death.

This kind of verbal isolation, this refusal to hear a woman, causes her thought process to turn in upon itself, to deteriorate, degenerate, to become disassociated from reality. Never intellectually or emotionally secure in the first place, she feels herself slipping beyond the pale. She keeps pounding at the door.

And what is her husband's response? He understands in some crude way what is happening to her, what he is doing to her, but he is so power-oriented he cannot stop. Above all, men must remain in control; it's either him or her. The worse she becomes, the more convinced he is that the coin must not be turned. And thence springs anew his fear of women, like the white's fear of blacks. We tend to forget that witches were burned in our own country not too long ago, in those heroic days before the founding fathers. That each day somewhere in our country women are raped and /or killed just for kicks or out of some perverted sense of retribution. And we never even consider the ten thousand innocent women annually murdered by men who refuse to legalize abortion. The fear and hatred must be deep indeed to take such vengeance.

But back to the husband. We all know that marriage is far from solitary confinement for a woman. Of course, the husband talks to her. The questions are, how often, what does he say, and how does he say it? He parries this plea for conversation, which he understands thoroughly, until bedtime or near it and then, exhausted and exasperated, he slaps down his book or papers, or snaps off the TV, or flings his shoe to the floor if he is undressing, and turns to his wife saying, "Oh, for Christ's sake, what is it you want to talk about?"

Now he has just used all of his big guns. He has shown temper which threatens violence. He has shown an exasperated patience which threatens eventual divorce. He has been insulting and purposely misunderstanding. Since she is not burning with any specific communiqué, since she is now frightened, hurt, angry, and thoroughly miserable, what is she to say? I'll tell you what she does say: "Forget it. Just forget it. If that's the way you are going to respond, I don't want to talk with you anyway."

This may bring on another explosion from him, frightening her still further. He may say something stupid like, "You're crazy, just crazy. All day long you keep telling me you've got to talk to me. OK, you want to talk to me, talk. I'm listening. I'm not reading, I'm not working, I'm not watching TV, I'm listening."

He waits sixty silent seconds while the wife struggles for composure, and then he stands up and announces that he is going to bed. To rub salt in the wound, he falls to sleep blissfully and instantly.

Or, playing the part of both cops in the jailhouse interrogation scene, he may, after the first explosion, switch roles. In this doubletake he becomes the calm and considerate husband, remorseful, apologizing, and imploring her to continue, assuring her he is interested in anything she has to say, knowing full well the limitations of what she can say under the circumstances. Predictably, done in by the tender tone, she falls in with the plot and confesses. She confesses her loneliness, her dependence, her mental agony, and they discuss *her* problem. Her problem, as though it were some genetic defect, some personal shortcoming, some inscrutable psychosis. Now he can comfort her, avowing how he understands how she must feel, he only wishes there were something he could do to help.

This kind of situation, if continued in unrelieved manner, has extreme consequences. Generally the marriage partners sense this and stop short of the brink. The husband, after all, is trying to protect and bolster his frail ego, not drive his wife insane or force her suicide. He wants in the home to be able to hide from his own inner doubts, his own sense of shame, failure, and meaninglessness. He wants to shed the endless humiliation of endless days parading as a man in the male world, pretending a power, control, and understanding he does not have.

All he asks of his wife, aside from hours of menial work, is that she not see him as he sees himself. That she not challenge him, but admire and desire him, soothe and distract him. In short, make him feel like the kind of guy he'd like to be in the kind of world he thinks exists.

And by this time the wife asks little more really than the opportunity to play that role. She probably never aspired to more, to an equalitarian or reality-oriented relationship. It is just that she cannot do her thing if it is laid out so baldly; if she is to be denied all self-respect, all self-development, all help and encouragement from her husband.

So generally the couple stops short of the brink. Sometimes, paradoxically enough, by escalating the conflict so that it ends in divorce, but generally by some accommodation. The husband encourages the wife to make some girlfriends, take night courses, or have children. And sooner or later, if she can, she has children. Assuming the husband has agreed to the event, the wife's pregnancy does abate or deflect the drift of their marriage, for a while anyway.

The pregnancy presents to the world visible proof of the husband's masculinity, his potency. This visible proof shores up the basic substructure of his ego, the floor beyond which he cannot now fall. Pathetically, his stock goes up in society, in his own eyes. He is a man. He is grateful to his wife and treats her, at least during the first pregnancy, with increased tenderness and respect. He pats her tummy and makes noises about mystic occurrences. And since pregnancy is not a male thing and he is a man, since this is cooperation, not competition, he can even make out that he feels her role is pretty special.

The wife is grateful. Her husband loves her. She is suffused with happiness and pride. There is at last something on her side of the division of labor which her husband views with respect, and delight of delights, with perhaps a twinge of jealousy.

Of course, it can't last. After nine months, the child is bound to be born. And there we are back at the starting gate. For many women, giving birth must be like a bad trip with the added feature of prolonged physical exhaustion. Sometimes it takes a year to regain one's full strength after a messy Caesarian. Sometimes women develop post-parturitional psychosis in the hospital. More commonly, after they have been home awhile they develop a transient but recurring state called the "Tired Mother Syndrome." In its severe form it is, or resembles, a psychosis. Women with this syndrome complain of being utterly exhausted, irritable, unable to concentrate. They may wander about somewhat aimlessly, they may have physical pains. They are depressed, anxious, sometimes paranoid, and they cry a lot.

Sound familiar? Despite the name, one doesn't have to be a mother to experience the ailment. Many young wives without children do experience it, particularly those who, without an education themselves, are working their husbands' way through college. That is to say, wives who hold down a dull eight- or nine-hour-a-day job, then come home, straighten, cook, clean, run down to the laundry, dash to the grocery store, iron their own clothes plus their husbands' shirts and jeans, sew for themselves, put up their hair, and more often than not type their husbands' papers, correct the spelling and grammar, pay the bills, screw on command, and write the in-laws. I've even known wives who on top of this load do term papers or laboratory work for their husbands. Of course, it's insanity. What else could such self-denial be called? Love?

Is it any wonder that a woman in these circumstances is tired? Is it any wonder that she responds with irritability when she returns home at night to find her student husband, after a day or half-day at home, drinking beer and shooting the bull with his cronies, the ring still in the bathtub, his dishes undone, his clothes where he dropped them the night before, even his specific little chores like taking out the garbage unaccomplished?

Is it any wonder that she is tempted to scream when at the very moment she has gotten rid of the company, plowed through some of the mess, and is standing in a tiny kitchen over a hot stove her husband begins to make sexual advances? He naively expects that these advances will fill her with passion, melting all anger, and result not only in her forgetting and forgiving, but in gratitude and renewed love. Ever heard the expression, "A woman loves the man who satisfies her?" Some men find that delusion very comforting. A couple of screws and the slate is wiped clean. Who needs to pay for servants or buy his wife a washing machine when he has a cock?

And even the most self-deluded woman begins to feel depressed, anxious, and used when she finds that her husband is embarrassed by her in the company of his educated, intellectual, or Movement friends. When he openly shuts her up; saying she doesn't know what she is talking about, or emphasizes a point by saying it is so clear or so simple even his wife can understand it.

He begins to confuse knowledge with a personal attribute like height or a personal virtue like honesty. He becomes disdainful of and impatient with ignorance, equating it with stupidity, obstinacy, laziness, and in some strange way, immorality. He forgets that his cultivation took place at his wife's expense. He will not admit that in stealing from his wife her time, energy, leisure, and money, he also steals the possibility of her intellectual development, her present, and her future.

But the working wife sending her husband through

DRAWING BY DIANE LOSCH

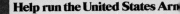

Women. Don't let my uniform get you uptight.
I always wear it when I do the housework. Makes me
feel more comfortable, more *me* as a housewife.

You know, underneath the military veneer, I really
believe women are somehow more gentle than men.

Now war is something that goes against woman's nature.
I agree.

I think we should get out of Vietnam.

I'm against the system, whether it's ABM or IBM.

I want R.O.T.C. and CBW stopped.

The military-industrial complex has existed long enough.

I wish people would stop saying that my politics are
motivated by my emotions. That makes it sound so easy.
Nobody bothers to listen.

Now men they really have to think a lot before taking
a stand. Refusing the draft is like refusing manhood.
Peace and non-violence come much easier to us because of
our roles as mothers and wives.

That's what everyone said when I resigned from the
Women's Army Corps in protest against our involvement
in Vietnam. "Woman's nature," they all said. Everyone
was so understanding.

A week later I resigned from my husband. This time
they said I was sick.

I learned a lot in the Women's Army Corps. Like,
you can't seriously expect young men to stop serving
(and dying) in the Army while you yourself spend your
life serving in the home.

You say "it's a dirty war." You're angry because
those who call the shots, the big shots, get others to do
the dirty work and the killing for them. I'm angry too.
But who gets to do the dirty work at home?

Cleaning and killing. That's what makes us so feminin
And them so masculine.

Sure. There's a certain division of labor which keeps
people in their place. That's why McNamara (Mac the Kni
sits on top of the World Bank.

I'm not kidding sister.

If you don't believe me, join the Women's Army Corp
and find out.

The Pentagon begins at home.

ACTUAL U.S. ARMY AD BROUGHT TO A HIGHER LEVEL OF STRUGGLE BY FLORIKA

ACROSS

2. Symbol of plastic America (2 words) The star of this show.
6. In Memoriam: leader of the Vietnamese revolution.
7. Masc. Spanish word for the
8. Average measurement is 35½" at this pageant. (sl)
12. Out. (Rhymes with cash)
13. Derogatory term for a woman with "loose morals".
14. Bible's stupid caricature of a disobedient woman.
15. Use this to chop wood.
16. Train (abbrev.)
18. Jack the ___ per.
19. What a man looks for in a woman.
22. Woman are ___.
25. When you flirt you act ___.
27. You ask God for "His" forgiveness with this.
29. What the contestants have to do all day long.
32. Opposite of war.
33. What you feel if you don't "have" a man.
35. Abbrev. for pop. soap opera, As ___.
36. Fate worse than death.
38. Businessmen capitalize on the Miss Amer. Image. That is the correct word.
43. A member of most oppressed group in our soc.
44. Cleavage
45. Everyone has it.
47. We are all ___ in the struggle.
48. What Miss America does for Toni.
50. Who's bored here?

DOWN

1. Best birth control device
2. The family martyr
3. Female beast of burden(other than woman)
4. A woman is supposed to be a ___ of strength for ever one but herself. Or syn. for body of water.
5. Imprisoned in a girdle
9. Girl raped by Jupiter in his cloud disguise.
10. "Love is a tender ___".
11. What's on the minds of the judges.
17. This year's pageant is a ___ of all the others that came before it.
20. ___ against the wall Miss America.
21. Get a little of this for #31 down.
23. Fill in lly. We don't want to make this too hard.
24. This is laden with mascara, liner, shadow, pencil and false lashes.
26. We would like to interrupt this show to remind you there's a war in ___.
28. Back
30. Army cop
31. ___ and order!
34. Patriarchial Egyptian son god.
37. Women are given token freedoms in ___ of a full life.
38. One of American women's main roles(rhymes with name of famous crossword artist)
39. In our society men are expected to be active. women ___.

Down con't.
41. Men have a "natural" ___ to women's work.
42. Join the women's liberation movement for a new ___ on life.
45. "To ___ or not to Be".
46. Are you glad you aren't Miss America?
49. The American Dream is a big, fat ___.

CROSSWORD PUZZLE BY WOMEN'S LIBERATION, SPRINGFIELD, MASS.

Atlantic City, 1968: First mass demonstration and action by Women's Liberation. *Top*, picketing and guerrilla theater on the boardwalk. *Above*, disruption of live telecast of Miss America Pageant.

First WITCH action in New York, Halloween, 1968. "Up Against the Wall Street." WITCH Coven hexes and disrupts *opposite page*, brokerage firm, *above right*, Chase Manhattan Bank, *below right*, Morgan Guaranty Trust. The Stock Market slumped five points after the hexing.

PHOTO BY LOUISE BROTSKY

Above, Chicago WITCH hexes
the Transit Authority for raising
the subway fare.

Right, Washington, D.C. WITCH
hexes billion-dollar corporation,
United Fruit Company for "slave-
labor practices abroad and sex
discrimination in hiring at home."

Opposite page, Grinnell College
(Iowa) students stage a nude-in to
confront a representative from
Playboy magazine speaking on
"The Playboy Philosophy." They
demanded that he also take off *his*
clothes. He fled.

PHOTO BY MARILYN SALZMAN WEBB

Opposite right, Women's Liberation guerrilla theater at the Bridal Fair, New York.
Disruptions of merchandise shows for brides took place all over the U.S. in 1969.

Opposite below, Protest against the firing of Marlene Dixon, radical, feminist, and
teacher, at the University of Chicago, 1968. A major riot followed, and university
buildings were seized and held by students.

PHOTO BY BILL NOWLIN/LNS—NY

PHOTO BY HENRY WILHELM/EAST ST. GALLERY, GRINNELL, IOWA

Above right and below, Mass
demonstration to abolish all
abortion laws, New York City, 1970.
Such demonstrations took place all
across the country in 1969–70.

Above, Women's Liberation march,
"Free Our Sisters! Free Ourselves!"
to free Black Panther women in
New Haven, Conn., 1969. The
Panther women were in prison,
pregnant, and being denied proper
food and medical care.

school has no monopoly on this plight. It also comes to those who only stand and wait—in the home, having kiddy after kiddy while their husbands, if they are able, learn something, grow somewhere.

In any case, we began this diversion by saying that women who are not mothers can also suffer from the "Tired Mother Syndrome." Once a mother, however, it takes on a new dimension. There is a difference of opinion in the medical and sociological literature with regard to the genesis of this ailment. Betty Friedan, in the sociological vein, argues that these symptoms are the natural outgrowth of restricting the mind and body of these women to the narrow confines of the home. She discusses the destructive role of monotonous, repetitive work which never issues in any lasting, let alone important achievement. Dishes which are done only to be dirtied the same day, beds which are made only to be unmade the same day. Her theory also lays great emphasis on the isolation of these women from the large problems of society and even from contact with those concerned with things not domestic, other than their husbands. In other words, the mind no more than the body can function in a strait jacket and the effort to keep it going under these circumstances is indeed tiring and depressing.

Dr. Spock somewhat sides with that theory. The mainline medical approach is better represented by Dr. Lovshin who says that mothers develop the Tired Mother Syndrome because they are tired. They work a sixteen-hour day, seven days a week. Automation and unions have led to a continuously shortened day for men but the work day of housewives with children has remained constant. The literature bears him out. Oh, it is undoubtedly true that women have today many timesaving devices their mothers did not have. This advantage is offset, however, by the fact that fewer members of the family help with housework and the task of child care, as it is organized in our society, is continuous. Now the woman puts the wash in a machine and spends her time reading to the children, breaking up their fights, taking them to the playground, or otherwise looking after them. If, as is often said, women are being automated out of the home, it is only to be shoved into the car chauffeuring children to innumerable lessons and activities, and that dubious advantage holds only for middle and upper-class women who generally can afford not only gadgets but full- or part-time help.

One of the definitions of automation is a human being acting mechanically in a monotonous routine. Now, as always, the most automated appliance in a household is the mother. Because of the speed at which it's played, her routine has not only a nightmarish but farcical quality to it. Some time ago, the *Ladies' Home Journal* conducted and published a forum on the plight of young mothers. Ashley Montague and some other professionals plus members of the *Journal* staff interviewed four young mothers. Two of them described their morning breakfast routine.

One woman indicated that she made the breakfast, set it out, left the children to eat it, and then ran to the washing machine. She filled that up and ran back to the kitchen, shoved a little food in the baby's mouth, and tried to keep the others eating. Then she ran back to the machine, put the clothes in a wringer, and started the rinse water.

The other woman stated they had bacon every morning so the first thing she does is put the bacon on and the water for coffee. Then she goes back to her room and makes up the bed. "Generally, I find myself almost running back and forth. I don't usually walk. I run to make the bed." By that time the pan is hot and she runs back to turn the bacon. She finishes making the children's breakfast and if she is lucky she gets to serve it before she is forced to dash off and attend to the baby, changing him, and sitting him up. She rushes back, plops him in a little canvas chair, serves the children if she has not already done so, and makes her husband's breakfast. And so it goes through the day. As the woman who runs from bed to bacon explains, "My problem is that sometimes I feel there aren't enough hours in the day. I don't know whether I can get everything done."

It's like watching an old-time movie in which for technical reasons everyone seems to be moving at three times normal speed. In this case it is not so funny. With the first child it is not as severe.

What hits a new mother the hardest is not so much the increased workload as the lack of sleep. However unhappy she may have been in her childless state, however desperate, she could escape by sleep. She could be refreshed by sleep. And if she wasn't a nurse or airline stewardess she generally slept fairly regular hours in a seven- to nine-hour stretch. But almost all babies returning from the hospital are on something like a four-hour food schedule, and they usually demand some attention in between feedings. Now children differ, some cry more, some cry less, some cry almost all of the time. If you have never, in some period of your life, been awakened and required to function at one in the morning and again at three, then maybe at seven, or some such schedule, you can't imagine the agony of it.

All of a woman's muscles ache and they respond with further pain when touched. She is generally cold and unable to get warm. Her reflexes are off. She startles easily, ducks moving shadows, and bumps into stationary objects. Her reading rate takes a precipitous drop. She stutters and stammers, groping for words to express her thoughts, sounding barely coherent—somewhat drunk. She can't bring her mind to focus. She is in a fog. In response to all the aforementioned symptoms she is always close to tears.

What I have described here is the severe case. Some mothers aren't hit as hard, but almost all new mothers suffer these symptoms in some degree and what's more, will continue to suffer them a good part of their lives. The woman who has several children in close succession really gets it. One child wakes the other, it's like a merry-go-round, intensified with each new birth, each childhood illness.

This lack of sleep is rarely mentioned in the literature relating to the Tired Mother Syndrome. Doctors recommend to women with newborn children that they attempt to partially compensate for this loss of sleep by napping during the day. With one child that may be possible, with several small ones it's sort of a sick joke. This period of months or years of forced wakefulness and "maternal" responsibility seems to have a long-range if not permanent effect on a woman's sleeping habits. She is so used to listening for the children she is awakened by dogs, cats, garbage men, neighbors' alarm clocks, her husband's snoring. Long after her last child gives up night feedings, she is still waking to check on him. She is worried about his suffocating, choking, falling out of bed, etc. Long after that she wanders about opening and closing windows, adjusting the heat or air conditioning, locking the doors, or going to the bathroom.

If enforced wakefulness is the handmaiden and necessary precursor to serious brainwashing, a mother—after her first child—is ready for her final demise. Too tired to comprehend or fight, she only staggers and eventually submits. She is embarrassed by her halting speech, painfully aware of her lessened ability to cope with things, of her diminished intellectual prowess. She relies more heavily than ever on her husband's support, helping hand, love. And he in turn gently guides her into the further recesses of second-class citizenship.

After an extended tour in that never-never land, most women lose all capacity for independent thought, independent action. If the anxiety and depression grow, if they panic, analysis and solution elude them.

Women who would avoid or extricate themselves from the common plight I've described, who would begin new lives, new movements, and new worlds, must first learn to acknowledge the reality of their present condition. They have got to reject the blind and faulty categories of thought foisted on them by a male order for its own benefit. They must stop thinking in terms of "the grand affair," of the love which overcomes, or substitutes for, everything else, of the perfect moment, the perfect relationship, the perfect marriage. In other words, they must reject romanticism. Romance, like the rabbit at the dog track, is the illusive, fake, and never-attained reward which for the benefit and amusement of our masters keeps us running and thinking in safe circles.

A relationship between a man and a woman is no more or less personal a relationship than is the relationship between a woman and her maid, a master and his slave, a teacher and his student. Of course, there are personal, individual qualities to a particular relationship in any of these categories, but they are so overshadowed by the class nature of the relationship, by the volume of class response, as to be almost insignificant.

There is something horribly repugnant in the picture of women performing the same menial chores all day, having almost interchangeable conversations with their children, engaging in standard television arguments with their husbands, and then in the late hours of the night, each agonizing over what is considered her personal lot, her personal relationship, her personal problem. If women lack self-confidence, there seems no limit to their egotism. And unmarried women cannot in all honesty say their lives are in much greater measure distinct from another's. We are a class, we are oppressed as a class, and we each respond within the limits allowed us as members of that oppressed class. Purposely divided from each other, each of us is ruled by one or more men for the benefit of all men. There is no personal escape, no personal salvation, no personal solution.

The first step, then, is to accept our plight as a common plight, to see other women as reflections of ourselves, without obscuring, of course, the very real differences intelligence, temperament, age, education, and background create. I'm not saying let's now create new castes or classes among our own. I just don't want women to feel that the movement requires them to identify totally with and more-over love every other woman. For the general relationship, understanding and compassion should suffice.

We who have been raised on pap must develop a passion for honest appraisal. The real differences between women and between men and women are the guideposts within and around which we must dream and work.

Having accepted our common identity, the next thing we must do is get in touch with each other. I mean that abso-lutely literally. Women see each other all the time, open their mouths, and make noises, but communicate on only the most superficial level. We don't talk to each other about what we consider our real problems because we are afraid to look insecure, because we don't trust or respect each other, and because we are afraid to look or be disloyal to our husbands or benefactors.

Each married woman carries around in her a strange and almost identical little bundle of secrets. To take, as an exam-ple, perhaps the most insignificant, she may be tired of and feel insulted by her husband's belching or farting at the table. Can you imagine her husband's fury if it got back to him that she told someone he farted at the table? Because women don't tell these things to each other, the events are considered personal, the woman may fantasize remarriage to mythical men who don't fart, the man feels he has a personal but minor idiosyncrasy, and maledom comes out clean.

And that, my dear, is what this bit of loyalty is all about. If a man made that kind of comment about his wife he might be considered crude or indiscreet; she's considered disloyal —because she's subject, he's king; women are dominated and men are the instruments of their domination. The true objective nature of men must never become common knowledge lest it undermine in the minds of some males but most particularly in the minds of women the male right-to-rule. And so we daily participate in the process of our own domination. For God's sake, let's stop!

I cannot make it too clear that I am not talking about group therapy or individual catharsis (we aren't sick, we are oppressed). I'm talking about movement. Let's get together to decide in groups of women how to get out of this bind, to discover and fight the techniques of domination in and out of the home. To change our physical and social surroundings to free our time, our energy, and our minds—to start to build for ourselves, for all people, a world without horrors.

WOMEN IN THE

PROFESSIONS:

FIVE SHORT PERSONAL

TESTIMONIES

WOMEN IN MEDICINE*
Miriam Gilbert, R.N.

From the time when Florence Nightingale was called a
camp follower up to the present day, male chauvinism has
reared its irrational head, and the battle of the sexes has been
waged in the most inappropriate arena I can imagine: the
centers of healing.

In hospitals where the concept of the medical team has
begun to be accepted as the only efficacious approach to any
patient's problem, the female nurse is not often likely to
come into daily contact with the problem of sex discrimination. The team is concerned only with how well each member is utilizing the knowledge and skills pooled for the
patient to draw upon during the healing process. This approach, unfortunately, is the exception.

* Most "women in medicine" are nurses, not doctors—so it was thought more
realistic to have the following article than any on the same subject by a female
doctor.—Ed.

In most working situations, the female nurse is still, in this country, subjected to a series of both subtle and obvious attempts on the part of male doctors to make sure that she is constantly reminded of what her "place" and her "role" are supposed to be. The place, of course, is behind the man; and the role is in most men's thinking a happy mixture of hospital wife, mistress, mother, and housekeeper.

In medicine, as elsewhere, there is a game being played between men and women. However, the stakes here are very high: they are the lives of momentarily nonactive participants, the patients. How is this game played and what effect does it have on those most victimized? To begin with, medicine is male-dominated and has been for centuries. There seems to be no evidence, no matter how great the need for doctors in this country may be, that men are willing to risk loss of this dominance by allowing, much less encouraging, more women to enter their realm. U.S. Department of Labor statistics for 1968 show that only 6 percent of all doctors in the nation are women.

Statistics from the same source show that of the three million women employed in professional and technical occupations, 70 percent work as full- or part-time nurses or teachers. This would indicate that women are well suited for the medical field. Why have they "chosen" to be nurses rather than physicians? Have they?

Most nurses would adamantly say, yes, they have freely chosen this profession, and in some cases this may be so. It is hard to know. For after spending all of her formative years in a male chauvinist society, a young woman with an inclination toward medicine, knowing that females with this inclination go into nursing, may feel she has made a free choice when she follows suit.

Given a situation in which no sex discrimination existed in any field of medicine, how many aspiring young women would become doctors and how many young men nurses? (As an aside, I have seen many men who, in my opinion, are third-rate doctors and would, unquestionably, have been first-rate nurses if they, too, had not been victimized by a double standard.)

Questions may be asked, hypotheses may be made, but the situation remains stagnant. Medicine is a microcosm of the society at large. The sex game is played; the patient is the ball. This cannot, of course, occur in moments of high crisis when intellectual and technical excellence take the forefront and all are, for the moment, asexual. But the moment the crisis has passed, the male doctor asserts his maleness and the female nurse moves from a position of total equality to that of sexual object. Thereafter, one of the primary functions of the nurse is to appeal to and flatter the male ego in order to best fulfill the needs of the patient.

The kind and degree of obsequiousness required to achieve this aim is dependent upon the strengths and weaknesses of the man as a man and a physician. It happens that when this male-doctor-ego is threatened, errors occur. A request voiced too aggressively by a nurse may not be answered for hours; the same request made passively usually gets an immediate response.

There is the problem of the nurse who happens to have a high degree of professionalism and does not respond to a doctor's flirtatious approach. If he is insecure or not highly skilled to begin with, she runs the risk of this situation leading to the doctor conveniently "forgetting" to write an order she needs. It will, of course, eventually be written, after the nurse has had the inconvenience of tracking him down to remind him. It is not unheard of for a nurse who knows a standard dose of a medication, and knows, too, that the doctor who must order it doesn't like her, to ask for another drug or dose in order to get what she knows he would prescribe if a nurse more to his liking asked. This may seem unbelievable, but, sadly, it happens.

Then there is the nurse who asks a doctor for advice and/or instruction she feels it is imperative to receive, and gets an inappropriate reply such as, "Come up to my apartment and I'll show you." A shocker like that leaves her staring in mute fury or, if she is articulate, making a rejoinder that she considers unworthy of professionals dealing with one another.

In its more subtle forms this condescension comes out in a nurse's notes not being read at all, or being read derisively; and, of course, a doctor with this attitude can choose to ignore an observation or a suggestion regarding a patient until either a male nurse or another doctor comes up with the same thing and redirects his attention to it.

It does not take long for even the most naive new graduate to notice that a male nurse will, in most cases, be treated with greater respect by most male doctors, regardless of his ability.

The adequate doctor or nurse will not allow emotional responses to interfere in over-all treatment for any length of time. In my view, any lapse in treatment due to this cause should not exist. It hurts the patient, it hurts the nurse; eventually it hurts the doctor.

The nurse who is aware of role-playing is in constant conflict. The best medical care, which is her responsibility to provide, is often bought at the expense of her own self-esteem. When self-respect is lost, even for a moment, any human being must do something to regain it. The highly competent and long-experienced nurse will attempt to ignore the undermining of her professionalism without castigating the doctor. The more insecure nurse invariably resorts to a superior, sneering attitude that is highly reminiscent of teen-aged girls' clubs. This further polarizes nurses and doctors. The concept of the medical team, which has proven to be the most effective method of treatment, deteriorates. Two of the most vital members are alienated by sex bias.

This does not happen when the physician is a female. There seems to be a continuance of mutual respect from the crisis situation to the daily routine. Only those nurses who are highly resentful and envious of the female physician will treat her with animosity.

It is generally acknowledged that good diagnosis, which may be synonymous with good medicine, is based upon keen observation—when men are doing the observing; when women are, it is most often called intuition. Women, for their own survival, have become notoriously adept in this area and recognize and respect it in one another. The value of this ability in medicine is inestimable.

The long-range goal of breaking through all the walls of male supremacy in medicine will be achieved at exactly the same pace social revolution occurs in all other areas.

In the interim, there is the matter of the professed goal of the male medical hierarchy, which is to find more people to help "alleviate pain and suffering." If they really were honest about this, they would encourage and attempt to develop talent wherever they found it.

Free education could be provided to anyone with the ability and earnest desire to start as an aide, progress to a nurse, and eventually become a doctor. This would destroy the caste system established by orthodox medicine and eventually lead to sexual integration and total medical team-work.

"A HOUSE IS NOT A HOME": WOMEN IN PUBLISHING

Laura Furman

A friend of mine who works for a New York publishing house explained to me that publishing is the gentlemanly profession. She meant by this that publishing has been traditionally for gentlemen and ladies, a very right occupation for members of the educated middle and upper classes. For young lady graduates of Eastern women's colleges, a job in a New York publishing house seems like a logical and easy extension of the academic life, a pleasant and respectable career.

I like making books, and I enjoy the work itself. What I found not only unsatisfactory but enraging was the attitude which I saw and felt existed toward women, an attitude that has been confirmed by numerous other women in publishing whose specific experiences were different from mine. Recently I heard of a white woman who was hired by a house as an editor. Her previous position with another house had been a good one, she was a talented and professional woman, and the second firm was apparently pleased to hire her. When the discussion of salary began she told the man who was hiring her that she didn't necessarily want a raise immediately, but that she wouldn't take a cut in pay. Unashamedly, her future employer said, "But women simply don't make that much money." She replied, "If I were a black man, you wouldn't dare say that."

I had dropped out of college for a year, and for nine months of that year had worked at a publishing house as a production editor in the college text department. When I finally graduated from college, I went to New York and got a job as assistant to the senior editor of a small publishing house. She had worked there for many years and I recognized in her numerous other women I had met in publishing. She was intelligent, sophisticated, well educated, conscientious—and she was a martyr. She was a martyr not because she worked hard, but because she worked hard in a vacuum. She had gone as far as she would go in the house, and she was resigned to it, if more conscious of it than other women in the same position might have been. She was very good at her job, but the work was without pleasure or satisfaction, save the brief moment when the bound books arrived—and then the books were quickly scrutinized for possible slip-ups, mistakes, or negligence.

It is not maliciousness or obsessiveness that at least initially limits pride in one's work. In publishing, women are kept "in the home." They work at a craft and learn the best way to make a manuscript into a book. There are many women like the woman I described who have worked in publishing for years, and who act and work as martyrs. They give the impression that without them the house would cease to function, and their attachment to the house and to the books becomes something more than attachment to a job. To the women who make books, books are something more than a better brand of corn flakes, packaged brightly and attractively, to be sold for the profit of the owner of the house. There is, as yet, no union of women in the publishing industry, and the fight for better salary, a full chance to advance and work as one is best able to is kept on a personal, "family" basis.

Women are allowed to craft the books, and even to promote them, but the really public life of the book is left to the male salesmen, who take the perfected product into the outside world. Once the book is a book, it is no longer any part of the job or concern of those who have made it—it is a better brand of corn flakes, something for the menfolk to tend to and profit from while the little women remain in the house to care for the next book.[1]

The reasons women hold such positions are many, not the least of which is the desire on the part of women to prove themselves as good as men, never to complain, never to refuse to do anything. Another reason is the attitude of the men in publishing. I can easily see that it would be gratifying for a normal, ambitious, American man who is pressured by the demands of his chosen job—to keep sales high, to know which books to publish when, which can be pushed and which will be quiet but steady sellers, and in some way

---

1. A family chart of most houses would place white males at the highest levels at least of decisionmaking, because men are the owners, the managers, and the top editors. Women and other oppressed groups begin appearing further down—down also in salary and power—as head copy editors, copy editors, production managers, production assistants, secretaries, to the point in one avant garde house where the mailroom is run by one Puerto Rican, one black, and one Irish Catholic.

how to scoop the competition and get the best-seller or the latest controversial issue before the rival houses do, for such is the show-biz quality of modern American publishing—for such a man to have someone there, female, obedient, preferably pretty, well educated, and kindly, to make dentist appointments, come along to lunch with a difficult author, do his correspondence, make his phone calls, see to reservations for authors at hotels, restaurants, and airlines, locate a hard-to-find book for his wife, remember everything, and to just be there and willing to do anything. The position of such men is not a totally enviable one, and they receive not only sympathy from their female helpers but loyalty. Not only would the house fall down if such a saintly lady left, but so would her favorite male in the place. But where is the satisfaction for the *woman*, whether the woman be a demiexecutive or a filing clerk? She certainly isn't receiving the salary the man is, or the power (however shared) to make decisions that will affect the publishing program of the house. If she is very useful where she is, that is usually where she will stay, lapping up second-hand sunbeams. That the woman's possibilities are much more severely limited than she deserves for her intelligence, hard work, and professional experience, does not occur to most men in publishing or any industry; and if one woman is rebellious and "demanding" she leaves that house and is replaced by another willing, professional woman.

With women and other minority groups tending the home fires, and men hustling the books along to their fates and profiting from them, publishing continues to function, if a bit hysterically. It will probably continue to do so as a profession until people come to resent being treated so automatically as separate functionaries, until women begin to protest the ease with which they themselves accept from first to last positions of lesser power and lesser salary, but equal pressure. One day at work I looked up at my desk lamp and saw that a fellow worker had put up a little sign that said: Change or Die. Some of us are trying to change, for the alternative is indeed a kind of death—accepting the daily overlooking, the distance between the quality of the work we have put into the book and the quality of the treatment we receive for such work. I changed. I quit.

WOMEN AND TELEVISION

Sheila Smith Hobson

I had always wanted to be a journalist—to be more accurate, a reporter (that was before I realized the supposed distinctions between a reporter and a journalist). Why? Only God knows. It was, I have to admit, a pretty wild ambition for a little black girl on the West Side of Chicago in those days (these days, too). I guess things like travel, quest for truth, name in print, etc., really turned me on. Even before I had ever heard or understood the word "Establishment," I was all bogged down in it.

All the way through high school I wrote. You know, "the only way to be a writer is to write." On the surface that little platitude seemed to be oh so true. I didn't know then and not for some time to come that it implied a lot of other things, too. Like the only way to be a successful (read: in the money) writer (read: hack) is to write (read: not what you believe, but what is expected and what you're told).

I got into New York University's communications program (fondly called in those days TMR: television, motion pictures, and radio)—and was instantly hooked. The subject matter and everything else one needs to know (according to film and television schools) was easy enough and actually very interesting most of the time. But one thing wasn't taught to me and the other three "girls" in the program: How to survive in a high-pressure business like television *as women.* Since there were no women instructors (which I now think is indicative of what lay ahead), I guess I shouldn't have expected any on-the-side consulting. But it was offered. It came from male instructors who, eyeing you suspiciously, asked why the hell a woman wanted to go into such a male-dominated area, and who told you you'd never make it anyway so better to quit and become an editorial assistant or get married. Well, since I had already been an editorial assistant and didn't know anyone to marry, I didn't have anything to drop out *to*. Despite what was thought (I was the only black girl and one of two blacks in the grad program) about my motives for being in an all-white male environment and wanting to go even further into it, I was going to do what I was going to do.

What about my other sisters in sex? Well, with one exception, they were all dumb, affable enough kids. Hard-working, smiling, little talent. They really grooved with the boys. Any typing to be done? They did it. Any simple-minded nothing work to be done? They did it. And so on. One other "chick" was a damn good writer. She had a head. She stood her ground. In time she became one of the boys. Now my situation was different. I didn't go grinning all over the place and that really threw them off. What the hell is that black chick all about. Business, baby. I had a trade to learn and I had to learn it well.

It took me some time (Master's degree and all) to finally get into television. For seven months I walked the whole of New York City. Letters, résumés, interviews, the whole scene. The same thing everywhere. Nothing. Nothing for inexperienced people. Nothing for women. Nothing for black women. Hey, I was once told, didn't I dig the fact that most of the chicks in research and production assistant (PA) positions were white? Hey, I was told many times, don't you know that Jewish chicks have cornered the market? Hey, I was told until I was sick to my stomach, don't you understand that this is a really tough business for women? And besides, do you see any black women around? Any black anything? I dug it.

I was already sick of the whole rotten business that said

you had to be white, preferably male, preferably WASP. I was sick of the no-talented, barelegged, miniskirted, preferably WASP, but often Jewish babes whose only function in the business (as outlined by unwritten hiring codes) was to provide a little during/after hours amusement for the three-hundred-dollar suited, "suave," with-it TV execs. I was sick of it, but I was going to get into it—because the *Man* said I couldn't.

I got in. I started on the educational circuit. The so-called educational, liberal, cultural end of the business. I gained the experience I needed to move on. I also gained more bitterness. In television the golden ladder to success is the heaped-up bodies and spirits and integrities of other people. All those put-down books written about the industry are true. My one objection is that they are all overdramatized. Hustling for the tube is hardly dramatic. It is a daily grind. The same garbage over and over again—until someone drops out of the race or until someone is dropped out of the race.

And what of the women who are in the business? PA's forever. What a thrill! Typing, fetching, or making coffee, delivery girl, office girl, and sexpot all rolled into one. The fellows never had it so good. Better than home! And you know what? These babes, for the most part, take it. They're thrilled to be connected with that exciting, glamorous world in any capacity. I'm in television, you know. Oh! Do *you* know? Well, I guess I shouldn't put them down because they *know* their place in that particular man's world. They're welcome to their place. Frequently, it's the casting couch. The office and studio hanky-panky *et al* were not for me. I had a "double burden" (as it was once inaptly put by a well-meaning white chick). What she meant was that I was a woman *and* black. Do tell! I also had (or should I say have) brains. But, I guess I wasn't smart enough because if I had been I would have been long gone from the world of Take 1, Take 2, Fade out, Dissolve.

Anyway, I moved up, or something like that. I went over to the big time of educational television, NET. I was working on a "black" (pardon the word) show called "Black Journal." NET set my TV career back three years. I clipped newspapers for the better part of my brief stay with them. My brain was picked—clean. And my womanhood and blackness was constantly insulted. That's not particularly new, but the manner was. Here I was working for the first time in my life with other blacks in television. Black men too, who for once weren't mail boys. I guess for about one day I thought it was something else. And it was. Something else. Something entirely else.

The color had been (for the time being) tinted a discrete color of black, but it was still television. This time television in a different disguise. (It has many.) The disguise was now the liberal, give them a break, let's train them for the summer at NET. Hell, most of us were about as trained as we needed to be. What we needed was some real, fruitful work. Well, the same scene existed there. Girl PA's and one or two associate producers. (How liberal! They actually had women associates. In fact, they had several woman producers, too. How extra liberal! So I thought, until I saw the stuff these chicks turned out.) Again, they were just fronts. The same way we blacks were fronts. I suppose I was an extra added attraction. Needless to say, it was an experience that didn't end well.

My next step "up" produced the same type of situation, but worse in many other ways. I had *arrived*, at a local network station. I was working on an all-black show (which nowadays seems to be just about the only outlet for blacks, male and female).

We had to be constantly on our toes against the Man there. All those black shows seen on your TV screens in the last two years are hardly the result of an industry that has seen the light. No, indeed! In a sense they are all a cop-out for the industry. Something that appeases the natives. Holds off the FCC and makes it seem that TV has finally come around to programming for all the people. Watch your television screen closely this season. It will be conspicuously empty of "soul" shows and black-oriented shows. (Of course, with the possible exceptions of Diahann Carrolls and Bill Cosbys. That type of soul sells and besides, you can even forget that they are black.) Television has given the niggers a *whole* season. What do *those* people want?

Did you ever look at black women on television? Closely? Really look! Note: complexions are usually fair to slightly brown. Hair? Straight, of course. Ever see a natural coiffed black chick interviewing, reporting the news, or leading a panel discussion outside of a black show? (Certain so-called black shows are hung-up on bright chicks, too.) Features? Thin, fine, near white. Ever see a black, natural-haired, broad-featured chick on your tube with a local or network station? If so, your set's not picking up good old U.S. of A. programming.

A black on-camera woman has to be not too black in looks, thought, and image. It just doesn't go. She gets weaker material than other women. She's not to be taken seriously on camera or off. The medium is the message. Give other black women something to make them think they've arrived. Something they can associate with. How many black women associate with a Diahann Carroll, a Joan Murray, or any of the other black-white women? Women who, in a slightly darker way, exemplify all the virtues of white American womanhood and supposed beauty. Am I putting down the appearance of the black on-camera woman? Yes and no.

Yes, because I object (to put it mildly) to a double cop-out. You get your token woman and your token black in one *foul* swoop. You use that "black" woman as your front to other blacks. What more do you want? You've got *your* black woman, Charlie.

No, because the black woman always belonged there and in any other segment of this society. She deserves to be there in a normal everyday presentation because first, she is black, and second, she, too, is a woman.

And what of the abilities of these black women on television? Despite what I really think about talent being the only true criterion, I think they are no better or no worse than the other women—white—seen on the tube. The point is that the general level of all women on television is low. And I really think it is meant to be that way (by the industry). Smart, personable women turn people off. Everybody knows that. Why in the hell don't they know their place? Why must they compete? Why? Simply, because it is only natural for intelligent, talented people to want to do their damnedest. Women have never been exempt from this one truth. If you've got it (really got it now), flaunt it.

The solution? Is there really any? There's talk of a revolution. A social revolution. It has started and is progressing. Television, one way or the other, is going to be a part of that revolution. And it is going to be an unwilling part. Television exists in this country for two reasons: money and audiences. Money puts the physical productions on the air, but audiences keep them there and keep the flow of money coming.

Women, black and white, and black people in general are going to have to revolt against the boob tube. They're going to have to say we want what we want or else no watchee. No spendee our bread for your insipid products. No lionizing of your poor, untalented, insulting superstars. Women are going to have to tear themselves away from the hypnotic effects of the glowing screen and click it off. They're going to have to write letters, picket, bitch about what is being poured down their throats. And they're going to have to persist in these efforts. Television is one of the strongest industries in this country. It has forgotten about audiences. It laughs at all those stupid dopes out there—unsophisticated, gullible, unfulfilled. It laughs all the way to the bank with your money. The point is who is allowed to have the last laugh.

If women who work for the industry and women who watch the results of that industry in their homes are so weak, so complacent, so convinced of their own inadequacies, well, the industry will continue in its pap production. If the blonde freak who makes hundreds of thousands of dollars a year by proclaiming "Take it off, take it all off" is *your* soul sister, you deserve it. If the sweet, near white, straight-haired black "chick" who arches her back in the best of Vogue fashion stances for the telephone company is *your* soul sister (or *a* soul sister), you deserve it. If some fumbling, mumbling, pretty little thing is the type of woman you want representing you on the news or anywhere else on the tube, you deserve it. *You may deserve it.* Frankly, I don't, nor do millions of my other black soul sisters. We've taken misrepresentation (along with our black men) long enough. If our flat noses, kinky hair, and black skin are not needed in television, on- *and* off-camera, then neither is our money to buy its products or our eyes to watch the insistent garbage. If white women are pleased with what is happening on the TV screen, well . . . what's that laughter I hear?

WOMEN IN THE MILITARY

Lt. Susan Shnall

When I first thought about doing an article on women in the military, I wanted to provide reasonable suggestions for a change in the armed forces system that would give females positions of responsibility and control. However, my gut reaction is one of repugnance to the entire system; any attempt at reform would still leave a brutal and destructive organization, the existence of which negates the individuality and humanness of its members. The professed purpose of the United States military is to maintain the peace, but its methods toward this goal are destructive and have resulted in the promotion of suffering and death of foreign peoples, as well as of its own.

Why do women "join up"? For a number of reasons, most of them indicative of the inferior position women are placed in in civilian life: enlisted women are taken mostly from high school, for example, and they join because of an unhappy family situation (young men are more readily permitted to run away from home and "sow their wild oats" for a year or so, but the restrictions on young women are much tighter), or because of the "career shill"—the lies about travel, a free education, a glamorous life, and "no orders unless you ask for them." (Enlisted women are not urged to go on to become officers—most women officers go in straight out of college, and they *go in* as officers.)

Many poor women and black women join the military to gain some modicum of education or to learn a skill (while earning a living wage) that they would be unable to acquire in civilian life. Frequently, nursing students join to finish their schooling, because scholarships are scarce and they would have to abandon their chosen field otherwise. The irony is that many women find that the education is hardly free, and frequently have to serve an extra term before they can acquire the very thing they joined for.

My own experiences with the military were as a female member of the Navy Nurse Corps at Oak Knoll Naval Hospital in California.

My initial contact with the Navy was with an attractive female recruiter who seemed to be in a position of leadership in the Nurse Corps, an organization I had thought was separate from the military and which functioned autonomously. As my enlistment was processed, I became familiar with members of the armed forces in other areas. Because I wore a peace symbol, I had to have an extra interview to determine my suitability as a member of the military. The session consisted of an interrogation by a male line officer who questioned me closely on U. S. foreign policy and decided that I would be able to function appropriately in the Navy.

About one-and-a-half years later, at Newport, Rhode Island, I attended Officers Indoctrination School as part of an orientation to the military. At this time I was again investigated, but apparently for a more serious reason: my "peace activities" were under surveillance by the Office of Naval Investigation. The questioning lasted five hours and was conducted by two male officers. When I refused to sign a statement, a third man was brought in to frighten me. The case was referred to the executive officer of the base and sent on to files in Washington, D.C., without ever being seen by a female officer.

Active confrontation with the military occurred in October, 1968, when I decided I could no longer remain a passive dissenter. A march and rally against United States involvement in Vietnam was being planned for that month. To help publicize the activity, I organized and led in uniform a leaflet "bombing" mission on various military installations in the Bay Area on October 10, 1968. We dropped thousands of leaflets, advertising the march, from an airplane onto Treasure Island, Yerba Buena Island, Oak Knoll Hospital, and the U.S.S. *Ranger* (an aircraft carrier). The day after, the Commanding Officer of Oak Knoll promulgated a general Navy regulation prohibiting the wearing of the uniform at a public demonstration. On October 12, I wore my Naval uniform to the march. Several days later I was called in to see the admiral. Waiting for me in his office were the heads of various hospital services—all men except for the head nurse. The charges were drawn up by a man, read by a man, processed by men, and witnessed by men. The enlisted man who also wore his uniform in the march was treated somewhat differently: he was awakened in the middle of the night while he was home on leave, taken into custody, and placed in confinement. Two obvious reasons for the different arraignments are 1) sex, and 2) rank. The Navy was very careful in its handling of my case because I was a female officer.

A couple of months later, I was tried for my "crimes" by a general court-martial board composed of five men and one woman, all of whom were line officers not connected to the health professions. This was considered to be trial by my peers. The sentence could have been a maximum of five years at hard labor, forfeiture of pay, and dismissal from service. Because I am a female my sentence was relatively light: six months' forfeiture of pay, six months at hard labor, and dismissal from service. Because of a Naval policy that any woman sentenced to confinement for one year or less would not be obliged to serve it, I am not serving time. Michael Locks, the airman who was tried on similar charges, received a sentence of one year at hard labor which he is currently serving at a military "rehabilitation" center.

When I returned to duty at the hospital after the court martial, I was placed on a pediatrics ward.[1] While there, I was called in to see the commanding officer and given a direct order not to convert people to my way of thinking while on duty. Three weeks later, I was again called to see the admiral who informed me that I had disobeyed his order and would be placed in an area of the hospital where I would have no contact with enlisted personnel, whom I had been influencing. There was no evidence to support his accusation, and, as a result, the matter was quietly dropped after an intensive investigation of all my co-workers. I am now working on a female surgery ward at the order of a man who had consulted neither the area superviser nor the chief nurse —a purely arbitrary decision by the controlling authority.

An attempt toward equalization of the sexes is made by the armed forces in the area of promotions for Nurse Corps officers. Those characteristics of importance to this promotion include: intelligence, leadership ability, loyalty, responsibility, reliability. These traits are important as they relate to one's passivity to and acceptance of the military system. A close friend of mine was called to see the commanding officer of the hospital and told that she was irresponsible, unreliable, not dependable, disloyal, and provided poor leadership ability because of her pacifist "political ideas."

1. My case is now going through an automatic appeal process.

It has been only recently that promotion of women to the higher rank of captain has been possible for more than one female. More billets have been opened for Nurse Corps officers to reach the rank of commander and captain. However, there are no female admirals and the relative number of higher ranks available to women is far below that for men.

The chief nurse at Oak Knoll is a captain in rank. Her position *should* include control and placement of nurses in that hospital. As a nurse, she should be familiar with the needs of the hospital areas and the capabilities of the nurses. With the help of area supervisors, she should be able to effectively place people under her jurisdiction. But who does that authority rest with? The commanding officer.

One of the more degrading procedures in the military is that of inspection. As an officer, I have to stand inspections infrequently. At this event, we are organized into our separate groups: male enlisted, female enlisted, male officer, female officer. We must stand at attention as a male inspecting officer looks us over to determine our fitness for duty.

Women in the military are not allowed to have dependents under the age of eighteen years. We are not able to claim our husbands as dependents even if they are attending school and have no source of income. Only if the men are completely physically or mentally dependent upon their wives for existence are they declared to be dependents and eligible for an allowance from the armed forces. Our male counterparts in the system, on the other hand, receive allotments for their respective spouses and children, along with complete medical coverage for the entire family. One nurse who protested this inequality was told: "If the Navy had wanted you to have a husband, they would have issued you one."

At this point I feel it is an obvious fact that the military is controlled and operated by men for their benefit. Women, regardless of rank, are in subservient positions in that any authority or responsibility they may have is ultimately under male control. As one who would not cooperate with the

System, I have felt very strongly the attempt at male manipulation of my life. Ironically, because of this chauvinistic attitide and policy on females, the military was not able to punish me and, in a sense, the System defeated itself.

THE TRIALS OF LOIS LANE:
WOMEN IN JOURNALISM

Lindsy Van Gelder

Everybody's seen the flicks: Bogart or Gable with a press card in his fedora, catching the killers and whipping out his deadline exclusive. Guys in green eyeshades yelling "Scoop." Hot tips, hard drinking, and undercover disguises. The cub reporter sneaking into the jury room, rifling the waste basket, and stuffing the secret ballots into his trench coat pocket. *The Daily Planet. The Flash. The Front Page.*

This is the mythology of American journalism, one of the last preserves of the Hemingway-style masculine mystique.

Newspapers have changed a great deal since the days when reporters functioned largely as cops without badges. Today we have press secretaries and public relations men, and our biggest everyday occupational hazard is getting clobbered by a television camera at a press conference. But the myths live on. The newspaper city-room is still the place where you sit in your shirtsleeves, flick your cigarettes on the floor, and keep a bottle in the desk drawer. You can even yell "shit" at the top of your lungs, and no one will be offended.

When a woman becomes a doctor or a lawyer, she is a doctor or a lawyer; when she joins the ranks of the press, she is a news*man*, a desk*man*, a rewrite*man*, or a copy*boy*. (The latter job, the traditional ladder to becoming a reporter, involves schlepping cartons of sandwiches, wallowing in carbon paper and assorted other menial tasks, and many papers won't hire girls for the "heavy work," effectively nipping their careers in the bud.) But most journalism-bound women have worse problems. My own experiences are fairly typical.

In 1964—the year Congress gave us our latest set of rights —the editor of the now defunct *New York World-Telegram & Sun* turned me down for a summer reporter's post because I was a female and would no doubt run off and get married my first day on the job. I must have believed in the gospel of Norman Vincent Peale in those days—I carefully prepared a chart showing that a far greater proportion of men had left the paper in recent years, for the Army or higher paying jobs elsewhere, than had nubile women. The editor wasn't impressed. Women, he pointed out, are a "distraction" in the city room. Other men apparently can make it through the day without raping their secretaries, but the virility of newspapermen is such that temptation has to be kept out of reach.

Then there was the *Wall Street Journal.* When I applied for a summer journalism training program, the first woman to do so, the director regarded me sadly and told me that I just didn't *look* like a newspaperman. "Perhaps," he mused, "if you cut your hair short and gained about twenty-five pounds . . ."

Among the male physical specimens hired in my stead, one is now a clergyman, another is a teacher, and a third is a VISTA worker. To this day, I'm certain any of them could wallop me in a Newspaperman Look Alike Contest.

But my favorite adventure was at the *New York Daily News,* which operates an internship program for college graduates. I remember the editor in charge beaming over my résumé and saying that I might even be "overqualified" for the program. Then he noticed that I was married. A walking womb. All those eggs tumbling down the tubes every single month just begging to be fertilized.

Ever rational, I told the editor I was on the Pill and planned to stay that way for some time to come. Anyway, my husband and I both believed in working motherhood. "Honey," the editor said cavalierly, "that's no way to talk. A pretty little thing like you ought to be home having a baby every year!"

Things went downhill from there faster than a speeding spermatozoa, and finally the editor fired his ultimate challenge at me: "What would you, as a girl, do if we sent you to cover a *race riot* in *Harlem???*" When I said I'd go, my friend was quick with his triumphant reply: "Well, we wouldn't send you there anyway!" *Nyah, nyah, nyah nyah nyah.* End of argument. End of interview. I got on the subway and went downtown to file a complaint with the State Human Rights Commission.

At the hearing, the editor testified that his decision not to hire me had nothing to do with my ovaries. No, the problem was that my husband worked for a rival paper. (He was in fact employed at that time by an evening paper that did not compete with the *News'* morning circulation.) Obviously, I would race home from the *News* every day and blab secrets to the enemy over the dinner table. Why hadn't he told me all this at the interview? Because he was being a "gentleman"—"protecting" me from all sorts of nasty marital resentments and things. No matter that lots of *News* employes had relatives on other papers. I lost the case.

These are the hard-luck sagas of only one woman. One friend of mine, now a top feature writer for a Chicago paper, came to the offices of *Look* magazine a few years ago with a Master's degree in journalism. She was offered the post of receptionist. When she declined the honor, the personnel manager glowingly assured her, "But you'd be an *editorial* receptionist. You'd have a chance to meet real writers!"

The list goes on. But the funny part of it is that I don't know a single woman journalist who has been handicapped by her sex once she did get the job. It's true that a lot of the traits required for reporting—aggressiveness, coolness under pressure, and self-reliance—are bred out of women in this society. From time to time, you *do* have to dodge flying bottles, trip over corpses, and all the rest of the Hollywood bit. In the long run, however, it's the stereotyped female traits that get the story.

One of the biggest changes in journalism over the past decade has been the broadened base of people who get into the news. In the old days reporters spent most of their time with people who were used to dealing with the press—cops, politicians, celebrities, etc. Now these types have hired spokesmen. Today's newsmakers are students, blacks, workers, welfare recipients, junkies, taxpayers, parents, teachers, soldiers, and marchers. And they don't have to talk to the press unless they feel like it.

Getting people to trust you—as opposed to shoving a microphone in their faces—is where responsible journalism is at today. You've got to have compassion, and all those other "female" virtues. Risking a faceful of MACE to tell what *happened* at a demonstration is not enough. You also have to tell what was *going on*—which usually means a rap with the demonstrators and really trying to see why they're there, whether they're liberating buildings or voting for Wallace.

Even in the standard press situations, the feminine stereotype can be turned to a reporter's advantage. If a politician calls on me at a press conference because he thinks I'm going to ask a noncontroversial dumb-broad question, that's his problem. If a guy gives me a story because he thinks I'm a cute little thing, I won't argue. But just try to tell all this to a hiring editor who equates good journalism with the ability to impersonate cops.

Another serious hang-up of the male press (underground, as well as Establishment, I might add) is its coverage of the women's movement. On the rare occasions when women's liberation makes the news—usually only because the media hope someone will be burning a bra—the male reporters act like Ringling Brothers has just come to town. Just look at all those freaky dykes, smirk smirk. Some of 'em aren't even bad looking.

Several months ago, for example, I covered a demonstration at the Plaza Hotel, where the National Organization for Women was attempting to integrate a businessmen-only dining room. The place was mobbed with newsmen, asking cute questions of the far-too-patient feminists, and breaking each other up with loud, clever sallies. Amid the general hilarity, I saw a television newsman thrust his microphone at a working female wire-service reporter to inquire, "And what do *you* think of all this?" The young woman put him down politely. I would very much like to have seen him try the same routine on a black reporter at a Black Panther rally.

The parallel between women and blacks in journalism is worth noting. Until the mid-Sixties, news of the black community was virtually ignored by the press, and black reporters numbered a handful. An astonishing proportion of the early civil-rights stories in New York were covered by, of all things, white Southern journalists, the feeling being that they were the next best thing to Negroes.

Then, as the value of black news accelerated, people like SNCC and the Panthers did a wicked thing. They started banning honkies from their press conferences. *Tsk tsk*, said all the editors as they madly hired up every black journalist they could find. Some of the white reporters were a little annoyed. But what do you know—it turned out that those niggers weren't so stupid after all. Some of them could even cover nonracial stories.

Come the women's revolution, an awful lot of talented women are going to be hauled away from their steno pads, research jobs, and fashion columns—to explain it in print.

THE SECRETARIAL PROLETARIAT

Judith Ann

As a child, I had the highest ambitions for myself. I was bright in school and full of energy. I can remember at the age of about fifteen, feeling like the world was at my disposal; there was nothing I couldn't do once I turned my mind to it. I had my heart set on the Foreign Service—perhaps I'd be a United States Senator—or else maybe a movie director—at any rate I always imagined myself in positions of power, with control over my environment, making creative decisions.

I went to college, although I wasn't sure I wanted to—I was so eager to take on the world that college seemed sort of a waste of time. Besides, although schoolwork came easily to me, I didn't like it. I was told I was "sensitive" and "perceptive"—nice things to be, and much more suitable for a girl than solid achievement. I swallowed that kind of claptrap, and found myself, as I grew older, actually getting

86

less and less smart. By the time I was a sophomore in college, I was literally incapable of rigorous intellectual work. I attended most of my classes, because I enjoyed listening to the professors, but I didn't do any homework. The avid bookworm of my childhood became a complete nonreader. I didn't write a single paper that year, and even ceased making up excuses for not handing them in. I spent examination periods lost in sexual fantasies, daydreaming of the mythical Man who would rescue me from this misery and give meaning to my life. By the time I flunked out, I was beaten down and felt worthless. My childhood ambitions seemed like a joke.

I pulled myself together with the consolation that it didn't matter anyway if I flunked out. After all, I was only a girl —I couldn't be drafted and there was no need really to plan a career; I resolved to take a job, any job, prove to the world that I was not really a failure, and in the meanwhile, devote my energies to husband-hunting. I went to live with my parents in Hartford, Connecticut, the insurance capital of the nation, and two days later I started work as a rater in an insurance company. The personnel manager was benevolent. I had done well on the intelligence tests, and I seemed sincere in my desire to mend my ways, and they really *wanted* to give me a good position, but young girls so often leave the company after a short time, and of course with my record of failure . . .

Rating actually turned out to be one of the best jobs available to women in the company, except for secretaries and a few special categories of "clerical support." Raters, in fact, had exactly the same qualifications and background as underwriters, a prestigious group with a good deal of responsibility. The only difference in qualifications was that raters were women and underwriters were men. The floor I worked on sheltered both raters and underwriters. It was a large room with maybe seventy desks, all in rows. The underwriters, with telephones on each desk, were on one side of the room; raters, without telephones, were on the other side. A solid wall of high filing cabinets separated the two areas.

The working day was from 8:00 A.M. to 4:00 P.M. We had to be in our seats with our coats hung up by eight sharp, when a bell rang to start us to work. We were allowed to start cleaning up at about 3:35, and then we sat at clean desks with purses in hand from 3:45 to 4:00, when the bell rang again and we bolted the building. We had a short coffee break about half-way through the morning, and then 45 minutes for lunch. (The work day was thus officially 7¼ hours long; we were not paid for lunch period.) Since the whole floor went to lunch at the same time, it was easily and duly noted if you were even one minute late getting back. On paydays (every other Friday) we got an extra half-hour for lunch—a state law so that employees could go to the bank. Paydays were also special because of the "quarter pool." This was voluntary, of course, but each payday nearly every employee on our floor put a quarter in the pool and his name in the hat. I played the quarter pool every payday I was there, and although I never won, I spent a lot of time planning what I would do with the approximately fifteen dollars if I ever did win. The quarter pool, the World Series, and an astronaut voyage (a few people brought in transistor radios and were allowed to play them very quietly the morning of splash-down) were the only breaks in office routine.

We went to the ladies' room, in groups of two or three, twice a day, after coffee break and again in the middle of the afternoon. Talking (in low tones and small quantities) with co-workers was allowed only with neighbors directly to the side or front or back—even cater-corner was not permitted. (This rule applied to coffee break as well.) The atmosphere was similar to that of elementary school. We were even called "girls," not women, no matter what our ages. We had no rights, only duties. Each employee was allowed five sick days per year; after that you were docked—or fired. There was no severance pay.

The work itself was completely routinized, mindless toil. You got a stack of policies in the morning and you spent the day referring to a set of rate schedules and computing the rates on a Calculator—an adding machine that also multiplies and divides. Your work was then checked by a co-worker and rechecked by the supervisor, and then sent out to the typists. The typists were off somewhere on another floor; I never found out where for sure. Typing was even more lowly work than rating, so a rater never even met, much less mingled with the typists.

This isolation by hierarchy of the different levels of female clerical labor (secretaries, raters, typists, file clerks, in that order) was a very potent tool in the hands of management. By giving some units a sense of false privilege and all units a feeling of rivalry with their sisters, we were effectively kept from any cross-unit solidarity or even sympathy, which would have been very threatening indeed to management.

Within the rating unit itself, however (and I suppose it was the same all over), there was a very warm feeling among the workers. Particularly the young unmarried raters developed strong friendships with each other and we often spent time together after working hours. We all hated our jobs, hated our supervisors, and spent long hours bitching about the conditions and plotting when and how we would quit. We also talked about what kind of jobs we would get instead —it was universally agreed that a small office with several men and only one or two girls would be a vast improvement over the rows and rows of women and the female supervisor that we now had to deal with. My friend Ann did leave while I was there. She went to an insurance agent's office. It was a small office, and she was clerical assistant to the three or four salesmen; in the insurance world, this was the *crème de la crème* of female employment, and the rest of us back at the old job were very envious.

The other subject we talked about even more consistently was men. Of course, we assumed that all this talk about future "better jobs" was only conditional on our single status, and it was our firm belief that at the end of all present suffering lay the final reward: marriage. We talked and thought about men constantly. If an unmarried underwriter looked at one of us cross-eyed, we would discuss the implications for an entire lunch hour. If one of us got a letter from a boy (usually in the Service or away at college) or, glory be, had a date, it provided us with conversation for days. Two or three of the girls were engaged and we discussed their wedding plans—and the terrifying, glorious "first night"— daily. We were all virgins, and the repressed sexuality of these vibrant young girls was almost tangible in the atmosphere. Since the work was so routinized, I found myself able to indulge in sexual fantasies eight straight hours a day —a vast improvement over the quality of my fantasies during exams at college, because, since here I could do my work at the same time, there was less anxiety attached to them. This is in fact one of the most oppressive aspects of female clerical work: since the working conditions were so bad and our daily life so dull, the only bright spots in our lives were our relationships or hoped-for relationships with men. We sought refuge from our oppression as working women in the male supremacist institutions of dating and marriage, and in escapist consumerism of make-up and pretty clothes.

Despite the atmosphere, the young raters were a high-spirited bunch, and our life-force could not be completely repressed. Nancy especially was full of fun, and her rebellious antics kept us almost sane. In fact, although her work was always accurate and quickly done, she was consistently passed over for raises and very nearly fired because she was a "discipline problem." But they had even gotten through to her, on a deeper level. Although she was constantly attacking and making fun of the supervisor, an absurd tragic spinster who wore a blonde wig (we were always hatching elaborate schemes to sneak up behind and snatch off the wig when she wasn't looking), Nancy nonetheless had internalized a profound respect for male authority; she spoke in awed tones of the floor's Big Boss who had his own office in the back of the room; she admired his apparel, his bearing, his kindly (i.e., patronizing) way of dealing with employees. In fact, we all agreed that we would much rather work for him than for the female supervisor, and that having a woman boss was one of the worst aspects of the job.

What we didn't realize was that the supervisor was exploited, too. She had spent thirty years with the company to achieve this title, and she still had two or three male bosses immediately over her. In order to gain this crumb of recognition, she had had to sell out her humanity.

Because the young raters were "hard to handle" and had a high turnover rate (we had nothing to lose by job-hopping, and the myth of the "better job" kept us moving often), the company didn't like us much. There were continual rumors that soon they would stop hiring so many young women and instead hire older, more desperate women, who could be intimidated with greater ease and who would probably stay a long time. Management had good reason for wanting workers to stay a long time—that way they could get away with paying lower salaries. Several girls who had been working there for two years longer than me, and getting regular salary increases every six months, were still making less than my starting salary. I started at $60.00 a week; this was in 1965. We could not afford apartments, of course, and usually lived with our parents. Even so, expenses were high. Alice, who, like me, took home less than $50.00 a week, was making time payments on a second-hand car, and gave her parents $25.00 *a week* for room and board. When I protested to her that this seemed unfairly high, she replied that she didn't mind; her parents were saving her rent money in a special account to pay for her wedding. Alice was married that summer with a lovely wedding and got pregnant on her honeymoon; no one in the office ever heard from her after that.

I worked at the insurance company for six months, saving

my money and making plans with a girlfriend to move to New York City, where I felt sure that my glamorous destiny would finally materialize. I was nineteen, and my work success (I was a very good rater) and the fact that I was about to leave my parents' home and protection had somewhat revived my basically independent spirit. Surely in New York, the most exciting city in the world, there would be an outlet for my creative energies. My old adolescent optimism surged. I was bursting to *do things*, to move, to grow, to be alive. A week after I arrived in New York, I found a job at a bank . . .

At The Bank, I was an assistant in the Investment Research Division. I had my own phone and my own In and Out box. Compared to the insurance company, this was already a real prestige job! Again, there were rows of desks, only this time there were more partitions, *and* the rooms were integrated! Men and women sat side by side. I soon learned, however, that here the segregation was simply more subtle. With the exception of the Big Bosses (in private offices), their secretaries, and the (all female) typing pool, the Investment Research Division was divided into two distinct categories, investment analysts and investment assistants. The analysts were men, and the assistants were women, mostly young girls just out of college. (There were other hierarchical distinctions among the male analysts— officers-of-the-bank, junior vice-presidents, trainees, and the like—but the women were consistently assistants.)

I wasn't happy at The Bank. The people were dull and stuffy and the rules were almost as bad as at the insurance company, but the worst thing about the job was that there was really no work for me to do. To this day, I can't think of why they hired so many assistants, unless it was so that the analysts might be able to refer to us ("My assistant will look into the matter," etc.) on the telephone. Well, there *were* some things I was responsible for—a scrapbook of clippings from the *Wall Street Journal*, a few charts of stock prices that I had to keep current, a little filing, errands—but most of the time I had to *look* busy, one of the most oppressive job functions I've ever performed.

I think that people like and need productive work, and when we're not allowed any, we make up games to make what we have to do seem productive. Filing, for example, was a task I really hated, but I spent many hours working out an elaborate and unique filing system, so that nobody could find things except me and I could feel I was at least of *some* use around the office.

Since it was so boring to just sit there and shuffle papers, any excuse to leave my desk was a treat, and I thus fell into sex-related servant-type tasks to the benefit of my boss. The pencil-sharpener was located at the other end of the office near a window, so I sharpened his pencils several times a day. In the afternoons I gladly offered to go to the deli for coffee and cokes for my co-workers, so that I could escape the office for a few minutes. I was happy to do Xeroxing for anybody, since the Xerox machine was on another floor, and sometimes you even got to wait on line and chat with other employees. The most minor errand was an excuse to wander the halls, "accidentally" get on the wrong elevator and explore a floor I hadn't seen before (it was a large building), or even just stand at a window and watch new construction across the street. I was always aware that my boss ought to be able to do these kinds of dumb errands for himself, but at the same time I didn't mind doing them for him, since it was more fun than sitting at a desk. Executives are always saying, "These girls [clerks and secretaries] like their jobs, they don't mind doing things for me. Furthermore they're lazy and don't want to get ahead." But it's not true. Willingness to go on dumb errands and "laziness" are resistance tactics.

The other thing I hated about The Bank was my isolation from the other women working there. The comradery of the rating unit was the one thing that had kept me sane there, and I found at The Bank that it was much harder to make friends. I thought at first that this was because I was now in New York, where things were tough, as opposed to Hartford, my home town. But in fact the reason was that The Bank job was a slightly more prestigious level of clerical work than rating. Raters were already so low on the totem pole that we had nothing to lose from human friendships with our sisters; but the "better" the job, the stiffer the competition—and the more isolation from your sisters. Work relationships at The Bank were "personalized" in a perverted way: you worked for one or two men and your loyalties were to them, not to the other women workers.

By the time I got to my third, and most recent, job (I am here discussing only my three major job experiences; I have also worked, for short periods, as a waitress, a flower-wrapper in a florist shop, a free-lance typist), I had begun to be conscious of women's oppression, and was involved in the political movement for women's liberation. It was therefore with a sharp sense of irony that I began work as a secretary in the editorial department of a leading bridal magazine. The more than $5 billion a year bridal industry, for which this magazine is a publicist and mainstay, is one of the largest institutionalized oppressors of women, since it reinforces the societal dictum that a woman must marry and find her identity through her husband and children, or else face life with no identity at all, as an "unwanted spinster."

But besides being an institutional oppressor of all women, the bridal magazine was oppressive on a daily basis to me and the other women working there. Paying lip service to the fact that it was, after all, a "women's magazine," the company hired mostly women on the editorial staff (as opposed to the other magazines published by the same company, where, for the most part, the only visible women were secretaries and clerks). In fact, of the seventeen or so members of the editorial staff, all were women, except for one man—that one man was the Editor-in-Chief, and I was his secretary. While responsibility for the editorial content of

The Magazine was nominally in the hands of the various (female) editors, in fact, every editorial decision was either reviewed or instigated by the Editor-in-Chief, who ruled absolutely by inspiring the staff with fear of the nearly violent temper tantrums he was given to when crossed. He was a temperamental man, unsure at the outset of his own masculinity, and he vented his hostility toward women by taking it out first on the (female) staff, and finally on the readers of "his" magazine, universally referred to as "our little readers" or "those dumb girls."

The isolation here was even worse than at The Bank. An editorship on a women's magazine is among the best jobs society offers to women, so each editor jealously guarded her own modicum of prestige, and the competitive atmosphere was really unbearable. At some point or another I heard each of them say that she would much rather work in an office with men and that she couldn't stand "these bitches." This hatred of other women, which was really self-hatred, made it easy for the Editor-in-Chief to divide and conquer. He would craftily make and break alliances with each of the editors in turn, keeping the whole office in a frenzy of suspense, all of us desperate to stay in his favor. I was titularly the only secretary in the department, but in actuality all of us women, no matter how fancy the title, were treated like secretaries by the Editor-in-Chief. I must say, though, that this consciousness was not really shared by the female editors. They clung like mad to the few privileges they as editors had over me, a secretary.

The Editor-in-Chief was himself answerable to yet another force of The Magazine—the advertising staff, and finally the advertisers themselves. In fact, it is a common joke around these consumer or trade magazines that "editorial is the poor relation of advertising." It is the advertisers who really determine the editorial content of the magazine: good advertisers get lots of editorial credit; infrequent or unreliable advertisers get little or none. By extension, it is the advertising (male) principle which governs the content of the so-called women's magazines.

At The Magazine, I had finally achieved the highest job rung available to girls of limited education or, for that matter, to most girls, no matter what their education. I was a private secretary. As a child, watching the television show "Private Secretary" with Ann Sothern, I had often day-dreamed about the glamorous and sexy life a New York secretary leads . . .

Well, I knew that I was letting myself in for such basically uncreative tasks as typing letters, filing, and opening mail. After all, I was a realistic girl, I needed bread, and I was prepared to sell my skills and labor to survive—I had done it before and I didn't expect this job to be much different from the others. I must confess, however, that I was not prepared for what I soon discovered was the bulk of a private secretary's work: balancing my boss's checkbook; making his coffee in an electric coffee-pot and then washing the pot and cups; dusting his office; Xeroxing his income-tax records; even at one point washing baseboards. It seemed incredible to me at first that a human being, very much like myself in appearance and basic needs, seemed incapable of the simplest tasks: sharpening his own pencils or answering his own phone. I finally realized, however, that it was probably not that the tasks themselves were so physically debilitating to my boss; the degrading division of labor was just the quickest way of enforcing the sexual hierarchy in employment, just a way of saying, "You're shit and I'm King."

The telephone mystique is even more complicated than that, of course. The secretary answers the phone and the caller asks to speak to the boss. Immediately, the caller knows that the boss is important enough to have a secretary. The secretary then asks for the caller's name and asks him to hold while she checks to see if the boss is "in." Now the game begins in earnest. The importance of the boss relates directly to the length of time the caller is made to wait before speaking to him; the importance of the caller is inversely proportional to that same length of time. And if, after a respectable period, the secretary returns to the phone and says that the boss is "in conference," then the caller knows that the boss is *really* important, and the caller himself had better watch his step, start using Listerine or something, because he's obviously on the way down in the reliable scale of telephone values. The secretary (or secretaries—and you can imagine the delicacy of situations in which *both* parties have secretaries; I have known cases in which a single phone conversation involved days, even weeks, of maneuvers and countermaneuvers) is, of course, essential to the corporate telephone ethic. I began to wonder if, without her, the whole corporate structure would not collapse. I have often wanted to do a census on exactly how many women it takes to keep one corporate executive alive: there's his mother, wife, usually a mistress, and a daughter or so, secretary, maid, waitresses, numerous cleaning women, clerks, operators . . . What if we all went on strike?

I endured daily humiliation at The Magazine for nearly a year; then finally, with the support and encouragement of my sisters in women's liberation, and inspired by a particularly offensive office situation which all the women had been complaining about for some time, I sent around a signed memo to the female employees on my floor, which read:

> As we all know, the door to the sixth floor Ladies' Room is locked. At the moment, it is so *well* locked that we can hardly get into it. The lock is in fact broken and requires complicated manipulation to open it. Besides this, the keys which we were all individually given are easily and continually being lost—or stolen by otherwise honest women made desperate by a sudden emergency. For pregnant women (of whom there are several now employed on the sixth floor) the specter of the Ladies' Room Lock holds real terror. In other words, the situation is intolerable.
>
> The reason for our difficulties, we are told, is that the sixth floor is only partially leased by the company. Apparently, the lavatory door is kept locked in order to keep the employees of other firms from using our toilets. I should think that their bathrooms must be in pretty ghastly condition if it is felt that those employees are so desperate to use ours. Surely no one

thinks that our lavatory is so clean and beautiful that we really need fear its defacement by outside agitators. Why should we not share our bathrooms with those less fortunate than we?

Furthermore, I have recently uncovered an astonishing piece of news—*the men's room door is not locked.* This is blatant discrimination against women—although it is only a more obvious manifestation of the discrimination against women which pervades this whole society and which is easily seen in the hiring practices of this company. (How many male secretaries have you met up with lately? And even at the bridal magazine, where mostly women are employed, and the content is geared especially toward women, the Publisher and Editor-in-Chief are men.)

Women! Let us unite for the attainment of our just demands! The toilets belong to the people! No more locks on any lavatory door! No more discrimination against women, in bathroom locks, or hiring practices, or any other area!

Retribution was swift and final; I was fired within a half-hour. My boss ran up to me in a rage, and shouted: "You're just a secretary—you can't do this!" His first concern, apparently, was the challenge I had made to his authority. His second concern was that people might find out about it, specifically the president of the company, and he might be made a laughingstock or worse. Implicit in this concern of his was the fact that he was held responsible for all my actions; as his secretary, I was merely an extension of him, a reflection of his glory or failure. The assumption was that the only reason I had been able to take an independent action was that he had failed to keep me in line properly.

Getting fired was a liberating experience. The Unemployment Board agreed with me that my dismissal was unfair, and they're supporting me until I find another job. But moments of vindication like this are brief, and I know that when my Unemployment Insurance runs out and I have to go back to work, things will be just as bad.

I can no longer fool myself with the fantasy that working conditions might improve at my next job. Each of my past jobs has been, by society's standards, "better" than the last, and each has been dehumanizing in its own way. I can't find my liberation through a "personal solution"; personal solutions do not exist in an inhuman society. I need a movement to help me find political solutions to these problems, which are societal problems, not personal problems.

The companies I worked for—insurance, banking, bridal magazine—all would be totally unnecessary in a society that served human needs rather than the profit motive. They should not even exist. I can't have my liberation without destroying them and the profit motive altogether.

Although we work at desks instead of on assembly lines, female clerical work is very much like factory labor in its exploitative nature. But unlike factory workers, we don't even have unions. The Bosses make a false separation between "blue collar" and "white collar" workers, because it's in their interest to keep us clerical workers from organizing to demand better wages, better working conditions, day-care for our children—or maybe even a revolution. And the unions which now exist don't do much good for the workers either; in fact, many of them are racist and sexist institutions in themselves.

Another thing that has kept women workers from organizing is that we are prevented from finding an identity through our work. There are several reasons for this. First of all, the work we are assigned, as women, is the lowest level, most meaningless and degrading work available in the society—who wants to identify as a file clerk? Second, all work in a capitalist society is alienating to the workers because the workers do not benefit from the fruits of their own labor—we sell our labor, while management reaps the profits and makes the identification with what we have produced. Third (and perhaps most important), as women we are allowed to identify not through production, achievement, and action, but through men. When you're bored and miserable all day at work, flirtation and role-playing with men begins to sound like fun. Marriage and staying at home with the children seem like liberating alternatives to the kind of jobs we can get. But we soon find out that that's a myth. When we marry, we only exchange our status as a worker for status as domestic slave labor—we do the cooking, cleaning, child-rearing (all important productive tasks) and we get no wages at all, only patronizing security and protection and perhaps a weekly allowance from a benevolent master. And we don't always even get to stay at home. Many working women *are* married (I was married during my last job; since my husband was sick at the time, I was the sole support of the household, on a salary that was half what my husband could make with the same qualifications). Then we have *two* full-time jobs instead of just one—underpaid clerical worker and unpaid housekeeper. In this way, they keep us just too damn *busy* to organize!

Maybe some readers of this article will think that I was unusual among clerical workers because I knew that I was being exploited and rebelled against it. Maybe some of you think that most clerical workers accept and even like their lot and don't care about changing it. But it's not true. Everywhere I worked the women at the bottom knew that they were underpaid and overworked, denied job security and the possibility of advancement, exploited by male supremacy and a class system. And everywhere we rebelled in a thousand small ways—taking extra time in the ladies' room, misfiling important letters, "forgetting" to correct typos.

What we must do now is resist collectively instead of in isolation. We have feared that by speaking out against our oppression we might lose our lousy jobs and thus our livelihood, which does happen if we speak out alone. We have feared that maybe our present conditions are just the way things are and can't be changed. But these and other fears can be overcome through collective actions and solidarity. We can pool our financial resources to reduce the danger of summary firings; we can share our child-rearing responsibilities to free each other's time for action. We can support each other emotionally and become sisters in oppression and, finally, in victory.

THE HALLS OF ACADEME

The Women's Caucus, Political Science Department, University of Chicago

Several of our professors have made these comments—some of them in jest—without realizing how damaging comments like these are to a woman's image of herself as a scholar:

"I know you're competent and your thesis advisor knows you're competent. The question in our minds is are you *really serious* about what you're doing."

"The admissions committee didn't do their job. There's not one good-looking girl in the entering class."

"Have you thought about journalism? I know a lot of women journalists who do very well."

"No pretty girls ever come to talk to me."

"Jane Jacobs' book *The Death and Life of Great American Cities* is the only decent book I've ever read written by a woman."

"Any girl who gets this far has got to be a kook."

"They've been sending me too many women advisees. I've got to do something about that."

"I hear I'm supposed to stop looking at you as a sex object."

"We expect women who come here to be competent, good students but we don't expect them to be brilliant or original."

Student: "No, I wouldn't stop teaching if I had children. I plan to work all my life."

Professor: "But of course you'll stop work when you have children. You'll have to."

Professor to student looking for a job: "You have no business looking for work with a child that age."

WOMEN AND THE WELFARE SYSTEM

Carol Glassman

Welfare is one of our society's attempts to preserve the traditional role of woman as childbearer, socializer, and homemaker. Early in the twentieth century there was growing concern for the victims of "laissez-faire" capitalism. Laws were passed dealing with workmen's compensation, regulation of work conditions, and limitations on child labor. Prominent among the "victims" were female heads of families. Since the system only provided for women as secondary wage earners, they and their children suffered from extreme poverty. In addition to economic discrimination, these women suffered from the lack of community facilities to share the burdens of socializing children. Thus faced with the failure of the system to allow women to support their families through employment, the legislature chose as a solution the creation of a "substitute man." This man was the Social Security Act of 1935.

The act provided for federal participation in a nationwide program of direct economic assistance to the elderly, to the blind, and to dependent children. The law defined a dependent child as "under sixteen without parental support because of death, disability, or continued absence of a parent, and living in his own home with certain near relatives." The liberal rhetoric of the day claimed that if the state took over the burden of financial support, the woman would be freed to perform her "natural" and needed tasks of child care and housekeeping.

For its recipients, the welfare system carried with it most of the hazards of "housewife and mother," and few of the rewards. Domination by a husband was replaced with control over every aspect of a woman's life by the welfare agency. Strangers could knock at any hour to pass judgment on her performance as mother, housekeeper, and cook—as well as her fidelity to the welfare board. The welfare board, like a jealous husband, doesn't want to see any men around who might threaten its place as provider and authority. An ex-client describes this attitude when she says, "The welfare never tried to find out what you wanted to do. All they was trying to find out was, did you have another man . . . and that bugged me! I used to ask them, 'just because you was on the welfare didn't mean you didn't have to have friends, or couldn't have associates.'"

More powerful and efficient than any husband, the welfare board keeps a running file on all its wives. Case records include such things as evaluations of a welfare woman's housekeeping, her ability to budget her small income and pay her bills, and her "moral standards." Likewise, she is often scorned for activities that take her outside her home.

While the extent of man-hunting by the welfare board varies, one finds evidence of it in many case records. One narrative states that the case worker noticed a man's razor and brush while using the john. He then proceeded to question the woman, check the closets for men's clothing, talk to neighbors, etc. Another record contained letters written by the client to a male friend. The man's mother had turned them over to the case worker, telling her to have the client leave her son alone. The case worker then reports that she lectured the client on her behavior, adding that the client was rumored to be a prostitute. For most welfare women there has been no pattern according to the sex or race of the case worker to indicate what they should expect. The "bad" case workers have been both men and women, black and white.

Another client tells how she was treated on the first visit of her case worker: "She came in. She looked around, she looked in my closets. She went in so far as to look in my closet, and she said, 'Why are you going on welfare with such beautiful furniture.' She even suggested, 'Why don't you have a man keep you?' " Thus the welfare "husband" who provides support and authority does not allow another male to provide sex and companionship.

Throughout the welfare department one finds the combined view that poverty is due to individual *fault* and that *something is wrong with women who don't have men.* Over and over one hears said, "If they didn't have problems they wouldn't be on welfare." (Poverty, a discriminatory job market, inadequate community facilities are, of course, not the problem.) The official version of the attitude toward welfare women is presented in a check-off form used in New Jersey as part of the regular three-month check done on welfare women. (All other categories of assistance—Old Age, Blind, Disability—are checked on once a year.) The form (on which the case worker must check the description that suits the client) contains such captions as: "Disorganized due to mother's inability to function"; "Repeatedly without money, food—due to inability to plan, immaturity, compulsive or unwise spending"; "Threat of eviction or cut off of utilities—reason: indifference or inexperience re: financial obligations"; "Exploitation resulting from illiteracy, physical or mental condition or behavior problem of parent." Always the problem lies in the woman herself and not in the society.

For most women, welfare is synonymous with a loss of control over their lives. From her first encounters she is given the message, "You do what we say!" Vague, but widespread rumors about how welfare can have your kids taken away, or have your check cut off, go unquestioned. As most women come to welfare after a series of marital difficulties or after a losing struggle to support themselves and their kids through employment, they feel defeated and easily cowed. Led to believe that the welfare board has the right to delve into every aspect of their lives, few women will challenge the specific actions of a case worker. One of the early welfare-rights organizers tells of an experience that led her to action:

I was down at the welfare office and I seen how she used to treat some of the people. She started out with me, but it didn't work. I don't think she'd think I'd just accept it. About three women come in there and she treated them like, really, they wasn't nothing. I walk out behind these women and ask them how they like Mrs. X [the case worker] They said she was awful! She had all these threatening letters she sent to different people: "If you don't come to the welfare office on such and such a day, your check will be held up on the first of the month," or "If you don't report to the office your check will be cut." After going out signing petitions to get rid of her we found that most of these people she cut off welfare were still entitled to welfare. And furniture—one girl didn't even have a bed to sleep in and she [Mrs. X] told her welfare didn't give furniture, the money had run out for furniture.

The power of the consumer is largely taken out of the hands of the welfare woman. Direct payments by the welfare board to doctors, dentists, and druggists, while of some advantage to her, still deny her the influence of a "private" patient. Food stamps, used by many poor women in food shopping, label her as poor and powerless in the marketplace. While the school free-lunch program forbids labeling of its recipients, the child's mother is labeled when buying her dinner at the supermarket. Likewise, the welfare board has direct contact with the welfare woman's landlord in order to verify the rental fee. As budgets vary according to rental, size of family, and the age of the oldest child, welfare women can't be "trusted" to give the correct figure. The landlord is thus informed that his tenant is on welfare. If she fails to pay her rent he calls the board, regardless of what services he has failed to perform. This means a visit from the case worker, who either subtly or directly pressures her to pay the rent. As federal regulations prevent the woman from being told how to spend her money, local administrations and individual case workers have found various means of getting the job done. In Essex County (N.J.) the client is told if she doesn't pay her rent she must return it to the welfare, regardless of housing-code violations or other problems. A grocery store in Newark which encouraged women to buy on credit, padded their bills, and then used the case workers as bill collectors, was closed down for this practice by a welfare-rights boycott in which nineteen people were arrested. A woman married for thirteen years talks of her reaction to first going on welfare:

> Men would approach you and proposition you. The sales people would look at you, always trying to sell you something, coming by with some gimmick. The landlord was exploiting on you, they was always putting their foot in your door. Doctors treated you differently 'cause you were on the welfare. All these things I started to notice. I had a really good pediatrician that I had taken all my children (seven) to when I had my husband. As soon as he found out I was on welfare, he told me he didn't take people on welfare. He knew me good; it made me feel just awful. I started to notice then that things were different when you were on welfare.

A woman who separates from her husband has full responsibility for the socialization of their children. This situation often puts her on welfare. Her husband is responsible for some support, but the System allows him to live on a much higher standard, without restrictions on with whom and how he lives, without a ceiling on his income, and without someone telling him how to spend his money. He also has no other responsibilities for the care of the children. When the woman applies for welfare, his income is evaluated to determine his "capacity to support." According to the evaluation charts, a single man can earn $310 per month before he has a capacity to give his family any money. Yet on a welfare budget this amount supports a woman and three children. As a man's income goes up, the amount he can keep after support goes up. The woman's income stays static. While the Domestic Relations Courts are less lenient (especially to poor black men), a man brought in on a non-support complaint still has only to meet his payments and keep his address active. He has no other restrictions or responsibilities.

Old notions about "illegitimacy" and the immorality of mothers of "out of wedlock" children are prevalent throughout the welfare system. On the abovementioned check-off form a caption reads, "O.W. children: 1st pregnancy; 1st child; repeated pregnancies and/or children. Conditions that foster illegitimacy." Under a proposed solution it reads, "Improving environmental conditions seriously contributing to illegitimacy." Unwed mothers are required to bring paternity suits against the fathers of the children. At a pre-court interview with the welfare board's legal staff the woman is asked degrading and guilt-inducing questions—Where did you meet the man? When did you first have intercourse? How often? Where? Did you continue after you became pregnant? Did he suggest any "medicines" or "treatments" to promote abortion? Did he suggest a doctor? Did you ever pose as man and wife to friends? What are his favorite pool halls and taverns? Did he offer marriage? Many women tell of being threatened in court with jail or with the loss of their children for having O.W. kids. Juveniles are particularly vulnerable. One hears stories of young girls who are forced in court to swear not to have intercourse again. Another example is a sixteen-year-old daughter of a welfare woman who became pregnant by her boyfriend, who was a few years older. Although they planned to marry, they wanted to wait until they could save enough money to set up an apartment and get a solid start. When the baby was born the boy contributed to her support regularly. Yet in court they were told if they didn't marry she would be sent away as a juvenile delinquent and he would be jailed for contributing to the delinquency of a minor. They married.

It is the woman who is ultimately held responsible for pregnancy. While not being allowed to have control over her body, she is nevertheless held responsible for its products. Recently, birth-control information has become more accessible, but still scarce. Abortions are illegal. Married women can't have their tubes tied without their husband's consent.[1]

The welfare system insists that when a man and woman live together they do so as a "family." Regardless of whether they are married or whether he is the father of any of her children, if they live together he must play the role of "family breadwinner" (with some supplementation from the welfare depending on his income). A welfare woman can only live with a man if she is willing to allow him to support her and her children and thereby be "husband" and man of the house. She cannot choose a relationship with a man who is not the father of her children, in which he has no rights or responsibilities toward the children. She cannot live with him just to meet her needs for sex and companionship.[2]

But while preventing new or "non-family" forms of living together, the system is also an enormous deterrent to the traditional forms. It is usually beyond the means and desire of a poor or working-class man to take on the responsibility of a woman with children who are not his. The example of Mrs. Y is illustrative. Divorced with two children, her ex-husband had remarried and was now the father of several other children. Although he was under court order to support his first family, he could barely manage his second on his lowpaying job. Thus Mrs. Y was on welfare. She met Mr. Z, a night watchman and janitor, and married. They bought furniture on credit and tried to make a go of it. Her welfare check was drastically cut. For over a year they were underbudgeted because the case worker never bothered about, or didn't know how to take into account, Mr. Z's expenses. But even with the correction he was under enormous economic pressure which he could only

1. See "Double Jeopardy: To Be Black and Female" by Frances Beal, p. 340.—
—Ed.
2. See "Does the Law Oppress Women?" by Diane Schulder; p. 139——Ed.

see as due to the two children who weren't his. The marriage lasted another year till finally he left the house. Mrs. Y's welfare grant went back up. Had Mr. Z stayed and been ill or out of work, the welfare would not have met his needs or expenses, because he was not the father of any of the children.

From its inception, welfare has been both an economic band-aid and a fortifier of traditional family roles. The 1961 amendments which instituted the Aid to Families of Dependent Children with Unemployed or Underemployed Parents (AFDC-UP) was a further step in this same direction. AFDC-UP provided welfare assistance to two-parent families whose male member was unemployed or underemployed. Having already recognized in 1935 that the economy did not provide for female breadwinners, the 1961 amendments recognized that the same conditions existed for many groups of men. The welfare system was thus expanded to include another group of economic victims and to keep them living in families. Welfare becomes an artificial economic base for the family.

"I think it's the System, really! I think it's a big racket in one sense for them to keep people on welfare rather than give them jobs. Because it keeps somebody happy! I don't know who! I can't figure it out!" An answer to this question posed by an ex-welfare woman lies in an understanding of the capitalistic exploitation of the economic underclass of woman. As stated elsewhere, most women work at only part-time or seasonal jobs to supplement their husbands' incomes. In seasonal factories, as office temporaries, as holiday or rush-hour sales help, or as domestic help, employers are able to use this "surplus labor" of women, getting rid of it when no longer needed, and not paying a living wage. The welfare system as "husband" also allows his wives this role. The toy industries of New Jersey are typical examples of this system. Hiring large numbers of women on a seasonal basis, paying the minimum wage, these factories draw a large number of welfare and other poor women. Since the wages are so low that even single women have trouble living on them, so low that wages often are lower than a full welfare grant, the women remain on welfare. In essence, the welfare system subsidizes them to work for a non-living wage, much to the profit of management. Clearly, it's the industry which is on welfare!

The welfare system has also been used to depress wages in these industries. Until recently, the "extra" money a welfare woman could get from working was static. She would not benefit from a wage increase as the welfare would just deduct it from her grant. Likewise the women who work without reporting it are not going to take part in a movement for higher wage or better conditions, for fear of getting caught.

A similar if reverse situation exists with regard to rentals. As rent is a variable in a welfare budget, the woman neither gains nor loses from increases or decreases. Slumlords have been quick to skyrocket rents for downtrodden and unkept housing. This leads to a situation of high rentals in welfare areas which are an enormous hardship on the working poor and a deterrent to women who wish to make it on their own. A welfare mother puts it this way:

> They know that if people are working for low wages they won't be able to pay these high rents. Now, they don't want a rent control because the landlord can really get fat off the welfare mothers. The average low-income working man, who has a family of four or five children, he wouldn't be able to feed the children and pay all this high rent. This is exploitation! They seem happier having separated families on welfare. You hear the people in the suburbs hollering about taxpayers' money going to welfare mothers. If they really wanted to do something about welfare, about how much money they put in, they would worry a little bit about where the money actually *went*, how much was actually given to the welfare mother. And when they found out that she got only a small portion of that money maybe they wouldn't scream so loud.

Most woman see their being on welfare as the fault of their personal histories and not as a socially determined result. Even black women, who often see welfare as generally connected to racism and poverty, still place great emphasis on the effects of their personal experiences—a bad marriage, the wrong man, leaving school, etc. One woman, who had tried to support her two daughters on her own, tells how long strenuous hours of work and severe problems with babysitters led to illness for one daughter, until finally she decided to stop working and apply for welfare. Still she views it as her own failure, not as a problem of an economy that doesn't provide a living "family" wage for its female workers, or have adequate provisions for child care and socialization by other than the biological mother.

Many women place the blame on their men. Having counted on a man to stay with and support the family, a woman may view with great hostility his failure to do either or both. "I blamed him . . . or between the two of us . . . no, I blamed *him!* If he had give me the certain amount of money he was supposed to give me I wouldn't have got on welfare in the beginning." But regardless of why they got on, most woman feel they can't get off welfare.

White welfare women, as compared to their black sisters, are much more in retreat from the world due to the absence of the male. Coming mostly from working-class or lower-middle-class backgrounds, they compensate for their exclusion from production and their seeming failure as wives with a heavy investment in the raising of their children. They view welfare as a disgrace and their own lives as failures and thus seek self-expression through their children. Many live on welfare for years without telling their families or friends. In one case a divorced woman would not even tell her teen-age children. Fear of, or actual experiences of abuse, ridicule, or exploitation cause them to internalize this negative view of themselves and retreat further into their shells. Therefore, they have little or no contact with each other and provide no mutual assistance. Unlike many black women, they are usually unwilling to fight for their rights and are more easily cowed. As one white welfare woman describes it, welfare was the last resort. "There was nothing else I could do. There really wasn't. I felt ashamed. Not guilty, but ashamed. Till this day I've told very few people that I'm on welfare . . . just ashamed."

Coming from a society with some history of fatherless families, black welfare women are less imbued with the value of the "little woman" and are more at home in somewhat aggressive and independent roles than the whites. While most black welfare woman have attempted marriages, they are less likely to see their failure as an end to their own roles as sexual and reproductive adults. They find "purpose" in the raising of their children, but rarely retreat and live through them. Black welfare woman have taken steps toward cooperative action, aided by the more social and communal nature of their communities. Thus, while the white women remain very isolated, the blacks move more freely through the local social centers, and this makes them more able to develop a life independent of their home and family.

Forced into institutionalized poverty, and living, involuntarily or by choice, on their own, welfare women still must seek men as providers. Since many women find it impossible to live on welfare budgets, they seek boyfriends or unreported work to supplement their income. An ex-welfare client relates her experiences:

> I met a friend of mine. Well, he had a good job and he helped me out financially. So I really didn't depend entirely on welfare at first . . . Then after he lost his job and didn't have that supplemental income, then I really found out what it was like to be on the welfare. Because you would almost be on starvation. And they say you can manage . . . but I know I'm a pretty good budgeter. But I found by the time I paid the landlord his rent, telephone bill, public service, and bought a little food, I didn't have nothing left.

For others the answer is doing domestic work or factory work without reporting their income to the welfare board. Such a supplemental income means the woman is able to live, but still not get out of poverty. It also means living with the fear of getting caught.

For many women, the welfare is a terrible economic and social trap. Those with small or numerous children are constantly tied to the house and kids with no means of getting out or relaxing. Working gets them nowhere and often complicates their financial state with less time to do economical shopping, cooking, sewing, etc. The burdens of work, kids, babysitters, and welfare are enormous. Depression, helplessness, and a downward spiral are not unknown to welfare women. Many feel trapped.

Staying home always bored me. I never liked to stay home. I liked to work. Staying home definitely had an effect on me because I had to get into the same category as other welfare mothers who just sat home and did nothing but watch television, etc. But I didn't like that, I always liked to be doing something . . . I got into it for a while, started to drink more. I had given up. I felt that there was no way out of this kind of a welfare situation.

Older women advise the young girl to go out into the world and be independent. "I think it's better for a young girl to go out and work than to be stuck on welfare. Once you get on welfare you kinda lose sight of the world, you get into your own little world. She would get more out of life by going to work and being independent." However, the reality is not so simple. The welfare woman who made the above statement has only one child, yet has lived in poverty, working almost full-time *and* receiving a full welfare grant. The lack of independence she felt on welfare led her to an active role in organizing other welfare women.

Many women have gained independence and strength from the lessons of their personal experiences as well as the "toughening" process of being on welfare. Having had to fight many battles, having borne many hardships on their own, and having lived for long periods without a man, they will never go back to dependent and subservient relationships. "I would like in a husband a man I could meet halfway. I wouldn't want him to do some things I've seen men do for women. I would like him to treat me as a woman, not as a little puppet. Then I don't want one to be mean to me. And I certainly don't want one that's too dominating, telling me everything to do, where I can go, what I can wear, what I should eat! This I can't stand." They search, often consciously, for a greater equality and mutual independence in their relationships and a more active and productive role in the society. "Up until two years ago I would have told my daughter her only goal in life would be to be a housewife and a mother. Not today, oh no, heavens no. First have pride in yourself and be somebody. Then worry about marriage after you've accomplished something and once you know who you are." It is particularly from this group of women that the welfare-rights movement has grown.

The welfare-rights movement began in the early Sixties with small groups of women getting together to help each other deal with the welfare system. In many cities these groups were connected to SDS organizing projects or OEO community action ventures or groups like CORE. As an outgrowth of work done by the Poverty Rights Action Center, in 1967 the National Welfare Rights Organization was established. It does not see itself as a woman's movement, rather, it is a movement that happens to have as its constituency mostly women. Because of this view, welfare-rights movements rarely describe or analyze the welfare problem as a women's problem but rather as part of the national problems of poverty and racial oppression. While pushing nationally for a guaranteed annual income and an end to repressive controls over clients' lives, they do not concern themselves with the role of women in the economy or the status of the family. The organization, which is 99 percent women, has as its head a male executive director. Yet all its national officers are women. Local leadership is female. In cities and towns across the country women meet, work, and fight together against an oppressive system. Thus the welfare-rights movement is fertile ground for developing and spreading an analysis of the welfare system that sees it as part of the larger problem of women's oppression.

The experience of involvement in the welfare-rights movement has for many women brought out an independence and militancy long supressed. As a welfare-rights activist put it: "I'm the same person I always was but the welfare rights brought it out." The personal experiences of these women have taught them that they can't get by on an identity of wife and mother. They have had to come out of their homes and take an active part in the world around them. The experience is telling. They want a better deal but they don't want to go back home. As the movement for women's liberation spreads out from the middle class and into other sectors of the society, the welfare-rights women are its potential base among the female poor.

TWO JOBS: WOMEN WHO WORK IN FACTORIES

Jean Tepperman

When people in the Movement talk about women who work in factories, they ask whether these women are exploited basically as *workers* or as *women.* You can answer that only if you divide up what happens in an artificial way. A movement for the liberation of factory women would have to take a whole new form, one which dealt with the problems together, in a way that traditional male unionism or traditional middle-class feminism cannot. The movement would have to attack exploitation on the job and in the home simultaneously to win changes that would make a real difference. I have this personal vision of a factory women's movement that would fight against the plant, wage a campaign for state-supported day-care centers, abortions, etc., and all of whose members would take a pledge to do only 50 percent of the housework at home—all this backed up by support squads of women trained in Karate.

I came to this conclusion by trying to sort out and describe my experience working in two factories for five
weeks each, in Chicago during the summer of 1968.

The woman who worked next to me on the line at Nadir
was named Pat. She had two children and two grand-
children, and she would talk to me about them, about getting her hair done, and about cooking. Every morning, just
before the bell rang to start work, she would give me a little
"well, here we go" look. One morning she said, "Every day
you think you can't possibly hate it any more, and then the
next day you hate it more."

Then the bell rang and it was like going underwater and
holding your breath for two hours (until the break). I
worked on an assembly line of about forty women. I put two
little things on wires into something else, with wire-cutters.
After a while I found out what the little things were, but I
never found out what they used for.

We had two ten-minute breaks and half an hour for lunch.
Bells rang all the time—women who had been there for a
while finally learned what each of them meant. The plant
was very big and cavernous—about a thousand people
worked on the day shift. The look of it, the cafeteria, and
the bells all seemed very familiar. I realized that Nadir was
like high school or, even more, it was what high school had
been approximating.

I started at $1.97 an hour, but there was a small bonus for
doing more than the quota (no one ever told me what the
quota was). The real pressure was to keep your pile of unfinished work from getting so big that the supervisor noticed.
I worked so fast it was like losing consciousness. Everything
hurt—blisters, back, safety glasses pinched—mostly shooting pains all over. I asked people if it got better after a while.
They said no, it always hurt.

The speed-up on my line was especially bad, and the
women complained a lot. One black woman kept saying, "I

thought slavery went out a long time ago." She would joke, "I'm gonna go find out about these hippies over on Wells Street. They don't believe in working. If this keeps up, I'll go be a hippie."

Most of the jobs in the plant were like mine, a series of the same ten or so motions all day. All the men I knew who were factory workers admitted that the women had the worst jobs, and that they (the men) would go crazy if they had to do that stuff.

My other job was in the Mary Ann Baking Company, which had about one hundred people on my shift (4 to 12 P.M.), only eight or so women. It was a smaller, more friendly plant; mostly everybody was Greek, there were no bells, and we didn't do the same thing all day (although each job was pretty bad). Mainly I stood and placed various sticky pastries on a conveyor belt that fed them into a machine where they were wrapped individually for vending machines. This job involved a lot of bending and one had to move quickly because the machine went so fast. But the other job was worse: scooping rolls off a tray with a big paddle and placing them in cute little blue-and-white boxes. There you had to bend from the waist at a peculiar and painful angle; some women stood in that position four hours a day.

When there was no work packing (the women's job), we helped the bakers, who were all men. The room where they worked was light, and cool, and quiet—no machines. Except for a very few things which required strength, we did everything they did, on the days we helped them. It was much more pleasant work. One day a girl told me that we weren't supposed to be doing this, because we were only getting paid for wrapping. Baking was higher-paid work because it was considered a skill.

This illustrates how women are discriminated against in wages. The going wage for women in Chicago factories was $2 an hour or less, but the factories don't need to pay women less for the same work—they have something better. They give women the worst, most debilitating jobs (no exercise, just aches and pains), then pay them less because the job has a lower classification. One version of this was true at Nadir, where *all* the production workers at my plant were women —so they were all paid the same, at the going women's wage. The other version was true at the bakery—the men had "skilled" jobs (which we could do too), more pleasant work and conditions—so of course they got paid more.

There was only one *type* of job women did in the factories —the fast, picky shitwork. Promotion, while difficult for uneducated factory men, was impossible for women, in my experience. Training was expensive and virtually impossible to manage if you had children—also most skills were men's prerogatives. It was possible at Nadir to be promoted to a sort of line-boss position, but these women worked hard at production in addition to being on call to supply materials and deal with problems that came up. Our line boss was a black woman named Betty—she talked all the time, and expressed very ambivalent feelings about her allegiance— one Monday morning she announced, "I'm through working my guts out for nothing, I'm just gonna take it easy," but next day she was acting as the boss-proxy ("If these older women can work in this heat, you can too").

So, almost without exception, the factory women were working for very little (Mary Ann's $2.40 was considered exceptionally good pay), at jobs like these. Contrary to what experts told me before I went to work, the women are not all old, or black, or immigrants. Most of the women at Nadir were young—about a third of them were white. This meant to me that being stuck in this kind of job is not an anachronism nor a peculiar result of racial discrimination, but a real possibility for a large number of young women—especially if they happen to have children too early to get any specialized training. The lack of promotion not only limits the possibilities for the future; it means that all of the bosses are men.

I think the most important thing about the male boss is

his ability to inspire fear. He can flirt some girls into working faster, but that's secondary. I think most people in
America are more afraid of and obedient to male authority
than to female. This is true of men as well as women—but
women have a habit of obedience to men. I think the companies know this. The work that the bosses do could certainly
be done by women promoted from the line—but I don't
think those women could as effectively intimidate their sisters into working fast (which is the boss's real job).

Our ability to get around the boss by flirting with him did
not mitigate any of this. In the first place, it worked both
ways; in the second place, it was part of the job, if job is
defined as "what you have to do to avoid getting fired." This
was especially true at first. At Mary Ann you couldn't join
the union for six weeks—at Nadir it was three months.
Before that you had no job security—the boss could fire you
any time. (Also at Nadir there were regulations—like if you
missed more than *two days* during that whole three months,
you were automatically fired.)

At Mary Ann there were a number of women's jobs, but
people didn't have regular assignments—the foreman or
supervisor (both men) could take you off one job and put you
on another for no reason. This was why the older women
did the worst and heaviest jobs—because it all depended on
how much the bosses like you, and they liked young, pretty
girls the best. There was always one girl who was the supervisor's favorite—when I was there a new girl was edging out
the old favorite, and there was a lot of bitterness about that.
There was a real sexual competition among the younger
women for Tommy's attention. But Tommy came around
to all of us, put his arm around us, patted us on the ass, etc.
Proprietarily.

The same was true of the supervisor at Nadir, but he was
more sophisticated. He was flirtatious, kind and paternal,
and threatening, in turn. It was all in terms of male-female
roles, but was more obviously directed toward getting us to
work harder.

Many women, especially at Nadir, were aware of the injustice of their situation—they were angry all the time. It seemed like there could have been a militant union movement, but there wasn't. When I got there, Nadir was in the middle of a series of elections between the established union and another. In all the discussion about it, I got an idea of what the word "union" means at Nadir.

It doesn't have anything to do with the anger women at Nadir felt all day against what was happening to them. "Union" is an office where some men in suits work. Your relationship to that "union" is like car insurance. It is compulsory for you to pay a certain amount of money each year to these people. You do it because you are forced to, and also because you have a vague feeling that without it you would be even worse off. The way most people chose between the unions was to compare prices (union dues) against the product (the list of union promises, adjusted by how much you felt they were lying).

One day I asked a black woman in the cafeteria if she thought there ever *could be* a union in America that wasn't really working for the boss. She looked startled and said no. I never heard anyone say any different at Nadir.

At Mary Ann people felt more positive toward the union because "it got them" more money. On the other hand, the main grievance that people talked about was the unfair way of assigning tasks, and that was never considered a problem that the union would have anything to do with. It was dealt with in practice by rivalry (mostly sexual) among the women.

The women I worked with had to deal with more extreme exploitation in work and wages, than men did, as well as the capitalist-male authority system in the plant. They also had to do everything else women are supposed to do.

Most of them felt they had to look "right"—at 10:00 P.M. in the bakery, when it was well over 90° in the plant, many women did their hair and put on make-up at break time.

Many of them had their hair done professionally every week. Sometimes it was good, because it helped their morale, but mostly it seemed to me like an additional burden.

The main thing, however, is that mostly everyone was married—I was the only person there without children. Often that means spending most of your paycheck on a babysitter; it *always* means that before or after eight hours spent as I have described, all the women are home taking care of children, cooking, and cleaning *things*—houses, clothes, etc. I understood from talking to the women that almost no husbands *ever* did *any* of this (they were too tired from working eight hours a day).

My best friend at Mary Ann sometimes used to talk about that. She thought it wasn't fair, but sort of felt it was cute and masculine that her husband refused to "help her," as she put it. One reason she wasn't angry was that he was good with the baby, which meant that after Sally did all the physical work involved in child care, her husband played with the baby some.

Frequently women said that "it's like having two jobs." They knew they worked too hard. But the only alternative they could formulate was that husbands "help out" in emergencies, like pregnancy. Few women ever questioned that the housework and child care was "their job" and they just had to do it, regardless of the other demands on them as workers and wives.

Although the situation remained, and the women seldom questioned its basic outlines, they were not passive victims. They fought all the time. Just doing their "two jobs" was a fight in itself, but they also fought to defend themselves against extreme demands. Especially at Nadir, this was directed against the company and the boss; people on the line were always announcing, "This is a hard job and I can't do it no faster." In both factories, many women kept telling me, "Don't let anybody push you around."

They kept close watch of the pennies and half-minutes to see that the company wasn't getting away with anything. This could have been militance, but it was mostly individual, and therefore accepted the company's rules as given. The concrete results you could get with this kind of bitching were minimal, but I think it was important, because it was a way the women preserved their feeling that they were fighting back and not completely helpless.

One week when I was at Nadir it was very hot. By Tuesday afternoon girls began fainting from heat and overwork. There was rumored to be a rule that they were supposed to let us go home if it got too hot, so anger built up against the company. The Spanish-speaking girls were the least subdued by the place; they always kept up a kind of opera of comments, which sometimes became chants ("I want to go home" fugues). That week when someone fainted they would start wailing "*Boooo*" in long, spooky up-and-down tones that sounded like a siren and reminded me of the women's cry in the *Battle of Algiers.* After a while the black, and finally the white women, picked it up; it kept getting longer and louder each time. It felt daring to do it —the bosses kept coming around trying to get us to stop.

This kind of psychological warfare was important at Nadir; on the other hand it never boiled over into a walkout. It was a defiance that didn't believe it could change anything—but still, an assertion of dignity.

Once in the cafeteria I heard two older women talking about how they "stood up to the boss." One told about a successful act of petty revenge she had taken against her boss, after which she remembered, "He says, Frances, you're my problem child, and I says, I'm not your child, I'm a woman."

The women's commitment to their children was a major cause of conflict over things like taking time off to take a kid to the hospital. That had been the issue with Frances, and also with Maria, a young Puerto Rican woman who came to work the same time I did. Maria was never picky-militant; she could sort of rise above factory values because her main identity was elsewhere, as a wife and mother. Her baby had a club foot and she used to take days off to take him to the clinic. She told me, "I don't care what he says. My baby comes first. If he fires me, there's other factories."

This is the other main way women defend themselves against being ground down by the factory: motherhood gives them a feeling of moral strength in confronting it. In a limited way, the "two jobs" could be played off against each other. If Maria was fired, her husband would support her until she got another job.

The woman who lived downstairs from me had held many jobs during her life, always taking off about two years in between to have a baby. This wasn't exactly leisure, but at least the sporadic pattern was in some sense less deadening than doing unbroken factory work for forty years. On the other hand, Mrs. Russell's husband had a good job. Many women work all their lives, taking off only a few months or less for each baby. And for all working women, these "advantages" rest on the fact of at least double exploitation during most of their adult lives.

As I learned more about the factory and the women working with me, I used to get a very strong feeling at closing time at Nadir.

Everybody stopped working at the appropriate bell, gathered up their things, and waited. There were at least three hundred women on my floor, so there were a lot of time clocks for punching out, all along the center aisle. When the closing bell rang, everyone literally ran to punch out. Afterward, I was caught up in the whole mass of women leaving the plant.

I used to look around at them, knowing in my own sore muscles that they had just finished eight hours of being pounded down physically and psychologically, seeing them all rush out now to do the next job: brightly colored summer clothes, talking and laughing; white, black, Spanish, young, and old. So beautiful and so strong—if only all of them would look around at each other and see that power.

WOMEN AND THE CATHOLIC CHURCH*

Dr. Mary Daly

The eight-year-old girl who asks why there can't be altar girls and who senses that there is something wrong with the reasons proposed by her elders has most likely just encountered for the first time that problem which—if she is a bright and somewhat religiously inclined little girl—will cross her consciousness many more times: the problem of women and the Catholic Church. The effect of such a first realization is immeasurable. If there is an appearance of satisfaction with the reasons given, necessarily inadequate because there is no adequate reason, this is not to say that the effect of such an experience is not harmful, even crushing. To be considered inferior because of personal defects is difficult, but it is bearable if there is some hope of improvement. To be rejected from activities for which one is obviously suited because of some fictional "ontological difference" is crushing because of its hopelessness and irrationality. The significance of such an experience cannot be conceptualized or verbalized by an eight-year-old, for whom, after all, so many things are mysterious, including multiplication tables. She can't yet suspect that what she is up against is that crude, cruel, and arrogant illogic which may be summed up in the famous line: "All men are equal, but some are more equal than others."

Despite the mindshrinking effects of such conditioning,

*In this article, the author borrows substantially from an essay which she had previously written under the title, "Antifeminism in the Church," published by IDO-C (Information Documentation on the Conciliar Church), no. 68–44. The document was translated into French, German, Spanish, and Italian.
Copyright © 1970 by Mary Daly

many today are coming to see the Catholic Church as a powerful enemy of female liberation. A mountain of evidence can be marshaled in support of this conviction. Yet it should be recognized that the situation always has been laden with ambiguity. In fact, the history of Christian ideology and practice concerning women has been a history of contradictions. In the documents of Scripture, church fathers, popes, and theologians throughout the centuries we find an astonishing contrast between, on the one hand, the teachings concerning the value and dignity of the human person and, on the other hand, an all-pervasive misogynism and downgrading of women as persons. Moreover, there has been a strange polarity between the glorification of Woman as a symbol, often identified with the person of Mary, and the underestimation of concrete existing women. The symbolic glorification often has served to mask the depreciation and oppression of the feminine half of the human species.

It is true that the Church is not the only cultural institution responsible for the oppression of women. Moreover, it would be unrealistic to expect that Christians could have been far in advance of their times; it is understandable that they have always had the same limitations as other men of their times. The irony is that in Christian ideology the stamp of divine approval has been put upon these limitations. The imposition of alienating sexual stereotypes and roles upon human beings has been justified as conformity to an immutable "divine plan" clearly known through revelation.

It was not Catholic ideology but the industrial revolution which led to feminine emancipation. The official Catholic reaction in the nineteenth and twentieth centuries to the movement for emancipation manifested the persistence of the conflict between the Christian concept of women as persons, made to the image of God, and the notion, imbedded in tradition, that they are inferior, derivative beings. In the writings of Leo XIII, Pius XI, and Pius XII, there is no resemblance to the misogynistic tirades of some of the fathers, nor is there a literal reassertion of the Thomistic teaching that woman is a "misbegotten male." However, a strong resistance to the emancipation movement is in evidence in these papal writings, together with ambiguous concessions to the modern situation. The tension between the desire to retain women in their subordinate situation and the recognition of demands for some adaptation is reflected in ambivalent terminology. Thus Pius XI affirmed an "equality in dignity" between husband and wife, but effectively negated any serious understanding of this by asserting the necessity of "a certain inequality." He wrote: "True emancipation will not involve false liberty and unnatural equality with the husband." It is evident that the adjectives in this sentence effectively neutralize the meaning of the nouns. In the copious utterances of Pius XII the same sort of devices are operative. The use of such expressions as "spiritual motherhood" permitted some expansion of the traditional role, with serious limitations.

An encouraging sign of change in official attitudes came with Pope John's *Pacem in Terris,* which conveys an authentic recognition of the equality of women and of the fact of their oppression. The spirit of Pope John is discernible also in Vatican II's Pastoral Constitution on *The Church in the Modern World.* Despite signs of regression in more recent years, the ideological breakthrough has been made. In addition, articles in the press and the appearance of numerous books and articles on the problem of women in the Church have caused a rather widespread awakening in the popular consciousness.

The existence of the problem of antifeminism in the Church, then, is coming to be recognized: pious euphemisms are losing their potency to disguise the reality of injustice. Widespread discussions of such issues as birth control, the emerging nun, and women clergy have brought out into the open the conflicts between an ancient ideology and the realities of existence in today's world. The eradication of antifeminism is coming to be recognized as one of the great tasks which the Church now faces. It is imperative, therefore, that we attempt to analyze the nature of the problem before us. Otherwise, the public discussion may become sterile and beside the point, and there may be needless repetition of the mistakes of the past.

The Problem of Stereotypes

Although there has been progress toward acceptance of women as persons with rights equal to those of men, stereotypes concerning their supposed "nature" continue to reappear in contemporary Catholic writings. The "eternal feminine" symbol, which continues to recur in religious writings, stands in stark opposition to the qualities of a developing, authentic person, who will be unique, self-critical, self-creating, active, and searching. In contrast to these authentic personal characteristics, the Eternal Woman is said to have a vocation for surrender and secrecy; hence the symbol of the veil. Self-less, she achieves not individual realization but merely generic fulfillment in motherhood, physical or spiritual. She is said to be timeless and conservative by nature. She is shrouded in "mystery," because she is not recognized as a genuine human person.

The stereotype serves to support antifeminine bias. Characteristically, those who adhere to the symbol of the eternal feminine, accepting as normative for women the cluster of qualities implied in this symbol, are opposed to any radical practical measures which will end sexual discrimination. Thus, for Gertrud von le Fort, the feminist movement had a "tragic" motivation. Catholic authors of recently published books in the "eternal feminine" tradition continue to oppose the idea of women having authority or becoming "too intellectualized" on the grounds that they then become "defeminized." Criticism of this sort is always directed toward those who fail to conform; never is it directed to the assumptions of the ideology itself.

A striking effect of the "eternal feminine" ideology, then, is insensitivity to injustice. The dehumanizing effects of exclusive male headship are passed over. So too, the effects of inferior education and opportunity are ignored, while energy is expended in describing the imagined evils of equality. It is particularly ironic, therefore, that the Church, which should be leading the way in matters of social justice, should be perpetuating this pattern of thinking and consequent behavior.

The complexity of the problem is indicated by the fact that many women themselves seem to justify insensitivity to the "feminine problem." Some of them have been ardent promoters of the "eternal feminine" (Gertrud von le Fort, Ida Gorres, Phyllis McGinley). More important perhaps, the majority of women have never protested their relegation, in theory and in social fact, to subhuman categories. This can only be understood when it is recognized that there are psychological mechanisms at work here which are profoundly damaging to the capacity for self-understanding, for creative activity, and for sensitivity to one's own predicament and that of others.

Help in understanding the situation of women comes from the psychoanalytic theory of repression and projection. Since certain feelings and attitudes are not permitted by society to have expression (at least not by the superior or ruling caste), these are often projected to disadvantaged persons or whole groups. Thus, the Jews in Germany and Negroes in the United States and South Africa have served as receptacles for the repressed problems of the majority in those societies. This, of course, requires the corresponding mechanism of introjection, by which the "inferior" accepts the role imposed upon him. Just as a Negro child actually becomes the "lazy nigger" which the white citizens want him to be, so also do girls accept a limiting and stunting role for themselves in a society which expects this of them. This whole process of "role psychology" or "self-fulfilling prophecy" involves a vicious circle. Since the members of an oppressed or minority group do in fact become inferior in just the way society desires, the prejudice is reinforced. They appear to be living evidence that the stereotype is grounded in "nature."

There can be no doubt about the harmfulness of the mechanisms we have described. Just as this is true in the case of racial discrimination, so it is also true in the case of sexual discrimination. Recent empirical psychological studies confirm the impression that the effects of self-fulfilling prophecy upon girls are subtly destructive. The imposition of passive self-images can seriously hinder intellectual creativity. Moreover, there is evidence both from sociological research and from psychoanalysis that the imposition of the feminine mystique is profoundly damaging to the man-woman relationship.

Divine Approval

It is important to give particular attention to this phenomenon as it manifests itself within the context of the Church, where the problematic is quite special. Let it be granted that the fallacies which are both cause and effect of the "eternal feminine" are by no means peculiar to Catholic apologetes. They are prominent in the myths of advertisers, in the theories of some educators and of doctrinaire Freudian psychologists, and in the operative philosophy of the editors of most women's magazines. However, there is a special problem when this surrounds itself with an aura of alleged divine approval. Often, for example, such terminology as "God's plan" or "Mary the model of all women" is used to support claims about women and the man-woman relationship for which there is no conclusive argument. Catholics have been very susceptible to this kind of mystification, particularly because of indoctrination in an underdeveloped theology, and because of static and traditionalist notions of faith and revelation.

The Church clearly has the duty to free human beings

from bondage to infantile images of the self and the species. Although the "chains" of sexual prejudice are invisible and psychological, their coercive strength is nonetheless real. In view of the psychological and sociological data now at our disposal, it is meaningless to support the "eternal feminine" on the basis that many people, including many women, are satisfied with it in theory and in practice. Not least among the demonic aspects of sexual discrimination is the blindness which it brings about.

By sexual discrimination the Church has been wounded in its structures, for it has deprived itself of the gifts and insights of more than half its members. It has been grievously hurt in its members of both sexes, for in a society which welcomes and fosters prejudice, not only is the human potential of the subject group restricted but the superordinate group also becomes warped in the process. A radical change of thought and of atmosphere is needed both in theory and in practice.

Not Needed: A "Theology of Woman"

It is most important that breadth of vision be sustained in our attempts to purify religious thought of its ancient antifeminine bias. In order that a radical reform can be achieved, it is necessary to opt for a definite rejection of that approach which is suggested by the expression "theology of woman." What is implied in this approach is the fallacious assumption that "woman" is a distinct species that can be understood apart from the other sex. It is based upon the unproved supposition that there is an innate psychological complementarity. Attempts to develop a "theolgy of woman" are inevitably disastrous because they naively assume the sex images of a patriarchal culture infallibly correspond to "nature" and to God's will.

The prejudice implied in this type of thinking becomes evident when one tries to state the corresponding formula: "theology of man (male)." It is significant that whereas the idea of a "thelogy of woman" is often proposed, few would seriously suggest that there should be a "theology of man." Since men have been seen as having the fullness of human nature, they do not appear to pose a special problem. By contrast, women, who have not yet achieved this status, are looked upon as "mysterious." Because of its assumptions, a "theology of woman" helps to perpetuate and lend support to this androcentric situation. Since it places the sexual differentiation above personhood, it contains a built-in distortion. Moreover, it assumes that one sex can be understood apart from the other, as if it were a complete "essence"— and thus the problematic of sexuality itself is misconstrued. In fact, the sexual differentiation can be understood only within the category of relation. Men and women as they are, are the products of complex social relations in an ongoing historical process.

The dynamics of human personality and social relationship need to be studied from a radically evolutionary point of view. Rather than a "theology of woman," we need to see develop an analysis of the man-woman relationship which rejects as alienating to both men and women the idea of a sexual hierarchy founded upon "nature" and defined once and for all. This much needed analysis will recognize that the relationship between the sexes is subject to evolutionary change, that its forms must vary according to the conditions of diverse historical periods and according to individual differences. Any conception of "the common good" which would diminish the potential of one sex for the sake of the other will be excluded from such an analysis. Instead, it will stress personal liberty and growth, which must be seen not as opposed to, but as essential to, love and commitment. It will reject the old obsession with sex roles, in order to focus upon the problems of persons in relation to others. It will strive for authenticity, recognizing the ambiguity of concrete reality, which cannot be contained in abstractions.

Unfortunately, however, the social environment of the theologian can present formidable obstacles to the eradication of androcentric bias in his thought processes. The ancient prejudices could not persist in doctrine if they were not given support and apparent justification by the actual condition of women both within the Church itself and in the secular milieu. Just as a regressive theology serves to justify and perpetuate harmful social conditions, so also such conditions in ecclesiastical and civil society prevent the kind of insight which would lead to the construction of a dynamic and liberating theological anthropology. It is important that we turn our attention to the problem of changing these conditions.

Normative Principles for Changing Women's Situations in the Church

Men and women exist in dynamic relationship to each other. In the past, we have been chained to the wheel not only of biological processes but also of psychological mechanisms whose nature was not understood. In our time, the developing sciences, particularly psychology and anthropology, have given us insight into the mechanisms which have been crippling us. Moreover, advancing technology has provided us with a situation in which, for the first time in history, we have the necessary leisure, mobility, and control of our environment to experiment on the basis of this insight. We should strive, therefore, toward a level of confrontation, dialogue, and cooperation between the sexes undreamed of in the past, when the struggle for biological survival of the species and numerical multiplication had to take precedence over any attempt at a qualitative development of relation between men and women as persons. The directing principle of our thoughts and plans concerning the future relations of men and women in the Church and society should be commitment to providing the possibility of ever more profound, complete, dynamic and humanizing relationships.

It should be self-evident that if the level of dialogue and

cooperation between men and women which we are seeking is to be attained, and if the vicious circle of imposed roles and of self-fulfilling prophecy is to be overcome among the people of God, then all automatic exclusion from any Church office or function on the basis of sex is to be eradicated.

Discrimination should be eliminated on all levels. On the parish and diocesan levels, wherever boards and councils of laymen are established, women should be represented, significantly and proportionately, not merely by a few token appointments. They should be in key positions in the national and international Catholic organizations. The talents of gifted and highly trained women specialists should be sought out and used in influential and decisionmaking roles within the Church. Competent women are now to be found in relevant areas of specialization such as theological research and teaching, sociology, political science, psychology, educational administration, business administration, journalism, law, social work. Such specialists should be recruited for post-conciliar commissions and other organizations which may be set up to continue the work begun by the Vatican Council.

As far as the liturgy is concerned, as the laity participate more actively it is necessary to insist upon equally active participation by both sexes. If men serve as lectors and acolytes, if they preach and distribute Holy Communion, then women should be encouraged to do the same. Moreover, it would be inconsistent to stop here in the process of eradicating discrimination. Honesty and consistency demand that the issue of women clergy be raised and courageously acted upon.

The Issue of Women Priests

The whole problem of this situation of women in the Church comes to focus in the question of women priests. Far from being a peripheral issue, their exclusion from the official ministry reflects and symbolizes the deep distortion which is present on all levels of the man-woman relationship in the Church. What is at stake here is nothing less than the character and quality of this relationship in the Church of the future. As long as qualified persons are excluded from any ministry by reason of their sex alone, it cannot be said that there is genuine equality of men and women in the church. It is senseless to point to the rising position of the laity in the Church and argue that women are therefore attaining equality. So long as the Church maintains a significant distinction between hierarchy and laity, the exclusion of women from the hierarchy is a radical affirmation of their inferior position among the people of God. By this exclusion the Church is saying that the sexual differentiation is —for one sex—a crippling defect which no personal qualities of intelligence, character, or leadership can overcome, In fact, by this policy it is effectively teaching that women are not fully human and conditioning people to accept this as unchangeable fact.

Often those who argue that the question of women priests has surfaced prematurely are projecting feelings of resistance within themselves. Often, too, the argument that it is "too soon" is rooted in the belief that this is a peripheral and even a trivial issue, having little to do with the real problems of men and women. This reveals a narrowness of vision. It betrays ignorance of the fact that exclusion of women from the hierarchy not only reflects but serves to perpetuate a restrictive style of man-woman relationship because of what it *says* symbolically about that relationship. It is not a question primarily of whether women clergy are needed to fill out the ranks, nor of any "special talents" they might bring. Rather, the problem we are dealing with is the problem of the liberation of human beings from a *conditioning* which is disastrous.

At the opposite pole from the position we have just analyzed is the attitude which supposes that the ordination of women will be a panacea for the problem of ecclesiastical misogynism. The experience of Protestant Churches which have ordained women should help to remove this delusion, for it has revealed that their ordination does not guarantee the eradication of discriminatory attitudes and practices. The problems involved in relations between the sexes are deep and complex. Advances in particular areas of the social organism will not be very effective in the long run unless they are accompanied and supported by over-all social developments.

Evolving Church Structures and the Man-Woman Relationship

We should realize, then, that the problem of women's situation in the Church is intricately bound up with the whole problem of changing structures. It would be foolish to become fixated upon presently existing forms of Church life, since much that we now associate with "the Church" is doomed to disappear. On the other hand, an attitude of quietism is not desirable either. If one is concerned about problems of injustice, it is not enough simply to "wait and see" what will happen. It is important to work within the given situation, to correct imbalance in present structures as much as possible, while at the same time thinking and working creatively in the direction of future developments. Thus, for example, the exclusion of girls from serving Mass in parish churches should be protested, despite the fact that the practice of having Mass servers already seems a quaint anachronism. It would be foolish to lose too much energy on this issue, in view of the whole spectrum of truly radical change taking place. Yet, for as long as the practice continues, there is injustice in sexual discrimination on this plane, and indeed the act of protesting this may contribute to the whole climate of questioning and re-thinking which is necessary for more radical changes. The same reasoning is applicable to the question of women priests.

An already widespread consciousness of the fact that radical transformations must take place in the Church is indeed

one reason for the lack of concern among some liberal thinkers about the issue of women in the hierarchy. The very
existence of a hierarchy seems like a dead remnant of an
earlier stage of human evolution. Class distinctions of the
past which were expressed in hierarchical patterns of society—distinctions which lasted for thousands of years—
have largely faded away. The structures of the Church
which reflected this hierarchical vision of the world still
remain, but modern man tends to experience them as either
suffocating or irrelevant. For this reason some see the question of women priests as already anachronistic, a kind of
clinging to the past. At the same time, many experience an
anxiety about the half-recognized fact of the disappearing of
hierarchical structures. This is why the women priests issue
sometimes evokes violent and irrational responses.

It is important, then, when thinking of the problem of
women in the ministry, to be aware that the whole idea of
priesthood is shifting radically. Modern theologians, recognizing that the idea of a separate and superior priestly caste
is no longer viable, have stressed the fact that the clergy
exist in order to serve, and not to accumulate prestige and
honors. Indeed, the ancient notion of the priest as a
"sacred person," an object of veneration, is coming to be
seen as both unacceptable and harmful—unacceptable to the
mature, harmful to those who have been held back in a state
of psychic infantilism because of it. The priest is coming to
be seen as a presence in the world rather than overseer, as
brother rather than father. The shift is toward democratization.

Most significant about the changing conception of the
priest is the fact that he is coming to see himself in terms
of a mission to the world, in terms of a life task, which
requires dialogue and cooperation with his fellow men. The
fact that these are two-way processes works in favor of realistic self-assessment on the part of priests. Their temptation
to accept false prestige and undeserved privileges, and the

inclination of people to bestow these upon them, are diminished when professional competence is seen to be more important than symbolic roles.

All of this is very important for the problem of the man-woman relationship in the Church. The new emphasis upon service and cooperation has helped precipitate the widespread identity crisis of priests, who have discovered that they are less qualified to serve the community than many competent laymen. In this age of specialization, many priests find themselves in the position of nonprofessional dabblers in a variety of fields, such as theology, teaching, public speaking, social work, counseling psychology, recreational leadership, and business administration. Work in any of these areas can be better handled by nonclerical specialists, whether men or women, than by clergy who are not adequately prepared. Recognition of this is bringing about an atmosphere conducive to the re-thinking of the meaning of ministry. Clerical caste is becoming less and less meaningful, and there is emerging a realization of the fact that there does exist a diversity of ministries. Competent women as well as men are already in these various ministries, in positions of leadership and responsibility.

The Church of the future may be envisioned as a community based upon "charismatic ministries." In order that it be transformed into a more adequately human social order there will have to be a continuing development away from symbolic roles identified with fixed states of life, toward functional roles freely assumed on the basis of personal qualifications and talents. Such a development in the direction of democratization and specialization will offer hope for realization of a higher level of dialogue and cooperation between men and women. We are witnessing the beginning of this already.

It must be acknowledged that there are many who do not share this hope. Viewing the Church as basically irrelevant, they argue that those who are concerned with the problem of the eradication of sexual discrimination should concentrate their energies upon the secular milieu rather than upon the Church. It is argued that if truly equal educational, professional, and political opportunities are offered to women in the secular milieu, and if the mystique of the "eternal feminine" can be eradicated from other cultural institutions, the Church cannot do too much harm, and eventually will be forced to change.

This objection has to be taken seriously. It may well be that it is in some ways more important to give attention to structures other than those of the Church itself. But there is more involved than a problem of priorities. In the end, we come to the question: Is the Church as such worth bothering about? A clear and unambiguous answer cannot be given to this. There is a demonic aspect to the Church's structures, but there are also signs of hope that its negative, life-destroying elements can be transformed. They will not be transformed, however, without the cooperation of men and women. Insofar as the Church diminishes the possibility for this cooperation by crushing the potentiality of women, it diminishes and warps its own life. Since the Church is a powerful cultural institution this warping process affects—and infects—the whole of society. It affects millions who do not personally identify themselves with the institutional Church. For this reason it should be a major focus of concern for all who are committed to the female liberation movement.

DOES THE LAW OPPRESS WOMEN?*

Diane B. Schulder

Introduction

Law is a reflection and a source of prejudice. It both enforces and suggests forms of bias. In earlier times, the United States Constitution blatantly described the black man as three-fifths of a man and the Supreme Court decided that black people did not qualify as "citizens." That black people have been thought of and treated as chattel is clear from a reading of the laws. An understanding of the attitudes toward women and the objective facts of women's oppression can similarly be found in an examination of the laws.

Sometimes, prejudices linger on long after corrective legislation is passed or decisions rendered—such as the 1954 Supreme Court (*Brown*) decision requiring desegregation of schools. Sometimes, oppressive laws remain on the books although public opinion has moved ahead of them—such as the abortion laws.

In the 1960's, most respected legal minds would, at least theoretically, profess the view that black people should be treated as citizens, as people, as equals, and not denied equal opportunity or equal protection under the laws. Not so for women! Goals, nature, and function are still very much in dispute. Technological advances, the economic structure, and the political situation have reached a point now, however, that permit women to examine the thinking in this area more carefully, and to analyze the supporting rationalizations and mythology.

In the following pages I touch on some of the legislation,

---

*This article is based on the outline of what will be the first law-school seminar on sex discrimination in U.S. history, to be taught by Diane B. Schulder at New York University.—Ed.
Copyright © 1970 by Diane B. Schulder

court decisions, administrative practices, and underlying rationale that support this discrimination.[1]

Civil Rights

Dr. Benjamin Spock was tried in June 1968 for conspiring to aid draft resistance. Would the case have been decided differently if he, a man of peace and the world's foremost baby doctor, had not been tried by an all-male jury? Leonard Boudin, his attorney, discovered that it had been the practice of the jury clerk in the federal court in Boston to take a list of the population, which is evenly divided between men and women, and to send jury eligibility questionnaires to approximately three times as many men as women.[2] Along the way, additional administrative hankypanky led, eventually, to a very lopsided jury panel and, in this case, to a jury devoid of women. This practice (although in existence for years) had never before been challenged.

The law has never been partial to women serving on juries. The rule at Common Law was that juries were composed of "twelve good men." One exception was made, however: when a pregnant woman faced execution, a jury of twelve women was convened to decide whether she should be executed *before* or *after* giving birth to her child. (Some commentators add that a jury of twelve men was convened simultaneously, anyway, to stand by and make sure the women reached the right decision.)

To the present day, the United States Supreme Court has not ruled it unconstitutional for women to be excluded from a jury.[3]

In 1879, when the Supreme Court ruled it was unconstitutional to exclude Negroes from state juries, it hastened to add:

1. Space permits the presentation of selected examples only.
2. *U.S.* v. *Spock* (1968), Record at 456–474. See also, Brief of Defendant-Appellant, Spock, in United States Court of Appeals for the First Circuit, at 49ff.
3. But, *cf. White* v. *Crook*, 251 F. Supp. 401 (N.D. Ala. 1966).

> A state may prescribe . . . the qualifications of its jurors . . .
> *It may confine the selection to males*, to freeholders . . .[4]

In one of its more recent pronouncements on the subject, in 1961, the Supreme Court dealt with a Florida statute that allows women on a jury only if they go to the Courthouse and request to be put on a special list. The procedure for men is automatic. The number of women on the Florida juries had been, of course, negligible. The Court said:

> At the core of appellant's argument is the claim that the nature of the crime of which she was convicted peculiarly demanded the inclusion of persons of her own sex on the jury. She was charged with killing her husband by assaulting him with a baseball bat . . . The affair occurred in the context of a marital upheaval involving, among other things, the suspected infidelity of appellant's husband, and culminating in the final rejection of his wife's efforts at reconciliation. It is claimed, in substance, that women jurors would have been more understanding or compassionate than men in assessing the quality of appellant's act and her defense . . .[5]

The Court dismissed her pleas and upheld her conviction by an all-male jury. In this instance, the Court found it convenient to minimize differences between men and women (as jurors).[6]

Not mentioned in the opinion was a recent study by Professor Hans Zeisel of the University of Chicago showing that jurors do vote differently, based on whether they are old or young, black or white, men or women. The Court justified its ruling in the Florida case by saying that "woman is still regarded as the center of home and family life."[7]

4. *Stauder* v. *U.S.*, 100 U.S. 303 (1879), at 310.
5. *Hoyt* v. *Florida*, 368 U.S. 57 (1961), at 58.
6. Cf. *Ballard* v. *U.S.*, 329 U.S. 187 (1946). Therein, Justice Douglas, in a case finding exclusion of women in *federal* juries to be illegal although not unconstitutional, stated: "But if the shoe were on the other foot, who would claim that a jury was truly representative of the community if all men were intentionally and systematically excluded from the panel. The truth is that the two sexes are not fungible; a community made up exclusively of one is different from a community composed of both . . . " (at 193, 194).
7. *Hoyt* v. *Florida, supra*, at 62.

There are many other areas of civil rights that could be studied. Women are not covered in the public accommodations section of the Civil Rights Act nor does the law currently protect them from being discriminated against by schools or universities. A group of women law students at New York University Law School, as recently as 1969, had to petition their school to open the Root-Tilden scholarships, $3,500 yearly stipends which had formerly been restricted to "young men who showed promise of being outstanding members of the Bar."[8] Dorms, of course, are still segregated, and colleges pretend to be able to exercise much more authority over its women than its men students.[9] Needless to say, women did not secure the right to vote until the Nineteenth Amendment in 1920—sixty-five years after it had been granted to people of any race.[10]

Myths built up to perpetuate the inferior status of women and black people are similar:

> As in the Negro problem, most men have accepted as self-evident, until recently, the doctrine that women had inferior endowments in most of those respects which carry prestige, power, and advantages in society, but that they were, at the same time, superior in some other respects. The arguments, when arguments were used, have been about the same: smaller brains, scarcity of geniuses and so on. The study of women's intelligence and personality has had broadly the same history as the one we record for Negroes. As in the case of the Negro, women themselves have often been brought to believe in their inferiority of endowment. As the Negro was awarded his "place" in society, so there was a "woman's place." In both cases the rationalization was strongly believed that men, in confining them to this place, did not act against the true interest of the subordinate groups. The myth of the "contented

8. See The Women's Rights Committee, "Fair and Equal Treatment for Women at New York University Law School" (1969).
9. The *Linda LeClair* case, for example, would never have happened to a male student at Columbia University.
10. In many countries the fundamental right to vote is still withheld from women. See Kanowitz, "Sex-based Discrimination in American Law," 11 St. Louis L.J. 293 (1967) at 294.

woman," who did not want to have suffrage or other civil rights and equal opportunities, had the same social function as the myth of the "contented Negro."[11]

Employment

Presented below are some key quotes from a few of the older United States Supreme Court cases. I would like the reader to see the source material, and to experience the process whereby the Court's prejudices become ossified into law and practice. Judges in those days were most honest, direct, and expansive about expressing their prejudices. *Moreover, the Supreme Court has not since overruled itself as to rights due women under the United States Constitution.* Some lower courts have ruled otherwise.[12] Legislation has improved. But practice remains.

As with many of the pernicious laws relating to women, judges explain their reasoning as being "protective" of women. In 1908, in upholding an hour-limitation statute for working women, the Supreme Court stated:

That woman's physical structure and the performance of maternal functions place her at a disadvantage in the struggle for subsistence is obvious. This is especially true when the burdens of motherhood are upon her. Even when they are not, by abundant testimony of the medical fraternity, continuance for a long time on her feet at work, repeating this from day to day, tends to injurious effects upon the body, and, as healthy mothers are essential to vigorous offspring, the physical well-being of woman becomes an object of public interest and care in order to preserve the strength and vigor of the race.

Still again, history discloses the fact that woman has always been dependent upon man. He established his control at the outset by superior physical strength, and this control in various forms, with diminishing intensity, has continued to the present.

11. Jan Myrdal, *An American Dilemma*, cited in Eastwood and Murray, "Jane Crow and the Law, Sex Discrimination and Title VII," 34 Geo. Wash. L. Rev. 232 (1966), at 234.
12. See, e.g., *Rosenfeld* v. *Southern Pacific Co.*, 37 LW 1089 (Cent. D. Cal., 1968).

As minors, though not to the same extent, she has been looked upon in the courts as needing especial care that her rights may be preserved. Education was long denied her, and while now the doors of the schoolroom are opened and her opportunities for acquiring knowledge are great, yet even with that and the consequent increase of capacity for business affairs it is still true that in the struggle for subsistence she is not an equal competitor with her brother. Though limitations upon personal and contractual rights may be removed by legislation, there is that in her disposition and habits of life which will operate against a full assertion of those rights . . . looking at it from the viewpoint of the effort to maintain an independent position in life, she is not upon an equality . . . she is properly placed in a class by herself . . . It is impossible to close one's eyes to the fact that she still looks to her brother and depends upon him. Even though all restrictions on political, personal, and contractual rights were taken away, and she stood, so far as statutes are concerned, upon an absolutely equal plane with him, it would still be true that she is so constituted that she will rest upon and look to him for protection: that her physical structure and a proper discharge of her maternal functions—having in view not merely her own health, but the well-being of the race—justify legislation to protect her from the greed as well as the passion of man. The limitations which this statute places upon her contractual powers, upon her right to agree with her employer as to the time she shall labor, are not imposed solely for her benefit, but also largely for the benefit of all . . .

We have not referred in this discussion to the denial of the elective franchise of the state of Oregon, for while that may disclose a lack of political equality in all things with her brother, that is not of itself decisive. The reason runs deeper and rests in the inherent difference between the two sexes, and in the different functions in life which they perform.[13]

In 1948, the Supreme Court reaffirmed its protective approach, in not allowing a woman to be a bartender unless she was "the wife or daughter of the male owner." The Court explained:

The fact that women may now have achieved the virtues that men have long claimed as their prerogatives and now indulge in vices that men have long practiced, does not preclude the

13. *Muller* v. *Oregon,* 208 U.S. 412 (1908), at 421–423.

states from drawing a sharp line between the sexes, certainly in such matters as the regulation of liquor traffic. *The Constitution does not require legislatures to reflect sociological insight, or shifting social standards, any more than it requires them to keep abreast of the latest scientific standards.*[14]

In 1963, many Congressmen tried to block the Equal Pay Act, the purpose of which was to give people, regardless of sex, equal pay for equal work. In 1964, when Congress was debating Title VII of the Civil Rights Act, forbidding discrimination in hiring, certain Southern Congressmen decided on a tactic to defeat the entire bill—add a clause prohibiting discrimination because of "sex" as well as a clause prohibiting discrimination because of "race"! Real supporters of women's rights opposed the amendment, in an effort to save the bill. Congressmen, generally, considered it some sort of obscene joke.[15]

In a polite understatement as to the present over-all condition of women and employment, the Committee on Private Employment of the President's Commission on the Status of Women noted:

Although women in the work force have a somewhat higher-than-average schooling than men, they, more generally than men, work in jobs far below their native abilities or trained capabilities. Barriers to women's employment and to their occupational progress generate feelings of injustice and frustration.[16]

The recently established Equal Employment Opportunity Commission should not have been surprised (as it was) to find that at times 50 percent of the complaints it received were from women.[17]

14. *Goesart* v. *Cleary,* 335 U.S. 464 (1948), at 466 (italics mine).
15. See Caroline Bird, *Born Female, or The High Cost of Keeping Women Down* (New York: David McKay, 1968), chapter 1.
16. President's Commission on the Status of Women, *Report of the Committee on Private Employment* (1963).
17. Caroline Bird, *Born Female,* pp. 205–206, 268. Her information comes from various newspaper articles and the *First Annual Report* of the Equal Employment Opportunity Commission, House Document No. 86, for the year ending

Recently, a study was conducted of all women law school graduates of the years 1956–1965.[18] Approximately half of the women stated that they had been the object of discrimination by employers. Average income differed sharply, based on sex:[19]

PRESENT INCOME

(Average income in 1964, by Years Since Graduation)

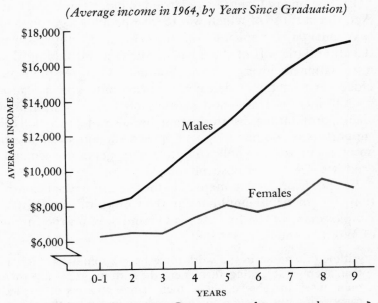

How has the Supreme Court treated women lawyers? In an opinion that might sound to some like a parody of sexism written by the Women's Liberation Movement, the Court upheld state legislation barring women from the practice of law.

A married woman from Illinois attacked the state law that forbade her from practicing law, and the Supreme Court answered her thusly:

June 30, 1966.
18. White, "Women in the Law," 65 Mich. L. Rev. 105 (1967) at 1068.
19. White, *ibid.*, 1055. Contrary to expectation, full-time employed married women earned significantly more money than did the unmarried women. White, *ibid.*, 1067. Reprinted by permission of Professor James J. White.

The claim of the plaintiff, who is a married woman, to be admitted to practice as an attorney and counselor-at-law, is based upon the supposed right of every person, man or woman, to engage in any lawful employment for a livelihood. The Supreme Court of Illinois denied the application on the ground that, by the common law, which is the basis of the laws of Illinois, only men were admitted to the bar . . .

The claim that (under the Fourteenth Amendment of the Constitution, which declares that no state shall make or enforce any law which shall abridge the privileges and immunities of citizens of the United States) the statute law of Illinois, or the common law prevailing in that state, can no longer be set up as a barrier against the right of females to pursue any lawful employment for a livelihood (the practice of law included), assumes that it is one of the privileges and immunities of women as citizens to engage in any and every profession, occupation, or employment in civil life.

It certainly cannot be affirmed, as an historical fact, that this has ever been established as one of the fundamental privileges and immunities of the sex. On the contrary, the civil law, as well as nature herself, has always recognized a wide difference in the respective spheres and destinies of man and woman. Man is, or should be, woman's protector and defender. The natural and proper timidity and delicacy which belongs to the female sex evidently unfits it for many of the occupations of civil life. The constitution of the family organization, which is founded in the divine ordinance, as well as in the nature of things, indicates the domestic sphere as that which properly belongs to the domain and functions of womanhood. The harmony, not to say identity, of interests and views which belong, or should belong, to the family institution is repugnant to the idea of a woman adopting a distinct and independent career from that of her husband. So firmly fixed was this sentiment in the founders of the common law that it became a maxim of that system of jurisprudence that a woman had no legal existence separate from her husband, who was regarded as her head and representative in the social state; and, notwithstanding some recent modifications of this civil status, many of the special rules of law flowing from and dependent upon this cardinal principle still exist in full force in most states. One of these is, that a married woman is incapable, without her husband's consent, of making contracts which shall be binding on her or him. This very incapacity was one circumstance which the Supreme Court of

Illinois deemed important in rendering a married woman incompetent fully to perform the duties and trusts that belong to the office of an attorney and counselor.

It is true that many women are unmarried and not affected by any of the duties, complications, and incapacities arising out of the married state, but these are exceptions to the general rule. *The paramount destiny and mission of woman are to fulfill the noble and benign offices of wife and mother.* This is the law of the Creator. And the rules of civil society must be adapted to the general constitution of things, and cannot be based upon exceptional cases.

The humane movements of modern society, which have for their object the multiplication of avenues for woman's advancement, and of occupations adapted to her condition and sex, have my heartiest concurrence. But I am not prepared to say that it is one of her fundamental rights and privileges to be admitted into every office and position, including those which require highly special qualifications and demanding special responsibilities . . . in my opinion, in view of the peculiar characteristics, destiny, and mission of woman, it is within the province of the legislature to ordain what offices, positions, and callings shall be filled and discharged by men, and shall receive the benefit of those energies and responsibilities, and that decision and firmness which are presumed to predominate in the sterner sex.

For these reasons I think that the laws of Illinois now complained of are not obnoxious to the charge of abridging any of the privileges and immunities of citizens of the United States.[20]

Twenty-two years later, a Miss Belva Lockwood was denied entry to the bar in Virginia. In its opinion this time, the Supreme Court decided that it is reasonable for a state court to find that a "woman" is not a "person":

It was for the Supreme Court of Appeals to construe the statute of Virginia in question, and to determine whether the word *"person"* as therein used is *confined to males*, and whether women are admitted to practice law in that Commonwealth. Leave denied.[21]

---

20. *Bradwell* v. *Illinois*, 83 U.S. (16 Wall) 130 (1872), at 140–142.
21. *In re Lockwood*, 154 U.S. 116 (1894), at 117 (italics mine).

Marital Relationship

In 1966, a bank in Texas got a raw deal. The Supreme Court found fit to uphold the Texas law providing that a married woman did not have the capacity to enter into a binding contract (and, therefore, the bank could not collect the $4,-000 she had promised to pay it).

In a dissenting opinion, Justice Black stated:

> The Texas law of "coverture" . . . rests on the old common-law fiction that the husband and wife are one. This rule has worked out in reality to mean that though the husband and wife are one, the one is the husband. This fiction rested on what I had supposed is today a completely discredited notion that a married woman, being a female, is without capacity to make her own contracts and do her own business . . . It seems at least unique to me that this Court in 1966 should exalt this archaic remnant of a primitive caste system to an honored place among the laws of the United States.[22]

Can a woman keep her own name upon remarrying? It seems that in some places she can if she has her husband's permission, but an Illinois court, in 1945, refused to let a woman vote in her maiden name, holding:

> The facts that a married woman practiced law for some years, became widely known as an attorney in her neighborhood, took active part in political activities thereof, was admitted to practice in various courts, and had certificates issued to her in her maiden name, were irrelevant on question of her statutory duty to cancel her registration under such name and reregister in her husband's surname in order to preserve her right to vote.[23]

Additionally, the Common Law tradition of loss of her legal personality when a woman marries, has raised, among others, the issues of right to a separate domicile; capacity to sue and be sued; change in citizenship upon marriage to an alien, cause of action for "loss of consortium" to one spouse only. Today, controversies center around men claiming to be discriminated against in the laws of alimony and child

22. *U.S.* v. *Yazell*, 382 U.S. 341 (1966), at 361.
23. *Peo* v. *Lipsky*, 327 Ill. App. 63, 63 N.E. 2d 642 (1945).

custody. "My wife sued to divorce me, and I had to pay for her lawyer!" complained a man recently. (There seems to be a trend among young women today not to request alimony if they can possibly afford not to.) Rights and obligations in marriage are currently under serious reconsideration.[24] Whether it is fair, or even wise—for children, husband, and wife—that the woman have complete responsibility as caretaker of the children is also being reconsidered.[25]

A supposed breakthrough was made in French law in February 1966, after heated debate. As a result of this new French law, "a wife, without asking the permission of her husband, can take a job or open a checking account. The husband can no longer simply choose housing without consulting his wife, nor make all the decisions about the children's education."[26]

Changes in the law cannot take place without changes in societal structure.[27]

Welfare Law

" . . . we have two systems of family law . . . different in origin, different in history, different in administration, different in orientation and outlook."—one for the rich and for the poor.[28]

One of the most flagrant abuses in recent years has been the searching of homes to find out if a welfare mother was having a sexual relationship and, if she was, then cutting her off welfare. The rule came to be known by various names,

24. Sayre, "A Reconsideration of Husband's Duty to Support and Wife's Duty to Render Services," 29 Va. L. Rev.857 (1943); Paulson, "Support Rights and Duties Between Husband and Wife," 9 Va. L. Rev. 709 (1956).
25. See Philip Roth, *Portnoy's Complaint* (New York: Random House, 1969).
26. *New York Times*, 2 February 1966. For n   65–570 due 13 Juillet 1965, [1965] J. O. 6044 (1); Recueil Dalloy Sirey, 31 Août 1965, p. 233; effective on February 1, 1966.
27. For a brilliant discussion of how women's roles change in the course of revolutionary struggle, see Frantz Fanon's *Studies in a Dying Colonialism* (New York: Grove Press, 1967).
28. Ten Broek, "California's Dual System of Family Law," 16 Stan. L. Rev. 257 (1964).

such as "substitute father" or "man in the house" rule. There was never, of course, any "woman in the house" rule. Raids to check out the situation were conducted as follows:

> Much more generally used than mass arrests are night calls, popularly known as "night raids," "bed checks," and "operations week-end." They may be made at the home of only one recipient but often they are a mass operation. The purpose is usually to determine whether there is an unreported man in the home of the recipient—whether he be husband, father, stepfather, or man assuming the role of spouse—whose presence may, on the one hand, determine eligibility or the amount of the grant, and on the other hand constitute an element in the crime of welfare fraud or theft. Such calls are frequently made between 10:00 P.M. and 4:00 A.M. The normal procedure is this: Investigators working in two-man teams approach the front and back of the house simultaneously and ring the doorbell; the investigator identifies himself, asks to be admitted, not specifically to look for a man or to make a routine check of the conditions of the home and the children; once inside, the investigator admits his partner and the two then conduct a minute search of the house looking into the children's and mother's bedrooms, in and under the beds, the attic, cellar, shower, closets, drawers, and medicine chest, searching for a man or evidence of his presence. Adults and children in the home are interviewed, notes taken, and sometimes signed statements are secured without explanation of their intended use.[29]

In the case which finally destroyed the "substitute father" theory rule,[30] a lawyer representing a welfare mother questioned a case-work supervisor:

> Q: Now, the regulation provides: " . . . though not living in the home regularly, he visits frequently for the purposes of cohabiting." What is your understanding of what the term "regularly" means in that provision?
> A: Well, I think it means on a continuing basis.
> Q: In other words, though not living in the home, on a continuing basis?

29. Ten Broek, "California's Dual System of Family Law, 17 Stan L. Rev. 257 (1965) at 667, 668.
30. This rule (which operated to deprive indigent women of a sex life), deems the men with whom she is fucking to be her children's "father" (although he is not). Ergo, he has to support them. Ergo, they are cut off welfare.

A: Yes.

Q: If a man is not living in a home on a continuing basis, but visits the house once a month for the purpose of cohabiting, is that, so far as your understanding of the regulation, sufficient to be presumptive evidence of a substitute father?

A: Well, I think it would depend upon the intent of the persons involved, whether they intended to have a continuing relationship or not.

. . .

Q: How would you go about finding this out? . . .

A: Well, I think that the worker would talk with the mother and also with the father if it were indicated.

Q: What kind of questions would be asked?

A: Well, how she felt about the man, what her intentions were, whether she intended to keep on with her relationship, or whether it was just a casual thing, or whether it had meaning.

. . .

Q: Assuming, now, that the mother and the substitute parent said that, although they cohabited only once every two months, they intended to do this on a permanent basis: would that be a basis for a *prima facie* presumption that the substitute parent rule should apply?

A: . . . we never have had an actual case that I can recall where they said it was once a month; but I assume that if it were considered permanent, as you say, that it would be considered a substitute parent.

Q: And that would be irrespective of whether the sexual relationship was in the home or outside of the home—is that right?

A: Yes.

Q: And so, if parties engaged in sexual relations once every two months outside of the home, but told you that they intended to continue to do this, it would be sufficient to warrant that they be denied aid under the regulation?

A: Now, do you mean with the same man, or do you mean different men?

Q: With the same man.

A: I would think that they would consider that—

Q: —*prima facie*—

A: —a marital relationship, if they continued to do this.

Q: Would your answer be the same if it were once every four months, and if the woman and the substitute parent told you that they intended to have these sexual relationships once every four months?—would that be sufficient *prima facie* proof to deny aid?

A: I believe I would have to call the State Department on that and see what they say about that.[31]

Criminal Law

Legislation and case law still exist in some parts of the United States permitting the "passion shooting" by a husband of a wife;[32] the reverse, of course, is known as homicide. Italy, on December 20, 1968, abolished a law under which a woman could be jailed for adultery for one year, while her husband could be unfaithful with impunity.[33] On December 12, 1968, the United States Supreme Court considered the case of a girl who was imprisoned for "lascivious carriage." It considered the constitutionality of a 1905 Connecticut law authorizing imprisonment of young women if they are "in manifest danger of falling into habits of vice or leading a vicious life.[34] Thus, we see sex discrimination in the very definition of crimes.[35] Laws also exist providing for different lengths of jail sentences for the same crime, de-

31. See *King* v. *Smith*, 329 U.S. 309 (1968). The above questioning was in a deposition taken on March 9, 1967. Martin Garbers, Esq., is questioning Jean M. Johnson, casework supervisor of Aid to Dependent Children in Dallas County.
32. See, N.M. Stat. Ann. sec. 40A–2–4(7) (Repl. 1964); Texas Penal Code art 1220 (Vernon's 1961); Utah Code Ann. sec. 76–30–10 (5) (1953); *State* v. *Williams*, 47 Utah 320, 168 pll04 (1917). See also the film *Adam's Rib*.
33. *New York Times*, 20 December 1968.
34. See *New York Times*, 12 December 1968.
35. The criminal prosecution of witches is not very common today, but it was at one time, and there are many volumes of legal writing on the subject. Why were most of the convicted witches women? Is it because religious and political heresy, or even independence of opinion, is less to be tolerated in women than men? Some groups are now researching the proposition that witches were actually early women revolutionaries. A book written in England in 1680 by Sir Robert Filmer would seem to support this conclusion. The book is entitled *The Freeholders Grand Inquest*. Its summary includes a review of the following subjects: Observations upon forms of Government; Directions for obedience to governors in dangerous and doubtful times; Observations on Anarchy; An advertisement to the jury-men of England, touching witches; Observations upon: Aristotle's *Politiques*, Hobbes's *Leviathan*, Milton against Salmasius, Grotius, *De Jure Belli & pacis*; The Anarchy of a limited or mixed Monarchy; A difference between an English and Hebrew witch.

pending on whether the perpetrator is male or female.[36]

More studies are needed in the area of criminal law and criminology to determine why some crimes are committed more often by men (e.g., violent crimes, shootings) and other crimes by women (e.g., shoplifting). Studies should also be conducted concerning comparative treatment inside jails. A counselor working with imprisoned women drug addicts told me recently that it is much more difficult working with female prisoners, partly because it is less possible to train them for work after release that would pay reasonably well. A woman confined for three years at one of these "rehabilitation centers" wrote to me on June 21, 1968:

> On May 27, 1968, I *volunteered* to Manhattan Rehabilitation Center [a center for drug addicts] . . . I volunteered to this program under the assumption that I would receive professional psychiatric and medical care at all times. I have found, much to my disappointment, that I receive very little medical care and no psychiatric treatment whatsoever.
> I have also found myself locked up in a building that was condemned by the Fire Department as a fire hazard.
> As a mere drug user, I understand I am legally considered "sick," yet here I am treated as a hardened criminal.
> For many reasons I feel this Center would be detrimental, not supplemental, to my health.[37]

In the area of sex and reproduction, the law has an effect on women more directly than on men. In many states, dispensing birth-control information is a crime. Thus, Bill Baird, for example, faced five years in jail in Massachusetts, for handing someone a can of "contraceptive" foam. Under recent New York abortion laws, a person who performed an abortion on another was guilty of a felony, and a woman who submitted herself to an abortion was guilty of a misdemeanor.[38] The abortion Statutes are in a section of the

36. See *Commonwealth* v. *Daniels*, 37 L. W. 2064 Pa. Sup. Ct. 7/1/68 (reversing L.W. 2004).
37. Letter to Diane B. Schulder, Esq. (italics mine) See also Father Daniel Egan S. A., *The Junkie Priest* (New York: Pocket Books, 1965), for a description of the life of drug addiction and prostitution.
38. N. Y. Penal Law, Section 125.40. The only exception was when it was neces-

New York Penal Law entitled "Homicide, abortion, and related offenses."

One of the areas where the criminal law operates most discriminatorily relates to prostitution. In New York City, policemen actively entrap women and then charge them with prostitution. A defendant (who was acquitted) testified to a typical example:

> He came up behind me first and asked me was I going out, and I really didn't have too much to say to him at first, and then he started walking alongside me and we both started a small conversation, and I told him that he looked like a police officer, and he told me that he wasn't, he was a shoe salesman or something from Minnesota, and he showed me some identification . . . It was like a name tag with a plastic covering over it or something. He took it out of his jacket pocket. He was wearing a suit and carrying a valise . . . Then there was a lot . of other small talk and then he told me that he was spending twenty dollars . . .[39]

The officer testified:

> I hailed a cab and we got into the cab, and she said, "Driver, go along Seventh Avenue," and as we drove away I said to the driver, "Forget about that, driver, take me to the 18th Precinct."[40]

A directive was issued, not too long ago, to policemen in New York City not to entrap male homosexuals; no such relating to female prostitutes. Nor, of course, do policewomen in disguise try to entrap businessmen seeking to exploit the indigent women who walk the streets.

In a recent pronouncement, a Criminal Court judge characterized the women prostitutes as "hardened criminals"

sary to save the mother's life.
39. Trial Transcript, *Peo* v. *Dixon*, trial in N.Y. Criminal Court, Part 1C, on July 18, 1968, at p. 14ff.
40. *Peo* v. *Dixon*, *supra*, at 3. Policemen often testify in court that women approach them and ask, "Do you want to get laid?" This is often a lie, used to secure a conviction, and frequently judges will close their eyes to this tactic. There have been speculative rumors, as well, that some vice squads participate in vice with their arrestees.

and said "one could not equate their activity with that of their customers."[41] This, despite the fact that New York law states that prostitutes and their customers are guilty of equal violations.[42] The New York District Attorney's office has also chosen not to prosecute the men customers.[43] Both deterrence and fairness, however, would be served if this were done. In another country, a strikingly successful campaign in the suppression of prostitution was carried out as follows:

> Whenever officers raided a place of vice—whether it was a house, a tavern, or simply a dark street—they were to take down the names, addresses, and place of employment of all men found there. The customers were not to be arrested. But on the following day, and for a specified period, those men would have their names and identifying information posted in a public place, under the heading "Buyers of the Bodies of Women." These lists were to be prominently displayed outside public buildings or on factory bulletin boards.[44]

Other countries, such as England, have legalized prostitution.[45] As has been suggested before (but not practiced), "The stigma and consequence of crime must . . . be either removed from the woman or affixed to the man."[46]

Conclusion

Thus, prejudice (the mythology of class oppression) is ensh-

41. *New York Times*, 27 January 1968.
42. N.Y. Penal Law, Sections 230ff. The New York law making it an equal offense for the man who participates was added in 1967. The stated purposes of this new addition are "deterrence" and "fairness."
43. An attorney friend of mine noted recently that if the police were too successful in deterrence, big business conventions would cancel out of New York City and go elsewhere.
44. Carter, *Sin and Science* (1945) at 56–57, describing action in the Soviet Union.
45. Another judge in the New York Criminal Court believes this is the proper solution. See *New York Times*, 27 January 1969.
46. Abraham Flexner, *Prostitution in Europe* (New York: Century Co., 1914), p. 103. As Flexner says (p. 107): " . . . as a matter of history, no proposition aiming at punishment of prostitution has ever involved both participants. The harlot has been branded as an outcast and flung to the wolves: she alone,—never the man, her equal partner in responsibility."

rined in laws. Laws lead to enforcement of practices. Practices reinforce and lead to prejudice. The cycle continues ... Women who feel oppressed, women involved in the fight for women's liberation, are not paranoid. Their feelings of oppression are not imaginary. Indeed their oppression, in more areas than generally realized, is built into the law.

ii

THE INVISIBLE WOMEN:

PSYCHOLOGICAL AND

SEXUAL REPRESSION

BARBAROUS RITUALS

Woman Is:

———kicking strongly in your mother's womb, upon which she is told, "It must be a boy, if it's so active!"

———being tagged with a *pink* beaded bracelet thirty seconds after you are born, and wrapped in *pink* blankets five minutes thereafter.

———being confined to the Doll Corner in nursery school when you are really fascinated by Tinker Toys.

———wanting to wear overalls instead of "frocks."

———learning to detest the words "dainty" and "cute."

———being labeled a tomboy when all you wanted to do was climb that tree to look out and see a distance.

———learning to sit with your legs crossed, even when your feet can't touch the floor yet.

————hating boys—because they're allowed to do things you want to do but are forbidden to—and being told hating boys is a phase.

————learning that something you do is "naughty," but when your brother does the same thing, it's "spunky."

————wondering why your father gets mad now and then, but your mother mostly sighs a lot.

————seeing grownups chuckle when you say you want to be an engineer or doctor when you grow up—and learning to say you want to be a mommy or a nurse, instead.

————wanting to shave your legs at twelve and being agonized because your mother won't let you.

————being agonized at fourteen because you finally have shaved your legs, and your flesh is on fire.

————being told nothing whatsoever about menstruation, so that you think you are bleeding to death with your first period, *or*:

————being told all about it in advance by kids at school who titter and make it clear the whole thing is dirty, *or*:

————being prepared for it by your mother, who carefully reiterates that it *isn't* dirty, all the while talking just above a whisper, and referring to it as "the curse," "being sick," or "falling off the roof."

————feeling proud of and disgusted by your own body, for the first, but not last, time.

————dying of shame because your mother makes you wear a "training bra" but there's nothing to train, *or*:

————dying of shame because your mother *won't* let you wear a bra and your breasts are bigger than other girls' your age and they flop when you run and you sit all the time with your arms folded over your chest.

————feeling basically comfortable in your own body, but gradually learning to hate it because you are: too short or tall, too fat or thin, thick-thighed or big-wristed, large-eared or stringy-haired, short-necked or long-armed, bowlegged, knock-kneed, or pigeon-toed—*something* that *might* make boys not like you.

————wanting to kill yourself because of pimples, dandruff, or a natural tendency to sweat—and discovering that commercials about miracle products just lie.

————dreading summertime because more of your body with its imperfections will be seen—and judged.

————tweezing your eyebrows/bleaching your hair/scraping your armpits/dieting/investigating vaginal sprays/biting your nails and hating that and filing what's left of them but hitting the quick instead.

————liking math or history a lot and getting hints that boys are turned off by smart girls.

————getting hints that other *girls* are turned off by smart girls.

————finally getting turned off by smart girls, unconsciously dropping back, lousing up your marks, and being liked by the other kids at last.

————having an intense crush on another girl or on a woman teacher and learning that that's unspeakable.

————going to your first dance and dreaming about it beforehand, and hating it, just *hating* it afterwards: you didn't dance right, you spilled the punch, you were a wallflower in anguish (*or*: you were popular but in anguish because your best *friend* was a wallflower); you said all the wrong things.

————being absolutely convinced that you are a clod, a goon, a dog, a schlep, a flop, and an utter klutz.

————discovering that what seems like everything worthwhile doing in life "isn't feminine," and learning to just *delight* in being feminine and "nice"—and feeling somehow guilty.

————masturbating like crazy and being terrified that you'll go insane, be sterile, turn into a whore, or destroy your own virginity.

————getting more information any way you can, and then being worried because you've been masturbating clitorally, and that isn't even the "right way."

————swinging down the street feeling good and smiling at people and being hassled like a piece of meat in return.

————having your first real human talk with your mother and being told about all her old hopes and lost ambitions, and how you can't fight it, and that's just the way it is: life, sex, men, the works—and loving her and hating her for having been so beaten down.

————having your first real human talk with your father and being told about all *his* old hopes and lost ambitions, and how women really have it easier, and "what a man really wants in a woman,"—and loving him and hating him for having been beaten down— and for beating down your mother in turn.

————brooding about "how far" you should go with the guy you really like. Will he no longer respect you? Will you get—oh God—a "reputation"? Or, if not, are you a square? Being pissed off because you can't just do what *you* feel like doing.

————being secretly afraid that you'll lose your virginity to a tampon, but being too ashamed to ask anyone about it.

————lying awake wondering if a girl really *can* get pregnant by the sperm swimming *through* her panties.

————having a horrible fight with your boyfriend who keeps shouting how *he's* frustrated by not "doing it" —it never occurring to him that *you* might be climbing walls, too, which you maybe don't even dare to admit.

————finally screwing and your groin and buttocks and thighs ache like hell and you're all wet and maybe bloody and it wasn't like a Hollywood movie at all but jesus at least you're not a virgin any more but is this what it's all about?—and meanwhile he's asking, "Did you come?"

————discovering you need an abortion, and really learning for the first time what your man, your parents, and your society think of you. Frequently paying for that knowledge with your death.

————finding that the career you've chosen exacts more than just study or hard work—an emotional price of being made to feel "less a woman."

————finding that almost all jobs open to you pay less for harder work than to men.

————being bugged by men in the office who assume that you're a virginal prude if you don't flirt, and that you're an easy mark if you are halfway relaxed and pleasant.

————learning to be *very tactful* if you have men working

"under you." More likely, learning to always be working under men.

——becoming a woman *executive*, for God's sake, and then being asked to order the delicatessen food for an office party.

——finding out how difficult it is to get hold of "easily accessible" birth-control information.

——chasing the slippery diaphragm around the bathroom as if in a game of frisbee the first time you try to insert it yourself, *or*:

——gaining weight, or hemorrhaging, or feeling generally miserable with the Pill, or just freaking out at the scare stories about it, *or*:

——going on a cross-country car trip in a Volkswagen, during which the Loop or the Coil becomes dislodged and begins to tear at your flesh.

——wondering why we can have live color telecasts of the moon's surface, but still no truly simple, humane, safe method of birth control.

——going the rounds of showers, shopping, money worries, invitation lists, licenses—when all you really wanted to do was live with the guy.

——quarreling with your fiance over whether "and obey" should be in the marriage ceremony.

——secretly being bitched because the ceremony says "man and wife"—not "husband and wife" or "man and woman." Resenting having to change your (actually, your father's) name.

——having been up since 6:00 A.M. on your wedding day seeing family and friends you really don't even like and being exhausted from standing just so and not creasing your gown and from the ceremony and reception and traveling and now being alone with this strange man who wants to "make love" when you don't know that you even *like* him and even if you did you desperately want to just sleep for fourteen hours, *or*:

————*not* getting married, just living together in "free love," and finding out it's just the same as marriage anyway, and you're the one who pays for the "free."

————playing the role to the hilt, cooking special dishes, cleaning, etc.—and knowing you'll *never* make it as *Good Housekeeping*'s "ideal," *or*:

————"dropping out" together to a "hip, groovy" commune—and cooking brown rice instead of Betty Crocker.

————having menstrual cramps each month quite normally, cramps and/or headaches and/or nausea that would put a "normal" man out of commission for two weeks—and going on with your job or chores, etc., so no one will be inconvenienced.

————finding out that you're bored by your husband in bed.

————faking an orgasm for the first time: disgust, frustration—and relief (because he never even knew the difference).

————feeling guilty for not having an orgasm: *what* is wrong with *you*?

————finding out that *you* bore *your* husband in bed. Getting desperate—where have *you* failed?

————wanting desperately to know what special things he wants you to do to him in bed—and being afraid to tell him what you'd want him to do; or telling him hints that he promptly forgets for ever after.

———wanting to be the power behind the throne and finding out either that he's not a great man after all, or that he doesn't need your support.

———being jealous and hating yourself for showing it.

———hating certain books that you might have loved—all because he read them first and told you all about them. Feeling robbed. This goes for movies, too.

———wanting to go back to school, to read, to join something, do something. Why isn't home enough for you? What's wrong with *you*?

———coming home from work—and starting *in* to work: unpack the groceries, fix supper, wash up the dishes, rinse out some laundry, etc., etc.

———feeling a need to say "thank you" when your guy actually fixes *himself* a meal now that you're dying with the 'flu.

———getting pregnant, hearing all the earth-mother shit from everyone, going around with a fixed smile on your terrified face.

———having men on the street, in cabs and busses, no longer (at least) regard you as an ogle-object; now they regard you as Carrier Of The Species.

———knowing there must be some deep-down way to enjoy this that maybe women in some "primitive" tribe feel, but being elephantine, achy, nauseated—and *kvetched* at having to be cheerful.

———wanting your husband with you, or wanting natural childbirth, and either he won't, or the doctor or hospital won't—and you're on your own, *or*:

———maybe you're lucky and he's not afraid or disgusted

and the doctor approves and you go through it together and it's even beautiful—and you hear another
woman screaming in solitary labor next door.

————feeling responsible for *more* lives—your kids' as well
as your man's—but never, never your own life.

————learning to hate other women who are: younger,
freer, unmarried, without children, in jobs, in school,
in careers—whatever. Hating yourself for hating
them.

————trying desperately not to repeat the pattern, and
catching yourself telling your daughter one day that
she "isn't acting like a lady," or warning your son
"not to be a sissy."

————knowing that your husband is "playing around" and
wanting to care, but not even being able to.

————being widowed, or divorced, and trying to get a
"good" job—at your age.

————claiming not to understand the "revolt" of your kids,
but understanding it in your gut and not being able
to help being bitter because you think it's too late for
you.

————still wanting to have sex but feeling faintly ridiculous
before your husband, let alone other men.

————being patronized and smirked over by your own children during the agonizing ritual of widowhood dating.

————getting older, getting lonelier, getting ready to die—
and knowing it wouldn't have had to be this way,
after all.

IT HURTS TO BE ALIVE AND OBSOLETE: THE AGEING WOMAN

Zoe Moss

What, fat, forty-three, and I dare to think I'm still a person? No, I am an invisible lump. I belong in a category labelled *a priori* without interest to anyone. I am not even expected to interest myself. A middle-aged woman is comic by definition.

In this commodity culture, we are urged and coerced into defining ourselves by buying objects that demonstrate that we are, or which tell us that they will make us feel, young, affluent, fashionable. Imagine a coffee table with the best-sellers of five years ago carefully displayed. You giggle. A magazine that is old enough—say, a *New Yorker* from 1944 with the models looking healthy and almost buxom in their padded jackets—or a dress that is far enough gone not to give the impression that perhaps you had not noticed fashions had changed, can become campy and delightful. But an out-of-date woman is only embarrassing.

The mass media tell us all day and all evening long that we are inadequate, mindless, ugly, disgusting in ourselves. We must try to resemble perfect plastic objects, so that no one will notice what we really are. In ourselves we smell bad, shed dandruff, our breath has an odor, our hair stands up or falls out, we sag or stick out where we shouldn't. We can only fool people into liking us by using magic products that make us products, too.

Women, especially, are commodities. There is always a perfect plastic woman. Girls are always curling their hair or ironing it, binding their breasts or padding them. Think of the girls with straight hips and long legs skulking through the 1890's with its women defined as having breasts the size of pillows and hips like divans. Think of the Rubens woman today forever starving and dieting and crawling into rubber compression chambers that mark her flesh with livid lines and squeeze her organs into knots.

If a girl were to walk into a party in the clothes of just five or six years past, in the make-up and hairstyle of just that slight gap of time, no one would want to talk to her, no man would want to dance with her. Yet what has all that to do with even a man and a women in bed? This is not only the middle class I am talking about. I have seen hippies react the same way to somebody wearing old straight clothes.

It is a joke, but a morbid one. My daughter has a girlfriend who always laughs with her hand up to her mouth because she is persuaded her teeth are yellow, and that yellow teeth are hideous. She seems somber and never will she enjoy a natural belly laugh. Most young girls walk around with the conviction that some small part of their anatomy (nose, breasts, knees, chin) is so large or so small or so misshapen that their whole body appears to be built around that part, and all of their activities must camouflage it.

My daughter is a senior in college. She already talks about her "youth" with a sad nostalgia. She is worried because she is not married. That she has not met anyone that she wants to live that close to, does not seem to figure in her anxiety. Everything confirms in her a sense of time passing, that she will be left behind, unsold on the shelf. She already peers in the mirror for wrinkles and buys creams and jellies to rub into her skin. Her fear angers me but leaves me helpless. She is alienated from her body because her breasts are big and do not stand out like the breasts of store mannequins. She looks twenty-one. I look forty-three.

I want to beg her not to begin worrying, not to let in the dreadful daily gnawing already. Everyone born grows up, grows older, and ages every day until he dies. But every day in seventy thousand ways this society tells a woman that it is her sin and her guilt that she has a real living body. How can a woman respect herself when every day she stands before her mirror and accuses her face of betraying her, because every day she is, indeed, a day older.

Everything she reads, every comic strip, every song, every cartoon, every advertisement, every book and movie tells her that a woman over thirty is ugly and disgusting. She is a bag. She is to be escaped from. She is no longer an object of prestige consumption. For her to have real living sexual desires is obscene. Her touch is thought to contaminate. No man "seduces" a woman older than him: there is no conquest. It is understood she would be "glad for a touch of it." Since she would be glad, there can be no pleasure in the act. Either this society is mad or I am mad. It is considered incredible that a woman might have had experiences that are valuable or interesting and that have enriched her as a person. No, men may mature, but women just obsolesce.

All right, says the woman, don't punish me! I won't do wrong! I won't get older! Now, if a woman has at least an upper-middle-class income, no strong commitments such as a real career or a real interest in religion or art or politics; if she has a small family and hired help; if she has certain minimal genetic luck; if she has the ability to be infinitely fascinated by her own features and body, she may continue to present a youthful image. She can prolong her career as sexual object, lying about her age, rewriting her past to keep the chronology updated, and devoting herself to the cultivation of her image. Society will reward her greatly. Women in the entertainment industry are allowed to remain sexual objects (objects that are prestigful to use or own—like Cadillacs) for much of their lives.

To be told when you have half your years still to wade through and when you don't feel inside much different than you did at twenty (you are still you!—you know that!), to be told then that you are cut off from expressing yourself sexually and often even in friendship, drives many women crazy—often literally so.

Don't tell me that it is human nature for women to cease to be attractive early. In primitive society a woman who is still useful—in that by all means far more humane definition than ours—will find a mate, whom she may share as she shares the work with his other wives. Black women are more oppressed on the job and in almost every other way in this society than white women, but at least in the ghetto men go on assuming a woman is sexual as long as she thinks so too.

Earlier mythology in which "the widow" is a big sex figure, French novels in which the first mistress is always an older woman, the Wife of Bath, all reinforce my sense that there is nothing natural about women's obsolescence.

I was divorced five years ago. Don't tell me I should have "held on to my husband." We let go with great relief. Recently he has married a woman in her late twenties. It is not surprising he should marry someone younger: most people in this society are younger than my ex-husband. In my job, most of the people I meet are younger than I am, and the same is true of people who share my interests, from skiing to resistance to the war against Vietnam.

When my daughter was little I stayed home, but luckily for me I returned to work when she entered school. I say luckily, because while I believe my ex-husband has an obligation to help our daughter, I would never accept alimony. I can get quite cold and frightened imagining what would have happened if I had stayed home until my divorce, and then, at thirty-eight, tried to find work. I used to eat sometimes at a lunchroom where the rushed and overworked waitress was in her late forties. She had to cover the whole room, and I used to leave her larger tips than I would give someone else because to watch her made me conscious of women's economic vulnerability. She was gone one day and I asked the manager at the cash register about her. "Oh, the customers didn't like her. Men come in here, they want to see a pretty face."

I have insisted on using a pseudonym in writing this article, because the cost of insisting I am not a cipher would be fatal. If I lost my job, I would have an incredible time finding another. I know I will never "get ahead." Women don't move up through the shelves of a business automatically or by keeping their mouths shut. I could be mocked into an agony of shame for writing this—but beyond that, I could so easily be let go.

I am gregarious, interested in others, and I think, intelligent. All I ask is to get to know people and to have them interested in knowing me. I doubt whether I would marry again and live that close to another individual. But I remain invisible. I think stripped down I look more attractive on some abstract scale (a bisexual Martian judging) than my ex-husband, but I am sexually and socially obsolete, and he is not. Like most healthy women my face has aged more rapidly than my body, and I look better with my clothes off. When I was young, my anxiety about myself and what was to become of me colored all my relationships with men, and I was about as sensual as a clotheshanger. I have a capacity now for taking people as they are, which I lacked at twenty; I reach orgasm in half the time and I know how to please. Yet I do not even dare show a man that I find him attractive. If I do so, he may react as if I had insulted him: with shock, with disgust. I am not even allowed to be affectionate. I am supposed to fulfill my small functions and vanish.

Often when men are attracted to me, they feel ashamed and conceal it. They act as if it were ridiculous. If they do become involved, they are still ashamed and may refuse to appear publicly with me. Their fear of mockery is enormous. There is no prestige attached to having sex with me.

Since we are all far more various sexually than we are supposed to be, often, in fact, younger men become aware of me sexually. Their response is similar to what it is when they find themselves feeling attracted to a homosexual: they turn those feelings into hostility and put me down.

Listen to me! Think what it is like to have most of your life ahead and be told you are obsolete! Think what it is like to feel attraction, desire, affection toward others, to want to tell them about yourself, to feel that assumption on which self-respect is based, that you are worth something, and that if you like someone, surely he will be pleased to know that. To be, in other words, still a living woman, and to be told every day that you are not a woman but a tired object that should disappear. That you are not a person but a joke. Well, I am a bitter joke. I am bitter and frustrated and wasted, but don't you pretend for a minute as you look at me, forty-three, fat, and looking exactly my age, that I am not as alive as you are and that I do not suffer from the category into which you are forcing me.

MEDIA IMAGES I: MADISON AVENUE BRAINWASHING—THE FACTS

Alice Embree

A Parable

Shortly after the turn of the century, America marshaled her resources, contracted painfully, and gave birth to the New Technology. The father was a Corporation, and the New Technology grew up in the Corporate image.

During the 1940's when the New Technology was in its adolescence, America went to war. She returned victorious and technology was made a war hero. A mythology grew up around the new hero describing America's greatness as her ability to harness the New Technology to commercial production. Revolution was used with careless abandon to describe technological innovation—the corollary being that no other kind of revolution was necessary.

There was the automobile revolution; the television revolution; even detergent revolutions. Each new innovation accelerated changing patterns of social relationships and created new patterns. For example, urban centers were built around automobiles, and television altered traditional family life. In short, the social fabric was being shredded and rewoven. But the new technology remained in the hands of corporations and the basic relationship between the producer and consumer remained unchanged. No political revolution was taking place. Instead, Americans became more and more passive observers of the entire technological process and more passive consumers of its corporate by-products. No one could tell General Motors, for instance, that Fords and Chryslers were sufficient and that GM should turn over its corporate assets to some other endeavor. The machinery was geared to commercial production, and people had to be put in gear to consumption. The war hero had opened up a new front—the domestic marketplace.

In the hands of corporations, the new technology quickly transformed America into the land of Mass Production, Mass Distribution, and Mass Consumption. The technology of wireless communication and transistors gave birth to a Mass Media. It became possible to create Instant Nation where before there had been regions and communities. Individual Americans were forged into a Mass. Decentralized information sources gave way, and a national media—newspapers, magazines, radio, and television—was beamed at that Mass.

The creation of an undifferentiated Mass was more than just a technological by-product. It was a corporate necessity. The first corporate imperative is profit: mass markets are needed for that profit. Humans must breathe, but corporations must make money. Their life rhythm is regulated by their annual reports to stockholders. If they fail to grow each year, if they fail to make more and more money, the spell is broken; they turn back into pumpkins with only their incorporation papers left.

The new Mass Media understood the process well. After all, they were corporations too. They shaped people into one-dimensional receivers of communication—people who were more easily channeled into roles of unprotesting consumers.

Women in America occupy a special position in the American consumer economy; they are exploited in a particular way, just as their exploitation takes on a particular form in the society at large. In the technological economy, women are particularly alienated. Men, at least, are brought up to have some kind of working knowledge of the technological produce that surrounds them: they can repair automobiles, they have a rudimentary understanding of electrical appliances, etc. But, more important, men occupy the jobs that put them in touch with the assembly line and managerial work of the new technology. Women are traditionally brought up to know only the skills of the household. Cooking, sewing, cleaning are eighteenth- and nineteenth-century skills, not contemporary ones. That is not to say that the traditional work of women is not important or that it doesn't have contemporary trappings. But women's roles are especially divorced from the overriding mythology of a highly technological America. Women are the neglected orphans of the technological age.

An exception to this general rule should prove the point. During World War II, when the men went off to wage war, the economy needed more production-line workers. Women were mobilized into the vacuum. The image of women projected through the mass media shifted drastically. Shoulder pads came in. There were more advertisements for the women's branches of the armed services, more pictures of women working alongside men. In fact, the new propaganda was that women were dull mothers if they didn't have roles outside the home. The accent on cosmetics dropped. Women were encouraged to give up their frilly accessories and nylons for the war effort. The wartime image that was projected was a far cry from the fashion plate mirage projected in the "You've come a long way, baby" ads for Virginia Slim cigarettes. In fact, Eleanor Roosevelt, one of the images of wartime competency, is the reverse image of a soft-spoken Jacqueline Kennedy or non-speaking Pat Nixon.

It should be remembered, in this context, that the media men had gone to war, too. Many of the men who are now in charge of "peacetime" image-creation in the mass media spent the wartime years in the Office of War Information and the Psychological Warfare Division of the army. (William Paley, now chairman of the board of Columbia Broadcasting System, was deputy chief of the Psychological Warfare Division). When the war was over, the corporations and the mass media retooled for the new war on the domestic market. The new staging grounds became livingrooms, newsstands, and supermarkets. Psychological warfare was declared on the domestic consumer. Like a battlefield commentator, *Forbes Business Magazine* (self-described as The Capitalist Tool) describes the competition for placement on the supermarket shelf in the soap industry: "Because shelf space is so important, P&G (Procter and Gamble) goes after its share with all the precision and force of a military invasion" *(Forbes,* 15 April 1969).

As the corporate need for expansion presses onward, it becomes necessary to intensify the penetration of the domestic market. Advertising is the means for that increased penetration. The function of advertising has changed from the simple display of products and presentation of information to the creation of needs. The bizarre consequence is the created "need" for electric toothbrushes, wigs, false eyelashes, an infinite variety of special cleansers —all in an economy that still has not solved the elementary problem of poverty. In 1890, total advertising expenditures in the United States were a mere $360 million. By 1920 they had increased to nearly $3 billion, by 1950 to $5.7 billion, and by 1966 they had skyrocketed to $16.5 billion. The very existence of the mass media is dependent on this income. In fact, it could almost be argued that the articles in magazines and programs on television are simply a device to keep the advertisements and commercials from bumping loudly together. The message of the media is the commercial.

Roughly 20 percent of TV air time is given over to commercials. *Time* magazine (12 July 1968) gives the following statistics: "This year two thousand advertisers will pour $3.1 billion into television advertising—twice the budget of the poverty program." The news of war in Vietnam is interspersed with ads for cigarettes; on the day Robert Kennedy died, Walter Cronkite wrapped up the latest bulletins on the assassination in time for a mouthwash ad. Or take the prestigious *New York Times* as an example. Remove the ads from its respected news coverage and its content would be quartered; it would look positively skimpy instead of overwhelming. Or consider another *Time* statistic: "As it is, the cost of a one-minute commercial—rehearsals, filming, reshooting, dubbing, scoring, animation, printing—runs to an average of $22,000 or about five times more than a minute of TV entertainment." *Newsweek* (26 May 1969) credits the commercial with even more: "It isn't art, but it's artful—which is more than can be said for many of the tasteless, saccharine, and irritating programs supported by the sponsors." Furthermore, the examples are legion of networks sacrificing important news coverage to their regular schedule so that the valuable commercials won't be pre-empted. If we are to judge America's mass media by its own priorities, its message is obvious: *consume!*

But an assessment of the mass media which only takes into account its economic backbone would be too superficial. The special media—the favorite child—of technological America is television. It is the most highly centralized of the mass media (reaching 95 percent of the nation's homes) and the most commanding in terms of attention required. It deserves special consideration. Regardless of whether its programming is labeled "entertainment," "news," or "public affairs" it is known for its reduction to the "lowest common denominator." This phrase has been misunderstood and an inferiority complex has settled onto the unconsulted mass. It does not mean that some kind of assessment is made of the mass mentality and that shows are geared to the worst of it. "The lowest common denominator" refers to the effort required of the *broadcaster.* The least the broadcaster can do and still reach a mass audience is what is screened.

The mass media is a twentieth-century twin to the mass education system. The target of corporate technology is an ever more homogeneous mass which is viewed as a market. As communities deteriorate in the wake of this dynamic, as family life disintegrates and churches lose their traditional importance, these two institutions—mass education and mass media—stand out as the chief socializers of young people, the chief value-setters and image-creators. Just as the present educational system fragments knowledge and divides it into courses rather than presenting an integrated whole, TV programming makes artificial distinctions between its news, public affairs, entertainment, and commercial messages. In reality, those things together comprise the media message in the same way that the process of education—more than the individual lectures—comprise the educational message. Just as students are converted into numbers in large bureaucratized educational institutions and into input categories for huge corporations, TV viewers are converted into objects of mammoth media institutions over which they have no control. In fact, these two key institutions are converging: the major textbook producers for the national educational market and the major educational filmmakers are being bought up by the mass media corporations. The "knowledge industry" is becoming big business for the media firms, and they are creating new systems for education which will include their own new technological produce: closed circuit TV's, language labs, slide projectors, combination print and film learning-programs, etc.

Television news is careful to divide things into small and easily digestible particles. There is no integrated or comprehensible world view presented. Everything is safely middle class. Poverty and discontent only show up briefly on short newsclips and even these are made safe by an "objective," unruffled, and fatherly announcer. The "entertainment" functions primarily as a diversionary tactic from real human problems. Everything is reduced to a personal level, in the same way that sociology and psychology courses accentuate an individualized view of society rather than concentrating on the structural or institutional problems: the problem with marriages is that wives can't get along with husbands, not that society generates unmanageable conflicts; the problem on the campuses is that children can't get along with parents, not that the educational system (not to speak of the society at large) is impossible to live a full life in.

The mass media molds everyone into more passive roles, into roles of more frantic consuming, into human beings with fragmented views of society. But what it does to everyone, it does to women even more. The traditional societal role for women is already a passive one, already one of a consumer, already one of an emotional nonintellectual who isn't supposed to think or act beyond the confines of her home. The mass media reinforces all these traits.

Television programming exists in a time, rather than a space spectrum. Printed media can add pages, but television has twenty-four hours (no more or less) to fill each day. The normal daytime routine for men is a job; for women it is taking care of the home and/or children. So, the nine-to-five television schedule is geared particularly to women. Consider it for a moment. From Captain Kangaroo to several comedies, a few minutes of news at noon (men might be watching during their lunch breaks), and then an afternoon predominated by soap operas and a few game shows. The media provides trivia and comedy for diversion from serious matters, while constantly pounding in the message of consumption. Stay slim, don't have bad breath or underarm odor, have long eyelashes, buy an endless assortment of products for the home, become a blonde, become a more beautiful brunette, smoke a woman's cigarette, smoke a man's cigarette. If you do all these things, you can capture a boyfriend, get married, stay happily married, and be a good hostess to boot. Simultaneous with the commercial messages, you are pelted with a series of soap operas which portray anything but happy marriages and game shows which show newlyweds making fools of themselves and women getting hysterical over money.

The soap operas themselves—the kitchenette version of the "adult" horse opera—deserve a special study. Aside from simply diverting energy to a fantasy family's worries, they reinforce the image of male-dominated women. Like all TV programs, they are safely middle class. Women are almost always pictured as housewives and mothers (an occasional interior decorator or nurse may be thrown in to take care of the divorcée category). Children are always either independent teen-agers or cute infants. Demanding four-year-olds or schoolchildren aren't part of the fantasy family's routine. But most interesting are the male roles portrayed. Soap-opera men are a special strain of middle-class culture. They are almost always shown in professional roles, usually as doctors or lawyers. These are specialized careers in which there is a clear relationship of dominance through expertise, and they are always male roles on TV. The men who work in bureaucratic jobs pushing papers around all day aren't part of the fantasy. Neither are insurance salesmen, car salesmen, factory-workers, or truck drivers. There is never any mention of the husband who works at an uncreative or boring job. There is rarely any mention of a woman who has work outside the home. The formula for the shows are infinite interpersonal conflicts. Collective struggles are taboo. The realities of urban riots, the draft for the war in Vietnam, labor-union struggles, insurgent political groupings, etc., don't intrude upon the fantasy. The question of a new and collective identity for women can't be raised, for it would completely destroy the soap opera's formula.

With the soap-opera image being broadcast into the collective female consciousness, the question of decisionmakers in the media must be raised. The mass media, like most of corporate America, is male-dominated. Its throbbing technology-maze broadcast centers do not house women employees—other than occasional secretaries. Women are rarely seen as announcers, news reporters, or emcees, although they are constantly objectified as actresses and models. The hierarchy of corporate decisionmaking doesn't include women. And you can be sure that the few exceptions are carefully inculcated into the overriding ideology of profitmaking. It was this doctrine of commercial expediency which kept Columbia Broadcasting System from preempting their regular schedule to show the Fulbright hearings on the war in Vietnam in 1967. Fred Friendly, who was working with the News Division at CBS at the time, quit over that decision. CBS broadcast an "I Love Lucy" rerun instead of the Senate hearings—not because the rerun was part of television folklore, but because the commercials surrounding it involved money. Friendly reports in his book, *Due to Circumstances Beyond Our Control,*[1] that one of the unpublicized reasons for the CBS decision was the fact that housewives, not "opinion leaders," were tuned in at that hour, and housewives weren't interested in Vietnam. Housewives were thus summarily disenfranchised, and the soap operas went on uninterrupted.

An obvious question is why soap operas are called soap operas. The answer is that they sell soap. Procter and Gamble is the largest single advertiser on television, spending close to $81 million on commercials in 1968. Procter and Gamble, in fact, spends more on advertising than any other corporation in the world. The next four largest TV advertisers are General Foods, Colgate-Palmolive, Coca Cola, and Lever Brothers. Three of the top five sell soap and one more sells soap pads. That is why soap operas exist. Women are said to make 75 percent of all family consumption decisions. For advertisers, that is why women exist. The real media messages about women come through in the advertising done by corporations dependent on the female market. This

1. New York: Random House, 1967.

includes not just manufacturers of products for the home, but the cosmetics manufacturers, the women and children apparel manufacturers, drug manufacturers, and more. But, for the moment, the soap industry deserves attention.

Soap marketing is a highly competitive business depending almost completely on the creation of new consumer needs: from regular detergents to low-sudsers, to pre-soaks to enzyme-action washing products; from regular bath-soaps to deodorant soaps; from stannous fluoride toothpastes to the new cosmetic (bright teeth) toothpastes. *Forbes* describes the Procter and Gamble world view (15 April 1968): "One Harvard grad recalls his on-campus interview with a P&G recruiter several years back. 'We sell products that aren't much different from anyone else's,' the recruiter told him. 'We sell them because someone will buy them, not because they are socially good. If we could put s——t in a box and the customer would buy it, we'd sell it.' " (The word is shit.)

Procter and Gamble mastered the selling technique long ago. It started as a maker of soaps and candles in 1837 and, according to *Forbes* again, "grew fat on Union Army orders during the Civil War." In 1879 it introduced Ivory Soap. It also produced the big seller Tide in 1946. Gleem and Crest, Zest and Safeguard, Prell and Head and Shoulders are also Procter and Gamble products. It recently diversified into the food business with Duncan Hines Cake Mixes, Big Top Peanut Butter, Folger's Coffee, and Crisco.

One of the prevailing myths in the consumer economy is that the consumer has a choice. The endless parade of products across the TV screen are meant to give the illusion of a highly competitive economy which, because of the competition produces quality products. Procter and Gamble doesn't care whether you choose Dash, Tide, Duz, Bold, Oxydol, Cascade, Cheer, or Ivory Soap, as long as you choose one of them. General Foods doesn't care if you choose Yuban, Sanka, Maxim, or Maxwell House so long as you choose one of them. And so on. The soap operas with their countless commercials all produce consumers for a handful of corporations.

Another prevailing myth of the consumer economy is that the new innovations create leisure time for the consumer. This is especially true of the housewife consumer. The special cleaners for windows, floors, carpets, sinks, toilets, furniture, etc. are supposed to release women from household drudgery. (Fantastik is "the spare time that comes in a spray cleaner bottle.") In actuality, they impose a highly elaborate routine on that drudgery. Cleaning the house becomes more and more a highly specialized routine linked to the consumption of highly specialized cleaning products. The cosmetics industry follows the same pattern. From the old image demanding only a dab of powder and lipstick, a new image is imposed, including a highly intricate process for making-up eyes—eyeliner, mascara, false eyelashes, remade eyebrows, etc. By introducing new layers of cosmetics each year, the industry increases rather than lessens the amount of time needed to comply with the latest in cosmetics fashion. The American woman is not only tied to the image created for her by the mass media and their consumption-minded commercials; but that image itself ties her into a routinized rather than a liberated role.

"Woman must be liberated to desire new products."

Those are the words of a market-research executive. (Not liberation for a new collective identity, not for more life-fulfilling roles, but for commodities.) The most telling critiques of the mass media are the words of their own market-minded specialists. When the media men talk to themselves as they do in their trade publications, they are most honest. They have succeeded in reducing everyone to the role of consumer object. But women are not only particularly exploited because of their special consumer role; we are doubly used as sexual objects to sell products. Any magazine, practically any commercial, provides examples—some in the grossest possible forms—and they need little comment. The lingerie ad "Be Some Body" isn't just a cute play on words. It is precisely the advertising message: a woman is supposed to be a *body*, not a *person*—a decorated body. If she can successfully manage that transformation, then she can market herself—for a man. The commercial creates commercialized people in its own image; and the marketed commodities create people who think of themselves as marketable commodities.

Women's magazines are the special vehicle in the printed media for the message of commercialized women. The following text appeared in *Advertising Age* (21 April 1969) alongside a photo of a Beautiful Blonde modeling the "nude look" in see-through fashions.

"But mother . . . underwear would hide my fashion accessories."

It wasn't long ago that all exposure was indecent. Today it's vogue. Admittedly spunky. But not spurned even in the safe suburbs.

How did it happen?

Magazines.

Magazines turned legs into a rainbow. Magazines convinced a gal she needed a flutter of fur where plain little eyelashes used to wink.

Magazines have the power to make a girl forget her waist exists. And the very next year, make her buy a belt for every dress she owns.

They can move a fashion trend from Paris to the papa-mama store as fast as somebody can sew it up.

Magazines help distressed damsels remake their wardrobes, faces, hair, body. And sometimes their whole way of being.

And the ladies love it. And beg for more.

When she gets involved with herself and fashion, in any magazine, she's a captive cover to cover.

And you can be sure she's looking at everything. Right down to the tiniest ad.

Think about that the next time you want to tell her what you have to sell.

The above was an advertisement for the Magazine Publishers Association. After its graphic description of the power of the magazine over women ("She's a captive cover

to cover"), the inscription which appears in the *Ladies'*
Home Journal ("Never Underestimate the Power of a
Woman") seems a little ludicrous. Over fifty million women
purchase a woman's magazine every month. That is practically three-quarters of the entire adult female population.
The women's magazines provide a captive audience for
women-minded advertisers.

The women's magazines vary from *Seventeen,* which is
mostly ads and very occasional copy aimed at the "youth
market," to the classier *Ladies' Home Journal* which is aimed
at the young-suburban-hostess market, to the true confession and true romance variety which is aimed at a lower-
class market. There is a strict class hierarchy to the
magazines. The more glossy the paper, the more middle-
and upper-class the readership; the more newsprint, the
lower in class the audience. Most of the magazines are edited by men. (*McCall's* just appointed the first woman editor
since 1921.) And nearly all the magazines are part of mammoth publishing empires. *Cosmopolitan, House Beautiful,*
Bride and Home, Harper's Bazaar, and *Good Housekeeping*
are all publications of the Hearst Corporation, headed by
William Randolph Hearst, Jr. *Seventeen,* along with *TV*
Guide, is part of the publishing empire of Walter Annen-
berg, the new Nixon-appointed ambassador to England,
whose media business also includes the *Philadelphia Inquirer*
and the *Daily Racing Form. Redbook* and *McCall's* are part
of the business empire of Norton Simon. Simon also has the
major interests in two supermarket suppliers, Hunt Food
and Industries (catsup, etc.) and Canada Dry. It is obvious
from their own propaganda (*Glamour* is the "Biggest Fashion Selling Magazine") that the function of the women's
magazines is to reach the woman as consumer, rather than
the woman as thinker. The articles on how to apply cosmetics or how to set a table provide a convenient packaging
device for the all-important ads.

As the war rages in the domestic marketplace, the trade
publications of the media man and the market surveys of the

advertising agencies carry on the work of battlefield intelligence. The advertising agencies themselves are rarely public companies (they don't offer stock to the public) so their affairs are by nature more private than other kinds of companies; their views of the American consumer are like classified military reports. *Advertising Age*—not a commonly read publication—ran two interesting articles (23 December 1968) on campaigns launched against the American consumer of cigarettes. Both dealt with the crucial issue of marketing on the basis of sex.

The Virginia Slim ads which picture fashion-plate models marching across the TV screen with the "voice over" singing "You've come a long way, baby" were the subject of one of the articles. The commercial is perhaps one of the most horrifying for women interested in *real* women's liberation, not liberation to desire more products. But the Leo Burnett Co., which dreamed it up, won the Clio award for the best over-all advertising campaign of the season. (The Clio awards are Madison Avenue-created prizes for Madison Avenue-created products.) *Advertising Age* reports that Virginia Slim sales have provided the parent company, Philip Morris, Inc. with sales of 1.3 billion cigarettes in the first three months of national distribution. The Burnett agency and Philip Morris, Inc., have had considerable success in marketing cigarettes with a specific gender. They also dreamed up the Marlboro "Tattoo" campaign, establishing Marlboros as a male cigarette. According to one of Burnett's vice-presidents, "When it comes to cigarets, we're all a little bi-sexual." Someday, when sex is not a useful marketing tool, women may look back on the Virginia Slim commercial and say, "We've come a long way."

But *Advertising Age* is even more explicit in its survey of the female market mentality in its article on the advertising campaign for Silva Thin cigarettes: "How to Get a Woman's Attention: Ignore Her." The Silva Thin commercials, in case you hadn't noticed, were built around several situations, but the plot-line never varied. An unsmiling man

with dark glasses loves his "impossible cigaret"—and hates
women. He was pictured deserting (women) on desolate
highways, ocean liners, mountain tops, etc. if they dared to
touch his cigarettes. This not-so-subtle sadism, according to
Advertising Age, "may yet go down in marketing history as
one of the most brilliant creations of advertising pundits."
The main character:

> is the epitome of the modern-male-on-the-prowl who picks his
> women the way you'd pick your hors d'oeuvre off a smorgas-
> bord table; they are merely to satisfy his momentary appetite.
> He is obnoxious, arrogant and quite possibly incurably selfish
> . . . Woman (an important market for this cigaret) especially dig
> the scene of "The Impossible Cigaret." Psychologically, they
> seem to feel right at home with the situations. They quite
> willingly put themselves in the place of the suffering heroine.
> The makers of this campaign demonstrate a shrewd insight into
> the emotional makeup of today's woman. Using what appears
> to be a masculine approach in their advertising, they are reach-
> ing the very core of their feminine audience. The hero in the
> Silva Thins commercials appears to be just what the doctor
> ordered. His strength lies in his aloofness. Ignoring practically
> every role of etiquette, he summarily puts his girlfriend in her
> place, and exactly where so many women would unconsciously
> like to be. The Silva Thins commercials, bold as they may be
> in their approach, are an open proclamation to the American
> public that it's still the male who rules the roost, or should be.
> Here the woman is presented with a boyfriend figure who
> dominates instead of being dominated. While he makes no at-
> tempt to make out with her—in fact if anything he takes the
> opposite tack—he establishes a relationship that pleases her
> feminine instinct . . . It's easy to change cigarets. It's not so easy
> to change the fundamental psychology of woman.

Advertising Age even makes the following prediction: "Our
guess is that the appeal of Virginia Slims—which claims that
its cigaret is made for women to permit them to assert their
independence at last—will not be as successful as that of
'The Impossible Cigaret.' "

America's technology has turned in upon itself; its corporate form makes it the servant of profits, not the servant of
human needs. The mass media *could* be used to make that

technology understandable. Instead of just Galloping Gour-
mets, there could be television shows that explain automobiles, airplanes, traffic systems, etc. The fact that it is almost
impossible to imagine an interesting show on that subject
illustrates how far astray we have been taken as a people—
and how thoroughly manipulated into passive roles we are
as women. Instead of liberating people through leisure time
and real knowledge about the surrounding environment,
the technology has been used to wage war on the domestic
consumer.

The warlike effort unleashed in the name of consumption
has produced a strange imagery—especially for women.
The theme of containment and control runs through most
imagery—especially for women. The theme of containment and control runs through most of the ads and commercials aimed at the female market. From the girdle
manufacturers who claim: "Girls with full figures have
gained control" to the yogurt ad which says: "It's a delicious
kind of self-control," the subliminal message is one of con-
taining and controlling. It is almost a warlike image which
brings to mind the real war going on in Vietnam. The
"Conspiracy of Dirt and Germs" must be fought wherever
it appears and must be conquered. Sometimes it is most
explicit. A Biz commercial with bugle music in the background proclaims that it "wins the war against dirt and
stains." An ad for Pine West cleaner says: "If you want to
live in New York, you've got to fight dirty." It is not too
surprising. Revlon, which manufactures cosmetics, also
manufactures arming devices for Army firebombs. The
Lever Brothers Company, which penetrates the domestic
market and produces enzyme cleaners to attack dirt biologically, has a Defense Department contract to study the "Alteration of the Penetrability of Skin" for Edgewood
Arsenal. Edgewood is the major chemical warfare center,
and the results of that study will most likely be used to
penetrate Vietnamese skin with poisonous chemicals.[2]

2. Revlon information from *Commerce Business Daily.* Lever Brothers information

Ultimately the imagery turns in upon itself. Just as the real warrior falls victim to his role and becomes a product of war, so the one who contains must ultimately be trapped by the weapons of containment and thus contained. Ice Blue Secret is for "a woman's extra feelings," but it is so those extra feelings won't betray her with their stickiness. The logic behind the commercial is that the extra feelings weren't legitimate; if they were, you wouldn't have to fear betrayal. The logic behind cosmetics is that the real you isn't enough. Feelings, dirt, hair must be controlled. The underlying message is one of self-control ("preventive warfare"), self-imposed passivity. The mass-media-created woman must have a fragmented grip on reality, must view herself not as the controller of the technology surrounding her, but as the one controlled. Her life must be routinized, her thoughts must be in terms of commodity. She must be the object, not the subject, of her world.

MEDIA IMAGES 2: Body Odor and Social Order

Florika

The aerosol spray container reveals that the roles of the policeman and the middle-class housewife are interchangeable.

The aerosol spray, both as a weapon and as a product, has created a new distinction in social behavior: between the rioters and the consumers. Between those who have to be controlled and those who've learned to control themselves.

The police have defined as well as sanctified the function of the aerosol weapon, but it is the housewife (the consumer), with her toy aerosol, who routinizes and normalizes its use. Through the medium of weapon-toy identification, the ad men encourage the housewife to believe that

from *1968 Research and Development Directory of Government Data Publications.*
Copyright © 1970 by Florika

germs are a substitute for human targets.

As the aerosol spray equates the drudgery of housework to that of police-work, it also reduces rebellious people to the level of germs. And what has become for the middle-class housewife an acting out of mindless routine, is to the potential victim a rehearsal for his humiliation.

The emergence of nonlethal weapons, i.e., gadget weapons, means a reinforcement and consolidation of control over a society already manipulated through gadget saturation. As a side effect it may cause traditional centers of law enforcement to disintegrate and render blatant repression obsolete.

The so-called breakdown of law and order is actually a credibility gap produced in no small measure by the aerosol spray weapon itself. Unquestionably, a face squirted with chemical MACE feels the pain all too credibly. But to anyone outside the immediate sphere of conflict, to see a fully armed policeman—gun on hip, club in hand, badge number shining on TV, trained to do the job—cringing behind the spray trigger for fear of spraying himself, spoils the image of his so-called masculinity.

The transplantation from home to precinct of the aerosol container is producing some undesirable side effects, at least in the public mind. It has done much to emasculate the nature of armed force and psychologically it has castrated the policeman.

The message of the aerosol spray is instant control, i.e., a condition of push-button readiness to meet any given contingency.

The spray forms an invisible, protective shield. This is a recurring image and theme used in aerosol advertisement which is in essence the heart of the Cold War policy of containment.

Sweating, stinking, germ build-up, flying insects, are all specific contingencies which are countered with the aerosol technique of flexible response and mobility.

The mass production of aerosol sprays not only enlarged

the microscopic and made it "visible"; it also magnified the puritan eye into a reactionary outlook.

The obsession with dirt, like the fear of communism, is the product of eyeing the world through the peephole of the aerosol can. And the American consumer, in trying to spray back and contain an impinging and elusive environment (enemy), has unknowingly been inside a psychological container himself.

Aerosol advertisement is extremely revealing. It has taken over the function of relating the individual to society, and interpreting society to the individual. In the case of deodorant sprays, it even pits the individual against himself.

Right Guard, for example, is a deodorant: "the perfect family deodorant." The product is promoted as a Super Ego, "the Protector," who alternately threatens—"Don't leave your family unguarded"—and reassures—"twenty-four-hour protection for the whole family."

The real social antagonisms that exist within the family, or between society and the family, which are portrayed in spot commercial deodorant dramas, are cleverly diagnosed as "perspiration problems."

Right Guard's formula, then, is to neutralize the conflict between body odor and social order by providing total sanitation through individual sterilization. It also assures each member maximum security from contact with all the rest —"Nothing touches you but the spray."

Right Guard—in its totality of concept, name, and function—is an environmental mechanism for controlling the middle class, the way the National Guard is an armed force for quelling rebellious minorities.

Right Guard even stops "wetness" too, because it regulates your emotions—which are a cause of wetness. Internal surveillance without telltale leakage—"Get it today."

The duty of every Right Guard is to whisper inside the middle-class ear, "contain yourself!"

Another group of antipersonal products are the hair sprays. Hair sprays are the "special forces" for dealing with the problem of hair-do sabotage. The threat of overthrowing the hair-do structure comes from the alliance between nature as an external liberating force and the natural movement of the hair itself. For this reason advertising lauds the merits of a hair spray by juxtaposing its capacity to hold a hair-do in place against the disintegrating powers of rain and wind.

Hair spray also acts as an invisible screen to prevent humidity from infiltrating and subverting an orderly coif into an unruly jungle.

Hair sprays are experts at "holding power." The labels even advise women on the degree of control she thinks she needs: "light" for the swinging natural look, "regular" for those who want to be sure, and "extra" for frizzy, unmanageable fly-away hair.

One commercial for *VO-5* hair spray shows two young "starlets" in the process of getting drenched by a "Hollywood rainstorm." The viewer is told that the blonde uses *VO-5* with "myrol," the brunette another favorite brand. "Watch!" Naturally, *VO-5* is the victor. The brunette's favorite hair spray could not prevent a total hair-do washout. Test proves: "*VO-5* hair spray with myrol holds [you] even in a Hollywood rainstorm."

The duel between nature and hair spray over the pretty, fragile hair-do is the ad man's recipe for selling hair-spray romance to the twentieth-century woman. Being desirable to a man, or dependent on him, becomes a stimulant for desiring a product. Hair sprays must respond to every woman's dream of a knight who will take her out of suburbia and into chivalry. The ad man caters to feudal myths as a panacea for a futile life.

You needn't always be the target.

You can go on the offensive. Extend the perimeter of defense.

Vietnam has sometimes been called the "War of the Mosquito." It is fought with aerosol technology—defoliants and herbicides.

The War of the Mosquito is also being waged right in the backyards of suburbia. With *Raid Yard Guard.*

The voice of God speaks to you over the tube: "Deep in a bug-infested jungle, two scientists are testing *Raid Yard Guard* against another leading spray."

After *Raid Yard Guard* has been proven king of the beasts, the jungle scene ends. Back to a friendly lawn somewhere in suburbia where Tarzan's family of four is about to settle down to a picnic dinner. The kiddies are playing, Tarzan is flipping over the medium-rare, charcoal-broiled burgers (with go-together-burger-buns toasting nearby) and Jane—what is Jane doing?

Jane is spraying the entire area with *Raid Yard Guard.*

The voice of God again: "Keeps out bugs, seals in protection. Get outdoor living with indoor comfort. Get *Raid Yard Guard,* the jungle-tested bug-killer."

If *Raid Yard Guard* doesn't do the job, you can try *Black Flag* insecticide—"Kills bugs on contact!"

Don't let pests, flying insects, and outside agitators drive you buggy. But if they do break through your perimeter of defense, retreat into the science-fiction environment called home: the man's castle.

Step over the threshhold. You've just entered the "Invisible World" of *Lysol.*

The ad man is waiting for you, arms open: "The Invisible World surrounds every man, every woman, every child, every day of his life . . . It's a world of germs you can't see. It's a world of odors you can't see. It's the world *Lysol Spray* was made for . . . Also in new Purse and Travel size for use away from home. It kills the ugly things you can't see."

The Invisible World, like mysticism and religion, has always been used to obscure and protect those powerful few in the real world. Advertising is the invisible hand which blesses the faithful consumer.

Out of the lowest form of life, bacteria, it has created the image of conspiracy. In true Cinderella fashion, a metamorphosis takes place: the microbe is transformed into a subversive agent. Confronted with the presence of The Invisible World the consumer takes up the holy *Lysol* spray on behalf on the Free World.

Biologically, the "invisible" power of germs came to an end in the nineteenth century with Pasteur's germ theory of disease. Their threat today is no longer really physical, but political.

Unconsciousness creates invisibility. Desires and fears which we are not aware of are turned into germs which we cannot see. Germs have become a symbolic enemy. The basis for germ phobia is the fear of contact. What makes it political is that the consumer culture converts this germ phobia into a middle-class hallucination of the "masses."

The Cold War reveals the phobic character of the aerosol products and their culture. The policy of containment is the reaction induced by the powerful few in their phobic subjects. Political paranoia is a symptom not so much of the Cold War mentality but of the routine of everyday life where neurosis is skillfully substituted for class consciousness. The more we try to control the movement of microbes, the less likely we are to realize that we ourselves have become the objects of control.

With *Lysol*, they make it easier to "adjust" to your dehumanization. Being turned into an animal (i.e., a mindless creature) is OK so long as you remain docile. Otherwise they use *Lysol* on you.

In the arsenal of aerosol products there is a new disinfectant spray cleaner on your supermarket shelf. *Clean & Kill.* The brand name is the solution.

Why do you need this new weapon which "zips through dirt and zaps household germs?" Because: "Dirt & Germs are buddies." "*Clean & Kill* cleans and cleans right down to the germs. It leaves every surface so germ-free you could eat off it!"

With *Clean & Kill* you can formulate foreign policy at the push of a button—do a man's job with a woman's touch.

With *Clean & Kill* you can participate in the defense of

your country without leaving the house.

With *Clean & Kill* you're honoring those commitments you made when you took the vow.

With *Clean & Kill* you're mobile. You've got options. You can contain bacterial unrest before it spreads. You can snuff out mildew and subversion, the leading causes of Staph and Stress. You can wipe out dirt and ignorance (which breed crime and germs), right off your kitchen floor.

Clean & Kill. Keeps your house germ-free, while it helps Standard International keep the world free. They make it, sister.

Psssst!

Isn't it about time we let them do their own cleaning and killing?

THE POLITICS OF ORGASM

Susan Lydon

Tiresias, who had been both man and woman, was asked, as Ovid's legend goes, to mediate in a dispute between Jove and Juno as to which sex got more pleasure from lovemaking. Tiresias unhesitatingly answered that women did. Yet in the intervening 2,000 years between Ovid's time and our own, a mythology has been built up which not only holds the opposite to be true, but has made this belief an unswerving ideology dictating the quality of relations between the sexes. Woman's sexuality, defined by men to benefit men, has been downgraded and perverted, repressed and channeled, denied and abused until women themselves, thoroughly convinced of their sexual inferiority to men, would probably be dumfounded to learn that there is scientific proof that Tiresias was indeed right.

The myth was codified by Freud, as much as by anyone

else. In *Three Essays on the Theory of Sexuality*, Freud formulated his basic ideas concerning feminine sexuality: for little girls, the leading erogenous zone in their bodies is the clitoris; in order for the transition to womanhood to be successful, the clitoris must abandon its sexual primacy to the vagina; women in whom this transition has not been complete remain clitorally-oriented, or "sexually anaesthetic" and "psychosexually immature."

> The fact that women change their leading erotogenic zone in this way, [Freud wrote] together with the wave of repression at puberty, which, as it were, puts aside their childish masculinity, are the chief determinants of the greater proneness of women to neurosis and especially to hysteria. These determinants, therefore, are intimately related to the essence of feminity.

In the context of Freud's total psychoanalytic view of women—that they are not whole human beings but mutilated males who long all their lives for a penis and must struggle to reconcile themselves to its lack—the requirement of a transfer of erotic sensation from clitoris to vagina became a *prima facie* case for their inevitable sexual (and moral) inferiority. In Freud's logic, those who struggle to become what they are not must be inferior to that to which they aspire

Freud wrote that he could not "escape the notion (though I hesitate to give it expression) that for women the level of what is ethically normal is different from what it is in men . . . We must not allow ourselves to be deflected from such conclusions by the denials of the feminists, who are anxious to force us to regard the two sexes as completely equal in position and worth."

Freud himself admitted near the end of his life that his knowledge of women was inadequate. "If you want to know more about femininity, you must interrogate your own experience, or turn to the poets, or wait until science can give you more information," he said; he also expressed the hope that the female psychoanalysts who followed him would be able to find out more. But the post-Freudians adhered rigidly to the doctrine of the master, and, as in most of his work, what Freud hoped would be taken as a thesis for future study became instead a kind of canon law.

While the neo-Freudians haggled over the correct reading of the Freudian bible, watered-down Freudianism was wending its way into the cultural mythology via Broadway plays, novelists, popular magazines, social scientists, marriage counselors, and experts of various kinds who found it useful in projecting desired images of women. The superiority of the vaginal over the clitoral orgasm was particularly useful as a theory, since it provided a convenient basis for categorization: clitoral women were deemed immature, neurotic, bitchy, and masculine; women who had vaginal orgasms were maternal, feminine, mature, and normal. Though frigidity should technically be defined as total inability to achieve orgasm, the orthodox Freudians (and pseudo-Freudians) preferred to define it as inability to achieve vaginal orgasm, by which definition, in 1944, Edmond Bergler adjudged between 70 and 80 percent of all women frigid. The clitoral *vs.* vaginal debate raged hot and heavy among the sexologists—although Kinsey's writings stressed the importance of the clitoris to female orgasm and contradicted Bergler's statistics—but it became clear that there was something indispensable to the society in the Freudian view which allowed it to remain unchallenged in the public consciousness.

In 1966, Dr. William H. Masters and Mrs. Virginia E. Johnson published *Human Sexual Response,* a massive clinical study of the physiology of sex. Briefly and simply, the Masters and Johnson conclusions about the female orgasm, based on observation of and interviews with 487 women, were these:

1) That the dichotomy of vaginal and clitoral orgasms is entirely false. Anatomically, all orgasms are centered in the clitoris, whether they result from direct manual pressure ap-

plied to the clitoris, indirect pressure resulting from the thrusting of penis during intercourse, or generalized sexual stimulation of other erogenous zones like the breasts.

2) That women are naturally multi-orgasmic; that is, if a woman is immediately stimulated following orgasm, she is likely to experience several orgasms in rapid succession. This is not an exceptional occurrence, but one of which most women are capable.

3) That while women's orgasms do not vary in kind, they vary in intensity. The most intense orgasms experienced by the research subjects were by masturbatory manual stimulation, followed in intensity by manual stimulation by the partner; the least intense orgasms were experienced by women during intercourse.

4) That the female orgasm is as real and identifiable a physiological entity as the male's; it follows the same pattern of erection and detumescence of the clitoris, which may be seen as the female equivalent of the penis.

5) That there is an "infinite variety of female sexual response" as regards intensity and duration of orgasms.

To anyone acquainted with the body of existing knowledge of feminine sexuality, the Masters and Johnson findings were truly revolutionary and liberating in the extent to which they demolished the established myths. Yet four years after the study was published, it seems hardly to have made much of an impact at all. Certainly it is not for lack of information that the myths persist; *Human Sexual Response*, despite its weighty scientific language, was an immediate best-seller, and popular paperbacks explicated it to millions of people in simpler language and at a cheaper price. The mythology remains intact because a male-dominated American culture has a vested interest in its continuance.

Dr. William Masters had searched for a woman co-worker for his research because, as he said, "No male really understands female sexuality." Before Masters and Johnson, female sexuality had been objectively defined and described by men; the subjective experience of women had had no part in defining their own sexuality. And men defined feminine sexuality in a way as favorable to themselves as possible. If woman's pleasure was obtained through the vagina, then she was totally dependent on the man's erect penis to achieve orgasm; she would receive her satisfaction only as a concomitant of man's seeking his. With the clitoral orgasm, woman's sexual pleasure was independent of the male's, and she could seek her satisfaction as aggressively as the man sought his, a prospect which didn't appeal to too many men. The definition of normal feminine sexuality as vaginal, in other words, was a part of keeping women down, of making them sexually, as well as economically, socially, and politically subservient.

In retrospect, particularly with the additional perspective of our own time, Freud's theory of feminine sexuality appears an historical rationalization for the realities of Victorian society. Culture-bound in the Victorian ethos, Freud had to play the role of *pater familias.* Serving the ethos, he developed a psychology that robbed Victorian women of possible politics. In Freud's theory of penis envy, the penis functioned as the unalterable determinant of maleness which women could symbolically envy instead of the power and prestige given men by the society.It was a refusal to grant women acknowledgment that they had been wronged by their culture and their times; according to Freud, woman's lower status had not been conferred upon her by men, but by God, who had created her without a penis.

Freud's insistence on the superiority of the vaginal orgasm seems almost a demonic determination on his part to finalize the Victorians' repression of feminine eroticism, to stigmatize the remaining vestiges of pleasure felt by women, and thus make them unacceptable to the women themselves. For there were still women whose sexuality hadn't been completely destroyed, as evidenced by one Dr. Isaac Brown Baker, a surgeon who performed numerous clitoridectomies on women to prevent the sexual excitement which, he was convinced, caused "insanities," "catalepsy," "hysteria," "epilepsy," and other diseases. The Victorians had needed to repress sexuality for the success of Western industrialized society; in particular, the total repression of woman's sexuality was crucial to ensure her subjugation. So the Victorians honored only the male ejaculation, that aspect of sexuality which was necessary to the survival of the species; the male ejaculation made women submissive to sex by creating a mystique of the sanctity of motherhood; and, supported by Freud, passed on to us the heritage of the double standard.

When Kinsey laid to rest the part of the double standard that maintained women got no pleasure at all from sex, everyone cried out that there was a sexual revolution afoot. But such talk, as usual, was deceptive. Morality, outside the marriage bed, remained the same, and children were socialized as though Kinsey had never described what they would be like when they grew up. Boys were taught that they should get their sex where they could find it, "go as far" as they could. On the old assumption that women were asexual creatures, girls were taught that since they needed sex less than boys did, it was up to them to impose sexual restraints. In whatever sex education adolescents did manage to receive, they were told that men had penises and women vaginas; the existence of the clitoris was not mentioned, and *pleasure* in sex was never discussed at all.

Adolescent boys growing up begging for sexual crumbs from girls frightened for their "reputations"—a situation that remains unchanged to this day—hardly constitutes the vanguard of a sexual revolution. However, the marriage-manual craze that followed Kinsey assumed that a lifetime of psychological destruction could, with the aid of a little booklet, be abandoned after marriage, and that husband and wife should be able to make sure that the wife was not robbed of her sexual birthright to orgasm, just so long as it was *vaginal* (though the marriage manuals did rather reluctantly admit that since the clitoris was the most sexually sensitive organ in the female body, a little clitoral stimulation in foreplay was in order), and so long as their orgasms were *simultaneous*.

The effect of the marriage manuals of course ran counter to their ostensible purpose. Under the guise of frankness and sexual liberation, they dictated prudery and restraint. Sex was made so mechanized, detached, and intellectual that it was robbed of its sensuality. Man became a spectator of his own sexual experience. And the marriage manuals put new pressure on women. The swing was from repression to preoccupation with the orgasm. Men took the marriage manuals to mean that their sexuality would be enhanced by bringing women to orgasm and, again co-opting feminine sexuality for their own ends, they put pressure on women to perform. The endorsement by the marriage manuals of the desirability of vaginal orgasm insured that women would be asked not only, "Did you come?," but also, "Did you conform to Freud's conception of a psychosexually mature woman, and thereby validate my masculinity?"

Rather than being revolutionary, the present sexual situation is tragic. Appearances notwithstanding, the age-old taboos against conversation about personal sexual experience still haven't broken down. This reticence has allowed the mind-manipulators of the media to create myths of sexual supermen and superwomen. So the bed becomes a competitive arena, where men and women measure themselves against these mythical rivals, while simultaneously trying to live up to the ecstasies promised them by the marriage manuals and the fantasies of the media ("If the earth doesn't move for me, I must be missing something," the reasoning goes.) Our society treats sex as a sport, with its record-breakers, its judges, its rules, and its spectators.

As anthropologists have shown, women's sexual response is culturally conditioned; historically, women defer to whatever model of their sexuality is offered them by men. So the sad thing for women is that they have participated in the destruction of their own eroticism. Women have helped make the vaginal orgasm into a status symbol in a male-dictated system of values. A woman would now perceive her preference for clitoral orgasm as a "secret shame," ignominious in the eyes of other women as well as those of men. This internalization can be seen in the literature: Mary McCarthy's and Doris Lessing's writings on orgasm do not differ substantially from D. H. Lawrence's and Ernest Hemingway's, and even Simone de Beauvoir, in *The Second Sex,* refers to vaginal orgasm as the only "normal satisfaction."

Rather than working to alleviate the pressure on them, women have increased it. Feeling themselves insecure in a competitive situation, they are afraid to admit their own imagined inadequacies, and lie to other women about their sexual experiences. With their men, they often fake orgasm to appear "good in bed" and thus place an intolerable physical burden on themselves and a psychological burden on the men unlucky enough to see through the ruse.

One factor that has made this unfortunate situation possible is ignorance: the more subtle and delicate aspects of human sexuality are still not fully understood. For example, a woman's ability to attain orgasm seems to be conditioned as much by her emotions as by physiology and sociology. Masters and Johnson proved that the orgasm experienced during intercourse, the misnamed vaginal orgasm, did not differ *anatomically* from the clitoral orgasm. But this should not be seen as their most significant contribution to the sexual emancipation of women. A difference remains in the *subjective* experience of orgasm during intercourse and orgasm apart from intercourse. In the complex of emotional factors affecting feminine sexuality, there is a whole panoply of pleasures: the pleasure of being penetrated and filled by a man, the pleasure of sexual communication, the pleasure of affording a man his orgasm, the erotic pleasure that exists even when sex is not terminated by orgasmic release. Masters and Johnson's real contribution was to stress an "infinite variety of female sexual response." One should be able to appreciate the differences, rather than impose value judgments on them.

There is no doubt that Masters and Johnson were fully aware of the implications of their study to the sexual liberation of women. As they wrote, "With orgasmic physiology established, the human female now has an undeniable opportunity to develop realistically her own sexual response levels." Two years later this statement seems naive and entirely too optimistic. Certainly the sexual problems of our society will never be solved until there is real and unfeigned equality between men and women. This idea is usually misconstrued: sexual liberation for women is wrongly understood to mean that women will adopt all the forms of masculine sexuality. As in the whole issue of women's liberation, that's really not the point. Women don't aspire to imitate the mistakes of men in sexual matters, to view sexual experiences as conquest and ego-enhancement, to use other people to serve their own ends. But if the Masters and Johnson material is allowed to filter into the public consciousness, hopefully to replace the enshrined Freudian myths, then woman at long last will be allowed to take the first step toward her emancipation, to define and enjoy the forms of her own sexuality.

"KINDER, KUCHE, KIRCHE" AS SCIENTIFIC LAW: PSYCHOLOGY CONSTRUCTS THE FEMALE*

Dr. Naomi Weisstein

It is an implicit assumption that the area of psychology which concerns itself with personality has the onerous but

*Paper read at Davis, University of California meeting of the American Studies Association, October 26, 1968.

necessary task of describing the limits of human possibility. Thus when we are about to consider the liberation of women, we naturally look to psychology to tell us what "true" liberation would mean: what would give women the freedom to fulfill their own intrinsic natures.

Psychologists have set about describing the true natures of women with an enthusiasm and absolute certainty which is rather disquieting. Bruno Bettelheim of the University of Chicago, tells us that:

> We must start with the realization that, as much as women want to be good scientists or engineers, they want first and foremost to be womanly companions of men and to be mothers.[1]

Erik Erikson of Harvard University, upon noting that young women often ask whether they can "have an identity before they know whom they will marry, and for whom they will make a home," explains somewhat elegiacally that "Much of a young woman's identity is already defined in her kind of attractiveness and in the selectivity of her search for the man (or men) by whom she wishes to be sought . . ."[2] Mature womanly fulfillment, for Erikson, rests on the fact that a woman's ". . . somatic design harbors an 'inner space' destined to bear the offspring of chosen men, and with it, a biological, psychological, and ethical commitment to take care of human infancy."[3] Some psychiatrists even see the acceptance of woman's role by women as a solution to societal problems. "Woman is nurturance . . . ," writes Joseph Rheingold, a psychiatrist at Harvard Medical School, ". . . Anatomy decrees the life of a woman . . . When women grow up without dread of their biological functions and without subversion by feminist doctrine, and therefore enter upon motherhood with a sense of fulfillment and altruistic sentiment, we shall attain the goal of a good life

1. Bruno Bettelheim, "The Commitment Required of a Woman Entering a Scientific Profession in Present Day American Society," *Woman and the Scientific Professions,* MIT symposium on American Women in Science and Engineering, 1965.
2. Erik Erikson, "Inner and Outer Space: Reflections on Womanhood," *Daedelus* (93), 1964.
3. *Ibid.*

and a secure world in which to live it."[4]

These views from men of high prestige reflect a fairly general consensus within psychology: liberation for women will consist first in their attractiveness, so that second, they may obtain the kinds of homes, and the kinds of men, which will allow joyful altruism and nurturance.

Business does not disagree. If views such as Bettelheim's and Erikson's do indeed have something to do with real liberation for women, then seldom in human history has so much money and effort been spent on helping a group of people realize their "true potential" . . . :

> Mother, for a while this morning, I thought I wasn't cut out for married life. Hank was late for work and forgot his apricot juice and walked out without kissing me, and when I was all alone I started crying. But then the postman came with the sheets and towels you sent, that look like big bandanna handkerchiefs, and you know what I thought? That those big red and blue handkerchiefs are for girls like me to dry their tears on so they can get busy and do what a housewife has to do. Throw open the windows and start getting the house ready, and the dinner, maybe clean the silver and put new geraniums in the box. *Everything to be ready for him when he walks back through that door.*[5]

It is an interesting but limited exercise to show that psychologist's ideas of women's nature fit so remarkably the common prejudice and serve industry and commerce so well. Just because it's good for business doesn't mean it's wrong. What we will show is that it *is wrong*; that there isn't the tiniest shred of evidence that these fantasies of servitude and childish dependence have anything to do with women's true potential; that the idea of the nature of human possibility which rests on the accidents of individual development or genitalia, on what is possible today because of what happened yesterday, on the fundamentalist myth of sex-organ causality, has strangled and deflected psychology so that it

4. Joseph Rheingold, *The Fear of Being a Woman* (New York: Grune & Stratton, 1964), p. 714.
5. Fieldcrest advertisement in the *New Yorker* (1965), Italics mine.

is relatively useless in describing, explaining, or predicting humans and their behavior.

It then goes without saying that present psychology is less than worthless in contributing to a vision which could truly liberate—men as well as women.

My central argument, then, is this. Psychology has nothing to say about what women are really like, what they need and what they want, essentially, because psychology does not know. I want to stress that this failure is not limited to women; rather, the kind of psychology which has addressed itself to how people act and who they are has failed to understand, in the first place, why people act the way they do, and certainly failed to understand what might make them act differently.

The kind of psychology which has addressed itself to these questions has been in large part clinical psychology and psychiatry. Here, the causes of failure are obvious and appalling: Freudians and neo-Freudians, Adlerians and neo-Adlerians, classicists and swingers, clinicians and psychiatrists in general have simply refused to look at the evidence against their theory and their practice, and have used as evidence for their theory and their practice stuff so flimsy and transparently biased as to have absolutely no standing as empirical evidence. But even psychology which conforms to rigorous methodology (academic personality research) has gone about looking at people in such a way as to have limited usefulness. This is because it has been a central assumption for most psychologists of human personality that human behavior rests primarily on an individual and inner dynamic, perhaps fixed in infancy, perhaps fixed by genitalia, perhaps simply arranged in a rather immovable cognitive network. But this assumption is rapidly losing ground as personality psychologists fail again and again to find consistency in the assumed personalities of their subjects[6] and as the evidence demonstrates that what a person

6. J. Block, "Some Reasons for the Apparent Inconsistency of Personality," *Psychological Bulletin* (70) 1968.

does and who he believes himself to be, will in general be a function of what people around him expect him to be, and what the over-all situation in which he is acting implies that he is. Compared to the influence of the social context within which a person lives, his or her history and "traits," as well as biological makeup may simply be random variations, "noise" superimposed on the true signal which can predict behavior. To summarize: the first reason for psychology's failure to understand what people are and how they act, is that clinicians and psychiatrists, who are generally the theoreticians on these matters, have essentially made up myths without any evidence to support these myths; the second reason for psychology's failure is that personality theory has looked for inner traits when it should have been looking at social context.

Let us turn to the first cause of failure: the acceptance by psychiatrists and clinical psychologists of theory without evidence. If we inspect the literature of personality, it is immediately obvious that the bulk of it is written by clinicians and psychiatrists, and that the major support for their theories is "years of intensive clinical experience." This is a tradition started by Freud and taken up by even his most vehement adversaries. Freud's "insights" occurred during the course of his work with his patients. Now there is nothing wrong with such an approach to theory *formulation*; a person is free to make up theories with any inspiration which works: divine revelation, intensive clinical practice, a random numbers table. However, he is not free to claim any validity for his theory until it has been tested and confirmed, and theories are treated in no such tentative way in ordinary clinical practice. Consider Freud. What he thought constituted evidence violated the most minimal conditions of scientific rigor. In *The Sexual Enlightenment of Children*, the classic document which is supposed to demonstrate empirically the existence of a castration complex and its connection to a phobia, Freud based his analysis on the reports of the father of the little boy, himself in therapy, and a devotee of Freudian theory. I really don't have to comment further on the contamination in this kind of evidence. It is remarkable that only recently has Freud's classic theory on the sexuality of women—the notion of the double orgasm—been actually tested physiologically and found just plain wrong. Now those who claim that fifty years of psychoanalytic experience constitute evidence enough of the essential truths of Freud's theory should ponder the robust health of the double orgasm. Did women, until Masters and Johnson, believe they were having two different kinds of orgasm? Did their psychiatrists cow them into reporting something that was not true? If so, were there other things they reported that were also not true? Did psychiatrists ever learn anything different than their theories had led them to believe? If clinical experience means anything at all, surely we should have been done with the double orgasm myth long before the Masters and Johnson studies.

But certainly, you may object, "years of intensive clinical experience" is the only reliable measure in a discipline which rests its findings on insight, sensitivity, and intuition. The problem with insight, sensitivity, and intuition, is that it can confirm for all time the biases that one started out with. People used to be absolutely convinced of their ability to tell which of their number were engaging in witchcraft. All it required was some sensitivity to the workings of the devil.

Years of intensive clinical experience is not the same thing as empirical evidence. The first thing an experimenter learns in any kind of experiment which involves humans is the concept of the "double blind." The term is taken from medical experiments, where one group is given a drug which is presumably supposed to change behavior in a certain way, and a control group is given a placebo. If the observers or the subjects know which group took which drug, the result invariably comes out on the positive side for the new drug. Only when it is not known which subject took which pill, is validity remotely approximated. In addition, with judgments of human behavior, it is so difficult to precisely tie down just what behavior is going on, let alone what behavior should be expected, that one must test again and again the reliability of judgments. How many judges, blind, will agree in their observations? Can they replicate their own judgments at some later time? When, in actual practice, these judgment criteria are tested for clinical validity, then we find that the judges cannot judge reliably nor can they judge consistently: they do no better than chance in identifying which of a certain set of stories were written by men and which by women; which of a whole battery of clinical test results are the products of homosexuals and which are the products of heterosexuals[7] and which, of a battery of clinical test results *and* interviews (where questions are asked such as "do you have delusions" and "what are your symptoms?"[8]) are products of psychotics, neurotics, psychosomatics, or normals. Lest this summary escape your notice, let me stress the implications of these findings. The ability of judges, chosen for their clinical expertise, to distinguish male heterosexuals from male homosexuals on the basis of three widely used clinical projective tests—the Rorschach, the TAT, and the MAP, was *no better than chance*. The reason this is such devastating news, of course, is that clinicians and psychiatrists assume sexuality to be of fundamental importance in the deep dynamic of personality; if what is considered gross sexual deviance cannot be caught, then what are psychologists talking about when they, for instance, claim that the basis of paranoid psychosis is "latent homosexual panic?" They can't even identify what homosexual anything is, let alone "latent homosexual panic." More alarming, expert clinicians cannot be consistent on what diagnostic category to assign to a person, again on the basis of both tests and interviews; a number of nor-

---

7. E. Hooker, "Male Homosexuality in the Rorshach," *Journal of Projective Techniques* (21), 1957.
8. K.B. Little and E.S. Schneidman, "Congruences among Interpretations of Psychological Test and Anamnestic Data," *Psychological Monographs* (73) 1959.

mals in the Little and Schneidman study were described as psychotic, in such categories as "schizophrenic with homosexual tendencies" or "schizoid character with depressive trends." But most disheartening, when the judges were asked to rejudge the test protocols some weeks later, their diagnoses of the same subjects on the basis of the same protocol, differed markedly from their initial judgments. It is obvious that even simple descriptive conventions in clinical psychology cannot be consistently applied; that these descriptive conventions have any explanatory significance is therefore, of course, out of the question.

As a student in a graduate class at Harvard, some years ago, I was a member of a seminar which was asked to identify which of two piles of a clinical test, the TAT, had been written by males, and which of the two piles had been written by females. Only four students out of twenty identified the piles correctly, and this was after one and a half months of intensively studying the differences between men and women. Since this result is below chance, that is, this result would occur by chance about four out of a thousand times, we may conclude that there *is* finally a consistency here; students are judging knowledgeably within the context of psychological teaching about the differences between men and women; the teachings themselves are simply erroneous.

A frequent argument is that the theory may be scientifically "unsound" but at least it cures people. There is no evidence that it does. In 1952, Eysenck reported the results of what is called an "outcome of therapy" study of neurotics which show that, of the patients who received psychoanalysis, the improvement rate was 44 percent; of the patients who received psychotherapy, the improvement rate was 64 percent; and the patients who received no treatment at all, the improvement rate was 72 percent. These findings have never been refuted; subsequent studies have confirmed the negative results of the Eysenck study.[9] How can clinicians

9. F. Barron and T. Leary, "Changes in Psychoneurotic Patients with and without

and psychiatrists then, in all good conscience, continue to practice? Largely by ignoring these results and being careful not to do outcome-of-therapy studies. The attitude is nicely summarized by Rotter: "research studies in psychotherapy tend to be concerned more with some aspects of the psychotherapeutic procedure and less with outcome . . . to some extent, it reflects an interest in the psychotherapy situation as a kind of personality laboratory."[10] Some laboratory.

Thus, we can conclude that since clinical experience and tools can be shown to be worse than useless when tested for consistency, efficacy, agreement, and reliability, we can safely conclude that theories of a clinical nature advanced about women are also worse than useless.

I want to turn now to my second major point, which is that, even when psychological theory is constructed so that it may be tested, and rigorous standards of evidence are used, it has become increasingly clear that in order to understand why people do what they do, and certainly in order to change what people do, psychologists must turn away from the theory of the causal nature of the inner dynamic and look to the social context within which individuals live.

Before examining the relevance of this approach for the question of women, let me first sketch the groundwork for this assertion.

In the first place, it is clear that personality tests never yield consistent predictions; a rigid authoritarian on one measure will be an unauthoritarian on the next.[11] But the reason for this inconsistency is only now becoming clear,

Psychotherapy," *Journal of Counseling Psychology* (19) 1955; A.E. Bergin, "The Effects of Psychotherapy: Negative Results Revisited," *Journal of Counseling Psychology* (10) 1963; R.D. Cartwright and J.L. Vogel, "A Comparison of Changes in Psychoneurotic Patients During Matched Periods of Therapy and No-therapy," *Journal of Counseling Psychology* (24) 1960; C.B. Traux, "Effective Ingredients in Psychotherapy: An Approach to Unreveling the Patient-Therapist Interaction," *Journal of Counseling Psychology* (10) 1963; E. Powers and H. Witmer, *An Experiment in the Prevention of Delinquency* (New York: Columbia University Press. 1951).

10. J.B. Rotter "Psychotherapy," *Annual Review of Psychology* (11) 1960.

11. J. Block, *op. cit.*

and it seems overwhelmingly to have much more to do with the social situation in which the subject finds himself than with the subject himself.

In a series of brilliant experiments, Rosenthal and his co-workers have shown that if one group of experimenters has one hypothesis about what they expect to find, and another group of experimenters has the opposite hypothesis, both groups will in fact obtain results in accord with their hypotheses.[12] The results obtained are not due to mishandling of data by biased experimenters; rather, somehow, the bias of the experimenter creates a changed environment in which subjects actually act differently. For instance, in one experiment, subjects were to assign numbers to pictures of men's faces, with high numbers representing the subject's judgment that the man in the picture was a successful person, and low numbers representing the subject's judgment that the man in the picture was an unsuccessful person. One group of experimenters was told that the subjects tended to rate faces high; another group of experimenters was told that subjects tended to rate the faces low. Each group of experimenters was instructed to follow precisely the same procedure: they were required to read a set of instructions to subjects and to say nothing else. For the 375 subjects run, the results showed clearly that those subjects who performed the task with experimenters who expected high ratings gave high ratings; those subjects who performed the task with experimenters who expected low ratings gave low ratings. (The results would have happened by chance about one in one thousand times.) How did this happen? The experimenters all used the same words; it was something in their conduct which made one group of subjects do one thing, and another group of subjects do another thing.

12. R. Rosenthal and L. Jacobson, *Pygmalion in the Classroom: Teacher Expectation and Pupil's Intellectual Development* (New York: Holt, Rinehart & Winston, 1968); R. Rosenthal, *Experimenter Effects in Behavioral Research* (New York: Appleton-Century Crofts, 1966).

The concreteness of the changed conditions produced by expectation is a fact, a reality: even with animal subjects, where there can be no verbal communication, in two separate studies[13] those experimenters who were told that rats learning mazes had been especially bred for brightness obtained better learning from their rats than did experimenters believing their rats to have been bred for dullness. In a recent study, Rosenthal and Jacobson extended their analysis to the natural classroom situation. Here, they tested a group of students and reported to the teachers that some among the students tested "showed great promise." Actually, the students so named had been selected on a random basis. Some time later, the experimenters retested the group of students; those students whose teachers had been told that they were promising showed real and dramatic increments in their I.Q.'s as compared to the rest of the students. Something in the conduct of the teachers towards the "bright" students made them brighter.

Thus, even in carefully controlled experiments, and with no outward or conscious difference in behavior, the hypotheses we start with will influence enormously the behavior of another organism. These studies are extremely important when assessing the validity of psychological studies of women. Since it is fairly safe to say that most of us start with hypotheses as to the nature of men and women, the validity of a number of observations on sex differences is questionable, even when these observations have been taken under carefully controlled conditions. Second, and more importantly, the Rosenthal experiments point quite clearly to the influence of social expectation. In some extremely important ways, people are what you expect them to be, or at least they behave as you expect them to behave. Thus, if women, according to Bruno Bettelheim, want first and foremost to

13. R. Rosenthal and K. L. Fode, "The Effect of Experimenter Bias on the Performance of the Albino Rat," (Harvard University, 1961); R. Rosenthal and R. Lawson, "A Longitudinal Study of the Effects of Experimenter Bias on the Operant Learning of Laboratory Rats," (Harvard University, 1961).

be good wives and mothers, it is extremely likely that that is what Bruno Bettelheim (and the rest of the society) want them to be.

There is another series of social psychological experiments which points to the inescapable, overwhelming weight of social context in an extremely vivid way. These are the obedience experiments of Stanley Milgram,[14] concerned with the extent to which subjects in psychological experiments will obey the orders of unknown experimenters, even when these orders carry with them the distinct possibility that the subject is killing somebody.

In Milgram's experiments a subject is told that he is adminstering a learning experiment, and that he is to deal out shocks each time the other "subject" (in reality, a confederate of the experimenter) answers incorrectly. The equipment appears to provide graduated shocks ranging upwards from 15 to 450 volts; for each four consecutive voltages there are verbal descriptions such as "mild shock," "danger, severe shock," and finally, for the 435 and 450 volt switches, simply a red XXX marked over the switches. Each time the stooge answers incorrectly the subject is supposed to increase the voltage. As the voltage increases the stooge begins to cry in pain; he demands that the experiment stop; finally, he refuses to answer at all. When he stops responding, the experimenter instructs the subject to continue increasing the voltage; for each shock administered, the stooge shrieks in agony. Under these conditions, about 62.5 percent of the subjects administered shock that they believed to be possibly lethal.

No tested individual differences between subjects predicted which of the subjects would continue to obey, and which would break off the experiment. When forty psychiatrists predicted how many of a group of one hundred subjects would go on to give the maximum shock, their predictions were far below the actual percentages; most

14. Stanley Milgram, "Liberating Effects of Group Pressure," *Journal of Personality and Social Psychology* (1) 1965.

expected only one-tenth of 1 percent of the subjects to obey to the end. But even though psychiatrists have no idea of how people are going to behave in this situation (despite the fact that one of the central phenomena of the twentieth century is that people have been made to kill enormous numbers of other people), and even though individual differences do not predict which subjects will obey and which will not, it is easy to predict when subjects will be obedient and when they will be defiant. All the experimenter has to do is change the social situation. In a variant of Milgram's experiment, two stooges were present in addition to the "victim;" these worked along with the subject in administering electric shocks. When these two stooges refused to go on with the experiment, only ten per cent continued to the maximum voltage. This is critical for personality theory. It says that the lawful behavior is the behavior that can be predicted from the social situation, not from the individual history.

Finally, an ingenious experiment by Schachter and Singer[15] showed that subjects injected with adrenalin (which produces a state of physiological arousal in all but minor respects identical to that which occurs when subjects are extremely afraid) became euphoric when they were in a room with a stooge who was acting euphoric, and became extremely angry when they were placed in a room with a stooge who was acting extremely angry.

To summarize: if subjects under quite innocuous and non-coercive social conditions can be made to kill other subjects and under other types of social conditions will positively refuse to do so; if subjects can react to a state of physiological fear by becoming euphoric because there is somebody else around who is euphoric, or angry because there is somebody else angry; if students become intelligent because teachers expect them to be intelligent, and rats run mazes better because experimenters are told that the rats are bright, then

15. S. Schachter and J.E. Singer, "Cognitive, Social, and Physiological Determinants of Emotional State," *Psychological Review* (69) 1962.

it is obvious that a study of human behavior requires first and foremost, a study of the social contexts within which people move, the expectations as to how they will behave, and the authority which tells them who they are and what they are supposed to do.

Two theories of the nature of women, which come not from psychiatric and clinical tradition, but from biology, can be disposed of now with little difficulty. The first argument notices social interaction in primate groups, and observes that females are submissive and passive. Putting aside for a moment the serious problem of experimenter bias,[16] the problem with the argument from primate groups is that the crucial experiment has not been performed. The crucial experiment would manipulate or change the social organization of these groups, and watch the subsequent behavior. Until then, we must conclude that, since primates are at present too stupid to change their social conditions by themselves, the "innateness" and fixedness of their behavior is simply not known. As applied to humans, the argument becomes patently irrelevant, since the most salient feature of human social organization is its variety; and there are a number of cultures where there is at least a rough equality between men and women.[17] Thus, primate arguments tell us very little.

The second theory of sex differences argues that since females and males differ in their sex hormones, and sex hormones enter the brain, there must be innate differences in "nature."[18] But the only thing this argument tells us is that there are differences in physiological state. The prob-

16. For example, H.F. Harlow, "The Heterosexual Affectional System in Monkeys," *The American Psychologist* (17) 1962. After observing differences between male and female rhesus monkies, Harlow quotes Lawrence Sterne to the effect that women are silly and trivial, and concludes that "men and women have differed in the past and they will differ in the future."

17. Margaret Mead, *Male and Female: A Study of the Sexes in a Changing World* (New York: Mentor, 1955).

18. D.A. Hamburg and D.T. Lunde, "Sex Hormones in the Development of Sex Differences in Human Behavior," in Maccoby, ed., *The Development of Sex Differences* (Stanford: Stanford University Press, 1966), pp. 1-24.

lem is whether these differences are at all relevant to behavior. Recall that Schachter and Singer[19] have shown that a particular physiological state can itself lead to a multiplicity of felt emotional states, and outward behavior, depending on the social situation.

In brief, the uselessness of present psychology with regard to women, is simply a special case of the general conclusion: one must understand social expectations about women if one is going to characterize the behavior of women.

How are women characterized in our culture, and in psychology? They are inconsistent, emotionally unstable, lacking in a strong conscience or superego, weaker, "nurturant" rather than productive, "intuitive" rather than intelligent, and, if they are at all "normal," suited to the home and the family. In short, the list adds up to a typical minority group stereotype of inferiority: if they know their place, which is in the home, they are really quite lovable, happy, childlike, loving creatures.[20] In a review of the intellectual differences between little boys and little girls, Eleanor Maccoby[21] has shown that there are no intellectual differences until about high school, or, if there are, girls are slightly ahead of boys. At high school, girls begin to do worse on a few intellectual tasks, such as arithmetic reasoning, and beyond high school, the achievement of women now measured in terms of productivity and accomplishment drops off even more rapidly. There are a number of other, nonintellectual tests which show sex differences; I choose the intellectual differences since it is seen clearly that women start becoming inferior. It is no use to talk about women being different but equal; all of the tests I can think of have a "good" outcome and a "bad" outcome. Women usually end up at the "bad" outcome. In light of social expectations

19. S. Schachter and J.E. Singer, *op. cit.*
20. H.M. Hacker, "Women as a Minority Group," *Social Forces* (30) 1951.
21. Eleanor E. Maccoby, "Sex Differences in Intellectual Functioning," in Maccoby, *op. cit.*

about women, what is surprising is not that women end up where society expects they will; what is surprising is that little girls don't get the message that they are supposed to be stupid until high school; and what is even more remarkable is that some women resist this message even after high school, college, and graduate school.

I began with remarks on the task of discovering the limits of human potential. Until psychologists realize that it is they who are limiting discovery of human potential, by their refusal to accept evidence, if they are clinical psychologists, or, if they are rigorous, by their assumption that people move in a context-free ether, with only their innate dispositions and their individual traits determining what they will do, then psychology will have nothing of substance to offer in this task. I don't know what immutable differences exist between men and women apart from differences in their genitalia; perhaps there are some other unchangeable differences; probably there are a number of irrelevant differences. But it is clear that until social expectations for men and women are equal, until we provide equal respect for both men and women, our answers to this question will simply reflect our prejudices.

A Theory on Female Sexuality

Mary Jane Sherfey, M.D.

No doubt the most far-reaching hypothesis extrapolated from biological data is the existence of the universal and physically normal condition of women's inability ever to reach complete sexual satiation in the presence of the most intense, repetitive orgasmic experiences, no matter how produced. Theoretically, a woman could go on having orgasms indefinitely if physical exhaustion did not intervene. It is to be understood that repetitive orgasms leading to the satiation-in-insatiation state will be most apt to occur in parous [1] and experienced women during the luteal phase[2] of the menstrual cycle. It is one of the most important ways in which the sexuality of the primate and human female differs from the primate and human male at the physical level; and this difference exists only because of the female's capacity to produce the fulminating pelvic congestion and edema. This capacity is mediated by specific hormonal combinations with high fluid-imbibing action which are found only in certain primates and, probably, a very few other mammalian species.

I must stress that this condition does not mean a woman is always consciously unsatisfied. There is a great difference between satisfaction and satiation. A woman may be emotionally satisfied to the full in the absence of *any* orgasmic expression (although such a state would rarely persist through years of frequent arousal and coitus without some kind of physical or emotional reaction formation). Satiation-in-insatiation is well illustrated by Masters' statement, "A woman *will usually* be satisfied with three to five orgasms . . ." I believe it would rarely be said, "A man will usually be satisfied with three to five ejaculations." The man *is* satisfied. The woman *usually wills* herself to be satisfied because she is simply unaware of the extent of her orgasmic capacity. However, I predict that this hypothesis will come as no great shock to many women who consciously realize, or intuitively sense, their lack of satiation . . .

It seems that the vast majority of cases of coital frigidity are due simply to the absence of frequent, prolonged coitus. This statement is supported by unpublished data which Masters and Johnson are now accumulating. Following this logical conclusion of their previous research, they began treating a series of couples with severe, chronic frigidity or

1. "Parous" describes women who have had at least one child.—Ed.
2. The luteal phase is the post-ovulatory phase of the menstrual cycle.—Ed.

impotence. All had received prior medical and, often, psychiatric treatment to no avail. For the women, none of whom had ever experienced orgasms after five or more years of marriage, treatment consisted of careful training of the husband to use the proper techniques essential to all women and the specific ones required by his wife. In many cases this in itself was sufficient. In the others, daily sessions were instigated of marital coitus followed by prolonged use of the artificial phallus (three to four hours or more). Thus far, with about fifty women treated, every woman but one responded within three weeks at most and usually within a few days. They began at once to experience intense, multiple orgasms; and once this capacity was achieved after the exposure to daily prolonged coitus, they were able to respond with increasing ease and rapidity so that the protracted stimulation was no longer necessary. It is too early for thorough follow-ups, but initial impressions are most favorable.

Should these preliminary findings hold, an almost total biological etiology of coital frigidity will be proved. The inordinate sexual, orgasmic capacity of the human female will fall in line with that of the other higher primates—and the magnitude of the psychological and social problems facing modern mankind is difficult to contemplate.

Historical Perspective and Cultural Dilemma

The nature of female sexuality as here presented makes it clear that, just as the vagina did not evolve for the delivery of big-headed babies, so women's inordinate orgasmic capacity did not evolve for monogamous, sedentary cultures. It is unreasonable to expect that this inordinate sexual capacity could be, even in part, given expression within the confines of our culture; and it is particularly unreasonable to expect the delayed blooming of the sexuality of many women after the age of thirty or so to find adequate avenues of satisfaction. Less than one hundred years ago, and in many places today, women regularly had their third or fourth child by the time they were eighteen or nineteen, and the life span was no more than thirty-five to forty years. It could well be that the natural synchronization of the peak periods for sexual expression in men and women has been destroyed only in recent years.

These findings give ample proof of the conclusion that neither men nor women, but especially not women, are biologically built for the single-spouse, monogamous marital structure or for the prolonged adolescence which our society can now bestow upon both of them. Generally, men have never accepted strict monogamy except in principle. Women have been forced to accept it; but not, I submit, for the reasons usually given.

The human mating system, with its permanent family and kinship ties, was absolutely essential to man's becoming —and remaining—man. In every culture studied, the crucial transition from the nomadic, hunting, and food-gathering economy to a settled, agricultural existence was the beginning of family life, modern civilization, and civilized man. In the preagricultural societies, life was precarious, population growth slow, and infanticide often essential to group survival. With the domestication of animals and the agriculture revolution, for the first time in all time, the survival of a species lay in the extended family with its private property, kinship lineages, inheritance laws, social ordinances, and, most significantly, many surviving children. Only in that carefully delineated and rigidly maintained large-family complex could the individual find sufficient security to allow his uniquely human potentialities to be developed through the long years of increasingly helpless childhood—and could populations explode into the first little villages and towns.

Many factors have been advanced to explain the rise of the patriarchal, usually polygamous, system and its concomitant ruthless subjugation of female sexuality (which necessarily subjugated her entire emotional and intellectual life).

However, if the conclusions reached here are true, it is conceivable that the *forceful* suppression of women's inordinate sexual demands was a prerequisite to the dawn of every modern civilization and almost every living culture. Primitive woman's sexual drive was too strong, too susceptible to the fluctuating extremes of an impelling, aggressive erotism to withstand the disciplined requirements of a settled family life—where many living children were necessary to a family's well-being and where paternity had become as important as maternity in maintaining family and property cohesion. For about half the time, women's erotic needs would be insatiably pursued; paternity could never be certain; and with lactation erotism, constant infant care would be out of the question.

There are many indications from the prehistory studies in the Near East that it took perhaps five thousand years or longer for the subjugation of women to take place. All relevant data from the 12,000 to 8,000 B.C. period indicate that precivilized woman enjoyed full sexual freedom and was often totally incapable of controlling her sexual drive.[3] Therefore, I propose that one of the reasons for the long delay between the earliest development of agriculture (c.

3. "Today it is unfashionable to talk about former more matriarchal orders of society. Nevertheless, there is evidence from many parts of the world that the role of women has weakened since earlier times in several sections of social structure." The evidence given here lends further support to this statement by J. Hawkes and L. Woolley. See *History of Mankind, Vol. I: Prehistory and the Beginnings of Civilization* (New York: Harper & Row, 1963). However, I must make it clear that the biological data presented support only the thesis on the intense, insatiable erotism in women. Such erotism could be contained within one or possibly several types of social structures which would have prevailed through most of the Pleistocene period.

I am indebted to Prof. Joseph Mazzeo of Columbia University for calling my attention to the fact that the first study on the existence of a pre-Neolithic matriarchal society was published in 1861: Bachofen's *Das Mutterrecht.* (Basel: B. Schwabe, 1897). Indeed, Bachofen's work remains an unsurpassed, scholarly analysis of the mythologies of the Near East, hypothesizing both a matriarchal society and the inordinate erotism of women. His entire thesis was summarily rejected by twentieth-century anthropologists for lack of objective evidence (and cultural bias). On several scores, the ancient myths have proved more accurate than the modern scientists' theories. I suspect this will be another instance in which the myths prove faithful reflections of former days.

12,000 B.C.) and the rise of urban life and the beginning of recorded knowledge (c. 8,000–5,000 B.C.) was the ungovernable cyclic sexual drive of women. Not until these drives were gradually brought under control by rigidly enforced social codes could family life become the stabilizing and creative crucible from which modern civilized man could emerge.

Although then (and now) couched in superstitious, religious and rationalized terms, behind the subjugation of women's sexuality lay the inexorable economics of cultural evolution which finally forced men to impose it and women to endure it. If that suppression has been, at times, unduly oppressive or cruel, I suggest the reason has been neither man's sadistic, selfish infliction of servitude upon helpless women nor women's weakness or inborn masochism. The strength of the drive determines the force required to suppress it.

The hypothesis that women possess a *biologically determined*, inordinately high, cyclic sexual drive is too significant to be accepted without confirmation from every field of science touching the subject. Assuming this analysis of the nature of women's sexuality is valid, we must ask ourselves if the basic intensity of women's sexual drive has abated appreciably as the result of the past seven thousand years of suppression (which has been, of course, only partial suppression for most of that time). Just within the very recent past, a decided lifting of the ancient social injunctions against the free expression of female sexuality has occurred. This unprecedented development is born of the scientific revolution, the product of both efficient contraceptives, and the new social equality and emotional honesty sweeping across the world (an equality and honesty which owe more to the genius of Sigmund Freud than to any other single individual). It is hard to predict what will happen should this trend continue—except one thing is certain: if women's sexual drive has not abated, and they prove incapable of controlling it, thereby jeopardizing family life and child care, a return to the rigid, enforced suppression will be inevitable and mandatory. Otherwise the biological family will disappear and what other patterns of infant care and adult relationships could adequately substitute cannot now be imagined.[4]

Should the hypothesis be true that one of the requisite cornerstones upon which all modern civilizations were founded was *coercive* suppression of women's inordinate sexuality, one looks back over the long history of women and their relationships to men, children, and society since the Neolithic revolution with a deeper, almost awesome, sense of the ironic tragedy in the triumph of the human condition.

Summary

Recent embryological research has demonstrated conclusively that the concept of the initial anatomical bisexuality or equipotentiality of the embryo is erroneous. All mammalian embryos, male and female, are anatomically female during the early stages of fetal life. In humans, the differentiation of the male from the female form by the action of fetal androgen begins about the sixth week of embryonic life and is completed by the end of the third month. Female structures develop autonomously without the necessity of hormonal differentiation. If the fetal gonads are removed from a genetic female before the first six weeks, she will develop into a normal female, even undergoing normal pubertal changes if, in the absence of ovaries, exogenous hormones are supplied. If the fetal gonads are similarly removed from a genetic male, he will develop into a female, also undergoing normal female pubertal changes if exogenous hormones are supplied. The probable relationship of the autonomous female anatomy to the evolution of viviparity is described.

4. On the contrary, communal family structures, with men *and* women sharing child care, are not only imaginable, but already in experimental practice.—Ed.

From this surprising discovery of modern embryology and other biological data, the hypothesis is suggested that the female's relative lack of differentiating hormones during embryonic life renders her more sensitive to hormonal conditioning in later life, especially to androgens, since some embryonic and strong maternal estrogenic activity is present during embryonic life. This ready androgen responsivity provides the physiological means whereby androgen-sensitive structures could evolve to enhance the female's sexual capacity. In the primates, the marked development of the clitoral system, certain secondary sexual characteristics including skin erotism, and the extreme degree of perineal sexual edema (achieved in part by progesterone with its strong androgenic properties) are combined in various species to produce an intense aggressive sexual drive and an inordinate, insatiable capacity for copulations during estrus.[5] The breeding advantage would thus go to the females with the most insatiable sexual capacity. The infrahuman female's insatiable sexual capacity could evolve only if it did not interfere with maternal care. Maternal care is insured by the existence of the extreme sexual drive only during estrus and its absence during the prolonged postpartum anestrus of these animals.

The validity of these considerations and their relevance to the human female are strongly supported by the demonstration of comparable sexual physiology and behavior in women. This has been accomplished by the research of Masters and Johnson, and a summary of their findings of the actual nature of the sexual response cycle in women is presented. Their most important observations are:

A. There is no such thing as a vaginal orgasm distinct from a clitoral orgasm. The nature of the orgasm is the same regardless of the erotogenic zone stimulated to produce it. The orgasm consists of the rhythmic contractions of the

5. Estrus is that time when a female animal, because of the hormonal milieu, is capable of conception and desirous of copulation. Strictly speaking, true estrus does not occur in the human female.—Ed.

extravaginal musculature against the greatly distended circumvaginal venous plexi and vestibular bulbs surrounding the lower third of the vagina.

B. The nature of the labial-preputial-glandar mechanism which maintains continuous stimulation of the retracted clitoris during intravaginal coition has been described. By this action, clitoris, labia minora, and lower third of the vagina function as a single, smoothly integrated unit when traction is placed on the labia by the male organ during coitus. Stimulation of the clitoris is achieved by the rhythmical pulling on the edematous prepuce. Similar activation of the clitoris is achieved by preputial friction during direct clitoral area stimulation.

C. With full sexual arousal, women are normally capable of many orgasms. As many as six or more can be achieved with intravaginal coition. During clitoral area stimulation, when a woman can control her sexual tension and maintain prolonged stimulation, she may attain up to fifty or more orgasms in an hour's time.

From these observations and other biological data, especially from primatology, I have advanced four hypotheses:

1. The erotogenic potential of the clitoral glans is probably greater than that of the lower third of the vagina . . . The evolution of primate sexuality has occurred primarily through selective adaptations of the perineal edema and the clitoral complex, not the vagina.

2. Under optimal arousal conditions, women's orgasmic potential may be similar to that of the primates described. In both, orgasms are best achieved only with the high degree of pelvic vasocongestion and edema associated with estrus in the primates and the luteal phase of the menstrual cycle in women or with prolonged, effective stimulation. Under these conditions, each orgasm tends to increase pelvic vasocongestion; thus the more orgasms achieved, the more can be achieved. Orgasmic experiences may continue until physical exhaustion intervenes.

3. In these primates and in women, an inordinate cyclic

sexual capacity has thus evolved leading to the paradoxical state of sexual insatiation in the presence of the utmost sexual satiation. The value of this state for evolution is clear: with the breeding premium going to the primate females with the greatest pelvic edema, the most effective clitoral erotism, and the most aggressive sexual behavior, the satiation-in-insatiation state may have been an important factor in the adaptive radiation of the primates leading to man—and a major barrier to the evolution of modern man.

4. The rise of modern civilization, while resulting from many causes, was contingent on the suppression of the inordinate cyclic sexual drive of women because (*a*) the hyper-hormonalization of the early human females associated with the hypersexual drive and the prolonged pregnancies was an important force in the escape from the strict estrus sexuality and the much more important escape from lactation asexuality. Women's uncurtailed continuous hypersexuality would drastically interfere with maternal responsibilities; and (*b*) with the rise of the settled agriculture economies, man's territorialism became expressed in property rights and kinship laws. Large families of known parentage were mandatory and could not evolve until the inordinate sexual demands of women were curbed.

Finally, the data on the embryonic female primacy and the Masters and Johnson research on the sexual cycle in women will require amendations of psychoanalytic theory. These will be less than one might think at first sight. Other than concepts based on innate bisexuality, the rigid dichotomy between masculine and feminine sexual behavior, and derivative concepts of the clitoral-vaginal transfer theory, psychoanalytic theory will remain. Much of the theory concerning the "masculine" components of female sexuality will also remain but will be based on a different biological conception. Certainly, much of present and past sexual symbolism will take on richer meanings.

It is my strong conviction that these fundamental biological findings will, in fact, strengthen psychoanalytic theory and practice in the area of female sexuality. Without the erroneous biological premises, the basic sexual constitution and its many manifestations will be seen as highly moldable by hormonal influences, which in turn are so very susceptible to all those uniquely human emotional, intellectual, imaginative, and cultural forces upon which psychoanalysis has cast so much light. The power of the psychic processes will stand the stronger. Therefore it may be safely predicted that these new biological findings will not "blow away" Freud's "artificial structure of hypotheses" but will transpose it to a less artificial and more effective level.

In any event, and regardless of the validity of my own conclusions, it is my hope that this presentation of recent major contributions from biology and gynecology bearing on female sexual differentiation and adult functioning will aid in the integration of psychological and biological knowledge and will provide a firm biological foundation upon which all future theories of female psychosexuality must rest.

A PSYCHIATRIST'S VIEW: IMAGES OF WOMAN— PAST AND PRESENT, OVERT AND OBSCURED*

Natalie Shainess, M.D.

Who is Eve? What has she looked like, what has she really been? What reveals her true nature—is there anything timeless about it?

At the outset, let us remember that man and woman are interdependent. In the balance and movement of their relationship, each affects the other, and is in turn altered by the other's actions, goals, beliefs, demands. In looking back to

---

*Presented at a meeting of the Association for the Advancement of Psychotherapy, January 25, 1968. Excerpted from *American Journal of Psychotherapy,* January 1969, pp. 77-97.

the roots of past or recent views of woman, she must be understood in terms of the confines of the life that man has allowed her . . . Of course, in a more primitive state, and early in history, the family was dyadic—mother and child; and woman managed well in a life similar to other mammals, as Briffault described in *The Mothers.*[1] Bachofen[2] and Engels[3] accounted for male ascendency in terms of changing religious beliefs—but this takes us too far afield. Yet these introductory remarks may serve to indicate that this paper will be devoted largely to woman's sociocultural circumstances.

Masculine Attitudes Toward Women

Undoubtedly, men tend to have a self-serving perspective on women. Helen Bacon,[4] in a superb paper considering the role of women as indicated from Sophocles' Oedipal tragedies, pointed out that in classical Greece, woman's only public function was in religious cult. Pericles proclaimed that "A woman's glory is in not departing from her woman's nature, which is to have no fame in the world of men whether for praise or blame." It is the author's thesis that psychoanalysts have shared in such views of woman, failing to consider woman as a totality, a human being. It is comforting to be reminded by Professor Bacon that Socrates braced himself to meet almost overwhelming waves of ridicule, as he set forth three revolutionary proposals: 1) equality of the sexes in intellectual and political activities, 2) equality of the sexes in sex relationships, and 3) the idea that philosophers should be rulers. What is needed is an image, perhaps not of what is "normal," but what is *ideal,* what

1. Robert Briffault, *The Mothers* (New York: Macmillan Co., 1959).
2. J.J. Bachofen, *Das Mutterrecht* (Basel: Benno Schwabe, 1948).
3. Frederick Engels, *The Origin of the Family* (New York: International Publishers, 1942).
4. Helen Bacon, "Woman's Two Faces: Sophocles' View of the Tragedy of Oedipus and His Family," in Jules H. Masterman, ed., *Science and Psychoanalysis*, vol. 10 (New York: Grune & Stratton, 1966), pp 10-27.

woman might be if she had full opportunity to develop and use her resources. Often what has been assumed to be pathologic, is the very thing that is healthiest in her; or if not that, has formed the core of her self and her humanness . . .

What was Sophocles[5] saying about Antigone, who defied Creon to give her brother ritual burial, and who was buried alive in punishment? Was she an aggressive defiant person, or a noble one, living her life philosophy? How should we regard Euripides' Medea[6], enraged and vengeful, in reaction to betrayal and deceit?

Perspective

In order to provide a framework, since much that follows may skip from one spot to another, the following ideas are basic:

Women have lived throughout much of history as a devalued subgroup.

Freud's postulates about women provided both information and misinformation. He was unable to distinguish between the culturally derived and the biologic substrate of feminine personality and sexuality.

Freud's thinking not only had its roots in Jewish theology, but was a direct extension of the New Testament and the thinking of St. Thomas Aquinas.

At the beginning of this century, women began to emerge as people, but their path has not been a direct one, and has perhaps turned back upon itself. There have been both a positive desire to emerge and a need to rebel. Unfortunately, technologic change has assisted the second and less benign force.

In spite of the fact that the pendulum seems to have swung to so-called freedom for women at this time, our society is still reluctant to accept authenticity in women —it is even more suspect in them than in men.

5. Sophocles, *Three Theban Plays* (New York: Oxford University Press, 1956).
6. Euripides, *Medea* (New York: Oxford University Press, 1952).

Cultural patterns of femininity (and masculinity) are becoming constricted and rigidified.

Women—and men—are increasingly in discordance with their biologic natures, and are losing purpose in life, in terms of meaningful affective ties, and sharing the life of the young. Another way of putting this is that women are increasingly losing contact with their inner selves—their sentience—and as a result, become further alienated from meaningful living.

In the generally progressive alienation of our times, we are back to the laws of the jungle, but without the gratification of biologic fulfillment. This applies to women to a greater degree than to men.

The basic attitudes and assumptions made about women influence approaches in treatment. Inability to see woman as a total person may have serious consequences in treatment.

Woman: a Subgroup

Women have existed as a subgroup, a subculture since their dyadic mother-child family structure altered to include men as husband and father, in a social as well as biologic sense. From earliest times, women's bodies have been used and abused, bought and sold, burned out into premature old age —not in terms of life primeval, but life in so-called civilization. Only recently, in historical perspective, have women organized in any sense as a group.

Josh Greenfeld, [7] a writer, commented on another subgroup—the Jews. He noted that they were "to that manner born: the eternal sufferer, the perennial fall-guy." But in the face of gloom, the Jew developed laughter as a shield. It was "a very special form of laughter—insider's laughter, the pick at the scab, rub at the wound, snort at the disease— privileged laughter reserved only for victims." The Negro

7. Josh Greenfeld, "Review of *A Bad Man* by Stanley Elkin," *New York Times Book Review*, 15 October 1967.

also developed a particular kind of laughter, turned in upon himself, yet striking in telling fashion at the white man . . .

How is it that there is no specifically feminine humor, even humor that picks at the wound or—should one say— womb? Perhaps because women have not lived apart in a ghetto, where closeness and interchange encourage this. No doubt the ghetto of the red-light district must have its own humor of sorts, but it seems not to have reached out by grapevine into the workaday world.

Women have reacted in different ways to the pressures of the roles laid down for them by men. When having no alternatives, they have submitted and become slaves—and even Uncle Toms. Men have often possessed everything but their secret thoughts. It is interesting to note that after World War II, where one consequence of American victory was increased contact with the Japanese, American men were particularly taken with Japanese women—their selflessness, submissiveness, and gracious subservience apparently offered all men could ask—and I know of a number of American enterprises established in Japan, of which not the least of the advantages were sojourns for several months a year with Japanese ladies—Madame Butterflies. Yet it is out of the oriental culture that a Madame Nhu erupted—a symbol, a revelation of the ugly hatred and resentment, the reactive cruelty festering under the kimono, walking on bound feet, lying under the smirk to their dictators. But, of course, dictators are not interested in the feelings of their slaves, only in their behavior. Nor do they speculate about what free gifts, willingly given, might offer.

The Freudian Woman

Freud's theories of feminine psychology have been by now well documented, and also well criticized. Yet it is necessary to call attention again, quite briefly, to Freud's basic theories[8] about women. His major great contribution was

8. Sigmund Freud, "Physchological Consequences of Anatomical Distinction be-

recognition of woman's dual sexual role. In a biologic sense, it is woman's first task to attract and have a sexual relationship with a man . . . The second task is that of producing children and assuming the mothering role. One must agree with Freud that to some extent, anatomy is destiny . . . Yet this is an oversimplification. As we have become removed from simple earthy ties, and freed from haphazard and continuous reproduction, women are also freed to utilize their resources in more complicated ways.

Freud's other concepts of femininity are much more open to question.

He considered women defective, since born without a penis, and felt that motherhood was a compensation for this deficiency. He took the penis-envy complaints of his patients quite literally, and also theorized that women were naturally passive, masochistic, and had weaker superegos than men. Those women who suffered from penis envy and masculine protest were all—*res ipsa loquitur*—neurotically sick, and aggressiveness became the hallmark of the illness. Actually, femininity and masculinity can be defined very simply: ideally, they are the psychic and behavioral components of optimal biologic function. But optimal function is not necessarily expressed quantitatively, but rather qualitatively. Further, this optimal function results from mastery of the individual's social, as well as sexual, circimstances. Since Freud's views have so greatly influenced the thinking and our treatment of women, their roots in Judeo-Christian tradition warrant further exploration.

One cannot help but wonder how much Freud's Jewish background contributed to his views, whether religiously pursued or not. It is a religion in which the orthodox Jew daily thanks God for making him a man; and whose religious life is filled with actual and ritual taboos separating the sexes . . .

Thomas Aquinas, in the *Summa*⁹, asks a number of philo-

tween the Sexes," "Female Sexuality." "Three Contributions to the Theory of Sex." "Case of Dora," in *Collected Papers* (London: Hogarth Press, 1950).

sophical questions, in his Articles on the Production of Woman:

Should woman have been made in the first production of things? He answers: No, since the female is a misbegotten male, and nothing misbegotten should have been made in the first production of things.

Since subjection and limitation are the result of sin, therefore it was said to woman: Thou shalt be under man's power (man apparently did not sin) . . .

He asks if the image of God is found in every man. Yes, it is; but this does not apply to woman, since she was made in the image of man, not God . . .

A Sexual Trauma Redefined

The case of Dora is an example in which Freud's male-oriented views may have led him along false paths. Freud either failed to perceive, or relegated to insignificance, the intense erotic coloration of her family surroundings, and the distorting web in which she was caught, as her father's sacrifice on the altar of his own sexual relationship with his friend's wife. He was not averse to trading Dora as a consolation prize. Freud also made nothing of the bitterness and psychosomatic symptoms of Dora's mother, and their effect upon the girl. In such circumstances, Dora may indeed have had erotic and seductive fantasies, as Freud insisted; but there is little real evidence of them in his report—and it seems a sign of incredible strength and health that Dora finally quit analysis. Freud's treatment amounted to a veritable attack—possibly a consequence of his eagerness to validate his theories.

An excerpt from the case history is illuminating: Dora was to have spent a few weeks with the family "friends"— the K.'s, and with her father. He unexpectedly had to leave for a brief time, and Dora declared that she was leaving with

9. St. Thomas Aquinas, "Articles on the Production of Woman," in *The Summa Theologica* (New York: McGraw-Hill, 1964).

him, and did indeed do so. This strange behavior (Freud's term) was explained by Dora as following an "improper proposal" by Herr K. However, Dora's father reported to Freud that he doubted this and considered it a fantasy of Dora's. He stressed his ties of friendship to Frau K., and his not wanting to cause her pain (apparently his daughter's pain was of considerably less significance). Dora reported to Freud that at one point, unexpectedly alone with Herr K., he suddenly clasped her and pressed a kiss upon her lips. Freud considered this a sexual trauma—but only in the sense that it surely must have called up a distinct feeling of sexual excitement in the girl. That it might have been unwelcome, or experienced as a frightening or devastating outrage did not occur to him—nor that sexual *revulsion* might be its consequence, rather than erotic stimulation. He did some analytic "script-writing" for Dora, telling her that she had slapped Herr K. as a seductive provocation, was jealous and revengeful. He commented at one point: "Dora listened to me without any of her usual contradictions, and said goodbye warmly." It is interesting that this was the point at which Dora ceased coming, and Freud regarded it as "an unmistakable act of vengeance." It was also at this time that he observed for the first time, but without any real insight, that Dora's father was "not entirely straightforward." Freud did not note the failure in fathering, the failure to offer support and protection to the daughter—nor was he aware that his own role reinforced Dora's view of fathers—and men—as attackers and betrayers.

Self-Realization or Neuroticism?

Classic views of feminine psychology strongly persist today, many promulgated by women analysts, and they seem to be prevailing over the meaningful rebellion of Karen Horney[10], of Clara M. Thompson[11]. Again the analogy of

10. Karen Horney, "Flight from Womanhood," *International Journal of Psychoanalysis* 7:324 (1926).

Uncle Tom comes to mind, and following this path for a moment, it suggests how theoretical bias may affect treatment. At a recent meeting devoted to the theme of dissent, a Negro analyst[12] pointed to the analyst's blind spot, in studying only the dissenters, but not the people or ideas dissented against. How valid a perception! Yet this same analyst presented a case history of a woman patient who was a civil-rights activist, stating that whenever she left his office to attend a meeting, she would cry; and when, one day, she had to leave her session early to attend a particularly important rally, she pleaded with him to understand, and not be angry at her early departure. He offered her an interpretation: "You defend yourself against feeling like a woman by going out and fighting like a man." (Perhaps a castrating slap on the cheek?)

It is hard to believe that an analyst today would feel that a woman has no place in the affairs of the world. But more important—is it possible that her tearful plea for understanding related to the fact that she was asserting her integrity as a person, in supporting the rights of all human beings, black and white? Her analyst was confronted with a value-choice—in following classic concepts of femininity, may he not also have been expressing countertransference in relation to a prejudice of his own, namely: "I don't need help from my inferiors—from women!" Perhaps this also suggests the validity of a study of male values in relation to female patients . . .

Misinterpreted Myths

Some of the previous examples relate to differing aspects of sexual integrity and illustrate the lack of clarity in values

11. Clara M. Thompson, "Cultural Pressures in the Psychology of Women," *Psychiatry* 5:331 (1942); "The Role of Women in this Culture," *Psychiatry* 4:1 (1941); "Penis Envy in Women," *Psychiatry* 6:123 (1943).
12. Charles Pinderhughes, "Psychodynamics and Therapy of Civil Rights Activists." Midwinter meetings of the American Academy of Psychoanalysis, New York City, December 3, 1967.

and recognition of authenticity in society. It applies also to the treatment approach to women. Another example comes to mind.

THE GIFTED WOMAN

For years, and until quite recently, a drug company ran an ad for tranquilizers, featuring a picture of Atalanta, and describing her as a belligerent huntress symbolizing rejection of femininity. Their ad was headed: Femininity? No, Thank You! But in point of fact, the story of Atalanta is quite other. It is a story of a richly endowed woman—one not only the equal but the unfortunate superior of most of the available men. She is known for slaying centaurs—a symbolic rejection of men who are "half beast." Her father attempts to protect her from marriage with an inferior, placing the condition that to win her hand, her suitor must defeat her in a race. Meilanion wins, but only by throwing down three golden apples which she stops to pick up— apples given him by Aphrodite, goddess of love. Thus, Meilanion wins by a ruse—pardonable, since resorted to out of love— and so is able to conquer her. One could also say she was outsmarted, and so *did* find her match—a "happy ending," since women of integrity want to marry men they can respect.

THE DAMAGED WOMAN

Devereux reviews the myth of Kainis, who was raped by Poseidon, and offered the fulfillment of a wish, in restitution.[13] She asks to be changed into a man, becoming Kaineus, refusing to worship the gods, but revering his spear instead. Devereux interprets this as the award of a penis in compensation for rape. Curiously, he ignores Kainis' statement that she wishes to be invulnerable. She may indeed worship the power of the man, but her refusal to worship the gods might best be interpreted as a

13. George Devereux, "The Awarding of a Penis as a Compensation for Rape," *International Journal of Psychoanalysis* 18:398 (1957).

feeling that they have failed her—she can no longer trust them.

Implications for Treatment

There is yet another area where choices must be made, in the treatment of women. Medical literature, and also the medical grapevine, makes many comments about women's seductiveness. Some of it may be valid. But again, perhaps Freudian theorizing has given added credence to woman's unfair use of her wiles, and little attention has been focused upon man—who perhaps is not quite the helpless creature he is inclined to consider himself (but only in very special circumstances!). At a recent APA colloquium on teaching of psychiatric principles to nonpsychiatric physicians, a colleague reported his discussion with a gynecologist, who claimed that a hospitalized patient was "extremely seductive, and did not even wear a robe" when he was there. What came to light was that somehow this physician seemed, quite by chance, to find that between 12:00 P.M. and 1:00 A.M. was the only time he could make his rounds to this particular patient—and, of course, his visit found her, predictably, in her nightgown.

To follow along with the idea of feminine seductiveness —one can find some surprising things in the current GAP report on *Sex and the College Student.*[14] Perhaps the author's vision has been sharpened by some astonishing and unbeautiful situations which came to her attention from her practice. Those who have read this report are aware that it contains several examples of sexual involvements between male teachers and female students, and in all instances except one, the onus was placed upon the girl. Here is an excerpt from one case:

> At a small party in the instructor's apartment, Betty, a junior, became intoxicated, and the teacher had intercourse with her after the party. *He thought little about it,* and was surprised and

14. Group for the Advancement of Psychiatry, *Sex and the College Student,* Report #60. New York 1965.

distressed to be summoned by the dean. The girl had reported him, saying that her condition made it impossible for her to protest effectively. He said he had not used force, believed the girl had been an active participant, and finally indignantly protested that he had been framed.

What is the real issue? If one expects responsibility, or maturity—to whom does one look first, student or teacher? Why make the inference that the student is to blame? Should a teacher be so casual about sexual relations with a student? Of several reports, the only instance in which responsibility was laid at the door of the teacher was one in which the teacher was a woman—and a Lesbian. And here one might be more inclined to suspect the student's willing participation.

What about out-of-wedlock pregnancies—beyond the obvious reasons, why is attention focused almost exclusively on the girl? What about the abortion problem—is it necessarily a sign of illness or destructiveness when a woman wants an abortion? May it not be an attempt to master her life circumstances and function more adequately? How does it happen that a myth of guilt feelings after abortion has grown so large and been readily accepted—and to what extent, if indeed it does occur, is it iatrogenically induced? It was with a sense that the millenium has come, that the author heard three outstanding psychiatrists[15] state that they had never seen a woman seriously disturbed as the consequence of a legal abortion, and found little evidence of guilt. With regard to understanding sexual problems in women . . . and in addition to the confusion of changing sexual codes, and women's assertion of their own right to sexual pleasure[16], rather than continuing to accept the role of accessory to male need[17]—we are torn between beliefs

15. John M. Cotton, Robert W. Laidlaw, and Arthur Peck, "Report at Workshop on Demography and Population Planning, Panel on Abortion." Divisional Meeting of the American Psychiatric Association, New York City, November 18, 1967.
16. Natalie Shainess, "The Problem of Sex Today," *American Journal of Psychiatry*, 124:1026 (1968).
17. Natalie Shainess, "A Re-assessment of Feminine Sexuality and Erotic Experience," in J. H. Masserman, *Science and Psychoanalysis*, vol. 10, pp. 56-74.

relating to classic analytic concepts on the one hand, in which it is assumed that many, if not all, women are not biologically equipped for orgastic response[18], and on the other, the view that it is a strictly mechanical thing and can be achieved by all[19]. Further, what will happen to women, and to the family, as sex is taken so casually that it has no emotional context whatsoever, and men feel less responsibility and involvement, both within and outside of marriage? Is it progress for women—or for men—that, as has been reported[20] "There has been little actual increase in sexual activity—it is simply that men have switched from the prostitute to the girl next door?"

What kind of help was offered to the eight-year-old Argentinian victim of rape, recently in the news[21] as the youngest mother, at nine, on record, who was given so-called psychologic preparation before delivery? What was the nature of this "preparation"? What help, *other* than a quick and merciful abortion, followed by good supportive care of every kind, could have had some reparative effect?

Sinclair Lewis, in his classic, *Main Street*[22], documented the plight of a gifted young woman who married a Western doctor, and was destroyed by a society permitting wives only a rigidly fixed position, and accepting nothing original, nothing different, nothing intellectual from them, and not even permitting them to work. But, many will say, times have changed. Today, women vote, they work (although holding fewer high-level posts than a decade or two ago),[23] they have considerable wealth, they are freed from household drudgery, they are increasingly free of unwanted

18. Marcel Heiman, "Sexual Response in the Female," *Psychoanalytic Quarterly*, 30: 615 (1961).
19. William H. Masters and Virginia E. Johnson, *Human Sexual Response* (Boston: Little, Brown, 1966).
20. Sex and the College Girl. Symposium on Changing Sex Behavior. Presented at a meeting of the Association for the Advancement of Science, New York City, December 26, 1967.
21. "Argentine Girl, 9, Gives Birth to Boy," *New York Post*, 19 October 1967.
22. Sinclair Lewis, *Main Street* (New York: Harcourt, Brace, 1961).
23. Caroline Bird, *Born Female* (New York: David McKay, 1968).

pregnancies—and it has even been proposed that legislation should provide for a "social menopause" at age twenty-eight, because of the population explosion. Women have been emancipated, and they are sexually more free as well (though what they will reap from this remains to be seen, and there are indications that it may offer ultimately more pain than pleasure). Undoubtedly, there are some women who have developed expansively under all these circumstances. For a large number, is this freedom myth—or reality? Women are increasingly taking to drinking as an escape, and will do virtually anything to evade the confines of their homes.

In an article in *Harper's*, titled: "The New American Female," and subtitled: "Demi-Feminism Takes Over," Marion Sanders[24] points to the schizophrenic split in women's image of their own roles. She cites the amusing Phyllis McGinley, who "writes sermons in praise of domesticity, or 'nesting,' " while noting also that Betty Friedan,[25] wrote a "shrill, humorless polemic" on the position of American women, and their "social disease"—the "problem that has no name." This has been referred to as the "Salvation through Job" gospel. She quotes David Riesman as observing that women should find it possible to "lead full multidimensional lives without mounting the barricades at home or abroad."

The author finds herself in a curious position. She would ask David Riesman: Who likes to live behind barricades? Like walls, as Robert Frost suggested, something there is that doesn't love them. On the other hand, she believes that woman is the pillar of the family—the source of love and care. There are no easy substitutes. But escape is no answer. It seems that the rewards of an affluent society turn bitter as gall in the mouth. Women do not any longer know what to do with a home, how to use it, how to enjoy it, what to devote themselves to, as mothers. Society places little value

24. Marion K. Sanders, "The New American Female," *Harper's*, July 1963.
25. Betty Friedan, *The Feminine Mystique* (New York: W.W. Norton, 1963).

on these things, and few rewards. As we have become a thing-oriented, impulse-ridden, narcissistically self-preoccupied people, we are increasingly dedicated to the acquisition of things, and cultivate little else. There is no nurture for the spirit. Besides, a freely roaming husband does not promote comfort and security at home . . . Marya Mannes has commented on women's plight in "The Roots of Anxiety in Modern Woman":

> What I call the destructive anxieties are not the growth of women's minds and powers, but quite the contrary: the pressures of society and the mass media to make women conform to the classic and traditional image in men's eyes. They must be not only the perfect wife, mother, and home-maker, but the ever-young, ever-slim, ever-alluring object of their desires. Every woman is deluged daily with urges to attain this impossible state . . . The real demon is success—the anxieties engendered by this quest are relentless, degrading, corroding. What is worse, there is no end to this escalation of desire . . . The legitimate anxiety—am I being true to myself as a human being?—is submerged in trivia and self-deception.[26]

If there is a solution for women, it will come from a better set of values, education, and society's help. It requires the recognition that nature has demanded much of them. To pursue interests beyond the home is an added burden, not an escape; and it demands great responsibility: it should be taken seriously by women, *and* society. It calls for an excellence upon which a high value should be placed, if there is concern about bettering the human condition. And finally, it calls upon the psychiatrist to be more perceptive—perhaps more generous—in his interpretation of feminine behavioral expressions.

Most of the theoretical concepts relating to feminine psychology were evolved by men, who have tended to have a self-serving perspective on women, and have taken for granted the superior position they have occupied in most

26. Marya Mannes, "The Roots of Anxiety in Modern Woman," *Journal of Neuropsychiatry*, 5:412 (1964).

societies. Women also have tended to accept their allotted place.

Freud's views also reflected a phallocentric bias (first recognized by Ernest Jones), and have remained relatively unchallenged by woman analysts. In many instances, these concepts have led to misunderstanding of feminine behavior, the tendency being to interpret some instances of self-assertion and efforts at mastery as rejection of femininity. The great writers have been more perceptive about women, at times, than psychoanalysts, and have understood and accepted woman's drive to be an equal human being . . . Psychiatrists are urged to examine some of their own prejudices and think more searchingly in interpreting feminine behavior.

Consideration of Eve has necessitated wandering far in time and space. Perhaps what has been presented is no more substantial than changing wave patterns upon the sea. Hopefully, it may stimulate further thought—a search beneath the surface. Let us join forces in trying better to understand Woman, in permitting her to be herself, realize her best potential. We can try to meet the Bard's challenge: "Let us not, to the marriage of true minds, admit impediments."

UNFINISHED BUSINESS: BIRTH CONTROL AND WOMEN'S LIBERATION*

Lucinda Cisler

Because women have wombs and bear children, and because technical control of the reproductive function has always been imperfect—as it still is today—society has ultimately always defined woman as a childbearer—that is, as she relates to children and to men, rather than as an individual.

Since her basic function has been to bear children, whatever "extra" activities the culture and the economy have allowed her to pursue, anything that alters social control over her reproductive capacities is deeply and fundamentally threatening to societal and individual psyches: different reproductive roles are *the* basic dichotomy in humankind, and have been used to rationalize all the other, ascribed differences between men and women and to justify all the oppression women have suffered.

Without the full capacity to limit her own reproduction, a woman's other "freedoms" are tantalizing mockeries that cannot be exercised. With it, the others cannot long be denied, since the chief rationale for denial disappears.

This is one very practical reason why the older movements for women's liberation could not go beyond hollow token gains; medical technology had not yet developed effective contraception and safe abortion techniques (nor had male law and custom placed a high priority on such developments). Women wanting to be something besides reproducers had to choose sexual abstinence, masturbation, or homosexuality, trust to luck and crude birth-control methods, or rely on hired substitutes to take care of the resulting children.

(The implicit linking of bearing the young with *rearing* the young raises all the basic questions about who should best care for children. These cannot be dealt with here, but a single comment may be appropriate: if women—in the present state of medicine—must carry pregnancies for nine months and then bear the children, one might ask why should men not then care for the infants during the next nine months, as their fair contribution? Social cooperation could then take over.)

In earlier times, even information on the poor alternatives to childbearing then available, let alone the actual devices, was kept from the general public by political and religious forces that even wrote this repression into law. At any rate, the earliest non-folk method of contraception that the industrial revolution produced was for the use of men: the condom, made possible by perfecting the vulcanization of rubber. And, of course, there was always withdrawal *(coitus interruptus)*, although religion proscribed it as the "sin of Onan." The nineteenth-century decline in the European birthrate has been attributed to the widespread use of withdrawal, especially among urban working people. With the industrial revolution these people flowed into the cities at a tremendous rate, and the density of cities has always been a stimulus to information exchange. Imagine the trust that women had to have in their men's good intentions—and agility! Even today, it is estimated that withdrawal is the most commonly used contraceptive technique in England. (Abortion is the world's most common birth-control method, chiefly because billions of people still have little access to other methods.)[1] The recent shift to woman-controlled means of contraception was, on balance, a good thing; but it is a mixed blessing: now many men resent women for "defending" themselves, or seek to blame them for the failures that occur.

Folk methods of birth control, both contraception and abortion, had been the province of midwives, witches, and "wise women" for centuries, and many of these underground methods were highly effective for their day. The women who attended other women in childbirth were frequently the outcasts of society who could get no other work: the delivery of a pregnant woman was not considered a "sacrament" but a dirty business, since anything having to do with the femal genitalia was fearsome and unclean.[2] Then came the rise of a special profession of medicine; and

---

1. On withdrawal: Ernest Havemann, *Birth Control*, (New York: Time-Life Books, 1967), p. 35. On abortion: Association for Voluntary Sterilization, Inc. (AVS), *The Case for Voluntary Sterilization*, New York: AVS, August 1968, p. 9.
2. Madeline Gray, *The Normal Woman* (New York: Scribner's, 1967), p. 299. Madeleine Riley, *Brought to Bed* (New York: A. S. Barnes, 1968), Chapter 4, *passim*.

when contraceptive knowledge did become available, it was carefully placed in the hands of doctors—mostly males, one hardly need add—where it remains, by and large, today.

One has an oppressive sense of *déjà vu* in reading old accounts (written as recently as the early Thirties) of "permissible indications" for doctors to give out contraceptive advice and materials: a huge family; the mother's health at a breaking point; a history of having borne defective children; the threat of her death if childbirth recurs—all very fine reasons, but a *woman's own* simple wish not to bear any more (or even any) children is conspicuously not on these tedious lists. They were dusted off and wheeled out again for the public when "abortion law reform" began to be a barely respectable topic of discussion a few years ago. Once again, men were to mete out carefully their information and skills to "deserving" women only—deserving women being those who had done their duty by bearing X number of *Kinder*, wearing themselves out by caring for these children, and perhaps facing disability or death if they had to continue. In short, if a woman is a *victim* she may qualify for that which is her right as a *person.* And this possibility of death is deplored more because it would deprive the family of a worker-mother than because it would deprive a person of life itself. Once more, women are valued in relation to other people's needs rather than as themselves.

An "undeserving" woman—sometimes called a "frivolous" woman—is one who is concerned with her own self-interest and actively seeks to preserve it by deciding she does not want to bear a child. That this self-assertion might coincide with the goals of a good society is an idea that few seem to entertain.

Contraception

Most people seem to think that there are no laws against contraception left on the books in this country, but that is not the case: only 40 percent of the states have no laws limiting the distribution or display of contraceptives.[3] The rest forbid young people or unmarried people access to contraception, or say that distribution to anyone must be through doctors or licensed pharmacists. Puerto Rico's law, for obvious religious reasons, lists the same old "indications" as those one must read over and over in abortion law "reform" proposals. (Women who think men have a special advantage because they are able to buy condoms from vending machines in some states are misled: in fact, such distribution is forbidden in many states and tightly regulated in others. Of course, there is no reason why women should not be able to buy foams or other non-prescriptive contraceptives from vending machines; the laws on condoms were made before foams were developed, or we would doubtless see these as-yet-nonexistent machines banned too.)

Those who are sanguine about these laws, considering them dead letters, only reveal their blissful middle-class state of mind: not only can such laws be used as cop-outs when, for instance, college women demand that university health departments provide them with contraceptive services, but they have also been used to keep poor women from having access to public birth-control clinics.

Quite recently, Massachusetts turned down about 30 million dollars in federal aid because it would have had to comply with federal stipulations that age and marital condition be no barrier to the receipt of birth-control services. And because he displayed a contraceptive pill before a Boston University audience in 1967, birth-control worker Bill Baird was arrested and had to fight all the way through the entire Massachusetts judicial system: his conviction—and the law against display—were overturned two years later by the state Supreme Court. He could have been jailed for five years.

At the same lecture he perpetrated another "Crime Against Chastity" (the actual name of the law), when he

---

3. Planned Parenthood Federation of America, Inc., *Laws Relating to Birth Control and Family Planning in the United States,* New York: Planned Parenthood, 1968 (mimeo.).

handed a can of contraceptive foam to a twenty-two year-old "girl." Unfortunately, although his chief crime was not being a pharmacist with a doctor's prescription in hand (although foam is non-prescriptive), the fact that the woman was not married proved, significantly, to be the most distressing fact for the courts to deal with: "promiscuity" would run rampant if single people could keep from having babies. Baird's conviction was upheld and at this writing he is on his way to the U.S. Supreme Court to test the rights of single women to protect themselves.

Those who imagine that this problem was taken care of by the famous *Griswold* decision of 1965, whereby the federal Supreme Court struck down Connecticut's astounding law against *using* contraceptives, are mistaken again: this case was argued, and won, on the grounds that doctors were being hampered in their practice of medicine and that the right of *marital* privacy was being violated. Once more the Sanctity of the Home was preserved, the rights of single people were deemed of no legal consequence, and young women go on lying about their age and their marital status in order to get what they need—if they know where to go in the first place, or what to ask for.

There are those, too, who believe devoutly that "the Pill" is 100 percent effective—for the women who can use it safely. Because it is easy to accuse a woman of not taking it when she should, failures are explained away as the patient's fault ("you know these women: no good with numbers"). Oddly enough, most women seem to have one or two friends who can count but who somehow got pregnant on the Pill anyway. Still, even the drug companies admit there is a failure rate of anywhere from .1 percent to 1 percent;[4] with 6 million women taking the Pill in the United States today, they have at least 6,000 surprises every year, and probably more.

The debate about the dangers of the Pill goes on, with

---

4. For examples, see Havemann, *op. cit.*, pp. 58–59, and *Consumers Union Report on Family Planning*, Mt. Vernon, N.Y.: Consumers Union, 1966, p. 26.

many pros and cons from doctors and little decisive data for women to go on. There are recurrent authoritative rumors that devastating reports will soon appear, revealing all sorts of horrible statistics about the high incidence of circulatory ailments and other disabilities among women who take the Pill. A recent British study has indicated that these rumors are more than scare stories, and a few similar reports have appeared in the United States, but only in professional journals: the medical profession must ruminate at length before revealing that such a setback has occured. It could also be that we are kept waiting for the news until a "really good" new Pill is developed and the pharmaceutical manufacturers tool up for it, thereby preserving their high quotations on the stock market.

A pro-feminist male doctor who works with pregnant teenagers has said in conversation, however, that he believes pills should be freely available over the counter, with simple directions and counterindications clearly printed on the container, as for so many other drugs, and that pills remain a prescriptive substance because doctors hate to relinquish control over their women patients' bodies.

The intrauterine devices (IUD's or "loops") are quite effective, too: they fail 1.5 percent to 3 percent of the time.[5] But many women's bodies reject these plastic shapes, and the most effective, larger varieties are not suitable for women who have never borne children. Many doctors will not even insert the small ones in single women, giving a variety of excuses that sometimes have less medical than moral justification. The same doctor quoted above has suggested that M.D.'s prefer to prescribe the Pill even in cases where a loop might be more suitable or where the woman is not enthusiastic about the Pill: if an IUD fails to prevent conception, the woman's foolishness can hardly be blamed,

5. U.S. Department of Health, Education, and Welfare, Food and Drug Administration, Advisory Committee on Obstetrics and Gynecology, *Report on Intrauterine Contraceptive Devices* (Washington: U.S. Government Printing Office, January 1968).

and imperfect medical technology must take the rap. Of course, in any case, the woman has to take the real rap—an unwanted baby or a dangerous illegal abortion—because the obvious insurance of safe, legal abortion isn't available.

What happens when women are used to test new contraceptive methods? If they were using no contraceptive before the experiment, they are probably better off than they were to begin with, but if the method doesn't work for some members of a large experimental population, they have no abortion fail-safe guarantee. Purity of "motivation" (i.e., desperation) must be preserved, it seems, to ensure that the experiment is not contaminated.

Whatever the real story about the Pill, its failures, and its side-effects, the fact remains that a good many women don't trust it and have gone back to that antique rubber mechanism, the diaphragm with cream or jelly. They know it does nothing odd to their body chemistry, it lasts for quite a while, and there is a curious psychological advantage (commonly considered a drawback) to the fact that they must exercise choice each time they use it. But some women, younger ones especially, seem to feel that all is lost if they can't use pills or IUD's (or can't get anyone to prescribe them): the Pill and the loop have been so successful, and so oversold, that women who have grown up in the Sixties sometimes imagine that other methods couldn't possibly work, or would be too hard to use, and they fall back on withdrawal (trust), some crude form of rhythm, or sheer luck.

It is surprising how few women know what contraceptive foam is, and that it can be bought over the counter, or that it works a great deal better than trust or luck. Here and there condoms still exist, too, and are quite effective; in fact, a condom and foam used together are very safe indeed, and are a quite readily available combination.[6]

Technology is not God, and will not provide salvation, but if one of its most highly touted products isn't available,

6. Havemann, *op. cit.*, p. 56.

settling for second- or third-best is still preferable to passivity. Yet because women are programmed to trust what society says is The Way, and because they are programmed to feel that sex isn't really very nice after all, they are easy prey to fatalism and often fail to seek out individual alternatives.

A recent article cast depressing light upon the practice of pill-taking among young single women.[7] Instead of the old practice of demanding that his girlfriend be a virgin, a certain kind of young man has now turned the Pill into an instrument of control: a bad girl is one who is already taking the Pill when she goes out with him, while a good girl waits (or pretends to wait . . .) for him to suggest it and even has him get the Pill supply for her. Passivity wins again, and self-protection is devalued. How different is this sad pattern, among bright, well-educated young women, from the proverbial fatalism of poor women—who, when they do assert themselves, must sometimes hide their pills at other women's houses so their husbands won't find them? Women have been taught to fear freedom and to shun it when by chance it comes their way.

An entire book could, and should, be written on the psychology of contraception: it would treat the place of fatalism, of power relations and communication between man and woman, of basic attitudes toward sexuality, of hostility, aggression, and punishment in the sex act, and much more. Lee Rainwater and his colleagues begin to do this quite well in their two books;[8] unfortunately, they deal only with married people and only implicitly with female oppression. What they discovered can hardly be summarized here; they did, however, find that people who enjoyed sex practiced contraception successfully and so enjoyed sex still more and thought it a fine thing. These couples also talked together more about contraception and sex, and had much more

7. *Eve*, April 1969.
8. Lee Rainwater and Karol K. Weinstein, *And the Poor Get Children* (Chicago: Quadrangle, 1960); Lee Rainwater *et al.*, *Family Design* (Chicago: Aldine, 1965).

"egalitarian" marriages (and fewer children) than other couples had. What is cause and what is effect here is left to the reader to decide, but the relative equality between the sexes seems to be a major causal factor, as one would imagine.

But the study of family power relations and contraceptive practices cannot tell us everything we need to know. There is a profound fear of woman's sexual potential behind the continuing insistence that (for women) sexuality and reproduction are inseparable. The physical fact is that in women these functions are potentially *more* distinct than they are in men: as Masters and Johnson pointed out quite explicitly—in a passage that seems to have been printed in invisible ink, judging from the attention paid it—the clitoris is unique in that it is the only organ in human anatomy whose purpose is exclusively that of erotic excitation and release.[9] It is the multi-functional penis—carrier of both semen and of sexual nervous response (among other things)—that in every sexual act is simultaneously procreative and erotic. Can men's unconscious realization of these truths, as well as their understandable desire to believe what is most convienient for their own needs in intercourse, underlie the stubborn orthodox-Freudian insistence that the seat of "mature" female sexuality must be the vagina? When an oppressed group has a profound natural advantage like this one (a special erotic organ), the dominant group cannot rest until it has convinced most of the subordinate ones that they are in fact disadvantaged in this way as in all others. How terrible if erection and intromission prove not to be the *sine qua non* of everyone's sexual pleasure! They must also be made the unswerving center of woman's life if sperm is to meet egg as frequently as possible: her capacity to conceive is periodic, while man's capacity to inseminate is continuous.

In *The Dangerous Sex*,[10] a cross-cultural and historical

9. William H. Masters and Virginia E. Johnson, *Human Sexual Response* (Boston: Little, Brown, 1966), p. 45.
10. H. R. Hays, *The Dangerous Sex: The Myth of Feminine Evil* (New York: Putnam, 1964; Pocket Books, 1965).

study, H. R. Hays analyzes men's fear of the sexual nature of women and their elaborate manifestations of this fear in the form of exclusively male institutions, legitimized by force or by the threat of it. So much for the "male bond"[11] of the primitive hunting band or the primitive board-room. Obviously, if women "by nature" were primarily passive breeders, there would be no need for the rococo superstructure of oppression that is implacably devoted to keeping them in their "natural" place.

But technically speaking, constantly improving birth-control methods are what is creating the revolutionary separation of sexuality from reproduction: "is creating" because no contraceptive method *is* yet perfect and because access to birth control is still guarded by those who know the most effective power is the exclusive possession of knowledge and skills.

Sterilization

It is revealing that most people do not seem to know that only two states, Connecticut and Utah, have even the mildest laws restricting access to sterilization, and that in thirty or more states Blue Cross–Blue Shield and Medicaid programs will even cover some of the costs.[12] Their ignorance probably stems in part from the fact that they confuse compulsory sterilization—with its overtones of Nazism, insane asylums, homes for the feeble-minded, and punishment of social transgressors like criminals and unwed mothers—with the voluntary kind, which two million Americans have chosen and 100,000 more choose each year.[13]

But it must also be explained by the fact that the same absurd hospital committees sit upon requests for both abortion and sterilization, although no such system is legally

11. Lionel Tiger, *Men in Groups* (New York: Random House, 1969).
12. Association for Voluntary Sterilization, *Blue Cross-Blue Shield and Medicaid Insurance for Voluntary Sterilization* (revised), New York: AVS, March 1969 (mimeo.)
13. AVS, *The Case for Voluntary Sterilization*, p. 3.

required for sterilization any more than it is for abortion (in those states that have not yet been blessed with the dubious benefits of abortion "reform" legislation). To sterilize a man is a simple office procedure, called vasectomy; to sterilize a woman is a major abdominal operation. But because of the automatic identification of reproductive matters with woman (the breeder)—an identification reinforced by the woman today usually being the one to employ contraceptives—and also because a tremendous number of men confuse fecundity with potency, somehow an operation on the woman is thought of first when a couple is considering sterilization and knows little about it. She is also the machine, so it is with her mechanism that the technician "naturally" tinkers.

Still, this is by no means to say that a woman should be dissuaded from seeking sterilization if she chooses to have it; given the failures of contraceptives and the cruel problems she must face if she wants an abortion, it is an ideal solution for many women. For those who hesitate to cut off their reproductive potential entirely, reversible operations for both sexes are being perfected and have already reached a high degree of success. Thus the main objection many people have to sterilization is beginning to be met. As it is now, however, even those operations intended to be permanent can fail to prevent conception: one vasectomy in 100 fails, and one in 250 salpingectomies is ineffective.[14]

If a woman does seek such an operation, she is most unlikely to be successful, unless she is over thirty and has done her duty by producing six, or sometimes only four, living children. Without her husband's consent her search is almost certain to be fruitless, since she is attempting to turn off the machine that belongs to him. It's just too bad if she's twenty-two and has five children and a husband afflicted with *machismo*, or if she has simply decided she'd prefer to have no children at all. Her own decision is considered frivolous unless a gang of medical people happens to

14. Alan F. Guttmacher, "Sterilization," *The Nation*, April 6, 1964.

agree with it. All this, again, is *not* part of a code of laws but part of an institutionalized system that must be destroyed even as repressive laws on contraception and abortion are done away with.

It is curious that many Catholic women seek to be sterilized, although, like other good birth-control methods, the procedure is counter to Church teachings. Perhaps this is because it is easier to confess one single, final big sin than to keep appearing in the confessional week after week saying, "Father, I sinned seven times: I took my pills." It is also easier than learning higher mathematics in order to play the losing game of Vatican Roulette (rhythm). These reasons— and the repressive Puerto Rican birth-control laws—may help explain why so many Puerto Rican women have had *La Operación* (notice the grammatic parallel with "the" Pill). Somewhere between a fifth and a third of the Puerto Rican women in New York City have been sterilized.[15]

While many women who want this operation ask in vain, unnecessary hysterectomies are being performed on others who may not want them at all. There are estimates that as many as 80 per cent of all hysterectomies are "unnecessary surgery." The estimators do not say whether "unnecessary" sometimes means that the woman just asked for it (at the time she was having a baby, for instance), but this speculation is doubtful. Judging from the accounts of women who have been "granted" hospital abortions—if they will "in return" agree to be sterilized—there are more instances of surgery as punishment than one might at first imagine. Punishment for what? For bothering the doctors by asking for an abortion ("*She* won't be back"); for not wanting to have a child and daring to do something active about it; for sexuality itself. This situation has hardly been examined yet, but surely deserves a closer look than it can be given here.

15. Lawrence Podell, "Fertility, Illegitimacy, and Birth Control," no. 6 in the series *Families on Welfare in New York City,* New York: City University of New York, Center for Social Research, 1968, p. 9. [Also see p. 340 of this book, "Double Jeopardy: To Be Black and Female," by Frances Beal, for an analysis of the racism in many birth-control programs.—Ed.]

Abortion

> It is at her first abortion that woman begins to "know." For
> many women the world will never be the same.
> —Simone de Beauvoir, *The Second Sex*[16]

The existence of anti-abortion laws in this country is well
known: most state laws say that a woman may not legally
have an abortion unless the pregnancy endangers her life.
Of course, since the death rate from childbirth and the
complications of pregnancy is about ten times as great as the
death rate from clinically performed abortions,[17] one might
say that any woman's life is always more endangered, statistically speaking, by carrying a pregnancy to term than by
having a good abortion! Still, it should be her choice to
make, whether she wishes to risk the dangers of childbirth
or follow the safer course of abortion.

The "reasoning" behind these laws will be considered in
greater detail later in this section. But first we should set up
a context of facts.

Just how many abortions there are, how many women
have them, who they are, and how many die from bad ones
—all these key statistics are hard to determine: illegal acts
are unreported because they're illegal. Still, a few basic
figures are generally agreed upon by those who study the
issue.

About 1,000,000 abortions are probably performed every
year in the U.S., although some say as many as 2,000,000
and others say as few as 200,000.[18] No one knows for sure
whether the widespread use of the Pill, with its low failure
rate, has kept this old figure of 1,000,000 stable in an increas-

16. Paris: 1949 (New York Bantam, 1968, p. 464).
17. Eastern European abortion figures from Lawrence Lader, *Abortion* (In-
dianapolis: Bobbs-Merrill, 1966), p. 17; 1966 U.S. maternal death figures from
Statistical Abstract of the United States, 1968 edition, p. 55.
18. See Alan F. Guttmacher in Foreword to Jerome E. Bates and Edward S.
Zawadzki, *Criminal Abortion* (Springfield, Ill.: Charles C. Thomas, 1964). See also
sources cited by Roy Lucas on page 731 of his "Federal Constitutional Limitations
on the Enforcement and Administration of State Abortion Statutes," *The North
Carolina Law Review, XLVI, June 1968, pp. 730-778.*

ing population, or whether the number has even grown because a larger proportion of young women are engaging in non-marital sex (which is less likely to involve contraception than sex within marriage). The main idea is that there *are* lots of abortions every year—about one for every four live births—and that only about 10,000 of them are "legal" —something like one in 100.[19]

Various calculations will show that about one American woman in four will have had an abortion by the time she reaches menopause.[20] Of course, no one knows how many other women want abortions they can't get, but we do know there are 300,000 out-of-wedlock births here annually, most of them unwanted by the woman involved, and that various surveys have found large numbers even of married women daring to admit that they didn't want their last child—or two, or three.

One frequently sees assertions that 70 percent, or 80 or 85 percent, of the women who get abortions are married women. Aside from the fact that ovaries and a uterus are not wedding presents but things all women possess, one must also realize that about 85 percent of all women of reproductive age *are* married and so tend to be more exposed to pregnancy than single women are. Those who worry about irrelevancies like the marital status of aborted women reveal their concern with establishing the "respectability" of abortion rather than with establishing justice for all women.

When one begins to think of the public attention paid to various social issues that involve the oppression of a group because of its physical attributes, an interesting analogy appears. About one in eight Americans has the direct expe-

19. Christopher Tietze, in "Therapeutic Abortions in the United States," *American Journal of Obstetrics and Gynecology*, CI, July 15, 1968, pp. 784–787, calculates that there were about 8,000 legal abortions in the U.S. annually from 1963 to 1965; but this figure pre-dates the slight easing of restrictions that "reform" laws brought.
20. Acknowledgements to Dr. Christopher Tietze and James Clapp for developing this conclusion, which mirrors the early findings of the Kinsey researchers in Paul Gebhard *et al.*, *Pregnancy, Birth and Abortion* (New York: John Wiley and Sons, 1959), pp. 93–94.

rience of being black and feels the oppression that goes with that experience; about one in eight Americans has the direct experience of having an illegal abortion, and feels the oppression that goes with *that* experience. Need we compare the amount of publicity given to each of these two brands of oppression to see that the bondage experienced by women as a physical class commands about as little interest from the media, government study groups, lawmakers, and citizens as the racist evil of slavery did before the abolitionist movement arose 150 years ago?

Another statistic that is bandied about for all the right reasons—but with much unwarranted confidence—is the figure of 10,000 U.S. abortion deaths per year. A study made in the 1930's,[21] before the development of antibiotics made even illegal abortion less deadly than it used to be, came up with this number of 10,000 deaths; but it is no longer anywhere near the truth and has no place in any serious discussion of abortion. The most accurate current estimates are that 500 to 1,000 deaths occur each year because of septic abortions, and this range takes false reporting strongly into account.[22] Of course, no one knows for sure how many women die from causes *related* to real or imagined unwanted pregnancies—like suicide (notoriously underreported anyway), murder, or automobile "accidents" (how many of these are really suicide or murder?). Still, the truth is our best weapon, and fifty women dead is too many to "accept" for such a simple operation as abortion. In fact, botched abortions are the leading cause of deaths associated with pregnancy.[23]

Who are the American women who die? As one might expect, they are usually the poor, the uninformed, the black,

21. Frederick J. Taussig, *Abortion, Spontaneous and Induced,*(St. Louis: C. V. Mosby, 1936).
22. Christopher Tietze and Sarah Lewit, "Abortion," *Scientific American*, CCXX, January 1969, p. 23.
23. Keith Monroe, "How California's Abortion Law Isn't Working," *The New York Times Magazine*, December 29, 1968. See also AVS, *The Case For Voluntary Sterilization*, p. 9.

and the Spanish-speaking women: in a recent three-year period, 79 percent of New York City's abortion deaths occurred among black and Puerto Rican women; the abortion death rate was 4.7 times as high for Puerto Rican women, and 8 times as high for black women, as for their white sisters.[24] It is obvious that poor women have almost no access to information about legal or safe illegal abortion sources, to friendly doctors who do abortions, or to the money to pay the exorbitant charges involved.

$300 to $1,000 is the going rate, regardless of "legality," for a procedure that ought not cost more than $25, and so might just as easily be free. One either pays it out in bits and pieces to the various psychiatrists, obstetricians, and hospitals involved in the Byzantine process of obtaining the coveted prize of a legal abortion, or else pays a lump sum of several hundred dollars to an illegal abortionist. One almost pays the illegal practitioner more willingly, knowing that fewer people will be prying into and keeping records of this private decision, and that the outlaw must pay off the cops and his lawyers in order to stay in business. Still, it is the woman (and often enough her man) who must in the final analysis pay the 2,000 percent markup. And forget asking Blue Cross to repay you, even if your operation was "legal."

If something goes wrong with a fifty-dollar—or a five-hundred-dollar—illegal abortion, and a woman lands in the hospital, as much as $10,000 worth of hospital facilities, time, and personnel may be devoted to saving her from death.[25] When we hear complaints that legal abortion will overtax our already beleaguered medical resources, we must remember how many women could safely be aborted for $10,000—and on an outpatient basis at that. The tax money that pays for the medical heroics to save poor women could be used instead to set up clinics to care for *all* women who want abortions.

24. Edwin M. Gold, *et al.*, "Therapeutic Abortions in New York City: A 20-Year Review," *American Journal of Public Health*, LV, July 1965, pp. 964–972.
25. Personal communication from Bernard N. Nathanson, M.D.

What about sterility? Is it often caused by badly performed abortions? While some East European countries report a certain incidence of post-abortion sterility, one's capacity for recovery even after simple operations depends to a major extent on one's general health; and the average woman in these countries is not in the best physical condition when she has her abortion. The Kinsey researchers here found fewer than 3 percent of the women they studied reported any bad physical consequences from their abortions—even though most of them had been performed in the 1920's and 1930's and all but about 6 percent had been illegal.[26] It is interesting to speculate that some of the sterility we hear about already existed before the abortion and was falsely attributed to the abortion: not a few women rush to abortionists in understandable panic, even before knowing for sure whether they are really pregnant; and not a few abortionists take their money to perform unneeded operations.

HOW ABORTIONS ARE DONE

There are several tried-and-true methods of doing an abortion, some more suitable for early stages of pregnancy and some better used in the later stages.

Dilatation and curettage (D & C) is still the technique most commonly used in the United States by medically trained practitioners, whether their practice is legal or illegal. Outlaw abortionists will usually refuse to perform a D & C beyond the tenth or eleventh week of pregnancy, and so will doctors performing legal abortions in a hospital setting—although with the proper medical resources standing by it can sometimes be done as late as the fourteenth or fifteenth week. When a D & C is performed, a woman is administered a general or local anesthetic (if she is "legal" or lucky), her cervix is dilated with a graduated series of instruments, and her uterus is scraped with a surgical knife —a curette—which removes the products of conception.

26. Gebhard *et al., op. cit.,* p. 196.

The skill of the operator is important here, because a mis-handled curette can puncture the uterine wall and injure surrounding organs, or cause massive hemorrhage that can lead to death. The operator must also be sure to remove all fetal material; otherwise, what is left in the uterus can produce serious, sometimes deadly, infection. Still, the chief danger of this essentially minor procedure is from the anesthetic, to which the woman may have a violent reaction. This partly explains why some illegal abortionists do not administer anything stronger than aspirin or Darvon to their patients: they do not know a woman's medical history, have no access to emergency help if she does react, and so fear that she may die from the medication they would otherwise give her. Some, of course, also don't want her to be groggy, in case the premises are suddenly raided; some don't want to spend the money for effective medication; and some are not averse to witnessing her pain.

Despite their relative simplicity as surgery, D&C's do require the skill of a doctor for their safe performance; but, because practice in "legal" D & C's is hard to come by, a doctor who has lost his license because he has done thousands of successful abortions, illegally, may in fact be far more skilled than an OB affiliated with a "respectable" hospital (that is, one with a low abortion rate). When we get abortion laws repealed, perhaps crash courses will have to be given to medical students and veteran physicians by some of the skilled outcasts they now cut dead socially and professionally.

But another, simpler method, the uterine aspirator (the "vacuum" or "suction" technique), is now being used more and more by a few forward-looking illegal abortionists, some less hidebound U.S. hospitals, and many hospitals and clinics in those countries where abortion in early pregnancy is legal. The apparatus works on the same principle as a vacuum cleaner—although, as abortion activist Lana Phelan says, "Don't use your Hoover, ladies: it won't fit!" At the outset, the cervix needs to be dilated only slightly, thus reducing and sometimes even eliminating the need for anesthetic and its attendant risks. Then a tubular curette, with a hole in the side of its tip, is introduced into the uterus. The curette is attached to a tube, a vacuum pump, and a receptacle; a slight negative air pressure loosens the fetus, which is sucked through the hole and passes down the tube into the receptacle. The entire process takes about two minutes (as opposed to an average of twenty minutes for an uncomplicated D & C), and even when anesthetic is used the woman can "go under" and come out again in fifteen minutes or so. Although, like the D&C, the aspirator is usually used in the early stages of pregnancy (as well as to clean up after incomplete abortions), its relative safety and simplicity mean that it can be and is employed on pregnancies as late as sixteen weeks.[27] Less blood is lost than with a D & C, the smaller cervical dilation is less painful and traumatic, and there is less damage to the uterine wall and fewer complications.[28] And, perhaps most important of all, paraprofessionals can easily be trained to use it, freeing doctors to practice more complex and "interesting" kinds of medicine.

If the aspirator is such an improvement over the conventional D & C, why then is it not used more often in this country? The reluctance of doctors and hospitals here to adopt this method is sometimes attributed to general medical conservatism about new techniques of any kind; but this explains little. New pharmaceuticals and devices are adopted quite eagerly in most branches of medicine, especially when they do a job more quickly and safely than older methods, and especially when they can be used by trained non-physicians. Even the Pill was adopted rapidly, despite a decided lack of sufficient preliminary safety-testing.[29] But

27. Antonin Cernock, "Experience with Intrauterine Suction for Artificial Termination of Early Pregancy," a paper presented before the Second Conference on Fertility and Contraception, State University of New York at Buffalo, October 31–November 1, 1966.
28. Dorothea Kerslake and Donn Casey, "Abortion Induced by Means of the Uterine Aspirator," *Obstetrics and Gynecology*, XXX, July 1967, p. 41.
29. See, for example, Morton Mintz, *The Pill: An Alarming Report*, 1969, and

doctors are perhaps more loath to take on new methods of doing jobs they don't expecially want to do ("I went to med school to learn how to deliver babies, *not* how to do abortions!"), and many of them half-consciously want to keep the practice of abortion at a scarce, handicraft level rather than make it available on an efficient mass basis.

Then, too, a technique that can fairly simply be employed by a paraprofessional is no longer under the physician's control—although one would imagine that a doctor reluctant to perform such "dirty work" himself would be glad to turn over the task to someone else. In fact, this will have to happen when we get repeal, since there are not and will not be enough M.D.'s coming out of school to fill the demand for medical care in general, and the use of paramedical people for all sorts of simple procedures is on the increase throughout medicine: for example, nurses' aides now do many tasks that nurses used to perform, and nurses have taken over many of the doctors' routine duties.

The same observations can be made about physical facilities: many D & C's and most aspirator abortions can easily be done on an outpatient basis, in birth-control clinics within or easily accessible to a hospital, thus making this care more readily available to women who want it and freeing the more elaborate facilities of the hospitals' gynecological departments for really serious procedures.

There will always be some need for abortion in the later stages of pregnancy, and two major techniques exist now to handle these cases. One is hysterotomy, which is analogous to a Caesarean delivery: the woman is anesthetized, an abdominal incision is made, and the fetus is removed. This older method is rather serious surgery, and the scar left by the incision can weaken the uterus and create problems during later pregnancies. A newer method is the injection of a hypertonic solution of saline or glucose through the abdominal wall into the amniotic sac, after first withdraw-

Barbara Seaman, *The Doctors' Case Against the Pill* (New York: Peter Wyden, 1969).

ing some of the amniotic fluid. This instillation technique kills the fetus and induces labor in the pregnant woman; although a delicate procedure, it is not such a major one as hysterotomy, requires much less anesthetic, and leaves no uterine scar.[30] It complements the use of the aspirator in that it can be used at any stage of pregnancy from about the sixteenth week up to term. (It cannot safely be used earlier partly because the fetal "target" is too small.)

Besides these four major methods—two old, and two relatively new—some other ways of producing abortion are either covertly or openly being used. One of these is usually thought of as a contraceptive, but its mode of action may well be that of an abortifacient. This is the IUD. While popular literature usually claims that no one quite knows how IUD's work, there is good evidence that at least certain varieties prevent the uterine implantation of fertilized eggs and speed their passage out of the body.[31] Advertisements in the medical press for various types of IUD's always list "pregnancy" as one of the primary "counterindications" for inserting an IUD; most doctors and clinics insist that a woman be menstruating when she comes to them for a loop —explaining that her cervix is most dilated at that time and so insertion is easier.

But if a woman is asking for an IUD it is obvious that she isn't interested in being pregnant just then. In fact, some doctors and some clinics do quietly ignore this "counterindication" and insert an IUD anyway. There are ways of getting around medical people who don't ignore it, however, and *The Abortion Handbook for Responsible Women* describes these devious means in gross and vivid detail.[32] It is also interesting to note that several medical centers—such

30. J. J. Sciarra *et al.*, "Induction of Labor by the Intra-Amniotic Instillation of Hypertonic Solutions," *Bulletin of the Sloane Hospital for Women*, X, Summer 1964.
31. "Loop Found to Interfere in Blastocyst Implantations," *Ob. Gyn. News*, IV, September 15, 1969, p. 46.
32. Patricia T. Maginnis and Lana Clarke Phelan, *The Abortion Handbook for Responsible Women* (North Hollywood: Contact Books, 1969), pp. 143-149.

as Brooklyn's Downstate [in New York]—are training nurse-midwives to insert loops for contraceptive purposes; these paraprofessionals may be able to use their skills more widely when the laws against abortion are repealed.

Another method that has some currency is the injection of massive doses of hormones shortly after possible conception has taken place—again producing a "spontaneous" abortion. This technique should not be confused with the hormone shots many doctors will administer to help speed up the arrival of an abnormally late period in a worried but unpregnant patient. Some women falsely think they've had an abortion, when they begin to menstruate (and some doctors encourage this belief, and charge accordingly).

One physician who has been administering abortifacient shots at a major teaching hospital seems to think that he is preventing abortions (awful things!) and providing his patients with "contraception after the fact."[33] Other people don't want to listen to evidence that the IUD is probably an abortifacient; and the "morning-after" pill, now being worked on so hopefully by the Swedes and others, is often listed as a new "contraceptive." The point of all this is that even many well-meaning medical people are scared of the idea of abortion and don't like to use that taboo word for anything *they* are involved in. Although it is always sad when people are afraid to give things the right names, whether something "is" contraception or abortion is actually of little consequence in evaluating the result: the goal is the prevention of an unwanted birth, and whatever will achieve this aim safely and surely we can simply call "birth control" and be done with it.

In fact, the astute Dr. Garrett Hardin has pointed out that the most popular "contraceptive" measure of the future will probably be some kind of abortifacient: as he says, "It is one of the psychological weaknesses of contraception that it requires the rational anticipation of an abrogation of reason

33. Quoted in C. P. Gilmore, "Something Better than the Pill?" *The New York Times Magazine*, July 20, 1969, pp. 6ff.

—which affronts both the logician and the poet in us."[34]

The methods just described are more "acceptable" medically than several others that are employed by considerable numbers of desperate women. Some are fairly effective, but carry quite dangerous side-effects along with their efficacy. Folk methods, such as coat hangers, knitting needles, soap solutions, catheters, and other uterine irritants, have worked upon occasion, but far more often result in the serious injury or the death of both the fetus and the woman. The digital method—whereby a woman manipulates her own cervix with her finger until labor contractions begin and the fetus is expelled—has certainly worked for some women, but can take as long as five weeks to do the trick and may not work even then. California's intrepid Patricia Maginnis used to give classes in the digital method, more to illustrate what lengths the *status quo* drives us to than actually to recommend this technique, but she no longer conducts these classes. The detailed and almost incredible accounts she has received from women who aborted themselves this way leave one with an exhausted feeling that to succeed with the digital techinque you must be very patient, very determined, very acrobatic, and have both long fingers and a properly placed cervix even to begin. New non-handicraft methods *must* be developed for women to use on themselves.

What might be called an underground medical technique is the use of aminopterin—also known as methotrexate—a substance used in the treatment of blood disorders such as leukemia. When taken in massive doses at about the tenth week, it destroys the white blood cells of the fetus and "spontaneous" abortion results. Although at least one hematologist's wife has used this method on four or five different occasions, and is alive to tell the tale, aminopterin affects the pregnant woman's white blood cells, too, leaving her disastrously susceptible to any passing infection. Ami-

34. "The History and Future of Birth Control," *Perspectives in Biology and Medicine,* Vol. X, No. 1, Autumn 1966.

nopterin is not recommended to those who value their health.

GETTING AN ABORTION—BY HOOK OR BY CROOK

These are some of the technical aspects of abortion—but how does one actually obtain the prize of a safe one? Some illegal ones, when they are done by experienced, skilled doctors, are quite safe, and the well-informed, well-heeled woman who carefully comparison-shops the alternatives she may hear of through friends, can often find one. She may consult one of the referral services now burgeoning across the United States, or she may go to some foreign country where the practice (if not always the law) is more accepting of reality than in America: Mexico or Japan if she is from the West, Puerto Rico, England, or (the newest) eastern Europe if she is from the East. Many women, however, distraught and all too aware that time is of the essence, run to the first source they hear of, fearful that they will find nothing better if they ask around (and understandably fearful *of* asking around). Nancy Howell Lee found that even the highly intelligent, well-educated woman whose abortion quests she studied, tended to do exactly this, often with tragic results.[35]

A tiny number of other women with courage, knowledge, cash, and connections, are able to get "legal" abortions by playing games (usually psychiatric) with hospital committees. These games are pretty much the same in all fifty states; whether or not a state has "reformed" its abortion laws, it is the hospitals that differ: some will do "rubella" [German measles] abortions, some "suicide" abortions, some both—but none do as many as they could, even under present law.

Those few states that have "reformed" their abortion laws (ten, at this writing) have merely codified and institutionalized the unspoken definition of women as creatures too feebleminded to decide for themselves that they want an

35. *The Search for an Abortionist* (Chicago: University of Chicago Press, 1969).

abortion. Even for the few "good reasons" for which one can legally seek abortion, one must ask permission in *any* state, from a hospital panel of doctors (usually male), who ponder one's case and then decide Yes or No. They protect themselves and their hospital from scandal (by keeping the number of winners as small as possible), and from economic distress (by okaying several times as great a proportion of "therapeutic" abortions for prosperous women as for poor women, five times as many for whites as for blacks, and twenty-six times as many as for Puerto Ricans).[36]

Of course, a woman can't be *too* feebleminded or she will not have the information or the initiative to subject herself to what the English feminist Stella Browne once called "insolent inquisitions and ruinous financial charges."[37] By "granting" more hospital abortions—and by quietly providing more informal nonlegal ones out of hospital—to educated women with some money, the medical establishment in effect buys off some of the most articulate potential protestors against this form of oppression.

Any woman fortunate enough to be considered "deserving" of safe medical care may still be subjected to various indignities by the hospital staff and bureaucratic procedures. She may be placed in the maternity department, sometimes as near the nursery as possible so that a parade of nurses with babies is sure to pass by constantly; nurses may abuse her verbally and by action or inattention; her trip to surgery may be the cynosure of all eyes because the foot of her stretcher has a card on it reading "T.A." (for "therapeutic abortion") in large letters; and so on. The chances of this kind of treatment are greater if she is unmarried.

Even if she successfully completes the long journey to surgery, she is not home safe: someone in charge may cancel her "permission" for abortion as she is on the threshold

36. Gold *et al., op. cit.,* pp. 966, 968.
37. Quoted in *The Abortion Problem* (Proceedings of the Conference held under the auspices of the National Committee on Maternal Health, Inc., at the New York Academy of Medicine, June 19 and 20, 1942.) (Baltimore: Williams and Williams, 1944).

of release from her problem. A black woman in the New York City area who had contracted rubella during the first three months of her pregnancy applied successfully for a "therapeutic abortion" because of the high risk that the fetus would be deformed—an excellent and very respectable, though illegal, ground. She entered the hospital and was about to undergo surgery when a doctor in authority ordered that the operation not proceed. She later bore a child with multiple deformities of the senses and the brain, and she and her husband sued the hospital for damages. At this writing, the final disposition of *Stewart vs. Long Island College Hospital* is still pending.

In mid-1969, after a Washington, D.C., woman was told to leave D.C. General Hospital just as her "approved" operation was about to begin, the hospital and health officials' offices were picketed and sat-in on by a coalition of women's liberation groups, welfare women, and the Medical Committee for Human Rights; they demanded that such oppressive practices stop and that women be provided with the medical care they needed. One can foresee many similar active protests occurring everywhere as women begin to find their voices and band together to protect their own interests. It is important to remember, too, that the existence of abortion and sterilization committees (which also hamper *physicians'* right to practice medicine freely), the requiring of husband's or parent's consent, and other indignities visited upon women seeking legal abortions are *not* required by law, but are only "practices"—except in those few states with the dubious benefits of "reform," where they have been written into the new laws.

SOME ASSUMPTIONS AND PRESUMPTIONS OF THE LAW

Returning to the older laws, which forbid abortion except to preserve the woman's life, we must ask why they were instituted in the first place. One lawyer, Cyril C. Means, Jr., in tracing the history of the New York State anti-abortion law,[38] asserts that the origin of that 1828 law—and of the others similar to it that were enacted later in other states— lay in a wish to protect women from the grave dangers of nineteenth-century surgery, not in a wish to limit their control of their bodies. He argues that such laws are now unconstitutional because abortion is now safer than child- birth and so the original reason for the laws no longer exists.

Leaving aside for a moment these assumptions that women should be "protected" from choosing dangerous courses of action and that their rights depend upon the then-current state of technology, one may question whether protection was indeed the entire reason for abrogating women's old common-law right to abortion. It is very hard to believe that abortion was safer than childbirth in 1728, yet no law seemed necessary then. And at the same time the anti-abortion law was introduced in the New York State legislature, a similar bill was proposed that would have limi- ted *all* surgery to cases where the patient's life was endan- gered without it. Why was abortion dealt with separately, and why did the legislature pass the anti-abortion bill while defeating the similar bill limiting general surgery? Means offers the rather unsatisfying explanation that, unlike most surgery, abortion is sought under extreme social and eco- nomic pressure, which can—in the words of *The New York Times* (1863)—drive "thoughtless women . . . rash mortals into an undesirable eternity."[39]

Of course, we all want to see childbirth become as safe as possible, but what happens if it once again is made less risky than abortion? So anti-abortion laws then suddenly become "constitutional" again, or do women have the inalienable right to take calculated risks in the interest of self-determi- nation?

It is unfortunate, if not potentially disastrous, that the

---

38. "The Law of New York Concerning Abortion and the Status of the Foetus, 1664-1968: A Case of Cessation of Constitutionality," *New York Law Forum*, Vol. XIV, No. 3, Fall 1968, pp. 411-515.
39. *Ibid.*, quoted at p. 506.

1969 California Supreme Court decision overturning that state's pre-"reform" law was based in part on this "protective" view of the state's interest in regulating abortion. The *People vs. Belous* decision will provide an important precedent for the many other cases now challenging state abortion laws, and undoubtedly the fallacious argument that might be called "contingent constitutionality" will be used in each one.

This argument is closely linked philosophically with another one, that proposes some sort of time limit up to which abortion may be "allowed": up to twelve weeks, five months, six months, "quickening," "viability," or some other magic date after conception. Thus the woman and her fetus revert to state ownership after a particular point in time, even though such a point is impossible to determine: conception takes place sometime within about thirty-six hours of intercourse (whenever that was), so when is twelve weeks *after* conception? What is "quickening" but an old religious concept devised by men who wished to keep close track of their product's progress? Only the woman herself knows for sure when a fetus first moves in the uterus, and only she can decide if she believes some important point of no return has been reached beyond which she does not want an abortion. (The mental state of some unwillingly pregnant women is so disturbed, in fact, that they will deny that they *are* pregnant until "quickening" at last makes them realize that they are indeed carrying a fetus—one they emphatically do not want to carry to term.)

And what about "viability"? Again, women's right to abortion is curtailed by tying her to the current state of medicine: viability is usually defined, quite cavalierly and imprecisely, as the capacity of the fetus to survive outside the woman's body. For how long? With what heroic medical assistance and devices? Recent developments in technology now permit fetal surgery (not always on wanted fetuses) and will soon permit inovulation—the removal of a fertilized egg or of a fetus from one woman and its implantation in another—and even extrauterine gestation. How soon will it be before a twelve-week-old, or a one-week-old, fetus can be considered "viable"? Women's right to abort *cannot* hinge on the state of technology, and we are left with the inescapable conclusion that the only event in the sequence of pregnancy that can be assigned a specific time is birth itself, at the time that it occurs. All else is mystique and conjecture.

THE ACCELERATING MOVEMENT FOR CHANGE

Only a handful of courageous people dared to question the American abortion laws publicly before the late 1950's. Most of those who did could not conceive of the laws being abolished within the foreseeable future, and so they began to discuss and work for "reform" of the existing laws. In 1959, this tiny movement was given a certain respectability and new impetus by the American Law Institute, which brought forth a new model penal code; part of this code recommended a new set of abortion statutes that would allow a woman to have a legal abortion if she presented any of these three now-classic reasons: (1) evidence that her pregnancy resulted from rape or incest; (2) evidence that the fetus would develop into a seriously deformed child if brought to term; (3) evidence that continuation of the pregnancy would result in grave impairment of her own mental or physical health.

Each of these is, it goes without saying, a perfectly *sufficient* reason for any woman to want an abortion, but the three magic ALI grounds soon came to be taken as the *necessary* conditions for "justifiable" abortion. Every so often someone would suggest that young girls under a certain age, or women suffering significant "socioeconomic" hardships, also be eligible for abortion. A few voices even reminded the public that, compelling and dramatic though such grounds were, they applied to only a tiny percentage of the hordes of women who actually *had* illegal abortions every year simply because they didn't want the pregnancy to continue.

Respectable organizations and religious denominations, eminent individuals in medicine, law, and public life (most of them well-meaning men), and concerned writers on medical and social issues began to come out for abortion law "reform"; panels of "experts"—usually all-male and always carefully balanced between proponents and opponents of change—began to appear at a few public meetings and on one or two daring radio and TV programs; ALI-type bills began to be introduced in state legislatures; and in 1966, Colorado became the first state to pass a "reform" law—in the face of strenuous opposition from the Catholic hierarchy and other seats of reaction. The proponents of change always pictured women as victims—of rape, or of rubella, or of heart disease or mental illness—never as possible shapers of their own destinies.

Great things were expected of "reform": the illegal abortion racket would die, only wanted, healthy children would be born, and we would all be happy. Of course it didn't turn out like that: "reform" states were afraid of becoming "abortion mills" and their hospitals began, probably unconstitutionally, to refuse help to anyone who didn't come from their state or even from their city; the more prosperous women who used to fly to foreign parts or to New York City for illegal abortions could now stay closer to home and be attended by the family doctor, while poor women often didn't even know the new law existed, much less how to stretch it for their own purposes; city women tended to get more legal abortions than women served only by the smaller, more conservative town or rural hospitals; and we were hardly much happier.

People began to see the unsatisfying results of "reform" (most of it even less permissive than the ALI proposals) in Colorado and the other early states, such as California and North Carolina, and in such countries as England and Sweden; but citizens' groups still formed everywhere to press earnestly for "reform," hoping now that it might be "a step in the right direction"—toward outright repeal.

Some organizations began to make statements in support of repeal: the Humanists, the Unitarians, and the National Organization for Women led the way. But very few people yet realized that "reform" and repeal are actually fundamentally incompatible ideas—although in 1969 the prestigious Group for the Advancement of Psychiatry did issue a report, commendably entitled "The Right to Abortion: A Psychiatric View," in which they supported repeal and *opposed* "reform."

Proposals for "reform" are based on the notion that abortions must be regulated, meted out to deserving women under an elaborate set of rules designed to provide "safeguards against abuse." At least the old laws require only the simple, if vague, test of danger to life, whereas the new bills make it quite clear that a woman's own decision is meaningless without the "right" reasons, the concurrence of her family, and the approval of a bunch of strange medical men. Repeal is based on the quaint idea of *justice:* that abortion is a woman's right and that no one can veto her decision and compel her to bear a child against her will. All the excellent supporting reasons—improved health, lower birth and death rates, freer medical practice, the separation of church and state, happier families, sexual privacy, lower welfare expenditures—are only embroidery on the basic fabric: *woman's right to limit her own reproduction.*

It is *this* rationale that the new woman's movement has done so much to bring to the fore. Those who caution us to play down the women's-rights argument are only trying to put off the inevitable day when the society must face and eradicate the misogynistic roots of the present situation. And anyone who has spoken publicly about abortion from the feminist point of view knows all too well that it is *feminism*—not abortion—that is the really disturbing idea.

Remember the lesson Aileen Kraditor has drawn from

the women's suffrage movement: when arguments from *expediency* began to replace the earlier argument from *justice* as the basis for woman's right to vote, the movement's original breadth of force was lost, and the only gain it made *was* the vote.[40]

Despite all this, the words reform and liberalization and modernization all sound as if they must stand for good things, and many people still confuse them with *repeal:* after all, repeal *is* a kind of reform, in the broader sense. The media continue to get the two ideas mixed up and perpetuate the public's confusion. Public-opinion polls have repeatedly posed the wrong questions to their samples ("In what circumstances would you allow a woman to have an abortion?"), reinforcing the presumptuous notion that someone has a right to disallow a woman to choose, and getting the same tiny percentages "favoring liberalization," again and again. Usually they have not even offered repeal as an alternative choice. This is like asking, "Do you favor freeing a slave when his bondage is (1) injurious to his health, (2) . . . ?", instead of asking "Can you justify involuntary servitude under any conditions?" Some of those sophisticated in the ways of opinion research seem to find such direct questions "biased," and the older kind "objective"— but all language implies certain values, by its very nature, and old biases sometimes look like "objectivity" just because they're so familiar.

One in four American women has already expressed her opinion by actually getting an abortion, and they and the rest of the public have now begun to respond to better questions with the answers they really feel—the ones reflected in their actions. A Louis Harris poll conducted in the spring of 1969 showed that 64 percent of a nationwide sample believed that the decision on abortion should be a private one. Sixty percent of the Catholics in the sample agreed; the upheaval in the Church seems to be affecting Catholic lay

40. *Ideas of the Woman Suffrage Movement, 1890–1920*(New York: Columbia University Press, 1965).

people's views on abortion as well as on contraception.[41]
Modern Medicine magazine and the Ortho Pharmaceutical
Company took polls among physicians in 1969, and both
found a majority favoring repeal, with little difference between younger and older doctors. Previous surveys that
posed restrictive questions rarely came up with percentages
as large as 20 percent "favorable," say, to granting an abortion to a married woman with more children than she
wanted.

Thus the real question is not, "How can we justify abortion?" but, "How can we justify compulsory childbearing?"
The right questions will elicit real responses.

At last the change in expressed public opinion has begun
to have real effects: two repeal bills were introduced into
state legislatures in 1969, the first in New York State and the
second in Wisconsin. Organized grass-roots support for repeal has begun to grow at an exciting rate, especially among
the mass of women, who were never particularly excited
about "reform" because they realized that it had almost
nothing to do with their interests or with the situatons they
were likely to find themselves in. Women are now demanding to be heard in the public hearings and "expert" panels
on abortion from which they had earlier been excluded, and
it is making a difference. Legislators at a February 1969
New York State hearing, preparing to listen to the "expert"
testimony of fourteen men and a nun, were shocked when
women from repeal groups, NOW, and women's liberation
groups picketed and then disrupted the session, shouting,
"*We* are the real experts!" But many women everywhere
rejoiced, whether silently or vociferously. Since Redstockings' [a New York women's liberation group] "panel of
experts" openly related their own abortion experiences a
month later at a New York City church, similar panels of
women have begun to testify in many places.

Following the early lead of a few intrepid individuals on
the East and West Coasts who announced in public that

41. "Changing Morality: The Two Americas," *Time*, June 6, 1969, p. 27.

they would help women find abortions, more and more "above-ground" referral services have been set up across the country (see the section on Abortion Counseling Informaton in the Appendices of this book). Even some Planned Parenthood affiliates are now making quiet referrals, and some women's liberation groups have enlisted the cooperation of individual doctors and radical medical groups in trying to provide "first aid" to women in their localities. In fact, most people active in the abortion movement are very quickly faced with requests for referral information, and most begin to give it.

Many women, and some men, too, have been drawn into activism after getting help from someone in the movement. Thus the movement is strengthened by the addition of those who join it for the most telling reasons: the recognition of their own self-interest and of the need for *concerted* action for change. While the existence of open referral services provides direly needed help to women *now* and contributes to the public awareness that abortion is no longer a taboo subject, the services are at best a stop-gap measure that only aid the informed few while the movement struggles toward the real goal.

Test cases challenging the constitutionality of state abortion laws have recently been entered in several state and federal courts, some of them mounted on behalf of women's right to have abortions, some on behalf of physicians' right to practice medicine freely, and some on behalf of people's right to give abortion counseling; most of these are civil cases, and seek to upset the present danger-to-life laws. Although hopes are high that the cases will be decided with decisions striking down the law, those who believe they are now the *only* route to repeal, and that the intransigent legislatures can be forgotten, are on the wrong track.

While these cases are pending, the legislatures must be told to vote only for total repeal, and must be kept from passing *any* new legislation short of that. The passage of new "reform" bills would moot the cases now in court, since they are challenging only the existing laws—and sometimes not even all the relevant statutes at that. The *Belous* case in California was a criminal case (Dr. Leon Belous was charged with referral, under the old state law), but the decision did not overturn California's 1967 "reform" law. Had "reform" never been passed, California would now have repeal. New court actions now have to be mounted there to challenge *that* law. So the many states lucky enough to have escaped "reform," so far, have better prospects of achieving repeal through court action than do the small number of "reform" states.

The recent precedents on which many of the arguments in the test cases are based, however, do not offer women unmixed blessings. As was mentioned earlier, the *Belous* decision relied heavily on Means's argument that abortion laws became unconstitutional when abortion became safer than childbirth—an argument that retains a protective, paternalistic view of women. And in the recent *Vuitch* decision in the District of Columbia, Judge Gerhard Gesell hedged round his blow at the D.C. law with statements that a woman has a right to an abortion at least in the *early stages of pregnancy*, and with suggestions that Congress draft a new law that provides different regulations for the various phases of pregnancy. The impertinence of this "reasoning" has been explored earlier, too.

Proposals to place the question before the voters in referendums are also being heard—sometimes from legislators who do not want to deal with this "delicate" subject, prefer to pass the buck to the citizenry, and hope thereby to delay the awful day when repeal will actually come. The very idea of putting a civil-rights issue to a public vote is the highest form of presumption. Perhaps on the same ballot they should also ask whether the voters would like to keep the Bill of Rights or not.

There is no royal road to repeal and universal access to abortion: legislators balk; judges and physicians hem and haw; demonstrations and disruptions, however many consciousnesses they raise, change only a small part of the picture; and referral services provide good first aid, but only to a few and on a custom-made basis, when *what is needed is a mass solution*—which can come only when "legal barriers" no longer provide excuses for medical establishmentarians. All routes are imperfect, but all *must* be used if the goal—safe, readily available abortion for any woman who wants it—is to be achieved.

How Can We Achieve the Freedom to Limit Our Own Reproduction?

There are three major areas of society where the attack must be made: the legal framework, the superstructure of medical practices, and the infrastructure of public knowledge and attitudes. Here are some ideas for activities in each of these spheres:

LAW

1. Demand that your legislators repeal all laws limiting access to contraception, sterilization, or abortion, and that they actively oppose any measures that restrict that access in *any way*. This includes the repeal of the anti-abortion statutes masquerading under the name "reform." Repeal is analogous to abolition in the anti-slavery movement: it *is* only a beginning, but it is an absolutely necessary prerequisite that will clear the field for truly widespread change.
2. Demand positive legislation requiring money, personnel, facilities, and publicity for easily accessible birth-control services, as well as for research into new and better techniques of contraception and abortion.
3. Offer support, for those challenging present anti-birth-control laws in the courts, with your voice, your vote (where judges are elected), your pocketbook, or—if you are in an organization that can undertake court action—with *amicus curiae* briefs.

MEDICINE

1. Look at the provision of birth-control services in context: the necessity for a complete overhaul of the system of medical economics, practice, and delivery.

2. Get medical people to recognize their professional obligation to *serve* the public rather than to *control* its health.

3. Demand that hospitals and physicians abolish hospital abortion and sterilization committees and "quotas," provide more contraception and abortion services *now*, and base their reputations on how well they perform these public health functions—even if they consider such action civil disobedience. If everyone does it, who will arrest them? We need more doctors like Nathan Rappaport, William Jennings Bryan Henrie, J. Paul Shively, Leon Belous, and the late C. Lee Buxton.

4. Urge physicians, nurses, and other medical personnel to work actively for repeal and for new attitudes, both as citizens and within their medical organizations.

5. Work for the admission of more women into medicine and urge women doctors to take leading roles in fighting for repeal.

6. Work with radical medical groups, like the Medical Committee for Human Rights and the Student Health Organization, so that they will make birth-control care a keystone of their battle to change the whole medical system.

7. Insist that the best new methods of contraception and abortion be used, that paramedicals be trained to provide them, and that research be stepped up to discover still better and safer techniques—especially abortion methods that women can use themselves.

8. Insist on the humane treatment of all those seeking birth-control care, private and clinic patients alike, in hospitals, local clinics, and Planned Parenthood centers.

9. Urge that hospitals and government set up a network of local public birth-control clinics whose existence is widely and continuously publicized.

10. While these services should of course be available at no charge as quickly as possible, insist in the meantime that Blue Cross, Medicaid, and other college, private, and public health-insurance plans provide full coverage for pregnancy-related treatment to all policy-holders, regardless of their marital status.

11. Students: demand that college health centers offer as full a range of birth-control services as possible to all members of the campus community.

12. Demand that pregnancy tests be easily available from laboratories and that the results be reportable directly to the woman herself, without her having to use a doctor as a middle-man.

13. Demand that abortion after-care centers be set up now to provide checkups and treatment for women who have had illegal abortions.

PUBLIC ATTITUDES

Changing them through providing public information and through personal and group action:

1. Speak to others from your own experience with contraception and abortion, and supplement your testimony with accurate informaton about the larger picture: statistics, however dry they seem, are the aggregate of many personal experiences. Explore and discuss the possibilities for what *can* and should be in the future. Set all that you say in the larger context of women's liberation.

2. Demand that the media publicize completely and accurately the present birth-control situations, as well as the growing mass movements to change it and the gains that are made along the way. Constantly insist that they recognize and clarify, for instance, the difference between abortion law repeal and "reform."

3. Insist that the facts about and the prospects for birth control be thoroughly taught to everyone in school sex-education courses (and that "sex-role" instruction be abolished).

4. Demand to be heard at public hearings, panels, and in media presentations about abortion and other facets of birth control.

5. Support or set up organized or individual abortion and contraception referral services that provide good emergency information in a broad feminist context. Remember that public announcement of a service entails tremendous responsibility and takes up most of the time of those involved in it: you must keep up-to-date on the status of abortionists—their quality, location, prices, attitudes, whether they are on tap or "on vacation," and so on. Most services have problems with feedback: urge the women who come to you to report their experiences to you afterward, and to join the repeal movement. Their problem is *not* individual but social, and women have been programmed to expect and even to accept incredible treatment when they seek an abortion: outrageous prices, doctors who accompany unanesthetized D & C's with lectures on the woman's "morality," even sexual assaults (before *or* after the operation). This is particularly striking evidence of woman's oppressed mental state when one realizes that those who even know about and use referral services are by definition more well-informed and self-assertive than the average abortion-seeking woman. Encourage open protest and elicit sisterly feeling.

6. Pressure existing birth-control groups—like Planned Parenthood, with its feminist origins—to stop compromising, to realize the radical nature of what they are, or should be, doing, and to use their considerable resources to act *now*: by making abortion referrals, offering pregnancy tests, serving teenagers with contraceptive services, and providing abortion after-care. The existing network of clinics can be an ideal pilot project for the larger system that must be established.

7. Regardless of whether you believe in the present legislative system, write letters to legislators and other public figures demanding that they support radical changes *now*.

This may sound boring, but it does have an important impact; and remember: reactionaries and bigots write lots of letters. If you are literate, you should, too.

8. *Organize* to deal publicly with repressive religious, political, and medical forces, whether they are individuals or organizations, in as many different ways as you and your group can think of: angry letters, speeches, articles, books, and media appearances; pickets, sit-ins, and occupations of their premises; and on and on—always drawing attention to the misogynistic basis of the "reasoning" they present and countering it with the unassailable argument: justice for women.

"Planned Parenthood" and Birth Control: A Critical Aside [42]

Despite its feminist roots in the intrepid acts and thoughts of Margaret Sanger, Planned Parenthood has increasingly lost sight of its radical origins and narrowed its vision for the sake of short-term gains in respectability. Considering the tremendous odds facing the birth-control movement until recently, one can certainly understand these tactics, and even forgive them; but the long-term price was a sacrifice of the early pioneering and questioning spirit.

To begin with a significant semantic observation, Planned Parenthood was at first called the "Birth Control League," and its purpose was to provide wide access to "birth control" information and devices. It was interested in freeing women and in the good of the larger society. Over the strenuous opposition of Margaret Sanger herself, it somehow became "Planned Parenthood," and the movement began to call its concern "family planning." The implications of euphemism should be self-evident, but some of them need enumeration.

---

42. After completing this section, the author came across two excellent articles that also make some of these points, in slightly different ways: Kingsley Davis' "Population Policy: Will Current Programs Succeed?" *Science*, CLVIII, November 10, 1967, pp. 730–739, and Alice Rossi's "Abortion and Social Change," *Dissent*, XVI, July–August 1969, pp. 338–346.

"Family planning" and "planned parenthood" carry a distinct connotation that you should get busy and plan a family—plan to be a parent—and if you aren't doing it, why aren't you? (If you are not even part of a family—that is, if you're single—then perhaps you won't be welcome at all, as indeed you still are not at many of the affiliate clinics.) This focus on *family*, in its redundant support of attitudes that already saturate the culture, necessarily left little place for the interests of the individual woman or of the larger society.

In Planned Parenthood materials woman was, and is, portrayed as a Mother (as distinguished from a person with reproductive capacities who may or may not be affiliated with a family unit), and "Let us help you plan your next child" became a common phrase of invitation: even "Let us help you plan your *first* child" would be preferable, since it is the arrival of the first child that forces the greatest alteration in the lives of most women and most couples. In any case, the emphasis is on "accepting" the "next child," when women's programmed fatalism hardly needs such reinforcement.

The exclusive emphasis on "private" *family* decisions also pretends that these individual acts somehow do not aggregate into a social act of tremendous importance, and that each family should be as large as its own private financial and psychological resources can support, with no thought given to the far more extensive social resources that must support the large families of the prosperous and the (presumably) small families of the poor.

If the old words and the old broad-gauge attitudes had been retained, several now-embarrassing problems might not have arisen. Americans now have by far the highest "ideal" of family size in the western world: four children; and, as you might guess, women have learned their lesson well and embrace the "ideal" in greater proportions than do men. If every country's population is to achieve a zero growth-rate—and this must happen soon, regardless of the more equitable economic systems we may and should devise—then nearly half of all women would have to remain childless if those who did bear children were to have the "ideal" four. Of course there are many reasons for this personally imperialistic American attitude, but the privatism officially encouraged by Planned Parenthood has surely been a major factor: only very recently have they officially recognized that perhaps America, like India and Peru, should slow down.

"Birth control" can easily mean, as it has throughout this essay, the entire panoply of methods that prevent the birth from occurring: contraception, sterilization, and abortion. But the desire of the early birth-control movement to prevent abortion (which in the pre-antibiotic era meant far more death and disability than it does today) led to an overblown emphasis on contraception as the *only* proper birth-control method, rather than as the most desirable, given the then-current state of technology. The fear of losing hard-won respectability through greater religious and political harrassment also contributed to this tactic, wherein abortion of any kind was not merely ignored but actively vilified. (Similar observations may be made about Planned Parenthood's attitude toward sterilization—at least until recent gingerly changes of policy were made.)

Thus the public began mistakenly to think that "birth control" = contraception, and that abortion was somehow the evil *opposite* of contraception rather than a *complement* to it.

Because of the long silence on what remedies should safely exist if contraception fails—or isn't used—and because of the emphasis on the woman as the accepting mother rather than on Sanger's feminist vision of woman as a free and separate individual, it took great wrenching and pulling for Planned Parenthood finally to emerge, late in 1968, with a statement somewhat grudgingly supporting abortion law repeal. One of the great worries that they share, ironically, with many of those who resist making abortion available to all women who want it, is that women who have free access to abortion will suddenly give up contraception and rush into doctor's offices clamoring for D & C's. Planned Parenthood's president, Dr. Alan Guttmacher, has expressed such a concern on repeated occasions. This fear may stem partly from an idea that women, after all, are not "planners" at heart (although contraception is one of the few areas in which females are not punished for displaying unfeminine rationality), and partly from an unacknowledged recognition that despite their "accepting, motherly instinct," women don't always want so much "family."

Ideally, of course, technologies must be developed that will require a decisive act only when one wishes to *invite* conception: only then can the phrase "planned parenthood" become more than a euphemistic mirage. Until that happens—and probably even after it happens—"birth control," in its real sense, is a perfectly good phrase. Let's use it.

Afterword

The technology of birth control, like all technology, is in itself value-free: *people* impute meaning to it; *people* determine the uses to which it will be put and the consequences of those uses. This is why women must enter actively into the process of defining the values that surround birth-control technology. Will new developments simply make us more efficient sex machines in a world of unchanged sexist domination? The old economy of work is beginning to give way to a new economy of relative leisure—at least for some people, in some countries. Will women now cease being instruments of production only to become equally passive instruments of diversion? Or will birth control help liberate us by freeing us, for the first time, to realize our full human potential and with it to change society?

Look into the developments in reproductive research that

are now on the horizon, such as prenatal sex-choice, [43]consider the implications, and let *your* voice be heard.

THE HOOKER

Ellen Strong

I think perhaps I ought to begin this chapter by saying that, based on my experiences, there is not as much difference between the hooker and the non-hooker as one might expect. In many ways the condition and dynamics of the hustler in American society parallels (in an exaggerated way, of course) the condition of women in general in this society. I intend to discuss several aspects of "the life," based on both personal experience as well as some philosophical concepts, but I think this basic premise should be kept in mind. There have been many books written which purport to deal with "the life," but none that I've come across which attempt to approach it from a radical orientation, whatever that really means. Perhaps I'm lucky; I had my radical training before becoming a hustler, so that even while involved in the drug, hustling, and homosexual life, I still was able to understand some of the dynamics of it. Of course, I could also turn that around and ask myself: if I knew so damned much, how the hell did I get involved? But that's a whole different issue, not terribly relevant to the question at hand.

American society has always been one of contradictions. This, I'm sure, is no great surprise to anyone. However, based as it is on the Calvinist code, it creates some glaring and rather painful consequences. In other cultures, years ago, the courtesan occupied a position that commanded

43. For a provocative but incomplete view of this topic, see Amitai Etzioni, "Sex Control, Science, and Society," *Science*, September 13, 1968, pp. 1107-1112.

respect, love, and adoration. She was even an integral part of many of the religious rites of the Greeks. Temples had their prostitutes, and one of the most beautiful sections of any Grecian city was that in which the homes of the wealthier courtesans stood. Whatever may be said about ancient Greece and their social and political system, at least they never attempted to make sex the forbidden, guilt-ridden subject it later became. Another interesting thing about the ancient courtesans was that they were more than sex merchants. They were educated, talented women, as well versed in all the arts as in the art of love. In the Eastern nations, too, the role of the courtesan was a much honored one. But enough history. Suffice it to say that in contemporary American society, due to the double standard of verbalized and behavioral values, the prostitute is forced into the societal definition and self-definition of a deviant.

As a result of woman's position in society, it is certainly understandable that the profession attracts a great many women who are hung-up, either economically, sociologically, or psychologically. Nor is the prostitute so difficult to understand, in terms of the input in our society. Open any so-called women's magazine, and one finds countless articles saying basically the same thing. Get what you can from a man and then "be nice" to him—but first, make sure that he's willing to provide you with those eminently desirable status symbols, ranging from the fur coat, ring, or necklace, to a box of chocolate-covered cherries. From the time a girl is old enough to go to school, she begins her education in the basic principles of hustling. Now there is certainly some conflict there, because on the one hand she is being taught, verbally, to value love, self-worth, pride, compassion, and humanness, while on the other hand she is receiving distinct messages from those around her (from parents on down through her favorite television personalities) that the really important goals are economic ascendancy and status acquisition, and that she, a female, can acquire all these things if she plays her hand right. So, in reality, all the hustler has done is to eliminate the flowery speeches and put things where they're really at. Without the games, she will trade what is regarded as a commodity anyway, for what she wants. If you doubt that sex is regarded as a commodity by more than just those who patronize the hustler, listen to any conversation among a group of men when they get together, and hear the way they discuss women. This sounds like a blanket indictment of all men, which is the danger in all generalizations, but I think it holds enough truth to justify the assertion. There still exists a widespread belief that a woman is little more than a receptacle for some man's "come." The most painful thing about that particular attitude is that many women believe it as well. Rather than sharing love and sex, we have been taught to use it. And use it we do, in a wide variety of ways. I wish I could put all the blame for the sorry state of American womanhood on men, but, unfortunately, it wouldn't be true. We have to share the blame. While it's true that this society still works on the double standard, we, as women, have accepted this standard. Using her body as a commodity, or medium of exchange, enables the man to feel more "masculine" and define himself by his "superiority" to his mate, but it also services a need in the woman. She is able to trade on her "fragility" (and let me say at this point that 99 percent of the women I have known, hustler and non-hustler, are about as fragile as a steel pole) and her sex to receive all those goodies she has been taught to want and value. If she ever should, for whatever reason, begin to assert herself and find it frightening, she can always retreat into her weak and delicate number and find some big, strong man to protect her. All the prostitute has done is eliminate the bullshit.

She demands payment for services rendered and also is able, if she is not too defensive and closed, to receive some occasional good feelings as well. She is perhaps best equipped, better than the sociologists, psychologists, etc., to accurately recount the sexual behavior scale of our society. I think that in the years I went from call girl to street-corner hustler, I learned more about human psychology than I could have had I gone to school for the next twenty years. There is something unquestionably real in that aspect of the man that the hustler sees. It's usually stripped of its public image, its defenses, its need to perform or to look good, and whatever other layers of phoniness are part of his public face. It's quite an experience to turn a trick with a particularly objectionable individual, then open the newspaper the next morning and read about what a pillar of the community and upstanding family man said creep is. This experience, multiplied by a couple of thousand, can do much toward giving one a worm's eye view of the world around one. Despite the fact that intellectually I knew, well before I began hustling, that the pillars of our society were pretty much rotten at the core, there is nothing like some field research to make that knowledge become visceral rather than cerebral. There's nothing like screwing (and I mean screwing, not making love to) one of the Establishment's leading lights, and hearing the hate and filth pour out of his mouth, to give one an insight into the basis of our revered society. The Big Lie is quite clear to the hooker; the almost unbridgeable gap between what is verbalized and what is practiced becomes painfully obvious. For myself, after hustling for four or five years, even with the help of drugs, I found it impossible to look at any man other than as a trick. That's probably one of the biggest reasons I was in the gay life for several years. It took quite some time and work after I'd left hustling and drugs to begin to develop respect for a man, or even to be able to look at sex as something other than a tool. I'm sure my experience is not unique or unusual.

I remember that at the beginning, when I was about sixteen or so, it seemed quite glamorous and exciting. In thinking back and trying to analyze for myself why this was so, or rather why I didn't experience more difficulty in making the transition from "respectable" young girl to call girl, I came up with a couple of things. It seems to me that all my life I had been receiving the double message I men-

tioned earlier—that sex was a beautiful thing and using it as
a commodity was a No-No, *but* that the trappings of respectability and status ascendancy were far more important
than the means used to achieve them. This may be in part
because of, rather than despite, my radical upbringing, in
the sense that I early knew that those who were most respected were far from being those who most deserved respect. But that's only part of it. The far larger part had to
do, for me, with the constant societal input, via the mass
media, of the virtue of achieving rather than the means used
to achieve. Again, open any magazine, look at any television
commercial, and that double message is clearly transmitted.
So, despite the fact that intellectually I accepted the verbal
message, on a deeper, more meaningful level, I bought the
visceral one.

And my early experience in "the life" confirmed it. The
tricks brought to the encounters their own needs to romanticize the experience and lend it an aura of glamour—which
fit my needs completely. I was a success. I was treated with
courtesy, respect, and tact. The money was discreetly left
for me under the vase, or in an envelope, or slipped into my
purse. The conversation was witty and intelligent. The atmosphere was elegance itself. It was easy to disregard the
sexual aspects of the encounters as being almost irrelevant.
In many cases they were. Many times what was really important was the illusion in which we both participated.

It was only later, when I needed the money more and
started really devoting time and effort to the job, that I
began to experience feelings of disgust and revulsion.
Again, there was no traumatic change. It happened gradually, as the tricks began to treat me with less of the romantic
overlay, and more as a commodity, that my visceral rationale began to crumble. Intellectually, I could probably
still defend and justify hustling. Emotionally, what happened is that I became so turned off that I could no longer
even enjoy sex in a non-hustling situation. As the hustling
began to get bad, I had developed a habit of turning off my

feelings so that in some way the experience didn't touch me. What began to happen after a while, however, was that I became unable to turn the feelings back *on* after I finished work. It was a total and complete drag.

Of course, what I did then was build up a new rationale that allowed me to become a homosexual for several years. I was still able to enjoy sex with women, although I couldn't with men, and, more important, I was still able to fill my needs to be loved and involved. Without that, I don't know what I would have done.

The double standard is a bitch. That old saw still holds true. A man can lie all night in the gutter, get up the next morning, shave, wash his face, and demand respect, but a fallen women is unredeemable. Nathaniel Hawthorne wasn't far wrong. That scarlet letter becomes part of your self-definition. In my head I recognized that the difference between myself and my trick in terms of degradation was non-existent. But somewhere in my gut I bought that value construct. The hooker catches shit from all ends. She provides a service made necessary by the inbred hypocrisies and contradictions of the System, and then is condemned by that same System for her behavior. I remember reading a short story by Guy de Maupassant many years ago when I was very young that made an indelible impression on me, and this was, mind you, years before I ever began hustling. The story was titled "Boule de Suif" (Ball of Fat) and, as I remember, it tells of a young girl who was riding a train with a group of strangers and who, when stopped by the gendarmes, allowed her body to be used in order to provide food and freedom for the other passengers. Needless to say, upon completion of her act of charity or what-have-you, she was totally ostracized by the others for the remainder of the trip. The story was somewhat melodramatic, and I was very young and impressionable, but somehow it stuck with me and still seems to be reflective of reality. Isn't that basically what happens in our culture today?

For a wide variety of reasons, all of which have been amply discussed by the psychologists and sociologists, our society refuses to deal with the underlying problems that cause the symptoms of prostitution, addiction, etc., but rather chooses to shake the finger of scorn at the symptom and its practitioner. Of course, it is far easier to condemn and look askance at the prostitute as a deviant than to seriously consider the many factors that make her trade a necessary and flourishing one. Perhaps it's my own insanity, but I see very little difference in practice between the hustler and a large number of non-hustling women. I do, however, see a great difference *morally* between the hooker and the shrew who opts for a home in suburbia and the whole status-ascendancy-via-acquisition number. The hooker definitely comes out on top.

As I write, I keep on thinking about my original goal for this article, which was to write about the hooker from a radical perspective. The hooker is a hell of a subject to write about from any perspective, really. Although I was one for many years, what keeps on going through my head is something to the effect that I must have a hell of a lot of heart to sit down and try to write about hustling, especially since it has been done before and will be done again far more completely and successfully than I am now doing in this article. However, each time I read the shit purporting to be case histories, sociological analyses, or what have you, there has always been something missing, like some frame of reference from which to examine the issue, some vantage point—some *politics*. I have this big thing about hating to sound pedantic and self-righteous; it's probably a result of going to too many political meetings, conferences, and conventions, and hearing lengthy speeches on "The Woman Question," "The Role of the Woman in American Society," "Male Chauvinism in the Radical Movement," and their ilk. What I have against these discussions is a little difficult to explain. I certainly believe there is male chauvinism in the radical, as well as every other, movement. I certainly believe that, being a product of this culture and this society, I myself have adopted a number of those attitudes, no matter how hard I may have tried not to. But, somehow, being looked upon as a problem minority upsets me. I've never liked 90 percent white conferences that discussed "The Role of the Negro (Black, Third World, Chicano, etc.) in American Society," either. Nor all-student conclaves which analyze the role of the workers. Ad nauseum. I always sit in the audience, which is usually nowhere near a fifty-fifty break-down between men and women, and get the uncomfortable feeling that I'm being told how to feel and what to think by a group of men—with a token woman or so to make it look good—and that after it's over, we can all go back to being natural.

Yet my own analysis has to come greatly from my own personal experiences and insights. If anyone feels like extending what I say to a broader base, well and good, but I would rather speak for myself than for that generic term "hustler." And one final point I want to discuss is the radicalization (or nonradicalization, if you will) of the hustler or other self- and societally-defined deviants.

I remember when I was a junkie, the person I could never stomach was the ex-junkie. This wasn't, as might first be assumed, because he had "cleaned up" and was therefore a confrontation to me to do likewise, but rather because he seemed to embody all that I most hated in this society. He became "Super Clean." He'd seen the light, and now out-Puritaned the Puritans. The same is true, unfortunately, of the ex-hustler. At first I thought that the easiest group of people to radicalize would be those who had really had a worm's eye view of the bullshit that is handed down to us as gospel. After all, who has a better view of society as it really is than the junkie or the hustler? Sad, but it doesn't work that way. The double message again does its work. Rather than choosing to recognize and fight the contra-dictions and inequities of the society, the ex-hustler usually opts for acting out the verbalized behavioral code. Faced with the contradiction between what is spoken and what is practiced, she too often chooses to practice what is spoken, rather than to attempt to close the gap. Filled with guilt as we all were after any amount of time in "the life," we attempt to exorcise that guilt by shouldering the whole burden of blame, accepting the definition of "sick" or "deviant," and striving to become proper. This in the face of all the evidence that points to the need for radical change in our society.

I have discovered during the last four years in which I have been actively involved in working with ex-junkies and ex-hustlers that the few who have developed any radical consciousness are dynamite—they will stop at nothing to work for change—but that the huge mass is more truly representative of the conservative, oft-times reactionary spirit of our society than many "straight" people who have never had their exposure.

What does it all mean? I'm not sure. I don't have the answers. What I do have is a whole bunch of questions. Questions that must be answered by us, and soon. Questions that affect the entire direction of any movement for radical change and, obviously, are especially relevant to the fight for women's liberation. Questions that are essential to understanding the very nature of the struggle.

THE LEAST OF THESE: THE MINORITY WHOSE SCREAMS HAVEN'T YET BEEN HEARD

Gene Damon

Run, reader, right past this article, because most of you reading this will be women, and you are going to be sincerely concerned with women's rights, and you are going to be frightened when you hear what this is all about.

I am social anathema, even to you brave ones, for I am a

Lesbian and I represent an organization, The Daughters of Bilitis, Inc., working to give me, and the millions like me, the civil rights I don't have but intend to get. You see, society, or government, or current mores, or a church, none of these has the right to deny me my human rights, just because I share my home and bed with another woman.

In 1955, eight women met in the home of one of them, and formed the group now known as Daughters Of Bilitis (DOB). Their early ambitions suited that earlier time—a social group and the finding of a few answers to some of the problems Lesbians face in their daily lives. During the first year, from a membership low of six to a grand high of fifteen, they worked out the form of the organization. In a do-it-now-or-give-up effort, they rented a hall and began public discussions. They met their biggest adversary, *fear*, from the very people they wanted to help. Despite this, the discussion groups did flourish.

In October 1956, DOB began publishing its national magazine, *The Ladder*, with seventeen paid subscribers and a mailing list of two hundred professional people—charging $1.00 per year. *The Ladder*, the voice of the Lesbian in America, has grown in size and scope and is, today, a forty-eight page bi-monthly slick little magazine, containing nonfiction, fiction, poetry, news, personal reports through its letters column, book reviews, and a counselling column. Each issue reaches approximately 1,200 people. And with inflation it now costs $7.50 per year.

DOB, chartered during its first year of life as a nonprofit organization in the state of California, branched out into many arenas. Person-to-person work on a local level in California, and later in New York City, resulted in many local social, political, and religious communications that relieved conditions for Lesbians to some extent in those local areas. The organization conducted and assisted in many research projects during the year, dealing with Lesbianism from many aspects. It has maintained a library for research as well as recreation, from the beginning. Branching out, DOB leaders have been instrumental in founding organizations in connection with religious groups, most notably The Council On Religion And The Homosexual, in San Francisco.

Much of this work has been to obtain for Lesbians the sort of commonplace, ordinary, basic civil-rights most people, even disadvantaged heterosexual women, take for granted every day of their lives. There are a number of active chapters in the United States today.[1]

DOB has been the only boat for the exhausted and mistreated Lesbian to crawl onto, out of the flood of abuse and vituperative treatment handed out on a daily basis to anyone who is either daring or foolish enough to stand up and admit to homosexuality or, even accidentally, to be so branded. And it *is* a brand, ironically, in this "enlightened" age, a brand which carries public, private, social, job, and other discriminations of such idiotic proportions that the more intelligent tend to dismiss this sort of statement as impossible, as mere social pleading, with that popular phrase, "It can't happen here."

Well, it can and does happen here every day. For the crime (psychological, religious, social, or whatever) of preferring women in bed to men, a woman is automatically out of the human race . . . There are few exceptions to this, and those are the few women who are so set up monetarily and socially that they cannot be criticized. But since most people do not come out of silver gravy-servers, the majority of Lesbians have a rotten row to hoe. DOB leaders have felt this many times, when they have presented themselves for public viewing on television and radio shows, in front of college and university, and, yes, even high-school classes. . . It takes courage to march around with a picket sign, yes, but try walking around with one sometime favoring civil rights for homosexuals.

1. The largest and most active are the San Francisco (and National) group at 1005 Market Street, Room 208, San Francisco, California, 94103, and the New York City Chapter, at 141 Prince Street #2, New York, New York, 10012. The other chapters are in San Diego, and Los Angeles, with groups forming in Boston, Cleveland, Chicago, Denver, Miami, and Portland.

We have an unusual minority position. Some of the "true" ethnic minorities resent our considering ourselves a minority. For example, we do not share a common racial or a common religious background, nor, indeed, any common background except our one difference: we prefer our own sex, sexually and in every other way.

Even when we fight our way out of the load of Freudian and other psychoanalytic crap placed in our path, and even if we can altogether ignore the religious stigma attached to us without our consent, we have to live every day with the social stigma. Now telling yourself, intelligently, that such a stigma has its roots in the psychological and religious stigma does not ameliorate being loathed for something which is not, in fact, anyone else's business. You have, none of you, any more right to loathe me without knowing me, or anyone like me, without knowing her, than I have or you have to loathe a Jewish woman, a black woman, anyone.

Whether I do or do not conform to your standards of conduct is not your business, as long as I do not infringe on your right to exist, equally, freely. As a matter of fact, as we shall see, Lesbians tend to conform mightily in the hope, however futile, that if they are all upright and uptight, somehow they will be allowed to continue their second-class existence forever . . .

Many years ago, in an issue of *The Ladder*, a reader wrote to the effect that the only thing holding back the civil-rights movement of Lesbians was the many couples living alone together in "egoism à deux." Very sadly, it is as true today as it was then. We seldom march, seldom picket, but frequently do run away . . . to our shame, I might add. But a good look at our group condition, to some extent, explains this.

Steeped as we are, in an age and atmosphere of more and more learning in more and more fields, it is astonishing that so little accurate material is written about Lesbians. This is so even considering that women, in general, are ignored in all areas outside of entertainment, sexuality, and their "functions" of childbearing, homemaking, and husbandtending. There are hundreds of technical and scientific articles and many books are written, with almost no exceptions, by heterosexual men, and, with no exceptions, they are inadequate. There are also hundreds of subculture pornographic and pseudopornographic fiction and nonfiction studies, with no more bearing on homosexual women than these same materials have on heterosexual women.

When the Lesbian is discussed at all (as is almost always true, too, in discussions of heterosexual women), it is exclusively in terms of sexuality. It might even be disappointing to the audience to learn that this is one of the basic errors committed by researchers and pornographers alike.

First of all, Lesbians cannot be counted by any of the existing methods of statistical estimation, so long as these studies continue to be based on conscious sexual experience. In our male-oriented society we recognize that most men have some sexual outlet, that exceptions to this are extremely rare. In this same male-oriented society, with its double standards waving proudly in every arena, we still "accept" the erroneous premise that there are millions of women who have no sexual interests in life. These are the women who make up our vast sea of lifelong spinsters whose outward mannerisms and behavior quite rightly lead to the erroneous assumption that they are "sexless" beings. Most of the leaders of the DOB agree that countless hundreds of thousands of women who can never conform to Kinsey statistics, are still, whether expressed or not, Lesbians. We are also quick to agree that most of these women, faced with this announcement, would die of shock on the spot.

Our male-oriented society gives the right of sexuality and the expectations of it to the men. Therefore, it finds suggestible any two adult males living together for any length of time, unless they are quite noisily and openly heterosexual bachelors. On the other hand, anyone reading this article will be able to call to mind at once at least one example of the "New England Marriages" so common in every city and town: those households made up of two women who live together all of their lives in a social regime that apes traditional heterosexual marriage in all of its worst and best aspects. Quite bluntly, most of these women, freed of whatever inhibitions they might have, or possessed with something stronger in the way of sexual drive, would be overtly Lesbian. In other words, they would be among the women that this article is presumably limited to discussing.

Additionally, even among women who are quite consciously aware of their homosexuality, there is an enormous number who, in direct response to social pressure, do nothing about it—never, in fact, have more than a series of close friendships. The reasons for this basically fall into two categories. First, no sexual behavior outside of marriage is allowed in this country in "respectable" social groups. This is particularly felt in the single-women preserves: the teacher, the librarian, the research assistant, etc. It is even more strongly felt by those women who have "dared" to become lawyers, doctors, business executives, any sort of wheel in any field. There is no way of determining what the costs are, but surely some of these thousands of women suffer to some extent having to make the choice of no sex.

Saddest of all, there are those who know their homosexual leanings and reject them as unclean and unfit. They are victims of what must be the best and longest advertising campaign in history, simply that homosexuality is perverted, wrong, bad, evil, despicable, and every other loaded word you can conceive of.

These three groups—combined with the hidden thousands of homosexual couples who live alone, without any friends among their own kind, and who "pass" as heterosexual leftovers—far outnumber the visible portions of the homosexual society found in big city bars (whence we, unfortunately, obtain much of our "public" image).

I can make no claim to any scientific background, and nothing in this article in based on any such claim. My credentials are simply those of having been a Lesbian as long as I can consciously remember and having spent my adult life working in this field in an effort to obtain civil, social, moral, legal, religious . . . *total* rights for Lesbians. Beyond this, I have read, literally, hundreds of books and articles on the subject, both nonfiction and fiction. Ironically, while virtually nothing in nonfiction has dealt reasonably with the homosexual woman, a little of the fiction has. Again, in not only a male-oriented but a science-oriented society, art is excluded as a source of reference, however much it reflects, at any given period, life.

Recently a member of the New York Chapter of DOB was asked by a well-meaning heterosexual: "But what do Lesbians do in the daytime?" The overwhelming vicious-ness of a question like this will be lost on some of you, perhaps—but it is not lost on the Lesbian who has to reply patiently without losing her temper. (It might unsettle a few readers to learn that even the sexually oriented and unsym-pathetic studies of male homosexuals show that the homo-sexual male on the average has less sexual contact than the heterosexual male. But this is not really surprising when you consider that if something is not only illegal but liable to be punished by loss of life or limb [or only one's job, possessions, and money], it is a wee bit harder to come by in the marketplace than in the marriage bed.) Despite the heritage from Courbet's voluptuous "Sleepers," despite volumes of pornography and legitimate literature—all writ-ten by and for a male audience for the sexual inspiration of males—we have this heritage of a sexuality few of us can or even wish to live up to. The dull gray facts are so much less titillating. The extraordinary lack of extraordinary behavior in Lesbians. The commonplace day-by-day existence of most of them. The general lack of interest in their own civil rights.

From the beginning, DOB has had to battle the terror of "being on a mailing list." We have a security system that is so tight that I, as Editor of *The Ladder*, have no access to our mailing list; but there are still people, thousands of them, who are so afraid "Big Brother" will find out they are gay, that they run away from their only hope of getting freedom.

The one thing we can quite safely assume that is radically different in approach in this article from the others in this book is that we are dealing with a minority group that strives by most of its actions *not* to stir up the populace. We have been much closer to the fire and brimstone than most of you. You can be laughed at in public for advocating civil rights for white women, black women, for all women, but we can be fired and blackballed out of our jobs for life. We can be ostracized in a way that you cannot be even touched. We can be put in jail for our sexual preferences. Even the most respectable among us, who advocate nothing wilder than social and civil rights with the same obligations now granted automatically to heterosexuals, live with the daily danger of job loss. It is this fear that has most crippled the homophile community, both male and female—the constant fear of losing economic viability.

The Lesbian movement with a few exceptions concerns itself with obtaining the many restrictive, simple rights granted the heterosexual society—the right to marriage, divorce, protection of property, self-declaration without job loss or social discrimination—all very simple things taken for granted by heterosexual women (and some of them are striving to undo these things for themselves—especially in the area of marriage and divorce).

Certainly many of us are ardent feminists. Equally certainly many of the women's rights groups shun and fear Lesbians because of the "brand" they fear they will receive. It comes as no surprise whatever to the Lesbian civil-rights worker to find that she is, among some of these brave women's groups, once again, *persona non grata*.

Persecution of Lesbians is not limited to the social and employment arenas. Homosexual women in the Armed Forces have been treated with an exhaustive sadism since World War II. There is an enormous body of almost identical stories from women who have gone through the very special form of interrogation used by male officers on "suspects." The harrassment, entrapment, and mindwarping interrogation features filth and degradation to such a mindblowing extent, that once again it is the sort of thing that prompts the unknowing outsider to protest, "but surely that can't happen here." There is no way, of course, of determining the effect of this sort of thing on the mind of an eighteen- or nineteen-year-old girl, but we can guess.

The homophile movement in general consists of fifty or more organizations all over the U. S. and Canada. (There are several in England and the European countries as well.) Most of these groups are, ostensibly, mixed groups open to both male and female homosexuals and interested heterosexuals of both sexes. DOB is strictly a women's group, open to all women, twenty-one years of age and older, of whatever orientation. As you might expect, the organizations open to both male and female homosexuals practice the same sort of sexual denigration of women as does the heterosexual society at large. Women in these organizations are rare. When they *are* members, no matter how loyal, they seldom hold office, and if they do, it is, yes, secretary or treasurer. (As you might expect, these mixed groups are chaired by the men and "charred" by the women. Familiar story, ladies?) When you examine, however, the bond that should bind these people, the male and female homosexuals, it is simply intolerable to find the social prejudices reinforced here. The vast majority of these groups combine social and civil-rights work. (The only other solely Lesbian group in the United States is a local group in the San Francisco bay area, called Nova, which limits its activities to social events.)

In a recent issue of *The Ladder*, there appeared an article called "The Least Of These" which pointed out that the homosexual is the last totally persecuted minority group in the United States. This writer spoke of the Lesbian in this way:

We are, even more than the male homosexuals, the least of these. We are the Lesbians, the most hidden, the least noticed of any minority group. As homosexuals we share the dubious honor with the males of being the "last of the minority groups."

As Lesbians we are even lower in the sand hole; we are women (itself a majority/minority status) and we are Lesbians: the last half of the least noticed, most disadvantaged, minority.

NOTES OF A RADICAL LESBIAN

Martha Shelly

Lesbianism is one road to freedom—freedom from oppression by men.

To see Lesbianism in this context—as a mode of living neither better nor worse than others, as one which offers its own opportunities—one must abandon the notion that deviance from the norm arises from personal illnesses.

It is generally accepted that America is a "sick society." There is an inevitable corollary to this statement, which has not been generally accepted: that people within our society are all crippled by virtue of being forced to conform to certain norms. (Those who conform most easily can be seen as either the most healthy, because adaptable, or most sick, because least spirited.) Black people are struggling to free themselves, not only from white oppression, but from the roles of self-contempt that they have been forced to play. Women are struggling to liberate their minds from sick sexual roles. It is clear that the suffering, supposedly self-abasing black is not someone with a personal neurosis, but society's victim; and someone who has been forced to learn certain techniques for survival. Few people understand that the same is true of the self-abnegating passive housewife. Fewer still understand this truth about the homosexual.

These techniques of survival help us meet certain needs, at the price of others.

For women, as for other groups, there are several American norms. All of them have their rewards, and their penalties. The nice girl next door, virginal until her marriage— the Miss America type—is rewarded with community respect and respectability. She loses her individuality and her freedom, to become a toothpaste smile and a chastity belt. The career woman gains independence and a large margin of freedom—if she is willing to work twice as hard as a man for less pay, and if she can cope with emotional strains similar to those that beset the black intellectual surrounded by white colleagues. The starlet, call girl, or bunny, whose source of income is directly related to her image as a sex object, gains some financial independence and freedom from housework. She doesn't have to work as hard as the career woman, but she pays through psychological degradation as a sex object, and through the insecurity of knowing that her career, based on youthful good looks, is short-lived.

The Lesbian, through her ability to obtain love and sexual satisfaction from other women, is freed of dependence on men for love, sex, and money. She does not have to do menial chores for them (at least at home), nor cater to their egos, nor submit to hasty and inept sexual encounters. She is freed from fear of unwanted pregnancy and the pains of childbirth, and from the drudgery of child raising.

On the other hand, she pays three penalties. The rewards of child raising are denied her. This is a great loss for some women, but not for others. Few women abandon their children, as compared with the multitudes of men who abandon both wives and children. Few men take much interest in the process of child raising. One suspects that it might not be much fun for the average person, and so the men leave it to the women.

The Lesbian still must compete with men in the job market, facing the same job and salary discrimination as her straight sister.

Finally, she faces the most severe contempt and ridicule that society can heap on a woman.

When members of the Women's Liberation Movement picketed the 1968 Miss America pageant, the most terrible epithet heaped on our straight sisters was "Lesbian." The sisters faced hostile audiences who called them "commies," and "tramps," but some of them broke into tears when they were called Lesbians. When a woman showed up at a feminist meeting and announced that she was a Lesbian, many women avoided her. Others told her to keep her mouth shut, for fear that she would endanger the cause. They felt that men could be persuaded to accept some measure of equality for women—as long as these women would parade their devotion to heterosexuality and motherhood.

A woman who is totally independent of men—who obtains love, sex, and self-esteem from other women—is a terrible threat to male supremacy. She doesn't need them, and therefore they have less power over her.

I have met many, many feminists who were not Lesbians —but I have never met a Lesbian who was not a feminist. "Straight" women by the millions have been sold the belief that they must subordinate themselves to men, accept less pay for equal work, and do all the shitwork around the house. I have met straight women who would die to preserve their chains. I have never met a Lesbian who believed that she was innately less rational or capable than a man; who swallowed one word of the "woman's role" horseshit.

Lesbians, because they are not afraid of being abandoned by men, are less reluctant to express hostility toward the male class—the oppressors of women. Hostility toward your oppressor is healthy, but the guardians of modern morality, the psychiatrists, have interpreted this hostility as an illness, and they say this illness causes and is Lesbianism.

If hostility to men causes Lesbianism, then it seems to me that in a male-dominated society, Lesbianism is a sign of mental health.

The psychiatrists have also forgotten that Lesbianism involves love between women. Isn't love between equals healthier than sucking up to an oppressor? And when they claim we aren't capable of loving men, even if we want to —I would ask a straight man, in turn: are you capable of loving another man so deeply that you aren't afraid of his body or afraid to put your body in his hands? Are you really capable of loving women, or is your sexuality just another expression of your hostility? Is it an act of love or an act of conquest?

I do not mean to condemn all males. I have found some beautiful, loving men among the revolutionaries, among the hippies, and the male homosexuals. But the average man, including the average student male radical, wants a passive sex-object *cum* domestic *cum* baby nurse to clean up after him while he does all the fun things and bosses her around —while he plays either bigshot executive or Che Guevara —and he is my oppressor and my enemy.

Society has taught most Lesbians to believe they are sick, and has taught most straight women to despise and fear the Lesbian as a perverted, diseased creature. It has fostered the myth that Lesbians are ugly and turn to each other because they can't get that prize, that prince, a male! In this age of the new "sexual revolution," another myth has been fostered: the beautiful Lesbians who play games with each other on the screen for the titillation of heterosexual males. They are not seen as serious people in love, but as performers in the "let's try a new perversion" game.

Freud founded the myth of penis envy, and men have asked me "But what can two women do together?" As though a penis were the *sine qua non* of sexual pleasure! Man, we can do without it, and keep it going longer, too!

Women are afraid to be without a man's protection— because other men will assault them on the streets. And this is no accident, no aberration performed by a few lunatics. Assaults on women are no more an accident than are lynchings of blacks in Mississippi. Men have oppressed us, and like most oppressors, they hate the oppressed and fear their wrath. Watch a white man walking in Harlem and you will see what I mean. Look at the face of a man who has accidentally wandered into a Lesbian bar.

Men fear Lesbians because they are less dependent, and because their hostility is less controlled.

Straight women fear Lesbians because of the Lesbian inside them, because we represent an alternative. They fear us for the same reason that uptight middle-class people fear hip people. They are angry at us because we have a way out that they are afraid to take.

And what happens to the Lesbian under all this pressure? Many of my sisters, confused by the barrage of anti-gay propaganda, have spent years begging to be allowed to live. They have come begging because they believed they were psychic cripples, and that other people were healthy and had the moral right to judge them. Many have lived in silence, burying themselves in their careers, like name-changing Jews or blacks who passed for white. Many have retreated into an apolitical domesticity, concerning themselves only with the attempt to maintain a love relationship in a society which attemps to destroy love and replace it with consumer goods, and which attempts to completely destroy any form of love outside the monogamous marriage.

Because *Lesbian* has become such a vile epithet, we have been afraid to fight openly. We can lose our jobs; we have fewer civil rights than any other minority group. Because we have few family ties and no children, for the most part, we have been active in many causes, but always in secret, because our name contaminates any cause that we work for.

To the radical Lesbian, I say that we can no longer afford to fight for everyone else's cause while ignoring our own. Ours is a life-style born out of a sick society; so is everyone else's. Our kind of love is as valid as anyone else's. The revolution must be fought for us, too, not only for blacks, Indians, welfare mothers, grape pickers, SDS people, Puerto Ricans, or mine workers. We must have a revolution for *human rights*. If we are in a bag, it's as good as anyone else's bag.

Maybe after the revolution, people will be able to love each other regardless of skin color, ethnic origin, occupation, or type of genitals. But if that's going to happen, it will only happen because we make it happen—starting right now.

SEXUAL POLITICS (IN LITERATURE)

Kate Millett

I would ask her to prepare the bath for me. She would pretend to demur but she would do it just the same. One day, while I was seated in the tub soaping myself, I noticed that she had forgotten the towels. "Ida," I called, "bring me some towels!" She walked into the bathroom and handed me them. She had on a silk bathrobe and a pair of silk hose. As she stooped over the tub to put the towels on the rack her bathrobe slid open. I slid to my knees and buried my head in her muff. It happened so quickly that she didn't have time to rebel or even to pretend to rebel. In a moment I had her in the tub, stockings and all. I slipped the bathrobe off and threw it on the floor. I left the stockings on—it made her more lascivious looking, more the Cranach type. I lay back and pulled her on top of me. She was just like a bitch in heat, biting me all over, panting, gasping, wriggling like a worm on the hook. As we were drying ourselves she bent over and began nibbling at my prick. I sat on the edge of the tub and she kneeled at my feet gobbling it. After a while I made her stand up, bend over; then I let her have it from the rear. She had a small juicy cunt, which fitted me like a glove. I bit the nape of her neck, the lobes of her ears, the sensitive spot on her shoulder, and as I pulled away I left the mark of my teeth on her beautiful white ass. Not a word spoken.[1]

1. Henry Miller, *Sexus, The Rosy Crucifixion, vol. three.* (Tokyo: Keimeisha, undated pirated edition).

This colorful descriptive prose is taken from Henry Miller's celebrated *Sexus*, first published in Paris in the Forties, but outlawed from the sanitary shores of his native America until the Grove Press edition of 1965. The protagonist Val is recounting his seduction of Ida Verlaine, the wife of his friend Bill Woodruff. As an account of sexual passage, however, the excerpt has much in it of note beyond that merely biological activity which the narrator would call "fucking." Indeed, it is just this other content which gives the incident its value and character. First one must consider the circumstances and the context of the scene. Val has just met Bill Woodruff outside a theatre where Ida Verlaine is playing in Burlesque. After the rambling fashion of Miller's narrative this calls up the memory of the hero's sexual bouts with Ida ten years before, whereupon follow eleven pages of vivid reenactment.

As a friend of the family, Val is entitled to spend the night at the Woodruff house followed by breakfast in bed while husband Bill goes off to work. Val's device of extracting service from Ida is very important to the events which follow:

> She hated the thought of waiting on me in bed. She didn't do it for her husband and she couldn't see why she should do it for me. To take breakfast in bed was something I never did except at Woodruff's place. I did it expressly to annoy and humiliate her. [p. 248]

Miller has established the characterization of Ida even before this:

> Ida swallowed everything like a pythoness. She was heartless and insatiable. [p. 246] She was just exactly the way her name sounded—pretty, vain, theatrical, faithless, spoiled, pampered, petted. Beautiful as a Dresden doll, only she had raven tresses and a Javanese slant to her soul. If she had a soul at all! Lived entirely in the body, in her senses, her desires—and she directed the show, the body show, with her tyrannical little will which poor Woodruff translated as some monumental force of character. [p. 245]

Woodruff himself is given out as an uxorious fool: "The more he did for her the less she cared for him. She was a monster from head to toe." The narrator claims to be utterly immune to Ida's charms, but is subject to a coldly speculative curiosity:

> I just didn't give a fuck for her, as a person, though I often wondered what she might be like as a piece of fuck, so to speak. I wondered about it in a detached way, but somehow it got across to her, got under her skin. [p. 247]

In accord with one of the myths at the very heart of a Miller novel, the protagonist, who is always some version of the author himself, is sexually irresistible and potent to an almost mystic degree. It is therefore no very great surprise to the reader that Ida is now ripe for the picking. To return to the picking, then, and the passage quoted at length above. The whole scene reads very much like a series of stratagems, those aggressive on the part of the hero and those agreeable on the part of what custom forces us to designate as the heroine of the episode. His first maneuver is to coerce further service in the form of a demand for towels. This places Ida in the appropriate role of hostess and domestic.

The circumstance that Ida enters wearing a collapsible bathrobe and attired only in silk stockings is not only accommodating, but almost romancelike in flavor. It also fits in with the stereotypic clues set up before: "She was a lascivious bitch, frigid only because she had the heart of a whore" (p. 248). While the female reader might recall that one rarely wears stockings without the foundational assistance of a girdle or garter belt, it is rather more to the point to remember that classic masculine fantasy dictates as nudity's most appropriate single exception some gauzelike material, be it hosiery or underwear. This is borne out in the "art" and sex photography of the Forty-second Street variety as well as in the surrounding sea of pulp magazines.

Val makes his first move: "I slid to my knees and buried my head in her muff." The locution "muff" is significant because it is a clue to the reader that the ostensible humility of the action and the stance of petition it implies are not to be taken at face value. "Muff" is rendered in the colloquial of slang and carries the tone, implicit in the whole passage, of one male relating an exploit to another male in the masculine vocabulary with its point of view. Considerably more pertinent to the real tone of the action is the description which follows: "It happened so quickly she didn't have time to rebel or even to pretend to rebel." As the entire scene is actually a description not so much of intercourse, but of a certain kind of intercourse, or rather of intercourse in the service of power, "rebel" is a highly charged word. Val sees Ida already under his domination and is acting fast to forestall insubordination. The means of enslavement are to be her sensual need followed by her complete depersonalization in the relationship, completed with a rigorous control through humiliation, insult, and contempt.

The next remarkable event is that Val brings Ida into his element as it were, and places her in the distinctly ridiculous position of being in a bathtub with her clothes on. Again the language is significant of the tone, "I had her in the bathtub." The reader is also advised that credit should be given to the speaker for his speed and agility; Ida is swoshed into the tub in a trice. Now assuming all initiative he proceeds to divest his prey of her redundant bathrobe and throw it on the floor.

Now the virtues of stockings and nudity may be brought on for aesthetic delectation; they contribute to make Ida more "lascivious looking, more the Cranach type." The frail perfection of a Cranach nude had been mentioned earlier as Ida's comparable body type. The inspiration of juxtaposing the innocence and rarity of this image with the traditional "girlie" figure in silk stockings is an eminent bit of strategy. The word "lascivious" implies a deliberate sensuality and is depended upon a relish for the prurient and particularly for the degrading in sexual activity, which in its turn relies on the distinctly Puritanical conviction that sexuality is indeed dirty and faintly ridiculous. "Webster's defines "lascivious" as "wanton; lewd; lustful" or a "tendency to produce lewd emotions." The Cranach in question is most likely to be the delicate and rather morbid Eve of the Genesis Panel, now depreciated to a calendar girl.

Val now proceeds with a manner coolly self-assured and redolent of comfort: "I lay back and pulled her on top of me." What follows is purely subjective description. The hero has ceased to admire himself and is now lost in wonder at his effects. For the animal fireworks which ensue are Ida's, though produced by Pavlovian mechanism. Like the famous programmed dog, in fact "just like a bitch in heat," Ida responds to the protagonist's skilled manipulation with frenzied animalism. No evidence is ever offered to the reader of any such demoralizing failure of self-restraint in our hero; nor does his response ever degenerate to convulsions suitable to description in bestial terms. The implication is clearly one of steely self-composure contrasted to lower-life servility and insectlike vulnerability.

After the conventional manner of this order of description one position of intercourse must be followed in rapid succession with another less orthodox, and therefore of greater interest. Miller obliges the reader in need of accelerated stimulation with a quick instance of dorsal intercourse, preceded by a flitting interlude of fellatio. Rather more pertinent to the larger issues under investigation is the information that Ida is now so "hooked" that it is she who makes the first move: ". . . she bent over and began nibbling at my prick." The hero's "prick," now very center-stage, is still a hook and Ida metamorphosed into a very gullible fish. Aquatic imagery befits a bathroom scene.

Furthermore, positions are significantly reversed: "I sat on the edge of the tub and she kneeled at my feet gobbling it." The power nexus is clearly outlined. It remains only for the hero to coolly assert his victorious manipulation of what is now his object by the braggadocio of his final gesture, one of arrogant superordination: "After a while I made her stand up, bend over; then I let her have it from the rear."

What the reader is vicariously experiencing at this juncture is a nearly supernatural sense of power—should the reader be a male. For the passage is not only a vivacious and rather imaginative use of effect, circumstance, and detail to reproduce the excitations of sexual intercourse, it is just as obviously an account of masculine assertion of dominance over a docile, compliant, and rather unintelligent female. It is a case of sexual politics at the basic level of copulation.

Without question the most telling statement in the narrative is its last sentence: "Not a word spoken." Like the folk hero who never condescended to take off his hat, Val has accomplished the entire campaign, including its *coup de grâce*, without stooping to one word of human communication.

While still providing the sensual stimulation which we are to suppose is of such a preternatural order that Ida is utterly enslaved by it, the hero now moves to consolidate his position of power through a series of physical and emotional gestures of contempt. In answer to her question " '. . . you don't really like me, do you?' " he replies with studied insolence, " 'I like *this*,' said I giving her a stiff jab." His penis is now an instrument of chastisement, whereas Ida's genitalia are but the means of her humiliation.

The affair continues for several pages of diversified stimulation and likely fantasy from which two themes clearly emerge. The first is the hero's prowess and astonishing good luck in bed, the second and more relevant is the degree to which he is able to insult his partner. Each moment exalts him further and degrades her lower; a dazzling instance of the double standard. The figure of Ida Verlaine appeared to haunt Miller's imagination and she is so far still unfinished business. She has clearly not been humiliated enough and as an archetype of the shrewish and rebellious wife, as an example of the general frigidity and "uppityness" of the American female, she has not yet undergone a sufficient and exemplary punishment. It is not enough that the hero should discover her "whorish" nature and brng her to paroxysms of sensual capitulation, while congratulating himself on cuckolding her adulating husband. It remains still to expose and chastise her not only so the husband, a buddy, may have his revenge, but simply so that the proper status of male and female be made explicit. Here Miller's didactic nature intrudes and one is made to perceive the value of his frequent insistence that his is a deeply moral imagination.

The solution to Ida Verlaine appears in another of Miller's books, *Black Spring* of 1936.[2] Ida, here brusquely introduced as a "frigid son of a bitch" (p. 251), has been discovered at prostitution. Recalling her "heart of a whore" in the *Sexus* account, one is not surprised. Bill Woodruff's brilliant reaction when the news is passed along to him by another buddy is narrated at length and with obvious relish. The narrator, again a version of Miller, while recounting the following, chuckles over it as "cute":

> This night, however, he waited up for her and when she came sailing in, chipper, perky, a little lit up and cold as usual he pulled her up short with a "where were you to-night?" She tried pulling her usual yarn, of course. "Cut that," he said. "I want you to get your things off and tumble into bed." That made her sore. She mentioned in her roundabout way that she didn't want any of that business. "You don't feel in the mood for it, I suppose," says he, and then he adds:"That's fine because now I'm going to warm you up a bit." With that he up and ties her to the bedstead, gags her, and then goes for the razor strop. On the way to the bathroom, he grabs a bottle of mustard from the kitchen. He comes back with the razor strop and he belts the piss out of her. And after that he rubs the mustard into the raw welts. "That ought to keep you warm for to-night," he says. And so saying he makes her bend over and spread her legs apart. "Now," he says, "I'm going to pay you as usual," and taking a bill out of his pocket he crumbles it and then shoves it up her quim.[p. 253]

Miller's educational intentions in the passage are abun-

2. Henry Miller, *Black Spring* (Tokyo: Keimeisha, dated 1936), pirated edition. All page numbers refer to this edition.

dantly clear; it is an object lesson. Females who are frigid, e.g., not sexually compliant, should be beaten. Females who break the laws of marital fidelity must also be beaten, for the barter system of marriage (sex in return for security) may not be violated with outside trading. Rather more informative than this sober doctrine of the cave is the insight one gathers into Miller's own participation in the events he describes and its undeniably sadistic implication. This is closer to the sexual politic of the cock-pit than of the boudoir, but the latter often casts considerable light on the former.

"I have nothing in me," she said. "Do we go ahead?"

"Who knows," I said, "keep quiet."

And I could feel her beginning to come. The doubt in me had tipped her off, the adjuration to be quiet had thrown the bolt. She was a minute away, but she was on her way, and just as if one of her wily fingers had thrown some switch in me, I was gone like a bat and shaking hands with the Devil once more. Rare greed shone in her eyes, pleasure in her mouth, she was happy. I was ready to chase, I was gorged to throw the first spill, high on a choice, like some cat caught on two wires I was leaping back and forth, in separate runs for separate strokes, bringing spoils and secrets up to the Lord from the red mills, bearing messages of defeat back from that sad womb, and then I chose—ah, but there was time to change—I chose her cunt. It was no graveyard now, no warehouse, no, more like a chapel now, a modest decent place, but its walls were snug, its odor was green, there was a sweetness in those walls of stone. "That is what prison will be like for you," said a last effort of my inner tongue. "Stay here!" came a command from inside of me; except that I could feel the Devil's meal beneath, its fires were lifting through the floor, and I waited for the warmth to reach inside, to come up from the cellar below, to bring booze and heat up the licking tongues, I was up above a choice which would take me on one wind or another, and I had to give myself, I could not hold back, there was an explosion, furious, treacherous and hot as the gates of an icy slalom with the speed at my heels overtaking my nose. I had one of those splittings of a second where the senses fly out and there in that instant the itch reached into me and drew me out and I jammed up her

ass and came as if I'd been flung across the room. She let out
a cry of rage.[3]

The foregoing is a description of heterosexual sodomy
from Normal Mailer's *An American Dream.* The practice is
not only one of the book's primary attractions, it is so central to the action that one might even say the plot depended
on it. Mailer's hero, Stephen Rojack, has just finished murdering his wife and is now relieving his feelings by buggering his maid. The former occupation has achieved the rank
of a classic American fantasy, and two of our major novels
revolve about the event of a male murdering a female: Dreiser's *An American Tragedy* and Richard Wright's *Native
Son.* The second "improved" on the former by involving its
protagonist in the murder of two women, one white and
one black. Yet it is curious how no one, Wright included,
pays much heed to the second murder, that of a black servant woman named Mary, which is both more brutal and
more graphic. Dreiser did not identify with his murderer
but instead with the victim. It is pertinent to recall that he
designated the event a "tragedy," whereas Mailer has far
more ambiguously termed it a "dream." Wright did identify
with Bigger Thomas, but he did so for cogent reasons of
racial suffering and with an extremely intelligent understanding of those social forces in Bigger's life which had so
brutalized him as to make his crimes inevitable.

Mailer rather transparently identifies with his hero who
has little motive for the killing beyond the fact that he is
unable to "master" his mate by any means short of murder.
And the occasion of mastery is an explicable and clearly
sympathetic motive in Mailer's eyes. Rojack's immediate
provocation is a novel case of that antiquated posture known
as the outraged husband. Mrs. Rojack, to whom Mr. Rojack's many affairs are perfectly well known, has herself
found the temerity to advise him that since their separation
she too has indulged in extramarital associations. Moreover,

3. Norman Mailer, *An American Dream* (New York: Dial Press, 1964), pp. 45-46.
All page numbers will refer to this edition.

and here is where one must depend on the forceful role of sodomy in the book, she admits she has been enjoying this very activity as well with her new lovers. Now sodomy is a Specialty in which our hero takes personal pride. Though he boasts to her face that his mistresses far excel her in this performance, the notion that his wife might also commit sodomous adultery is evidently too severe a trial on his patience. The consequence of this final blow to his vanity, his sense of property and most material of all, his fancied masculine birthright of superordination, is that Rojack promptly strangles the upstart. But as Mrs. Rojack is that classic Celtic Sporting Woman one finds in books, it is not really easy work and Rojack is exhausted when he finishes. Yet, thereupon he experiences an epiphany of righteous joy and congratulates himself: "I was weary with a most honorable fatigue, and my flesh seemed new. I had not felt so nice since I was twelve. It seemed inconceivable at this instant that anything in life could fail to please"(p. 32).

It is time we got back to the maid.

Toying for an instant with the idea of simply murdering the maid as well as the mistress and rejoicing momentarily in his lately acquired supernatural powers, "I was ready to kill her easy as not, there was an agreeable balance in the thought that I was ready to kill anyone at this moment" (p. 42), Rojack decides instead to take her on. Three pages of sexual activity then intervene before a word is spoken, a detail repeatedly emphasized, and as the hero boasts, "It must have been five minutes before I chose to give her a kiss, but I took her mouth at last" (pp. 42-43). In doing so, he undertakes to absorb her soul, which is that of a German proletarian. It appears that Mr. Rojack's employee smells and it is chiefly through her odor that Rojack, a Harvard man, a college professor, a United States Congressman, a television personality, and the very recent widower of a rich woman comes upon the understanding outlined in the next statement:

But then, as abruptly as an arrest, a thin high constipated smell (a smell which spoke of rocks and grease and the sewer-damp of wet stones in poor European alleys) came needling its way out of her. She was hungry, and it could have spoiled my pleasure except that there was something intoxicating in the sheer narrow pitch of the smell, so strong, so stubborn, so private, it was a smell which could be mellowed only by the gift of furs and gems.[p. 43]

As her patron, Rojack is almost too repelled to continue: "it could have spoiled my pleasure." Then he decides that even this unworthy creature can serve him in some way: "I had a desire to skip the sea and mine the earth, a pure prong of desire to bugger, there was canny hard-packed evil in that butt, that I knew"(p. 44).

It is at this point that the first word is spoken; the servant resists the will of her master. But Ruta's "verboten" makes little impression on Rojack. He has convinced himself that her essence lies in her rectum and that it is a quality which might be convenient to him. As a newly arrived homicide, he is in immediate need of a bit of that canny lower-class self-preservation Ruta is presumed to contain. . . Furthermore, Rojack regards himself in the light of a moralist in search of wisdom and Ruta's anus can teach him evil. How evil resides in her bowels or why Ruta has a greater share of it than her master may appear difficult to explain, but many things are possible with our author.

In most of Mailer's fiction sexuality has such a mystical and metaphysical import that genitals acquire definite personalities. Ruta's "box" as Rojack refers to it, has very little to offer; nothing resides therein but "cold gasses from the womb and a storehouse of disappointments"(p. 44). In *An American Dream* sex is either a matter of class or a matter of nature. Ruta behaves like a guttersnipe: Deborah, the former Mrs. Rojack, like a cruel duchess. Cherry, the mistress Rojack later wins, has the virtues of nature, unavailable to poor Ruta, and excelling those of the privileged female who is now too dangerously insubordinate to stay alive. As the hero and a male, Rojack, of course, transcends such typology.

Finding more of Ruta's true serviceability to rely in her rectum, the hero disdains her vagina to continue rooting in her nether orifice. (Her name appears to be a cruel English pun on this: in German *"Rute,"* pronounced nearly the same as Ruta, refers both to the switch or birch of chastisement as well as to the penis, and perhaps more than mere linguistic coincidence is involved.) As her resistance renders her difficult to penetrate, Rojack hits upon the device of pulling her hair as an aid to his endeavors, noting with fastidious justification that it is dyed red: "I could feel the pain in her scalp strain like a crowbar the length of her body and push up the trap, and I was in, the quarter-inch more was gained, the rest was easy"(p. 44).

As a homicide of less than an hour's experience, Rojack hits on the glitteringly expedient rationale that in forcibly buggering his servant he is actually performing an act of patriotism because Ruta is a "Nazi." The reader may have some difficulty in accepting this; twenty-three years old and therefore a child during the war, it is extremely unlikely that Ruta is a fit subject for Rojack's instant justice . . . Rojack, a wizard at manipulative ethics, has arrived at what is—for him at any rate—a position of moral leverage.

Sodomy has a number of possible meanings in Rojack's mind: homosexuality (he confesses to Cherry that he has grave doubts about his suitability to heterosexual activity); a private and unorthodox species of sexuality at which he is an expert and over which he holds copyright (his motive in killing his wife); or forcible rape, which is an expression of contemptuous mastery. It is the last item in this series of associations which is reserved for Ruta.

Thoughout the rest of the passage Rojack entertains us with his contrasted impressions of Ruta's rectum, a "bank of pleasures," and her vagina, a "deserted warehouse, that empty tomb." But this ambidextrous virtuosity is not accomplished without certain misgivings. As one might expect, these are directed not at her pleasure, which is never the issue, but at Rojack himself. After all, he muses, her womb might contain "one poor flower growing in a gallery"—the hope of impregnation. It is for this reason, for having deprived her of the monumental aspiration of bearing his seed, a substance Rojack regards with reverential awe, that he feels obliged to advertise himself as a "great thief" (p. 45). . . Poor Ruta has missed the radiant opportunity of implantation by a higher power and he can only pity her in a hazy seignorial manner.

And magically, Ruta responds just as the relevant masculine fantasy would dictate. Her obsequious gratitude at being sodomized is outrageously gratuitous: "I do not know why you have trouble with your wife. You are absolutely a genius, Mr. Rojack" (p. 46). Accordingly, the final stages whereby this man has his will with his maid take place under the most cooperative and obliging conditions. Ruta now responds quite as masculine egotism might dictate: ". . . she was becoming mine as no woman ever had, she wanted to be part of my will" (p. 45). It would seem that she could want nothing better for herself, and at once her "feminine" and "true woman" instincts emerge and she acquires what her master relays as ". . . the taste of power in her eyes and mouth, that woman's look that the world is theirs" (p. 45). It is delusion of success most advantageous to her lord's purposes.

Sexual congress in a Mailer novel is always a matter of strenuous endeavor, rather like mountain climbing—a matter of straining after achievement. In this, as in so many ways, Mailer is authentically American. Rojack is presently doing very well at his cliff-face, but Ruta begins to waver. In the manner of a bearer to a rajah, she turns with guilty admission of possible failure "a little look of woe was on her face, a puckered fearful little nine-year-old afraid of her punishment, wishing to be good"(p. 45). In his vast composure, Rojack orders her to "keep quiet." Not only is he suspiciously more conscious than she of the state of her orgasm, he enjoys a complacent sadistic awareness of what "punishment" might ensue, if she isn't "good." The whole orgasm itself takes on elaborate configurations of the Lord and the Devil. The Devil is manifestly an anal force.

The chief function of this passage is to provide a vehicle for Rojack to commit his crime a second time in different circumstances. Given the often emphasized choice between the Devil (sodomy) and the Lord (procreation), or Death and Life, Rojack opts for Death a second time. Just as he refuses what we are asked to believe is a portentous existential opportunity to sweeten Ruta's womb with his magical semen (infallible in its power to bring about conception), so too does Rojack refuse the choice of acknowledging his crime, accepting responsibility for it, and going to prison.

After receiving his servant's congratulations on his dazzling performance, Rojack proceeds calmly to the next floor and throws his wife's body out of the window. He has elected to remain with the Devil and stay alive. Ruta has been a vessel of considerable utility. Through her, or rather through her "ass," the hero has made his major decision: to pass the murder off as an accident . . . In fact, Mailer's *An American Dream* is an exercise in how to kill your wife and be happy ever after.

The humanist convictions which underlie *Crime and Punishment* (the original and still the greatest study in what it is like to commit murder), may all go by the board. Both Dreiser and Dostoievsky gradually created in their murderers an acceptance of responsibilty for the violation of life which their actions had constituted and both transcend their crimes through atonement. Rojack has some singularity in being one of the first literary characters to get away with murder; he is surely the first hero as homicide to rejoice in his crime and never really lose his creator's support. Wright understood Bigger's crime while never condoning it and made of it a prototypic fable of life under a racist society. Mailer also appears to find in Rojack a symbolic figure whose crime is diagnostic of conditions in American society. But the condition appears to be simply an hostility between the sexes so considerable that it has reached the proportions of a war waged in terms of murder and sodomy. And Mailer is to be on the winning side, to which end he has created in Rojack the last warrior for a curious cause, none other than male supremacy. Rojack is a far cry from Wright's underdog of a Chicago slum, acting only through desperation in a novel that is both a plea for racial justice and a threatening vision of what may come to pass should the hope of justice fail. Rojack belongs to the oldest ruling class in the world, and like one of Faulkner's ancient retainers of a lost cause, he is making his stand on the preservation of a social hierarchy that sees itself as threatened with extinction. Mailer's *An American Dream* is a rallying cry for a sexual politic where diplomacy has failed and war is the last political resort of a ruling caste who feel their position in dread peril.

But while fate hangs in the balance, I should like to enter upon a short digression on the language of sexuality. In this article the word "sexuality" shall generally refer to sexual intercourse or related activity. Two ideas strike me—that the four-letter word derives from a puritanical tradition which is vigorously antisexual, seeing the act as dirty, etc. This in turn derives from a conviction that the female is sex and therefore both dirty and inferior to the intellectual and rational, and therefore masculine, "higher nature" of humanity. The error is not a matter of language but of attitude, and therefore I call this the semantics of sexuality, for semantics, the study of meaning, leads us to understand the motives language institutionalizes.

I recall James Joyce's dictum that the dynamic in literature is pornographic, basely utilitarian, and therefore not on the level of art. I disagree, for I see the function of true Erotica (writing which is pro-, not antisexual) as one not only permissible but worthy of encouragement and social approval, as its laudable and legitimate function is to increase sexual appetite just as culinary prose encourages other appetites. The East, in its customary wisdom, is finely aware of this. I also suggest that our criteria in judging works which deal in sexuality are not only feeble but slightly absurd. In our hurry either to condemn as "filth" or exalt as "naked honesty," we miss the point as to the book's persuasion on the issue of sex altogether. For our highly repressive and Puritan tradition has almost hopelessly confused sexuality with sadism, cruelty, and that which is in general inhumane and antisocial. This is a deplorable state of affairs. Nor did the pathology begin with Sade; he was merely its first and most cogent expositor. It has since taken on the aspect of a literary convention and a cultural fashion. It is partly toward this unfortunate habit of mind that my argument is directed, and which it will examine selectively through writers representative of a sexual hostility now grown into the condition of intellectual and emotional custom.

A few days later, when I met him near the docks, Armand ordered me to follow him. Almost without speaking, he took me to his room. With the same apparent scorn, he subjected me to his pleasure.

Dominated by his strength and age, I gave the work my utmost care. Crushed by the mass of flesh, which was devoid of the slightest spirituality, I experienced the giddiness of finally meeting the perfect brute, indifferent to my happiness. I discovered the sweetness that could be contained in a thick fleece on torso, belly and thighs and what force it could transmit. I finally let myself be buried in that stormy night. Out of gratitude or fear I placed a kiss on Armand's hairy arm.

"What's eating you? Are you nuts or someting?"

"I didn't do any harm."

I remained at his side in order to serve his nocturnal pleasure. When he went to bed, Armand whipped his leather belt from the loops of his trousers and made it snap. It was flogging an invisible victim, a shape of transparent flesh. The air bled. If he frightened me then, it was because of his powerlessness to be the Armand I see, who is heavy and mean. The snapping accompanied and supported him. His rage and despair at not being *him* made him tremble like a horse subdued by darkness, made him tremble more and more. He would not, however, have tolerated my living idly. He advised me to prowl around the station or the zoo and pick up customers. Knowing the terror inspired in by his person, he didn't deign to keep any eye on me. The money I earned I bought back intact.

This quotation, from Jean Genet's autobiographical novel, *The Thief's Journal*, is the first passage where the author's identification is with what it will be necessary to refer to here as the "female figure." Jean Genet is both male and female. Young, poor, a criminal and a beggar—he was female; the despised drag queen, the *maricone* (faggot), contemptible because the female partner of homosexual acts. Older, distinguished by fame, wealthy and secure, he became a male; though never ascending to the full elevation of the pimp or supermale. Sex assignment is not a matter of biological identity but of class or caste in the hierocratic state projected in Genet's novels. In the very perfection with which they ape and exaggerate the "masculine" and "feminine" of heterosexual society, his homosexual characters represent the deepest contemporty insight into its constitution and beliefs. Given that this homosexual caricature is grotesque, and Genet is fully aware of the morbidity of this pastiche, these homosexuals have unerringly penetrated to the essence of what heterosexual society imagines to be the character of "masculine" and "feminine," and thereby what contemporary thought takes to be the nature of male and female, and with it the proper relation of the sexes. Sartre's brilliant psychoanalytic biography of Jean Genet describes the sexual life of the pimps and queens, male and female figures in these terms:

> This is murder: submissive to a corpse, neglected, unnoticed, gazed at unmindfully and manipulated from behind, the girl queen is metamorphosed into a contemptible female object. She does not even have for the pimp the importance that the sadist attributes to his victim. The latter, though tortured and

4. Jean Genet, *The Thief's Journal*, trans. Bernard Frechtman (New York: Grove Press, 1964), p. 134.

humiliated, at least remains the focal point of her tormentor's concern. It is indeed she whom he wishes to reach, in her particularity, in the depths of her consciousness. But the fairy is only a receptacle, a vase, a spittoon, which one uses and thinks no more of and which one discards by the very use one makes of it. The pimp masturbates in her. At the very instant when an irresistible force knocks her down, turns her over and punctures her, a dizzying word swoops down upon her, a power hammer that strikes her as if she were a medal: "Encule!"[Faggot][5]

Sartre has given a description of what it is to be female as reflected in the mirror society of homosexuality. What then is it to be male? It is to be master, hero, brutal, and a pimp. Which is also to be irremediably stupid and cowardly. In the feudal relationship of male and female, pimp and queen, there is said to be an exchange of servitude for protection. Yet the pimp never protects his slave, but allows him/her to be beaten, betrayed, or even killed, responding only with ambiguous amusement. One may conclude, then, that only servitude is paid in the contract. One might be naturally curious to discover just what the drag queen does receive in return. The answer appears to lie only in the intensity of humiliation which constitutes identity in those who despise themselves. This, in turn, leads up to the reasons for such self-despair. With Genet they are quite explicit and he outlines them very clearly for us. A bastard, he was repudiated at birth and left at an orphanage; the double rejection of what can only be described as an error from inception. Adopted then by a family of narrow Morvan peasants, he was found stealing and sent to grow up in a children's prison. Entering there upon his last and final ostracism, he was subjected to forcible rape by older and stronger males. He had now achieved the lowest status in the world as he saw it; a perfection of opprobrium in being criminal, outlaw,

5. Jean-Paul Sartre, *Saint Genet: Actor and Martyr,* trans. Bernard Frechtman (New York: George Braziller, 1963), p. 125. In his footnote, Frechtman translates "Encule" as "one who gets buggered," but as English lacks such an expression he suggests "cocksucker" as the best equivalent of the insult.

and female. It remined only to study and refine his role, thus the wallowing in self-hatred which both Sartre and Genet describe as the "femininity" of the passive homosexual. He is feminine because ravished and subjected by the male; therefore he must study the slavish gestures of "femininity" that he may better exalt his master. As a criminal he is obliged to controvert every decency of the property-owning class not only through a life of larceny (material) but through one of betrayal (moral) as well. And as an outcast, his life's demeanor must be plotted both to imitate and to contradict every notion of the world beyond whose boundaries he lives in exile.

But having gone this far, having plunged himself this low in the scale of values, he further and carefully observes only that he may carefully and further desecrate them; Genet acquires the pride of the utterly abject. For such figures are also saints, and in the Barrio Chino of Barcelona as a young beggar and whore, Genet had attained this sanctity and the unshakeable self-respect of one who has truly nothing more to lose. Out of this sprang a wily urge to live. And for those who continue in downright ignominy, the will to live may very plausibly become the will to win. This whole cast of thought is generously supported by the French tradition wherein martyrdom is still the highest boon open to chivalrous imagination. The logic is one of mystic paradox, a Christian or Buddist asceticism, and as Sartre points out, it is a game where the loser wins.[6]

Genet's two great novels, *Our Lady of the Flowers* and *The Thief's Journal,* are tales of odium converted to grandeur. Together with the rest of his prose fiction they constitute Genet's painstaking exegesis of the barbarian vassalage of sexual orders, the power structure of "masculine" and "feminine" in a homosexual world of crime modeled with brutal frankness on the larger bourgeois heterosexual society, which is host to this parasitic existence.

But the explication is also a satire. By the insinuating

6. Sartre, *Saint Genet,* p. 124.

virtue of their deadpan earnestness, Genet's community of homosexuals call into ridicule the conventions they have so fervently adopted:

> As for slang Divine did not use it, any more than did her cronies, the other Nellys . . . Slang was for men. It was the male tongue. Like the language of men among the Caribees, it became a secondary sexual attribute. It was like the colored plumage of male birds, like the multi-colored silk garments which are the prerogatives of the warriors of the tribe. It was a crest and spurs. Everyone could understand it, but the only ones who could speak it were the men who at birth received as a gift the gestures, the carriage of the hips, legs and arms, the eyes, the chest, with which one can speak it. One day at one of our bars, when Mimosa ventured the following words in the course of a sentence " . . . his screwy stories . . . ," the men frowned. Someone said with a threat in his voice: "Broad acting tough."[7]

The virility of the pimp is a transparent egotism posing as strength. His "masculinity" is in fact the most specious of petty self-inflations and is systematically undermined by the true heroes of these adventures, the Queens. Though Genet is a great romantic and has created in Divine what is perhaps the last and possibly the most illustrious of those archetypal greathearted whores so dear to the French tradition, Genet is just as certainly a cold-blooded rationalist whose formidable analytic mind has fastened upon the most fundamental of society's arbitrary follies, its theory of sex as natural caste. One finds Genet's most pungent critique of sexual politics in the heterosexual system in his latest works for the theater, *The Blacks, The Balcony,* and *The Screens.*

What he has to tell this snug and pious enclave will hardly furnish it with such reassuring comfort as it has begun to feel the need of and takes as a balm from old retainers like Norman Mailer. Genet submits the entire social construct of "masculine" and "feminine" to a merciless scrutiny and concludes they are odious.

The Balcony is Genet's theory of revolution and counter-

7. Jean Genet. *Our Lady of the Flowers,* trans. Bernard Frechtman (New York: Grove Press, 1963).

revolution. The play is set in a brothel, whereby one may perceive the rigorous logic of the dramatist. Having studied human relationships in the world of pimp and faggot, Genet has come to understand how sexual caste supersedes all other forms of inegalitarian stratification: racial, political, or economic. *The Balcony* demonstrates the futility of all forms of revolution which preserve intact the basic unit of exploitation and oppression, that between the sexes, male and female, or any substitute for them. Taking the fundamental human connection, that of sexuality, to be the nuclear model of all the more elaborate social constructs growing out of it, he perceived that it is in itself not only hopelessly tainted but the very prototype of institutionalized inequality. Genet is convinced that in dividing humanity into two groups and appointing one to rule over the other by virtue of birthright, the social order has already established and ratified a system of oppression which will underlie and corrupt all other human relationships as well as every area of thought and experience.

The first scene, which takes place between a prostitute and a bishop, epitomizes the work much as it does the society it describes. The cleric holds power only through the myth of religion, itself dependent on the fallacy of sin, in turn conditional on the lie that the female is sexuality itself, and therefore an evil worthy of the condign punishment which is the Bishop's power. And so power circles around and around and around the hopeless mess we have made of sexuality. And money—for it is with money that the woman is purchased, and economic dependency is but another index of her bondage to a system whose coercive agents are not only mythical but actual. Delusions about sex foster delusions of power and both depend on the reification of woman.

That the Bishop is actually a gasman visiting the bordello's "chambers of illusions" so that he may, if only vicariously, partake of the power of the church, is itself a biting satire on the class system. Those males relegated to reading gas meters may still participate in the joys of mastery through the one human being any male can buy—the woman as whore. And the whore, one wonders, what can she buy? Nothing. Her "role" in the ritual theatre where sexual politic and social institution are so felicitously combined is merely to serve, to accommodate the ruling passions of her rentiers.

In the second scene, the whore is a thief and criminal (versions of Genet himself) so that a bank clerk may play at justice and morality. Her judge may order her whipped by a muscular executioner or grant her mercy in a transcendent imitation of the powers that be, powers reserved to other more fortunate males. The general of scene three, following his own notions of masculine majesty, converts his whore into his mount and plays at hero while her mouth bleeds from the bit. No matter which of the three leading roles of sinner, malefactor, or animal the male client may choose to mime his delusions of grandeur upon, the presence of the woman is utterly essential. To each masquerading male the female is a mirror in which he beholds himself. And the penultimate moment in his illusory but purchasable power fantasy is the moment when he as Bishop, Judge, or General "fucks" her as woman, as subject, as chattel.

The political wisdom implicit in Genet's statement in the play is that unless the ideology of real or fantasized virility is abandoned, unless the clinging to superordinance as birthright is finally foregone, all systems of oppression will continue to function simply by virtue of their logical and emotional mandate in the primary human situation. But, one might counter, what of the madame? As procuress, Irma, *The Balcony*'s able and dedicated administrator, may make money by selling other women, wherein it may be observed how no institution holds sway without collaborators and overseers. As Queen under the counterrevolution Irma may do nothing at all, for Queens do not rule. In fact, they do not even exist in themselves but die, as the Envoy graciously explains. Their function is to serve as figureheads and abstractions to males, just as Chantal, a talented former whore who moves for a moment toward human realization in the hope of the revolution, wavers, and is sold anew and converted into the sexual figurehead for the uprising when it becomes corrupt and betrays its radical ideals under the usual excuse of expediency. Thus, "in order to win" it adopts the demented consciousness of its opponent in a rotten recreation of all it had once stood against. In no time it has turned the rebellion into a suicidal carnival, an orgy of blood connected by the old phallic fantasy with "shoot and screw." Its totem is the ritual scapegoat of every army's beauty queen. When Chantal enters upon the nebulous territory of a primitive standard over whom males will tear each other apart, the irrelevant pretext projected as reward in a dog-eat-dog fight, the revolution passes irrevocably into counterrevolution.

Throughout *The Balcony* Genet explores the pathology of virility, the chimera of sexual congress as a paradigm of power over other human beings. He appears to be the only living male writer of first-class literary gifts to transcend the chauvinist myths of our era and contribute a useful critique of the heterosexual politic, pointing the way back to the true course of the sexual revolution, a path which must be explored if any meaningful social change is to come about. In Genet's analysis, it will be fundamentally impossible to change society without changing personality, as well as overturning institutions. Sexual personality as it has generally existed must undergo the most drastic overhaul.

If we are to be free at last, Genet proposes in the last scenes of the play, we must first break those chains of our own making through our blind acceptance of common ideas. The three great cages in which we are immured must be dismantled. The first is the potential power of the "Great Figures," the cleric, the judge, and the warrior, elements of myth which have enslaved consciousness in a coil of self-imposed absurdity. The second is the omnipotence of the police state, the only virtual power in a corrupt society, all other forms of coercion being largely psychological. Last, and most insidious of all, is the cage of sex, the cage in which all others are enclosed. For is not the totem of Police Chief George a six-foot, rubber phallus, a "prick of great stature"? And the old myth of sin and virtue, the myth of guilt and innocence, the myth of heroism and cowardice on which the Great Figures repose, old pillars of an old and decadent structure are also built on the sexual fallacy. (One is tempted to pun, phallacy.) As it is quite impossible to replace this corrupt and tottering edifice with the mirror of its depravity, *The Balcony*'s own bid for revolution inevitably fails, sours into the counterrevolution where the Grand Balcony, a first-class whorehouse, furnishes both costumes and actors for the new pseudo government.

Genet's play ends as it began.[8] Irma, turning out the lights informs us we may go home where all is falser than the theater's rites. The brothel will open again tomorrow for an identical ritual. The sounds of revolution begin again offstage, but unless the Police Chief is permanently imprisoned in his tomb and unless the new rebels have truly forsworn the customary idiocy of the old sexual politics, there will be no revolution. Sex is deep at the heart of our troubles, Genet is urging, and unless we eliminate the most pernicious of our systems of oppression, unless we go to the very center of the sexual politic and its sick delirium of power and violence, all our efforts at liberation will but land us again in the primordial stews.

8. One is tempted to comment upon how frequently in contemporary literature the circle presents itself as a figure of perfection. The symbol of an absurd closed-circuit, it is made use of in another first-rate play of our period, Ionesco's *The Bald Soprano*. There is much of the circular in Beckett, beyond question the greatest living writer in English. Unfortunately for this study, Beckett, in his brilliant obsession with the metaphysical, has transcended the question of sex altogether ["Perhaps I shall put the man and woman in the same story, there is so little difference between a man and a woman, between mine I mean."—*Malone Dies* (New York: Grove Press, 1956), p. 3].

iii

GO TELL IT IN THE

VALLEY:

CHANGING

CONSCIOUSNESS

RESISTANCES TO CONSCIOUSNESS

Irene Peslikis

Thinking that our man is the exception and, therefore, we are the exception among women.

Thinking that individual solutions are possible, that we don't need solidarity and a revolution for our liberation.

Thinking that women's liberation is therapy. This, whether or not you belong to the organization, implies that you and others can find individual solutions to problems, for this is the function of therapy. Furthermore, the statement expresses anti-woman sentiment by implying that when women get together to study and analyze their own experience it means they are sick but when Chinese peasants or Guatemalan guerillas get together and use the identical method they are revolutionary.

Thinking that some women are smart and some women are dumb. This prevents those women who think they're smart and those women who think they're dumb from talking to each other and uniting against a common oppressor.

Thinking that because we have an education privilege and can talk in abstracts we are somehow exempt from feeling oppression directly and talking about it honestly and, therefore, think of personal experience as something low on the ladder of values (class values).

Thinking that women consent to their own oppression (or that anyone does for that matter). This is a statement which puts the blame on the oppressed group rather than on the oppressor class which ultimately uses brute force to keep the oppressed where they are. It is an anti-women and anti-people statement.

Thinking that only institutions oppress women as opposed to other people. This implies that you have not identified your enemy, for institutions are only a tool of the oppressor. When the oppressor is stopped he can no longer maintain his tools and they are rendered useless. Present institutions and our feelings about them should be analyzed in order to understand what it is we want or don't want to use in the new society.

Thinking in terms of them and us. This implies that you are setting yourself off or apart from women (the people). In doing this you neglect to recognize your own oppression and your common interests with other people, as well as your stake in revolution.

Thinking that male supremacy is only a psychological privilege with "ego" benefits as opposed to a class privilege with sexual and economic benefits. The former implies a considerable amount of individual variation among men , therefore permitting you to find an individual solution to the problem.

Thinking that the relationships among men and women are already equal and thus immersing yourself in utopian fantasies of free love in spite of the fact that the objective conditions deny it. Love between men and women, free or unfree, is millennial, not real, and if we want it we will have to struggle for it.

Thinking you can educate the people. This implies that you are educated and you will get a revolution going by teaching other people what you know. Education does not bring on revolutions; but consciousness of our own oppression and struggle might. Unfortunately formal education and political consciousness do not usually coincide. Even formal education in Marxism-Leninism tends to make people think that they know more than they really know. When we think of what it is that politicizes people it is not so much books or ideas but experience.

WOMEN IN THE BLACK

LIBERATION MOVEMENT:

THREE VIEWS

DOUBLE JEOPARDY: TO BE BLACK AND FEMALE

Frances M. Beal (New York Coordinator: SNCC
Black Women's Liberation Committee)

In attempting to analyze the situation of the black woman
in America, one crashes abruptly into a solid wall of grave
misconceptions, outright distortions of fact, and defensive
attitudes on the part of many. The System of capitalism (and
its afterbirth—racism) under which we all live, has attempted by many devious ways and means to destroy the
humanity of all people, and particularly the humanity of
black people. This has meant an outrageous assault on every
black man, woman, and child who resides in the United
States.

In keeping with its goal of destroying the black race's will
to resist its subjugation, capitalism found it necessary to
create a situation where the black man found it impossible
to find meaningful or productive employment. More often
than not, he couldn't find work of any kind. And the black

woman, likewise, was manipulated by the System, economically exploited and physically assaulted. She could often find work in the white man's kitchen, however, and sometimes became the sole breadwinner of the family. This predicament has led to many psychological problems on the part of both man and woman and has contributed to the turmoil in the black family structure.

Unfortunately, neither the black man nor the black woman understood the true nature of the forces working upon them. Many black women tended to accept the capitalist evaluation of manhood and womanhood and believed, in fact, that black men were shiftless and lazy; otherwise they would get a job and support their families as they ought to. Personal relationships between black men and women were thus torn asunder and one result has been the separation of man from wife, mother from child, etc.

America has defined the roles to which each individual should subscribe. It has defined "manhood" in terms of its own interests and "femininity" likewise. Therefore, an individual who has a good job, makes a lot of money, and drives a Cadillac is a real "man," and conversely, an individual who is lacking in these "qualities" is less of a man. The advertising media in this country continuously informs the American male of his need for indispensable signs of his virility— the brand of cigarettes that cowboys prefer, the whisky that has a masculine tang, or the label of the jock strap that athletes wear.

The ideal model that is projected for a woman is to be surrounded by hypocritical homage and estranged from all real work, spending idle hours primping and preening, obsessed with conspicuous consumption, and limiting life's functions to simply a sex role. We unqualitatively reject these respective models. A woman who stays at home, caring for children and the house, leads an extremely sterile existence. She must lead her entire life as a satellite to her mate. He goes out into society and brings back a little piece of the world for her. His interests and his understanding of the world become her own and she cannot develop herself as an individual, having been reduced to only a biological function. This kind of woman leads a parasitic existence that can aptly be described as "legalized prostitution."

Furthermore, it is idle dreaming to think of black women simply caring for their homes and children like the middle-class white model. Most black women have to work to help house, feed, and clothe their families. Black women make up a substantial percentage of the black working force and this is true for the poorest black family as well as the so-called "middle-class" family.

Black women were never afforded any such phony luxuries. Though we have been browbeaten with this white image, the reality of the degrading and dehumanizing jobs that were relegated to us quickly dissipated this mirage of womanhood. The following excerpts from a speech that Sojourner Truth made at a Women's Rights Convention in the nineteenth century show us how misleading and incomplete a life this model represents for us:

> . . . Well, chilern whar dar is so much racket dar must be something out o'kilter. I tink dat 'twixt de niggers of de Souf and de women at de Norf all a talkin' 'bout rights, de white men will be in a fix pretty soon. But what's all dis here talkin' 'bout? Dat man ober dar say dat women needs to be helped into carriages, and lifted ober ditches, and to have de best place every whar. Nobody ever help me into carriages, or ober mud puddles, or gives me any best places . . . and ar'nt I a woman? Look at me! Look at my arm! . . . I have plowed, and planted, and gathered into barns, and no man could head me—and ar'nt I a woman? I could work as much as a man (when I could get it), and bear de lash as well—and ar'nt I a woman? I have borne five chilern and I seen 'em mos' all sold off into slavery, and when I cried out with a mother's grief, none but Jesus heard— and ar'nt I a woman?

Unfortunately, there seems to be some confusion in the Movement today as to who has been oppressing whom. Since the advent of Black Power, the black male has exerted a more prominent leadership role in our struggle for justice in this country. He sees the System for what it really is, for the most part, but where he rejects its values and mores on many issues, when it comes to women, he seems to take his guidelines from the pages of the *Ladies' Home Journal.* Certain black men are maintaining that they have been castrated by society but that black women somehow escaped this persecution and even contributed to this emasculation.

Let me state here and now that the black woman in America can justly be described as a "slave of a slave." When the black man in America was reduced to such an abject state, the black woman had no protector and was used and is still being used in some cases as the scapegoat for the evils that this horrendous System has perpetrated on black men. Her physical image has been maliciously maligned; she has been sexually assaulted and abused by the white colonizer; she has suffered the worse kind of economic exploitation, having been forced to serve as the white woman's maid and wet nurse for white offspring while her own children were starving and neglected. It is the depth of degradation to be socially manipulated, physically raped, used to undermine your own household—and to be powerless to reverse this syndrome.

It is true that our husbands, fathers, brothers, and sons have been emasculated, lynched, and brutalized. They have suffered from the cruellest assault of mankind that the world has ever known. However, it is a gross distortion of fact to state that black women have oppressed black men. The capitalist System found it expedient to oppress them and proceeded to do so without consultation or the signing of any agreements with black women.

It must also be pointed out at this time, that black women are not resentful of the rise to power of black men. We welcome it. We see in it the eventual liberation of all black people from this oppressive System of capitalism. Nevertheless, this does not mean that you have to negate one for the other. This kind of thinking is a product of miseducation; that it's either *X* or it's *Y*. It is fallacious reasoning that in order for the black man to be strong, the black woman has to be weak.

Those who are exerting their "manhood" by telling black women to step back into a submissive role are assuming a counterrevolutionary position. Black women likewise have been abused by the System and we must begin talking about the elimination of all kinds of oppression. If we are talking about building a strong nation, capable of throwing off the yoke of capitalist oppression, then we are talking about the total involvement of every man, woman, and child, each with a highly developed political consciousness. We need our whole army out there dealing with the enemy, and not half an army.

There are also some black women who feel that there is no more productive role in life than having and raising children. This attitude often reflects the conditioning of the society in which we live and is adopted from a bourgeois white model. Some young sisters who have never had to maintain a household and accept the confining role which this entails, tend to romanticize (along with the help of a number of brothers) this role of housewife and mother. Black women who have had to endure this kind of function are less apt to have these utopian visions. Those who project in an intellectual manner how great and rewarding this role will be and who feel that the most important thing that they can contribute to the black nation is children, are doing themselves a great injustice. This line of reasoning completely negates the contributions that black women have historically made to our struggle for liberation. These black women include Sojourner Truth, Harriet Tubman, Mary McLeod Bethune, and Fannie Lou Hamer, to name but a few.

We live in a highly industrialized society and every member of the black nation must be as academically and technologically developed as possible. To wage a revolution, we need competent teachers, doctors, nurses, electronics experts, chemists, biologists, physicists, political scientists, and so on and so forth. Black women sitting at home reading bedtime stories to their children are just not going to make it.

ECONOMIC EXPLOITATION OF BLACK WOMEN

The economic System of capitalism finds it expedient to reduce women to a state of enslavement. They oftentimes serve as a scapegoat for the evils of this system. Much in the same way that the poor white cracker of the South, who is equally victimized, looks down upon blacks and contributes to the oppression of blacks—so, by giving to men a false feeling of superiority (at least in their own home or in their relationships with women)—the oppression of women acts as an escape valve for capitalism. Men may be cruelly exploited and subjected to all sorts of dehumanizing tactics on the part of the ruling class, but they have someone who is below them—at least they're not women.

Women also represent a surplus labor supply, the control of which is absolutely necessary to the profitable functioning of capitalism. Women are consistently exploited by the System. They are often paid less for the same work that men do and jobs that are specifically relegated to women are lowpaying and without the possibility of advancement. Statistics from the Women's Bureau of the United States Department of Labor show that in 1967, the wage scale for white women was even below that of black men; and the wage scale for non-white women was the lowest of all:

White Males	$6704
Non-White Males	4277
White Females	3991
Non-White Females	2861

Those industries that employ mainly black women are the most exploitative in the country. The hospital workers are a good example of this oppression; the garment workers in New York City provide us with another view of this economic slavery. The International Ladies Garment

Workers Union (ILGWU) whose overwhelming membership consists of black and Puerto Rican women has a leadership that is nearly all lily-white and male. This leadership has been working in collusion with the ruling class and has completely sold its soul to the corporate structure.

To add insult to injury, ILGWU has invested heavily in business enterprises in racist, apartheid South Africa—with union funds. Not only does this bought-off leadership contribute to our continued exploitation in this country by not truly representing the best interests of its membership, but it audaciously uses funds that black and Puerto Rican women have provided to support the economy of a vicious government that is engaged in the exploitation and murder of our black brothers and sisters in our motherland, Africa.

The entire labor movement in the United States has suffered as a result of the superexploitation of black workers and women. The unions have historically been racist and male chauvinistic. They have upheld racism in this country and have failed to fight the white-skin privileges of white workers. They have failed to struggle against inequities in the hiring and pay of women workers. There has been virtually no struggle against either the racism of the white worker or the economic exploitation of the working woman, two factors which have consistently impeded the advancement of the real struggle against the ruling class.

The racist, chauvinistic, and manipulative use of black workers and women, expecially black women, has been a severe cancer on the American labor scene. It therefore becomes essential for those who understand the workings of capitalism and imperialism to realize that the exploitation of black people and women works to everyone's disadvantage and that the liberation of these two minority groups is a stepping stone to the liberation of all oppressed people in this country and around the world.

BEDROOM POLITICS

I have briefly discussed the economic and psychological

manipulation of black women, but perhaps the most out-landish act of oppression in modern times is the current campaign to promote sterilization of non-white women, in an attempt to maintain the population and power imbalance between the white "haves" and the non-white "have nots."

These tactics are but another example of the many devious schemes that the ruling class elite attempts to perpetrate on the black population in order to keep itself in control. It has recently come to our attention that a massive campaign for so-called "birth control" is presently being promoted not only in the underdeveloped non-white areas of the world, but also in black communities here in the United States. However, what the authorities in charge of these programs refer to as "birth control" is in fact nothing but a method of outright surgical genocide.

The United States has been sponsoring sterilization clinics in non-white countries, especially in India where already some three million young men and boys in and around New Delhi have been sterilized in makeshift operating rooms set up by the American Peace Corps workers. Under these circumstances, it is understandable why certain countries view the Peace Corps not as a benevolent project, not as evidence of America's concern for underdeveloped areas, but rather as a threat to their very existence. This program could more aptly be named the "Death Corps."

The vasectomy, which is performed on males and takes only six or seven minutes, is a relatively simple operation. The sterilization of a woman, on the other hand, is admittedly major surgery. This operation, (salpingectomy) must be performed in a hospital under general anesthesia.[1] This method of "birth control" is a common procedure in Puerto Rico. Puerto Rico has long been used by the colonialist exploiter, the United States, as a huge experimental laboratory for medical research before allowing certain practices

1. Salpigectomy: through an abdominal incision, the surgeon cuts both fallopian tubes and ties off the separated ends, after which there is no way for the egg to pass from the ovary to the womb.

to be imported and used here. When the birth-control pill was first being perfected, it was tried out on Puerto Rican women and selected black women (poor), as if they were guinea pigs to see what its effect would be and how efficient the Pill was.

The salpingectomy has now become the commonest operation in Puerto Rico, commoner than an appendectomy or a tonsilectomy. It is so widespread that it is referred to simply as *la operación. On the Island, 20 percent of the women between the ages of fifteen and forty-five have already been sterilized.*

And now, as previously occurred with the Pill, this method has been imported into the United States. These sterilization clinics are cropping up around the country in the black and Puerto Rican communities. These so-called "Maternity Clinics," specifically outfitted to purge black women or men of their reproductive possibilities, are appearing more and more in hospitals and clinics across the country.

A number of organizations have recently been formed to popularize the idea of sterilization, such as The Association for Voluntary Sterilization, and the Human Betterment (!!!?) Association for Voluntary Sterilization, Inc., which has its headquarters in New York City. Front Royal, Virginia, has one such "Maternity Clinic" in Warren Memorial Hospital. The tactics used in the clinic in Fauquier County, Virginia, where poor and helpless black mothers and young girls are pressured into undergoing sterilization, are certainly not confined to that clinic alone.

Threatened with the cut-off of relief funds, some black welfare women have been forced to undergo this sterilization procedure in exchange for a continuation of welfare benefits. Mt. Sinai Hospital in New York City performs these operations on its ward patients whenever it can convince the women to undergo this surgery. Mississippi and some of the other Southern states are notorious for this act. Black women are often afraid to permit any kind of necessary surgery because they know from bitter experience that they are more likely than not to come out without their insides. (Both salpingectomies and hysterectomies are performed.)

We condemn this use of the black woman as a medical testing ground for the white middle class. Reports of the ill effects, including deaths, from the use of the birth-control pill only started to come to light when the white privileged class began to be affected. These outrageous Nazi-like procedures on the part of medical researchers are but another manifestation of the totally amoral and brutal behavior that the capitalist System perpetrates on black women. The sterilization experiments carried on in concentration camps some twenty-five years ago have been denounced the world over, but no one seems to get upset by the repetition of these same racist practices today in the United States of America —land of the free and home of the brave.

The rigid laws concerning abortions in this country are another means of subjugation and, indirectly, of outright murder. Rich white women somehow manage to obtain these operations with little or no difficulty. It is the poor black and Puerto Rican woman who is at the mercy of the local butcher. Statistics show us that the non-white death rate at the hands of the unqualified abortionist is substantially higher than for white women. Nearly half of the child-bearing deaths in New York City are attributed to abortion alone and out of these, 79 percent are among non-whites and Puerto Rican women.

We are not saying that black women should not practice birth control. Black women have the right and the responsibility to determine when it is in *the interest of the struggle to have children or not to have them and this right must not be relinquished to anyone.* It is also her right and responsibility to determine when it is in *her own best interests* to have children, how many she will have, and how far apart. The lack of the availability of safe birth-control methods, the forced sterilization practices, and the inability to obtain le-

gal abortions are all symptoms of a sick society that jeopard-
izes the health of black women (and thereby the entire black
race) in its attempt to control the very life processes of
human beings. This is a symptom of a society that is attempting to bring economic and political factors into the
privacy of the bedchamber. The elimination of these horrendous conditions will free black women for full participation in the revolution, and thereafter in the building of the
new society.

RELATIONSHIP TO WHITE MOVEMENT

Much has been written recently about the white women's
liberation movement in the United States and the question
arises whether there are any parallels between this struggle
and the movement on the part of black women for total
emancipation. While there are certain comparisons that one
can make because we both live under the same exploitative
System, there are certain differences, some of which are
quite basic.

The white woman's movement is far from being mono-
lithic. Any white woman's group that does not have an
anti-imperialist and antiracist ideology has absolutely nothing in common with the black woman's struggle. In fact,
some groups come to the incorrect conclusion that their
oppression is due simply to male chauvinism. They therefore have an extremely antimale tone to their dissertations.
Black people are engaged in a life-and-death struggle and
the main emphasis of black women must be to combat the
capitalist, racist exploitation of black people. While it is true
that male chauvinism has become institutionalized in
American society, one must always look for the main
enemy—the fundamental cause of the female condition.

Another major differentiation is that the white women's
movement is basically middle class. Very few of these
women suffer the extreme economic exploitation that most
black women are subjected to day by day. This is the factor

that is most crucial for us. It is not an intellectual persecution alone; it is not an intellectual outburst for us; it is quite real. We as black women have got to deal with the problems that the black masses deal with, for our problems in reality are one and the same.

If the white groups do not realize that they are in fact fighting capitalism and racism, we do not have common bonds. If they do not realize that the reasons for their condition lie in the System and not simply that men get a vicarious pleasure out of "consuming their bodies for exploitative reasons" (this kind of reasoning seems to be quite prevalent in certain white women's groups), then we cannot unite with them around common grievances or even discuss these groups in a serious manner because they're completely irrelevant to the black struggle.

THE NEW WORLD

The black community and black women especially must begin raising questions about the kind of society we wish to see established. We must note the ways in which capitalism oppresses us and then move to create institutions that will eliminate these destructive influences.

The new world that we are attempting to create must destroy oppression of any type. The value of this new system will be determined by the status of the person who was low man on the totem pole. Unless women in any enslaved nation are completely liberated, the change cannot really be called a revolution. If the black woman has to retreat to the position she occupied before the armed struggle, the whole movement and the whole struggle will have retreated in terms of truly freeing the colonized population.

A people's revolution that engages the participation of every member of the community, including man, woman, and child, brings about a certain transformation in the participants as a result of this participation. Once you have caught a glimpse of freedom or experienced a bit of self-determination, you can't go back to old routines that were established under the racist, capitalist regime. We must begin to understand that a revolution entails not only the willingness to lay our lives on the firing line and get killed. In some ways, this is an easy commitment to make. To die for the revolution is a one-shot deal; to live for the revolution means taking on the more difficult commitment of changing our day-to-day life patterns.

This will mean changing the routines that we have established as a result of living in a totally corrupting society. It means changing how you relate to your wife, your husband, your parents, and your co-workers. If we are going to liberate ourselves as a people, it must be recognized that black women have very specific problems that have to be spoken to. We must be liberated along with the rest of the population. We cannot wait to start working on those problems until that great day in the future when the revolution, somehow, miraculously, is accomplished.

To assign women the role of housekeeper and mother while men go forth into battle is a highly questionable doctrine for a revolutionary to maintain. Each individual must develop a high political consciousness in order to understand how this System enslaves us all and what actions we must take to bring about its total destruction. Those who consider themselves revolutionary must begin to deal with other revolutionaries as equals. And, so far as I know, revolutionaries are not determined by sex.

Old people, young people, men, and women must take part in the struggle. To relegate women to purely supportive roles or purely cultural considerations is dangerous doctrine to project. Unless black men who are preparing themselves for armed struggle understand that the society which we are trying to create is one in which the oppression of *all* members of that society is eliminated, then the revolution will have failed in its avowed purpose.

Given the mutual commitment of black men and black women alike to the liberation of our people and other oppressed peoples around the world, the total involvement of each individual is necessary. A revolutionary has the responsibility of not only toppling those who are now in a position of power, but creating new institutions that will eliminate all forms of oppression. We must begin to rewrite our understanding of traditional personal relationships between man and woman.

All the resources that the black community can muster up must be channeled into the struggle. Black women must take an active part in bringing about the kind of society where our children, our loved ones, and each citizen can grow up and live as decent human beings, free from the pressures of racism and capitalist exploitation.

FOR SADIE AND MAUDE

Eleanor Holmes Norton

Some subjects are so complex, so unyielding of facile insight, that it will not do to think about them in the ordinary way. Black women—their lot and their future—is for me such a subject. Thus, the new crop of literature concerning women—attuned to the peculiar relationship between white women and white men in America—has inspired me much, but less than the poetry of the great black poet, Gwendolyn Brooks, who writes for me and about me. Take, for example Miss Brooks' poem "Sadie and Maude,"[1] a sad ballad which in a few stanzas touches in some intimate respect all of us who are black women:

> Maude went to college.
> Sadie stayed at home.
> Sadie scraped life
> With a fine-tooth comb.

1. Gwendolyn Brooks, *Selected Poems* (New York: Harper & Row, 1963). Copyright © 1970 by Eleanor Holmes Norton

She didn't leave a tangle in.
Her comb found every strand.
Sadie was one of the livingest chits
In all the land.

Sadie bore two babies
Under her maiden name.
Maude and Ma and Papa
Nearly died of shame.

When Sadie said her last so-long
Her girls struck out from home.
(Sadie had left as heritage
Her fine-tooth comb.)

Maude, who went to college.
Is a thin brown mouse.
She is living all alone
In this old house.

Sadie and Maude are blood sisters, each in her own way living the unrequited life of the black woman. Sadie has two children out of wedlock, but the Sadies of this world also include black women who have been married but have lost their husbands in America's wars against the black family. Maude "went to college"—or wherever black women have gone over the years to escape the perils of living the nearly predestined half-life of the black woman in this country. Maude, the "thin brown mouse," lives alone rather than incur Sadie's risks or risk Sadie's pleasures.

The difference in the lives of these two women cannot conceal the overriding problem they share—loneliness, a life lacking in the chance to develop a relationship with a man or satisfactory family relationships. The complexities of the problem facing black women begin to unfold. Not only must we work out an unoppressive relationship with our men; we must—we can at last—establish a relationship with them *de novo*.

In this respect, we conceive our mission in terms which are often different from the expressed goals of many white women revolutionaries. To be sure, our goals and theirs in their general outlines are the same, but black women confront a task that is as delicate as it is revolutionary. For black women are part of a pre-eminent struggle whose time has come—the fight for black liberation. If women were suddenly to achieve equality with men tomorrow, black women would continue to carry the entire array of utterly oppressive handicaps associated with race. Racial oppression of black people in America has done what neither class oppression nor sexual oppression, with all their perniciousness, has ever done: destroyed an entire people and their culture. The difference is between exploitation and slavery. Slavery partakes of all the worst excesses of exploitation—and more—but exploitation does not always sink people to the miserable depths of slavery.

Yet, black women cannot—must not—avoid the truth about their special subservience. They are women with all that that implies. If some have been forced into roles as providers or, out of the insecurity associated with being a black woman alone, have dared not develop independence, the result is not that black women are today liberated women. For they have been "liberated" only from love, from family life, from meaningful work, and just as often from the basic comforts and necessities of an ordinary existence. There is neither power nor satisfaction in such a "matriarchy." There is only the bitter knowledge that one is a victim.

Still, the stereotypic image of matriarchy has basic appeal to some black men who in their frustration may not see immediately the counterrevolutionary nature of such a battle cry. To allow the white oppressor to share the burden of his responsibility with the black woman is madness. It is comparable to black people blaming Puerto Ricans for competing with them for jobs, thus relieving the government of the pressures it must have to fulfill its duty to provide full employment. Surely, after hundreds of years, black men realize that imprecision in detecting the enemy is an inexcusable fault in a revolutionary.

But our problems only *begin* with the reconstruction of

the black family. As black men begin to find dignified work after so many generations, what roles will their women seek? Are black people to reject so many of white society's values only to accept its view of woman and of the family? At the moment when the white family is caught in a maze of neurotic contradictions and white women are supremely frustrated with their roles, are black women to take up such troubled models? Shall black women exchange their ancient insecurity for the white woman's familial cocoon? Can it serve us any better than it has served them? And how will it serve black men?

There is no reason to repeat bad history. There is no reason to envy the white woman who is sinking in a sea of close-quartered affluence, where one's world is one's house, one's peers one's children, and one's employer one's husband. Black women shall not have gained if Sadie and Maude exchange the "fine-tooth comb" and the "old house" for the empty treasures white women are today trying to turn in.

We who are black have a chance for something better. Europeans who came to this country struggled to be accepted by it and succeeded. Occasionally they changed America—for the better and for the worse—but mostly they took it as it was, hoping it would change them. Black people imitated this process pitifully, generation after generation, but were just so much oil on all that melting-pot water. Today we are close to being true outsiders, no longer desiring to get in on any terms and at any cost. Racial exclusion has borne ironic fruit. We are perhaps the only group that has come to these shores who has ever acquired the chance to consciously avoid total Americanization with its inherent, its rank, faults. On the road to equality there is no better place for blacks to detour around American values than in forgoing its example in the treatment of its women and the organization of its family life.

With black family life so clearly undermined in the American environment, blacks must remake the family unit, not imitate it. Indeed, this task is central to black liberation. The black male will not be returned to his historic strength—the foremost task of the black struggle today—if we do not recreate the strong family unit that was a part of our African heritage before it was dismembered by the slave-owning class in America. But it will be impossible to reconstruct the black family if its central characters are to be crepe-paper copies acting out the old white family melodrama. In that failing production, the characters seem set upon a course precisely opposite to ours. White men, in search of endless financial security, have sold their spirits to that goal and begun a steady emasculation in which the fiscal needs of wife and family determine life's values and goals. Their now ungrateful wives have begun to see the fraud of this way of life, even while eagerly devouring its fruits. Their even more ungrateful children are in bitter rejection of all that this sort of life signifies and produces. White family life in America today is less than a poor model for blacks. White family life is disintegrating at the moment when we must reforge the black family unit. The whole business of the white family—its softened men, its frustrated women, its angry children—is in a state of great mess.

But it would be naive to think that the temptatious aspects of this sort of life are incapable of luring black people into a disastrous mockery. The ingredients are all there. We are a people in search of what for us has been the interminably elusive goal of economic security. Wretchedly poor for three-hundred-fifty years in a country where most groups have fattened, we could come to see the pain of much of white family life as bearable when measured against the tortures we have borne. Our men, deliberately emasculated as the only way to enforce their servile status, might easily be tempted by a family structure which, by making them the financial head of the household, seemed to make them its actual head. In our desperation to escape so many suffering decades, we might trip down the worn path taken by so many in America before us.

If we are to avoid this disaster, the best, perhaps the only, place to begin is in our conception of the black woman. After all, the immediate tasks of the black man are laid out for him. It is the future role of the black woman that is problematical. And what she is allowed to become—or relegated to—will shape not simply her future but that of the black family and the fate of its members.

If she is forced into the current white model, she is doomed to the fate of "The Empty Woman" about whom Miss Brooks has also written:

The empty woman had hats
To show. With feathers. Wore combs
In polished waves. Wooed cats

If so, she will be unfit for the onerous responsibilities she must meet if the struggle for black freedom is to bring us out of our ancient bondage into a truly new and liberated condition.

In any case, it is too late for any group to consciously revert to old familial patterns of male dominance and female servility. Those roles have their roots in conditions of life that are rapidly disappearing, and especially so in this country. If the woman's place has historically been at home, it was at least in part because there was much work to be done there and, as the natural custodian of the children, it seemed logical for her to do it. But today there is neither so much work to be done there nor so many children. Do-it-all appliances and technology are making housework a part-time job, freeing millions of women to do something else. An increasing array of birth preventatives has released women from the unwanted multiples of children it was difficult to avoid in the past. The effect on the family of these work- and child-liberating phenomena will reverberate in ways we still cannot foresee.

Yet it is certain that the institution of the family will undergo radical alteration largely through the new roles women will have to seek. With birth preventatives and with world overpopulation, many couples will rethink whether it is wise to have children at all. And even though most may choose to have children, it is doubtful that it will any longer be prestigious or wise to have very many. With children no longer the universally accepted reason for marriage, marriages are going to have to exist on their own merits. Marriages are going to have to have to exist because they possess inherent qualities which make them worthy of existing, a plane to which the institution has never before been elevated. For marriage to develop such inherent qualities the woman partner, heretofore oriented toward fulfilling now outmoded functions, will have to seek new functions. Whether black or white, if American women are to find themselves, they must begin looking outside the home. This will undoubtedly lead them into doing and thinking about matters now pretty much reserved for men. Inevitably, women are going to acquire new goals and a new status.

We who are black are taking up the long delayed work of family-building at a historic moment in history. We embark upon this goal at a time when the family institution in America is in a state of great and undecided flux. This is fortunate happenstance, for had we been about this task in the years immediately following World War II, we might have fallen into the mold which today traps white families, and especially white women. As it is, we have a chance to pioneer in forging new relationships between men and women. We have a chance to make family life a liberating experience instead of the confining experience it more often has been. We have a chance to free woman and, with her, the rest of us.

STATEMENT ON BIRTH CONTROL

Black Women's Liberation Group, Mount Vernon, New York

Dear Brothers:

Poor black sisters decide for themselves whether to have a baby or not to have a baby. If we take the Pills or practice birth control in other ways, it's because of poor black men.

Now here's how it is. Poor black men won't support their families, won't stick by their women—all they think about is the street, dope and liquor, women, a piece of ass, and their cars. That's all that counts. Poor black women would be foolish to sit up in the house with a whole lot of children and eventually go crazy, sick, heartbroken, no place to go, no sign of affection—nothing. Middle-class white men have always done this to their women—only more sophisticated-like.

So when Whitey put out the Pill, and poor black sisters spread the word, we saw how simple it was not to be a fool for men any more (politically we would say men could no longer exploit us sexually or for money and leave the babies with us to bring up). That was the first step in our waking up! Black women have always been told by black men that we were black, ugly, evil bitches and whores—in other words we were the real niggers in this society—oppressed by whites, male and female, and the black man, too.

Now a lot of black brothers are into the new bag. Black women are being asked by militant black brothers not to practice birth control because it's a form of Whitey's committing genocide on black people. Well, true enough, but it takes two to practice genocide and black women are able to decide for themselves, like poor people all over the world, whether they will submit to genocide. For us, birth control is the freedom to *fight* genocide of black women and children.

Like, the Vietnamese have decided to fight genocide, the South American poor are beginning to fight back, and the African poor will fight back, too. Poor black women in the United States have to fight back, too. Poor black women in the United States have to fight back out of our own experience of oppression. Having too many babies stops us from supporting our children, teaching them the truth, or stopping the brainwashing, as you say, and from fighting black men who still want to use and exploit us.

But we don't think you're going to understand us because you are a bunch of little middle-class people and we are poor black women. The middle class never understands the poor because they always need to use them as you want to use poor black women's children to gain power for yourself. You'll run the black community with your kind of Black Power—You on top! The poor understand class struggle!

Signed by: two welfare recipients
two housewives
a domestic
a grandmother
a psychotherapist
and others who read, agreed, but did not
help to compose.

HIGH SCHOOL WOMEN:

THREE VIEWS

THE SUBURBAN SCENE

Connie Dvorkin

I was born March 4, 1955, in Doctor's Hospital in New York City. All my life I have lived in an unincorporated area of the town of Greenburgh, though my mailing address is Scarsdale and the school district is Edgemont, Greenburgh Union Free District No. 6. I am in the eighth grade and have been a pacifist and a vegetarian since October 1968. I live in a Republican stronghold and the conservatism that usually goes along with that is very evident here. My prison's name is Edgemont Junior-Senior High School, grades 7–12, with approximately 850 inmates. I am the so-called secretary of Edgemont Students for Action to which all the activist radicals and more radical liberals more or less belong.

I think I first heard of the Women's Liberation Movement on WBAI (Radio Free New York), most likely on "Radio Unnameable." Like Eldridge Cleaver in *Soul On Ice*,

I never realized how oppressed I was until someone brought it into the open. I wrote a letter asking for some literature on the Women's Liberation Movement that I could read. It was for a Social Studies report that never materialized. But that is irrelevant like school is. The important thing is that I read the stuff and immediately agreed with everything. Ironically the very night I was reading it I was babysitting and watching TV. The show, "I Love Lucy," was an episode where the two women were to be equal to the men for one night—no courtesies "due to a woman," no shit like that for *one* night, eating out at a restaurant—and they couldn't do it. They *had* to depend on their husbands. They couldn't face life out in front, they had to hide behind their husbands' names and souls. The kids I was sitting for laughed their asses off, and I realized that I would have, too, five months earlier.

Now, with awakened eyes, I could see all the brainwashing of my sisters that goes on at school. It starts almost the instant they are born, by their mothers, and by fathers encouraging the boys to take an interest in cars, baseball, etc., and discouraging girls. A girl I know who was always a "tomboy," now, in the compulsory intramural volley ball we have with the boys, always seems to hang back and doesn't seem as "boyish" as she always is. I feel particularly sorry for the snobs or society "chicks" of my grade. Everybody knows the type. They will probably never hear the gospel and if they do would never accept it. I once thought it was "fun" to wear miniskirts (I had a really good figure then, but no longer worry about that shit) and look good for boys and men generally. I rationalized, "Why not? It's fun and they like it." I read all the literature on women's liberation and still wore skirts. But then I heard about the momentous decision by the judge who said that principals could no longer tell girls what to wear, and I went up to my principal; he said he couldn't stop me, but he thought slacks "were in bad taste." Anyway, since that, I've worn dresses or skirts about five times—one time it was to the Passover Seder.

Since I began wearing pants I have discovered two things: 1) I feel more equal with boys, and 2) I no longer have to worry as to how my legs are placed and all that bullshit as I had to when I wore skirts. I no longer feel myself fighting other girls for the attention of boys, and am generally much more at ease with the world.

In seventh and eighth grade you have the trimester along with the regular report card. The trimester consists of three subjects—Music, Art, and Home Ec "for girls" and Shop "for boys." I began thinking about a groovy idea—taking Shop instead of Home Ec. So I talked it over with my mother (whom I consider far more liberal than my father) who sent a note off to the junior high girls' guidance counselor. She said I couldn't, but she didn't really tell me why. Then my mother sent a letter off to my principal, repeating that I wished to take Shop and could he please voice his opinion on that. Three weeks later his reply came back. I thought this was a deliberate delay tactic on his part. He is a very clever conservative always having this fantasy that he's on the students' side, which of course is bullshit. Anyway, in his letter he cited several reasons why I couldn't take Shop: 1) it was traditional that a girl took Home Ec, 2) there wouldn't be enough room in Shop for one more pupil, 3) the teacher in Shop would be overworked. He knew that we would go over him to the school supervisor, Dr. Larson, so he sent Larson a copy of his letter. I obtained an appointment with Dr. Larson five days before Home Ec was supposed to start. I explained to him my reasons why I didn't want to take Home Ec. I said I thought that the school system is the mold for people in this society and that in giving a course in Home Ec just for girls and Shop just for boys they were trying to mold girls into being "homemakers" and boys into what molds people thought define "masculinity." I was very impressed by the interview because Dr. Larson, outside of one understanding teacher, was the only school official who took me seriously and listened to me while discussing school affairs. Well, Dr. Larson passed on the request to the district superintendent, Dr. Russo. Larson sent me Xerox copies of the letter to Russo and Russo's letter to an official up at Albany, so I could trust him. Word was passed along to me that nobody in Albany wanted to touch the issue, and they finally sent down an edict that I could do what I wanted to.

While this was going on Home Ec and Shop had already started and I was given a Study Hall during the period that Home Ec/Shop was in. I requested this since I am a pacifist and do not believe in confrontation politics. I wasn't trigger-happy for a confrontation like many SDSers are. (I don't mean to offend any SDS people reading this. Some of my best friends are in SDS.)

The first day I started Shop I was very apprehensive about how the boys were going to react to me being in the class. I have two very good friends in that class (including Dr. Larson's son Mark), and they congratulated me on my success. One of the boys is very condescending toward me, always speaking in the patronizing, gentle voice that really makes me angry. "Connie, let me help you," they say. "Well! I just want to tell you—fuck you, damn it, and go home and stop farting out all that chickenshit, man, just quit it!" I say furiously, but silently. But Shop is fun if the "teacher" isn't paying attention because you can goof all you want to. One thing I realized when I walked into the room the first day was that I could *never* cut, because my absence would be too noticeable.

The whole scene at a suburban school I realize is different than a city school in many ways, of which the maybe most important is that Edgemont is very isolated from other schools and the things you hear about other schools are from either the *New York Times* (who believes them?) and the lower-county paper, the *Reporter Dispatch*, based in White Plains (truthfully called the Distorter Repatch). And you can guess from their nickname what they print. The whole middle-class values, including the meek, passive, "feminine" girl and the strong, overpowering, "masculine" boy are very evident here as in any suburb but especially here since Westchester is such a wealthy suburb-county. The whole bit with the school dances where the boys ask the girls helps brainwash girls and boys into thinking that girls' places in the social caste of a social life and school and elsewhere are lower than boys. As a girl, I often find myself tongue-tied when trying to argue points with older boys, but can talk with boys my age successfully.

I am sure some people when reading this will say, "But surely there's a contradiction in Connie being a pacifist and trying to break down the old definition of feminity as passivity!" I became a pacifist simply because I do not believe that wars solve anything but only create new ones such as new hates, refugees, etc. That is also why I think that Joan Baez is correct in saying all the New Left has is anger and that anger doesn't solve anything just as war doesn't. (I assume I am misquoting her out of context and putting things in her mouth that she never said.) My belief as a vegetarian has grown out of my belief as a pacifist and a lover of life.

ON DE-SEGREGATING STUYVESANT HIGH

Alice de Rivera

Before I went to John Jay High School I hadn't realized how bad the conditions were for students. One of the things that changed my outlook was being involved with the hostilities of the New York City teacher strikes in the fall of 1968. Students were trying to open the school and the teachers were preventing them. I was disillusioned by the low-quality, high-pay teaching we received afterwards, and soon became involved with expressing my discontent.

It was then I found that students had no rights. We had no freedom of the press: many controversial articles were

removed from the newspapers by the teacher-editors. We
were not allowed to distribute leaflets or newspapers inside
our school building, so that press communication was taken
away from us. We also had no freedom of speech. Many
teachers would put us down in class for our political ideas
and then would not let us answer their charges. If we tried
to talk with other students during a free period about political issues, we were told to stop. The school was a prison—
we were required by state law to be there, but when we
were there we had no rights. We had to carry ID cards and
passes. We could be suspended; we were considered guilty
before proven innocent.

It was this treatment which made me as a student want
to change the schools. When I talked to students from other
public high schools in the city, I found they had been oppressed within the schools in much the same way.

I have been writing about the student's plight in general
because it was my first encounter with oppression. It is such
a familiar experience to me now, that I think I can try to
define it. Oppression, to me, is when people are not allowed
to be themselves. I encountered this condition a second
time when I realized *woman's* plight in the high schools.
And for the second time I tried to help change the schools
so that I and other girls would not be hurt.

The first time it really occurred to me that I was oppressed as a woman was when I began to think of what I was
going to be when I was older. I realized I had no real plans
for the future—college, maybe, and after that was a dark
space in my mind. In talking and listening to other girls, I
found that they had either the same blank spot in their
minds or were planning on marriage. If not that, they
figured on taking a job of some sort *until* they got married.

The boys that I knew all had at least some slight idea in
their minds of what career or job they were preparing for.
Some prepared for careers in science and math by going to
a specialized school. Others prepared for their later jobs as
mechanics, electricians, and other tradesmen in vocational

schools. Some just did their thing in a regular, zoned high school. It seemed to me that I should fill the blank spot in my mind as the boys were able to do, and I decided to study science (biology, in particular) much more intensively. It was then that I encountered one of the many blocks which stand in the woman student's way: discrimination against women in the specialized science and math high schools in the city.

Many years before women in New York State had won their right to vote (1917), a school was established for those high-school students who wish to specialize in science and math. Naturally it was not co-ed, for women were not regarded legally or psychologically as people. This school, Stuyvesant High School, was erected in 1903. In 1956, thirty-nine years after New York women earned the right to vote, the school was renovated; yet no provision was made for girls to enter.

There are only two other high schools in New York which specialize in science and math: Brooklyn Technical, a school geared towards engineering, and Bronx High School of Science. Brooklyn Tech moved from the warehouse, where its male-only classes were started, into a modern building in 1933. It was renovated in 1960, yet still no provision was made for girls.

This left only Bronx Science. Bronx High School of Science is the only school where girls can study science and math intensively—it is co-ed. It became so in 1946, the year it moved into a new building. However, although it admits girls, it still discriminates against them; it admits only one girl to every two boys.

Out of these three schools I could try out for only one. This one, Bronx Science, is one and one-half hours travel time from my home. It presents very stiff competition because of the discriminatory policy which allows only a certain number of girls to enter, and also because all the girls who would otherwise be trying out for Stuyvesant or Brooklyn Tech have Bronx Science as their only alternative. I became disgusted with this, not only for my sake, but for all the girls who hadn't become scientists or engineers because they were a little less than brilliant or had been put down by nobody having challenged those little blank spots in their minds. After talking about it with my parents and friends, I decided to open up Stuyvesant and challenge the Board of Education's traditional policy.

I took my idea to Ramona Ripston, co-director of the National Emergency Civil Liberties Committee, and she accepted it warmly. Pretty soon I became involved in trying to get an application for the entrance exam to Stuyvesant filled out and sent. It was turned down and we—NECLC, my parents, and I—went to court against the principal of Stuyvesant and the Board of Ed.

The day on which we went to court was the day before the entrance exam was scheduled to be given. The Board of Ed granted me the privilege of taking the test for Bronx Science (which is the same as the one given for Stuyvesant), and the judge recognized that the results of this test would be used in another court hearing to resolve whether or not I would be admitted. Five days after the other students had received their results, we found out that I had passed for entrance into both Stuyvesant and Bronx Science.

We went to court again a couple of months later, in April. Our judge, Jawn A. Sandafer, seemed receptive to our case, but he reserved his decision. Later we were told that he wished an open hearing for May 13. This was a great break for us because if what the judge needed was public support, we had many important people who were willing to argue in my favor. However, on April 30 the New York City Board of Education voted to admit me to Stuyvesant High School in the Fall. The superintendent had wanted to continue the court fight.

This seemed a victory to us at first, but in actuality it would have been better if we could have continued the case and received a court order. We hoped to establish that public funds could not be used to support institutions of learning which discriminate against women. Such a ruling would have been the key to opening up the other sexually segregated high schools in New York City.

There are a great many battles yet to be fought. Aside from being discouraged to study for a career, women are discouraged from preparing for jobs involving anything *but* secretarial work, beauty care, nursing, cooking, and the fashion industry. During my fight over Stuyvesant, I investigated the whole high-school scene, and found that out of the twenty-seven vocational high schools in the city, only *seven* are co-ed. The boys' vocational schools teach trades in electronics, plumbing, carpentry, foods, printing (another example of Board of Ed traditional policy—there is hardly any work for a hand-typesetter today), etc. The girls are taught to be beauticians, secretaries, or health aides. This means that if a girl is seeking entrance to a vocational school, she is pressured to feel that certain jobs are masculine and others feminine. She is forced to conform to the Board of Education's image of her sex. At the seven co-ed vocational schools, boys can learn clerical work, food preparation, and beauty care along with the girls. But the courses that would normally be found in a boys' school are not open to girls. There are only two schools where a girl can prepare for a "masculine" job. Charles Evans Hughes High School in Manhattan is coed for teaching technical electronics. Newtown High School offers an academic pre-engineering course of study for boys and girls. However, this school is zoned for the Borough of Queens only.

In conclusion, there are three types of schools, twenty-nine in number, that the Board of Ed has copped out on. These schools are composed of the specialized science and math school Brooklyn Tech, twenty vocational schools which teach students their trade according to what sex they are, and the eight traditionally non-co-ed academic schools.

These eight academic schools are zoned schools which admit only boys or only girls. The argument against these schools is that "separate but equal" is not equal (as established with regard to race in the Brown Decision). The psychological result of the school which is segregated by sex —only because of tradition—is to impress upon girls that they are only "flighty females" who would bother the boys' study habits (as a consequence of girls not being interested in anything but the male sex). This insinuates immaturity on the part of girls—and certainly produces it in both sexes. A boy who has never worked with a girl in the classroom is bound to think of her as his intellectual inferior, and will not treat her as if she had any capacity for understanding things other than child care and homemaking. Both sexes learn to deal with each other as non-people. It really messes up the growth of a person's mind.

Out of the sixty-two high schools in New York City, twenty-nine are now sexually segregated. I believe that it is up to the girls to put pressure on the Board of Education to change this situation. I myself cannot live with oppression.

All girls have been brought up by this society never being able to be themselves—the school system has reinforced this. My desire at this time is to change the educational situation to benefit *all* the students. But I'm afraid changes *could* be made that benefited male students, leaving the status of females pretty much as it is. Female students share the general oppressive conditions forced upon everyone by the System's schools, plus a special psychological discrimination shown to women by the schools, the teachers, *and* their fellow students. So, since I don't want *my* issues to get swallowed up in the supposed "larger" issues, I'm going to make women's liberation the center of my fight.

EXCERPTS FROM THE DIARIES OF ALL OPPRESSED WOMEN

Women's Collective of the New York High School Student Union

When we decided to write this article on women's liberation, the person who approached us was under the impression that we would be almost totally liberated as women. Her reason for this feeling was that, in her experience, each younger section of the Movement had fewer and fewer hang-ups about the role of women, and therefore, as members of the high-school movement, we would naturally have the least. That statement really freaked us out.

While it is basically true that each new generation has fewer hang-ups, our experience has been that this is mainly true in a sexual context. We and our sisters are a lot less hung-up about sleeping with different people and we recognize that our need to fuck is a sexual need and we aren't concerned about the love bullshit routine. *But,* fucking when you feel like it isn't liberation. And the absence inside ourselves of the need to struggle to overcome that particular hang-up has freed our minds to cope with the real problems of women's liberation.

We have been trying to write this statement for a long time and it's really a bitch. We do have a real sense of oppression but we get caught up in fighting the more obvious manifestations of the exploitation of females in this society. Margarine ads that use bikini-clad girls to sell the grease, and toothpaste ads that tell us we will find it easier to catch a man after using that stuff, really fuck us up. They are so deeply ingrained in this society that even we who see them and who want to destroy them don't know what to do. So we freak out about shit like whether it is ethical for us to wash the dishes in our commune, as a visible reaction, but underneath we get really discouraged about how to even feel inside ourselves that what we are saying has validity and whether we really are stupid or whatnot.

What we see as the biggest obstacle to women's liberation is an internal hassle. All our lives we have been relegated to a second-class position. Now we have finally realized that that shits and that we have just as much fucking ability to lead really productive lives as men do.

As revolutionaries, we feel that no one can lead a really meaningful life if they cooperate with this screwed-up society, so we direct our energies into the Movement, where we are creating a new life-style that will liberate all peoples of both sexes. Movement work involves a whole lot of just plain talking to people on a personal level, trying to point out to them how they get fucked over no matter what they do.

All institutions fuck you up. Families fuck you up, school fucks you up, jobs fuck you up. And you even get fucked over by the stuff that is supposed to be there for your recreation.

For girls, getting over the initial hang-up about saying anything is a real impediment to our feeling worthwhile as a group, even in the Movement. All our lives we have been trained to assume a passive role. Even for those of us who are born into middle-class backgrounds where you are expected to go to college, any interest toward entering a career is entirely secondary to getting married and raising a family. Girls who reject this traditional role are generally regarded as cold and unfeeling.

When women join the Movement they have to build a whole new role for themselves, and it's fucking hard.

One situation that works against us in the Movement is that we are used to thinking that what we say isn't worth expressing or that somebody else who's been around longer (usually a guy) can express what we are feeling much better than we can. We have got to overcome that in ourselves. What we think *is* worth saying. Even if at first it's a little incoherent that's even good, 'cause we really *feel* the oppression that we're rapping about. It's because we've been oppressed that we don't say much.

The obvious manifestations of male chauvinism—women confined to cooking and cleaning—can be destroyed because people will eventually have to regard those tasks as mere shitwork that must be done as quickly and efficiently as possible so that our time will be free to attend to the more important responsibilities we have assumed. Raising children will be a radically different procedure than before. Children will not belong to one couple. Because the group has made a collective decision to have a child, it will assume the responsibility of raising a liberated person—*as a group.*

Without the specter of a meaningless life hanging over our heads, we women can be free to get our heads together and get over the hang-ups we would naturally have inside us.

One of the best things that has happened to us as women is that we are beginning to recognize that we all experience many of the same things. Getting together and rapping about hang-ups that have arisen as a result of our being females helps us to realize that we aren't shits, that we aren't docile and reticent because of something fucked up inside us, but it's like that because we have been *programmed* into that.

It's a really amazing experience when women first get together and begin talking about their hang-ups—all of those things you always think are your own personal faults turn out to be common. We've all been fucked over and show it.

As for "Girls Say Yes to Boys Who Say No" and "Pussy Power" and being sex bait for GI's but being told (by some males in the Movement) not to fuck with guys who aren't "good revolutionaries":

If there are guys whose politics we don't like, we can open our mouths and tell them so, instead of locking our legs.

Even in the Movement, where we and our brothers are trying to reshape our lives, we are met with very real obstacles. Many times, when we talk among ourselves, the guys refuse to admit that they still have male-chauvinist "tendencies." Because they have made the initial step of rejecting the society that maintains chauvinist distinctions, they feel that they have eradicated something that the society has actually ingrained in them since birth. And in a traditional life-style, girls tend to naturally assume the role reserved for them, even if they do feel that it is repressive, because males do not or will not realize that chores like cooking, cleaning, and raising children should be taken care of by both sexes.

A solution to this situation is the creation of a radically different life-style.

As part of our struggle, we have to liberate ourselves from the fucking educational system that has tried to destroy our minds by forcing us to think and write in linear forms. Therefore, we have just written a statement of our feelings and thoughts that can be regarded as excerpts from the diaries of all oppressed women.

COLONIZED WOMEN:

THE CHICANA

An Introduction

Elizabeth Sutherland

For many militants in the Women's Liberation Movement of this country today, the following comments of Enriqueta Vasquez may come as a shock and perhaps even seem like a cop-out—or "Tommish." But most of these women are white, middle-class in background, and in the majority of the population. They have little gut understanding of the position of women from a colonized—not merely oppressed —group.

For the woman of a colonized group, even the most political, her oppression as a woman is usually overshadowed by the common oppression of both male and female. Black and brown people in this country are fighting for sheer survival against the physical genocide of wars (including a high draft-rate), police brutality, hunger, deprivation—and against the cultural genocide of white Anglo institutions and values. The overused word "minority" becomes significant here; any colonized woman will feel an impulse toward unity with her brothers rather than challenge against them, but when the colonized group is the minority, as in the United States, this becomes even truer. The very growth of the white radical movement in this country during recent years is one reason why white women have begun to reject their roles in that movement. There is room for it, time for it, in a way that did not seem to exist before.

The sensitive woman from a colonized people also recognizes that many times it has been easier for her economically than for the men of her group. Often she can get a job where a man cannot. She can see the damage done to the men as a result, and feels reluctant to risk threatening their self-respect even further. This may be a short-range viewpoint involving false definitions of manhood, but it is created by immediate realities whose force cannot merely be wished away. It is also a fact that in many Chicano families, the woman makes many of the important decisions —not just consumer decisions—though the importance of her role will be recognized only privately. This may seem hypocritical or like a double-standard, but the knowledge of having real influence affects how the Chicana feels.

There is something else, and larger. It has been eloquently described by Maria Varela, now working in the Chicano movement of the Southwest:

> When your race is fighting for survival—to eat, to be clothed, to be housed, to be left in peace—as a woman, you know who you are. You are the principle of life, of survival and endurance. No matter how your husband is—strong but needing you to keep on, or weak and needing you for strength, or brutal and using you to keep his manhood intact—no matter what *he* is, your children survive and survive only through your will, your day-to-day battle against inimical forces. You know who you are. This is even more true when, as a woman, you are involved in battling the forces of oppression against your race. For the Chicano woman battling for her people, the family—the big family—is a fortress against the genocidal forces in the outside world. It is the source of strength for a people whose identity

is constantly being whittled away. The mother is the center of that fortress.

For the young, alienated Anglos, on the other hand, the family as it has functioned in the past often reflects a bundle of false values in a lying society of which she is part. Her position is almost the opposite of the Chicana's. And the family is but one example of how the culture or life-style of a colonized people becomes a weapon of self-defense in a hostile world—hostile to any signs of unity among them, hostile to their very existence. It is a weapon against the oppressor's tactic of "divide and conquer," with which he has sustained his rule these many centuries.

That life-style may have other roots as well, but to challenge it today means to risk being seen as the oppressor. "We don't want to become like the dominating Anglo women," you can hear Chicanas say. The comment shows a great lack of understanding of the Anglo woman's struggle, but it also reveals how deeply cultural integrity is interwoven with survival for a colonized people. The middle-class Anglo woman must therefore beware of telling her black or brown sisters to throw off their chains—without at least first understanding the origins and reasons for those "chains." And also without first asking themselves: are there perhaps some aspects of these other life-styles from which we, with our advanced ideas, might still learn?

At the same time, we can hope that women from colonized groups will listen with open minds to their Anglo sisters' ideas about women's liberation and then take another look at their own values. There is, for example, nothing worth preserving about the young Chicano male habit of fighting at a dance over some girl whom both hardly know—to prove their manhood. There is, on the other hand, much to be gained by examining the "Anglo-style" idea that authoritarianism—always male—does not merely oppress women but also the masses; that the struggle for "Power to the People" is intimately linked to the women's liberation struggle. In the present age of nationalism combined with the intensified repression of colonized peoples, such an open-minded exchange of ideas must be difficult. But for those who have moved on to revolutionary values, no other real choice exists.

Enriqueta Vasquez is a revolutionary, with her own tone of voice. Let Anglo women listen for her voice, not merely for echoes of their own.

THE MEXICAN-AMERICAN WOMAN

Enriqueta Longauex y Vasquez

While attending a Mexican-American conference in Colorado this year, I went to one of the workshops that were held to discuss the role of the Chicana—the Mexican-American woman, the woman of La Raza.[1] When the time came for the women to report to the full conference, the only thing that the workshop representative had to say was this: "It was the consensus of the group that the Chicana woman does not want to be liberated."

As a woman who has been faced with living as a member of the Mexican-American minority group, as a breadwinner and a mother raising children, living in housing projects, and having much concern for other humans plus much community involvement, I felt this as quite a blow. I could have cried. Surely we could at least have come up with something to add to that statement. I sat back and thought, Why? Why? Then I understood why the statement had been made and I realized that going along with the feelings of the men at the convention was perhaps the best thing to do at the time.

1. Literally, "The Race," a term referring to people in the United States who are descended from the American Indians and the Spanish colonialists; also carries the meaning, "a new breed."—Ed.

Looking at the history of the Chicana or Mexican woman, we see that her role has been a very strong one—although a silent one. When the woman has seen the suffering of her people, she has always responded bravely and as a totally committed and equal human. My mother told me of how, during the time of Pancho Villa and the revolution in Mexico, she saw the men march through the village continually for three days and then she saw the battalion of women marching for a whole day. The women carried food and supplies; also, they were fully armed and wearing loaded *Carrilleras.* In battle, they fought alongside the men. Out of the Mexican Revolution came the revolutionary personage "Adelita," who wore her *rebozo* crossed at the bosom as a symbol of the revolutionary women in Mexico.

Then we have our heroine Juana Gallo, a brave woman who led her men to battle against the government after having seen her father and other villagers hung for defending the land of the people. She and many other women fought bravely with their people. And if called upon again, they would be there alongside the men to fight to the bitter end.

Today, as we hear the call of La Raza and as the dormant, "docile," Mexican-American comes to life, we see again the stirring of the people. With that call, the Chicana woman also stirs and I am sure that she will leave her mark upon the Mexican-American movement in the Southwest.

How the Chicana woman reacts depends totally on how the *macho* Chicano[2] is treated when he goes out into the "mainstream of society." If the husband is so-called successful, the woman seems to become very domineering and demands more and more in material goods. I ask myself at times, Why are the women so demanding? Can they not see what they make of their men? But then I realize: this is the price of owning a slave.

---

2. *Macho* and *machismo*—a term used among the Mexican-Americans (and other Latins) as a sense of manhood, defining the behavior of the male as truly masculine according to how superior and dominating he acts.—Ed.

A woman who has no way of expressing herself and of realizing herself as a full human has nothing else to turn to but the owning of material things. She builds her entire life around these, and finds security in this way. All she has to live for is her house and family; she becomes very possessive of both. This makes her a totally dependent human. Dependent on her husband and family. Most of the Chicana women in this comfortable situation are not particularly involved in the movement. Many times it is because of the fear of censorship in general. Censorship from the husband, the family, friends, and society in general. For these reasons she is completely inactive.

Then you will find the Chicana whose husband was not able to fare so very well in society, and perhaps has had to face defeat. This is the Chicana who really suffers. Quite often the man will not fight the real source of his problems, be it discrimination or whatever, but will instead come home and take it out on his family. As this continues, his Chicana becomes the victim of his *machismo* and woeful are the trials and tribulations of that household.

Much of this is seen, particularly in the city. The man, being head of the household but unable to fight the System he lives in, will very likely lose face and for this reason there will often be a separation or divorce in a family. It is at this time that the Chicana faces the real test of having to confront society as one of its total victims.

There are many things she must do. She must: 1) find a way to feed and clothe the family; 2) find housing; 3) find employment; 4) provide child care; and 5) find some kind of social outlet and friendship.

1) In order to find a way to feed and clothe her family, she must find a job. Because of her suppression she has probably not been able to develop a skill. She is probably unable to find a job that will pay her a decent wage. If she is able to find a job at all, it will probably be sought only for survival. Thus she can hope just to exist; she will hardly be able to live an enjoyable life. Here one of the most difficult

problems for the Chicana woman to face is that of going to work. Even if she does have a skill, she must all at once realize that she has been living in a racist society. She will have much difficulty in proving herself in any position. Her work must be three times as good as that of the Anglo majority. Not only this, but the competitive way of the Anglo will always be there. The Anglo woman is always there with her superiority complex. The Chicana woman will be looked upon as having to prove herself even in the smallest task. She is constantly being put to the test. Not only does she suffer the oppression that the Anglo woman suffers as a woman in the market of humanity, but she must also suffer the oppression of being a minority person with a different set of values. Because her existence and the livelihood of the children depend on her conforming, she tries very hard to conform. Thus she may find herself even rejecting herself as a Mexican-American. Existence itself depends on this.

2) She must find housing that she will be able to afford. She will very likely be unable to live in a decent place; it will be more the matter of finding a place that is cheap. It is likely that she will have to live in a housing project. Here she will be faced with the real problem of trying to raise children in an environment that is conducive to much suffering. The decision as to where she will live is a difficult matter, as she must come face-to-face with making decisions entirely on her own. This, plus having to live them out, is very traumatic for her.

3) In finding a job she will be faced with working very hard during the day and coming home to an empty house and again having to work at home. Cooking, washing, ironing, mending, plus spending some time with the children. Her role changes to being both father and mother. All of this, plus being poor, is very hard to bear. On top of this, to have a survey worker or social worker tell you that you have to have incentive and motivations—these are tough

pressures to live under. Few men could stand up under such pressures.

4) Child care is one of the most difficult problems for a woman to have to face alone. Not only is she tormented with having to leave the raising of her children to someone else, but she wants the best of care for them. For the amount of money that she may be able to pay from her meager wages, it is likely that she will be lucky to find anyone at all to take care of the children. The routine of the household is not normal at all. She must start her day earlier than an average worker. She must clothe and feed the children before she takes them to be cared for in someone else's home. Then too, she will have a very hard day at work, for she is constantly worrying about the children. If there are medical problems, this will only multiply her stress during the day. Not to mention the financial pressure of medical care.

5) With all of this, the fact still remains that she is a human and must have some kind of friendship and entertainment in life, and this is perhaps one of the most difficult tasks facing the Mexican-American woman alone. She can probably enjoy very little entertainment, since she can not afford a babysitter. This, plus the fact that she very likely does not have the clothes, transportation, etc. As she cannot afford entertainment herself, she may very often fall prey to letting someone else pay for her entertainment and this may create unwanted involvement with some friend. When she begins to keep company with men, she will meet with the disapproval of her family and often be looked upon as having loose moral values. As quite often she is not free to remarry in the eyes of the Church, she will find more and more conflict and disapproval, and she continues to look upon herself with guilt and censorship. Thus she suffers much as a human. Everywhere she looks she seems to be rejected.

This woman has much to offer the movement of the Mexican-American. She has had to live all of the roles of her Raza. She has had to suffer the torments of her people in that she has had to go out into a racist society and be a provider as well as a mother. She has been doubly oppressed and is trying very hard to find a place. Because of all this, she is a very, very strong individual. She has had to become strong in order to exist against these odds.

The Mexican-American movement is not that of just adults fighting the social system, but it is a total commitment of a family unit living what it believes to be a better way of life in demanding social change for the benefit of humankind. When a family is involved in a human rights movement, as is the Mexican-American family, there is little room for a woman's liberation movement alone. There is little room for having a definition of woman's role as such. Roles are for actors and the business at hand requires people living the examples of social change. The Mexican-American-movement demands are such that, with the liberation of La Raza, we must have a total liberation. The woman must help liberate the man and the man must look upon this liberation with the woman at his side, not behind him, following, but alongside of him, leading. The family must come up together.

The Raza movement is based on brother- and sisterhood. We must look at each other as one large family. We must look at all of the children as belonging to all of us. We must strive for the fulfillment of all as equals, with the full capability and right to develop as humans. When a man can look upon a woman as human, then, and only then, can he feel the true meaning of liberation and equality.

"**Chung-kuo Fu nü**" WOMEN OF CHINA*

Charlotte Bonny Cohen

Chung-kuo CHINA

China is unique, remote. After four years of language study,
you might be able to read *Jen-min Jih-pao*, the *People's
Daily.* You can't get through to China by trying to fit it into
our categories. The Chinese people have their own way of
looking at the world. What the People's Republic of China
is can only be understood in terms of what the Chinese
people are—and were.

China is almost exactly the same size as the United States.
Its population is at least three times larger. It can't be uni-
formly described. I can talk only in generalities.

China had the world's oldest social institutions and the
world's longest male tyranny. The basic fact was poverty.

*I would like to acknowledge the assistance of Richard Sorich and the other
members of the 623 Kent Club. The inscription at the top of the page is a fac-
simile of Chairman Mao's calligraphy. It reads "women of China" (from *Peking
Review*)—C.B.C.

Someone has calculated: Between 108 B.C. and A.D. 1911, there were 1,828 famines in China.[1] Four-fifths of the population was peasant: rural subsistence farmers not far from starvation. The other fifth was urban upper-class landlords, members of the official elite, the educated, refined gentry. And then there was the Emperor.

The country was ruled by the official bureaucracy which fanned out from the royal center. But the administration hardly penetrated the villages of China. The system seems to have persisted of its own momentum, the cycles of planting and harvesting, birth, marriage, and death. There were peasant revolts and barbarian conquests occasionally devastating enough to topple the Emperor. Dynasties usually lasted several hundred years. The last, the Ch'ing, began in 1644 and ended in 1911.

The longevity of the imperial system was facilitated by China's isolation. Its stability was reinforced by Confucian ideology which emphasized correct behavior, the proper handling of relationships, adjustment to existing conditions. The family was the unit of economic existence and the matrix of social contact for the individual. Most often, several generations lived, worked, and survived together, sharing one kitchen. It was an *absolutely authoritarian* grouping: domination of the young by the old, females by the males.

It is the habits so deeply ingrained by the Chinese family system that the People's Republic confronts today. The role of women in New China is a reaction to what had happened to women in old China.

Hsiao Chou or *Hsiao Tsueh*   Little Unpleasantness or Little Mistake[2]

That was what baby girls might be named by their Chinese

---

1. Walter H. Mallory, *China, Land of Famine,* quoted in *The China Reader: Imperial China,* eds. Franz Schurmann and Orville Schell (New York: Vintage Books, 1967), p. 263.
2. Martin C. Yang, *A Chinese Village* (New York: Columbia University Press, 1945), p. 125.

peasant parents; only male children were welcomed.

Female inferiority was prescribed in the Chinese classical tradition. From the *Book of Odes:*

> Daughters shall be born to him . . .
> It will be theirs neither to do wrong nor to do good.
> Only about the spirits and the food will they have to think,
> And to cause no sorrow to their parents.[3]

And from the *Li Chi* comes this rule of obedience: "The woman always follows the man." There is in Confucianism a concept of respect and honor for the female as mother. And there have been powerful females in China's history— four Empresses including the one who finally brought the house down, the Empress Dowager. Nevertheless, the tradition was overwhelmingly one of female passivity.

Ideology derives from concrete conditions and helps rationalize and perpetuate those conditions. How do the Communists view their own past? According to Mao Tse-tung:

> A man in China is usually subjected to the domination of three systems of authority . . . As for women, in addition . . . they are also dominated by the men. These four authorities—political, clan, religious, and masculine—are the embodiment of the whole feudal-patriarchal ideology and are the four thick ropes binding the Chinese people, particularly the peasants. [4]

The overt forms of discrimination speak for themselves. A woman had no independent status, no property rights. She could not inherit; land and other holdings were divided equally among sons only. She was raised only to become an obedient wife in someone else's family. Still young, she would be sold as a bride to a man she had never seen. She acquired status in her new family only by bearing male children. She belonged to that family, whether her husband left her or died. Remarriage of widows was forbidden, divorce extremely rare. She lived in illiterate seclusion, physi-

3. Ann E. Wee, "Chinese Women of Singapore," in *Women in the New Asia,* ed. Barbara Ward (Paris: UNESCO, 1963), p. 384.
4. *Quotations from Chairman Mao Tse-tung: The Little Red Book* (Peking:Foreign Languages Press, 1963), pp. 294–295.

cally handicapped by bound feet which were no more than two or three inches long. She prepared meals for men and then ate separately after they had finished. She could have no occupation other than that connected with her sex—prostitute, marriage matchmaker, midwife, perhaps a sorceress.

Marriage epitomized female subjugation. "With marriage began the most personally humiliating and emotionally disturbing stage of a woman's life."[5] There was no eroticism involved—it was an affair of the *family*. Love between husband and wife occurred by chance or habit. The girl was brought—a stranger into a strange home—to bear children. She was terrified and often terrorized, frequently beaten by both her husband and her mother-in-law. Since status and security increased with age, as a mother-in-law, a woman took her revenge upon the younger women: a tradition of tyrannous mothers-in-law; perpetuation of the system.

But China was a class society. The gentry woman's life differed from the peasant woman's as much as wealth permitted. The gentry was caught up in its own ideology; there was great pressure to conform to the Confucian family pattern of male domination. Upper-class families tended to be larger, with a bevy of rival daughters-in-law. Bickering, jealousy, suspicion, and conflict characterized relations among the women.

Satisfaction of erotic desires was a male prerogative only. "Secondary wives," "parallel wives," concubines, and prostitutes were all acceptable institutions. Female slaves were also common. In any of these capacities, the woman was degraded by the gentry way of life.

The peasant families supplied the slaves and prostitutes for the upper classes. In a poor family, the birth of a daughter was often a curse. Female infanticide was practiced. A young girl must be sold as a slave or sold to a family as a "child bride,"and later be married to a man in the purchas-

5. C. K. Yang, *Chinese Communist Society: The Family and the Village* (Cambridge: MIT Press: 1959), p. 107.

ing family, often ten or fifteen years her senior.

A peasant daughter was often treated criminally. As a wife, however, she was in a slightly better position; out of economic necessity she had to labor. In the South, this meant actual field work. There, women's feet were not bound. In the North, the woman was burdened with heavy domestic labor. The peasant woman therefore had "more say and greater power of decision in family matters."[6] There was less difference between peasant husband and wife. He could not afford concubines or even prostitutes. The couple were stuck with each other and their mutual fate.

Gentry or peasants, mindless erotic objects or domestic slaves—women had little choice. The life situation of women reflected the nature of Chinese society: "In every society the degree of liberation of women is a natural criterion of general liberation" (Engels). It was clear that there would be no change in the status of women until the total structure of authority was broken and then rebuilt on a new basis. It was not at all clear that change would inevitably liberate the Chinese woman.

hsien sheng and *te mo k'e la szu hsien sheng*   Mister and "Mister Democracy"

The beginning of the end: In the latter half of the nineteenth century the institutional bones of the aged system began to crack. Western imperialism coincided with and hastened degeneration of the elite (opium heads, many of them). From 1850 on, China was ravaged from within and from without. Chinese society very quickly fell apart. Just as quickly, discontented, self-conscious people began to come up with new solutions. Women's rights became an issue, for the first time in China's history.

Rebellious Chinese were inspired by Western thought—Christianity, liberal democracy, scientific experimentation,

6. *Quotations from Chairman Mao*, p. 295.

pragmatism, then anarchism and communism. The mainstream of activity was the rebellion of youth against the Confucian system, especially its family patterns. The youth and women's movement were organic allies. Infused with Western concepts of equality and competitiveness, advanced Chinese women became bourgeois feminists. The fight for women's rights in China coincided with the suffragist movement in the United States.

The intensity of social upheaval meant that new ideas could hardly keep up with events. Demonstrations which brought young girls into the streets were more effective as a tool of social change than was propaganda. Here is a brief and oversimplified summary of this crucial period:

The Taiping Rebellion, one of the world's worst civil wars, lasted from 1850 to 1864. The social organization of the Taipings served as inspiration and model for future political movements. The Taipings' program was revolutionary: communal property, complete equality of men and women. Women fought in the Taiping army. Footbinding and prostitution were forbidden. Monogamy, based on mutual love, was instituted. The Taipings' ideas were early stirrings; the same program was to re-emerge later, because it responded to the desires of the people.

Disintegration and frustration increased simultaneously in the early years of the twentieth century. Sun Yat-sen began to organize a political movement which admitted its first female member in 1904. Upper-class families began to open schools for their daughters, an act of emancipation which was soon to produce a generation of feminist leaders.

During these early years, protest was unorganized and sporadic. A few women demanded freedom of marriage, a few insisted on being called Mister. One early activist, Ch'iu Chin, established the first *Chinese Women's Journal.* She also wrote poetry:

> May Heaven bestow equal power on men, women.
> Is it sweet to live lower than cattle?
> We would rise in flight yes! drag ourselves up.

She correctly linked women's freedom to the freedom of all the Chinese people, and so became a revolutionary. She was executed by the Court in 1907.[7]

In 1911 the Empire fell. Battalions of women fought in the revolution, demanding women's rights. Under Sun Yat-sen's guidance, the 1912 Republican constitution made provisions for female education.

The "May Fourth Movement," from 1917 to 1921, was an all-out attack on Confucianism.[8] It was a period of enthusiasm, a time of searching for a new culture. Again, Western thought seemed to provide immediate answers. "Mr. Democracy" and "Mr. Science" became popular solgans. Meanwhile women were being drawn to the urban areas to work in factories, a new proletariat release from the traditional bondage of the family. And more women were becoming educated.

On May 4, 1919, there occurred massive student demonstrations against China's humiliating treatment by the Western powers. Peking students organized a union—composed of both sexes—and street demonstrations, including men and women. Nationalism and anti-imperialism had taken their place next to anti-Confucianism, and the woman's movement was linked with both.

The young people demanded a "family revolution"—sex equality, freedom of marriage, freedom of association. In 1919, the student Mao Tse-tung wrote nine articles in thirteen days denouncing the old and "hailing the 'great wave of the freedom to love.' "[9] Tsai Chang, a schoolmate of Mao's, later to become a leading female Communist, writes: "I hated marriage . . . I wanted to study and not to marry. My brother and Mao Tse-tung also hated marriage and declared they would never marry . . . "[10]

7. Helen Foster Snow, *Women in Modern China* (Paris: Mouton and Co., 1967), pp. 93–96.
8. Much of the following discussion is based on an excellent account of the period: Chow Tse-tsung, *The May Fourth Movement* (Stanford: University of Stanford Press, 1967).
9. Stuart Schram, *Mao Tse-tung* (Baltimore: Penguin Books, 1966), p. 55.

The Republic was unable to assert Chinese national supremacy, unify the country, or satisfy the demands of its rebellious youth. The insufficiency of cultural attacks and feminist campaigns became apparent. At least one militant female, Hsiang Chin-yü, recognized this. She called the May Fourth Movement a "bourgeois fight of women against men" and declared that "the emancipation of women can only come with a change in the social structure which frees men and women alike."[11] With this aim, the Chinese Communist Party was founded in 1921. The Communists worked within the Kuomintang (KMT). Women became political organizers. At the 1924 plenary session of the KMT, three women were elected to key positions, sex equality was recognized, and a Woman's Emancipation Association was formed.

Within a very short span of time, the rights of Chinese women had become an important political issue; to actualize these rights required a restructuring of Chinese society. The Communists wanted total revolution; the Nationalists didn't. The split between them occurred in 1927.

fan tung   Reaction

In 1927, Chiang Kai-shek launched a counterrevolution within the ranks of the KMT. Chiang was a conservative Nationalist and militarist, close to the Confucian tradition. He was supported by a reactionary alliance of the old Confucian gentry and the new merchant middle class. The Communists saw the necessity of destroying the power base of gentry, bourgeoisie, and militarists. The Nationalists opposed basic social reform and therefore had to stop the Communists.

In their 1927 purge, Chiang and his supporters were particularly vindictive of the KMT female contingent. Women's rights was an important symbol of the total social

10. Snow, *Women in China*, p. 236.
11. *Ibid.*, p. 247

reform desired by the leftists. And, as reactionaries, the Nationalists must have viewed the ascendancy of the Chinese woman with disdain.

Under the KMT, Madame Liao Chung-kai had organized 1,500,000 women. In 1927, her Women's Department was destroyed and many of her organizers were tortured or imprisoned. Women's noses and breasts were cut off; a girl who had freely chosen her fiancé was tortured, then shot seventeen times. Before beheading other young women, KMT soldiers shouted at them: "You have your free love now!"[12] Hsiang Chin-yü (quoted earlier) was publicly executed—the revenge of the oppressed upon the oppressed. After 1927, women were no longer an active political force within the KMT.

Among the middle classes and conservative intellectuals, the loosening of family bonds and freedom of marriage continued as a concomitant of the urban bourgeois life-style. As a concession to his allies, Chiang promulgated a Civil Code in 1931, which incorporated the principles of monogamy, freedom of marriage, and equal rights to inherit property. However, the basic authoritarian family structure was to remain intact. It was essential to the System.

More important, no effort was made to enforce or even publicize the Code. It was a piece of paper sanctioning the urban elite's practices, meanwhile permitting the Confucianists to continue their way of life. In fact, the institutions of polygamy and concubinage flourished among Nationalist officials.[13] The Nationalists could not countenance political or social change; they were forced back on an inappropriate and increasingly hated ideological tradition, and therefore became isolated from the demands of the vast majority of the Chinese people.

At the same time, the class structure of Chinese society

---

12. *Ibid.*, p. 242.
13. Henry McAleavy, "Some Aspects of Marriage and Divorce in Communist China," in *Family Law in Asia and Africa*, ed., J. N. D. Anderson (London: Allen and Unwin Ltd., 1968), pp. 76–77.

was becoming even more stratified. In urban factories, KMT entrepreneurs were creating an oppressed proletariat out of millions of Chinese workers, many of them women and children. Their treatment in Shanghai factories is a notorious historical fact: an average work day of twelve hours, a six-day work week, an average wage of fifteen dollars a month.[14]

The Nationalists had alienated women activists. They were creating a mass of poor workers—male and female—and were doing nothing to relieve the burden of peasant poverty. Enlightened women were increasingly attracted to Communism. And the Nationalists were digging their own graves.

ai jen   beloved

A ten-year civil war began in 1927. After that, from 1937 to 1945, the Communists fought the Japanese. From 1945 to 1949, the Communists fought the Nationalists. The women's movement was nurtured by war.

The Communist leadership recognized the importance and potential of women as a political allegiance group. They agreed with Lenin:

> The experience of all emancipation movements shows that the success of the revolution depends on the extent to which the women participate in it.[15]

The Communists actively organized women. They emphasized political action as the means of attaining women's goals. At the same time, the women's movement was made an arm of the total Communist offensive. Equality was to be achieved by participation in the struggle to liberate the rest of China.

As early as 1924, the Communists had sponsored a Woman's Day demonstration whose slogans were "Down

14. R.H. Tawney, *Land and Labor in China* (Boston: Beacon Press, 1966), p. 146.
15. Quoted in *Chinese Toiling Women* (Peking: Foreign Languages Press, n.d.), p. 29.

with Imperialism," "Same Work Same Pay," and "Equal Education." Initial organization efforts, directed at factory workers, failed. In one of their own publications, the Party admitted their isolation from the majority of women workers. Why? "The false view still persists that *work among the women is less important than other Party work.*" Furthermore, "*There is no solidarity between the working men and working women.*"[16] A strike by women workers in a hair-net factory was not supported by the male Red Trade Union. The strike failed. The Communists had come up against deeprooted resistance to the equality of women. In the cities, Communism was foundering. In the rural areas, however, it began to flourish. Mao successfully redirected the Party's efforts to the countryside.

To the Red areas flocked a new breed of leaders, educated men and women who had already freed themselves from the traditional family patterns. (At age thirty-five, Mao began living with his second wife; both his first wife and his sister were executed by the Nationalists).

The Communist cadres found the peasant women receptive. Their oppression was conspicuous and unmitigated; their poverty pitiful. Few had even heard of the movement for women's rights or the Nationalist Code. In the liberated areas, women became the object of a special appeal.

In 1931, the Communists promulgated their own marriage regulations; marriage and divorce by mutual consent, free of charge; prohibition of tyrannous mothers-in-law, prostitution, infanticide, and footbinding; equal property rights. These provisions were enforced and supported by publicity and propaganda. The term *ai-jen* came into use among the husbands and wives of the leaders as an example to all of the new equality.[17]

Women were drawn into a broad organizational network of women's groups: Women's Associations, study groups,

16. *Ibid.*, pp. 25–26.
17. Edgar Snow, *The Other Side of the River* (New York: Random House, 1961), p. 377.

anti-Japanese societies, Young Communist Leagues, nursing schools. The Communist strategy was to gain allegiance through constant participation and to get support by giving people a sense of belonging. And women were mobilized for labor. Each of these policies was experimental—and successful. The experience in the liberated areas was to provide the basis for the social policy of the new regime.

People's war meant that women were needed. They were mobilized and in the process partially liberated. The essential task was struggle and survival. In that, women played a vital role.

Yet the resistance put up by both sexes to women's rights was and is a continuing problem. For the Chinese Communists, ideology is always ahead of practice.

I'd like to point to a specific case of the social problems encountered in one village, Long Bow, as described by William Hinton in *Fanshen.*[18] The most difficult problem in that village proved to be psychological—the attitude of both men and women about women. Male cadres at first used their prestige to get what the old system would have offered them—an abundance of women. Ideological resistance was even stronger among husbands and mothers-in-law. Both felt their own status threatened by the freeing of the young wife. The liberation of one group necessitated the liberation of all.

The struggle for ideological change in Long Bow in 1948 pinpoints the central social problem which confronted the Chinese Communists once they came to power: how to change people.

chieh fang   Liberation

WOMEN AND THE REVOLUTION

On the way to power in 1949, Mao wrote a poem whose last

18. New York: Vintage Books, 1966, pp. 225–230, 353–354. I highly recommend it.

line is: "The true way that governs the world of men is that of radical change."[19] Radical change begins, not ends, with the seizure of state power. The Communists see the process of social change in a unique way, and I'd like to present some of their views.

Revolution is very much a psychological process, the act of changing yourself. Mao's Marxism emphasizes the human will, that human nature is changeable. The material conditions of society determine *what kind* of people live there, but people can change their conditions and themselves. At the same time, there is an understanding of the force of deeply rooted habits. A change in political institutions and ideology can come overnight; changing human behavior takes generations.

How do you change?

> If you want to know the taste of a pear, you must change the pear by eating it.[20]

Participation, involvement, constant self-analysis, struggle with yourself. Perhaps the most important method is discussion and persuasion—*t'an pai* ("speak freely"), confess your backwardness, your inadequacies, and then make statements about your future behavior which you must begin to actualize. Eventually your whole personality can change, your way of looking at the world. Hopefully, that new world view is a realization of your role in the total collective of Chinese society, your *responsibility* to the Chinese people.

What are the internal goals of the Communist Party, under the guidance of Mao? Primarily, economic—bringing China out of poverty, piloting it from an underdeveloped to a prosperous nation. In order to accomplish this *and* in order to create communism, the party wishes to bring about vast changes in the domestic structure of everyday life.

19. Schram, *Mao*, p. 244.
20. Mao Tse-tung, "On Practice," 1937.

The policy toward the women of New China reflects these basic goals. Women are to be liberated from their traditional semi-existence, to go to work for the Chinese people. Over the last twenty years their role in the economy has varied with the economic requirements and capabilities of the nation. At the same time, because of the emphasis on voluntarism, women are continually encouraged to create new roles for themselves, to constantly innovate.

Changing consciousness means altering men's views of women and women's views of themselves—getting rid of the "feudal" attitudes and avoiding the growth of "bourgeois" ones. Here, the domestic situation is a focal point. Policy has varied. Sometimes Chinese women are treated as a special case, a disadvantaged group; at other times their struggle for emancipation is immersed in the general class struggle between the two viewpoints—bourgeois and proletarian.

When judging what the People's Republic is doing about women's liberation, you have to keep in mind the extreme poverty, scarcity, and economic backwardness of China, and the oppressive nature of the old society out of which the New China was painfully born.

The Marriage Law of the People's Republic of China

Another poem by Mao ends:

the mountain goddess, if she is still there,
will be startled to see her
world so changed.[21]

On May 1, 1950, the Communists put into effect a revolutionary Marriage Law. By many, it is considered to be second in importance only to the Constitution of the People's Republic. Here is a summary of its significant points:

---

21. "Swimming," in *Major Doctrines of Communist China*, ed., John Wilson Lewis (New York: W. W. Norton, 1964), pp. 321–322.

Chapter One; General Principles

Article 1	"the arbitrary and compulsory feudal marriage system, which is based on the superiority of man over woman . . . is hereby abolished. The new Democratic marriage system, which is based on free choice of partners, on monogamy, on equal rights for both sexes, and on the protection of the lawful interests of women and children, shall be put into effect."
Article 2	prohibits polygamy, concubinage, child bethrothal, interference with remarriage of widows, marriage by purchase

Chapter Two: Contracting of Marriage

Article 3	marriage by mutual willingness
Article 4	minimum marriage age: twenty for males, eighteen for females
Article 6	marriage requires only registering in person with the People's Government

Chapter Three: Rights and Duties of Husband and Wife

Article 7	"Husband and wife are companions living together and shall enjoy equal status in the home."
Article 8	"Husband and wife are in duty bound to love, respect, assist, and look after each other, to live in harmony, to engage in production, to care for their children, and to strive jointly for the welfare of a new society."
Article 9	both have the right to free choice of occupations and social activities
Article 10	both have equal rights to possession and management of family property
Article 11	both have the right to use their own family names
Article 12	both have the right to inherit property

Chapter Four: Relations between Parents and Children

Article 13	no infanticide
Article 15	illegitimate children have the same rights as lawful children. If the father can be identified, he must support the children.

Chapter Five: Divorce

Article 17	"Divorce shall be granted when husband and wife both desire it."
Article 18	A husband can't divorce a pregnant wife nor a wife

with a child under one year of age. This restriction does not apply to women.

(Chapters Six and Seven contain detailed regulations about divorce, especially the obligations of the ex-husband towards his wife and children.)

This document is the legal basis for the status of women in Chinese society. It represents a total effort to abolish each specific act of the traditional marriage system, and female inferiority. It is Communist ideology; the government is the ally of the woman in her fight for status and equal rights. Two specific points:

*1)*Women have equal rights *vis-à-vis* their husbands. *Marriage is an affair of the individuals*; the family can no longer interfere. Registration with the government constitutes marriage. The state replaces the domineering family as the unit which sanctions it. The *duty* of both husband and wife is to create a harmonious, stable family unit—that is their *obligation* to the state. *2)*Polygamy, as a class institution and as a common practice of the Nationalists, is particularly offensive to the new government. Similarly, prostitution was abolished quickly. In 1950, two-hundred brothels in Peking were closed, the whores given merit badges and re-educated for new roles.[22]

Labor Heroines and Free Marriage Models (1949–1953)

In 1949, China was a war-devastated country. The only conceivable goal was economic reconstruction; for women: help reconstruct, put into practice the Marriage Law. Women's rights meant the right to work, and through labor, women were to attain equality. "Women must work hard if they want to be equal with men," declared Teng Ying-chao, President of the All-China Democratic Women's Federation (A–CDWF). "People say that women are good for nothing, but we must now set an example to show them that we are good in everything."[23]

22. C. K. Yang, *Chinese Communist Society*, p. 62.
23. Teng Ying-chao, *The Women's Movement in New China* (Peking: Foreign Languages Press, 1952), p. 12.

The central task was defined as mobilizing women for work. And there was plenty of work to do. Women were to attain equality with men by undertaking previously unheard of tasks, by becoming labor heroines. A model worker who was extolled for being the first woman to engage in steel production, declared, "If men can do the job here, why can't I?"[24] A female train dispatcher, China's first, was proudly described as having the "sturdiness and well-developed muscles typical for the women of New China." In this early period of exuberance, the dignity of laboring for China was defined as an act of freedom—"Ah, only such women can be called liberated women." Female workers were singled out for their remarkable achievements, but *individual* pride was frowned upon.

Pulling women out of their feudal torpor was no easy job. Propaganda focused on the contrast between the old and the new societies. Women were encouraged to develop confidence, courage, self-respect, initiative, the attitude of overcoming all difficulties. Propaganda also emphasized the desirability of *belonging* to the new society. A case in point is a young woman previously caught up in her small world of husband, children, home. From her self-confession:

> . . . the gongs and drums of "liberation" woke me up like thunder in spring and I began to crawl out of the dirt . . . I am going to throw myself into the human current . . . I want to shout with millions of sisters . . . We want to be masters of the new society . . . We have to break the chains on our hands and create the garden of happiness for humanity.[25]

Solidarity, mastery, control of one's own destiny—a far cry from the traditional female servility. It was propaganda, but part of a very serious effort to reverse the course of female history in China.

The other policy goal of this early period was publication and implementation of the Marriage Law. The economic

24. *Women in China Today,* June 1953, p. 13.
25. C. K. Yang, *Chinese Communist Society,* pp. 125–126.

motivation was clear. From a report by the commission which drafted the Law:

> The breaking down of the old family basis and the introduction of the new mode of life are urgent and necessary, especially to promote the growth of the productive power of society.[26]

Female emancipation was linked to participation in labor which in turn was linked to freedom within family relations.

Models of free marriage were those women willing to fight against the resistance put up by their families. "This Way is Better," the propaganda shouted. "How Wang Kwei-lan Married the Man of Her Choice" is a story typical of the government's promotional campaign. Wang's mother refused to let her marry the man she loved. Wang became depressed. Then her boyfriend told her about the new Marriage Law. "That reference to the Marriage Law settled the question." To celebrate their engagement the couple "planned to outshine each other in raising their output, making progress in their studies and correcting their shortcomings."[27] Again there was that important connection between *equal rights* of husband and wife, and their mutual *obligations* to the state. To counteract the emphasis on the duties of family life, housewifery was played down: "Although I have many children, I will never make them an excuse for relaxing my efforts at work or study."

What was really happening? In some areas, women by the thousands were seeking divorces from their arranged-marriage husbands. At first the government encouraged the movement as an "expression of the revolutionary struggle against the remnants of feudalism."[28] The courts usually granted the women's requests; divorce suits began to clog up the judicial system. With the State as ally, women were seeking new freedom.

But there was resistance, especially from men—as cadres and as husbands. Domestic conflicts and violence flared up

26. Emily Cohen, "Women in Communist China" (1963), p. 7.
27. *Women in China Today,* October 1952, p. 3.
28. C. K. Yang, *Chinese Communist Society,* p. 72.

wherever the Marriage Law was propagandized. In many rural areas cadres, although officially Communist, invoked their powers to *prevent* free marriages. In Kwangsi province, for instance, ten women were ordered to be tortured and made the object of "struggle" meetings for their audacity in desiring to marry for love.[29] Communist methods of persuasion, confession, and re-education were turned back against the government, an example of the power of local forces in China's vast countryside. There is a great difference between the top and the bottom of the Chinese power pyramid.

The government began to correct the discrepancy between ideology and practice. Mass Marriage Law education campaigns were conducted for both officials and general population. March 1953 was designated Marriage Law Month. The drive to enlist the support of women was carried on by political tactics as well. The masses of women were to be mobilized. Organizational appeals were directed at daughters, then their mothers. Women were to be drawn into all campaigns. Female activists were brought into the lower echelons of government—village government, peasant associations, the people's representative councils (in 1951 at least 10 percent female).[30]

By 1953 it is true that only a small minority of women had been affected by Communist policy. A poor showing? It depends on how important you consider history.

Economy and Diligence (1954–1958)

The themes of the women's movement had been set forth —participation in production, equal rights, free marriage, a new social conscience. The year of 1954 seems to mark the beginning of a new period—that is, in terms of the official policy coming out of Peking. China is huge and diverse, and extremely decentralized. In some areas the Marriage Law

29. *Ibid.,* p. 37.
30. Snow, *Women in China,* p. 64.

had not yet even been introduced. Many stages of revolution were occurring at the same time.

The general line during this period was economic development. On International Working Women's Day, 1954, the A–CDWF issued a notice: only through the building of socialism will it become possible for women to be fully emancipated. And only through women's devotion to that task can socialism be built.[31] Women were being urged to throw themselves into the struggle for economic development *as a means to* the creation of the conditions for full emancipation—a step backward in ideology, the postponing of freedom, in order to create its material base. The mood had changed. Previously, model women were singled out for their individual achievements. Now the broad mass of women were to be mobilized for agricultural work, the backbone of the Chinese economy.

Mao issued specific directives: "It has become necessary to get the great mass of the women—who have never worked in the fields before—to take their place on the labor front."[32] The same articles outlined the obstacles to women's agricultural work: "The men were urged to get rid of their usual contempt for the woman's working ability, while the women were urged to give up their old idea that production was men's job only." This was official admission of ideological backwardness.

During this period, there is continual reference to the need to persuade women to accept the work assigned to them, and to leave their children in nurseries. Apparently, traditional life, although oppressive, offered the security of well-known routine. In the North, women had never engaged in field labor before. Now they were being "liberated"—asked to perform menial labor. Was this a new form of enslavement? The women had to learn that they were working, ultimately, for themselves.

31. *New China News Agency* (NCNA) (Peking), 3 March 1954.
32. "Women Joining in Production Solve the Labor Shortage," in *Socialist Upsurge in China's Countryside* (Peking: Foreign Languages Press, 1957) p., 285n.

Simultaneously, Women's Day proclamations focused more and more on the positive contributions of the housewife. A 1956 declaration:

> Women are the equals of men now and this has made for harmony in family life; and better family life in turn has helped both men and women to play a fuller part in society.[33]

The new policy emerged full-blown in early 1958. Women were called upon to "build the state and run the home with economy and diligence." Tsai Chang cautioned that "emulation should be mainly in creativeness and initiative, not in intensity of labor." This seemed to be a reversal of earlier policies which praised individual women for their productive bravado.

Why this simultaneous emphasis on the value of home life and the necessity of laboring? In 1954, China experienced a minor depression; putting women to work in the fields seemed essential. The campaign for economy and diligence was its counterpart—an austerity program. Essentially, though, the emphasis on the woman's role in the home reflected the actual conditions of Chinese society. There were few desirable jobs—industrial or otherwise—for urban females. The great majority of Chinese women were, in fact, housewives. Propaganda had to be correspondingly readjusted. The line became: be a socialist in your own home, emancipate yourself by your daily conduct.

Finally, the emphasis on women's domestic responsibilities was probably a reaction to the disruption caused by the Marriage Law. The regime was trying to consolidate its base; the family had to be restabilized and its value reaffirmed. The courts began taking a less conciliatory attitude toward divorce cases.

Housewives were being told to develop a new consciousness. Women's home life was to be neither "feudal" nor "bourgeois." The Party was trying to develop a new concept of the family. Marriage became a socialist political act.

33. NCNA (Peking), 7 March 1956.

The qualities desired in a spouse were correct political viewpoint and willingness to devote oneself to the socialist cause. Esteem became more important than romantic sentiments. A peasant "love" poem captures this new attitude:

> . . . treading together
> at the windlass that brought up water
> from the well below. At times
> he pushes faster and then she
> keeps pace—always the two
> in harmony.[34]

Divorce on the grounds of "incompatibility" was being denounced as bourgeois and disruptive of socialist development. Coordinated with this new concept of family life was a birth-control campaign, China's first. Young people were encouraged to marry late and postpone having children.

These trends suggest the difficulties of finding a new solution to the age-old problems of domestic life. Overemphasis on freeing wives had produced frustrated ambitions and unstable families. Overemphasis on home life reeked of the enforced confinement of traditional Chinese life and seemed to rationalize female inertia. The family in Communist China was in limbo. By their own policies, the Communists had sharpened the contradictions between the desire for women in the labor force and the importance of the female in the household. With one bold step that contradiction was about to be solved.

The Socialization of Housework (1958–1961)

> I have a good mother
> She works in the fields;
> She works so hard that the commune
> Has presented her with a red flower.
> Our mothers are all good.
> All are working
> For the benefit of our new country[35]

34. Felix Greene, *Awakened China* (Garden City, L.I.: Doubleday and Co., 1961), p. 176.

In 1958, China took a "Great Leap Forward." The outcome was the organization of city and countryside into communes. The commune was a sudden attempt to overcome past failures. For women this meant resolving the contradiction between the desire to work and the necessity of being a housewife. There was a change in the material conditions of society, a reforming of the relationship between base and superstructure. Women were to be freed from household labor.

This drastic change was imposed upon the women suddenly. Being a housewife would no longer be permitted. Marx, Engels, and Lenin were dusted off and brought in to convince the women. Lenin:

> . . . when women are busy at household chores they suffer inevitably . . . In order to liberate women thoroughly . . . it is necessary to have a public economy and to allow women to share in the performance of productive labor.[36]

There was trouble with the communes. They seem to have been an overenthusiastic leap into the future without some of the necessary preconditions. Many women probably resisted the campaign to release them. Severe economic problems also beset the country. With its typical flexibility, the Party took a step backward and reverted to lower-level organization; keeping those aspects of the commune which were desirable, and preparing the way for ultimate communization.

During the era of the communes, it was openly admitted that previously women had not been liberated in the home, the factory, or the fields. The commune was viewed as an immediately liberating step, a *new stage* in the emancipation of women, and a weapon to hasten the transition to communism, or full emancipation.

A commune is a cooperative organization for working

---

35. *Ibid.*, p. 57.
36. Henry J. Lethbridge, *China's Urban Communes* (Hong Kong : Pagoda Press, 1961), p. 16. See also NCNA (Peking), 29 February 1960.

and living. In the rural communes, women were brought into low-level agricultural work in order to release men for heavier productive labor. In the urban communes, housewives were organized into workshops, handicraft industries, and "satellite enterprises" around the state factories.[37] For the first time, women were paid directly (previously all wages had been given to the male in the family). Essential to both rural and urban communes were the public messhalls, nurseries, and kindergartens, which Lenin had affectionately called "the young buds of communism." In the more advanced communes there were service stations with staffs to perform household chores, do marketing and laundry. Many communes began to develop their own centers of life—post office, bank, barbershop, theater, school, food processing plant.

The Great Leap Forward was a campaign for total mobilization of man and womanpower, and a campaign to release the creative energies of all the Chinese people. Innovation and initiative were the required virtues. In the street workshops women were supposed to invent handicraft projects, discover new methods; in the country women were supposed to help increase the productivity of the Chinese economy.

In terms of both labor and life, the communes did in fact constitute a sudden break from the past. Women gained economic independence: they were paid for their work—an important aspect of self-sufficiency and self-respect. But the most important achievement of the communes was hailed as "the very profound change [which] had come about in the spiritual outlook of women."[38] This spiritual change was manifested in family relationships and a new social awareness.

A Party Resolution on the Peoples' Communes declared, "We stand for the . . . development of family life in which there is democracy and unity."[39] Propaganda literature in-

37. NCNA(Peking), 8 March 1959.
38. Greene, *Awakened China*, pp. 143–144.

sisted on the new equality within the home now that husband and wife both labored and brought home income. Women and men told stories about the improvement in their relationships; the sources of friction in family life were removed—a woman was no longer a slave in her home. Household activity was officially denounced as "stultifying." A *Jen-min Jih-pao* editorial on Womens' Day, March 8, 1959, insisted that "family life has become more harmonious and united, so that women have become mentally much more comforted."

The second change was the emergence of women from their mental shells: they became more daring and self-confident, they ran the workshops and filled many of the political positions within the commune organizational structure.

> Private life was decried as old-fashioned, women were mobilized for labor, and collective life supplanted home life. The street, not the home, became the focus of daily life.[40]

Along with their emergence from the confines of the home came an interest in politics, and a concern for national affairs.

All of these propaganda claims point to both the boldness of the new and the failures of the old. Up to 1958, most women had been secluded, self-interested, domesticated. Now, an immediate change in consciousness was supposed to accompany the alteration of material conditions.

Economic and political relations were collectivized, but social relations were not. Communes were instituted for more efficient production, not for enjoyment. The lack of emphasis on *social* communization probably helped account for the failure of the communes; they didn't seem to offer an acceptable alternative to family life.

In 1960, articles began to expound the new stern Commu-

39. Franz Schurmann, *Ideology and Organization in Communist China* (Berkeley: University of California Press, 1966), p. 392.
40. *China Youth Daily*, "Views on Marriage," in *The China Reader : Communist China*, eds. Franz Schurmann and Orville Schell (New York : Vintage Books, 1967), pp. 458–460.

nist morality which was accompanying communization:

> The very basic foundations for love between man and woman are common political understanding, comradeship in work, mutual help and mutual respect. Money, position, or . . . prettiness should not be taken into consideration for a right marriage because they are not reliable foundations for love.[41]

Divorce was looked down upon, considered frivolous. Extramarital sex was condemned, as were any other family deviations.

Communization was meant to *strengthen* the family and to *politicize* it, in effect, to create a new family form. Men and women were drawn together by common aims and political outlook, were married and became part of a commune. They each worked—for the family and for the Chinese people as a whole. At home they shared whatever minimal domestic work was required. They remained strictly loyal to one another and bore children who were raised communally. Father, mother, and children spent their evenings and days off together, passing most of the time in study, discussion, and improvement of their socialist outlook.

As an experiment, the communes were in many ways unsuccessful. Specifically, they failed to inspire people to adhere to the new domestic patterns. As a model, however, they remain the goal of the Chinese Communist Party. The renewal of class struggle in the ensuing years was meant to create a firmer psychological basis for future communization.

What Do Women Live For? (1962–1965)

Despite the boasts of the regime, Chinese women remained, above all, home-oriented. Liberation through labor had failed; liberation through release from housework had failed. Some areas of China were still under the influence of

41. NCNA (Peking), 8 March 1965.

the Confucian tradition. In the cities and elsewhere, however, a new form of confining ideology was springing up—materialism, the sufficiency of a happy home-life, the satisfaction of being a wife. Tainted ideas from the West. The Communists began another ideological campaign. And the day of women's ultimate liberation was put back one more step: emancipation required communism which now required the defeat of imperialism. Beginning in 1962, Women's Day proclamations were internationalist in tone, exhorting women to help defeat imperialism and linking women's emancipation to the struggle for world peace. Even communism was being relegated to a hazy future. Gone was the exuberance of the post-liberation era and the enthusiasm of the Great Leap Forward. The mood was one of struggle—with oneself, with the sluggish economy.

The old propaganda began reappearing: practice frugality and industry in the home, remember the bitterness of the past, develop revolutionary spirit, "show an iron determination to conquer all difficulties."[42] Women had not been inspired to activism. Worse, they were falling into the bourgeois pit, limiting their aspirations to happy homemaking. The women's problem was becoming a class problem.

Marriage Law propaganda was replaced. The focus was no longer women's *rights* but women's *attitudes.* Women were being asked, What should you live for? What is happiness?

How should a Chinese socialist woman conduct her life? First, she should marry late: "Once you get married, you are bound to be harnessed by household chores, and if you have children early, it would inevitably affect your work and study."[43] The Party was trying to postpone marriage, to keep young people unattached and revolutionary as long as possible. Second, the socialist woman should select her spouse on the basis of his ideology, character, the quality of his work, and the strength of his revolutionary ideas—"poli-

42. *Survey of China Mainland Magazines* (SCMM), 23 September 1963, p. 39.
43. SCMM, 9 December 1963, p. 24.

tics in command." Third, a female worker or cadre should put revolutionary work ahead of domestic responsibilities, lest people say to her children, "Just because of you, your Mama has lagged behind the others!"[44] As a housewife, the socialist woman must not be content merely with the "warm small family." Finally, the socialist woman must strive for self-assertion and independence, emancipate herself through her own efforts—"if one should depend on one's husband . . . the spiritual life will be empty and meaningless."[45]

Instead of communes it was now revolutionary spirit which would overcome the contradiction between labor and housework.

By late 1964, the problem was being stated even more clearly—"the question of women must be subordinated to the interests of the integral class struggle of the proletariat."[46] —i.e., there are only two conceptions of life, the bourgeois and the proletarian: there is only one struggle for liberation; there is no such thing as the women's question.

By 1965, the political criteria of a proper domestic relationship were made explicit:

> Only the beauty of political quality, sentiments, thinking, and the way of handling things represents the true and everlasting beauty. Love that is built on this basis will be evergreen.[47]

The deepset love is built on struggle. Through revolutionary attitudes domestic problems will solve themselves.

Men were criticized for desiring beautiful women; women were criticized for desiring rich husbands. Men were criticized for treating women equally at work, then lording it over their wives at home; women were criticized for remaining within the womb of materialism. Sound familiar?

44. "Translations of Political and Sociological Information on Communist China # 151," *Joint Publications Research Service,* 24 February 1964, p. 9.
45. Chang Ying, "Before and After Labor Participation," *ibid.,* p. 19.
46.–"How the Problem of Women Should Be Viewed," SCMM, 23 November 1964.
47. Wan Mu-ch'un, *Red Flag,* 28 October 1964, p. 18.

Communist ideologues were assuring women that proletarian attitudes would solve their problems. But what did that mean? To most women, very little. Jan Myrdal describes a North Chinese woman's typical plight—a double workload. She explains that "women work much more than men. We have two jobs: we work in the fields and in our homes."[48] The contradictions weren't really being resolved after all. And anti-socialist attitudes were cropping up all over. As in 1958, the solution was a great leap—this time in consciousness. An all-out effort to revitalize the Chinese revolution. The women's movement dissolved into class struggle.

ke-ming te nü-jen   Revolutionary Women (1966–1969)

> . . .learn to swim by swimming, learn to make revolution by making revolution.[49]

The first wall poster of the great proletarian Cultural Revolution was put up by a woman, Nieh Yuan-tzu. But there was no longer a women's movement: "Revolution differs according as it is true revolution or false revolution. It does not differ according to sex."[50]

Mao Tse-tung launched ideological war in order to rid the Chinese people of attitudes which were slowing the course of socialism: careerism within the Party, routinization within the bureuacracy, above all, bourgeois thought among the people. Mao wanted to shake up Chinese society. He was recreating revolution. And women, especially young women, were supposed to become revolutionaries. International Working Women's Day, March 8, began disappearing from the celebration calendar. In 1968 it was ignored.

Now when the question was asked, What is happiness? the answer was unambiguous: *happiness is serving the people.*

48. Jan Myrdal, *Report from a Chinese Village* (New York: Random House, 1965), p. 238.

49. *Peking Review,* 2 Septermber 1966, p. 17.

50. "Expose the Plot, Remove the Poisonous Weeds," SCMM, 31 October 1966, p. 28.

Revolutionary women were singled out for their contributions to that end. Wei Feng-ying, a worker-engineer, is one
of the Cultural Revolution's heroines. Her story is worth
relating because of its definition of the ideal revolutionary
female.

"I Shall Always Make Revolution and Always Be Loyal
to Mao Tse-tung's Thought:" in 1953 Wei took a job in a
factory. But she was tainted with bourgeois ideas. She
thought her job inferior, and was dissatisfied. One day she
wore a white blouse to work because her roommates had
called her factory dress unbecoming. Her foreman criticized Wei: white blouse today, fancy dress and hair oil tomorrow. In 1954, Wei began intensively studying Mao—"I
would write a quotation from Chairman Mao on my palm
and study it on the way [to work]." She was awakened to
the call to serve the people and became an activist in the
Cultural Revolution.

She discusses female problems: love, marriage, children.
"I put revolution first . . . After I met my husband concrete
problems came up . . . I could not let love affect my work
and studies. In this he fully agreed." Their courtship lasted
four years. "Although we did not often go out strolling
together and did not talk sweet nothings, our love was not
affected. On the contrary this made our love for each other
stronger . . . "

It was not until after marriage that Wei "realized what
running a home meant, and how much bigger the responsibilities of a wife were than those of the husband."

The couple drew up a four-point plan:

1. We must help each other and study Chairman Mao's works
in a planned way
2. We must both share the household work and not let it be a
burden on us
3. We must plan our spending, be frugal and diligent . . .
4. We must plan our family, continuously make revolution, and
advance.

After the birth of her first child, Wei was chided by her mother for ignoring the infant—"You think of making technical innovations at the expense of your baby." Wei pointed out that breast-feeding would mean a loss of three months' work that year. So Grandma agreed to bring up the baby with reassurances that she, too, was contributing to socialist construction.[51]

Wei has told her story at mass meetings all over China. She is a model of the contemporary conception of the Chinese liberated woman—revolutionary, independent, innovative, self-sacrificing, hard-working, companion to her husband, adequate as housewife and mother.

Against this model was set the bourgeois humanist ideals which had been advanced by Tung Pien, the editor of *Women of China*. In 1966, Tung Pien was denounced as a "black gang" element and expelled as editor of the magazine. She was accused of breeding the poisonous weeds that the purpose of revolution was to improve life, and that happiness consisted in the good life—good food and good clothes—"the founding of individual happiness on the suffering of the majority." She was also condemned for trying to keep women "intoxicated" within their "warm small family" world. One of her accusers, a young student, also denounced her for "making us stay all day long in the midst of 'love and marriage,' breaking our revolutionary will, and making China change its color, beginning with our generation."[52]

Like Liu Shao-ch'i, Tung Pien became the target and the scapegoat for all that was counterrevolutionary within each of the Chinese people. Denunciation of her was also self-denunciation, a repudiation of past behavior and an affirmation of the strength of new attitudes. There is a great contrast between the ideals set forth by Wei Feng-ying and those supposedly propagated by Tung Pien. A bourgeois

51. *Peking Review,* 2 December 1966, pp. 19–24.
52. "The Big Plot of False Discussion and Real Release of Poison," SCMM, 31 October 1966, pp. 22–28.

way of life sounds strangely out of place in contemporary China, still an economy of scarcity. But Red China is still very much a class society. It was that concrete awareness which Mao wished to give to the people, especially the youth.

Another aspect of the Cultural Revolution deserves mention. As in the years immediately after liberation, the family has once again become a focal point of struggle: one fourteen-year-old girl put up a big character-poster criticizing her mother.[53] In another family a proletarian revolutionary wife had the support of her husband and son, but was opposed by her sister. After a series of "bitterness" meetings —recalling the past—the family was reconciled, i.e., the sister was won over.[54] These stories are propaganda designed to encourage upheaval. As in the past, the restabilizing of the family situation will probably follow.

I have deliberately avoided discussion of the few female leaders in contemporary China. The two most powerful had been Tsai Chang and Teng Ying-chao, the wife of Chou En-lai. Both are veteran revolutionaries, but they are not representative of the mass of Chinese women. During the Cultural Revolution, Mao's third wife, Chiang Ching, emerged from obscurity to become one of its leaders. She is highly controversial. She has been Mao's loyal ally in a period of suspicion and chaos within the ruling elite. Yeh Chün, the wife of Lin Piao, has joined Chiang as the other female member of the Party Politburo. She is also there as Lin's wife rather than as an independent political figure. Finally, like her husband, Liu Shao-ch'i, American-born Wang Kuang-mei became a target of attack in the Cultural Revolution. She was denounced as bourgeois, especially her taste in clothes (cartoons caricatured her in miniskirts and jewelry).

The percentage of women on the Party's Central Committee—4.5 percent in 1956, about 8 percent in 1969—indi-

53. NCNA (Nanking), 5 March 1968.
54. NCNA (Shanghai), 12 March 1968.

cates that women are not yet a significant force in Chinese politics. Educational achievement is a more important indicator of women's rising status. In 1960, the percentage of females enrolled in full-time college programs was given as:

College Program	Percentage of Females Enrolled[55]
Engineering	18 percent
Medicine	42.2 percent
Agronomy	28 percent
Normal Studies	24 percent

But the problems of women's liberation are far from solved. When the Cultural Revolution subsides, consolidation will bring back the women's movement. Its goals will be geared to the general economic and social goals of the nation. But it will be grappling with the same problems which confronted the Communists in 1949—how to turn the female half of China into independent, productive individuals. Socialism, the material base for emancipation, will be built. Meanwhile there will be periodic attempts to leap to new stages of consciousness. The Chinese will keep trying to fight their past, two thousand years of female servitude. And as long as China remains revolutionary, the Communists will be fighting the equally oppressive forces created by class society.

China is not our model. Its needs and desires are very different from ours. Women are *told* what they should be and do—that's not the way it could be here. But Mao and the Chinese Communists do show us that society is changed by changing people's daily lives. Working side by side with men partially liberates women. Freedom—however you want it—comes from new ways of living together.

55. Snow, *Women in China*, pp. 177–178.

iv

UP FROM SEXISM:

EMERGING IDEOLOGIES

THE GRAND COOLIE DAMN

Marge Piercy

The Movement is supposed to be for human liberation: how come the condition of women inside it is no better than outside? We have been trying to educate and agitate around women's liberation for several years. How come things are getting worse? Women's liberation has raised the level of consciousness around a set of issues and given some women a respite from the incessant exploitation, invisibility, and being put down. But several forces have been acting on the Movement to make the situation of women actually worse during the same time that more women are becoming aware of their oppression.

Around 1967—the year of what the mass media liked to call the Summer of Love—there was a loosening of attitudes in the Movement just as there was a growing politicization among dropouts and the hippie communities. For a while, Movement people were briefly more interested in each other as human beings than is the case usually, or now. Movement men are generally interested in women occasionally as bed partners, as domestic-servants–mother-surrogates, and constantly as economic producers: as in other patriarchal societies, one's wealth in the Movement can be measured in terms of the people whose labor one can possess and direct on one's projects.

For a while, people were generally willing to put effort into their relationships with each other and human liberation was felt as something to be acted out rather than occasionally flourished like a worn red flag. People experimented with new forms of communities and webs of relationship reaching beyond the monogamous couple. Men and women were trying new ways of relating that would not be as confining, as based on concepts of private property and the market economy as the means by which we have learned to possess each other. Some of the experimenting was shallow, manipulative, adventurist, with little regard for consequence to the others involved; but some was serious and had a tentative, willed oppenness that allowed room for men and especially for women to grow whole new limbs of self and encounter each other in ways that made them more human.

It is not necessary to recount the history of the last two years to figure out what happened. Repression brings hardening. It is unlikely the Movement could have gone along with the same degree of involvement in personal relationships. An excessive amount of introspection and fascination with the wriggles of the psyche militate against action. One of the high schools in New York was effectively cooled by involving students in therapy groups and sensitivity training. But there is also a point beyond which cutting off sensitivity to others and honesty to what one is doing does not produce a more efficient revolutionary, but only a more efficient son of a bitch. We are growing some dandy men of steel nowadays.

The typical Movement institution consists of one or more

men who act as charismatic spokesmen, who speak in the name of the institution, and negotiate and represent that body to other bodies in and outside the Movement, and who manipulate the relationships inside to maintain his or their position, and the people who do the actual work of the institution, much of the time women. Most prestige in the Movement rests not on having done anything in particular, but in having visibly dominated some gathering, in manipulating a certain set of rhetorical counters well in public, or in having played some theatrical role. To be associated with a new fashion trend in rhetoric is better rewarded than is any amount of hard work on the small organizing projects that actually recruit new people and change their heads.

The Movement is an economic microcosm. Presumably the rewards will be bringing about a revolution changing this society into something people want to live in and which they have a chance of affecting, and which will get off the back of the rest of the world. But the day-to-day coin is prestige. Another short term reward is a modicum of power, largely to force other people out of some group, or to persuade that group to engage in one activity rather than another. A third type of power is over the channels of communication. These may be formal channels such as *New Left Notes*, the *Guardian*, underground papers, *Liberation News Service*, or other media. There is also power over informal channels of communication. A person may come to usurp the prestige of an organization simply by being the speaker on all public occasions or by representing that group to other Movement groups. That may be actually the only work he does, but what meager satisfactions can come from parading the name of his group before others, he will enjoy. At the least he will get a chance to travel a little. Lives in the movement are not exactly running over with pleasures, so that if you have spent all winter on the lower east side of New York, a trip to Rochester or Buffalo can look glamorous.

It is possible to build up power simply through insisting

or arranging that all of a particular kind of contact occur through you. The important thing is to keep all transfer of information or requests between any Dick and any Bill routed through you. That gives a look of busyness and importance. It can be a career in itself. There is a loss of information and energy, but strangely enough, good will is created with both Dick and Bill. Your phone will ring all the time and people call wherever you go, making manifest your importance before others. Almost all informal Movement contacts of this sort are between men. Especially in Ivy League schools, SDS chapters seem to act as fraternities, creating in-groups who respect and trust only each other.

If the rewards are concentrated at the top, the shitwork is concentrated at the bottom. The real basis is the largely unpaid, largely female labor force that does the daily work. Reflecting the values of the larger capitalist society, there is no prestige whatsoever attached to actually working. Workers are invisible. It is writers and talkers and the actors of dramatic roles who are visible and respected. The production of abstract analyses about what should be done and the production of technical jargon are far more admired than what is called by everybody shitwork.

Nor is the situation improved when the *machers* are competing to demonstrate their superior, purer, braver militancy, rather than their purer analysis. In an elitist world, it's always "women and children last." Only a woman willing and able to act like a stereotyped American frontier male can make herself heard.

The leader co-opts the work of his laborers. How many times a *macher* will say, "I have done," "I have made" when the actual labor was somebody else's. It is easy for the *macher* to pretend he has written a leaflet he glanced over, inserting the fashionable cant phrase of the week. I am aware that men in the Movement who are not domineering, highly verbal, manipulative, or hypercompetitive also turn into invisible peasant laborers. If there were no women at all in the male-dominated Movement, men not ready to stomp on others would end up playing many roles now filled by women. Which is to say that poor whites may be no better off economically than poor blacks, for the System oppresses them in some of the same ways.

We take this alloting of prestige for granted, in which we are an exact microcosm of the society we oppose. Work is shit. It is mindlessly done by unappreciated, invisible workers, and the results, the profits in prestige and recognition, are taken away. Truly, it is not necessary that work be shit even in the bowels of the beast. One of the things that really is true about visiting Cuba is discovering how proud people can be of their work—work they would be ashamed to do here. Because work is admired, and makes sense in a society that makes sense, it is social in the full meaning. All right, we cannot have little islands of revolutionary culture in the heart of the empire, but we can try a little harder not to reflect the ugliest aspects of the society we are presumably rejecting.

As the fight gets stiffer and we settle in for the long haul, as all of us accumulate enough experience of failure and look long and hard enough at the cost to ourselves of what we are trying to do, as we get older and go through our share of the nasties, there is an attitude that sustains many: *I am a professional revolutionary.* To take that kind of step in one's head and rhetoric is felt as a leap of commitment. It explains to the person and to others what he is doing. After all, he is acting quite differently from what was expected of him. He is failing to make it in any way he was taught all through growing up American to expect he would do (and to be scared he wouldn't do). So it turns out there is an answer. No, Ma, I'm not a bum. I'm a professional, like a doctor or a lawyer, like I was supposed to be.

One trouble: to be a professional anything in the United States is to think of oneself as an expert and one's ideas as semisacred, and to treat others in a certain way—professionally. Do you question your doctor when he prescribes in dog Latin what you should gulp down? The expert has expertise. Unfortunately he also often has careerism. He is giving up everything else, and he is not about to let some part-time worker (differentiation between part-time and full-time in the Movement is instructive and dangerous) challenge his prerogatives. Shall the professional revolution-ary haul garbage, boil potatoes, change diapers, and lick stamps? Finally, what opposes the professional is counter-revolutionary, even though it may be repressed by the power structure with the same zeal.

The incidence of violent brand-loyalty to one's own cur-rent dogma has risen. The word "cadre" as something to caress in the mouth and masturbate over has gone whoosh to the top of the pole in the last year. Cadre has meaning when a movement has really gone underground, when its members have been through training that has attempted to change their characters, when groups have shared violent and harrowing experiences over time so that they know they can trust each other. Cadre applied to the white Move-ment in the United States at this time is elitist bullshit. Our big problem is learning how to reach all kinds of people and we haven't invented any training yet that helps much on that score. People are working hard on projects scattered around the country, and here and there they are making headway in one or another enclave of the old or new work-ing class (or groups in motion are reaching out to them); or in high schools or the army or neighborhoods under stress such as the threat of urban renewal, things are happening; but experts are experts largely in manipulating current jargon.

Now common, ordinary, gross *chutzpah* is something that in this society sprouts more commonly from the egos of men than from the more shattered and battered egos of women. Women are not encouraged toward professional-ism in general, and we are certainly not in the Movement encouraged to gives ourselves too many airs. Suppose you, Woman Alice, unknown, unvouched for, unaccompanied, come wandering into a meeting and want to speak. The male supremacist will not even hear you. He may launch a sentence while you are in the middle of speaking, and probably he can simply drown you out. The male chauvinist will keep quiet while you speak and may even give a quick acknowledgment that some noise has occurred. He will patronize and move on. The male liberal will note your energy and will commiserate and then co-opt you. You will end up working for him, no matter what you think you are doing. When you oppose him, you will find out which side he is on.

With the professional comes his professional language. A predominantly student movement is a great soil for the growth of monstrosities of jargon. The use of scholarly Marxist jargon is exactly analogous to the use of any other academic jargon. It is a way of indicating that you have put in your time, read the right texts and commentaries, that you are an expert. It is one thing to learn from the long line of revolutionaries who have come before us: we must learn that history or caricature it. (With the factionalism, name-calling, and assumption of infallibility that has been growing lately, I sometimes get the impression of people role-playing as professional revolutionaries based on certain comic books in which that was how you could identify the Reds.) It is another thing to adopt the language of any of them, especially translated into lousy American. Now we have scholarly quarrels about the definition of key terms and the appreciation among the in-group of the way in which someone is handling them, as in any English or Sociology department. Such articles are written for a snobbishly defined audience of peers. The jargon covers up holes in the world. Most of us know damn little about how the society works and how people live, but rather than find out, we will adopt a jargon that stands between the observer and what he is trying to observe. Such articles fail to make our politics lucid to people on a level where they can become autonomous political thinkers and doers. If you have contempt for people and think they cannot know what they want and need, who the hell is the revolution for?

Women in the Movement, with a few outstanding exceptions, have trouble talking jargon. One source of unease is lack of practice. The phenomenon of a woman speaking in a meeting, and the meeting going on as if she had belched, is too widespread to need comment. Women don't generally practice on each other. Women are able at least on occasion to be more honest in talking about their lives together than men ever are: not always, not often, but it is a possibility. The mores of the society do not prevent women who trust each other from speaking about their sexual and emotional troubles. Much of this ability comes from our being taught to define our "careers" in terms of that part of our lives, so that it is shoptalk. In contrast, so much of what passes for communication between men and women are responses to signals given, the fulfilling of subtly or not so subtly indicated wishes, games of protection and mutual blackmail. The bases of many relationships are unspoken, not because they lie too deep for words, but because speaking about them would disgust. It would expose connection based on gross and subtle forms of lying and exploitation that could not bear examining aloud.

Sometimes women simply refuse to use jargon. I know one woman who grew up in the Old Left and who will not use language she associates with that type of life and politics. In the small group of organizers she operates in, her refusal is viewed by the male ideological clique as a pitiful weakness. She is crippled. If she cannot talk their language, they cannot hear her, although she speaks the language of the kind of workers they are attempting to organize. They cannot accept her criticisms or insights unless couched in their terminology. Not that that always produces acceptance.

I remember watching a girl at a council meeting a few years ago who was striking in all aspects. She spoke well in a husky but carrying voice, she was physically attractive, she had read her texts and had a militant Left position and an obvious sense of style. In her head she was on the barricades, and that excitement carried in her speeches. She had no impact. I heard many people giving précis of the council afterward, and no one singled her out to mention, although many of the issues she spoke to carried. She did not succeed in becoming part of that collective of *machers* who are always counting points with each other. If she had been sexually connected with any of the *machers* present, the odds on her achieving impact would have been much greater, for she would have been automatically present at the small caucuses and meetings where policy, unfortunately, originates.

Around that time, when I attended many women's liberation meetings I saw the whole thing as interesting primarily as an organizing tool: here was a way to organize women who could not be reached on other issues or in other organizing contexts. I am older than most Movement women, have a harder sense of myself, make a living off my writing and care about it, and have a good, longstanding, and non-possessive relationship with a man I trust politically and personally. It took me two *more* years of grisly experiences, of getting used and purged, to get my nose well rubbed into women's exploitation, to find out women's liberation was not talking about the other fellow, and to understand how much I had adopted male values to think of liberation as a *tool.* We are oppressed, and we will achieve our liberation by fighting for it the same as any other oppressed group. Nobody is going to give it to us because we ask, however eloquently. I once thought that all that was necessary was to make men understand that they would achieve their own liberation, too, by joining in the struggle for women's liberation: but it has come to me to seem a little too much like the chickens trying to educate the chicken farmer. I think of myself as a house nigger who is a slow learner besides. A tendency to believe quite literally in the rhetoric of Movement males is a form of naiveté that no woman can afford. Most Movement males' idea of women's liberation is something for their girlfriend to do to other women while they're busy in decisionmaking. That's her constituency to bring in.

Fucking a staff into existence is only the extreme form of what passes for common practice in many places. A man can bring a woman into an organization by sleeping with her and remove her by ceasing to do so. A man can purge a woman for no other reason than that he has tired of her, knocked her up, or is after someone else: and that purge is accepted without a ripple. There are cases of a woman excluded from a group for no other reason than that one of its leaders proved impotent with her. If a *macher* enters a room full of *machers*, accompanied by a woman and does not introduce her, it is rare indeed that anyone will bother to ask her name or acknowledge her presence. The etiquette that governs is one of master-servant.

Women come into the Movement for as many reasons as men do. It is not sufficient to speak of women as being recruited in bed, since their attraction to the man is usually as much to the ideas they hear him spouting, what they think he represents, and what they imagine their life with him will be, as it is to his particular body or personality. Movement men often project a very sexual image. What's behind that too often is, as with actors, narcissism, impotence, and a genuine lack of interest in anybody else except his hero, The Professional Revolutionary in the Mirror, and a small peer group whose opinions he values and whom he likes to shoot the bull with, much like ex-fraternity boys.

I've listened to the troubles of dozens and dozens of women and men in the Movement. There are a lot of lonely and a lot of horny women. Sex lives of women seem to fall into two patterns, both dreary. Domestic unions on the whole are formed young and maintained in hermetic dependency, until exchanged for others that appear almost identical. People seldom maintain relationships with any content without living together, though it happens. As in conventional marriages, the woman living with a man often finds her world constricted. She is his thing. She keeps house for him and plays surrogate mother, and often he talks to her no more than the tired businessman home from the office. Often the relationship is much like that of the woman living with a medical student and helping to put him through school. Of course, since the woman's intellectual energy is concentrated on that relationship, she may in fact dominate or manipulate or control the man, as is frequent in conventional marriages also.

The other model is the liberated woman: she can expect to get laid maybe once every two months, after a party or at councils or conferences, or when some visiting fireman comes through and wants to be put up. She may find she can work for years and even take part in planning demonstrations, and doing important research, and organizing without achieving recognition or visibility. There is a phenomenon I have noted, by the way: allowing for geographical variations, the list of men whom Movement women not living with anyone have gone to bed with is surprisingly repetitive. One is left to draw the conclusion that all the liberated (i.e., living alone) women have gone to bed with the same set of men, who would fit in one large room.

These serviceable males fall into two categories: those who make it clear that what they are doing is fucking, and those who provide a flurry of apparently personal interest, which fades mighty quick. The first category are on far fewer hate lists than the second. There are men in the Movement who have left women feeling conned and somehow used, emotionally robbed, in every city in the country. Rarely have I heard any man in the Movement judge any other man for that kind of emotional exploitation, and never so it could hurt him. The use of women as props for a sagging ego is accepted socially. Everybody sees it and everybody agrees that they don't. Scalp-hunting goes on on both sides of the sexual barrier, but the need to extract a kind of emotional conquest which is sometimes not even sexually consummated, out of woman after woman, seems exclusively the disease of male *machers*.

This sort of thing can even be called organizing. Many politicos spend their energies organizing inside the Movement, instead of into the Movement: hence the passionate concern with who is, and who is not, in the vanguard. Transferring the loyalties of worker-woman Lizzie from the research project of *Macher A* to the pamphlet project of *Macher B* is organizing.

The men who often get the most opposition from Movement women and are often publicly called male oppressors, are precisely those men who have the least skill at co-opting the labor of women: men with a bluff style, frontal attack, an obvious sense of their own competence, and a tactless assault on what they see as other's lack of it. They often succeed in rapid fashion in uniting some of the women in a caucus against them.

The style most rewarded is that of the manipulator: the person who makes use of the forms of workers' control and community decisionmaking to persuade others that they are involved in a "we" that is never out of his control. Given the careerism, in almost any Movement enterprise there is at least one person who feels a vested interest: that endeavor is his baby. If there were true workers' control, he might find himself ousted. Most Movement ventures exist hand-to-mouth, and the entrepreneur can always tell himself that a couple of weeks of financial chaos would wreck that precarious balance and run the enterprise into the ground. The rationale for retaining control may be political: the entrepreneur as professional revolutionary finds it necessary to keep political control of the little *Iskra*, lest the bourgeois revisionists get it into their slimy paws, or the soft minds of the shitworkers be led stray. The means to that control is seldom an obvious role as boss, for antiauthoritarianism is as deeprooted among women in the Movement as among men.

No, the successful entrepreneur uses all the forms of workers' control and collective decisionmaking. He may covertly despise these indirect, time-consuming methods. Or he may have contempt instead for those who attempt to work without them, and feel morally superior because of his attachment to the forms of participatory democracy. This distinction is equivalent to the different between the modes of the male supremacist and the male liberal: but both aim to retain control.

Methods vary. The *macher* may play off faction against faction or appear to float above petty quarrels. He may form sexual alliances, sabotage others, repeat gossip, start rumors, flatter, sow suspicion, retain the switchboard-control central function, flirt, listen to troubles, pay attention. Since most people in this society are dreadfully lonely, a little attention is a pungent tool. But he must always keep the others from combining.

On one Movement staff where I worked, there was one *macher,* a couple of other males who did not challenge his hegemony, plus a two-thirds majority of women. Whenever we threatened to form an alliance on anything that mattered, the *macher* would begin jiggling the sexual balance of the group, pursuing publicly one of the staff or another until he had suceeded in creating a harem atmosphere in which all attention once again centered on him. He would use his confidant relationship to the staff members to persuade each to talk about the others, comments he would remember and reveal as if reluctantly at the proper moment. Even the fact that he was sexually involved with only one of the staff could be turned to moral advantage, for he would keep her in her place (on his right hand, just under the thumb) by constantly pointing out that he could in fact be involved with the others, by ignoring her in the office, and flirting and teasing, and creating a constant subsurface tizzy centering on his person. None of this, of course, was ever openly discussed. The superficial reality was business as usual, bureaucratic efficiency and personal relations kept out of the office. The effect was to make his position impregnable and enable him to dismiss whomever he chose.

The ability to dismiss from a collective is as important as the ability to recruit. One effective method is to stir up the workers so they themselves expel the person threatening the *macher's* power. If the expulsion is carried out in the name of workers' control or women's liberation, an expulsion whereby the entrepreneur's power is strengthened, the irony is complete. If the threat to the *macher's* power is a woman, he will probably carry out the expulsion himself. If he has recruited her sexually, he can expel her on the same basis. There is a false puritanism in never publicly permitting the allusion to relationships everyone knows about.

The male supremacist tends to exploit women new to the Movement or on its fringes. His concept of women is conventionally patriarchal: they are for bed, board, babies and, also, for doing his typing and running his office machines and doing his tedious research. By definition women are bourgeois: they are housewives and domesticators. A woman who begins to act independently is a threat and loses her protected status. He can no longer use her.

Such a man will sit at his desk with his feet up and point to the poster on his wall of a Vietnamese woman with her rifle on her back, telling you, "Now that is a truly liberated woman. When I see you in that role, I'll believe you're a revolutionary." He has all the strength of the American tradition of Huckleberry Finn escaping downriver from Aunt Polly, down through Hemingway where the bitch louses up the man-to-man understanding, to draw upon in defense of his arrogance. Not only are women losers, but for a woman to think of herself is bourgeois subjectivity and inherently counterrevolutionary. Now dear, of course you find your work dull. What the Movement needs is more discipline and less middle-class concern with one's itty-bitty self!

At times it may seem to women as if the only way to win their battle is to form some sort of women's brigades and achieve instant liberation by eliminating that whole part of life which hurts the most and competing with the men in meeting goals set by the male-dominated movement. But where women have fought beside their men, how often afterwards they have found themselves right back where they were before. It is easy for men to deal with women as quasi-equals, all soldiers together, during a long or short crisis, but inside their heads in all the old dominance/submission machinery and the old useful myths about mom and the playmate and good girls and bad girls.

The male liberal respects the pride of women. He has learned well the rhetoric of women's liberation and offers apparent partnership. He will permit small doses of spokesmanship roles, so long as his hegemony is not challenged. Because he is willing to listen on a basis of apparent equality to women who work with (for) him, he is in a better position to draw out higher quality labor. He is just as career-oriented and just as exploitative as the male supremacist, but he gives back enough tidbits of flattery and attention to make the relationship appear reciprocal by contrast with what goes on with bullier males, and he is by far the more efficient long-range co-opter.

Often a woman working with a male liberal will learn imperceptibly to accept a double standard for his behavior: alone with her when she is his equal; and with other *machers*, when he will pretend essentially not to know her. After all, he will gain no points by insisting others treat her as an equal. Further, if he acted as if the woman were of importance, he might lose some control over contacts essential in dominating his scene. Thus the woman will come to accept the master-servant manners in public, for the sake of the private relationship of equals. It can take her a long time to see that the public manner reflects the power realities.

The importance of male solidarity to enforce discrimination and contempt for women cannot be overemphasized. The man who goes in the face of this will find himself isolated. He will pay for betraying his caste. Men in this society reinforce each other's acted-out manhood in many small social rituals, from which the man who truly treats women as his equals will be excluded.

Neither can we over-emphasize our own acquiescence. As I said, I have been a house nigger in the Movement. Since I was first on my own as a skinny tough kid, nobody ever succeeded for long in exploiting me as a woman, until I came into the Movement. Then I lay down my arms before my brothers to make the revolution together. How much I swallowed for my politics I have only realized in the pain of trying to write this piece truthfully. I have also begun to see how many male structures I took into my head in order to make it in the male-dominated world. How often in writing this I have been afraid, because I have incorporated so much male thinking that I can hear the responses I am going to get. Finally I have come to see how separated from my sisters I have been at times to preserve one or another superexploitative relationship with one or another male *macher*. As a house nigger how much worse treatment of other women I have watched and satisfied my conscience with vague private protestations to the professional revolutionary in question: nothing that would get him angry at me, you can be sure.

Two inhibitions have acted on me constantly. One inhibition occurred in relationships where work and sexual involvements overlapped. I have not been able to keep tenderness and sensual joy from being converted into cooperation in my own manipulation. One takes the good with the bad, no? The good is loving and the bad is being used and letting others be used. One holds on to good memories to block perceptions that would rock the boat. Yet always what was beautiful and real in the touching becomes contaminated by the fog of lies and half-truths and power struggles, until the sex is empty and only another form of manipulation.

The other, stronger inhibition comes from having shared the same radical tradition, rhetoric, heroes, dates, the whole bloody history of class war. It is pitifully easy for radical women to accept their own exploitation in the name of some larger justice (which excludes half the world) because we are taught from childhood to immolate ourselves to the male and the family.

Once again in the Movement, oppression is becoming something for professionals to remove from certifiably oppressed other people. When I am told day in and day out to shut up because our oppression pales beside the oppression of colonialized peoples and blacks, I remember half of them are women too, and I am reminded of my mother telling me to eat boiled mush because the Chinese were starving and would be glad to have it. When people are unhappy, no one can tell them their pain is unimportant. The ruling class isn't dissatisfied: they are healthy, well-fed, live in beauty, enjoy their own importance: fun-loving cannibals. Our men aren't dissatisfied either.

It is true some oppression kills quickly and smashes the body, and some only destroys the pride and the ability to think and create. But I know no man can tell any woman how to measure her oppression and what methods are not politic in trying to get up off her knees. The answer does not lie in trying to be the token woman or in trying to learn quickly how to manipulate or shove around those who manipulate us. Certain of any oppressed group can always rise from that group by incorporating the manners and value system of the oppressed, and outwitting them at their own rigged game. We want Something Else.

We are told that our sense of oppression is not legitimate. We are told women's liberation is a secondary issue, to be dealt with after the war is won. But the basis of women's oppression is economic in a sense that far predates capitalism and the market economy and that is woven through the whole fabric of socialization. Our claims are the most radical, for they entail restructuring even the nuclear family. Nowhere on earth are women free now, although in some places things are marginally better. What we want we will have to invent ourselves.

We must have the strength of our anger to know what we

know. No more arguments about shutting up for the greater good should make us ashamed of fighting for our freedom. Even since private property was invented, we have been waiting for freedom. That passive waiting is supposed to characterize our sex, and if we wait for the males we know to give up control, our great-grand-daughters will get plenty of practice in waiting, too. We are the fastest growing part of the Movement, and for the next few years it would be healthiest for us to work as if we were essentially all the Movement there is, until we can make alliances based on our politics. Any attempts to persuade men that we are serious are a waste of precious time and energy; they are not our constituency.

There is much anger here at Movement men, but I know they have been warped and programmed by the same society that has damn near crippled us. My anger is because they have created in the Movement a microcosm of that oppression and are proud of it. Manipulation and careerism and competition will not evaporate of themselves. Sisters, what we do, we have to do together, and we will see about them.

INSTITUTIONALIZED OPPRESSION *vs.* THE FEMALE

Florynce Kennedy

People who have trouble accepting the thesis that women are an oppressed group might be somewhat placated by my theory of the *circularity of oppression.* It should be noted, from the jump, that there can be no really pervasive system of oppression, such as that in the United States, without the consent of the oppressed. People who have not withdrawn consent usually deny that they are oppressed. It follows. However, although the concept of circularity fails to suggest that some groups are far more restricted, segregated, boycotted, ostracized, and insulted than others, it does succeed in suggesting one reason for the uncomfortably solid basis for the male backlash.

Men are outraged, turned off, and wigged out, by threats that women might withdraw consent to oppression, because they—men—subconsciously (and often consciously) know that they—men—are oppressed. Women, as they loudly proclaim their rejection of further oppression, will arouse men to turn upon the established order. First, women will ignore or take care of the male backlash by any means necessary. In acknowledging their oppression, women will do well to reject their own roles in the hierarchy of institutionalized oppression.

At least one answer to the failure of any number of people, especially women, to accept as a fact the contention that women are oppressed, might lie in their experience of having been the victim of an oppressive woman, i.e., women being utilized as agents for oppressors.

Women are frequently oppressive in one-to-one situations. In those cases the oppressees tend to be their children, other family members, especially husbands, superintendents, or other domestic or nonpolitical public servants, e.g., waiters.

I see our society, however defined, as an excellent example of institutionalized oppression. *Where a system of oppression has become institutionalized it is unnecessary for individuals to be oppressive.* So it is that where blacks are concerned (there we go again analogizing women and black people; it's too perfect to ignore) whites can say, "But I never feel the slightest prejudice!" So, also, a man may say, "I'd hire a woman art director in a minute!"

Even if thousands of white male personnel directors made such declarations, such is the System that the overwhelming majority of art directors in major advertising agencies would be white and male. Just by nobody doing nothing the old bullshit mountain just grows and grows. Chocolate-covered, of course. We must take our little teaspoons and get to work. We can't wait for shovels.

It may be the church, the husband, the TV series, or a sister-in-law who persuade the pregnant woman that she should run for cover the second she dons a maternity dress. Surely the personnel director does not decree that she hover over the crib, the creeper, the crawler, and the cuddly until puberty. Women in their brainwashed consentual condition frequently act out their role of hovering mother without any noticeable pressure from anyone. Note "noticeable."

Dictates, from so many sources that you couldn't even count them, wind like soft cotton-candy fiberglass to bind the woman to the BPBP status—Barefoot-Pregnant-and-Behind-the-Plow. Although the BPBP status of peasant days now translates into various updated versions, there is little doubt that sex and the female ability to bear children is a frequent rationalization for ever so many of the (at least) fifty-seven varieties of rationale for oppressing women. What difference does it make whether the rationalizations arise from suspicion, tradition, or competition? It's women's job to put their power to work to slow it down or break it up.

Very usually consent to oppression is obtained by the issuance of a license to oppress. Since not all women seek a license to oppress, and since children are frequently the objects for women's oppression and not all women have access to children, consent is sometimes obtained through the ennoblement of suffering and sacrifice. Quite often, women consent to the system of oppression in exchange for a Vaseline-dispensing franchise. The franchise for dispensation of Vaseline is not wholly distinguishable from the honor of sacrifice and suffering, but has the added dimension of giving the female a superior status. She ministers to the suffering natives in her role as missionary, nun, or nurse, in exchange for which she suffers a second-class treatment from male missionaries, priests, or doctors. But she is so superior to the natives, novitiates, sinners, and bedridden that she glides serenely through the bullshit as if it were a field of daisies.

Coalitions of welfare spies, euphemistically dubbed social investigators, with welfare victims, called clients, is a good example of salutary coalition of the oppressed.

The concepts of *horizontal hostility* and *dumping* are an integral part of the circularity of oppression in an institutionalized system. Horizontal hostility may be expressed in sibling rivalry or in competitive dueling which wrecks not only office tranquility or suburban domesticity but also some radical political groups and, it must be sadly said, some women's liberation groups. Considerable headway toward a refocussing of hostility *upward* can be seen in the New York State area where broad coalitions of women's liberation groups joined with such victimized pioneers as Bill Baird and Dr. Nathan Rappaport to demand, not reform, but repeal of abortion laws. Yet upon sober consideration, horizontal hostility is most understandable. Oppressed people are frequently very oppressive when first liberated. And why wouldn't they be? They know best two positions. Somebody's foot on their neck or their foot on somebody's neck. Rednecks and poor white trash have traditionally dominated the Ku Klux Klan in the South, even as racist social workers and schoolteachers have infiltrated the ranks of those assigned to babysit the black communities in the North. To avoid these destructive effects of horizontal disruptiveness, women need some minimal political and/or social awareness of the pathology of the oppressed when confronted by divide-and-conquer experts. How else would it be so easy for Jews—who have never been placed in concentration camps by black people, or kept out of country clubs by black people, or pushed out of upstate resorts by black people—to fall for the line that black anti-Semitism was a greater threat to them than the Establishment's divide-and-conquer techniques?

Similarly, even as they huddle together in the cold, damp atmosphere of their new-found liberation, and until they don the cozy raiment of "How beautiful we!" women who have rejected the Establishmentarian goodies (pink mops, wigs, women's magazine romances, a door-held-open and miniskirts) often clash with each other before they learn to share and enjoy their new-found freedom. Some direct their hostility understandably to male counterparts rather than vertically toward the institutions that program us all, e.g., the media and the church.

A lack of a sense of considerable worth is another reason for horizontal hostility, consent to oppression, and the circularity of oppression. Values are learned at the parents' knee, at the laundromat, at church, at club meetings, and on TV networks. One Establishmentarian device, usually resorted to in newspapers and TV or other mass media is to show women sacrificing and suffering. She quits her job so that she can follom *him* to South America or some such place.

Women are dirt searchers; their greatest worth is eradicating rings on collars and tables. Never mind real-estate boards' corruption and racism, here's your soapsuds. Everything she is doing is peripheral, expendable, crucial, and non-negotiable. Cleanliness is next to godliness.

She quits her job to have a baby. Magazine articles ponder the question of whether a wife can be a mother *and* a career woman. Never any problem being a *wife, hostess, chauffeur, gardener, cook, home typist, nurse, seamstress, social secretary, purchasing agent,* and/or *baby-manufacturing machine.* A woman may be discouraged from studying law. "The books are *so* heavy." But do they weigh more than a six-month-old baby? TV commercials reduce the female worth by depicting the young wife crying over sink spots and water marks on goblets. What will his mother say? Make a good pudding so's you'll be loved. Get a good strong deodorant! Women get so excited, they smell! Poor dears.

Men are scarcely less peripheral and irrelevant in their day-to-day or weekend activities than women. They should be prepared to join with women to force society to liberate everybody from irrelevant, peripheral, societal bullshit. But for the foreseeable future some women will act as if getting in on the corruption is more desirable than ending it.

Freud was at his most fraudulent (forgive, I couldn't help it) when he talked about women's frustrations and hostility in terms of "penis envy." One would have thought that even the most pompous and fatuous of asses would have gathered that women were less interested in standing at urinals than in standing on an equal basis before the bar of justice! As with most, if not all systems of injustice and institutionalized oppression, the law had a leading role in oppressing women. It still has.

Some considerable time ago, anachronistic laws depriving women of most, if not all, civil and property laws were rewritten or repealed. But try to rent an apartment without a husband's(or some man's) signature. I can't begin to tell how many times a woman, separated from her husband, had to get him to sign a lease or help her get a charge account. Brothers or fathers often have to co-sign or countersign auto loans or chattel mortgages. This comes as a superirony, when, as is occasionally the case, the woman in question earns more, or has a longer, and/or more impressive work record.

As a rule, of course, the men, especially if they're white, do have the better jobs and the more impressive work record. That's because of sex bigotry, the buddy system, and various other below-the-belt Establishmentarian characteristics.

Women with really good jobs and connections are often kowtowed to, like the "Negro" who has "made it." Women who know what's good for them lapse into old role styles when they really need or desperately want something, like an apartment, or a part in a play, or a really cool job.

The kind of female who doesn't pull punches even to get an important Precious becomes known as strident, strong, a ball-breaker, or crazy. If they survive the ridicule, sarcasm, hostility, demotions, and demerits, such women frequently fare better than the pliables. But the casualty rate is high.

Survivors of the gamut often are among those most impatient with feminism or female liberation. They scrambled their way up and why can't anybody else? Such women are gleefully quoted by the Establishment, even as the "Uncles" Roy Wilkins and Bayard Rustin are widely quoted when they take black activisits to task or defend pig Establishmentarians.

I predict that the Harriet Van Hornes who sniff at such beautiful zaps as the 1968 women's liberation demonstration against the Miss America Pageant, or the hollow, bewigged, superchic Pamela Masons who seem so bright and brittle until they have to deal with the matter of women's liberation, will meet with less tolerance than the Uncle Toms and the white maggots who feed off the few edibles in the garbage dump that the civil rights "fight" turned out to be.

Just as the students bypassed some of the turn-the-other-cheek, beat-me-daddy-eight-to-the-bar bullshit that black people grooved on, so, I predict, women will begin almost where the students left off, and *they* are starting more fires than get into the papers.

Some of the same reasons might account for the speed with which the women's movement will take off, once it taxies the field for a season or two. Students and women, unlike black people, didn't see themselves as oppressed, therefore when they were niggerized they didn't respond with a shuffle and a "S'cuse me, boss." Of course, black students are in the vanguard of the student movement. This, if my theory is right, is because they knew they were scheduled for oppression and withdrew their consent: "Hell, no, we won't go," "No Vietnamese ever called me Nigger," etc. So black students were indeed not representative of the black community, or the shit would have hit the fan a long time ago.

But women are doers, and dreamers, and activists by the nature of their permissible roles. They do most of the buying, most of the lying ("Honey, call them and say I have to see an out-of-town client on the weekend"; "Dear, say I have a virus"—Hangover Hal; "Say we'll send the rent in on Friday"; "Change the appointment 'til next week") and a major portion of the hassling: with the landlord, merchants, family, etc. Women are more ready than most for the liberation struggle. We have only to direct our hostility from the vertical *down* (the kids, the merchants, the family, co-workers, and other women), and the horizontal—to the vertical *up*. According to my *modus operandi* this means systems and institutions less than people.

Kicking ass should be only where an ass is protecting the System. Ass-kicking should be undertaken regardless of the sex, the ethnicity, or the charm of the oppressor's agent. As the struggles intensify, the oppressor tends to select more attractive agents, frequently from among the oppressed.

It is for this reason that I have considerable difficulty with the sisterhood mystique: "We are all sisters," "Don't criticize a 'sister' publicly," etc. When a female judge asks my client where the bruises are when she complains about being assaulted by her husband (as did Family Court Judge Sylvia Jaffin Liese), and makes smart remarks about her being overweight, and when another female judge is so hostile that she disqualifies herself but refuses to order a combative husband out of the house (even though he owns property elsewhere with suitable living quarters)—these judges are not my sisters. And if the same pair of female Family Court judges concurred in decisions to return a three-year-old child to her mother and stepfather only a few months before the child's body was recovered from the river and her stepfather accused of her death? (Foster parents had pleaded to keep the child and had pointed to the evidences of physical abuse to no avail.) No, these judges are not my sisters. Such females, in my opinion, are agents of an oppressive System, which the Family represents without a doubt.

Every form of bigotry can be found in ample supply in the legal system of our country. It would seem that Justice (usually depicted as a woman) is indeed blind to racism, sexism, war, and poverty.

Dean Willis Reese, a lanky man who talks with a lisp in a shrill voice and walks with a switch, hastened to assure me that I was being refused admission to Columbia Law School in 1948 not because I was black, but because I was a woman. I leaned on the ethnic angle, saying that some of my more cynical friends thought I was being discriminated against because I was a Negro (we weren't saying "black" in those days), and in any case it felt the same. Law-school admissions opened the door just wide enough for *me*, but not for my friend Pat Jones, who was a Barnard graduate, with a slightly higher law aptitude level and slightly lower undergraduate average, but white.

Many senior partners, or hiring partners in Establishment law firms still have the nerve to say they don't normally hire women. Some, perhaps most, firms will accept a woman if she is in the upper percentile of her law school class. (So, also, they'll accept supersmart Jews.)

Of course, the law schools assist by screening out the women and the blacks "from the gitgo." Nowadays the tokens have become a trickle. Much of the clash of black students on campus and the predictable upcoming clashes involving women is due to the "expectancy gap" which prevails when a bigot decides to go straight. The crabgrass liberal-bigot anticipates a good sport, a dazzled recipient with damp hands and misty eyes near to overflowing with gratitude—but is confronted by a cool, if not coldly suspicious, potential foe—a creditor sullenly receiving a miniscule payment of an unconscionably late I.O.U. Black students now—and female students in seasons to come—will break up the bank.

THE POLITICS OF HOUSEWORK

Pat Mainardi

> Though women do not complain of the power of husbands, each complains of her own husband, or of the husbands of her friends. It is the same in all other cases of servitude; at least in the commencement of the emancipatory movement. The serfs did not at first complain of the power of the lords, but only of their tyranny.
> —John Stuart Mill, *On the Subjection of Women*

Liberated women—very different from women's liberation! The first signals all kinds of goodies, to warm the hearts (not to mention other parts) of the most radical men. The other signals—*housework*. The first brings sex without marriage, sex before marriage, cozy housekeeping arrangements ("You see, I'm living with this chick") and the self-content of knowing that you're not the kind of man who wants a doormat instead of a woman. That will come later. After all, who wants that old commodity anymore, the Standard American Housewife, all husband, home and kids. The New Commodity, the Liberated Woman, has sex a lot and has a Career, preferably something that can be fitted in with the household chores—like dancing, pottery, or painting.

On the other hand is women's liberation—and housework. What? You say this is all trivial? Wonderful! That's what I thought. It seemed perfectly reasonable. We both had careers, both had to work a couple of days a week to earn enough to live on, so why shouldn't we share the housework? So I suggested it to my mate and he agreed—most men are too hip to turn you down flat. "You're right," he said, "It's only fair."

Then an interesting thing happened. I can only explain it by stating that we women have been brainwashed more than even we can imagine. Probably too many years of seeing television women in ecstasy over their shiny waxed floors or breaking down over their dirty shirt collars. Men have no such conditioning. They recognize the essential fact of housework right from the very beginning. Which is that it stinks. Here's my list of dirty chores: buying groceries, carting them home and putting them away; cooking meals and washing dishes and pots; doing the laundry, digging out the place when things get out of control; washing floors. The list could go on but the sheer necessities are bad enough. All of us have to do these things, or get some one else to do them for us. The longer my husband contemplated these chores, the more repulsed he became, and so proceeded the change from the normally sweet considerate Dr. Jekyll into the crafty Mr. Hyde who would stop at nothing to avoid the horrors of—*housework*. As he felt himself backed into a corner laden with dirty dishes, brooms, mops, and reeking garbage, his front teeth grew longer and pointier, his fingernails haggled and his eyes grew wild. Housework trivial? Not on your life! Just try to share the burden.

So ensued a dialogue that's been going on for several years. Here are some of the high points:

"I don't mind sharing the housework, but I don't do it very well. We should each do the things we're best at."
Meaning: Unfortunately I'm no good at things like washing dishes or cooking. What I do best is a little light carpentry, changing light bulbs, moving furniture (*how often do you move furniture?*).
Also Meaning: Historically the lower classes (black men and us) have had hundreds of years experience doing menial jobs. It would be a waste of manpower to train someone else to do them now.
Also Meaning: I don't like the dull stupid boring jobs, so you should do them.

"I don't mind sharing the work, but you'll have to show me how to do it."

Meaning: I ask a lot of questions and you'll have to show me everything everytime I do it because I don't remember so good. Also don't try to sit down and read while I'm doing my jobs because I'm going to annoy hell out of you until it's easier to do them yourself.

"We used to be so happy!" (Said whenever it was his turn to do something.)

Meaning: I used to be so happy.

Meaning: Life without housework is bliss. (*No quarrel here. Perfect agreement.*)

"We have different standards, and why should I have to work to your standards. That's unfair."

Meaning: If I begin to get bugged by the dirt and crap I will say "This place sure is a sty" or "How can anyone live like this?" and wait for your reaction. I know that all women have a sore called "Guilt over a messy house" or "Household work is ultimately my responsibility." I know that men have caused that sore—if anyone visits and the place *is* a sty, they're not going to leave and say, "He sure is a lousy housekeeper." You'll take the rap in any case. I can outwait you.

Also Meaning: I can provoke innumerable scenes over the housework issue. Eventually doing all the housework yourself will be less painful to you than trying to get me to do half. Or I'll suggest we get a maid. She will do my share of the work. You will do yours. It's women's work.

"I've got nothing against sharing the housework, but you can't make me do it on your schedule."

Meaning: Passive resistance. I'll do it when I damned well please, if at all. If my job is doing dishes, it's easier to do them once a week. If taking out laundry, once a month. If washing the floors, once a year. If you don't like it, do it yourself oftener, and then I won't do it at all.

"I *hate* it more than you. You don't mind it so much."
Meaning: Housework is garbage work. It's the worst crap
I've ever done. It's degrading and humiliating for someone
of *my* intelligence to do it. But for someone of *your* intelligence . . .

"Housework is too trivial to even talk about."
Meaning: It's even more trivial to do. Housework is beneath
my status. My purpose in life is to deal with matters of
significance. Yours is to deal with matters of insignificance.
You should do the housework.

"This problem of housework is not a man-woman problem!
In any relationship between two people one is going to have
a stronger personality and dominate."
Meaning: That stronger personality had better be *me*.

"In animal societies, wolves, for example, the top animal is
usually a male even where he is not chosen for brute
strength but on the basis of cunning and intelligence. Isn't
that interesting?"
Meaning: I have historical, psychological, anthropological,
and biological justification for keeping you down. How can
you ask the top wolf to be equal?

"Women's liberation isn't really a political movement."
Meaning: The Revolution is coming too close to home.
Also Meaning: I am only interested in how *I* am oppressed,
not how I oppress others. Therefore the war, the draft, and
the university are political. Women's liberation is not.

"Man's accomplishments have always depended on getting
help from other people, mostly women. What great man
would have accomplished what he did if he had to do his
own housework?
Meaning: Oppression is built into the System and I, as the

white American male receive the benefits of this System. I don't want to give them up.

Postscript

Participatory democracy begins at home. If you are planning to implement your politics, there are certain things to remember.

1. He *is* feeling it more than you. He's losing some leisure and you're gaining it. The measure of your oppression is his resistance.
2. A great many American men are not accustomed to doing monotonous repetitive work which never ushers in any lasting let alone important achievement. This is why they would rather repair a cabinet than wash dishes. If human endeavors are like a pyramid with man's highest achievements at the top, then keeping oneself alive is at the bottom. Men have always had servants (us) to take care of this bottom strata of life while they have confined their efforts to the rarefied upper regions. It is thus ironic when they ask of women—where are your great painters, statesmen, etc? Mme. Matisse ran a millinery shop so he could paint. Mrs. Martin Luther King kept his house and raised his babies.
3. It is a traumatizing experience for someone who has always thought of himself as being against any oppression or exploitation of one human being by another to realize that in his daily life he has been accepting and implementing (and benefiting from) this exploitation; that his rationalization is little different from that of the racist who says "Black people don't feel pain" (women don't mind doing the shitwork); and that the oldest form of oppression in history has been the oppression of 50 percent of the population by the other 50 percent.
4. Arm yourself with some knowledge of the psychology of oppressed peoples everywhere, and a few facts about the animal kingdom. I admit playing top wolf or who

runs the gorillas is silly but as a last resort men bring it up all the time. Talk about bees. If you feel really hostile bring up the sex life of spiders. They have sex. She bites off his head.

The psychology of oppressed people is not silly. Jews, immigrants, black men, and all women have employed the same psychological mechanisms to survive: admiring the oppressor, glorifying the oppressor, wanting to be like the oppressor, wanting the oppressor to like them, mostly because the oppressor held all the power.

5.   In a sense, all men everywhere are slightly schizoid—divorced from the reality of maintaining life. This makes it easier for them to play games with it. It is almost a cliché that women feel greater grief at sending a son off to war or losing him to that war because they bore him, suckled him, and raised him. The men who foment those wars did none of those things and have a more superficial estimate of the worth of human life. One hour a day is a low estimate of the amount of time one has to spend "keeping" oneself. By foisting this off on others, man gains seven hours a week—one working day more to play with his mind and not his human needs. Over the course of generations it is easy to see whence evolved the horrifying abstractions of modern life.

6.   With the death of each form of oppression, life changes and new forms evolve. English aristocrats at the turn of the century were horrified at the idea of enfranchising working men—were sure that it signaled the death of civilization and a return to barbarism. Some working men were even deceived by this line. Similarly with the minimum wage, abolition of slavery, and female suffrage. Life changes but it goes on. Don't fall for any line about the death of everything if men take a turn at the dishes. They will imply that you are holding back the Revolution (their Revolution). But you are advancing it (your Revolution).

7.   Keep checking up. Periodically consider who's actually *doing* the jobs. These things have a way of backsliding so

that a year later once again the woman is doing everything. After a year make a list of jobs the man has rarely if ever done. You will find cleaning pots, toilets, refrigerators and ovens high on the list. Use time sheets if necessary. He will accuse you of being petty. He is above that sort of thing—(housework). Bear in mind what the worst jobs are, namely the ones that have to be done every day or several times a day. Also the ones that are dirty—it's more pleasant to pick up books, newspapers etc. than to wash dishes. Alternate the bad jobs. It's the daily grind that gets you down. Also make sure that you don't have the responsibility for the housework with occasional help from him. "I'll cook dinner for you tonight" implies it's really your job and isn't he a nice guy to do some of it for you.

8.   Most men had a rich and rewarding bachelor life during which they did not starve or become encrusted with crud or buried under the litter. There is a taboo that says that women mustn't strain themselves in the presence of men: we haul around 50 pounds of groceries if we have to but aren't allowed to open a jar if there is someone around to do it for us. The reverse side of the coin is that men aren't supposed to be able to take care of themselves without a woman. Both are excuses for making women do the housework.

9.   Beware of the double whammy. He won't do the little things he always did because you're now a "Liberated Woman," right? Of course he won't do anything else either . . .

I was just finishing this when my husband came in and asked what I was doing. Writing a paper on housework. Housework? he said, *Housework?* Oh my god how trivial can you get. A paper on housework.

Little Politics of Housework Quiz

The lowest job in the army, used as punishment is: a) working 9–5; b) kitchen duty (K.P.).

When a man lives with his family, his: a) father b) mother does his housework.

When he lives with a woman, a) he b) she does the housework.

A) his son b) his daughter learns preschool how much fun it is to iron daddy's handkerchief.

From the *New York Times*, 9/21/69: "Former Greek Official George Mylonas pays the penalty for differing with the ruling junta in Athens by performing household chores on the island of Amorgos where he lives in forced exile" (with hilarious photo of a miserable Mylonas carrying his own water). What the *Times* means is that he ought to have a) indoor plumbing b) a maid.

Dr. Spock said (*Redbook* 3/69): "Biologically and temperamentally I believe, women were made to be concerned first and foremost with child care, husband care, and home care." Think about: a) *who* made us b) why? c) what is the effect on their lives d) what is the effect on our lives?

From *Time* 1/5/70, "Like their American counterparts, many housing project housewives are said to suffer from neurosis. And for the first time in Japanese history, many young husbands today complain of being henpecked. Their wives are beginning to demand detailed explanations when they don't come home straight from work and some Japanese males nowadays are even compelled to do housework." According to *Time*, women become neurotic: a) when they are forced to do the maintenance work for the male caste all day every day of their lives or b) when they no longer want to do the maintenance work for the male caste all day every day of their lives.

SOCIAL BASES FOR SEXUAL EQUALITY: A COMPARATIVE VIEW*

Karen Sacks

What kind of society does not oppress or exploit women? The two are not synonymous. Exploitation, or work for the society without power in the society, exists only in class societies. But women are oppressed, treated as wards of men, in nonclass as well as class societies. In our society, a woman's place is in the home, in the kitchen, and in the bedroom: to keep men's bellies and souls full; to buy the gadgets, goods, and status symbols that reflect her man's abilities as provider; to raise the kids. Many women in the Movement see our oppression as stemming from being the consumers of the commodities that make the capitalist system survive. To the extent that we deck up our homes, families, and bodies like Astor's pet horse, the oppressive society can continue. I would like to argue that though all women face this kind of oppression, the main reason for its perpetuation lies in the System's need to "superexploit" working women, and put them in competition with men to keep both down. If *all* women have to be treated as the social inferiors of men, that's just too bad. For us to truly liberate ourselves, we must end the System that oppresses all of us to exploit some of us.

Once we end exploitation, what are the conditions necessary to end our oppression? Looking at Mbuti and Iroquois societies suggests that we need a complete reorganization of "work," a radically different kind of division of labor. If they can do it, so can we.

Though anthropology is not supposed to look at other

*Many people's ideas and criticisms went into this article. I would like to thank Carol Andreas, Peter Bertocci, Arturo Biblarz, Terry Bohnhorst, Judith K. Brown, Sharon Brown, Bill Sacks, Carleton W. Smoth, Judy Williams, and Elizabeth Zelman for their help.—K.S.

societies through Western eyes, it has failed to do its job in looking at the status of women in non-Western societies. Most anthropologists assume that women are universally the social inferiors of men. A reputable British anthropologist, male, assesses the evidence as follows:

> I find it difficult to believe that the relative positions of the sexes are likely to undergo any considerable or lasting alteration in the forseeable future. Primitive [sic] societies and barbarous [sic] societies and the historical societies of Europe and the East exhibit almost every conceivable variety of institutions, but in all of them, regardless of the form of social structure, men are always in the ascendancy and this is perhaps the more evident the higher the civilization.[1]

He goes on to attribute the cause of women's social inferiority to "deep biological and psychological factors."[2]

Margaret Mead has demonstrated that differences of social roles and sexual temperament are culturally conditioned.[3] She argues that it is the society which creates particular ideal male and female personalities. A society may make women and men temperamentally different, or it may pay little attention to sex-typing and create instead a "human" personality. Women, like men, are "basically" anything the society makes them. If Mead is right, and I think she is, then for women to merely fight men would be to miss the point. The point is to change the social order that produces male supremacists.

But a lot of anthropologists discount Mead's argument because in the societies she writes about, it is men who publicly hold political authority. Though this does not come through strongly in her writing, men's trading ventures are economically vital to New Guinea societies and political power accompanies this economic importance. Parallel arguments can be made for Samoan chiefs (male).

1. E. E. Evans-Pritchard, *The Position of Women in Primitive Societies* (New York: The Free Press, 1965), p. 54.
2. *Ibid.*
3. Margaret Mead, *Sex and Temperament in Three Savage Societies.* (New York: Apollo, 1967); *Male and Female* (New York: Mentor Books, 1955).

Anthropologists often argue that in so-called primitive societies, a woman's childbearing and childrearing responsibilities keep her from holding equal political power with men, though they are not sure why. Though no man has ever borne a child, women sometimes hold as much or more political power than men, so this notion is false. Two non-class societies, Iroquois and Mbuti Pygmies, can be used to suggest what it takes for women not to be oppressed in a *non*exploitative society.

In her paper, "Economic Organization and Female Status Among the Iroquois," Judith K. Brown demonstrates that a group of Iroquois women, the matrons, have power over the major productive resources of the society as well as over the distribution of food and wealth.[4] Women do most of the agricultural work and they do it cooperatively. Men hunt, but this is an activity which contributes less to the actual food supply than agriculture, which takes them away from the village often for many months at a time, and in small groups. In Iroquois society women have an enormous amount of decisionmaking power in the domestic, political, and religious spheres of life.

> Economic reality was institutionalized in giving the matrons the power to nominate Council Elders, to influence Council decisions, and a voice in the conduct of war and the negotiation of treaties; by giving them also the power to elect "keepers of the faith" and to serve in that capacity; and by giving them authority over households.[5]

In the society of the Mbuti Pygmies of the Congo, men and women share equally in the process of decisionmaking. But here there are *no* positions of authority, economic privilege, or institutionalized forms of charismatic leadership in the society. Decisions affecting the group are made collectively. Mbuti society is egalitarian but hardly anarchic.[6] I

4. *Ethnohistory*, in press.
5. *Ibid*.
6. Information on the Mbuti in this paper comes from Colin Turnbull, *Wayward Servants* (New York: Natural History Press, 1965) and "The Mbuti Pygmies of the Congo," in *Peoples of Africa*, ed. James L. Gibbs Jr. (New York: Holt, Rinehart

would like to deal with the Mbuti in a little more detail to illustrate what seem to be the necessary conditions for the liberation of women.

In Mbuti society the subsistence base is hunting and gathering wild vegetable food in the Congo rain forest. Food is plentiful and with the economic organization they have, not much time is required to get it. Leisure is a major occupation. Each band of about thirty families has its own territory which is "owned" by the band as a whole. No one has monopoly or ownership of any part of it. The means of production—nets, spears, digging sticks—can be made by anyone. The division of labor is by age and sex, with age being more important. The old people and some older children watch the young children, while the adult men and women (and infants) go out for the hunt. Men's and women's subsistence contributions, through different, depend on each other and are done collectively. The men set up a large semicircle of nets and kill game driven into the nets; women act as beaters, and gather wild plants as well as. By informal sharing, the catch is distributed fairly equally. Two things are important: *1)* subsistence is a collective venture, no single married couple can make it on its own; *2)* both men and women's contributions must be made together.

As to family life, women gather leaves for huts, build the huts, and do the cooking, while men gather poles for the huts, and make their nets and spears. But these jobs are also done by either sex if it is handier. Both care and take responsibility for children (except nursing infants). What is more, children call all women and men in the band by the same term they use for mother and father. They expect the same treatment from them, and they get it. The de-emphasis of the sex division of labor can be seen in the terms of reference and address for different members of the band. There are only five: grandparent (sex unimportant), father-mother (sex unimportant), sibling, child, in-law.

and Winston, 1965).

Sex may be less important than age in determining how one categorizes people, but sex and sex relations are a very important part of life. The Mbuti have enormous pre- and postmarital sexual freedom, by our standards, and they enjoy it openly. But this does not fit some Victorian scholars' views of primitive promiscuity. Though children expect maternal and paternal treatment from all adults in the group, everyone knows who his real father and mother are and feels closer to them. This family lives together, eats together, and goes visiting together (often for long periods of time). Marriage is a matter of personal choice, but subject to consent of the band which is concerned with economic abilities and sociability of the prospective member. The group has no coercive power, though.

In terms of economic decisionmaking, men and women have an equal say, since their work is equally important and interdependent. Decisions are made by informal consensus and there is no coercion beyond shame or ridicule—except the supreme coercion: the knowledge that cooperation is necessary for survival. This cooperation is achieved without punitive laws or sanctions, and without any loss of "individuality."

There are other "egalitarian" societies where men are dominant over women. But Mbuti society differs from these in several ways: *1*) it is a society of abundance; *2*) men and women are equal producers of subsistence and their work is coordinated; *3*) subsistence is a collective venture. Given the necessary job of any society to keep its members alive, the crucial decisions of social life come down ultimately to economic decisions. Where all men and women are equal and *interdependent* in terms of subsistence production, this equality between sexes extends to other aspects of social life: sex, marriage, consumption.

It is necessary to emphasize that it seems to be the organization of subsistence *production*, not consumption, that is crucial in determining dominance. Childbearing or childrearing is even less important than consumption. Women do that in all societies, but we are generally not the equals of men; children are for the future, and power is based on current actual relations, not potential.

But in our society, there is one big stumbling block that prevents us from being equal to and interdependent with men in economic production, and thereby making it possible to end our oppression. Our immediate problem is capitalism's need to exploit its workers. Though women were oppressed before capitalism, male dominance and family relations have been transformed by capitalism to fit its needs for ever increasing profit. Here ownership of productive resources and technology is monopolized by a few who do not work at production, or even day-to-day management of production. We discover that it is not work, but ownership (these were inseparable in Mbuti society) that gives decisionmaking power. In our capitalist society, profit for the owners rather than the meeting of the social needs of the majority is the major criterion for what goods and services will be produced, for whom, and when. From Domhoff and the many Movement analyses we can see that the government is controlled by and acts on behalf of the corporate owners.[7] So we have a class society made up of: *1)* owners who hold political and economic power; *2)* full-time workers who produce the goods and services, but who hold little or no legitimate power. There is a third group from the point of view of power and production that women, black people, and other "minority" groups are put into. Unlike Mbuti society, not all of us who are able to work are allowed or expected to do all the types of work which we are able to do; or we are not expected to work at all. Black people are largely restricted to low-paid manual labor and allowed to work for fairly short periods of time. Racism and a miseducational system are used to justify and promote these restrictions. Ideally, women are not supposed to work at all after marriage and children, though in fact many do work.

7. G. William Domhoff, *Who Rules America?* (New Brunswick, N.J.: Prentice-Hall, 1967).

Male chauvinism and lack of child-care facilities are used against women in the same way that racism is used against black people. All work is exploitative in capitalist society. The wages of one worker are not enough to support most families in the governmentally defined "modest" manner, even if that worker is a white male. Racial and sexual oppression make the exploitation much more profitable, and also are used to make black people and women into reserve, part-time, and superexploited workers. Though they grossly underestimate, Labor Department unemployment rates can be used to show the extent to which women and black people are a reserve army of labor:

Unemployment Rates, September, 1967*

	White Male	Nonwhite Male	White Female	Nonwhite Female
Age 20-64 years	1.7	2.9	4.6	8.2
Age 16-17	10.1	32.5	12.9	43.7
Age 18-19	8.9	18.8	11.1	31.0

We can have a better perspective on women as a labor reserve when we see that women make up 51 percent of the population, but only 35 percent of the labor force. [8]

Black people are superexploited in that they earn (by sex) less than whites; women are superexploited in that we earn less than men, given equal education in both cases.

Median Income by Educational Attainment, 1965††

	White Men	Nonwhite Men	White Women	Nonwhite Women
Less than 8 years	$2571	$1988	$ 909	$ 824
8 years	3912	2619	1211	1252
1-3 years high school	4365	2804	1238	1018
4 years high school	5976	3784	2425	1944
Some college	7257	4892	2999	3530

*U.S. Department of Labor, *Handbook on Women Workers,* 1965.
8. Marilyn Salzman Webb, "Women Face Oppression as Workers," *Guardian,* 15 March 1969.
††Detroit NOW, *op. cit.*

These restrictions on who can be a producer of the society's goods and services keep workers divided and in competition among themselves for a slice of the pie controlled by the owners—a competition that makes for very thin slices and a lot of uncut pie in the hands of the owners.

The man-job–woman-home ideology, like racism, is used to perpetuate a reserve army of temporary labor which can be used to keep wages down. Women are the last hired, first fired, least organized, most transient, and least skilled group in the labor force. Contrary to popular propaganda, most women do *not* work to buy "those little extras." They work to survive. Over half the women in the labor force in March 1964 were the sole breadwinners for their families.[9]

It is necessary to look a little more closely at the relationship of the man-woman conflict within working-class family structure to the class conflict of capitalist society. In the family, production and consumption come together. The wage earner produces the capitalists' profit and his or her family realizes this profit through consumption. For the capitalist, a society made up of a lot of nuclear families is a joy. It means a lot of workers and a lot of consumption units. The more workers on the labor market, the lower the wages and the higher the profit. With small nuclear families, consumption is more inefficient than in a cooperative living arrangement or in an extended family situation, for example. Thus, the market is large.

The "ideal" American family has one breadwinner: the husband. But many ideal American male workers are not earning enough to keep their families out of hock, or, to do so, they must work such long hours that they are seldom home long enough to enjoy the fruits of their labor. This situation forces many women to look for work to supplement their husband's income and to buy some time for him to be with the family. Thus, many married women who work do so out of real economic needs. Wives whose hus-

9. Webb, *op.cit.*

bands earned between $3,000 and $5,000, were the highest percentage of working wives (39 percent) in the labor force. Those whose husbands earned between $5,000 and $7,000 ran a close second (38 percent).[10] In working, married women often get a good bit of resistance from their husbands, who would rather kill themselves than have their socially defined ego flattened. They also have all sorts of guilt feelings about being separated from their children, which their husbands reinforce.

A woman's childraising responsibilities are the excuse given by the capitalists for assigning women to a superexploited position. Since infants and children are economically unproductive, the capitalists see no reason to have day-care centers; they cost money. Children are a woman's responsibility and if she wants to enter a man's world (as many women must), *she* had better figure out something on her own. But that something in this society means separation from the children for most of their waking day, as well as accounting for a good bit of the money a woman earns.

The family ideal is fine for the owners. Men and women are pitted against each other in competition for wages. Women are made to feel out of place in a work situation, treated less seriously, and given less pay for equal work. This is justified by the "well-known fact" that women do not stay on the job for long. So despite the work or career plans of any individual woman, certain types of work are reserved for us as a group: the most underpaid in any given category of work. Women do not put up with this kind of situation any longer than they absolutely must. But in quitting, we only reinforce the woman-home ideology, and help perpetuate the System.

It is a vicious circle. We are frustrated in seeking roles where we are more than wards of our men (present or expected). Yet it is economically difficult to be maintained as social adornments, as well a being psychologically crippling to women and destructive to man-woman relations

10. Webb, *ibid.*

within the family. So long as men and women accept the notions of no work for women, a superexploited status in the social production sphere of life, and woman's sole responsibility for childraising, we doom both of our sexes to rotten pay for a lot of work at the family level.

In broader perspective, it helps perpetuate an exploitative society, one where the material needs of a large percentage of the population are not met. If Colin Turnbull's description of Mbuti society is accurate, there are probably (proportionately) fewer malnourished Mbuti than Americans. So much for the glories of "higher civilization."

So far I have focused mainly on the economic exploitation of women, yet it is pretty clear that a lot of the oppression we feel as women goes way beyond the economic sphere of exploitation, though derived from it. Evans-Pritchard, in dealing with the economics of the Nuer, a largely pastoral society in the southern Sudan, said that cattle are the material links along which social relations flow. For the United States the situation is reversed. We would have to say that social relations are the links along which material goods flow. This is an enormous difference in emphasis. With the Nuer, the quality of life is primary; with us, commodities are primary.

We have a very complex division of labor, based on a complex technology, but extending to all areas of social life. We interact with a large number of people, but with each of them for very specific purposes. Consequently, the strength of interpersonal ties is weak. Our primary ties are to objects and since our relationships with people are for a specific purpose, people become means to attaining or producing things. We relate to functions rather than to people. A person is defined by the things he or she possesses, or by the status of the very specialized economic functon he, but not she, holds in the society.

It seems that the whole notion of individualism also helps legitimize this inhuman System. One becomes an "individual" by defining oneself as different from (and therefore superior to) others. This is done by having as little in common as possible with the largest number of people possible, by minimizing shared or shareable experiences. The results are a turning inward, and relating to objects. This approach to life can be seen as a justification of the kinds of relations which must predominate in a capitalist society: functionally specific, hierarchical relations.

Women's oppression, because it is not based on ability or ownership criteria, needs a lot of ideological bulwarking. Thus we find male-supremacist attitudes and institutionalizations extended way beyond the productive spheres of life to define *completely* our place in society. Since status and power stem from productive relations, and since women are not supposed to be in these, we are inferior wherever we are. There are other chapters in this book which demonstrate our subservient positions in religious, professional, service, *ad infinitum* institutions.

But this view seems to be contradicted by women's dominant position in the family. Family functions and women's functions are almost synonymous. We are the consumers, childraisers, and sex objects of the society. The family is supposed to be the place where one can find relief from the commodity relations that dominate the rest of the society. What is important here is the closeness of interpersonal relations, maximizing shared experiences. The "temperamental" qualities necessary for these kinds of relations (warmth, supportiveness, other-directedness, etc.) are the proper qualities for women to have.

But if our functions and "temperaments" are supposed to dominate the family, we have to realize that these qualities are fighting a losing battle in a capitalist society. First of all, the family as an institution is hardly a repository of social power. It must respond to the productive and political forces over which it has no control. Consumption is limited by income. Childraising is secondary to school after children are about five years old. We still have a sexual double standard.

Just as family functions rank low in this society, so too does the "womanly" emphasis on human interpersonal relations, as opposed to "manly" commodity relations. These latter are reinforced by the larger society, which takes up most of the time of the family. One or both parents are separated from the children and involved in specific-purpose, hierarchical commodity relations. Nonworking mothers relate to little children and seldom to another adult. Preschool children relate to one adult and few other children. Once in the classroom, they too are involved in these specific-purpose, hierarchical relations. The members of a family must spend most of their time apart if the unit is to survive, so shared or shareable experiences are gravy for those who can afford to buy the time for them. In a sense then, the home situation actually does prepare children for their pretty grim adult life in capitalist society.

For a woman there is tremendous conflict. All education, work experience, sexual and social experimentation, in short all direct relations with other adults become socially secondary once she is married. On the one hand we are supposed to be adults to children, but on the other, we are children in the eyes of the society. Like children, it is "adults" (males) that tell us what we may and may not do with our bodies. Male-dominated institutions tell us who we may or may not go to bed with, and under what conditions we may or may not bear children. To our husbands or men, we are commodities to be used in the battle ("on our behalf ") for socially defined success. Though in this battle, unless he is a capitalist, he too is a commodity (and the goods and services our commodity produces, we consume).

The position of woman as child is buttressed by defining women in terms of family functions and qualities. The family, like woman, is a passive institution; it is *acted on* by dominant economic and political forces. Like women, it is at the bottom of the institutional pecking order. Therefore "womanly" qualities cannot really predominate even here so long as the members of the family do not have these qualities buttressed by the material survival aspects of the society. This situation really gets ridiculous. Given socially defined temperamental differences for men and women, American women are not even allowed to be what the society insists a woman should be. We are forced to become part-man (inferior man at that) in that: *1*) the overwhelming majority of women do not spend their lives at home, and *2*) even for those that do, commodity relations and hierarchical relations extend into the family. In this society, sex-typing of temperament cripples men as well as women as long as it is used to divide men and women to serve a System which exploits both men and women.

What are the necessary conditions for the liberation of women? From the Iroquois and Mbuti situations, what seems crucial is not contribution to subsistence itself, but how that contribution is made. In the case of the Iroquois, women's agricultural work required a lot of cooperation, but men's work did not. Women held as much or more power than men. If, as in Mbuti society, nature is abundant, women's work is part of a collective effort and is an indispensable part of the execution of the men's role in food production; then there is no sexual domination in the society.

But the Iroquois and Mbuti are not class societies. In a class society these subsistence factors are overridden by another set of considerations. Class societies are run by and for one class through the exploitation of other classes and groups. Here sex is a "natural" difference that can be used to keep the exploited divided. In societies without bottle feeding, infants and mothers are pretty inseparable. As long as a woman's place is with the children, she wants peace and bread. Within the family focus, women can be used as a force for the status quo. Unlike men, they are buffered from direct exploitations by the ruling class. In our own class society this division of ruled men *vs.* ruled women is made worse by the use of women as a part-time reserve labor force.

Many men accuse women who are fighting against our own oppression of wanting to be men. We know that is false, but it is necessary to spell out why. The social definitions of men and women in this society restrict both sexes. As in Mbuti society we want both men and women to be able to put equal emphasis on close interpersonal relations with both adults and children. But it is not our industrial technology which distinguishes us from the Mbuti here. Quite the contrary. With bottles, child-care facilities, reorganization of the structure of work, there is no reason why women cannot participate equally with men. Like the Mbuti, we too have the technological basis for an economy of abundance. We have then the material bases for sexual equality. What is standing in the way of their realization is the nature of the economic relationships in our society—private ownership and the profit system.

So where do we go? First of all our movement is not growing up in a vacuum. Since World War II, there has been a change in perspective on the part of people who are opposed to the destructiveness of the capitalist system. Prior to World War II, Marxists saw the main force for revolution as being the American working class. This perspective has had to be broadened in the light of the anti-imperialist revolutions which have grown up since that time. The peoples of the Third World are rebelling against the economic superexploitation and caste oppression imposed on them by capitalism. Increasing numbers of American black people are seeing their own position in the United States in the same manner. And now, women in the Movement are beginning to see many symptoms of oppression in common with both groups. These symptoms derive from the fact that all three are exploited to a greater extent than white, male, American workers, and that a "caste" ideology which affects nonworkers in these groups, is used to justify this. Just as the peoples of the imperialized nations must destroy the source of their exploitation and oppression, capitalism, so too must we. We must fight the sexual aspect of divide-

and-rule in our roles as wives, mothers, middle- or working-class women.

It is social justice that the peoples of the many different cultures altered or destroyed by imperialism should now be in the forefront of those seeking to overthrow this system, and their cultures provide us with guidelines and possibilities for new and more human ways of life. Perhaps for the first time in human history we are faced with the possibility of a pan-human, nonexploitative society. Abundant production is possible given our technology and there is a real need for all peoples, women and men, to unite, if we are to defeat the numerically tiny, but very powerful forces in opposition to our needs.

SELF-DEFENSE FOR WOMEN

Susan Pascalé, Rachel Moon, Leslie B. Tanner

Women are attacked, beaten, and raped every day. By men. Women are afraid to walk certain streets after dark, and even afraid to walk into buildings where they live. It's about time that we as women got strong in order to defend ourselves! Two of us (ages twenty-nine and forty-three) and three children decided to learn Karate. We went to watch a class before signing up and if we hadn't been so determined, the class (consisting of about twenty-five frighteningly strong men) would have scared us into quitting before we started. We had yet to learn how really weak we were.

One reason for taking Karate, other than strictly learning self-defense, was a matter of health—women seem to smoke more than men, and certainly we never give our bodies physical exercise except for cleaning house, chasing kids, and fucking. Both of us smoked too much and hadn't moved in over ten years. Another reason for one of us getting into

Karate was the fact that she has three children and the family structure being what it is, she had hopes that if she and her children took Karate together it might relieve some of the emotional bullshit that goes on, not only between children but also between the mother and children.

In the middle of August the five of us (two women, one girl aged fifteen, and two boys, ages eleven and six) started classes.

Psychological Oppression

When we went to our first class, we huddled in a corner, feeling inferior and somehow as though we were trespassing. The men stood directly in front of the mirrors, totally unself-conscious, to practice. We, after three months, are still self-conscious. Interestingly, the fifteen-year-old girl is not. She has not yet been completely conditioned to be "feminine." We have discussed this among ourselves and feel it must stem from numerous causes: we are conditioned to see ourselves other than as a tough puncher—we don't really want to see ourselves looking like that, and yet we do want to. We see our little fists in the mirror, and they look like shit. We punch with our left hand, and it looks and feels like a piece of spaghetti. We are totally unaccustomed to looking in the mirror, contemplating our own gorgeous muscles. It makes us feel like fools. We are conditioned to feel that what we're doing is unfeminine. We have been taught to be passive all our lives—even for the two of us, who were sportswomen and dancers, the punching is just a little too much.

A corollary of this is falling into "female" patterns as a sort of defense against feeling inadequate. When being instructed in small groups, or working out with each other, we often start laughing, playing around, and not really doing it seriously. This attitude has become particularly noticeable now that we have begun, after three months, to learn Kumite (or free fighting). Up to this time we have really been punching air, and not engaging in actual combat. This is tremendously difficult: not only do we laugh as a protective mechanism, but we also tend to do the traditional womanly thing of backing away and covering our faces. It is our first instinct not to fight back.

The trouble is, even now, after actually learning how to punch, we don't really want to punch at men. The first thing we think about is: "But I don't want to hurt him." Then we realize that this is really a traditional feminine cover-up for the truth which is that we are afraid of men. Women have always known that to hit a man seriously means risking getting killed. We have acknowledged these "feminine attributes" to ourselves, and we try every day to overcome them. It is clear that the longer our attitudes persist, the less we learn.

Male Chauvinism in the Dojo, or "We Are All Brothers Here"

NON-TRICKY, OBVIOUS FORMS OF MALE CHAUVINISM

Our experiences, as women, at the Dojo (the place where you learn and practice Karate) have shown us how very deep and oppressive the attitudes of men are towards women. We have been tolerated to the point that we have sometimes felt like the "Invisible Woman." The men treat us with a patronizing air that seems to say they wish we weren't there.

The first and most obvious example of discrimination is that women are charged only half price. We don't know the actual reason for this, perhaps it's because we're considered only half-persons, or because the teacher feels guilty because he figures we'll never learn Karate anyway. We decide to take advantage of this form of oppression, and have not yet challenged it.

Secondly, the Sensei (Teacher) originally addressed the class as "Gentlemen." We let this pass for a couple of days, thinking it would take him a lesson or two to get used to us.

But he continued and we confronted him, stating that we didn't care how he wished to address us, just as long as our existence was recognized, either as "ladies" with "gentlemen," or as "women" with "men," or just a part of "everybody." The Sensei admitted his oversight and agreed to make amends.

Throughout the next week he continued to address everyone as "gentlemen," and we confronted him again, calling him "Mrs." and explaining that if he didn't like that, we didn't like being called "gentlemen." He apologized and said he would stop it. In the next few lessons he occasionally let one or two "gentlemen" slip but usually no more than once per lesson.

Then, quite recently, Sensei got angry at the class and let loose a loud: "Don't punch like that. It's too weak. You're punching like girls!" (Obviously the worst insult that can be given to a man.) At one time, we probably wouldn't have been insulted by this, thinking that he couldn't possibly mean us. The fifteen-year-old girl didn't understand our anger: we explained that any insult toward women is an insult to *us*, since we *are*, in fact, women.

Immediately after class we went to the Sensei with the words, "Remember, don't punch like a . . ."which he interrupted with, "Yes, I know, I'm sorry. I realized the minute I said it." We replied, "If women punch weak, it's precisely because of such male attitudes."

Finally, after three and a half months of attending the Dojo four to six times a week, a breakthrough came at least on this issue. Sensei let a "gentlemen" slip from his mouth and after a slight hesitation, followed it with "and ladies." Whether this will remain a permanent feature in the Dojo remains to be seen, but because two more women will soon be in our class, it probably will. Our feeling has been that we may not be able to change these men's attitudes, but at least we don't have to hear them. This much at least is relatively easy to win.

TRICKY, UNOBVIOUS FORMS OF MALE CHAUVINISM

Much more difficult to identify, and hence to combat, is the deep-seated, unobvious male chauvinism in the Dojo. While knowing that close to 100 percent of the men have traditional attitudes, this is complicated, first, by the fact that the Karate code says that women should be trained on an equal basis with men.

In Karate no distinctions are made in instruction between men and women. We are expected to do everything the men do: to learn the positions as fast and to do them as well. We have been rewarded on that assumption. We have advanced in rank beyond some men who were ahead of us when we started. (We are now advanced white belts and by December we should have our green belts.) It seems to be simply a matter of time spent working in the Dojo. We can say categorically that it is possible to participate in a mixed Dojo on physical considerations. Woman entering a male Dojo should watch that they are not discriminated against by having less demanded of them. Women taking Karate with an all-women's group should check their instruction against all-male or mixed classes.

The only real difficulty we had was with push-ups. None of us could do more than one or two, when we started. We are now doing fourteen or sixteen, at least. Twenty are done in every class and we are expected to work up to this number. If anyone tells you that women should not do push-ups, you can tell them that you certainly should and will. Or just tell them they're full of shit.

Second, male chauvinism is masked by the fact that the code of the Dojo is that everyone be treated with great respect and humility, regardless of rank. The slogan is: "We are all brothers." We are treated *very politely*, formally, and respectfully. In terms of human relationships, however, we are avoided as much as possible because the Sensei and all the other men in the Dojo know how to treat us only in the traditional sense, i.e., as sex objects. Since we have not allowed ourselves to be treated as sex objects, we are not "women" in their eyes. And obviously we are not brothers. Hence we are in some undefined, neuter area. We are *invisible!*

Third, it is very difficult to figure out whether we are being treated in a certain manner because we are beginners (and weak) or because we are women. The men have tried to avoid all physical contact with us. It's a mind-blower! When we need a partner for sit-ups (which means entangling our legs with theirs), they immediately try to find someone other than one of us, using the excuse (when questioned directly) that we're too light-weight or too weak. When Sensei makes the rounds to test our "stance," by touching the "butt" and thigh muscles, he just doesn't touch ours. After three months he finally did touch the fifteen-year-old's "butt," but he still avoids us older women like the plague. It seems clear that twenty-five-year-old Sensei cannot see us as other than females who can be touched for one purpose and one purpose only.

Finally, the actual free-fighting exercise we do is ridiculous. One man refused to make any contact at all, and stayed at least five feet away, punching at the air. Nobody can learn to fight if they're invisible. The rationale that's given is that we're still too weak to defend ourselves. One male member of the Dojo told us that a lot of the men take us as a sort of joke, and that we must be very careful, for if we think we'll "show them" by really giving them some good strong punches, they then might retaliate far beyond what we can handle at this stage and really beat us up badly. He advised playing it soft until we could handle rough dealing. This is an obvious case of oppression. Men think we're a joke until we prove otherwise, at which point they're out to demolish us.

We seem to have only scratched the surface of the male chauvinism in the Dojo. This is so partly because we never intended to make the Dojo an area of attack. It is very difficult to carry on any fight in the Dojo because of the traditional authoritarianism which we accepted in order to get our training. Male chauvinist attitudes have been attacked only when *blatant* and when we felt directly offended. We don't know what changes the future will bring. As we get stronger and more confident, issues of male chauvinism which are murky to us now because of our own insecurities, will become clear, and may necessitate a real fight. The men probably will do anything (within reason) to protect the traditional "brotherhood" of the Dojo.

Positive Aspects and Implications for Women's Liberation

1. Karate has indeed affected the attitude the children have toward each other, and toward their mother. They no longer fight and throw sneak punches at each other the way they used to, but use Karate, bowing to each other, and being courteous and thoughtful of each other. The fifteen-year-old girl is getting very strong and is feeling confident enough to walk city streets alone, after dark. Let her speak for herself:

   There are several reasons why I wanted to learn the art of self-defense. The two most important reasons were 1) in the society we live in today I feel a great need for women to be strong 2) Karate and Kata (dance forms) are really most beautiful and exciting. In the very beginning I felt inhibited, but not because I am a woman (as did my mother and friend). It was because being a white belt in the Dojo you get treated like "brand new beginners." I didn't know that much about Karate but as the months passed I began to feel confident. At the end of three months I was put up against men to do free fighting. I felt inferior again, basically because I had never fought before; also again it was the feeling of low rank and less experience. All in all, I feel I am getting stronger, and I feel all women should get strong and learn to fight.

2. Karate has made us feel much healthier and stronger than we were before (we've even cut our smoking in half). Stronger hands and arms enable us to do things we usu-

ally rely on men to do, such as carrying heavy loads from the store.

3. Karate gets us out of the house three nights (or days) a week, and because we like it, it becomes something we'll do *no matter what.* It's good for freeing us from household chores/waiting around for a man to call/waiting around for the man to come home/waiting around because the man *is* home/creating a good reason why a man must fit his schedule into ours, i.e., see us when *we're* available/or take care of his own children three nights a week!

4. Karate has mentally increased our confidence in ourselves as human beings. Simone de Beauvoir says, "Not to have confidence in one's body is to lose confidence in oneself" (*The Second Sex*).As a result of Karate, we are gaining confidence in our bodies and are going through some fantastic changes in terms of our feelings of self-worth. Our confidence has increased not only in confrontations with "dirty old men" in the streets, but in non-physical confrontations with our own men and society in general. We do feel as though we have more control over our own lives because of our new potential physical power.

5. After participating in a few women's liberation actions, we see more clearly than ever the need for women to get strong. We demonstrated against blatant sexual exploitation of women in front of the Electric Circus [a discotheque] on the Lower East Side of New York City, and we almost went sprawling several times as people tried to trip us. We wished then that we were Black Belts so we could defend ourselves. Recently we helped take over a panel at Cooper Union that was going to discuss Abortion —a panel consisting of four men! The men gave up the stage very quickly to the women, but shortly after came back on stage and slowly removed four mikes (that were switched off anyway) from the speakers' table, acting all the time as if no one were there. Invisible again! The men

should have been forcibly escorted off the scene. We were not strong enough to confront them and make them meet our demands.

Women's liberation has a long, tough, political fight before it, and our oppression, which is ultimately maintained by force, can only be overcome by force. Women will be needed as fighters.

Finally, Simone de Beauvoir says that "Violence is the authentic proof of each one's loyalty to himself, to his passions, to his own will; radically to deny this is to deny oneself any objective truth, it is to wall oneself up in an abstract subjectivity; anger or revolt that does not get into the muscles remains a figment of the imagination. It is a profound frustration not to be able to register one's feelings upon the fact of the world." This we agree with completely. But she continues, "It remains true that her physical weakness does not permit woman to learn the lessons of violence." This we categorically reject. We, once as physically weak as any average female, *are* learning the lessons of violence, and learning them well. We strongly recommend that anyone else who is interested do the same.

Women must get strong!

FEMALE LIBERATION AS THE BASIS FOR SOCIAL REVOLUTION

by Roxanne Dunbar

The present female liberation movement must be viewed within the context of international social revolution and within the context of the long struggle by women for nominal legal rights. The knowledge that is now available, gained in past struggles, makes the current women's movement more scientific and potent. Black people in America and Vietnamese people have exposed the basic weakness of the system of white, Western dominance which we live under. They have also developed means of fighting which continually strengthen themselves and weaken the enemy. The dialectics of liberation have revealed that the weak and oppressed can struggle against and defeat a larger enemy. Revolutionary dialectics teach that nothing is immutable. Our enemy today may not be our enemy next year, or the same enemy might be fighting us in a different way tomorrow. Our tactics must be fitted to the immediate situation and open to change; our strategy must be formed in relation to our overall revolutionary goals. Black Americans and the Vietnamese have taught, most importantly, that there is a distinction between the consciousness of the oppressor and the consciousness of the oppressed.

I.

Women have not just recently begun to struggle against their suppression and exploitation. Women have fought in a million ways in their daily, private lives to survive and to overcome existing conditions. Many times those "personal" struggles have taken a self-destructive form. Almost always women have had to use sex as a tool, and have thereby sunk further in oppression. Many women still believe in the efficacy of fighting a lone battle. But more and more women are realizing that only collective strength and action will allow us to be free to fight for the kind of society that meets basic human needs. Collective activity has already had an enormous effect on our thinking and on our lives. We are learning not to dissipate our strength by using traditional methods of exerting power—tears, manipulation, appeals to guilt and benevolence. But we do not ignore what seem to be the "petty" forms of female oppression, such as total identification with housework and sexuality as well as physical helplessness. Rather we understand that our oppression and suppression are institutionalized; that all women suffer the "petty" forms of oppression. Therefore they are not petty or personal, but rather constitute a widespread, deeply rooted social disease. They are the things that keep us tied down day to day, and do not allow us to act. Further, we understand that all men are our policemen, and no organized police force is necessary at this time to keep us in our places. All men enjoy male supremacy and take advantage of it to a greater or lesser degree depending on their position in the masculine hierarchy of power.

It is not enough that we take collective action. We must know where we have come from historically and personally, and how we can most effectively break the bonds. We have identified a system of oppression—*Sexism*. To understand how sexism has developed and the variety of its forms of suppression and mutations, female liberation must, as Betsy Warrior puts it, "re-examine the foundations of civilization."

What we find in re-examining history is that women have had a separate historical development from men. Within each society, women experience the particular culture, but on a larger scale of human history, women have developed separately as a caste. The original division of labor in all societies was by sex. The female capacity for reproduction led to this division. The division of labor by sex has not put a lighter physical burden on women, as we might believe, if we look only at the mythology of chivalry in Western ruling class history. Quite the contrary. What was restricted for women was not physical labor, but mobility.

Because woman's reproductive capacity led to her being forced into sedentary (immobile, not inactive) life, the female developed community life. Adult males were alien to the female community. Their job was to roam, to do the hunting and war-making, entering the community only to leave again. Their entrances and exits probably disrupted normal community life. What hunters experienced of the community were feasts and holidays, not day-to-day life. At some point, when women had developed food production and animal domestication to the point of subsistence, hunters began settling down. However, they brought to the community a very different set of values and behavioral patterns which upset the primitive communism of the community.

In a very real sense, the hunter was less civilized than the female. He had little political (governing) experience. The experience of the hunter had led him to value dominance; he had become unsuited for living as equals in the community, because he knew only how to overpower and conquer the prey. Other masculine values, formed in the transient existence as hunters, included competition (with the prey) and violence (killing the prey). Hunters developed a taste for adventure and mobility. They developed technical skills and a sense of timing and accuracy and endurance. Though hunters worked together and developed a sense of brotherhood, their brotherhood developed outside community life.

Gradually in some cases, but often through violent upheaval, former hunters took over female communities, suppressing the female through domination and even enslavement. The political base for the taking of power often came from the secret male societies formed by men in reaction to female control of community institutions.

As societies became more affluent and complex, life was rationalized and ordered by introducing territoriality, or private property, and inheritance. Patrilineal descent required the control of a female or a number of females to identify the father. The offspring served as labor as well as fulfilling the function of transcendence for the father (the son taking over), and females were used for barter, as were cattle. This then led to the dominance of the male over a wife or wives and her (his) offspring. The female, like the land, became private property under masculine dominance. Man, in conquering nature, conquered the female, who had worked with nature, not against it, to produce food and to reproduce the human race.

II.

In competing among themselves for dominance over females (and thereby the offspring) and for land, a few males came to dominate the rest of the male population, as well as the entire female population. A peasant laboring class developed. Within that laboring class, males exploited females, though the male peasant had no property rights over females (or land). The landlord could take any young girl or woman he wanted for whatever purpose, and the peasant was not allowed to "protect" "his" woman.

The pattern of masculine dominance exists almost universally now, since those cultures where the pattern developed have come to dominate (colonize) pre-literate societies, and have introduced patterns of private property and nationalism. The Western nation-states, which have perfected colonialism, were developed as an extension of male dominance over females and the land. Other races and cultures were bought and sold, possessed, dominated through "contract" and ultimately through physical violence and the threat of destruction, of the world if necessary. We live under an international caste system, at the top of which is the Western white male ruling class, and at the very bottom of which is the female of the non-white colonized world. There is no simple order of "oppressions" within this caste system. Within each culture, the female is exploited to some degree by the male. She is classed with the very old and very young of both sexes ("the women, children, and old men"). White dominates black and brown. The caste system, in all its various forms, is always based on identifiable physical characteristics—sex, color, age.

Why is it important to say that females constitute a lower *caste?* Many people would say that the term caste can only properly be used in reference to India or Hindu culture. If we think that caste can only be applied to Hindu society, we will then have to find some other term for the kind of social category to which one is assigned at birth and from which one cannot escape by any action of one's own; also we must distinguish such social categories from economic classes or ranked groups as well as understand their relationship.

A caste system establishes a definite place into which certain members of a society have no choice but to fit (because of their color or sex or other easily identifiable physical characteristics such as being aged, crippled, or blind). A caste system, however, need not at all be based on a prohibition of physical contact between different castes. It only means that physical contact will be severely regulated, or will take place outside the bounds deemed acceptable by the society; it means that the mobility of the lower castes will be limited. It means that whatever traits associated with the lower caste will be devalued in the society or will be mystified in some way.

Under the caste system in the Southern states, physical contact between black and white is extensive (particularly through white male sexual exploitation of black women). In the South under slavery, there was frequent contact between black "mammy" and white child, between black and white pre-adolescent children, and between white master and black slave women.

Between male and female, thousands of taboos control their contact in every society. Within each, there is a "woman's world" and a "man's world." In most, men initiate contact with women, usually for the purpose of exploitation. Women have little freedom to initiate contact with adult males. The same is true for black and white in America.

The clearest historical analogy of the caste status of females is African slavery in English-speaking America. When slaves were freed during the Civil War, the female slaves were included, but when the right to citizenship was in question, female blacks were excluded. To many, comparing the female's situation in general with that of a slave in particular seems far-fetched. Actually, the reason the analogy is indicated has to do with the caste status of the

African in America, not with Slavery as such.

Slave status in the past did not necessarily imply caste status by birth. The restriction of slavery to Africans (black people) in the English colonies rested on the caste principle that it was a status rightly belonging to Africans as innately (racially) inferior beings. (Of course, this was a rationalization on the part of the English, but it became a ruling ideology and was connected with the past.) If a person was black, he was presumed to be a slave unless he could prove otherwise. Caste was inclusive of the slave and free status, just as the caste status of females is inclusive of all economic classes, age, and marital status, though some are more "privileged" and some are more exploited, depending on the female's relationship with a male, or whether she has one or not.

Caste, then, is not analogous to slavery. In Rome, where slaves were not conceived of as innately inferior, and did not differ racially from the enslaving group, slaves did not form a separate caste when they were freed. While they were slaves, however, they had no rights to property nor any legal rights. The master had the power of life and death over his slaves, just as in the slave South. As far as the legal category of the slave as property went, Rome and America had the same social form. It was caste which produced the contrast between the effects of the two systems of slavery. It was the system of caste which gave African slavery in America its peculiarly oppressive character. That caste oppression is analagous to the situation of females both legally and traditionally. (When jurists were seeking a legal category for the position of African slaves in Virginia, they settled on the code of laws which governed wives and children under the power of the patriarch, the head of the family).

In order to understand the power relations of white and black in American society, of white imperialist America and the Third World, and of male and female in all human societies, we must comprehend the caste system which

structures power, and within which caste roles we are conditioned to remain.

Often, in trying to describe the way a white person oppresses or exploits a black person, or a man oppresses or
exploits a woman, we say that the oppressor treats the other
person as a "thing" or as an "object." Men treat women as
"sex objects," we say; slavery reduced black human beings
to "mere property," no different from horses or cattle. This
interpretation of caste oppression overlooks the crucial importance of the fact that it is human beings, not objects,
which the person in the higher caste has the power to dominate and exploit. Imagine a society becoming as dependent
upon cattle as Southern plantation society was upon black
people, or as men are upon women. The value of slaves as
property lay precisely in their being persons, rather than
just another piece of property. The value of a woman for a
man is much greater than the value of a machine or animal
to satisfy his sexual urges and fantasies, to do his housework,
breed and tend his offspring. Under slavery, the slave did
what no animal could do—planting and harvest, as well as
every other kind of backbreaking labor for which no machines existed. But the slave served a much larger purpose
in terms of power. It is convenient and "fun" for a man to
have satisfactions from "his woman," but his relation to her
as a *person*, his position of being of a higher caste, is the
central aspect of his power and dominance over her and his
need for her.

(A further example of the importance to the higher castes
of dominating human beings, not mere objects, is the way
men view their sexual exploitation of women. It is not just
the satisfaction of a man's private, individual, sexual urge
which he fantasizes he will get from a woman he sees. In
addition, and more central to his view of women, he visual-
izes himself taking her, dominating her through the sexual
act; he sees her as the *human* evidence of his own power and
prowess. Prostitution, however exploitative for the woman,

can never serve this same purpose, just as wage labor, however exploitative to the wage slave, could not have served the same purpose in Southern society that black slaves served.)

Black people fell under two patterns of dominance and subservience which emerged under slavery, and which are analogous to patterns of male-female relations in industrial societies. One pattern is the paternalistic one (house servants, livery men, entertainers, etc.). The second pattern is the exploitative pattern of the fieldhands. Among females today, housewives and women on welfare are subject to the paternalistic pattern. The exploitative pattern rules the lives of more than a third of the population of females (those who work for wages, including paid domestic work) in the United States. But it is important to remember that females form a caste within the labor force; that their exploitation is not simply double or multiple, but is *qualitatively* different from the exploitation of workers of the upper caste (white male).

Though the paternalistic pattern may seem less oppressive or exploitative for females, it is actually only more insidious. The housewife remains tied by emotional bonds to a man and children, cut off from the more public world of work; she is able to experience the outside world only through the man or her children. If she were working in public industry, however exploitative, she could potentially do something about her situation through collective effort with other workers.

However, even for women who hold jobs outside the home, their caste conditioning and demands usually prevail, preventing them from knowing even that they have the *right* to work, much less to ask for something more. Also, the jobs women are allowed to have are most often "service" and domestic ones, demanding constant contact with men and children. Females and blacks, even under the alienating capitalist system, are subject to the paternalistic pattern of caste domination every minute of their lives. White men, however exploited as laborers, rarely experience this paternalism, which infantilizes and debilitates its victims.

A caste system provides rewards that are not entirely economic in the narrow sense. Caste is a way of making human relations "work," a way of freezing relationships, so that conflicts are minimal. A caste system is a *social system*, which is economically based. It is not a set of attitudes or just some mistaken ideas which must be understood and dispensed with because they are not really in the interest of the higher caste. No mere change in ideas will alter the caste system under which we live. The caste system does not exist just in the mind. Caste is deeply rooted in human history, dates to the division of labor by sex, and is the very basis of the present social system in the United States.

III.

The present female liberation movement, like the movements for black liberation and national liberation, has begun to identify strongly with Marxist class analysis. And like other movements, we have taken the basic tools of Marxist analysis (dialectical and historical materialism) and expanded the understanding of the process of change. Our analysis of women as an exploited caste is not new. Marx and Engels as well as other nineteenth-century socialist and communist theorists analyzed the position of the female sex in just such a way. Engels identified the family as the basic unit of capitalist society, and of female oppression. "The modern individual family is founded on the open or concealed domestic slavery of the wife, and modern society is a mass composed of these individual families as its molecules." And "within the family, he (the man) is the bourgeois and the wife represents the proletariat." (Frederick Engels, *Origin of The Family, Private Property, and the State*).

Marx and Engels thought that the large-scale entrance of

women into the work force (women and children were the first factory workers) would destroy the family unit, and that women would fight as workers, with men, for the overthrow of capitalism. That did not happen, nor were women freed in the socialist revolutions that succeeded. In the West (Europe and the United States) where proletarian revolutions have not succeeded, the family ideology has gained a whole new lease on life, and the lower caste position of women has continued to be enforced. Even now when 40 percent of the adult female population is in the work force, woman is still defined completely within the family, and the man is seen as "protector" and "breadwinner."

In reality, the family has fallen apart. Nearly half of all marriages end in divorce, and the family unit is a decadent, energy-absorbing, destructive, wasteful institution for everyone except the ruling class, the class for which the institution was created. The powers that be, through government action and their propaganda force, the news media, are desperately trying to hold the family together. Sensitivity, encounter, key clubs, group sex, income tax benefits, and many other devices are being used to promote the family as a desirable institution. Daniel Moynihan and other government sociologists have correctly surmised that the absence of the patriarchal family among blacks has been instrumental in the development of "anti-social" (revolutionary) black consciousness. Actually, in the absence of the patriarchal family, which this society has systematically denied black people, a sense of community life and collective effort has developed. Among whites, individualism and competitiveness prevail in social relations, chiefly because of the propagation of the ideology of the patriarchal family. The new sense of collective action among women is fast destroying the decadent family ideology along with its ugly individualism and competitiveness and complacency. Our demand for collective public child care is throwing into question the private family (or individual) ownership of children.

Yet, under this competitive system, without the family

unit and without the tie with a male, the female falls from whatever middle-class status she has gained from the family situation. She quickly falls into the work force or has to go on welfare. Such was the case for black slaves when a master voluntarily freed them, and when slavery was ended as an institution. In both cases, the "helplessness" is used as the rationale for continued domination. Lower caste status almost always means lower class status as well. For women who are supported by and gain the status of their husbands, working class status is always a potential threat, if they do not perform their wifely duties properly. However, many of these supported women have chosen to enter the work force in the vast pool of female clerical workers, in order to gain the economic independence that is necessary to maintain self-respect and sanity. On these jobs, women are still subjected to patterns of masculine dominance. But often on the less personal ground of workplace, a woman can begin throwing off the bonds of servitude.

IV.

How will the family unit be destroyed? After all, women must take care of the children, and there will continue to be children. Our demand for full-time child care in the public schools will be met to some degree all over, and perhaps fully in places. The alleviation of the duty of full-time child care in private situations will free many women to make decisions they could not before. But more than that, the demand alone will throw the whole ideology of the family into question, so that women can begin establishing a community of work with each other and we can fight collectively. Women will feel freer to leave their husbands and become economically independent, either through a job or welfare.

Where will this leave white men and "their" families? The patriarchal family is economically and historically tied to private property and, under Western capitalism, with the development of the national state. The masculine ideology most strongly asserts home and country as primary values, with wealth and power an individual's greatest goal. The same upper class of men who created private property and founded nation-states also created the family. It is an expensive institution, and only the upper classes have been able to maintain it properly. However, American "democracy" has spread the ideology to the working class. The greatest pride of a working man is that he can support "his" wife and children and maintain a home (even though this is an impossibility for many and means misery for most). The very definition of a bum or derelict is that he does not maintain a wife, children, and home. Consequently, he is an outcast. It is absurd to consider the possibility of women sharing with men the "privilege" of owning a family. Even though 5.2 million families are headed by females in this country, they gain no prestige from doing so. In fact, the family without a male head or support is considered an inferior family. A woman supporting her family actually degrades the family in terms of social status.

At this point in history, white working-class men will fight for nothing except those values associated with the masculine ideology, the ideology of the ruling class— family, home, property, country, male supremacy, and white supremacy. This force, the organized or organizable working class, has been vital in other social revolutions. However, because of the caste system which reigns here, the American democracy of white males, and the power of the nation in the world with which white workers identify, white male workers are not now a revolutionary group in America. Among the most oppressed part of the white working-class males—Irish, Italian, French Canadian (in the U.S.), Polish immigrants—the patriarchal Catholic church buttresses the masculine ideology with its emphasis on family. Even among lower caste (color) groups, Puerto Ricans and Mexican-Americans, the church reinforces masculine domination.

However, the women who "belong" to these men are going to revolt along with the women who belong to middle-class men, and women on welfare and women not yet in the cycle of marriage and family. Black women will probably continue to fight as blacks alongside black men with a reversal of the trend toward taking second place to the black man in order for him to gain his "due" masculine status according to the prevailing masculine ideology. When the white working-class man is confronted with the revolt of women against the family and the society, he will no longer have the escape valve of supremacy over those beneath him in the caste system.

V.

Feminism is opposed to the masculine ideology. I do not suggest that all women are feminists, though many are; certainly some men are, though very few. Some women embrace the masculine ideology, particularly women with a college education. But most women have been programmed from early childhood for a role, maternity, which develops a certain consciousness of care for others, self-reliance, flexibility, non-competitiveness, cooperation, and materialism. In addition, women have inherited and continue to suffer exploitation which forces us to use our wits to survive, to know our enemy, to play dumb when necessary. So we have developed the consciousness of the oppressed, not the oppressor, even though some women have the right to oppress others, and all have the right to oppress children. If these "maternal" traits, conditioned into women, are desirable traits, they are desirable for everyone, not just women. By destroying the present society, and building a society on feminist principles, men will be forced to live in the human community on terms very different from the present. For that to happen, feminism must be asserted, by women, as the basis of revolutionary social change. Women and other oppressed people must lead and structure the revolutionary movement and the new society to assure the dominance of feminist principles. Our present female liberation movement is preparing us for that task, as is the black liberation movement preparing black people for their revolutionary leadership role.

The female liberation movement is developing in the context of international social revolution, but it is also heir to a 120-year struggle by women for legal rights. The nineteenth-century feminist movement as well as its child, the women's suffrage movement, were comparatively modest in their demands. They fought from a basis of no rights, no power at all. In the first movement, women began fighting for the right of females to speak publicly for abolition of slavery. The cause of female rights and the abolition of slavery were inexorably linked. The early feminists did not see the family as a decadent institution. They wanted to find a way to force men to share responsibility in the institution they created by supporting their families. They saw alcohol as an enemy of family solidarity.

With the end of slavery, only black males received citizenship. Black women and white women remained unenfranchised. Women then began the long struggle for the vote. They felt they could make the large-scale and basic changes in society which they saw as necessary by their influence in politics. They believed that woman's political involvement would bring her out of privacy. Many of them questioned the very foundations of civilization, but their strategy and tactics for gaining the desired upheaval of their society revolved around political influence within the System.

In the process of their struggle, the feminists and suffragists opened the door for our present female liberation movement. They won not only the right to vote, but other legal rights as well, including the custodial rights to their children. More than that, women began to fight their oppression and lift up their heads. At the same time, working women were fighting their wage slavery. Women began to emerge from privacy and to know that they did in fact have rights for which they must fight. They gained confidence in the struggle, and asserted a new independence, which we all inherited.

We also inherited an understanding of the weakness of single issue tactics, and of "organizing" women around issues rather than teaching a complete analysis of female oppression. We learned that there is no key to liberation. We must fight on many fronts at once. Thanks to gains made by our feminist predecessors, though, we have the confidence to assert feminism as a positive force, rather than asking for equality in the man's world. We can demand that men change. We can consider leading a social revolution, not just working in supportive positions, and hope for the justness, benevolence, and change of heart of men. We can assert the necessity of industrializing all housework, and for right now to have school cafeterias open to adults as well as children. We can demand the extension of public education facilities and funds to include infant and child care. We can demand the development of maternal skills and consciousness in men. We can insist on the necessity for revolution to be based on the needs and consciousness of the most oppressed of women. We can revoke any privileges we have which divide us from other women.

We are developing necessary skills—self-defense and physical strength, the ability to work collectively and politically, rather than privately and personally, and the ability to teach our ideas to many other women in such a way that they then can become teachers as well. From these new relations and skills will be built the values of the new society. Right now they are our tools of struggle. Though we may work in isolated and difficult and dangerous situations, we can know our larger strategy and goals, and know that we are a part of a worldwide struggle for human liberation.

V

THE HAND THAT CRADLES THE ROCK: PROTEST AND REVOLT

POETRY

AS PROTEST

FOR WITCHES

Susan Sutheim

today
i lost my temper.

temper, when one talks of metal
means make strong,
perfect.

temper, for humans, means angry
irrational
bad.

today i found my temper.
i said,
you step on my head
for 27 years you step on my head
and though i have been trained
to excuse you for your inevitable

clumsiness
today i think
i prefer my head to your clumsiness.

today i began
to find
myself.

tomorrow
perhaps
i will begin
to find
you.

ELEGY FOR JAYNE MANSFIELD, JULY 1967

Karen Lindsey

she was a
sunday news centerfold
bosoms thrust toward subway-
rush men leaning on the
legs of pretty secretaries
always a bleeding
divorce or a beaten child,
she had a pink voice, and lived in a pink house.
no hints of a self
cringing away from sticky headlines
or an art groping beyond
barebreasted titters.

we used to have fun laughing at her.
when she lost her head, the joke turned sick.

A Chant for My Sisters

Marilyn Lowen Fletcher

        it's all right to be woman
dishwasher, big belly, sore back
swollen ankles

its all right to be woman
the listener the waiter/sailor's wife
patient
by the seashore/looking out

it's all right to be woman
coquette
        seductress
                conniving bitch

it's all right to be woman
a chant for my sisters
strong before me
harriet sojourner emma and rosa
harriet sojourner emma and rosa

a chant for my sisters
rifke sorel rochel & mary
yema ya yemaya yemaya yemaya

yemaya yemaya yemaya yemaya
oshun...................
oshun...................

a chant to my sisters
strong in battle
la bandita killing generals with zapata
maría in mexico and mississippi

haydee with the rest at moncada
a chant for my sisters
dead before i could meet them
victorious
in havana
and dien bien phu

MUST I MARRY

Lynn Strongin

Must I
marry
my body?

Shall I
be
the bride?
or groom?

Take it to bed,
lie beside
the pain . . .

As a bride I
in a white
nightgown.

Only, being broken,
there'd be no breaking in.

THE PLAYGROUND (A PROSE POEM)

Leah Fritz

The iron gate is high and there are points. But this is a public garden and therefore treeless. The women sit and sweat over their children in the summertime. The children run under the spray in bathing suits when the spray is on, but this summer there is a drought.

Hamlet is a play about remembrance, remembrance and death. "Pray love, remember." "Rosemary is for remembrance." "Remember me."

Woman, that strange creature, strives—to be, uniquely to be. What to be? Caught. In a cage. The bars of iron have tidy points to rip the little shins that climb. Alarmed. At the swellings. And the braces. At the cough. At the growing up. Alarmed. We gossip in the park. We watch the children play. This is mine to pass on to you. Remembrance. Pray, love. Remembrance of the dead, that you may die.

And did he scream at me? And did he say you don't know what you're talking about once too often? And did I kill him? Was it time for him to die? Did I grow tired of he said, she said, I said? And I discovered, it took a whole generation for me to discover, that I am right. So what do I tell you? Believe them, be safe. I don't know what that means.

Play with the ball. Leave me alone. I'm talking to the ladies. It is hot. You are hot too? Listen, I've never lied to you. I never will. Make of your life. It's not much I gave you. I found that out too late. Make a sandpile. Make a pie. Eat, *mein kind.*

These are the ladies that push you. Into the playground and out. In their suits and their slacks and their empty voices, you hear me talk to them to pass the time. You know it's foolish. Mama, come and play with me! I would be better off, but my depression, my morbid curiosity, sticks me to the bench.What will she say, this one, that I have heard before?

So I swear a vow of silence. Mute I stand in my black robes against the wall of iron spikes that the children chin on I have heard that talk before I will not listen to another word but buy the groceries and check out at the check-out counter pick up my stamps and go. Before I go, give me one kiss. Oh, you are so sweet. Pray, love. Pray love, remember.

SHE

Maria Ann Britton

she wears
her pain
like an ageing
dress.
      moves her
hips within
and smothers
in it's warmth
she cries for
freedom, discard
lady-like lace
to lose companionship.

DANCING THE SHOUT TO THE TRUE GOSPEL

OR

THE SONG MOVEMENT SISTERS DON'T WANT ME TO SING

Rita Mae Brown

I follow the scent of a woman
Melon heavy
Ripe with joy
Inspiring me
To rip great holes in the night
So the sun blasts through
And this is all I shall ever know
Her breath
Filling the hollows of my neck
A luxury diminishing death.

POEM

Jayne West

as i was walking along
    the gentleman to my left
addressed me as a fat-assed pig
feeling this comment to be neither

accurate nor appropriate
i reciprocated by calling him a
     lecherous old whore-monger
taking no pleasure in his most recently
     acquired appellation
he proclaimed me a
     bitch in heat
i said in reply
     that my condition was far more
     desirable
than his condition which was that of
     a mangy cock-sucker
he retorted with fuck you
whereupon i gasped admirably
and waddled on

SONG OF THE FUCKED DUCK

Marge Piercy

In using there are always two,
the manipulator dances with a partner who cons herself.
There are lies that glow so brightly we consent
to give a finger and then an arm
to let them burn.
I was dazzled by the crowd where everyone called my
     name.
Now I stand outside the funhouse exit, down the slide
reading my guidebook of Marx in Esperanto
and if I don't know anymore which way means forward
down is where my head is, next to my feet
with a pocketful of words and plastic tokens.

Form follows function, says the organizer
and turns himself into a paperclip,
into a vacuum cleaner,
into a machinegun.
Function follows analysis
but the forebrain
is only an owl in the tree of self.
One third of life we prowl in the grottos of sleep
where neglected worms ripen into dragons
where the spoilt pencil swells into an oak
and the cows of our early sins are called home chewing their
       cuds
and turning the sad faces of our childhood upon us.
Come back and scrub the floor, the stain is still there,
come back with your brush and kneel down
scrub and scrub again
it will never be clean.
Fantasy unacted sours the brain.
Buried desires sprout like mushrooms on the chin of the
       morning.
The will to be totally rational
is the will to be made out of glass and steel:
and to use others as if they were glass and steel.
We can see clearly no farther
than our hands can touch.
The cockroach knows as much as you know about living.
We trust with our hands and our eyes and our bellies.
The cunt accepts.
The teeth and back reject.
What we have to give each other:
dumb and mysterious as water swirling.
Always in the long corridors of the psyche
doors are opening and doors are slamming shut.
We rise each day to give birth or to murder
selves that go through our hands like tiny fish.
You said: I am the organizer, and took and used.
You wrapped your head in theory like yards of gauze

and touched others only as tools that fit to your task
and if the tool broke you seized another.
Arrogance is not a revolutionary virtue.
The manipulator liberates only
the mad bulldozers of the ego to level the ground.
I was a tool that screamed in the hand.
I have been loving you so long and hard and mean
and the taste of you is part of my tongue
and your face is burnt into my eyelids
and I could build you with my fingers out of dust
and now it is over.
Whether we want or not
our roots go down to strange waters,
we are creatures of the seasons and the earth.
You always had a reason and you have them still
rattling like dried leaves on a stunted tree.

ANONYMOUS POEM BY A SEVEN-YEAR-OLD WOMAN

A hen
is useful to men.

She lays eggs
between her legs.

TERROR

Martha Shelley

Terror is six ice glass splinters underneath your tongue
It is overdue bills
Time torn out of your side, bleeding bright pink.
It is not having cash for a drink
Or time to learn how the drink is
To really know it—sour on the side of your mouth,
      hot in your throat.

  Don't hurry it—
Terror is the now when he puts an insistent hand on my
  waist
And the wall of nothing stiffening between his nothing
     flesh my   nothing flesh

  Over too soon—
A drink to forget the fear of ancient contempt
And the Fist that rocked the cradle
Big as God, held over your head.
Thou shalt honor them, that thy days may be long . . .

(honor the cop that thy days may be long)

In the waiting room
  An off-white clock, faceless,
Saying too-late, deadline is past, so bang you're dead.
Trying to catch the curve of a bird,
But the bird won't hold still;
And the bird is my blood pumping out.

POEM

Janet Russo

I shall not allure you
    with dangling adornments
Nor entice you
    with painted face
Nor dazzle you
    with natty garments
I shall not please you
    with a veneer belying my thoughts
No, I shall not come to you cloaked in false beauty
    only to disillusion you later
I shall come bald.

GOING THROUGH CHANGES

Jean Tepperman

1
My head aches.
I love you.
How can you talk this way?
Afternoon light
falls gently in the parlor
you are groping—
the language is wrong.
Why don't you speak
Welsh/Swahili/Gaelic/Navajo?

You serve the man
drinks and dinner
then sit on his lap
and ask for a revolution—
just a little one
for being such a nice girl.
A plastic flower
grows out of my navel.
You are afraid
of what he will think of you.
I am afraid of you
when you talk like this.
You are ashamed of me.
You don't have nice friends.
I'm not a nice friend.
The honor system
sets its teeth in me.
I can't talk to you
I am failing us
again.

2

I used to get very big.
I used to be in rooms full of strangers
and questions made me into
China and Russia and Cuba
ten thousand teenage draft resisters
the history of the Communist Party
a lone terrorist in Oakland
the entire black population
and Marx and Engels.
I got so big
there were miles
from my mouth to your ear.
Today,
in my small natural body,
I sit and learn—

my woman's body
like yours
target on any street,
taken from me
at the age of twelve
like Venezuelan oil
with the same explanation
        You are ignorant
        let me show you
then sold back drop by drop
in pink-frosted bottles
by tiny merchants with big shadows
sitting behind the screens of Oz
and buying armies
with the profits.
I watch a woman dare
I dare to watch a woman
we dare to raise our voices
smash the bottles
learn.
Watch me learn to dare
my arms and legs feel awkward—
we came to ask your help.

3

I am not a lady
I live in an elevator
in a big department store America.
        "Your floor, lady?"
        "I don't have a floor,
        I live in the elevator."
        "You can't just live in an elevator".
They all say that
except for the man from *Time* Magazine
who acted very cool.
We stop and let people into
dresses, better dresses, beauty,

and on the top floor,
home furnishings and then
the credit office, suddenly stark
and no nonsense this is it.
At each floor I look out
at the ladies quietly becoming
ladies and I say "huh"
reflectively.
My hair is long and wild
full of little twigs and cockleburrs.
I visit the floors only for water.
I make my own food
from the berries and frightened rabbits—
I pray forgive me brother as I eat—
that grow wild in the elevator.
Once every three months,
solstice and equinox,
a cop comes and clubs me a little.
The man from *Time* says
I articulate my generation something
wobble squeegy squiggle pop pop
Yesterday pausing at childrens
I saw another lady
take off all her clothes
and go to live in #7.
We are waiting to fill
all thirteen.

THE JAILOR

Sylvia Plath

My night sweats grease his breakfast plate.
The same placard of blue fog is wheeled into position
With the same trees and headstones.
Is that all he can come up with,
The rattler of keys?

I have been drugged and raped.
Seven hours knocked out of my right mind
Into a black sack
Where I relax, foetus or cat,
Lever of his wet dreams.

Something is gone.
My sleeping capsule, my red and blue zeppelin,
Drops me from a terrible altitude.
Carapace smashed,
I spread to the beaks of birds.

O little gimlets!
What holes this papery day is already full of!
He has been burning me with cigarettes,
Pretending I am a Negress with pink paws.
I am myself. That is not enough.

The fever trickles and stiffens in my hair.
My ribs show. What have I eaten?
Lies and smiles.

Surely the sky is not that colour,
Surely the grass should be rippling.

All day, gluing my church of burnt matchsticks,
I dream of someone else entirely.
And he, for this subversion,
Hurts me, he
With his armoury of fakery.

His high, cold masks of amnesia.
How did I get here?
Indeterminate criminal,
I die with variety—
Hung, starved, burned, hooked!

I imagine him
Impotent as distant thunder,
In whose shadow I have eaten my ghost ration.
I wish him dead or away.
That, it seems is the impossibility,

That being free. What would the dark
Do without fevers to eat?
What would the light
Do without eyes to knife, what would he
Do, do, do without me?

HISTORICAL DOCUMENTS

**NOW (NATIONAL ORGANIZATION for WOMEN)
BILL of RIGHTS**

Adopted at NOW's first national conference, Washington, D.C., 1967

I. Equal Rights Constitutional Amendment

II. Enforce Law Banning Sex Discrimination in Employment

III. Maternity Leave Rights in Employment and in Social Security Benefits

IV. Tax Deduction for Home and Child Care Expenses for Working Parents

V. Child Day Care Centers

VI. Equal and Unsegregated Education

VII. Equal Job Training Opportunities and Allowances for Women in Poverty

VIII. The Right of Women to Control Their Reproductive Lives

WE DEMAND:

I. That the U.S. Congress immediately pass the Equal Rights Amendment to the Constitution to provide that "Equality of rights under the law shall not be denied or abridged by the United States or by any State on account of sex," and that such then be immediately ratified by the several States.

II. That equal employment opportunity be guaranteed to all women, as well as men, by insisting that the Equal Employment Opportunity Commission enforces the prohibitions against racial discrimination.

III. That women be protected by law to ensure their rights to return to their jobs within a reasonable time after childbirth without loss of seniority or other accrued benefits, and be paid maternity leave as a form of social security and/or employee benefit.

IV. Immediate revision of tax laws to permit the deduction of home and child-care expenses for working parents.

V. That child-care facilities be established by law on the same basis as parks, libraries, and public schools, adequate to the needs of children from the pre-school years through adolescence, as a community resource to be used by all citizens from all income levels.

VI. That the right of women to be educated to their full potential equally with men be secured by Federal and State legislation, eliminating all discrimination and segregation by sex, written and unwritten, at all levels of education, including colleges, graduate and professional schools, loans and fellowships, and Federal and State training programs such as the Job Corps.

VII. The right of women in poverty to secure job training, housing, and family allowances on equal terms with men, but without prejudice to a parent's right to remain at home to care for his or her children; revision of welfare legislation and poverty programs which deny women dignity, privacy, and self-respect.

VIII. The right of women to control their own reproductive lives by removing from the penal code laws limiting access to contraceptive information and devices, and by repealing penal laws governing abortion.

EXCERPTS FROM THE SCUM (SOCIETY FOR CUTTING UP MEN) MANIFESTO

Valerie Solanis

Life in this society being, at best, an utter bore and no aspect of society being at all relevant to women, there remains to civic-minded, responsible, thrill-seeking females only to overthrow the government, eliminate the money system, institute complete automation, and destroy the male sex.

It is now technically possible to reproduce without the aid of males (or, for that matter, females) and to produce only females. We must begin immediately to do so. The male is a biological accident: the Y (male) gene is an incomplete X (female) gene, that is, has an incomplete set of chromosomes. In other words, the male is an incomplete female, a walking abortion, aborted at the gene state. . . .*

Being an incomplete female, the male spends his life attempting to complete himself, to become female. He attempts to do this by constantly seeking out, fraternizing with and trying to live through and fuse with the female, and by claiming as his own all female characteristics—emotional strength and independence, forcefulness, dynamism,

Copyright © Valerie Solanis 1967–1968
* See "A Theory on Female Sexuality," by Dr. Mary Jane Sherfey, p. 220.—Ed.

decisiveness, coolness, objectivity, assertiveness, courage, integrity, vitality, intensity, depth of character, grooviness, etc.—and projecting onto women all male traits—vanity, frivolity, triviality, weakness, etc. It should be said, though, that the male has one glaring area of superiority over the female—public relations. (He has done a brilliant job of convincing millions of women that men are women and women are men.) The male claim that females find fulfillment through motherhood and sexuality reflects what males think they'd find fulfilling if they were female.

Women, in other words, don't have penis envy; men have pussy envy.

The male, because of his obsession to compensate for not being female combined with his inability to relate and to feel compassion, has made of the world a shitpile. He is responsible for:[1]

War
Niceness, Politeness, and "Dignity"
Money, Marriage and Prostitution, Work and Prevention of an
    Automated Society
Fatherhood and Mental Illness (fear, cowardice, timidity,
    humility, insecurity, passivity)
Suppression of Individuality, Animalism (domesticity and
    motherhood) and Functionalism
Prevention of Privacy
Isolation, Suburbs, and Prevention of Community
Conformity
Authority and Government
Philosophy, Religion, and Morality Based on Sex
Prejudice (racial, ethnic, religious, etc.)
Competition, Prestige, Status, Formal Education, Ignorance,
    and Social and Economic Classes
Prevention of Conversation
Prevention of Friendship and Love
"Great Art" and "Culture"
Sexuality
Boredom
Secrecy, Censorship, Suppression of Knowledge and Ideas, and

1. Note: Each item on the following list appears in the Manifesto as a heading of an explanatory sub-section.—Ed.

Exposés
Distrust
Ugliness
Hate and Violence
Disease and Death

. . . if a large majority of women were scum, they could acquire complete control of this country within a few weeks simply by withdrawing from the labor force, thereby paralyzing the entire nation. Additional measures, any one of which would be sufficient to completely disrupt the economy and everything else, would be for women to declare themselves off the money system, stop buying, just loot, and simply refuse to obey all laws they don't care to obey. The police force, National Guard, Army, Navy, and Marines combined couldn't squelch a rebellion of over half the population, particularly when it's made up of people they are utterly helpless without. . .

The conflict, therefore, is not between females and males, but between scum—dominant, secure, self-confident, nasty, violent, selfish, independent, proud, thrill-seeking, free-wheeling arrogant females, who consider themselves fit to rule the universe, who have free-wheeled to the limits of this "society" and are ready to wheel on to something far beyond what it has to offer—and nice, passive, accepting, "cultivated," polite, dignified, subdued, dependent, scared, mindless, insecure, approval-seeking Daddy's Girls, who can't cope with the unknown, who want to continue to wallow in the sewer that is, at least, familiar, who want to hang back with the apes, who feel secure only with Big Daddy standing by, with a big, strong man to lean on and with a fat, hairy face in the White House, who are too cowardly to face up to the hideous reality of what a man is, what Daddy is, who have cast their lot with the swine, who have adapted themselves to animalism, feel superficially comfortable with it and know no other way of "life," who have reduced their minds, thoughts and sights to the male level, who, lacking sense, imagination and wit can have value only in a male "society," who can have a place in the sun, or, rather, in the slime, only as soothers, ego boosters, relaxers, and breeders, who are dismissed as inconsequents by other females, who project their deficiencies, their maleness, onto all females and see the female as a worm.

But scum is too impatient to hope and wait for the debrainwashing of millions of assholes.

A small handful of scum can take over the country within a year by systematically fucking up the system, selectively destroying property, and murder:

scum will become members of the unwork force, the fuck-up force; they will get jobs of various kinds and unwork. For example, scum salesgirls will not charge for merchandise; scum telephone operators will not charge for calls; scum office and factory workers, in addition to fucking up their work, will secretly destroy equipment. scum will unwork at a job until fired, then get a new job to unwork at.

scum will forcibly relieve bus drivers, cab drivers, and subway token sellers of their jobs and run busses and cabs and dispense free tokens to the public.

scum will destroy all useless and harmful objects—cars, store windows, "Great Art," etc.

Eventually scum will take over the airwaves—radio and TV networks—by forcibly relieving of their jobs all radio and TV employees who would impede scum's entry into the broadcasting studios.

scum will couple-bust—barge into mixed (male-female) couples, wherever they are, and bust them up.

scum will kill all men who are not in the Men's Auxiliary of scum. Men in the Men's Auxiliary are those men who are working diligently to eliminate themselves, men who, regardless of their motives, do good, men who are playing ball with scum. . . .

Dropping out is not the answer; fucking-up is. Most women are already dropped out; they were never in. Dropping out gives control to those few who don't drop out; dropping out is exactly what the establishment leaders want; it plays into the hands of the enemy; it strengthens the system instead of undermining it, since it is based entirely on the non-participation, passivity, apathy, and non-involvement of the mass of women. Dropping out, however, is an excellent policy for men, and scum will enthusiastically encourage it. . .

scum will not picket, demonstrate, march, or strike to attempt to achieve its ends. Such tactics are for nice, genteel ladies who scrupulously take only such action as is guaranteed to be ineffective. . . . If scum ever marches, it will be over LBJ's stupid, sickening face; if scum ever strikes, it will be in the dark with a six-inch blade.

scum will always operate on a criminal as opposed to a civil disobedience basis, that is, as opposed to openly violating the law and going to jail in order to draw attention to an injustice. Such tactics acknowledge the rightness of the over-all system and are used only to modify it slightly, change specific laws. scum is against the entire system, the very idea of law and government. scum is out to destroy the system, not attain certain rights within it. Also, scum— always selfish, always cool—will always aim to avoid detection and punishment. scum will always be furtive, sneaky, underhanded (although scum murders will always be known to be such).

Both destruction and killing will be selective and discriminate. scum is against half-crazed, indiscriminate riots, with no clear objective in mind, and in which many of your own kind are picked off. . . .

After the elimination of money there will be no further need to kill men; they will be stripped of the only power they have over psychologically independent females. They will be able to impose themselves only on the doormats, who like to be imposed upon. The rest of the women will be busy solving the few remaining unsolved problems before planning their agenda for eternity and Utopia—completely revamping educational programs so that millions of women can be trained within a few months for high-level intellectual work that now requires years of training (this can be done very easily once our educational goal is to educate and not to perpetuate an academic and intellectual elite); solving the problems of disease and old age and death and completely redesigning our cities and living quarters. Many women will for a while continue to think they dig men, but as they become accustomed to female society and as they become absorbed in their projects, they will eventually come to see the utter uselessness and banality of the male.

The few remaining men can exist out their puny days dropped out on drugs or strutting around in drag or passively watching the high-powered female in action, fulfilling themselves as spectators, vicarious livers[2] or breeding in the cow pasture with the toadies, or they can go off to the nearest friendly neighborhood suicide center where they will be quietly, quickly, and painlessly gassed to death.

The sick, irrational men, those who attempt to defend themselves against their disgustingness, when they see SCUM barreling down on them, will cling in terror to Big Mama with her Big Bouncy Boobies, but Boobies won't protect them against SCUM; Big Mama will be clinging to Big Daddy, who will be in the corner shitting in his forceful, dynamic pants. Men who are rational, however, won't kick or struggle or raise a distressing fuss, but will just sit back, relax, enjoy the show, and ride the waves to their demise.

2. It will be electronically possible for him to tune in to any specific female he wants to and follow in detail her every movement. The females will kindly, obligingly consent to this, as it won't hurt them in the slightest and it is a marvelously kind and humane way to treat their unfortunate, handicapped fellow beings.

PRINCIPLES

(New York Radical Women)

We take the woman's side in everything.

We ask not if something is "reformist," "radical," "revolutionary," or "moral." We ask: is it good for women or bad for women?

We ask not if something is "political." We ask: is it effective? Does it get us closest to what we really want in the fastest way?

We define the best interests of women as the best interests of the poorest, most insulted, most despised, most abused woman on earth. Her lot, her suffering and abuse is the threat that men use against all of us to keep us in line. She is what all women fear being called, fear being treated as and yet what we all really are in the eyes of men. She is Everywoman: ugly, dumb (dumb broad, dumb cunt), bitch, nag, hag, whore, fucking and breeding machine, mother of us all. Until Everywoman is free, no woman will be free. When her beauty and knowledge is revealed and seen, the new day will be at hand.

We are critical of all past ideology, literature and philosophy, products as they are of male supremacist culture. We are re-examining even our words, language itself.

We take as our source the hitherto unrecognized culture of women, a culture which from long experience of oppression developed an intense appreciation for life, a sensitivity to unspoken thoughts and the complexity of simple things, a powerful knowledge of human needs and feelings.

We regard our feelings as our most important source of political understanding.

We see the key to our liberation in our collective wisdom and our collective strength.

No More Miss America!

August 1968

On September 7th in Atlantic City, the Annual Miss America Pageant will again crown "your ideal." But this year, reality will liberate the contest auction-block in the guise of "genyooine" de-plasticized, breathing women. Women's Liberation Groups, black women, high-school and college women, women's peace groups, women's welfare and social-work groups, women's job-equality groups, pro-birth control and pro-abortion groups—women of every political persuasion—all are invited to join us in a day-long boardwalk-theater event, starting at 1:00 p.m. on the Boardwalk in front of Atlantic City's Convention Hall. We will protest the image of Miss America, an image that oppresses women in every area in which it purports to represent us. There will be: Picket Lines; Guerrilla Theater; Leafleting; Lobbying Visits to the contestants urging our sisters to reject the Pageant Farce and join us; a huge Freedom Trash Can (into which we will throw bras,* girdles, curlers, false eyelashes, wigs, and representative issues of *Cosmopolitan, Ladies' Home Journal, Family Circle,* etc.—bring any such woman-garbage you have around the house); we will also announce a Boycott of all those commercial products related to the Pageant, and the day will end with a Women's Liberation rally at midnight when Miss America is crowned on live television. Lots of other surprises are being planned (come and add your own!) but we do not plan heavy disruptive tactics and so do not expect a bad police scene. It should be a groovy day on the Boardwalk in the sun with our sisters. In case of arrests, however, we plan to reject all male authority and demand to be busted by policewomen only. (In Atlantic City, women cops are not permitted to make arrests—dig that!)

*Bras were never burned. Bra-burning was a whole-cloth invention of the media —Ed.

Male chauvinist-reactionaries on this issue had best stay away, nor are male liberals welcome in the demonstrations. But sympathetic men can donate money as well as cars and drivers.

Male reporters will be refused interviews. We reject patronizing reportage. *Only newswomen will be recognized.*

The Ten Points

We Protest:

1. *The Degrading Mindless-Boob-Girlie Symbol.* The Pageant contestants epitomize the roles we are all forced to play as women. The parade down the runway blares the metaphor of the 4-H Club county fair, where the nervous animals are judged for teeth, fleece, etc., and where the best "specimen" gets the blue ribbon. So are women in our society forced daily to compete for male approval, enslaved by ludicrous "beauty" standards we ourselves are conditioned to take seriously.

2. *Racism with Roses.* Since its inception in 1921, the Pageant has not had one Black finalist, and this has not been for a lack of test-case contestants. There has never been a Puerto Rican, Alaskan, Hawaiian, or Mexican-American winner. Nor has there ever been a *true* Miss America—an American Indian.

3. *Miss America as Military Death Mascot.* The highlight of her reign each year is a cheerleader-tour of American troops abroad—last year she went to Vietnam to pep-talk our husbands, fathers, sons and boyfriends into dying and killing with a better spirit. She personifies the "unstained patriotic American womanhood our boys are fighting for." The Living Bra and the Dead Soldier. We refuse to be used as Mascots for Murder.

4. *The Consumer Con-Game.* Miss America is a walking com-

mercial for the Pageant's sponsors. Wind her up and she plugs your product on promotion tours and TV—all in an "honest, objective" endorsement. What a shill.

5. *Competition Rigged and Unrigged.* We deplore the encouragement of an American myth that oppresses men as well as women: the win-or-you're-worthless competive disease. The "beauty contest" creates only one winner to be "used" and forty-nine losers who are "useless."

6. *The Woman as Pop Culture Obsolescent Theme.* Spindle, mutilate, and then discard tomorrow. What is so ignored as last year's Miss America? This only reflects the gospel of our society, according to Saint Male: women must be young, juicy, malleable—hence age discrimination and the cult of youth. And we women are brainwashed into believing this ourselves!

7. *The Unbeatable Madonna-Whore Combination.* Miss America and Playboy's centerfold are sisters over the skin. To win approval, we must be both sexy and wholesome, delicate but able to cope, demure yet titillatingly bitchy. Deviation of any sort brings, we are told, disaster: "You won't get a man!!"

8. *The Irrelevant Crown on the Throne of Mediocrity.* Miss America represents what women are supposed to be: unoffensive, bland, apolitical. If you are tall, short, over or under what weight The Man prescribes you should be, forget it. Personality, articulateness, intelligence, commitment—unwise. Conformity is the key to the crown—and, by extension, to success in our society.

9. *Miss America as Dream Equivalent To—?* In this reputedly democratic society, where every little boy supposedly can grow up to be President, what can every little girl hope to grow to be? Miss America. That's where it's at. Real power to control our own lives is restricted to men, while women get patronizing pseudo-power, an ermine clock and a bunch

of flowers; men are judged by their actions, women by their appearance.

10. *Miss America as Big Sister Watching You.* The Pageant exercises Thought Control, attempts to sear the Image onto our minds, to further make women oppressed and men oppressors; to enslave us all the more in high-heeled, low-status roles; to inculcate false values in young girls; to use women as beasts of buying; to seduce us to prostitute ourselves before our own oppression.

NO MORE MISS AMERICA

LETTER TO OUR SISTERS IN SOCIAL WORK

WAR *(Women of the American Revolution)*

What is Illegitimate?
[law] "nullius fillius" . . . "nobody's child" . . .

[Encyclopedia Britannica, 1958 edition:]"Not to condemn illegitimacy would be to attach no special significance to marriage. Recognizing the great importance of marriage for social responsibility and stability and the corresponding dangers of non-marriage, the state makes marriage easy . . ."
Implication: The state makes nonmarriage a criminal undertaking and the children outcasts. So you thought marriage a pleasant religious tradition? The encyclopedia sets us straight on that marriage is an economic disposition of individuals into units beneficial to the state. What would happen to our economy if people didn't establish themselves in nuclear family units? They would stop spending millions on wastefully duplicated supplies of china, linen, furniture and appliances. And women would no longer constitute an unpaid labor force performing the socially valuable work of caterers to their husbands and child care for future citizens.

The Prevention of "Illegitimacy"

Obviously a first step towards abolishing the syndrome of shame, poverty and discrimination bound up with "illegitimacy" would be to end the branding of children as illegitimate. But what's in a name? Everyone knows about the high crime rate among "illegitimates." Doesn't that prove there's something behind it?

The significance of "fatherlessness" is social, not biological. In our society the "illegitimate" child is made to feel, every day, that his very existence is abnormal. If "fatherlessness" leads to crime then we would have to blame welfare regulations that make it impossible for poor fathers to stay near their children. But that is only another way of saying that criminals are a product of a society where vast wealth rests in the hands of a few.

Your Mother Wears Army Shoes

When will women social workers recognize our common bond with poor women, including unmarried mothers? We share with such women the common oppression of our sex. Every insult to a woman insults *you*.

All women should have the right to determine whether or not to have children. Women should stand together in demanding readily available birth-control information and free abortions for all who wish them. Any woman who chooses to have a child does so *legitimately*.

Women all over the world have not only been assigned a dependent social role for centuries: they have also been taught to like it. For ages we have subordinated ourselves willingly to childrearing and housekeeping, as if men do not have an equal interest in the performance of these essential jobs. The time has come for even those women fortuante enough to pursue a profession to recognize that they cannot be genuinely liberated so long as the mass of women remain sexually oppressed—and oppressed not only by the imposition of such insulting categories as "illegitimacy." Women must now join together to demand equal pay for equal work, subsidized child-care facilities, an end of the absurdification of woman in the mass media, and repeal of abortion laws.

HOW TO NAME BABY—A VOCABULARY GUIDE FOR WORKING WOMEN

Media Women—New York

If A Person Is:	Call Her	Call Him:
Ingratiating	Sweet	Ass-Licker
Supportive	Bright	Yes-Man
Intelligent	Helpful	Smart
Helpful	Good Girl	Helpful
Innovative	Pushy	Original
Insistent	Hysterical	Persistent
Tough	Impossible	Go-Getter
Cute & Timid	A Sweetheart	A Fairy
Sexy	A Piece	Handsome
Dumb	Not Too Bright	An Idiot
Plain Looking	Homely, Ugly	no comment
Successful	Ball-Breaker Up-Tight Hard Dame Bitch The Only Successful Woman I've Ever Met Who Isn't A——(Ball-Breaker, Up-Tight, Hard Bitch, etc.)	Successful

Politically Involved. . Over-Emotional . Committed

Supportive
Helpful
Ingratiating
Passive
Gentle............. A Real Woman. . A Minister's Son
Invisible .... Nice Chick..... Never Heard
of Him

Lilith's Manifesto—1969

Women's Majority Union (Seattle, Washington)

To his credit (although in hackneyed latter-day Marxist jargon unworthy of such a vivid writer) Eldridge Cleaver has
said again what needed saying—what has been said, again
and again, almost as often as it needed saying, until it has
become an incantation: We must root out all manifestations
of male chauvinism from the ranks of the vanguard party.
Hail Mary Mother of God blessed art thou among women
. . . We must root out all manifestations of male chauvinism
from the ranks of the vanguard party . . . andblessedisthe-
fruitofthywombJesus . . . Wemustrootoutallmanifestation-
sofmalechauvinismfromtheranksofthevanguardparty . . .
HareKrishna . . .This is where I came in.

Once upon a time, I have been told, there was a woman
in the then-vanguard party who felt a need deeper than that
of spot-welding a superficial unity around current issues.
She disappeared and has never been heard from since. Presumably the earth swallowed her, or maybe it was the East
River. At any rate, such foolhardy hubris was not repeated,
and radical women have since disciplined themselves, with
only minor grumblings ("bitchings"), to accept the incanta-

tion as a promissory note on pie to be granted in some future socialist sky, reward for humble performance of their allotted tasks in the kitchens of radical halls and at the typewriters of radical offices, or for zeal in organizing their fellow-women to support prevailing campaigns.

Well, damn it, I've no faith in the unity that's sought through yielding; and I'm not going to walk away, because I'm as much a part of this revolution as you are, and maybe, at this moment in history, more. Here I stand. You're going to have to cope with me, brother. *Now.*

Therefore Be It Manifest:

1. The biological dichotomy of sex needs no reinforcement by differential cultural mores. Whatever qualities pertain to humanity pertain to it as a species. If assertiveness, for example, is a virtue in man, it is a virtue also in woman; if forbearance is a virtue in woman, it is likewise a virtue in man. (If you, brother, can't get a hard-on for a woman who doesn't grovel at your feet, that's *your* hangup; and sister, if you can't turn on to a man who won't club you and drag you off by the hair, that's yours. Keep your hangups the hell out of this revolution.)

2. The mutilation of individual whole human beings to fit the half-size Procrustes' beds society assigns selectively to "men" and to "women" serves a purpose far more contrary to the pursuit of freedom than simple divisiveness: because *all* persons can be consigned to one or the other category and their personalities trimmed, by differential social experience, to fit the mold considered appropriate to their sex, *none* can escape; half the human race receives indoctrination and training in the exercise of dominance over others, while the other half receives reciprocal conditioning to servility, all being given to presuppose that a pattern of authority and submission to authority is the universal, inevitable, and biologically determined order of social relationships.

3. All known societies have thus utilized the clear and all-inclusive dichotomy of sex as the chief vehicle for early and continuous limitation on the essentially liberatory free play of human imaginings and aspirations, perverting a benign natural phenomenon to service of the social status quo. Bourgeois society only inherited this tradition—anti-revolutionary by definition—and modified it to suit the special needs and conditions of capitalism; socialist societies have done no more than modify it likewise to their ends. The pursuit of freedom demands that it be utterly transcended.

4. By the nature of revolution as such, not all the forces engaged in it are committed to its fullest possible consummation. That commitment, however, defines the vanguard, whatever other elements may, in the vicissitudes of movement, usurp or be displaced into its position. Should leadership be retained by forces of but limited vision, the revolution must be cut tragically short of its full potential, for commitment to the lesser goals such a pseudo-vanguard does envision will turn against the revolution at the very moment it stands poised to overreach them.

5. It is unthinkable that the revolution now in process be allowed to suffer such curtailment. Heretofore, disappointed survivors of a truncated revolution have known, at least, that the seeds of future revolt remained; no power was capable of exterminating them. The proliferating technology of biochemical manipulation now robs us of even that bitter consolation; no state power, capitalist or socialist, is to be entrusted with it; we can afford no less than total liberation. *This* revolution has got to go for broke: *power to no one, and to every one: to each the power over his/her own life, and no others.*

OUR STATEMENT

Women Against Daddy Warbucks (New York, 1969)

We did it.

We interfered with the the ability of the 13 uptown Manhattan draft boards to initiate the processing of men into numbers, into killing-machines, into corpses.

We acted together as women against the draft because conscription rests on women's accepted role as insulated comforter and supporter of its violence, as indeed does the violence of American society in general.

Those files were destroyed to decry the incredible continuation of death in Vietnam. Now, we bring file remains to Rockefeller Center to indict the insidious pattern by which American arms follow capital investment into the Third World.

We are here to make clear the connection between overseas corporate involvement and American military and political intrusions into the affairs of Asia, Africa, and Latin America. Corporations such as Dow, Standard Oil, Shell, and Chase Manhattan—with offices in Rockefeller Center —bear much responsibility for U. S. domination of those areas from which we profit. . .

If our action confuses you, think about what led to our decision. Consider how the draft controls by fear lives that might be inspired by hope. Consider the interdependence between corporation profits and military "protection" overseas. Consider the roles programmed for women by our society, accepted as insulation from social responsibility. Consider the real reasons why resources are wasted in arms competition while people are starving and homeless . . .

We are saying that profits are not worth lives, that peace does not come through war. Americans, men and women, must confront themselves with what their country is doing.

STATEMENT BY CHICAGO WOMEN'S LIBERATION

February 1969

During sit-ins and other protests at the University of Chicago over the firing of Professor Marlene Dixon, a radical feminist, for her political ideas:

What does women's freedom mean? It means freedom of self-determination, self-enrichment, the freedom to live one's own life, set one's own goals, the freedom to rejoice in one's own accomplishments. It means the freedom to be one's own person in an integrated life of work, love, play, motherhood: the freedoms, rights and privileges of first class citizenship, of equality in relationships of love and work: the right to choose to make decisions or not to: the right to full self-realization and to full participation in the life of the world. That is the freedom we seek in women's liberation.

To achieve these rights we must struggle as all other oppressed groups must struggle: one only has the rights one fights for. We must come together, understand the common problems, despair, anger, the roots and processes of our oppression: and then together, win our rights to a creative and human life.

At the U of C we see the *first large action, the first important struggle of women's liberation.* This university—all universities—discriminate against women, impede their full intellectual development, deny them places on the faculty, exploit talented women and mistreat women students.

AN EXEGESIS ON WOMEN'S LIBERATION

The Women's Caucus Within The Youth International Party (YIP)

When in the course of the progressive dialectic of history it becomes necessary for people oppressed by caste to off the nuclear family which stabilizes the capitalist, imperialist, military complex economy which of necessity and by its very nature causes the writing of male oriented reformist revisionist opportunist adventurist papers, a decent respect for the opinions of our sisters in struggle, compel us to assume the responsibility of the vanguard. The Women's Liberation Caucus within the Youth International Party, being through a rigorous analysis of the thoughts of Mao, Susan B. Anthony, Che, Lenin, and Groucho, considers itself bound by the historic necessity of becoming the vanguard party of the progressive women's revolution because we fly higher. A revolution being defined as the final process of the analysis of working class and petit bourgeois rivalries for parental and male support, one would therefore show that the Youth International Party, being suppressed in direct proportion to its support of the third world liberation struggles at home and back home, has the class and caste consciousness to off the class and caste barriers separating themselves from the ruling class and caste.

Revisionism teaches us that no sex is sexless until it submerges itself in the teachings of marxist leninist socialist thought in alliance with the regressive forces fostering social change among rank and file on the left.

Trade unionism and its militant allies among male chauvinists dare to struggle, dare to win, but only when cadres among fascist progressive rhetoric factionalism class assume solidarity with the oppressed peoples of the world. Marxist leninist cultural nationalism has no truck with the evil capitalist exploiters of the working class vanguard of the revolutionary process as exemplified in the question of women's liberation and its repercussions on the right wing revisionism shown by the proletariat. The Youth International Party is defined as such a party being both Youth, International, and a Party. This is not to assume, therefore, that the Trotskyite racism among sexist communoanarchists of the center leads to repression by the exploited class, but only given the analysis of Mao, page 398 of the red book, militant socialism is given to be all the power to the people and the liberation struggle among the class interest of the police state.

SCREWEE!

(Society for Condemning the Rape and Exploitation of Women, Etc., Etc.)

REDSTOCKINGS MANIFESTO

I After centuries of individual and preliminary political struggle, women are uniting to achieve their final liberation from male supremacy. Redstockings is dedicated to building this unity and winning our freedom.

II Women are an oppressed class. Our oppression is total, affecting every facet of our lives. We are exploited as sex objects, breeders, domestic servants, and cheap labor. We are considered inferior beings, whose only purpose is to enhance men's lives. Our humanity is denied. Our prescribed behavior is enforced by the threat of physical violence.

Because we have lived so intimately with our oppressors, in isolation from each other, we have been kept from seeing our personal suffering as a political condition. This creates the illusion that a woman's relationship with her man is a matter of interplay between two unique personalities, and can be worked out individually. In reality, every such relationship is a *class* relationship, and the conflicts between individual men and women are *political* conflicts that can only be solved collectively.

III We identify the agents of our oppression as men. Male supremacy is the oldest, most basic form of domination. All other forms of exploitation and oppression (racism, capitalism, imperialism, etc.) are extensions of male supremacy: men dominate women, a few men dominate the rest. All power structures throughout history have been male-dominated and male-oriented. Men have controlled all political, economic and cultural institutions and backed up this control with physical force. They have used their power to keep women in an inferior position. *All men* receive economic, sexual, and psychological benefits from male supremacy. *All men* have oppressed women.

IV Attempts have been made to shift the burden of responsibility from men to institutions or to women themselves. We condemn these arguments as evasions. Institutions alone do not oppress; they are merely tools of the oppressor. To blame institutions implies that men and women are equally victimized, obscures the fact that men benefit from the subordination of women, and gives men the excuse that they are forced to be oppressors. On the contrary, any man is free to renounce his superior position provided that he is willing to be treated like a woman by other men.

We also reject the idea that women consent to or are to blame for their own oppression. Women's submission is not the result of brainwashing, stupidity, or mental illness but of continual, daily pressure from men. We do not need to change ourselves, but to change men.

The most slanderous evasion of all is that women can oppress men. The basis for this illusion is the isolation of individual relationships from their political context and the tendency of men to see any legitimate challenge to their privileges as persecution.

V We regard our personal experience, and our feelings about that experience, as the basis for an analysis of our common situation. We cannot rely on existing ideologies as they are all products of male supremacist culture. We question every generalization and accept none that are not confirmed by our experience.

Our chief task at present is to develop female class consciousness through sharing experience and publicly exposing the sexist foundation of all our institutions. Consciousness-raising is not "therapy," which implies the existence of individual solutions and falsely assumes that the male-female relationship is purely personal, but the only method by which we can ensure that our program for liberation is based on the concrete realities of our lives.

The first requirement for raising class consciousness is honesty, in private and in public, with ourselves and other women.

VI We identify with all women. We define our best interest as that of the poorest, most brutally exploited woman.

We repudiate all economic, racial, educational or status privileges that divide us from other women. We are determined to recognize and eliminate any prejudices we may hold against other women.

We are committed to achieving internal democracy. We will do whatever is necessary to ensure that every woman in our movement has an equal chance to participate, assume responsibility, and develop her political potential.

VII We call on all our sisters to unite with us in struggle.

We call on all men to give up their male privileges and support women's liberation in the interest of our humanity and their own.

In fighting for our liberation we will always take the side of women against their oppressors. We will not ask what is "revolutionary" or "reformist," only what is good for women.

The time for individual skirmishes has passed. This time we are going all the way.

WOMEN: DO YOU KNOW THE FACTS ABOUT MARRIAGE?

Leaflet by The Feminists (written for a demonstration at the Marriage License Bureau, New York City, Winter 1969)

DO YOU KNOW THAT RAPE IS LEGAL IN MARRIAGE?

According to law, *sex* is the purpose of marriage. You have to have sexual intercourse in order to have a valid marriage.

DO YOU KNOW THAT LOVE AND AFFECTION ARE NOT REQUIRED IN MARRIAGE?

If you can't have sex with your husband, he can get a divorce or annulment. If he doesn't love you, that's *not* grounds for divorce.

DO YOU KNOW THAT YOU ARE YOUR HUSBAND'S PRISONER?

You have to live with him wherever *he* pleases. If he decides to move someplace else, either you go with him or he can charge you with desertion, get a divorce and, according to law, you deserve nothing because *you're the guilty party.* And that's if *he* were the one who moved!

DO YOU KNOW THAT, ACCORDING TO THE UNITED NATIONS, MARRIAGE IS A "SLAVERY-LIKE PRACTICE"?

According to the marriage contract, your husband is entitled to more household services from you than he would be from a live-in maid. So, why aren't you getting paid? Under law, you're entitled only to "bed and board."

When you got married, did you know these facts? If you didn't know, what did you *think* you were consenting to?

But these are the *laws*. If you *had* known the terms, would you have signed the contract?

Do You Resent This Fraud?

All the discriminatory practices against women are patterned and rationalized by this slavery-like practice. We can't destroy the inequities between men and women until we destroy marriage. *We must free ourselves. And marriage is the place to begin.*

THE FEMINISTS

- v -

THE MARRIAGE LICENSE
BUREAU OF THE
CITY OF NEW YORK

WHEREAS it is common knowledge that women believe the conditions of the marriage contract to be positive and reciprocal feelings between the two parties (known as "love and affection"); and

WHEREAS the marriage contract in fact legalizes and institutionalizes the rape of women and the bondage of women, both their internal (reproductive) and external (domestic labor) functions; and

WHEREAS the marriage contract, known as "license", fails to list the terms of that contract, a failure which would automatically nullify the validity of any other important contract

THEREFORE, WE, THE FEMINISTS, do hereby charge the city of New York and all those offices and agents aiding and abetting the institution of marriage, such as the Marriage License Bureau, of fraud with malicious intent against the women of this city.

September 23, 1969

WITCH

Following is a selection of leaflets, hexes, etc, from WITCH —a phenomenon in itself *within* the Women's Liberation Movement.

WITCH was born on Halloween, 1968, in New York, but within a few weeks Covens had sprung up in such diverse spots as Boston, Chicago, San Francisco, North Carolina, Portland (Oregon), Austin (Texas), and Tokyo (Japan). They're still spreading. A certain common style—insouciance, theatricality, humor, and activism, unite the Covens—which are otherwise totally autonomous, and unhierarchical to the point of anarchy.

Nor will any of their leaflets or statements elaborate on what that means.

Washington, D.C., WITCH—after an action hexing the United Fruit Company's oppressive policy on the Third World *and* on secretaries in its offices at home ("Bananas and rifles, sugar and death/War for profit, tarantulas' breath-/United Fruit makes lots of loot/The CIA is in its boot")— claimed that WITCH was "a total concept of revolutionary female identity" and was the striking arm of the Women's Liberation Movement, aiming mainly at financial and corporate America, at those institutions that have the power to control and define human life.

Chicago WITCH Covens showered the Sociology Department at the University of Chicago with hair cuttings and nail clippings after the firing of a radical feminist woman professor, and the Chicago Witches also demonstrated against a transit fare hike. They, as well as Witches in New York, San Francisco, North Dakota, and New England, disrupted local Bridal Fairs. The fluidity and wit of the Witches is evident in the ever-changing acronym: the basic, original title was Women's International Terrorist Conspiracy from Hell, but on Mother's Day one Coven became

Women Infuriated at Taking Care of Hoodlums; another group, working at a major Eastern insurance corporation, became Women Indentured to Traveler's Corporate Hell; still another set of infiltrators, working at Bell Telephone, manifested themselves disruptively as Women Incensed at Telephone Company Harrassment. When hexing inflationary prices at supermarkets, a Midwest Coven appeared as Women's Independent Taxpayers, Consumers, and Homemakers; Women Interested in Toppling Consumption Holidays was another transfigutory appellation—and the latest heard at this writing is Women Inspired to Commit Herstory.

For Rebellion Is As The Sin Of Witchcraft . . .
        —I Samuel, 15:23

New York Covens

WITCH is an all-women Everything. It's theater, revolution, magic, terror, joy, garlic flowers, spells, It's an awareness that witches and gypsies were the original guerrillas and resistance fighters against oppression—particularly the oppression of women—down through the ages. Witches have always been women who dared to be: groovy, courageous, aggressive, intelligent, nonconformist, explorative, curious, independent, sexually liberated, revolutionary. (This possibly explains why nine million of them have been burned.) Witches were the first Friendly Heads and Dealers, the first birth-control practitioners and abortionists, the first alchemists (turn dross into gold and you devalue the whole idea of money!). They bowed to no man, being the living remnants of the oldest culture of all—one in which men and women were equal sharers in a truly cooperative society, before the death-dealing sexual, economic, and spiritual repression of the Imperialist Phallic Society took over and began to destroy nature and human society.

WITCH lives and laughs in every women. She is the free

part of each of us, beneath the shy smiles, the acquiescence to absurd male domination, the make-up or flesh-suffocating clothing our sick society demands. There is no "joining" WITCH. If you are a women and dare to look within yourself, you are a Witch. You make your own rules. You are free and beautiful. You can be invisible or evident in how you choose to make your witch-self known. You can form your own Coven of sister Witches (thirteen is a cozy number for a group) and do your own actions.

Whatever is repressive, solely male-oriented, greedy, puritanical, authoritarian—those are your targets. Your weapons are theater, satire, explosions, magic, herbs, music, costumes, cameras, masks, chants, stickers, stencils and paint, films, tambourines, bricks, brooms, guns, voodoo dolls, cats, candles, bells, chalk, nail clippings, hand grenades, poison rings, fuses, tape recorders, incense—your own boundless beautiful imagination. Your power comes from your own self as a woman, and it is activated by working in concert with your sisters. The power of the Coven is more than the sum of its individual members, because it is *together.*

You are pledged to free our brothers from oppression and stereotyped sexual roles (whether they like it or not) as well as ourselves. You are a Witch by saying aloud, "I am a Witch" three times, and *thinking about that.* You are a Witch by being female, untamed, angry, joyous, and immortal.

Witches As Women's Hidden History

Chicago Covens

Like other oppressed groups, women have not been allowed to develop a consciousness of their own history. When we try to think of great women of history, we think of George and Martha, and who the hell was Martha anyway? We demand to learn about the history of women in the same way that we demand that history be the history of the people, not of the elites.

The history of women has been severely distorted. An excellent example of this is our understanding of witchcraft in Europe and America. We think of witches as malevolent old women, conspiring the death of their neighbors, and the debauchery of the civilized Christian world, leading us all to hell with the aid of Satan. Or else we do not take them seriously at all, but believe that witches never existed and that the trial and purges were isolated incidents particualr to a few small societies.

In fact, witchcraft was the pagan religion of all of Europe for centuries prior to the rise of Christianity, and the religion of the peasantry for hundreds of years after Catholicism prevailed among the ruling classes of Western society. The witchcraft purges were the political suppression of an alternative culture, and of a social and economic structure.

Before the middle ages, the people of Europe lived in societies which were small agricultural and pastoral groupings. They were a diminutive race which was driven into the hills and continued to live in small communal societies while Christianity took over the lowlands. These societies were matriarchal, had no private property, and no institution of marriage. Their god was a woman—Tana, the moon goddess. Tana was queen of heaven, the moon, and was a fertility goddess of rain and magic. Witch rituals were basically circular dances at night which worshipped the moon and the change of the seasons.

Unlike their counterparts in Christian culture, women were highly respected in witch societies; they were integral in the church hierarchy which also served the governmental needs of the people. Since there was no private property or marriage, women were not sold as chattel to their prospective husbands, as they have been throughout Western culture. Thus, during their forced conversion to Christianity, women fought to retain their rights as well as for a religion which recognized women as an important part of theology. The Catholics had tried slow conversion of the witches for many centuries and there is evidence that there was a mixing of beliefs going on increasingly. The cult of the Virgin Mary was emphasized by the popular demand of new converts who had been accustomed to worshipping a woman as the Supreme Deity. But numerous factors combined to make the continued existence of pagan rituals and beliefs intolerable: primarily, the black plague.

Death swept Europe in the thirteenth century, killing twenty-five percent of the population. A religious explanation of this was needed to calm the fears of the people. The plague was defined as the punishment of God to a people that tolerated heresy. But who was to define heresy? The witches blamed the plague on the Christians, who had deserted the old gods, and the Catholics blamed the witches. The stronger prevailed. The Christians were hierarchically organized, controlled the upper classes, the military, and the state governments throughout Europe. The witches were the peasants and lower classes, the hill tribes, and women. The scapegoat for the plague naturally became the local witch. As peasant revolts developed, "witchcraft" became a cry for the rest of the population to arm itself. The purges clearly assumed the nature of a class war.

However, the trial signaled more than an attempt to keep the people "in line." Women found themselves in a uniquely oppressive condition resulting from the cultural views implicit in Catholicism. The chief document used to suppress witchcraft, Kramer and Sprenger's *Malleus Maleficarum*, commissioned by the Pope in 1486, discusses the evil nature of women at length.

The main reason for woman's frequent alliance with evil is that "she is more carnal than a man, as is clear from her many carnal abominations . . . there was a defect in the formation of the first woman, since she was formed from a bent rib . . . And since through this defect she is an imperfect animal, she always deceives . . . To conclude: All witchcraft comes from carnal lust, which is in women insatiable."* Accordingly, the witch religion, known for its fertility rites, and the freedom of women, could not be tolerated if women were to be chaste and subservient to men in theology and in the home.

Even as the religion of witchcraft became suppressed, women fought hard to retain their former freedom. The Church understood that if its control was to be effective, the purge must be extensive and brutal. The insurgents were not easily smashed. Several authorities have estimated that from the fifteenth to the eighteenth centuries, *nine million witches* were executed for their alleged beliefs and crimes. (Persecution of witches was particularly brutal on the Continent. Torturing and burning effectively destroyed 900 witches in a single year in the Wurtzburg area, and 1,000 in and around Como. At Toulouse, 400 witches were put to death in a single day.)

Thus, the witch was chosen as a revolutionary image for women because they did fight hard and in their fight they refused to accept the level of struggle which society deemed acceptable for their sex. Finally, they were the center of motion both as agitators and as targets, as women today must assume positions of leadership if radical politics are to relate to the real oppression of people, and mutually, if women are to gain true equality in a revolutionary movement.

Confront the Whoremakers
At the Bridal Fair

February 1969   WITCH

Marriage is a dehumanizing institution—legal whoredom for women. *Confront* the perpetrators of our exploitation as women. *Confront* the institutions which make us pawns in

---

*See SCUM Manifesto (Solanis), on page 514, and "A Theory on Female Sexuality" (Sherfey), page 220, for more on insatiability.— Ed.

a male-dominated culture. *Confront* the structure which forces men into the dehumanizing roles of our oppressors. *Confront* the Bridal Fair, which encourages vulnerable young girls to be dutiful, uncomplaining, self-sacrificing, "loving" commodities on the marriage market, and well-packaged, fully automated, brand-conscious consumers. *Confront* the exhibitors of this commercial extravaganza: "Big Boys" of the world of business and finance who are at the same time enslaving and murdering our sisters and brothers in Asia, Africa, and Latin America.

Come witches, gypsies, feminists, students, our black and Puerto Rican sisters, professional women, housewives, welfare women—come all oppressed women of every age and marital status. Come to New York's first *and last* "Bridle Un-Fair."

Bring posters, brooms, costumes, consciousness, anger, witches' brews, love, bridal gowns, tambourines, hexes, laughter, solidarity, and alternatives.

We will create our own rituals and festivals, perform our own anti-fashion shows, meet each other and the brides-to-be attending the fair in self-defense against the common enemy. We will distribute WITCH "shoplifting" bags, share free cocoa and experiences, cast spells, celebrate guerrilla theater, and demand an *end* to the patriarchal structure and the profit-oriented society. *Bridal Fairs must not happen. Here's why:*

1. ALWAYS A BRIDE, NEVER A PERSON. Women were the first slaves, the first barter items way back when the monied economy and the patriarchal structure were just beginning. Ever since, the pressure has been on women to marry or face society's rejection as a spinster—a species of sub-human. A woman is taught from infancy that her only real goal in life is to fulfill the role of wife and mother of male heirs. She is allowed an identity only as an appendage to a man. An unmarried girl is considered a freak—a lesbian, or a castrating career girl, a fallen woman, a bitch, "unnatural,"

a frustrated old maid, sick. In the end, she begins to believe these innuendos herself, There is no way out—marry or die.

2. HERE COMES THE BRIBE. The corporations are quick to capitalize on our insecurities. Will I be a good housekeeper and cook? How do I keep my husband from having affairs with other women? Will his friends like me? Will I get along with my mother-in-law? Will I be a hindrance to his career? Will I lose my looks after the first baby? Will I be good in bed? Does he really love me?

Isolated from her sisters, who have been cast in the role of enemies and competitors in the desperate struggle for a husband, the bride is alone. She is alone in her suburb, or apartment, or job as a clerk-typist—dehumanized, with no resources. And she is manipulated—by the giant corporations who need consumers on which to unload their over-productivity, and who have one answer for the anxious women: *buy!*

Buy cosmetics and fancy clothes to be beautiful. Buy gourmet foods to win your way to a man's heart. Buy fashionable home furnishings to be respected in the community. Take a glamorous honeymoon to gain status at the office. Buy deodorant, to be "dainty" and "safe." Buy Virginia Slims to prove America's assertion that "you've come a long way, baby." And, after all this, is your life still lacking in meaning? Then give yourself a lift—spend an afternoon choosing what shade of flowered toilet paper is most *you*. With this drivel, the corporations transform our self-doubts and emotional needs into commodities and sell them to us at a profit.

3. YOU HAVE A FIEND AT CHASE MANHATTAN. The corporations exhibiting at this Bridal Fair include Chase Manhattan Bank—major investor in racist South Africa; International Coffee, which condemns its South American workers to poverty and slave labor; Aereonaves de Mexico, airline of a government which is now torturing, jailing, and killing thousands of students: J.P. Stevens, a fabric supplier with

large government defense contracts (Is J.P. Stevens making military uniforms and soldiers' shrouds at the same time as he is filling our hope chests with shoddy linens?). *Imperialism begins at home.*

4. THE RITUAL IS THE REALITY. Our wedding day is the "only" day in our lives. We commence, consummate, consume, and are consumed on that single day, having spent our childhood playing "house," and our adolesence filling hope chests with empty Hollywood–Madison Avenue dreams. The wedding ceremony is the symbolic ritual of our legal transference from father's property to husband's property. The name is changed from one man's to another's, and our role as chattel in a male's house remains the same. And this is the highlight of our lives, our only festival. *We will no longer celebrate this day of ignominy. We will create our own rituals and festivals—festivals of life, instead of death.*

Nor is that all. Although we resist society's demand for legal and commercial trappings to the simple act of living together, our alternative is *not* "not marrying" within this present sick, racist, sexist society. The so-called "sexual revolution" of the last decade has only made the pressures on women more subtle, and provided the greed-brokers with even more complicated means of insuring their consumptive hegemony over us.

SISTERS! Let us confront the whoremakers at the Bridal Fair (and at every bridal fair across the country) but more important, confront and overthrow the institutions of marriage and capitalism which make such bridal fairs possible!

WITCH Un-Wedding Ceremony

We are gathered together here in the spirit of our passion to affirm love and initiate our freedom from the unholy state of American patriarchal oppression.

We promise to love, cherish, and groove on each other and on all living things. We promise to smash the alienated family unit. We promise not to obey. We promise this through highs and bummers, in recognition that riches and objects are totally available through socialism or theft (but also that possessing is irrelevant to love).

We promise these things until choice do us part. In the name of our sisters and brothers everywhere, and in the name of the Revolution, we pronounce ourselves Free Human Beings.

Hex On Slavery

Boston Covens

DOWN WITH CHAINS

CHAINS ON BRAINS

SHACKLED BY

BEAUTY CLAIMS

HEX ON MASTERS'

EGO GAMES

FREE US FROM THE

AUCTION BLOCK

tote that bail
iron that shirt
don't call him
he'll call you
shut your mouth
don't think
smile for him
he's always right

HEX THAT GAME
LEARN TO FIGHT

AT & T (AMERICAN TELEPHONE AND TELEGRAPH) WANTS GIRLS—NOT WOMEN

WITCH *(Women Incensed at Telephone Company Harrassment) Leaflet:*

Last week, AT&T fired two typists who were tired of being "girls."

Definition: Girl—Young, inexperienced, easy to train, innocent, respectful, obedient, emotional—not logical, gay, frilly, frivolous, carefree, scatterbrain, good at details, petty, decorative, docile, sweet and passive, easy to manage.

HOW DOES A GIRL BECOME A GIRL?

A girl is born and her parents buy her pink and frilly (starchy and scratchy) things . . . but they really wanted a boy. They buy her dolls and doll houses, and tell her she must not play with her brother's erector sets.

While her brother is dreaming of becoming president, doctor, or astronaut, the little girl is told that she wants to be a secretary or a nurse—or an astronaut's wife.

At school: Girls are expected to be quiet and well behaved, while boys are expected to play rough and be wild. Boys are expected to ask questions and be logical—and girls to be diligent and good at details. Teachers, like parents, think it's important for boys to go to college to get a good job—but all a girl has to learn is how to be some man's good secretary until she's some man's good wife. And the danger that she might not be a wife is the worst threat of all, held over her to make her behave.

To get a man she has to be both sexy and sexless—because a man is supposed to be experienced when he marries, but a girl is supposed to be a virgin. If we're natural about sex, we're used by men and disgraced by society and made to feel ashamed and guilty ourselves. But if we're not natural about it, we're put down for that too, called uptight and frigid—and in fact do become afraid of our sexual feelings.

At the job: And finally we get to work, thinking that at last we've got the right to be women. But we discover AT&T treats us like girls just like we were treated in school.

CHILDREN:

DO NOT:

Talk with your neighbors
Wear your skirts too short
Wear culottes
Be late
Not wear stockings
Wear sandals that go between your toes
Put pretty things on your desks
Have fun pictures on your line-a-time
Go to the bathroom in two's
Leave hair in bathroom sink
Use too much toilet paper
Use correc-type
Use white-out—it might get on your clothes
Have fun at work—this is a place of business
Go to the bank at break
Smoke in typing room when you want to because
　　you see supervisor smoking
Question your supervisor
Waste time resting eyes or fingers
Laugh aloud
Act young (which you are)
Get pregnant without consulting supervisor
Stand when supervisor says sit
Sit when supervisor says stand
Discuss your rights as workers with each other
Discuss your paychecks
Stick together with your fellow workers

DO:

Fill out your work sheets and compete against each other
Carry a pass at all times
Accept everything the supervisor says
Take breaks (recess) on schedule
Produce, Produce, Produce so the company that
　　treats you so well can make more and more profits

HOW DOES A GIRL BECOME A WOMAN?

　　When she defines her own life and stops being controlled by
her family, her boyfriend, or her boss. When she learns to stand
up and fight for herself and other women—because she has

learned that her problems aren't just her own.
All over the world, girls are growing up . . .

Mother's Day Incantation

WITCH (Women Interested in Toppling Consumption Holidays)

Every year we set aside
a very special day
to remind you, Martyr Dear,
that *home* is where you stay.

Your family wants to thank you
for your martyrdom.
After all, without you
no *real* work would get done.

While hubby challenges the world
his wonders to perform
you cook his meals, clean his home
and keep his bedside warm.

Your children are your challenge,
in them your dreams are sown.
You've given up your own life
and live for them alone.

Now look upon your daughter
will she too be enslaved
to a man, a home, and family
or can she still be saved?

This is your real challenge—
renounce your martyrdom!
Become a *liberated mother*
a woman, not a "mom."

(card by Hellmark)

Conspiracy Against Women

WITCH (Women's Independent Taxpayers, Consumers, and Homemakers)

Double, bubble, war and rubble,
When you mess with women, you'll be in trouble.
We're convicted of murder if abortion is planned.
Convicted of shame if we don't have a man,
Convicted of conspiracy if we fight for our rights.
And burned at the stake when we stand up to fight.
Double, bubble, war and rubble,
When you mess with women, you'll be in trouble.
We curse your empire to make it fall—
When you take on one of us, you take on us all!

Pass the Word, Sister.

WITCH (Women Inspired to Commit Herstory)

6 sisters in prison.
3 sisters pregnant.
2 sisters almost in labor.
All have been accused
of conspiracy and murder.
None have been tried
or found guilty.
All 6 are black.
All 6 are Panthers.
All 6 are sisters.

CONFINEMENT: 1. The act
of shutting within an enclosure;
the act of imprisoning.
2. The state of being restrained
or obliged to stay indoors.
3. A woman's lying-in;
childbirth. —*Standard College Dictionary*

How does New Haven's Niantic State
Woman's Farm treat women
in confinement?
They are:
isolated from other prisoners;
denied sleep by the continual noise
of walkie-talkies
and constant bright lights;
denied their constitutional right
to prepare their case;
denied their legal right
to choice of counsel.

How does Niantic State
Woman's Farm prepare women
for their confinement?
They are:
denied their choice of doctors;
denied information about childbirth;
denied their choice of method
of childbirth; deprived of proper
diet, exercise, medication & clothing.

Rose Smith weighed 132 pounds
at the start of her pregnancy.
Now—7 months pregnant—
after Niantic's prenatal care,
Rose Smith weighs 133 pounds.

Guards will be there
when the babies are born.
Guards will be there
to take them away.
The State will decide
who's "fit" and who's "not fit"
to guard and be guardian
of mother and child.

Children oppressed:
on welfare, in orphanages,
in schools, in foster homes;
by poverty, by routine,
by racism, by male supremacy.
Therefore,
WITCH curses the State
and declares it unfit.

WITCH knows our suppressed history:
that women who rebel are not only
jailed, napalmed, & beaten,
but also
raped, branded & burned at the stake.

We women are:
in jail at Niantic
in the mud of Vietnam
in the slums of the cities
in the ghetto-sinks of suburbia
at the typewriters
of the corporations
at the mimeograph machines
of the Left
in the water at Chappaquidick
in the brutalizing beds of Babylon.

We are going to stop
all confinement of women.
WITCH calls down destruction
on Babylon.
Oppressors:
the curse of women is on you.
DEATH TO MALE CHAUVINISM.

SONGS

To be sung to the tune of "A Pretty Girl Is Like A Melody":

a) A pretty girl is a commodity
   With stock to buy and sell.
   When the market is high,
   Count up your shares
   In what she wears
   That pay you dividends.

b) A pretty girl in this society
   Is judged by looks alone.
   What you see on her face
   Is often the waste
   Of chemicals developed for the war.

To be sung to the tune of "Down by the Riverside":

a) We're gonna ask all our sisters here
   To come and join the fight
   To come and join the fight,
   To come and join the fight,
   We're gonna ask all our sisters here

554

To come and join the fight:
Don't be Miss America no more.

b) We're gonna tell all the ad men here
They've used us long enough, *etc.*

c) Now sisters companies want us to buy
So they control our taste, *etc.*
No Miss America no more.

Chorus:
We won't let 'em bend our minds no more, (*4 times*)
We're gonna be free from here on in,
We're gonna be free from here on in,
No Miss America no more!

Won't be no Miss America
Won't be no Miss America
Won't be no Miss America.
Ain't gonna be Miss America.
Ain't gonna be Miss America.
No Miss America no more.

To be sung to the tune of "Frère Jacques":

Who's Max Factor
Who's Max Factor
He fakes up
our make-up
Dirty old man
with the Hollywood tan
That's the man
we must ban.

What's the factor
the factor in Max
He's a bad actor
Woman de-tractor
Facts on Max
Hex on Max.

To be sung to the tune of "A Tisket, A Tasket":

Wall Street, Wall Street
Mightiest Wall of all street
Trick or treat
The corporate elite
Up against the Wall Street

Wall Street, Wall Street
Dirtiest Wall of all Street
Talk and fight
Research and destroy
Trick and treat
Means sure defeat
Up against the Wall Street

Wall Street, Wall Street
Crookedest street of all Street
Foreign exchange
Student exchange
Wife exchange
Stock exchange
Trick or treat
Up against the Wall Street.

VERBAL KARATE

(Statistical and Aphoristic Ammunition)

General

In terms of longevity, resistance to disease and stress, adaptability to environment and so on, the male is the weaker of the two sexes.
—Landrum B. Shuttles, M.D., Ph.D. (in *New York Magazine*)

Statistically, women drivers have less accidents than men do. —U.S. Department of Highways

Everyone agrees that little girls mature faster than little boys, physically, emotionally, and intellectually. The process evens out, however, and the boys move ahead in fact, interestingly enough, at the point of puberty—when the feminine role locks around the female child for life.

The average housewife works a 99.6 hour work-week.
—Chase Manhattan Bank

Women never have their own names. The "maiden name" belongs to one's father; the "married name" belongs to one's husband.

When faced with the "look at other species" argument and told about the inherent docility of female monkeys, ducks, bears, etc., *remember*:

The sex life of spiders is very interesting. He fucks her. She bites off his head.

It is the lioness who is the killer, *not* the king of the beasts.

Think about bees.

It is the male seahorse who gives birth—the female deposits her fertilized eggs in him and swims blithely off.

Marriage

The average bride spends over $3,000 to furnish her new home and $500 for apparel.

Brides spend an estimated *$5 billion* annually.

Weddings have increased from 1,302,000 in 1934 to an estimated 2,000,000 in 1968, with U.S. Department of Health, Education, and Welfare projections estimating 2,170,000 in 1970.

Each year brides outspend the other "big spenders" (women aged nineteen to twenty-five) by more than fourteen to one.

Wedding dresses alone are estimated to have a $50 million market potential and the trousseau market is put at $162 million.

—The above from *Brides Showcase International* Press Kit, Bridal Fair (New York 1969)

One out of three American marriages end in divorce.

Birth—and Abortion

To any man who says population control is a form of genocide, I say, ask any woman.
—Judith Hart, British Minister for Overseas
Development (at a Food and Agricultural Conference on
birth control)

Thirty million abortions a year are performed on the planet.

Fifty thousand abortions a year are performed in Great
Britain.

Between 1 and 1.5 million abortions a year are performed
in the United States.

Only 9,000 legal abortions are performed each year in the
United States. (Very recent figures may be slightly higher.)

There is one abortion for every four live births.

One-fourth of all the women in America have had illegal
abortions.

4.7 times as many Puerto Rican women, and 8 times as
many black women die of the consequences of illegal abortions as do white women.

In New York City the ratio of *legal* abortions to live births
is:
     5 times as high for whites as for non-whites
     2 times as high in private (profit) as in voluntary (non-
     profit) hospitals
     39 times as high in private as in municipal hospitals

In New York City, 80 percent of the women who die from
abortions are black and brown.

The death rate in the United States from abortions is 50–100
deaths per 100,000 operations.

In countries where abortion is legal, the death rate is 3 deaths per 100,000 abortions.

"In Hungary, where abortion is completely legal, the death rate averages less than 6 per 100,000. Contrast this with the deaths in the United States resulting from the removal of tonsils and adenoids—17 per 100,000—which is three times as great. Or the death rate from childbirth and its complications: 24 per 100,000. This figure, which applies only to the white population of the United States, is unusually low, but note: a pregnant woman who is considering abortion should realize that *childbirth, under the best circumstances, is four times as dangerous as a competently performed abortion.* Why is this fact not more widely publicized? I leave you to supply the answer."

—from a lecture by Garrett Hardin, April 1964

Working Women

Twenty-eight million women in America work at more menial jobs, at lower pay, and suffer higher unemployment than men.

Forty percent of all working-age women work. Women are thirty-five percent of the work force.

In 1900 the typical woman worker was twenty-six and single; now she is forty-one and married.

The 1968 unemployment rate for women was 4.8 percent; for men 2.9 percent.

In ten out of fourteen clerical and office jobs, men got higher pay than women—for identical work.

—from a study by the Equal Employment Oportunities Commission

As regards the myth about female absenteeism and turnover:

The Public Health Service shows men lose more days from work each year than do women—including days lost for pregnancy and childbirth. The 1966 average was: 5.9 days for men, 5.6 days for women.

In 1964 the median male income was $6,233
In 1964 the median female income was $3,710

In 1920 a higher proportion of women (15%) received Ph.D's than do today (12.6%). The number of women awarded Master's degrees is lower today than in 1930.

Over all, the median wage for women is only 60 percent of that for men. In specific industries or fields, women's wages compared to those of men in 1965 as follows:

Median Wages per Year

	Women	Men
Factory workers	$3,282	$5,752
Service industries	2,784	4,886
Sales	3,003	7,083
Clerical	4,237	6,220
Professional, technical	5,573	8,233
Manager, officials (executives)	4,516	8,658

The following figures explode the myth that women are among the richest people in the country:

	Women	Men
Earning less than $1,000 per year	33%	15.5%
Earning between $3-4,000 per year	13%	8.5%
Earning $10,000 or more per year	0.7%	10.0%

(The figures for 1965 are from Background Facts on women workers in the U.S., Women's Bureau, U.S. Department of Labor, May 1967.)

Department of Labor statistics (1965)

Annual Earnings:

White men	$6,375
Black men	$4,000
White women	$3,744
Black women	$2,642

In 1969, of the Americans who earned more than $10,000 a year, only 2% were women.

In the United States:

Engineers	1 percent are women
Lawyers	3 percent are women
Doctors	7 percent are women

Nearly one-fifth of employed women with a Bachelor's degree have jobs in such categories as clerks, factory workers, and cooks.

In the past ten years, women have lost fifty seats in state legislatures. There is one lone woman senator (Margart Chase Smith), and there are only ten congresswomen, compared with seventeen in 1960.

Clerical work is the single largest women's occupation. In 1960, 31% of all working women were secretaries, bookkeepers, stenographers, and clerk-typists. The next largest women's occupation is service work. Over 15% of working women are waitresses, cooks, bartenders, and hospital attendants, not including nurses. Fifty-five percent of all nonwhite working women hold service jobs, while only 19% of white working women are in this category. Seventeen percent of black women workers and 19% of white women workers are blue-collar workers: operatives, assemblers, and kindred workers in textile, garment, electrical, and other industrial plants. One fourth of professional women (in 1964) were in the health professions, the largest single occupation being nurses, followed by dental and medical technicians.

> —*1965 Handbook on Women Workers* published by the Women's Bureau of the Labor Department

Useful Quotes

If particular care and attention are not paid to the ladies we are determined to foment a rebellion and will not hold ourselves bound to obey any laws in which we have no voice or representation.

—Abigail Adams (in a letter to her husband, John, 1776)

All the reasonings of men are not worth one sentiment of women.   —Voltaire

It is only too obvious that a man has no obligation whatever to a woman who is considered brilliant. To such a woman a man can be ungrateful, treacherous, and even mean, and no one will think of taking her side.

—Madame de Staël

Shall 'man be free and woman a slave,' and idiot? says Shelley. Never! say I.

—Anna Wheeler (Irish patriot and rebel, 1825)

I married for ambition. Carlyle has exceeded all that my wildest hopes ever imagined for him, and I am miserable.

—Mrs. Thomas Carlyle

You forget too much/That every creature, female as the male,/Stands single in responsible act and thought,/As also in birth and death.

—Elizabeth Barrett Browning (*Aurora Leigh*)

I go for all sharing the privileges of government [suffrage] who assist in bearing its burdens. . . who pay taxes or bear arms, by no means excluding females.

—Abraham Lincoln, 1836

If I were asked . . . to what the singular prosperity and growing strength of that people ought mainly to be attributed, I should reply: to the superiority of their women.

—Alexis De Tocqueville (*Democracy in America*, 1840)

Will it be answered that we [feminists] are factious, discontented spirits, striving to disturb the public order, and tear up the old fastnesses of society? So it was said of Jesus Christ . . . So it was said of our forefathers . . . So it has been said of every reform.   —Frances D. Gage, 1851

In education, in marriage, in everything, disappointment is the lot of woman. It shall be the business of my life to deepen this disappointment in every woman's heart until she bows down to it no longer. —Lucy Stone, 1855

Women are declared to be better than men, an empty compliment which must provoke a bitter smile from every woman of spirit, since there is no other situation in life, in which it is the established order, and quite natural and suitable, that the better should obey the worse.
  —John Stuart Mill, 1869 (*The Subjection of Women*)

It is because of men that women dislike one another.
  —La Bruyère

Genius has no sex! —Madame de Staël

A woman . . . is expected to regard it as complimentary to be told that she is in any respect the equal of a man; I do not know how many times in my life I have been graciously informed that I have a masculine brain.
  —Barbara (Lady) Wootten

Man is willing to accept woman as an equal, as a man in skirts, as an angel, a devil, a baby-face, a machine, an instrument, a bosom, a womb, a pair of legs, a servant, an encyclopedia, an ideal or an obscenity; the only thing he won't accept her as is a human being, a real human being of the female sex. —D.H. Lawrence

Woman learns how to hate in the degree that she forgets how to charm. —Nietzsche

Women have served all these centuries as looking glasses possessing the power of reflecting the figure of man at twice its natural size. —Virginia Woolf

It is the easiest thing in the world to say every broad for herself—saying it and acting that way is one thing that's kept some of us behind the eight ball where we've been living for a hundred years. —Billie Holliday

Being an old maid is like death by drowning—a really delightful sensation after you have ceased struggling.
—Edna Ferber

Whatever ground woman manages to establish for herself, man abandons, denying its importance. —Jules Feiffer

It is a feudal attitude that attaches importance to men and slights women. —Mao Tse-tung

What we owe men is some freedom from their part in a murderous game in which they kick each other to death with one foot, bracing themselves on our various comfortable places with the other. —Grace Paley

Woman is the nigger of the world. —Yoko Ono

AND

Remember the dignity of your womanhood. Do not appeal, do not beg, do not grovel. Take courage, join hands, stand beside us, fight with us.
—Christabel Pankhurst (English suffragette, 1880–1958)

vi

APPENDIX

Bibliography*

Works of General Interest

Beauvior, Simone de. *The Second Sex.* New York: Knopf, 1953.
"Margaret Bennett" (pseud.) *Alice in Womanland, or the Feminine Mistake.* Englewood Cliffs, N.J.: 1967.
Bird, Caroline. *Born Female: The High Cost of Keeping Women Down.* New York: McKay, 1968.
Cassara, Beverly Benner, ed. *American Women: The Changing Image.* New York: Beacon Press, 1962.
Citizens' Advisory Council on the Status of Women. *American Women 1968*, U.S. Department of Labor, 1968.
Dunn, Nell, *Talking to Women.* New York: Ballantine Books, 1968.
Friedan, Betty. *The Feminine Mystique.* New York: Dell, 1963.
Harding, Esther. *Psychic Energy.* 2nd edition. Princeton, N.J.: Princeton University Press, 1965.
——. *The Way of All Women.* New York: Longmans Green, 1933.
——. *Women's Mysteries.* New York: Pantheon, 1955. Jungian books on the feminine psyche.
Herschberger, Ruth. *Adam's Rib.* New York: Pellegrini & Cudahy, 1948.
Lifton, Robert Jay. *The Woman in America.* Boston: Houghton Mifflin, 1965.
Mencken, H.L. *In Defense of Women.* New York: Knopf, 1922.
Merriam, Eve. *After Nora Slammed the Door.* Cleveland: World Publishing Company, 1964.

*Many of these books are currently available in paperback.

Mill, John Stuart. *On Liberty; On Representative Government; On the Subjection of Woman.* London: Oxford University Press, 1952.

Reid, Marion. *Woman, Her Education and Influence.* New York: Fowler's & Wells, 1848.

Rham, Edith de. *The Love Fraud.* New York: Clarkson N. Potter, Inc. 1965.

Russell, Dora. *Hypatia, or, Woman and Knowledge.* New York: Dutton, 1925.

Tarbell, Ida. *The Business of Being a Woman.* New York: Macmillan, 1912.

――――. Ida. *The Ways of Woman.* New York: Macmillan, 1915.

Thompson, William. *Appeal of One Half of the Human Race, Women, Against the Pretensions of the Other Half, Men, to Retain Them in Political & Thence in Civil and Domestic Slavery.* New York: Burt Franklin, 1825.

Wollstonecraft, Mary. *A Vindication of the Rights of Women.* New York: W.W. Norton, 1967.

Woolf, Virginia. *A Room of One's Own.* New York: Harcourt, Brace, 1929.

The Oppressed Majority

HISTORY

Abbott, Edith. *Women in Industry: A Study in American Economic History.* New York: D. Appleton & Co., 1928.

Adams, Mildred. *The Right to Be People.* Philadelphia: J.B. Lippincott, 1967.

Anthony, Susan B., Stanton, Elizabeth Cady, and Gage, Matilda Joslyn. *History of Women's Suffrage.* New York: Susan B. Anthony, n.d.

Aries, Philippe. *Centuries of Childhood: A Social History of Family Life.* New York: Knopf, 1962.

Banks, J.A. and Banks, Olive. *Feminism and Family Planning in Victorian England.* New York: Schocken Books, 1964.

――――. *Prosperity and Parenthood: A Study of Family Planning among the Victorian Middle Classes.* London: Routledge and Kegan Paul, 1954.

Beard, Mary E. *Woman as Force in History.* New York: Macmillan, 1946.

Brittain, Vera. *Lady into Woman: A History of Women From Victoria to Elizabeth II.* New York: Macmillan, 1953.

Dangerfield, George. *The Strange Death of Liberal England: 1910–1914.* New York: Putnam, 1961. See especially the section on the Pankhursts.

Dexter, Elizabeth A. *Career Women of America, 1776–1840.* Francestown, N.H.: M. Jones, 1950.

Diner, Helen. *Mothers and Amazons: The First Feminine History of Culture,* New York: Julian, 1965.

Ditzion, Sidney. *Marriage, Morals, And Sex in America— A History of Ideas.* New York: Bookman Associates, 1953.

Flexner, Eleanor. *A Century of Struggle.* Cambridge: Harvard University Press, 1959.

Grimké, Angelina. *Appeal to the Christian Women of the South.* New York: American Anti-Slavery Society, 1836.

Grimké, Sarah. *Letters on Equality of the Sexes and the Conditions of Women.* New York: Burt Franklin, 1838.

Hagood, Margaret. *Mothers of the South.* Chapel Hill: University of North Carolina Press, 1939.

Hirsch, A.H. *The Love Elite (The Story of Woman's Emancipation and Her Drive for Sexual Fulfillment.)* New York: Julian, 1963.

Irwin, Inez Hayes. *Angels and Amazons: 100 Years of American Women.* Garden City, L.I.: Doubleday & Co., 1933.

————. *The Story of the Woman's Party.* New York: Harcourt, Brace, 1921.

Kraditor, Aileen S. *Ideas of the Woman Suffrage Movement, 1890–1920.* New York: Columbia University Press, 1965.

————, ed. *Up From the Pedestal: Selected Documents from the History of American Feminism.* Chicago: Quadrangle Books, 1968.

Leonard, Drinker, and Holden. *The American Woman in Colonial and Revolutionary Times 1565–1800: A Syllabus with Bibliography,* Philadelphia, University of Penn. Press, 1962.

Lutz, Alma. *Crusade For Freedom: Women in the Anti-Slavery Movement.* Boston: Beacon Press, 1968.

Melder, Keith. "The Beginnings of the Women's Movement, 1800–1840." Unpublished dissertation, Yale University, 1963.

Morgan, Edmund S. *The Puritan Family.* Boston: Trustees of the Public Library, 1944.

Newcomer, Mabel. *A Century of Higher Education for Women.* New York: Harper & Row, 1959.

O'Meara, Walter. *Daughters of the Country: The Women of the Furtraders* New York: Harcourt, Brace, 1968.

O'Neill, William L. *Everyone was Brave: The Rise and Fall of Feminism in America.* Chicago: Quadrangle Books, 1969.

Pankhurst, Sylvia. *The Suffrage Movement: An Intimate Account of Persons and Ideals.* New York and London: Longmans Green, 1931.

Parker, Theodore. *Essays on Women.* Abolitionist.

Pinchbeck, Ivy. *Women Workers in the Industrial Revolution 1750–1850.* London: G. Routledge, 1930.

Plato. *The Republic.* Book 5: The Communal Rearing of Children.

Putnam, Emily James. *The Lady: Studies of Certain Significant Phases of Her History.* Chicago: University of Chicago Press, 1970.

Ramelson, Marian. *The Petticoat Rebellion.* London: Lawrence and Wishart, 1967.

Riegel, Robert E. *American Feminists.* University of Kansas Press, 1968.

Rogers, Katharine M. *The Troublesome Helpmate: A History of Misogyny In Literature.* Seattle: University of Washington Press, 1966.

Rougemont, Denis de. *Love in the Western World.* New York: Pantheon, 1956.

Scott, Anne Firer. "After Suffrage: Southern Women in the 20's". *J. Southern History*, XXX, August, 1964.
Sillen, Samuel, *Women Against Slavery*. New York: Masses and Mainstream, 1955.
Sinclair, Andrew. *The Better Half: The Emancipation of the American Woman.* New York: Harper & Row, 1965.
Sprague, William. *Women and the West.* Boston: Christopher, 1940.
Spruill, Julia C. *Women's Life and Work in the Southern Colonies.* Chapel Hill: University of North Carolina Press.
Weld, Theodore, Weld, Angelina Grimké, and Grimké, Sarah. *Letters of 1822–1844.* Gloucester, Mass.: P. Smith, 1965.
Woodward, Helen. *The Lady Persuaders.* New York: I. Oblensky, 1960.

ECONOMICS, LABOR, AND LAW

Baker, Elizabeth F. *Technology and Women's Work.* New York: Columbia University Press, 1964.
Baker, Melba. "Women Who Work." *International Socialist Review*, Summer 1962.
Beecher, Catherine E. *A Treatise on Domestic Economy.* Boston: Marsh, Copen, Lyon & Webb, 1841. An early advocate of household efficiency and mechanization through planning and technology.
Benjamin, Lois. *So You Want To Be a Working Mother!* New York: McGraw-Hill, 1966. Practical and individualistic "solutions" to the problem of being a working mother.
Boone, Gladys. *The Woman's Trade Union Leagues in Great Britain and the United States of America.* New York: Columbia University Press, 1942.
Brownlee, Jean. "Where Is the Professional Woman?" *Women Lawyers Journal*, Winter 1967.
Cussler, Margaret. *The Woman Executive.* New York: Harcourt, Brace, and World, 1958.
Engels, Frederick. *The Origins of Family, Private Property, and The State.* New York: International Publishers, 1942.
Fava, Sylvia. "The Status of Women in Professional Sociology." *American Sociological Review*, April 1960.
Fenberg, Matilda. "Blame Coke and Blackstone." *Women Lawyers Journal*, Spring 1948. A history of the legal status of women in America.
Flexner, Eleanor. *Century of Struggle.* Cambridge: Harvard University Press, 1959.
Francis, Phillip. *Legal Status of Women.* Dobbs Ferry, N.Y.: Oceana, 1963.
Gilman, Charlotte Perkins. *Women and Economics.* Magnolia, Mass.: Peter Smith, 1898. The problem of housework is treated with collective solutions. See also Gilman's other works on children, the home, and human work.
Ginsberg, Eli and Yohalem, Marie. *Educated American Women: Self-portraits.* New York: Columbia University Press, 1966.

Greenwald, Harold, M.D. *The Call Girl.* New York: Ballantine Books, 1958.

Hartman, Sylvia. "Should Wives Work?" *McCall's*, February 1969.

Hatterer, Lawrence J., M.D. *The Artist in Society: Problems and Treatment of the Creative Personality.* New York: Grove Press, 1966. See the chapter on "The Woman Artist."

Henry, Alice. *Women and the Labor Movement.* New York: George H. Doran Co., 1923.

Kanowitz, Leo. *Women and the Law: the Unfinished Revolution.* Albuquerque: University of New Mexico Press, 1969. "Law and the Married Woman." *St. Louis University Law Journal*, Fall 1967. "Sex-Based Discrimination in American Law: Law and the Single Girl." *St. Louis University Law Journal*, Spring 1967. "Title VII of the 1964 Civil Rights Act and the Equal Pay of 1963." *Hastings Law Review*, November 1968.

Mattfield, Jacquelyn A., and Van Aken, Carol G., eds. *Women and the Scientific Professions.* Cambridge: MIT Press, 1965. A symposium held at MIT; see especially piece by Rossi.

McVeety, Jean. "Law and the Single Woman." *Women Lawyers Journal*, Winter 1967.

Michael, Donald. *Cybernation.* Santa Barbara: Center for the Study of Democratic Institutions, 1965. The new meanings cybernation will bring to "work" and "leisure."

Morse, Nancy S., and Weiss, Robert S. "The Function and Meaning of Work and the Job." *American Sociological Review*, April 1955.

Murray, Pauli, and Eastwood, Mary. "Jane Crow and the Law: Sex Discrimination and Title VII." *George Washington Law Review*, 2(1965). A review of the legal status of women, especially in employment.

Mydral, Alva, and Klein, Viola. *Women's Two Roles: Home and Work.* London: Routledge and Kegan Paul, 1956.

National Manpower Council. *Womanpower.* New York: Columbia University Press, 1957. *Work in the Lives of Married Women.* New York: Columbia University Press, 1958.

Nye, F. Ivan, and Hoffman, Lois Wladis, eds. *The Employed Mother in America.* New York: Rand-McNally, 1963. Research findings which disprove the working-mothers-are-bad-mothers theory.

Pilpel, Harriet, and Zavin, Theodora. *Your Marriage and the Law.* Rev. ed. New York: Collier, 1965. Marital duties, responsibilities, and rights, as seen in American law.

Pressman, Sonia. "Sex Discrimination in Employment and What You Can Do About It." *Women Lawyers Journal*, Fall 1968. Sonia Pressman is one of the few advocates of women's rights and enforcement of Title VII on the EEOC.

Pruette, L. *Women and Leisure: A Study of Waste.* New York: Dutton, 1924.

Ruderman, Florence. *Child Care and Working Mothers.* New York: Child

Welfare League of America. Arrangements of women in seven American cities for day care, maternal employment.

Smith, Georgina. *Help Wanted: Female.* New Brunswick, N.J.: Rutgers, the State University Press, 1964.

Smuts, Robert W. *Women and Work in America.* New York: Columbia University Press, 1959.

U.S. Department of Labor, Women's Bureau. *The Fuller Utilization of the Woman Physician.* 1968.
Handbook on Women Workers.
Know Your Rights.
Leaflet # 10. A free list of Bureau publications.

White, James J. "Women in the Law." *Michigan Law Review,* April 1967.

SOCIOLOGY AND SOCIAL COMMENTARY

Bernard, Jessie. *Academic Woman.* University Park, Pa.: Pennsylvania State University Press, 1964. *Remarriage: A Study of Marriage.* New York: Dryden Press, 1956.

Bettelheim, Bruno. *The Children of the Dream: Communal Child-rearing and American Education.* New York: Macmillan, 1969. The kibbutz and American schools.

Callahan, Sidney. *The Illusion of Eve.* New York: Sheed and Ward, 1965.

Cohn, David L. *Love in America: An Informal Study of Manners and Morals in American Marriage.* New York: Simon and Schuster, 1943.

Coser, Rose. *The Family: Its Structure and Functions.* New York: St. Martins, 1964.

Daly, Mary. *The Church and the Second Sex.* New York: Harper and Row, 1968.

Flynn, Elizabeth Gurley. *Women's Place in the Fight for a Better World.* New York: New Century, 1947.
Women in the War. New York: Workers Library, 1942.

Goode, William J. *After Divorce.* Glencoe, Ill.: Free Press, 1956.

Goodman, Percival, and Goodman, Paul. *Communitas.* Rev. ed. New York: Vintage Books. A modern utopia.

Hacker Helen. *Women as a Minority Group.* Bobbs-Merrill Reprint Series in the Social Sciences. New York: Bobbs-Merrill.

Hawes, Elizabeth. *Men Can Take It.* New York: Random House, 1939. Illustrated by James Thurber.
Why Women Cry, or, Wenches With Wrenches. Clifton, N.Y.: Reynal and Hitchcock, 1943.

Henriques, Fernando. *Love in Action: The Sociology of Sex.* New York: Dutton, 1960.
———. *Prostitution and Society.* New York, Citadel, 1962.
———. *Stews and Strumpets: A Survey of Prostitution.* London: MacGibbon and Kee, 1961.

Henry, Jules. *Culture Against Man.* New York: Random House, 1963.

Hollingsworth, Leta S. "Social Devices for Compelling Women to Bear and Rear Children." *American Journal of Sociology, July 1916.*

Komarovsky, Mirra. *Blue-Collar Marriage.* New York: Random House, 1964.
————. *Women in the Modern World.* Boston: Little, Brown, 1953. Special attention is given to social pressures on educated women.
Mannes, Marya. *More in Anger.* Philadelphia: Lippincott, 1958.
Marcuse, Herbert. *Eros and Civilization.* Boston: Beacon, 1955.
Myrdal, Gunnar. *An American Dilemma.* 2 vols. New York: Harper and Row, 1941, 1944. A classic with a particularly important analogy between blacks and women (Appendix 5).
O'Neill, William. *Divorce in the Progressive Era.* New Haven: Yale University Press, 1967. A positive approach to divorce. See introduction and chapters on "The New Morality."
Pollak, Otto. *The Criminality of Women.* Philadelphia: University of Pennsylvania Press, 1950.
Reich, Wilhelm. *The Mass Psychology of Fascism.* New York: Orgone Institute Press, 1946.
Rham, Edith de. *How Could She Do That?* New York: Clarkson N. Potter, 1969. A study of female criminality.
Russell, Bertrand. *Marriage and Morals.* New York: Bantam Books, 1968.
Wieth-Knudsen, K. A. *Feminism: A Sociological Study of the Woman Question from Ancient Times to the Present Day.* London: Constable, 1928.

WOMEN IN OTHER COUNTRIES

Anér, Kerstin. *Swedish Women Today: A Personal Appraisal.* Stockholm: Swedish Institute for Cultural Relations with Foreign Countries, 1966.
Berreman, Gerald. "On the Role of Women." *Bulletin of the Atomic Scientist.* November 1966. A comparison of attitudes toward women in the United States and India.
Briffault, Robert. *The Mothers: The Matriarchal Theory of Social Origins.* New York: Macmillan, 1931.
Dahlström, Edmund, ed. *The Changing Roles of Men and Women.* London: Duckworth, 1967.
Hinton, William. *Fanshen.* New York: Vintage Books, 1968.
Hays, H. R. *The Dangerous Sex: The Myth of Feminine Evil.* New York: Pocket Books, 1965. An historical and crosscultural study of man's fearful fantasies about woman.
Leijon, Ana-Greta. *Swedish Women—Swedish Men.* Stockholm: Swedish Institute for Cultural Relations with Foreign Countries.
Levi-Strauss, Claude. *Tristes Tropiques.* New York: Atheneum, 1963.
Lewis, Oscar. *The Children of Sanchez.* New York: Vintage Books, 1961.
————. *La Vida.* New York: Vintage Books, 1965.
Linnér, Birgitta. *Sex and Society in Sweden.* New York: Pantheon Books, 1967.
Ludovici, L. J. *The Final Inequality.* New York: W. W. Norton, 1965.
Mead, Margaret. *And Keep Your Powder Dry.* New York: Morrow, 1943.
————. *Male and Female.* New York: Mentor Books, 1955.

————. *Sex and Temperament in Three Savage Societies.* New York: Apollo, 1967.

Patai, Raphael, ed. *Women in the Modern World.* New York: Free Press, 1967.

The Status of Women in Sweden: Report to the United Nations. Stockholm: Swedish Institute for Cultural Relations with Foreign Countries.

Snow, Helen. *Women in Modern China.* New York: Humanities Press, 1968.

Taylor, Grace. "Equal Rights for Women." *University of Florida Review,* Summer 1962.

"Vietnamese Women." *Vietnamese Studies* #10. Hanoi: Democratic Republic of Vietnam, 1966. Available from China Press and Periodicals, 2929 24 Street, San Francisco, California 94110.

The Invisible Woman

PSYCHOLOGY AND PSYCHIATRY

Freud, Sigmund. "Femininity" in *New Introductory Lectures on Psychoanalysis.* New York: W.W. Norton, 1965.

Fromm, Erich. *The Art of Loving.* New York: Bantam Books, 1967.

Goldberg, Philip. "Are Women Prejudiced Against Women?" *Trans-Action,* April 1968.

Hilliard, Marion. *Woman and Fatigue.* Garden City, L.I.: Doubleday, 1960.

Hinkle, Beatrice. "On the Arbitrary Use of the Terms 'Masculine' and 'Feminine'." *Psycho-analytic Review,* 7 (1920).

Horney, Karen. *New Ways in Psychoanalysis.* New York: W.W. Norton, 1939. See especially "Feminine Psychology."

Kirkpatrick, Clifford. "Inconsistency in Attitudinal Behavior with Special Reference to Attitudes Toward Feminism." *Journal of Applied Psychology,* (1936).

Klein, Viola. *The Feminine Character: History of an Ideology.* New York: International Universities Press, 1946, 1948.

Kurtz, Richard M. "Body Image—Male and Female." *Trans-Action,* December 1968.

Laing, R.D. *The Divided Self: An Existential Study in Insanity and Madness.* New York: Pantheon Books, 1969.

————. *The Politics of Experience.* New York: Ballantine Books, 1968.

LaPiere, Richard. *The Freudian Ethic.* New York: Duell, Sloan & Pearce, 1959.

Legman, Gershon. *The Rationale of the Dirty Joke: An Analysis of Sexual Humor.* New York: Grove Press, 1968.

Maslow, Abraham H. *Motivation and Personality.* New York: Harper and Row, 1954.

————. "Self-Actualizing People: A Study of Psychological Health" in *Self: Explorations in Personal Growth*, ed. Clark E. Moustakas. New York: Harper and Row, 1956.

————. "Self-Esteem (Dominance Feeling) and Sexuality in Women." *Journal of Social Psychology*, 16(1942).

Pearce, Jane, M.D. and Newton, Saul. *The Conditions of Human Growth.* New York: The Citadel Press, 1963.

Reik, Theodor, *Sex in Man and Woman.* New York: Bantam Books.

Ruitenbeek, Hendrik M. *The Male Myth.* New York: Dell Books, 1967.

Sampson, Ronald V. *The Psychology of Power.* New York; Pantheon Books, 1965.

Stoller, Robert J., M.D. *Sex and Gender: On the Development of Masculinity and Femininity.* New York: Science House, 1968.

Thompson, Clara B. *Interpersonal Psychoanalysis.* New York: Basic Books, 1964.

CONSUMERISM

Coleman, Richard P.; Handel, Gerald; and Rainwater, Lee. *Working-man's Wife: Her Personality, World, and Life Style.* New York: Oceana, 1959. A valuable market-research study of the blue-collar wife.

Hawes, Elizabeth. *Fashion Is Spinach.* New York: Random House, 1938.

————. *It's Still Spinach.* Boston; Little, Brown, 1954. Sensible accounts of fashion from a woman designer.

McLuhan, Marshall H. *The Mechanical Bride.* New York: Vanguard Press, 1951.

————. *Understanding Media.* New York: McGraw-Hill, 1964.

Riegel, R. "Women's Clothes and Women's Rights." *American Quarterly*, Autumn 1963.

Rudofsky, Bernard. *Are Clothes Modern? An Essay on Contemporary Apparel.* Chicago: Theobald, 1947. An architect asks for more rational apparel and points out the sadism of previous traditions in dress.

Veblen, Thorstein. "The Economic Theory of Women's Dress." *Popular Science Monthly*, November 1894.

Woolf, Janet. *What Makes Women Buy.* New York: McGraw-Hill, 1958.

SEX AND SEXUALITY

Brecher, Ruth and Brecher, Edward. *An Analysis of Human Sexual Response.* New York: New American Library, 1966. Recommended strongly; a very readable discourse on Masters and Johnson.

Bullough, Vern L. *The History of Prostitution.* New Hyde Park, N.Y.: University Books, 1964.

Chadwick, Mary. *The Psychological Effects of Menstruation.* New York: Nervous and Mental Disease Pub. Co., 1932.

Ellis, Albert. *The American Sexual Tragedy.* Rev. ed. New York: Lyle Stuart, 1962.

Ellis, Havelock. *Man and Woman.* New York: Houghton Mifflin, 1929.

Farewell, Nina (pseud.). *The Unfair Sex.* New York: Simon and Schuster, 1953. A bitter and funny treatment of feminine wiles.

Kinsey, Alfred C.; Pomeroy, Wardell B.; Martin, Clyde E.; and Gebhard, Paul H. *Sexual Behavior in the Human Female.* Philadelphia: Saunders, 1953.

———. *Sexual Behavior in the Human Male.* Philadelphia: Saunders, 1949.

Martino, Manfred F. de, ed. *Sexual Behavior and Personality Characteristics.* New York: Grove Press, 1966.

Masters, William H., M.D., and Johnson, Virginia. *Human Sexual Response.* Boston: Little, Brown, 1966.

Millett, Kate. *Sexual Politics,* New York: Doubleday, 1970.

Reich, Wilhelm. *The Function of the Orgasm.* New York: Noonday, 1961.

———. *The Sexual Revolution.* New York: Noonday, 1963. Important and original works on human sexuality by a seminal thinker.

Stearn, Jess. *The Grapevine.* London: MacFadden, 1965. A book on Lesbianism with many insights into women's roles in a more general way.

Stekel, Wilhelm. *Frigidity in Women.* London: Boni and Liveright, 1926.

Young, Wayland. *Eros Denied: Sex in Western Society.* New York: Grove Press, 1964.

CHILDBIRTH, ABORTION, AND BIRTH CONTROL

Day, Lincoln H., and Day, Alice Taylor. *Too Many Americans: Tomorrow's Issue.* Boston: Houghton Mifflin, 1964.

Dick-Read, Grantly, M.D. *Childbirth Without Fear: The Principles and Practices of Natural Childbirth.* New York: Dell Books, 1962.

Hardin, Garrett. "Abortion—or Compulsory Pregnancy?" *Journal of Marriage and the Family,* May 1968.

Himes, Norman A. *A Medical History of Contraception.* Rev. ed. New York: Gamut, 1963.

Karmel, Marjorie. *Thank You, Dr. Lamaze.* Philadelphia: Lippincott, 1959.

Lader, Lawrence. *Abortion.* Boston: Beacon Press, 1967.

Lee, Nancy Howell. *The Search for an Abortionist.* Chicago: University of Chicago Press, 1969.

Lucas, Roy. "Federal Constitutional Limitations on the Enforcement and Administration of State Abortion Statutes." *North Carolina Law Review,* June 1968.

Mead, Margaret, *et. al. The Peaceful Revolution: Birth Control and the Changing Status of Women.* Planned Parenthood-World Population, 1967.

Phelan, Lana Clarke, and Maginnis, Patricia T. *The Abortion Handbook For Responsible Women.* Los Angeles: Contact Books, (6340 Coldwater Canyon, North Hollywood, California), 1969. A recent book from two of the most active women in the abortion movement. Available by writing publisher at 7813 Beverly Blvd. in Los Angeles.

Phelan, Lana Clarke. "Abortion Laws: The Cruel Fraud." A reprint of a speech. Available from Society for Humane Abortion, Inc.

Rainwater, Lee, and Weinstein, Karol. *And the Poor Get Children.* Chicago: Quadrangle Books, 1960. An analysis of the relationship between marital power structures and attitudes toward sex and contraception.

Schenk, Roy U. "Let's Think About Abortion." *The Catholic World,* April 1968.

Go Tell It in the Valley

BIOGRAPHY AND AUTOBIOGRAPHY

Anderson, Mary. *Woman at Work.* Minneapolis: University of Minnesota Press, 1951. The autobiography of the head of the Women's Bureau.

Balabanoff, Angelina. *My Life as a Rebel.* n.d.

———. *Impressions of Lenin.* Ann Arbor: University of Michigan Press, 1968.

Beauvoir, Simone de. *Memoirs of a Dutiful Daughter.* Cleveland: World Publishing Co., 1959.

———. *The Prime of Life.* Cleveland: World Publishing Co., 1962.

———. *A Very Easy Death.* New York: Putnam, 1966.

Besant, Annie. *An Autobiography.* London: Fisher Unwin, 1893. The autobiography of a pioneer in birth control.

Chace, Elizabeth Buffum, and Lovell, Lucy Buffum. *Two Quaker Sisters.* New York: Liveright Publishing Co., 1937. A New England diary from the Abolitionist period.

Conrad, Earl. *Harriet Tubman: Negro Soldier and Abolitionist.* New York: International Publishers, 1968.

Day, Dorothy. *The Long Loneliness.* Image, 1952. The autobiography of the founder of the Catholic Worker movement.

Dell, Floyd. *Women as World Builders: Studies in Modern Feminism.* Chicago: Forbes & Co., 1913.

Deming, Barbara. *Prison Notes.* New York: Grossman, 1965.

Drinnon, Richard. *Rebel in Paradise.* Chicago: University of Chicago Press, 1961. A biography of Emma Goldman.

Duncan, Isadora. *My Life.* New York: Liveright & Co., 1933.

Fauset, Arthur. *Sojourner Truth, God's Faithful Pilgrim.* Chapel Hill, N.C.: University of North Carolina Press, 1938.

Flynn, Elizabeth Gurley. *I Speak My Own Piece.* New York: International Publishing Co., 1935.

Gilman, Charlotte Perkins. *The Living of Charlotte Perkins Gilman.* New York: Appleton, Century, Croft, 1935.

Goldman, Emma. *Living My Life.* 2 vols. New York: Knopf, 1931.

Hays, Elinor Rice. *Morning Star: A Biography of Lucy Stone.* New York: Harcourt, Brace, 1961.

578   Appendix

Ibarruri, Dolores. *They Will Not Pass: The Autobiography of La Pasionaria.* New York: International Publishers, 1966.
Jesus, Carolina Maria de. *Child of the Dark.* New York: Signet Books, 1964.
Lader, Lawrence. *The Margaret Sanger Story, and The Fight for Birth Conrol.* Garden City, L.I.: Doubleday, 1955.
Lerner, Gerda. "The Grimké Sisters from South Carolina: Rebels Against Slavery." Boston: *Atlantic Monthly,* 1967.
Lutz, Alma. *Created Equal.* New York: John Day Co., 1940. A biography of Elizabeth Cady Stanton.
———. *Emma Willard, Daughter of Democracy.* New York: Houghton Mifflin, 1929.
———. *Emma Willard, Pioneer Educator of American Women.* Boston: Beacon Press, 1964.
———. *Susan B. Anthony.* Boston: Beacon Press, 1959.
Marder, Herbert. *Feminism and Art: A Study of Virginia Woolf.* Chicago: University of Chicago Press, 1968.
Mora, Constancia de la. *In Place of Splendor.* New York: Harcourt, Brace, 1939. Autobiography during the Spanish Civil War.
McCarthy, Mary. *Memories of a Catholic Girlhood.* New York: Harcourt, Brace, 1957.
Mott, Lucretia. *Diary from England.* A nineteenth-century diary of a feminist.
Nettl, J.P. *Rosa Luxemburg.* 2 vols. Oxford: Oxford University Press, 1966.
Nin, Anais. *The Diary of Anais Nin.* 2 vols. New York: Harcourt, Brace, 1966.
Pankhurst, Emmeline. *My Own Story.* London: Eveleigh Nash, 1914.
Richardson, Dorothy. *Pilgrimage.* 4 vols. London: Dent, 1967.
Sanger, Margaret. *An Autobiography.* New York: W.W. Norton, 1938.
Wardle, Ralph. *Mary Wollstonecraft: A Critical Biography.* Kansas City: University of Kansas Press, 1951.
Webb, Beatrice. *My Apprenticeship.* London: Longmans Green, 1926.
———. *Our Partnership.* London: Longmans Green, 1948.
———. *Diaries 1912–1924.* London: Longmans, Green, 1952.
———. *Diaries 1924–1932.* London: Longmans, Green, 1956.

LITERATURE AND LITERARY CRITICISM

Aristophanes. *Lysistrata.*
Austen, Jane. All of her novels are highly recommended, but especially *Pride and Prejudice* and *Sense and Sensibility.*
Beauvoir, Simone de. *Force of Circumstance.*
———. *The Mandarins.*
———. *The Woman Destroyed.*
Dickinson, Emily. *The Complete Poems of Emily Dickinson.*
Dreiser, Theodore. *An American Tragedy.*
Eliot, George. *Middlemarch.*
———. *The Mill on the Floss.*

Ellmann, Mary. *Thinking About Women.* New York: Harcourt, Brace, 1968. Critiques of literature from a feminist point of view.

Farrar, Rowena. *A Wondrous Moment Then.* A novel of women in Nashville in World War I.

Flaubert, Gustave. *Madame Bovary.*

Hardy, Thomas. *Tess of the D'Urbervilles.*

Ibsen, Henrik. *A Doll's House.*

———. *Ghosts.*

James, Henry. *The Bostonians.*

———. *The Portrait of a Lady.*

Lessing, Doris. *Children of Violence.* A series of novels which includes: *Martha Quest; A Popular Marriage; A Ripple from the Storm; Landlocked.*

———. *The Grass is Singing.*

———. *The Golden Notebook.*

———. *The Habit of Loving.*

———. *A Man and Two Women.*

———. *Retreat to Innocence.*

Lowell, Amy. *Collected Poems*

McCarthy, Mary. *A Charmed Life.*

———. *The Company She Keeps.*

———. *The Group.*

Millett, Kate. *Sexual Politics.* New York: Doubleday, 1970.

Mortimer, Penelope. *The Pumpkin Eater.*

Paley, Grace. *The Little Disturbances of Man.*

Parker, Dorothy. *Collected Stories* and *Poems.*

Piercey, Marge. *Breaking Camp.* Middletown, Conn.: Wesleyan University Press, 1968.

Plath, Sylvia. *Ariel.* (Poems). New York: Harper and Row, 1966.

Sophocles. *Electra.*

Tolstoy, Leo. *Anna Karenina.*

———. *Resurrection.* A novel with some fine portraits of pre-Revolution women radicals.

Woolf, Virginia. *Mrs. Dalloway.*

———. *To the Lighthouse.*

———. *The Years.*

———. *Orlando.*

WOMEN AND REVOLUTION

Beauvoir, Simone de. *The Long March.* Cleveland: World Publishing Co., 1958.

Bebel, August. *Women in the Past, Present, and Future.* London: Modern Press, 1885.

———*Women and Socialism.* 1891.

Brown, Donald, ed. *Role and Status of Women in Soviet Russia.* New York: Columbia University Press, 1968.

Castro, Fidel. *Address to the Confederation of American Women.* 1966.

Chinese Women in the Great Leap Forward. Peking: Foreign Languages Press, 1960.

Cowell, Margaret. *Women and Equality.* New York: Workers' Library, 1942.

———.*Women's Place in the Fight for a Better World.* New York: New Century, 1947.

Fanon, Frantz. *Studies in a Dying Colonialism.* New York: Grove Press, 1967

———.*The Wretched of the Earth.* New York: Grove Press, 1965.

Goldman, Emma. "On Love" in *The Anarchists*, Horowitz, ed.

Greene, Awakened China. Garden City, L.I.: Doubleday, 1961

Hinton, William. *Fanshen.* New York: Vintage Books, 1968.

Inman, Mary. *Woman Power.* Los Angeles: Committee to Organize the Advancement of Women, 1942

Landy, Avrom. *Marxism and the Woman Question.* Toronto; Progress Publishing, 1943.

Lenin, V.I. *The Emancipation of Women.* New York: International Publishers.

———.*What is to be Done?*

Mao Tse-Tung. *On Practice.*

———.*Quotations from Chairman Mao.*

Myrdal, Jan. *Report from a Chinese Village.* New York: Vintage Books, 1967.

Shaw, George Bernard. *The Intelligent Woman's Guide to Socialism.*

Snow, Edgar. *The Other Side of the River: Red China Today.* New York: Random House, 1961.

Snow, Helen Foster. *Women in Modern China.* New York: Humanities Press, 1968.

The Woman Question. New York: International Publishers, 1951. Selections from Marx, Engels, Lenin, Stalin.

Writing from the Women's Liberation Movement

The following list includes not only specific works but also general resources for literature concerning women's liberation. For an extended list of Women's Liberation Movement literature write to Washington, D.C., Women's Liberation, c/o Wolfson, 1520 New Hampshire Avenue, N.W., Washington, D.C. 20036.

"American Women and the Radical Movement." *Revolutionary Age* 1:3. A special issue devoted to women, available (60 c) from Revolutionary Age, 3117 East Thomas, Seattle, Washington 98102.

Aphra: A Feminist Journal. Available ($1.00) from Elizabeth Fisher, 22 Cornelia Street, New York, New York 10014.

Association for the Study of Abortion (ASA), 120 West Fifty-seventh Street, New York, New York 10019. A newsletter is available as well as reprints and a bibliography.

Brown, Judith, and Jones, Beverly. *Toward a Female Liberation Movement.* Available (40c) from New England Free Press, 791 Tremont Street, Boston, Massachusetts 02118.

Cisler, Lucinda. *Women: A Bibliography.* Available (30c) from Lucinda Cisler, 102 West Eightieth Street, New York, N. Y. 10024.

California Conference on Abortion. (CCA) *Abortion Law Reform.* Speeches and symposia available from CCA, Box 526, Ross, California 94957.

Dunbar, Roxanne. *Female Liberation as the Basis for Social Revolution.* Available from Southern Female Rights Union, Box 30087, Lafayette Sq. Station, New Orleans, Louisiana.

Female Liberation Journal, Fall 1968, Spring 1969. Available ($1.00) from Female Liberation. 371 Somerville Avenue, Somerville, Massachusetts 02143.

Female Liberation Newsletter. Available (25c) from Nancy Hawley, 193 Hamilton Street, Cambridge, Massachusetts.

Freeman, Jo. "The New Feminists." *Nation,* 24 February 1969.

Hayden, Casey, *et al.* "Sex and Caste." *Liberation,* April 1966, December 1967. A discussion of women and the Movement.

It Ain't Me, Babe. Berkeley, California. Women's Liberation Newspaper. Available ($1.80 for six-months suscription) from Women's Liberation, 2398 Bancroft Avenue, Berkeley, California 94704.

Jordan, Joan. "The Place of American Women." Available (30c) from New England Free Press.

Joreen. *The 51% Minority: A Statistical Essay.* Available for 25c and a 6c stamp from Joreen, 816 East Fifty-eighth Street, Chicago, Illinois 60637.

Koedt, Anne. *The Myth of the Vaginal Orgasm.* Available for 10c from Anne Koedt, 97 Second Avenue, New York, New York 10003.

Lilith. Available ($1.00) from Women's Majority Union, 2021 East Lynn, Seattle, Washington 98102.

Limpus, Laurel. "Liberation of Women: Sexual Repression and the Family." *This Magazine is About Schools,* Spring 1969.

Mitchell, Juliet. "The Longest Revolution." *New Left Review,* November/December 1966. An important piece on the place women's role has held in the socialist movements.

Morton, Peggy. *Abortion Briefs.* Available from Peggy Morton, 52 Elgin, Toronto, Canada.

"On the Liberation of Women" *Motive Magazine,* March/April 1969. A special double issue with a number of important articles.

National Organization for Women (NOW), New York Chapter. *Token Learning: A Study of Women's Higher Education in America.* Available ($1.00) from Kate Millett, 307 Bowery, New York, New York 10003.

New England Free Press, 791 Tremont Street, Boston, Massachusetts 02118. Write for their extensive list (and prices) of Women's Liberation Movement articles and reprints.

Off Our Backs: Women's Liberation Newspaper published every other

week. One year's subscription ($6.00) from 2318 Ashmead Place,
N.W. Washington, D.C. 20009.
Neubardt, Selig. M.D.: *Contraception.* New York: Pocket Books.
New York Radical Women (NYRW). *Notes from the First Year.* June
1968. Available (50c) from Kathie Amatniek, 169 Sullivan Street,
New York, New York 10012.
Rat. Radical underground newspaper published every other week by an
all-women collective. One year's subscription ($6.00) from *Rat,* 241
East Fourteenth Street, New York, New York.
Seattle Radical Women (SRW). *Radical Women: Program and Structure.*
Available, for a contribution, from SRW c/o Severn 2940 Thirty-
sixth Avenue, Seattle, Washington 98144.
Seattle Women's Majority Union. *Lilith.* A magazine available (50c) from
WMU, Box 1895, Seattle, Washington 98111.
Society for Humane Abortion. Reprint list available, P.O. Box 1862, San
Francisco, California 94101.
Solanis, Valerie. *SCUM Manifesto.* New York: Olympia Press, 1968.
Spazm. Mixed Media Women's Newsletter. Available (75c) from Laura
X., 2325 Oak Street, Berkeley, California, 94708.
Tooth and Nail. Bay Area (California) Women's Liberation Journal. Avail-
able (25c each issue) from P.O. Box 4137 Berkeley, California
94704.
Up From Under. Woman's Liberation Magazine. Available (5 issues for
$2.50) from 339 Lafayette Street, New York, New York 10012.
Wells, Lyn. "American Women: their Use and Abuse." Available (35c)
from New England Free Press.
Women: A Journal of Liberation. Yearly subscriptions $5.00 for four issues.
Women, 3011 Guilford Avenue, Baltimore, Maryland 21218.

Films

The following films are recommended either for their insights into
women's problems or into the society that creates the problems.
(Also write for catalog from Women's Caucus, *Newsreel,* 28 West
Thirty-first Street, New York, New York.)

An American Tragedy.
Adam's Rib.
Gaslight.
Johnny Belinda.
Masculine-Feminine.
The Nun's Story.
The Queen.
Red Desert.
L'Avventura.
Salt of the Earth.
Two Women.
La Chinoise.

Weekend.
Most early Rosalind Russell films. Most early Katharine Hephurn films (especially *A Woman Rebels*).
Any Doris Day film,
etc.
etc.
etc.

Drop Dead List

Belfort, Bax, E. *The Fraud of Feminism.* London: Grant Richards, 1913. Anti, of course.

Bergler, Edmund and Kroger, William S. *Kinsey's Myth of Female Sexuality: The Medical Facts.* New York: Grune and Stratton, 1954.

Bonaparte, Marie, *Female Sexuality.* New York: Grove Press, 1965. Psychoanalytic; one chapter heading "The Essential Masochism of Women."

Bross, Barbara, M.D., and Gilbey, Jay. "How to Love Like a Real Woman." *Cosmopolitan,* June 1969.

Brown, Helen Gurley. *Outrageous Opinions.* New York: Avon Books, 1963

———. *Sex and the Office.* New York: Bernard Geis, 1964. The Game.

———. *Sex and the Single Girl.* New York: Bernard Geis, 1962. More of the Game and How to Play it.

Cosmopolitan Magazine. Any issue.

Deutsch, Helene. *The Psychology of Women.* New York: Grune and Stratton, 1944. To be adult, a woman must be narcissistic, masochistic and passive.

Dingwall, Eric John. *The American Woman.* London: G. Duckworth, 1956. Another tiresome attack.

Lundberg, Ferdinand and Farnham, Marynia F. *Modern Woman: The Lost Sex.* New York: Harper, 1947. Rabidly anti-feminist and psychoanalytic, but it has good appendices and a good bibliography of feminist literature and individuals' thoughts.

Montagu, Ashley. *The Natural Superiority of Women.* New York: Macmillan, 1968. Patronizing Pedestalitis.

Reage, Pauline. *The Story of O.* New York: Grove Press, 1966. This is supposed to be by a woman. It sounds more like a man's fantasy.

Robinson, Marie, M.D. *The Power of Sexual Surrender.* New York: Doubleday, 1959. Handbook for the Compleat Slave, a la Deutsch.

Ruark, Robert. *Women.* New York: New American Library, 1967. Another in the giant "know-your-enemy" category.

Winick, Charles. *The New People.* New York: Pegasus, 1968. The author is terribly upset about the "fading differences" between the sexes, and sees evidence, causes, and effects everywhere.

ABORTION COUNSELING INFORMATION DISTRIBUTED BY NATIONAL ORGANIZATION FOR WOMEN (NOW)

General comments:

1 Be as sure as you can that you ARE pregnant before seeking help from a counseling service. Try to have had an animal pregnancy test and get an internal examination from a doctor. Take the written results with you (a full "pregnancy workup" is unnecessary).

2 All services should try to determine whether you have the "grounds" —and the time!—for a legal abortion in your state or in another state: be sure to ask your doctor about this, even before asking the service. Practices may not always agree with laws. Your local Planned Parenthood clinic may also be able to advise you on this (some now help you find a sympathetic doctor for a pregnancy examination, and some even do referrals themselves).

3 Avoid using the word "abortion" in phone conversations with the services or with the doctors they refer you to; say you "have a problem," or something similar that still conveys your message. "Comparison shop": this may be the most important purchase of your life.

4 Some services have been able to force prices down somewhat, but of course they are still exorbitant: in the United States, $350–$1,000 (Costlier for pregnancies beyond 11 or 12 weeks); in Mexico, $200–$500, plus travel; in Puerto Rico, $600–$1000, plus travel; in Japan, $100 or so, plus TRAVEL (the only one of these countries where abortion on request is almost completely legal); in England, $200–$400, plus travel. *Do not go to a foreign country without having made firm arrangements in advance,* preferably through one of the services.

5 You will help other women tremendously if you will *report your experiences*—whether bad or decent—to your service or other referral source: too many women expect the worst and accept it passively. Providing feedback, and working actively for *total repeal of the laws* and for proper, reasonably-priced medical care for all women, is a major responsibility of those who join this "community"—to which perhaps *one-fourth of American women* belong. Change is up to YOU!

Abortion Counseling Service (ACS)
P.O. Box 9199, San Diego, California 92109
(714)233-4515

Run by a group of young women only for San Diego County residents; helps with legal abortions in that county. Arranges for discreet pregnancy tests and consultations with sympathetic physicians. Located at 1369 "B" Street, San Diego. ACS has an excellent newsletter that could serve as a model for other groups; $2.oo to be on the newsletter mailing list.

Association to Repeal Abortion Laws (ARAL)
P.O. Box 6083, San Francisco, California 94101
(415)387-6480

Patricia Maginnis and Rowena Gurner are the guiding lights of this service. For a $5.00 donation to ARAL they will send you very detailed advice and a list of abortion specialists—mostly in Mexico, but also in Puerto Rico and Japan. The list should always be freshly ordered: it is updated constantly for your safety. Help is available up through 7 months. A post-abortion care center and classes in various aspects of abortion are other ARAL activities.

Clergy Consultation Service (on Abortion/on Problem Pregnancies/etc.)

These services are located in several cities and are run by groups of ministers and rabbis. Each service generally counsels with women from its state or area only. Clergy services will soon be in operation in Chicago, Montreal, and other cities: write the National Clergy.Consultation Service on Abortion, 55 Washington Square South, New York City 10012; or call, weekdays between 9 a.m. and noon, 212-254-6314,, to find out whether there is someone available in your area. These services have recently received some foundation support for their work. Most of them maintain a tape-recorded message, reached at the phone numbers given below, that announces which 5 or 6 ministers and rabbis are available for counseling that week, and gives instructions on procedures to follow in setting up appointments with the one you choose. The CCS uses out-of-state doctors and foreign doctors (England, Puerto Rico, Japan), and provides help up to 22 weeks. Those over 12 weeks are generally referred to England. (The laws there are far from repealed, but some doctors are willing to interpret them liberally). The clergy services will ask you to bring with you a note signed by an obstetrician/gynecologist, stating

how many weeks pregnant you are: be *sure* to get this note before
contacting them and take it with you when you go.

Massachusetts (Boston)	(617) 527-7188
Ohio (Cleveland)	(216) 229-7423
Michigan (Detroit)	(313) 964-0838
California (Los Angeles)	(213) 666-7600
Pennsylvania (Philadelphia)	(215) 923-5141
Iowa	(515) 282-1738
Connecticut (New Haven)	(203) 624-8648
New Jersey (north)	(201) 933-2937
upper New York State	(607) 272-7172
New York City*	(212) 477-0034

*no message giving clergy list between 5 p.m. Friday and 9 a.m. Monday:
call on a weekday.

Parents' Aid Society
130 Main Street, Hempstead, Long Island, New York 11550
(516) 538-2626 or 437-2828

This service of Parents' Aid, a birth-control clinic, has been in operation
since before April 1967. Be sure to place all telephone calls person-to-
person to Bill Baird—a former drug-company executive who is the
founder and director: he is sometimes hard to reach because he travels
around the country lecturing, or because he may be in Massachusetts
seeing about his test case challenging their anti-contraceptive laws. Parents' Aid generally holds evening consultations at the clinic, usually on
the weekends. The clinic—which may move to new quarters soon—is a
block and a half from the Hempstead station of the Long Island Rail
Road, and is about one hour's ride from Penn Station in New York City.
Parents' Aid gives advice on both local and distant sources of help, and
tries to aid any woman who comes to them; women visiting the clinic
should try to bring the man involved, if possible. Joining Parents' Aid is
a good way to help the service meet its expenses. Contraceptive advice
and materials are also available.

Women's Assistance Tour
New York City   (212) 245-2569

A woman runs this air tour to an eastern European city that has excellent
medical facilities—and attitudes to match. You must have (1) a doctor's
note saying how many weeks pregnant you are (not over 12 weeks). (2)
a record of a current vaccination (available from your local department
of health or your doctor), and (3) a passport (you can get one in a week

for $12, in two days for $14). You leave on a Wednesday night plane, are met at your destination, and are back home Sunday evening. The total cost now is $800, if you leave from the east coast (more from points west), but volume may soon bring the price down to under $700. This includes: air fare, lodging in first-class hotels, meals, in-city transportation, medical care and post-abortion checkup, 24-hour English-language information service—and sightseeing! Phone for more data.

Great Britain:

Abortion is by no means completely legal in Britain, and many doctors are rather uncooperative as well. Earlier versions of this counseling sheet listed referral services in England. Unfortunately, these services are so overwhelmed by requests from English women that they are regretfully turning away foreign visitors who seek their help. In any case, do not go to England without first having made firm arrangements through an American source. And do not expect to have the abortion paid for under the National Health plan; things usually don't work out that way. Bring money.

For Information on Political & Other Action to get rid of present laws and practices, contact these groups:

1 National Organization for Women (NOW), whose National Abortion Task Force co-chairmen are:

Lana Clarke Phelan
3430 Orange Avenue
Long Beach, California 90807
(213) 424-4681

Lucinda Cisler
102 West 80 Street, Apt. 77
New York City 10024
(212) 799-0620

NOW's local chapters are active in the repeal movement, and the co-chairmen of the Task Force can tell you if there is a chapter in your area; they can also help you locate repeal groups and repeal-minded individuals near you, and give advice on starting a local group for abortion law repeal.

2 New Yorkers for Abortion Law Repeal (NYALR) P.O. Box 240, Planetarium Station New York City 10024. This statewide action group for New York has contacts throughout the country, and can help you form a local committee for repeal. A regular newsletter is available to members, as are brochures, reading lists, and other materials—such as buttons showing the "alpha" symbol of abortion law repeal (5 cents plus stamped envelope, or $4.00 for 100). Please send a stamped, self-addressed business-size envelope with your request for information. Out-of-state inquirers are welcomed.

Further Information on the Subject of Abortion:

1 *Books:* Read Lawrence Lader: Abortion (1966: Beacon paperback BP 264, $1.95), the best general source of information on the subject. Also see Selig Neubardt; MD: Contraception (Pocket Books 77025, $.95; in hard covers as A Concept of Contraception; 1967). Lana Clarke Phelan and Patricia Maginnis are the authors of The Abortion Handbook for Responsible Women (1969: Contact Books, Inc. 6340 Coldwater Canyon, North Hollywood, California). This book, a "survival kit" by women and for women, is available at some bookstores, or can be ordered for $3.00 from the publisher.

2. *Leaflets and reprints:* Write for the latest newsletter and current bibliography/reprint list from the Association for the Study of Abortion, 120 West 57 Street, New York City 10019. Reprints are 10 cents each. Especially good ones are those by Hardin (all of them—4 at this writing), Lucas, Monroe, Rossi, Schenk, Shainess, Simms, *Time* essay, White.

A reprint list is also available from the Society for Humane Abortion, P.O. Box 1862, San Francisco, California 94101. Enclose a stamped, addressed business-size envelope. Particularly good reprints (20 cents each): Rossi, ("Public Views . . ."), Phelan, Kerslake, Maginnis, Hardin. Mailing list: $2.00 a year.

Several pages of "Abortion Facts," with commentary and extensive references, are available for 25 cents from James Clapp, 607 East 12 Street, New York City 10009.

Recordings and tapes: LP record of 10 women describing their own abortion experiences: $3.50 from the Marin County Chapter of the California Committee for Legalized Abortion, Box 101, Kentfield, California 94904. Their supply of records may have run out, so it is best to write first and inquire.

Series of 5 hour-long tapes on various aspects of the issue (all repeal-oriented), for discussion groups (ask also about broadcast arrangements): contact James Clapp, 607 East 12 Street, New York City 10009 for details.

WOMEN'S LIBERATION MOVEMENT CONTACTS*

National:

Black Women's Liberation Committee
346 West 20th Street
New York City, N.Y. 10011

Daughters of Bilitis
141 Prince Street #2
New York City, N.Y. 10012

National Organization for
Women (NOW)
P.O. Box 114 Cathedral Station,
New York City, New York 10025

WITCH
P.O. Box 694
Stuyvesant Station
New York City, N.Y. 10009

Berkeley:

Women's Liberation
c/o Laura X
2325 Oak Street
Berkeley, California 94708

Boston

Bread and Roses
c/o *The Old Mole*
2 Brookline Street
Cambridge, Massachusetts

Female Liberation
371 Somerville Ave.
Somerville, Massachusetts

Atlanta

Women's Liberation
P.O. Box 7312
Station "C"
Atlanta, Georgia 30309

California

See Berkeley
Los Angeles
Oakland
San Francisco

Baltimore:

Women's Liberation
3011 Guilford Avenue
Baltimore, Maryland

Canada:

See end of list

*This list is by no means complete. It is merely an attempt to cover some of the groups in major cities, so that readers would have an outline, at least, of who to contact. Each group listed would be helpful in referring someone onto others in the area or region.—Ed.

Chicago:

The Women's Center
5406 South Dorchester
Chicago, Illinois 60615

Women's Liberation Center
2875 West Cermak (Room 9)
Chicago, Illinois

New Feminists Bookstore
1525 East 53rd Street
Room 503
Chicago, Illinois 60615

Cleveland:

Women's Liberation
c/o The Outpost
13037 Euclid Avenue
East Cleveland, Ohio 44112

Connecticut:

See New Haven

Detroit area:

Women's Liberation
c/o K. Sacks
Oakland University
Rochester, Michigan 48063

Durham:

Women's Liberation
P.O. Box 7378
College Station
Durham, North Carolina

Florida:

See Gainesville

Gainesville:

Women's Liberation
P.O. Box 1313
University Street
Gainesville, Florida 32601

Georgia:

See Atlanta

Grinnell:

Women's Liberation
c/o Molly Malcolm
Grinnell College
Grinnell, Iowa

Iowa:

See Grinnell

Kansas City:

Women's Liberation
721 West 16th Street
Kansas City, Missouri 64108

Los Angeles:

The Women's Center
1027 South Crenshaw
Los Angeles, California 90005

Michigan:

See Detroit and Ypsilanti

Missouri:

See Kansas City

Nashville:

Women's Liberation
P.O. Box 371
Nashville, Tennessee

Female Liberation
P.O. Box 12333
Nashville, Tennessee

New Haven:

Women's Liberation
86 Howard Avenue
New Haven, Connecticut

New Orleans:

Southern Female Rights Union
Box 30087
Lafayette Square Station
New Orleans, Louisiana

New York:

The Women's Liberation Center
36 West 22nd Street
New York, N.Y.

The Feminists
120 Liberty Street
New York, N.Y. 10006

Gay Liberation Front
Box 92, Village Station
150 Christopher Street
New York City, N.Y. 10014

High School Women's Coalition
711 Amsterdam Avenue
New York City, N.Y. 10025

Media Women
G.P.O. 1692
New York City, N.Y. 10001

New York Radical Feminists
P.O. Box 621
Chelsea Station
New York, N.Y. 10011

Older Women's Liberation (OWL)
c/o Schwartz
91 Bedford Street
New York City, N.Y. 10014

Redstockings
P.O. Box 748
Stuyvesant Station
New York City, N.Y. 10009

New Feminists Repertory Theater
c/o Dell'Olio
43 West 54th Street
New York City, N.Y.

Theater for Women's Liberation
c/o Ceballos
148 West 68th Street
New York City, N.Y.

Women's Liberation 55
c/o Klaus
40 West 83rd Street
New York City, N.Y. 10024

North Carolina:

See Durham

Oakland:

Women's Liberation
452 60th Street
Oakland, California

Ohio:

See Cleveland and Yellow Springs

Pennsylvania:

See Philadelphia

Philadelphia:

Women's Liberation
c/o Brewer
4911 Catharine Street
Philadelphia, Pennsylvania 19143

Sojourner Truth's Disciples
c/o Trumbule
1009 South St. Bernard Street
Philadelphia, Pennsylvania 19143

San Francisco:

Women's Liberation
Room 101
3740 25th Street
San Francisco, California 94110

Seattle:.

Women's Majority Union
Box 1895
Seattle, Washington 98111

Tennessee:

See Nashville

Washington, D.C.:

Women's Liberation
P.O. Box 13098
"T" St. Station
Washington, D.C. 20009

Washington State:

See Seattle

Yellow Springs:

The Women's Center
Antioch Union
Yellow Springs, Ohio 45387
(Also has information on
Dayton, Cincinnatti, etc.)

Ypsilanti:

Women's Liberation
c/o Meeropol
7 West Ainsworth
Ypsilanti, Michigan 48197

Canada:

Women's Liberation
Apt. 205
105 Water Street
Guelph, Ontario

Women's Liberation
c/o Ramsey
51 Maple Avenue
Toronto 287, Ontario

Notes on Sister Contributors

Frances M. Beal attended the University of Wisconsin and has a diploma in French History from the University of Paris. She lived in France for six years, where her two daughters, Anne and Lisa, were born. Since her return from abroad in 1966, she has worked with the Student Nonviolent Coordinating Committee and is presently on SNCC's national staff, working for SNCC's Black Women's Liberation Committee as the New York Cooordinator. She is employed by the National Council of Negro Women as a program specialist in the field of African and Afro-American History and Culture.

Maria Britton "I am for movement and revolving. You must consider the hell of revolution and be aware of everyone's heat, mainly your own. It passes."

Connie Brown was born and raised in Massachusetts. She went to college, then worked for a few years in an SDS community organizing project. She lives in New York, and is twenty-seven years old.

Rita Mae Brown was born "illegitimate" on November 28, 1944, in Hanover, Pennsylvania; the father was unknown, the mother left the infant at an orphanage. Adopted by a couple who took her to Florida when she was eleven years old, Rita distinguished herself at Fort Lauderdale High School by putting a dead fish in the ventilating system and by serving as Youth Governor (!) of Florida. She was thrown out of the University of Florida for civil-rights activities, hitchiked to New York City where she lived for weeks in an abandoned automobile before moving up in the world to a cold-water slum flat. She completed her B.A. at New York University and attended graduate school, but dropped out to do what she really cared about: writing, films, and building a counterculture to oppose the war-oriented, polluted male culture we now live in. A member of the Harriet Tubman Brigade of the Redstocking Sisterhood, she is a feminist.

Lucinda Cisler is a New York architect and city planner, with degrees from Vassar, Yale, and the University of Pennsylvania. She is active in Women's Liberation and in the National Organization for Women. In the area of birth control, she has worked with Parent's Aid Society, and is the national co-chairman of NOW's Task Force on Abortion, the secretary of NARAL (National Association for Repeal of Abortion Laws), an officer of New Yorkers for Abortion Law Repeal, and on the board of Zero Population Growth.

Charlotte Bonny Cohen was born September 21, 1943. She has been active in the Movement, and has also been active in Women's Liberation in New York, Boston, and San Francisco. She has written for and worked on a number of underground newspapers, and is currently living in New York.

Mary Daly holds a rather stunning string of seven degrees, three of which are doctorates (in religion, sacred theology, and philosophy). She is the author of *The Church and the Second Sex* (Harper and Row) which explores the history of anti-feminism in the Catholic Church. Shortly after the book's publication in 1968, Dr. Daly was fired from her teaching position in the theology department of Jesuit-run Boston College. After three months of tumult, a petition with 2,500 student and faculty signatures, and a march on the college president's office by 1,500 students, all in support of Dr. Daly, she was re-hired, with promotion and tenure. She is concerned with feminism and with the issue of freedom in the Church.

Gene Damon is in her thirties, and lives in the Middle West with a lifelong friend. A former librarian and public-relations advisor, in recent years she has made her living as a free-lance writer and bibliographer. Currently she is the editor of *The Ladder*, a magazine published by the Daughters of Bilitis, Inc., a Lesbian civil-rights organization.

Roxanne Dunbar was born in 1939 into a poor white family in Oklahoma. She married, attended college, and had a child—and then came to the Women's Liberation Movement after being involved in the Black Liberation Movement. She was one of the founders of Cell 16, Female Liberation, in Boston, and has written widely on women's oppression and strategy for liberation. She is now living in New Orleans, where she has founded the Southern Female Rights Union, her aim now being to return to her roots and work with poor white and black Southern women. She is an advanced student in Tae Kwon Do, a Korean form of self-defense.

Alice de Rivera won her battle to enter Stuyvesant High School in 1969, only to move away from New York with her family. (Her sisters profitted from her fight, however—there are other women students now at Stuyvesant.) She still writes poetry, likes music and science, and is involved in the Women's Liberation Movement.

Connie Dvorkin, as she notes in her article, was born March 4, 1955, in New York City. She has recently left high school to organize her summer camp around Women's Liberation.

Alice Embree attended the University of Southern California and the University of Texas. She has worked as a laboratory assistant, as a Peace Corps administrative assistant, as a computer coder, and as a temporary typist. She has been active in the civil-rights and free-speech movements in her native Texas, helped found the *Rag* (an Austin underground newspaper), and has written for a number of Movement publications. Recently she was on the staff of the North American Congress on Latin America (NACLA), doing research on American corporations, on the real-estate and banking interests of major universities, and on financial contributors to the Democratic Party.

Marilyn Lowen Fletcher Born Detroit. "Took things too seriously." Age 14 Rabbi told her "You'll never get a man because you're too intelligent."

1 1/2 years Best Progressive Woman's College. Escaped. 5 years in civil-rights movement in the South. Lives in New York City with photographer and Kabenga, their 19 month-old son. "All my work is dedicated to Barbara Christian, Mary Lee Jackson Kenyatta, Dorothy Gibbs, Loutishia Frierson, Mae Jackson, and other sisters whose strength makes me feel the millenium is at hand."

Florika is a woman who was born in Roumania who was once a girl who became a woman. She is with New Haven (Connecticut) Women's Liberation.

Leah Fritz describes herself as a "verbal terrorist" who has written for the over-and underground press, including the *Village Voice, Liberation,* and the *New York Free Press.* She is active in the drive for community control of schools, and in Women's Liberation. "The Playground" is a section of "The Swindle," a long prose poem about the class structure of Manhattan.

Laura Furman was born in New York City and is a graduate of Bennington College.

Miriam Gilbert worked at a variety of jobs including cess-pool digger, waitress, bookkeeper, and psychiatric aide prior to getting her nursing degree from Queens College in 1967 at the age of twenty-nine. A militant in the matter of human rights, she has not pledged allegiance to any one group involved in the women's movement, choosing, instead, to support any action which offer hope for positive results or dynamic statement. She is divorced, and plans to continue her medical education in Europe.

Carol Glassman was born and grew up in Brooklyn, New York, and went to Abraham Lincoln High School and Smith College ('64). She worked with SDS, the Newark Community Union Project, and the Essex County Welfare Board. She traveled with the American Delegation to the Bratislava, Czechoslavakia, Conference of Vietnamese and Americans in 1967. Currently living in Newark, she is working with local welfare-rights groups, and with other caseworkers in a group called Welfare Workers for Change.

Sheila Smith Hobson is married and lives in Manhattan. She is from Chicago; has a B.A. in journalism, and an M.A. in television writing and production. She has been an editor for a trade newspaper, and a staff editor for a publishing company; she has also worked as an assistant producer, researcher, and graphic coordinator at Channel 13 (in New York), National Educational Television, and WABC-TV. At present, she is doing free-lance writing, and, despite the tone of her article, she hopes to continue in television on a free-lance basis.

Beverly Jones was born July 24, 1927. She attended public schools in Chicago, the University of Illinois, and the University of Chicago. She received her B.A. with honors from the University of California (L.A.) in 1952, and her M.A. in psychology from the same school in 1953. She has been president of the League of Women Voters in Pensacola, Florida, and Vice-president of the Democratic Women's Club of Florida in 1963. In the fall of 1963, she founded and became the first president of the Gainesville (Florida) Women for Equal Rights, a civil-rights organization. She has been active in the peace and student movements; she is married to Marshall B. Jones and they have two children, Donald, age twelve, and Susan, age ten. She now lives with her family in Hershey, Pennsylvania.

Joreen is a Chicago-based free-lance writer and photographer who started that city's first Women's Liberation group in June, 1967. She was also the founder and first editor of the first national newsletter, the *Voice of the Women's Liberation Movement*. Still in Chicago, she is currently doing extensive research into women's situation and is compiling her own book of readings on women and the women's movement. She is also working with other Chicago women in the development of a training program for women who want to learn organizing and group skills.

Judith Ann lives and works in New York City, where she has been active in the Women's Liberation Movement for the past two years. She types sixty words per minute and is taking Karate lessons.

Florynce Kennedy is a well-known civil-rights lawyer who is active in both the Black Liberation Movement and the Women's Liberation Movement. She is Director of Media Workship, and also of Consumer Information Service in New York City, where she lives, and is a member of the Women's Liberation group called The Feminists. She was a delegate to the National Conference on Black Power, is a frequent visitor and lecturer on college campuses, and is currently, in addition to her other activites, teaching a course on "Institutionalized Oppression" at Alternate U. in New York.

Karen Lindsey was born in California in 1944. She attended Queens College in New York; her poems have appeared in numerous "little" literary magazines, and have also been published in *Where Is Vietnam?*, an anthology of anti-war poetry (Doubleday Anchor). Recently she was in charge of poetry programming at the non-commercial radio station WBAI, in New York City, where she lives.

Enriqueta Longauex y Vasquez is a Chicana—"Mexican-American," as some call it, though this is not a popular term in the current movement of Chicanos. Her knowledge of the Southwest is wide and varied. She was born and raised in Colorado, spent ten years in Denver and a year in Los Angeles, and since 1967 has been living in the small mountain village of San Cristobal, New Mexico (North of Taos), with her husband and two teenaged children. Her background includes five years of work in legal offices and a year on welfare; experience as the Director of the Skills Bank of Operation (Service Employment Redevelopment)—a program to help get Chicanos into jobs, together with many years of living in housing projects among the poor. At all times, she has been deeply involved with the Chicano community. Today, among other activities, she writes a regular column for the movement newspaper *El Grito Del Norte,* called "Despierten Hermanos" ("Wake Up, Brothers").

Susan Lydon is a free-lance writer active in Berkeley (California) Women's Liberation. She graduated from Vassar in 1965 and has published articles in *Ramparts,* the *New York Times, Rolling Stone, London Life,* and *The Times of London.* She lives in Berkeley and is currently at work on a book about sex and politics.

Pat Mainardi is a member of Redstockings and a painter. She attributes her insights into male culture to her mother, her grandmother, and her mother's four sisters. The seven women have collectively put in over two hundred years of housework and all that feeling, speaking, and sharing pain has resulted in "The Politics of Housework." May our daughters be spared.

Kate Millett, a sculptor and critic, is a graduate of Oxford who teaches at Barnard College, Columbia University. *Sexual Politics* is actually her doctoral dissertation, which will be published in 1970 by Doubleday (the article appearing here is extracted from the first chapter of that book). She is active in a number of Women's Liberation groups in New York.

Rachel Moon lives in New York, works as a community organizer, and occasionally writes for the radical press. She is active in the women's movement.

Zoe Moss is the pseudonym of a woman born on Cleveland, Ohio, in 1926. Her father was a Greek immigrant, and her mother Italian. Zoe was the second youngest of a family of seven. She lives alone in an apartment in Spokane, Washington, except when her daughter is with her. She works "backstage in retailing." What keeps her going, she says, are: anger, a small cabin in the Cascades, and a few 'friends who are interested in Women's Liberation.

Eleanor Holmes Norton, a civil-liberties lawyer educated at Antioch and Yale (M.A., LL.B.), is a civil-rights activist and legal advisor to SNCC's Black Women's Liberation Committee. While working at the American Civil Liberties Union, she established the Women's Rights Project there (to use the law to end discrimination). In March, 1970, she was appointed Chairman of New York City's Human Rights Commission by Mayor John Lindsay. Her husband, Edward, is also a lawyer who is happy to have a wife in the profession—and in both movements.

Susan Pascalé is fifteen years old. She lives in New York City, attends the High School of Art and Design, and is active in Women's Liberation.

Irene Peslikis is a member of Redstockings, and a painter. The ideas for "Resistances to Consciousness" came from a Redstockings group. She, as an individual, only put these ideas down on paper.

Marge Piercy's first book of poetry was published by Wesleyan University

Press in 1968 (*Breaking Camp*), and her second, *Hard Loving*, in September of 1969. Her first novel, *Going Down Fast*, was published by Trident (Simon & Schuster) in 1970. Her poems and stories have appeared in many magazines and anthologies, including *The Bold New Women*, edited by Barbara Alson, and *31 New American Poets*, edited by Ron Schreiber. She has been active in SDS since 1965, worked in the North American Congress on Latin America (NACLA), and was a founder of MDS (Movement for a Democratic Society) in New York. Since March of 1969, she has been working on the periodical, *Leviathan*, and has been active mostly in the Women's Liberation Movement.

Sylvia Plath was born in Boston, Massachusetts, in 1932. She attended Smith College, was a Fulbright Scholar to Cambridge (England), and while there met and married Ted Hughes, an English poet. She wrote a novel, *The Glass Bell*, and her first book of poems, *The Colossus*, appeared in 1961. Then came two children. "The Jailor," one of her last poems, is nonetheless not included in *Ariel*, the stunning collection of most of her last work (Harper and Row, 1966). She committed suicide on February 11, 1963—at thirty-one years of age. There was no movement for Women's Liberation at that time.

Janet Russo was born in San Francisco twenty years ago. She attends San Francisco State College, and is active in the peace movement, as well as in Women's Liberation.

Karen Sacks has been involved in Women's Liberation groups in Ann Arbor, Michigan, and at Oakland University for the past two years, and is currently teaching anthropology at Oakland University in Rochester, Michigan. She is working on her Ph.D thesis, is married, and has two children, ages three and one years old, respectively. She says, "It's a bitch to find time for everything."

Susan Schnall was born 9 March, 1943, in the Navy Hospital at Quantico, Virginia. She was named Susan Marina (after the Marine Corps) Levine. Her father, an attorney, joined the Marine Corps, and was killed on Guam during World War II. Raised by her mother, she attended Berkeley, got her B.S. in 1967 from Stanford, and married Peter Schnall about three weeks after she started work at Oak Knoll. She overcame her "overpowering fear of the military in 1968, and began acting out against it." Her case is now going through an automatic appeal process; meanwhile, she was returned to full duty.

Diane B. Schulder is a member of the New York Bar; L.L.B. 1964, Columbia University School of Law; B.S. 1964 Columbia (major: French Language and Literature; Phi Beta Kappa). She worked for two years with the Criminal Branch of the Legal Aid Society, and tried over a hundred cases. She has also worked on cases involving the right of soldiers and others to speak out against the war in Vietnam, including working with Leonard Boudin on the *Spock* case and the *Fort Jackson Eight* case, and on cases involving greater rights for artists. She is one of the lawyers handling the mass-plaintiff abortion lawsuit in New York (spring of 1970), in which women are suing the state for violating their Constitutional Rights. She is also teaching a seminar at New York University Law School, entitled "Women and the Law"—the first of its kind to be offered in a law school in the United States.

Jane Seitz attended college in Providence, New York, and Paris, and is currently an editor at Random House.

Natalie Shainess is a Diplomate of the American Board of Psychiatry and Neurology. She holds a Certificate in Psychoanalysis from the William Alanson White Psychoanalytic Institute, where she is a member of the faculty. She is a Lecturer in Psychiatry at Columbia University College of Physicians and Surgeons, a Fellow and former Trustee of the American Academy of Psychoanalysis, and former Assistant Clinical Professor of Psychiatry at the New York School of Psychiatry. Dr. Shainess is known for her writings in feminine psychology.

Martha Shelly is a graduate-school dropout who has been on an ego trip for twenty-six years. An admitted coward with liberal tendencies, she began working in the peace movement under her father's "assumed" name. She later joined the Daughters of Bilitis and helped found the Gay Liberation Front—never having made a dime out of any of it. Her friends think she is a socialist.

Dr. Mary Jane Sherfey has been a practicing psychiatrist for fifteen years. She interned at Payne-Whitney, at Cornell Medical School, where she later became an assistant professor. She is expanding her article into a book.

Valerie Solanis should be known primarily as an artist, not as someone who shot Andy Warhol. Her filmscripts and other writings have not received the attention they deserve. She is still being persecuted by police and "mental health" authorities for her "attempted murder" of Warhol, and has been in and out of prisons ever since. Interestingly enough, Norman Mailer was charged with the same crime when he almost fatally stabbed his wife. He was never imprisoned; all charges were dropped; his reputation was enhanced; he subsequently ran for Mayor of New York. Enough said—Ed.

Ellen Strong was born in New York City in 1941 and raised as a "red-diaper baby"—she was active in political activities when she was still quite young. Her formal education ended with a spectacularly unsuccessful first year at City College. From the time she was around sixteen years old, she began to experiment with the drug and hustling life, and shortly after leaving school began several extremely educational years as a junkie hustler. Emerging from this life in 1965 via Daytop Village, a therapeutic community in New York, she is now living and working in Chicago, and has resumed her activity and interest in the Movement.

Lynn Strongin's poems have appeared in a number of "little" magazines, including *Trace, The Goliards, Galley Sail Review, Confrontation, Bay Podium, Motive, Hiram Poetry Review* and *Illuminations.* Her work has also been published in *31 New American Poets,* edited by Ron Schrieber (Hill & Wang), and *The American Literary Anthology, 2* (Random House). She is living in California where she is an instructer in English at Mills College.

Susan Sutheim is a former regional staff member for New York SDS. She has written for a number of Movement publications, and was news editor for the *Guardian.* She has recently been most active in the Women's Liberation Movement.

Elizabeth Sutherland (Martinez) is a "tired old revolutionary writer-type," by way of SNCC, a couple of books (*Letters From Mississippi, The Youngest Revolution—Personal Report on Cuba*), and is now editing a Chicano movement newspaper, *El Grito Del Norte*—whose full-time staff and major columnists are all women—in New Mexico, yet.

Leslie B. Tanner lives in New York, is a "house slave," former burlesque dancer, mother of three, book designer, typist, and active in the school struggle.

Jean Tepperman worked with SDS in college, and then for JOIN Community Union in Chicago, 1966–68 (welfare, block organizing, internal, education). She worked in factories in 1968 and tried to go to graduate school for a while. She is now living in the Boston area, working for the underground newspaper *The Old Mole,* and for the women's movement (Newsletter, Karate, study group, Bread and Roses, actions, WITCH). Her poems have appeared in *Lion Rampant, Motive,* and *The Old Mole.* At age twenty-five, she has had "scattered employment," ranging from being a typist to doing anthropological research. She considers herself "urban semi-nomadic."

Lindsy Van Gelder is twenty-five years old and a graduate of Sarah Lawrence College (1966). She has worked around newspapers since she was fifteen, first as a stringer, and then as a copygirl for the *New York World Telegram,* later as a reporter at United Press International, and currently as a reporter at the *New York Post.* (She was recently fired from the *Post* for refusing a byline on an assignment which she thought was insulting to women—and later re-hired, after feminist protests and demonstrations of support on her behalf). She is active in the Women's Liberation Movement in New York, and is a member of Media Women and of the New York Radical Feminists.

Naomi Weisstein completed her NSF postdoctoral fellowship in mathematical biology at the University of Chicago, after obtaining her Ph.D in psychology from Harvard University in two and a half years. She was understandably surprised, therefore, that none of the twelve institutions to which she had been recommended for jobs would hire her. She is now Assistant Professor of Psychology at Loyola University in Chicago. She has been in SDS since 1965, in Women's Liberation since 1966, plays piano in a women's liberation rock group, holds a yellow belt in Karate —and is no longer surprised.

Jayne West lives in Boston, where she is active in Female Liberation. In addition to writing poems, she teaches Boston-area women the Korean martial art of self-defense, Tae Kwon Do, in which she herself is an advanced student.

Robin Morgan was born in Florida in 1941. She grew up in Mount Vernon, N.Y. and wanted, at age six, to become a doctor and a poet. The male-supremacist society destroyed the first ambition but couldn't dent the second; her poems have appeared widely in over- and underground publications, ranging from *The Yale Review* and *The Atlantic* to *Rat* and *Caw.* She interrupted finishing her first collection of poems, to be titled *War Games,* to edit this anthology. She was active in the male-dominated Left for about six or seven years, and has been working solely in the Women's Liberation Movement for the past three years. She wants to write, and work toward a worldwide women's revolution—whatever that takes.